This is the office copy
— not to be taken out
of the office — contains
corrections and is intended
ultimately for deposit in
the archives of the university

W.J.C.

PRINCETONIANS
1748–1768

PRINCETONIANS

=== 1748–1768 ===

A BIOGRAPHICAL

DICTIONARY

By JAMES McLACHLAN

PRINCETON UNIVERSITY PRESS
PRINCETON, NEW JERSEY
1976

Copyright © 1976 by Princeton University Press
Published by Princeton University Press,
Princeton, New Jersey
In the United Kingdom: Princeton University Press,
Guildford, Surrey

ALL RIGHTS RESERVED

Library of Congress Cataloging in Publication Data will
be found on the last printed page of this book

*Publication of this book has been aided by the
Whitney Darrow Publication Reserve Fund of
Princeton University Press, The Princeton University
Bicentennial Committee, and Princeton University*

This book has been composed in Linotype Baskerville

Printed in the United States of America
by Princeton University Press, Princeton, New Jersey

CONTENTS

LIST OF ILLUSTRATIONS

PREFACE

EVERY reference work presents unique problems in its composition. The present work is no exception. An outline of some of the difficulties encountered in designing and researching *Princetonians* may prove useful to its readers.

The construction of an accurate roster of Princeton's eighteenth-century matriculates was the first task. The determination of the names of all recipients of the A.B. presented no difficulties. The names are recorded in the manuscript minutes of the Board of Trustees, in the catalogues published by the College at irregular intervals from 1770 onward, and in almost annual accounts of the College's commencements that appeared in New York and Philadelphia newspapers beginning in 1748. Determination of the names of students who attended the College without graduating presented a problem. Unlike many European universities and some other American colleges, during the years 1747–1768 Princeton did not maintain matriculation registers; or, if it did, they have not survived. Moreover, Princeton's eighteenth-century records are very sparse. For instance, faculty records begin only in 1787. Many others were destroyed during the Revolutionary War; most of those that survived were consumed in a fire that gutted Nassau Hall in 1802. The names of Princeton's eighteenth-century non-graduates included in this volume were drawn from two main sources: President Aaron Burr's manuscript Account Book, 1753–1757, and miscellaneous sources, chief among them an extensive file of letters of inquiry accumulated during the twentieth century, now in the University Archives. These letters were written by people in every part of the United States, either requesting information about an ancestor known to have attended Princeton during the eighteenth century or suggesting that an ancestor had attended the College. All possible leads in this mass of correspondence were checked. The process proved almost worthless; only a few names of certain non-graduates were added to our list.

The most valuable manuscript source used in the preparation of *Princetonians* was the Account Book kept by President Aaron Burr. Acquired by the University Library early in the twentieth century, its provenance is not known. Burr began his accounts with page references to an earlier, lost, volume. In his Account Book he recorded the entry of various students to the College, the books they bought, and a wide

variety of miscellaneous expenses. Unhappily for the researcher, Burr
not only headed the College but also maintained a Latin grammar
school in his parsonage. His Account Book records the affairs of both
the College and the grammar school students, along with many other
matters. Unscrambling this mass of often cryptic notation was extremely time-consuming. Differentiation of the college and grammar
school students became possible when it finally was determined that
Burr had been at least moderately consistent in charging the grammar
school students for "schooling," and the college students for "tuition."
We were thus able to add several new names to the list of non-
graduates. (Sketches of non-graduates have been placed with the class
in which it appears they most probably belonged.) On balance, however, the bulk of newly discovered eighteenth-century matriculates
belongs to the classes later than those contained in this volume.

The second step in the research process was the assembling of reliable
biographical data for our subjects. Here we built upon the work of
three earlier scholars, George Musgrave Giger (A.B. 1841), Samuel
Davies Alexander (A.B. 1838), and Varnum Lansing Collins (A.B.
1892). Giger, successively professor of Mathematics, Greek, Latin, and
librarian of Princeton from 1854 to 1865, began in the mid-nineteenth
century a multi-volumned biographical dictionary of Princeton alumni,
culled largely from antiquarian sources. Giger's death in 1865 brought
the project to a halt, but his manuscript has been preserved in the
University Archives. Giger's work served as the basis for Samuel Davies
Alexander's *Princeton College in the Eighteenth Century*, a book that
since its publication in 1872 has been a major reference source for
early Princetonians. A Presbyterian clergyman who spent the larger
part of his ministry in New York City, Alexander found time to write
books on Scottish history and on the history of the Presbyterian
church in Ireland. Although he was a diligent antiquarian, Alexander's work is somewhat misleading. "These Sketches are not selected
from the great body of graduates," Alexander declared in his preface,
"but it is the whole number, just as they stand in the Catalogue, so
far as their history could be traced." The catalogue Alexander used to
establish his roster of eighteenth-century graduates is not known.
However, with no indication that he was doing so, Alexander consistently omitted from his work many graduates whose names appear in
the Trustees' Minutes, a source he otherwise used. For example, four
of the twelve A.B.s of the class of 1756 were omitted, three of the
twenty-two A.B.s of 1757 were omitted, and so on. Since information
on ministerial graduates of the College was usually available to

Alexander, the cumulative effect of his omissions was to make the early alumni body appear much more heavily clerical than was actually the case.

Foundations for the present volume were laid early in the twentieth century by Varnum Lansing Collins, from 1912 professor of French Language and Literature, and Secretary of the University until shortly before his death in 1936. Among his many other duties, Collins found time to write a fine history of Princeton (1914) and a two-volume biography of John Witherspoon (1925), which remains the major scholarly work on one of the College's more prominent presidents. At some time before 1906 Collins established individual files for every known Princeton matriculate and drew up a standard biographical data form that included a wide range of information that he hoped to gather for every alumnus. The culmination of this work was the *General Catalogue of Princeton University, 1746–1906*, published in 1908. The *General Catalogue* lists all degree recipients in alphabetical order within each class. It also includes a certain amount of biographical data on each alumnus, where available. Highly accurate for the nineteenth century, the *Catalogue* is less so for the eighteenth century. Many entries are merely names, and the careers assigned some alumni belong in fact to contemporaries of the same name.

Collins did not cease collecting information about Princetonians with the publication of his *General Catalogue* in 1908. From that time on he and his successors continued to add information to the individual alumni files. The information contained in these files varies widely in quantity and quality—some files contain no information, some are the result of excellent genealogical research, others consist of unidentified antiquarian scraps. In the preparation of this volume, all the material contained in these files was thoroughly checked and evaluated.

The work of Giger, Alexander, and Collins provided a starting point, but a starting point only, for the present volume. The main scholarly source used to research *Princetonians* was one created specially for the project, the "Master Bibliography." This consisted of five manuscript volumes listing every reference to every Princetonian found in a wide variety of sources, ranging from all standard biographical dictionaries to all references in all major American national, state, and local historical journals relevant to the period. Several thousand volumes were used in its preparation. Some indication of their nature is given in the list of abbreviations and in the "Sources" section that follows each sketch. To conserve space and to avoid needless repetition, a few basic references have been omitted from the "Sources" sections. For instance, the career of every clergyman in this volume has been checked against the listings in Frederick L. Weis's four volumes on the colonial clergy of America.[1] We have not, however, cited Weis's works in the "Sources" section of the sketches.

Each biography is mainly factual and narrative in form. An attempt has been made in every case to establish, when the information is available, the following facts: (1) place of birth; (2) date of birth; (3) father's name; (4) father's occupation; (5) father's economic status, as indicated by probate, will, or other records; (6) mother's maiden name; (7) college preparation; (8) date entered college, or class entered; (9) if non-graduate, date left college; (10) college awards and organizations; (11) further education; (12) degrees beyond A.B. and licenses; (13) occupation(s); (14) positions, and when they were held; (15) military service, if any; (16) political and governmental activities; (17) clubs and social organizations; (18) main residence(s); (19) religious denomination; (20) wife's (wives') maiden name(s) and date(s) of marriage(s); (21) number of children and connection, if any, with Princeton; (22) date of death; (23) place of death; (24) value of estate as indicated by will, probate records, or other sources; (25) number of slaves, if any, as indicated by 1790 Census, will, etc.; (26) publications, if any; (27) locations of manuscripts. If information in any of these categories is not included in the sketch, we have been unable to find it.

Many of the sketches, particularly those of subjects about whom little or no information has been discovered, do not indicate the scope of the research. For instance, we have been unable to identify John Harris, A.B. 1762. We have, however, constructed rough career profiles of approximately ten men of that name—any one of whom may have been the Princeton alumnus. We have also maintained "negative reference files" for all subjects—lists of sources consulted that have proved useless. If anyone should wish to carry research on the subjects in this volume further, he would do well to consult the research files for this volume, which are deposited in the Princeton University Archives.

In all dates before 1753, the year is begun on January 1, rather than in March, as was the usage before Great Britain adopted the modern calendar in 1752. Many changes in place names (and their spellings) and in boundaries have occurred in North America since the eighteenth century. For instance, the town of Princeton is now located in Mercer

---

[1] *The Colonial Clergy and the Colonial Churches of New England* (Lancaster, Mass., 1936); *The Colonial Clergy of Maryland, Delaware and Georgia* (Lancaster, 1950); *The Colonial Clergy of Virginia, North Carolina and South Carolina* (Boston, 1955); *The Colonial Clergy of the Middle Colonies* (Worcester, Mass., 1957).

County, New Jersey. In the period covered by this volume, Princeton was partly in Middlesex, partly in Somerset County, for the boundary between the two jurisdictions ran right down Nassau Street. In the 1750s, parts of what are now Orange County, New York, were included in Ulster County. We have attempted to refer to a jurisdiction by the name it bore at the time the events we are describing occurred. This has not been completely feasible in respect to presbyteries, whose boundaries were continually changing in response to population movements. In general, we have aimed for clarity rather than consistency.

Works of this nature inevitably contain errors of fact or omission. We have been guided by an adage of the late Clifford K. Shipton, author of a monumental fourteen volumes of *Sibley's Harvard Graduates*. "The secret of accomplishing anything in the historical field," Shipton once wrote, "is controlled superficiality and sloppiness."[2] While our emphasis has been on "controlled," we hope that readers of *Princetonians* will bring instances of superficiality or sloppiness to our attention by writing directly to the Princeton University Archives.

The 222 unsigned sketches were written by James McLachlan. Authorship of other sketches is indicated by the initials of the contributor following his sketch. Our gratitude to our research assistants is deep, and we would like to thank those who typed the manuscript in its various stages: Jane Serumgard Harrison, Joanne A. Weissman, Renee Hylton, and Jennifer Guberman. Our editor, Gail Filion, has aided us with her thoroughness.

Preparation of this volume was made possible by the generous cooperation of many individuals and institutions. We cannot name all of them, but we would like to express our gratitude to some here. We owe special thanks to the staff of the Princeton University Archives: Earle E. Coleman, Archivist; Edith Blendon, Acting Archivist; and their assistant, Diane Girvin. Past and present members of several divisions of Firestone Library have eased our task in countless ways, particularly Alexander P. Clark, Robert Fraser, Charles E. Greene, John Leypoldt, Jay Lucker, Ann Mann, Mardell Pacheco, Wanda Randall, Agnes Sherman, Eleanor Weld, and Susan B. White.

Several institutions outside Princeton were most helpful. We express special thanks to Gerald W. Gillette and the staff of the Presbyterian Historical Society, Philadelphia, and to Peter J. Parker and the staff of the Historical Society of Pennsylvania. We thank, too, the staffs of the

[2] Quoted by Lawrence A. Towner in his obituary of Shipton in the *AASP*, 84 (1974), 26.

following organizations: the Connecticut State Library, Hartford; the Maryland Historical Society, Baltimore; the Maryland Legislative History Project, Annapolis; the Massachusetts Historical Society, Boston; the Frick Art Reference Library, New York; the Genealogy and Local History Room, New York Public Library; the Manuscript Division, Alexander Library, Rutgers, The State University; the New Jersey State Library, Trenton; the New Jersey Historical Society, Newark; and the Genealogical Society of Pennsylvania.

Many individuals—genealogists, archivists, historians, and friends of the University—have contributed information, advice, and assistance. We extend particular thanks to the following: Charles B. Anderson '40, Whitfield J. Bell, Jr., William E. Benua '21, William R. Bishop, Jr. '39, Koert D. Burnham '26, Nelson R. Burr '27, Lewis D. Cook, James Dallett, Frederic E. Fox '39, John P. Furman '42, Malcolm Freiberg, George E. McCracken '26, Jerome Nashorn, Henry L. Savage '15, M. Halsey Thomas, Donald A. Sinclair, David Wise, and Arthur Zilversmit.

Preparations for this volume began in 1971. Professors Richard D. Challener and Lawrence Stone of the Princeton History Department lent their support. We are grateful to Professor Stone and the Executive Committee of the Shelby Cullom Davis Center for Historical Studies for providing seed-money, and to Shelby Davis '30 for his interest in the enterprise. William S. Dix, now Librarian Emeritus of the University, added his support and the resources of Firestone Library. Presidents Robert F. Goheen and William G. Bowen have been helpful in times of need. The contributions of many Princeton alumni sustained the work throughout. We cannot list all of them, and many do not wish to be listed, but our thanks must be extended especially to Nathaniel Burt '36, Levering Cartright '26, Peter H. B. Frelinghuysen '38, John K. Jenney '25, Joel B. Johnson '32, Wheaton J. Lane '25, Maurice D. Lee, Jr. '46, Richard W. Lloyd '28, Baldwin Maull '22, Adolph G. Rosengarten '27, Edward W. Scudder, Jr. '35, and Richard B. Scudder '35. Matching grants from the National Endowment for the Humanities have been particularly welcome. We are grateful too to Princeton University's Bicentennial Committee and to Princeton University Press for their part in making the publication of this volume possible.

A mere listing of the members of the Editorial Advisory Committee does not indicate properly their contribution to this volume. I am profoundly grateful to each member, and particularly to the chairman, W. Frank Craven.

INTRODUCTION

DURING the eighteenth century, approximately 1,268 men are known to have matriculated at the College of New Jersey, which often was called Princeton College long before its name was officially changed to Princeton University in 1896. Of this total, 919 received the bachelor's degree, while some 348 attended without graduating. This volume contains the biographies of approximately one-quarter of Princeton's known eighteenth-century matriculates, the 338 men who attended the College in its first 21 classes, those spanning the years 1748 through 1768. Of these men, 313 received their A.B., while another 25 matriculated in the College but did not complete their course.

Chartered in 1746, Princeton was the fourth college founded in the British colonies of North America, the earlier ones being Harvard (1636), William and Mary (1693), and Yale (1701). Princeton's charter of 1746 was granted by the acting royal governor of New Jersey, Andrew Hamilton, in the name of King George II, "for the Education of Youth in the Learned Languages and in the Liberal Arts and Sciences."[1] The original trustees of the College were three prominent New Yorkers—William Smith, Peter Van Brugh Livingston, and William Peartree Smith—and four Presbyterian clergymen—Jonathan Dickinson of Elizabethtown, New Jersey, who would serve as the College's first president, John Pierson of Woodbridge, New Jersey, Ebenezer Pemberton of New York City, and Aaron Burr of Newark, New Jersey, who would serve as the College's second president. A second charter, enlarging the board of trustees to thirteen, was granted in 1748 by Governor Jonathan Belcher, himself a warm supporter of the new institution.

The broader impulse that led to the founding of the College was the Great Awakening, a series of emotional religious revivals that stirred the colonies in the 1730s, reached a peak of mass participation with the intercolonial tours of the great English evangelist George Whitefield in 1739–1740, and then gradually ebbed. A complex movement, and one that is still not completely understood, the Awakening meant different things to the inhabitants of different regions. But everywhere it manifested itself in a striving toward a more direct and intense experience of the divine that had been usual in the various American religious denominations during the previous generation.

[1] Thomas J. Wertenbaker, *Princeton, 1746–1896* (Princeton, 1946), 397.

Revivalist preachers, itinerant and otherwise, placed heavy emphasis on the notion that a minister should have experienced a religious conversion of considerable emotional intensity. They even called into question the qualifications of clergymen seemingly not so blessed, among them many graduates of Harvard and Yale. This, not surprisingly, led to furious controversy in New England and in the middle colonies to schism in the Presbyterian Church.

Advocates of the Awakening came to be called "New Lights" or "New Sides," and within this group there was a further division between those who can be considered moderates and those who were described by contemporaries as "enthusiasts." Neither Jonathan Dickinson nor Aaron Burr were "enthusiasts." Yet both, along with their lay and clerical followers, believed strongly in a religion marked by personal, or "experimental," contact with God. They believed also in the necessity for a formally and traditionally educated ministry. Their ideal, in fact, combined two qualities sometimes thought to be antithetical to one another during the eighteenth century, one that might be summed up as "rational piety." This ideal was the main legacy of the Great Awakening to the new College.

The College of New Jersey began operations in Jonathan Dickinson's parsonage at Elizabethtown, New Jersey, in May 1747. Within a few months Dickinson died, and the College moved to the parsonage of Aaron Burr in nearby Newark. Over the following ten years it was Burr, more than anyone else, who laid a firm foundation for the infant institution's subsequent development. In these years students either lived with Burr and his wife (Esther Edwards Burr, daughter of the great New Light theologian Jonathan Edwards) or boarded in the homes of local residents. Many of the students were prepared for their higher studies at a Latin grammar school maintained by the College, first in Newark and later in Princeton.

With the completion of Nassau Hall the College moved in the fall of 1756 to its permanent location in the tiny village of Princeton. The move brought only tragedy to the Burr family. Worn out by years of overwork, President Burr fell ill and died in September 1757. The trustees shortly named his father-in-law, Jonathan Edwards, as his successor. Smallpox was abroad in New Jersey. Inoculated against the disease, Edwards contracted a severe case of it and died, having spent only a few weeks in his new post. The trustees then turned to Samuel Davies, leader of the Presbyterians in Virginia, who earlier had helped to raise funds in Britain for the construction of Nassau Hall. Davies arrived in Princeton on July 29, 1759. Unhappily, his term as president was also short; on February 4, 1761, he died at the age of thirty-seven.

Faced with the choice of still another president, the trustees turned closer to home. On May 21, 1761, they elected Samuel Finley as president. Master of an academy in Nottingham, Maryland, that had prepared many youths for the College, and an early leader of the Great Awakening in the middle colonies, Finley continued the tradition established by Burr and Davies. Under his management the student body saw its greatest expansion since the founding of the College. Finley's death on July 17, 1766, marked the end of an era in Princeton's early history. There followed a two-year interlude while the trustees sought, with ultimate success, to persuade the eminent Scottish divine John Witherspoon to accept the presidency. His arrival in time to preside over the commencement of September 1768 marks the beginning of another and especially significant era in the College's history.

From a very small beginning the College of New Jersey had become the third largest institution of collegiate rank in the British colonies, if the test be the number of bachelor's degrees awarded, as the following table indicates:

A.B. DEGREES AWARDED BY COLONIAL COLLEGES, 1748–1768[2]

	Harvard	Yale	Princeton	Other	Total
1748–50	65	75	19	—	159
1751–53	82	53	31	—	166
1754–56	69	72	42	—	183
1757–59	92	132	58	26	308
1760–62	113	104	46	46	309
1763–65	139	117	64	24	344
1766–68	124	90	53	45	312

Even more remarkable was the extraordinarily broad geographical area from which the College of New Jersey drew its students. Precise figures are not available, but it appears that in these years almost all of William and Mary's students came from Virginia, and perhaps over

2 The Yale figures are drawn from Dexter, *Yale Biographies*, I–II; the Harvard figures from *Harvard University: Quinquennial Catalogue of the Officers and Graduates, 1636–1925* (Cambridge, 1925). The "other" colleges were King's College (now Columbia University) and the College of Philadelphia (now the University of Pennsylvania), which respectively awarded approximately 85 and 56 A.B.'s in these years. See: *University of Pennsylvania: Biographical Catalogue of the Matriculates of the College . . . 1749–1893* (Philadelphia, 1894), and: M. H. Thomas, *Columbia University Officers and Alumni, 1754–1857* (New York, 1936). Although scores of students are known to have attended the College of William and Mary, it apparently did not award the bachelor's degree until 1776. See W. C. Eells, *Baccalaureate Degrees Conferred by American Colleges in the 17th and 18th Centuries* (Washington, D.C., 1958), 54. We are indebted to Jane E. Weber for the compilation of most of the figures used in this introduction.

90% of Harvard's from Massachusetts, while it has been established that at mid-century Yale drew approximately 75% of its students from Connecticut.[3] In striking contrast is the evidence in the following table of the provinces in which students were living at the time they enrolled at Princeton:

RESIDENCE OF PRINCETON STUDENTS AT TIME OF
ENROLLMENT, 1748–1768

New Hampshire	2	Delaware	6
Massachusetts/Maine	39	Maryland	17
Connecticut	43	Virginia	9
New York	50	North Carolina	4
New Jersey	89	South Carolina	2
Pennsylvania	40	Unknown	37

It is evident enough that the College of New Jersey was on the way to becoming a national institution well before there was a nation. Several circumstances contributed to the new college's attractiveness. First, it drew on a constituency created by the Great Awakening—"New Light" Congregationalists dissatisfied with Harvard and Yale in New England and "New Side" Presbyterians in the Middle and Southern colonies. Second, the College's location at the demographic center of the North/South axis of the colonies made it easily accessible. Third, Princeton seems to have been willing to admit students to advanced standing (i.e. directly into the sophomore or junior classes) more readily than Harvard or Yale. Last, and perhaps most important, for much of the period the College's tuition was the lowest among all American colleges,[4] while its final location in the small village of Princeton meant that other student expenses were apt to be lower than in the Boston area, New Haven, New York, Philadelphia, or Williamsburg. Yet, while Princeton's growth was impressive, it must be kept in perspective: throughout this period the College remained approximately half the size of either Harvard or Yale.

The absence of matriculation records leaves any definitive answer respecting the age at which students entered college or the length of time they spent there speculative. Their approximate age at graduation, however, can be determined, for this information is available for 262 of the 338 students in this volume. Although the notion that

[3] Dexter, *Yale Biographies*, II, 783.
[4] Beverly McAnear, "The Selection of an Alma Mater by Pre-Revolutionary Students," *PMHB*, 73 (1949), 429–40.

eighteenth-century college students were much younger than those of the twentieth century appears to be widespread, it is only a half-truth. Princeton did in fact graduate students ranging in age from 14 to 47. However, more students graduated at age 20 than at any other age, while the median age at graduation for all students was 21. The higher median was caused largely by students who went on to become clergymen. These were often poor youths who decided at a relatively advanced age to attend college for the ultimate purpose of qualifying for the ministry. Their median age at graduation was 24 years, in contrast to alumni who became businessmen, whose median age at graduation was 19.

As we have seen, intensive investigation has failed to discover many "drop-outs" from Princeton; once matriculated in the College, most students stayed the course. In this, Princeton resembled Harvard and Yale more than the College of Philadelphia or King's College. Surviving lists of matriculates at the Philadelphia and New York colleges suggest that one-third to one-half of the students did not complete their courses. The situation in those places resembled that at Oxford in the mid-eighteenth century, where 44% of the students left before receiving the A.B. Both the northern and the English institutions stand in sharp contrast to the College of William and Mary, where almost no one took the A.B.[5] Some of Princeton's drop-outs simply transferred to other colleges, where they received their degrees: two (Hanna '58 and I. Ogden '58) went to King's; three (Graham '60, Robbins '60, and Wheelock '65) went to Yale; five (Briggs '67, Morse '67, Knowles '68, Parker '68 and West '68) transferred to Harvard; and one (Walter Livingston '59) completed his education in England at Cambridge.

Contrary to a widely held notion, the majority of Princeton's alumni in this period did not become clergymen, although that occupation did claim the largest number of alumni, all told 158. Next came the 49 who became lawyers, and after them the 44 medical men. That 251 of the 338 alumni found their primary occupations as clergymen, lawyers or medical men suggests that the College in this period served above all else as a "pre-professional" school. It should not be assumed, however, that career lines were more well-defined in eighteenth century America than was actually the case. A clergyman, for example, might tend the sick and teach school or even farm, as well as fill a pulpit, and a lawyer rarely confined his activity to the practice of his profession. Nor should

[5] For Oxford, see Lawrence Stone, "The Size and Composition of the Oxford Student Body, 1580–1910," in Stone, ed., *The University in Society* (2 vols., Princeton, 1974), I, 95, Table 4.

it be assumed that the colonial college offered, in any modern sense of the term, pre-professional programs of study. Instead, all students shared a broad liberal arts program.

Although Princeton was founded under Presbyterian auspices, from the beginning it welcomed all students, "any different sentiments in religion notwithstanding," as its charter reads. In fact, Princeton attracted students from several different Protestant denominations. Of the 158 who went on to become clergymen, 97 filled Presbyterian pulpits, 41 became Congregational parsons, while the remainder were scattered between the Anglican, Baptist, Dutch Reformed, and Lutheran denominations. In pre-Revolutionary America there were no theological seminaries; prospective clergymen after college "read" divinity with an established clergyman. The median time between ministerial alumni's graduation and ordination was a bit over four years.

Prospective lawyers and medical men apparently faced a longer period of apprenticeship than did prospective clergymen. Information on this point is difficult to find, but from such evidence as is available for Princeton alumni it appears that prospective lawyers spent about 5.4 years between graduation and licensing, while an aspiring medical man spent 6.4 years either apprenticed to an established physician or in study at a medical school before setting up his own practice.

The occupations of Princeton alumni differed markedly from those of their fathers. The occupations of 152 fathers have been discovered. Of these, 31 were clergymen, 11 were lawyers, and 3 were medical men. In other words, while only 45 of these fathers were professionals, fully 251 of the sons took up professional occupations. As would be expected, most of the men (76) who sent their sons to Princeton were farmers. It seems safe to say that Princeton's primary function in American society at this time was to transform the sons of modest farmers into prospective clergymen, lawyers and medical men.

Princeton alumni settled in all parts of the American colonies. Although many alumni moved several times during their careers, the place where an individual stayed longest, or made the most significant contribution of his career, is known for 322 of the 338 subjects. Of these, 69 settled in New Jersey, 53 in New York, 45 in Pennsylvania, 40 in Massachusetts/Maine, and 33 in Connecticut. As for the other alumni, one at least found a home in each of the remaining original thirteen states as well as in Tennessee, Kentucky and Vermont. Three settled in the West Indies and one in Ireland. Many graduates did not return to the place, or even the province, of their birth. For some, new frontiers of settlement in New England, New York, Pennsylvania, and the southern provinces had a special attraction. One can only speculate as to how far the mingling of students drawn from an unusually broad geo-graphical area may have contributed to the settlement of alumni in an even broader geographical area.

The wide geographical dispersal of the alumni accounts in some measure for their extraordinary role in the public affairs of their time. By the end of 1775, 279 of the 338 men in this volume were still living. Of these only 8 (3%) became Loyalists, in contrast to Harvard, where 196 (16%) of the 1,224 alumni living in 1775 took the British side during the Revolution.[6] All told, 88 of the Princeton alumni assumed some office of military responsibility during the War for Independence, including the 35 who served as chaplains. No less than 9 of the 55 members of the Constitutional Convention of 1787 had graduated from Nassau Hall, and these 9 represented six different states. Five of the members of the Convention are found in this volume. In addition, this volume includes 21 men who served in the Continental Congress, 4 who lived to become members of the United States Senate, 7 who served in the House of Representatives, and 2 who became justices of the United States Supreme Court, one of them a Chief Justice. The contribution to leadership at the state and local levels of government was comparably impressive. Two alumni became the governors of their respective states, and more than 40 served in their state legislatures. Five men served as state attorney-general, three of them being the first to hold the office. Over one-third of the alumni at some time or other held public office, a figure including very few of the 158 who became clergymen.

The public record established by this generation of Princetonians suggests that they had absorbed something of the spirit of the exhorta-tions of their mentors at Nassau Hall. In 1760 President Samuel Davies delivered an oration to the students in words that might equally well have been spoken by his predecessors or successors. In that year Davies urged each of the seniors to become "the good, the useful, and public-spirited Man." Whether, Davies continued, the graduates planned to

appear in the sacred Desk . . . to make Men wise, good and happy; or whether you appear at the Bar, as Advocates for Justice, and the Patrons of the Opprest; or whether you practise the healing Art in the Chambers of Affliction . . . whatever, I say, be your Place, permit me, my dear Youth, to inculcate upon you this important Instruc-tion, imbibe and cherish a publick spirit. Serve your Generation. Live not for yourselves, but the Publick. Be the Servants of the Church; the Servants of your Country; the Servants of all.[7]

6 Samuel Eliot Morison, *Three Centuries of Harvard* (Cambridge, 1936), 147, n.1.
7 *Religion and Public Spirit. A Valedictory Address to the Senior Class, Delivered in Nassau-Hall, September 21, 1760* (Philadelphia, 1761), 6–7.

In 1768 John Witherspoon arrived from Scotland to assume Princeton's presidency. Under Witherspoon, the nature of the College would gradually change. In his administration Princeton's direct link with the heritage of the Great Awakening was decisively broken. Interrupted too was the steady stream of New England youths who had provided a quarter of the early undergraduates. Witherspoon would establish a new constituency for Princeton, one that while still centering on the middle colonies would draw much more heavily from the southern provinces and states. Although the character of Princeton would change in the years after 1768, the spirit of the College of Dickinson, Burr, Edwards, Davies, and Finley continued to make its contribution to the American experience through the careers of the men whose lives are recounted in the following pages.

ABBREVIATIONS AND SHORT TITLES
FREQUENTLY USED

AAS   American Antiquarian Society

AASP Proceedings of American Antiquarian Society

Adams Papers L. Butterfield et al., eds., *Diary and Autobiography of John Adams*

AHR American Historical Review

Alexander, *Princeton* S. D. Alexander, *Princeton College during the Eighteenth Century*

APS Proc. American Philosophical Society Proceedings

APS Trans. American Philosophical Society Transactions

Beecher, *Index of Presbyterian Ministers* W. J. and M. Beecher, *Index of Presbyterian Ministers: . . . , A.D. 1706–1881*

Bentley, *Diaries Diary of William Bentley*

Burr, MS Account Book Account Book kept by President Aaron Burr, 1753–1757, Manuscript Division, NjP

Burr, Esther, MS Journal Esther Edwards Burr, MS Journal, 1754–1757, Edwards Park Family Papers, CtY

Butterfield, *Rush Letters* L. H. Butterfield, ed., *Letters of Benjamin Rush*

CaNBA Public Archives of New Brunswick, Canada

CaOOA Public Archives Library, Ottawa

Clinton Papers H. Hastings and J. A. Holden, eds., *Public Papers of George Clinton*

CNJ College of New Jersey

Col. Rec. N.C. W. N. Saunders, ed., *Colonial Records of North Carolina*

CtHC Hartford Seminary Foundation Library

CtHi Connecticut Historical Society

CtY Yale University Library

DAB A. Johnson and D. Malone, eds., *Dictionary of American Biography*

Dexter, *Yale Biographies* F. B. Dexter, *Biographical Sketches of the Graduates of Yale College*

DLC Library of Congress

DNB L. Stephen and S. Lee, *Dictionary of National Biography*

DNLM National Library of Medicine

Doc. Col. Hist. N.Y. E. B. O'Callaghan and B. Fernow, eds., *Documents Relative to the Colonial History of the State of New York*

Doc. Hist. N.Y. E. B. O'Callaghan, ed., *Documentary History of the State of New York*

Dwight, *Travels* B. M. Solomon, ed., *Travels in New England and New York by Timothy Dwight*

Eager, *Orange County* S. W. Eager, *An Outline History of Orange County* (New York)

Fithian Journal, I J. R. Williams, ed., *Philip Vickers Fithian, Journal and Letters, 1767–1774*

Fithian Journal, II R. G. Albion and L. Dodson, eds., *Philip Vickers Fithian: Journal, 1775–1776*

Foote, *Sketches, N.C.* W. H. Foote, *Sketches of North Carolina, Historical and Biographical*

Foote, *Sketches, Va.* W. H. Foote, *Sketches of Virginia, Historical and Biographical*

Force, *Am. Arch.* Peter Force, ed., *American Archives . . . a Documentary History*

Giger, *Memoirs* G. M. Giger, MS Memoirs of the College of New Jersey, PUA

GMNJ Genealogical Magazine of New Jersey

Hageman, *History* J. F. Hageman, *History of Princeton and Its Institutions*

Hamilton Papers H. C. Syrett and J. E. Cooke, eds., *Papers of Alexander Hamilton*

Hatfield, *Elizabeth* E. F. Hatfield, *History of Elizabeth, New Jersey*

Heitman F. B. Heitman, *Historical Register of Officers of the Continental Army . . .*

Hening, *Statutes* W. W. Hening, ed., *The Statutes at Large . . . of Virginia*

Hist. Orange Cty. E. M. Ruttenber and L. H. Clark, *History of Orange County, New York*

JAH *Journal of American History*

JCC W. C. Ford et al., eds., *Journals of the Continental Congress, 1774–1789*

Jefferson Papers J. P. Boyd et al., eds., *Papers of Thomas Jefferson*

Jones, *Inns of Court* E. Alfred Jones, *American Members of the Inns of Court*

JPH *Journal of Presbyterian History*

JPHS *Journal of Presbyterian Historical Society*

Kegley, *Va. Frontier* F. B. Kegley, *Kegley's Virginia Frontier*

Lanc. Co. HSPA *Lancaster County Historical Society Proceedings and Addresses*

LMCC E. C. Burnett, ed., *Letters of Members of the Continental Congress*

Maclean, *History* John Maclean, *History of the College of New Jersey*

Madison Papers W. T. Hutchinson and W.M.E. Rachal et al., eds. *Papers of James Madison*

Maryland Wills A. W. Burns, comp., Abstracts of Maryland Wills

MdAn U.S. Naval Academy, Annapolis

MdHi Maryland History Society

MH Harvard University Library

MHi Massachusetts Historical Society

MHM *Maryland Historical Magazine*

MHS Col. *Massachusetts Historical Society Collections*

MHSP *Massachusetts Historical Society Proceedings*

MiD Detroit Public Library

Mills, *Life at Princeton College* W. J. Mills, ed., *Glimpses of Colonial Society and the Life at Princeton College, 1766–1773*

MiU-C William L. Clements Library, University of Michigan

MNtcA Andover Newton Seminary Library, Massachusetts

Moore, *Patriot Preachers* F. Moore, ed., *Patriot Preachers of the Revolution*

N New York State Library, Albany

NCHR *North Carolina Historical Review*

NcU University of North Carolina Library

NEHGR *New England Historical and Genealogical Register*

NEQ *New England Quarterly*

NhHi New Hampshire Historical Society

NHi New York Historical Society

NJA *New Jersey Archives*

NjHi New Jersey Historical Society

NJHS Col. *New Jersey Historical Society Collections*

NJHSP *New Jersey Historical Society Proceedings*

NjP Princeton University Library

NjPT Princeton Theological Seminary Library

NjR Rutgers Library, State University, New Brunswick

N.J. Wills *NJA*, v. XXIII–XXXXI

NN New York Public Library

NNNAM New York Academy of Medicine

NYGBR *New York Genealogical and Biographical Record*

NYHS Col. *New York Historical Society Collections*

New York Marriages Names of Persons for Whom Marriage Licenses Were Issued by the Secretary of the Province of New York Previous to *1784*

NYSHA Proc. New York State Historical Association Proceedings

N.Y. Wills Abstracts of Wills, NYHS Col., 1892–1906

P Pennsylvania State Library, Harrisburg

PHi Historical Society of Pennsylvania

Pilcher, *Samuel Davies* G. W. Pilcher, *Samuel Davies, Apostle of Dissent in Colonial Virginia*

PMHB Pennsylvania Magazine of History and Biography

PPAmP American Philosophical Society Library

PPC College of Physicians, Philadelphia

PPPrHi Presbyterian Historical Society

Presbyterian Encyclopaedia Alfred Nevin, ed., *Encyclopaedia of the Presbyterian Church in the United States of America*

Proc. N.J. Med. Soc. S. Wickes, *The Rise, Minutes, and Proceedings of the New Jersey Medical Society*

PUA Princeton University Archives

PYHi Historical Society of York County, Pennsylvania

Rec. Col. Conn. J. H. Trumbull and C. J. Hoadly, eds., *Public Records of the Colony of Connecticut*

Rec. Pres. Church Records of the Presbyterian Church . . . *1706–1788*

Rec. State Conn. C. J. Hoadly and L. W. Labaree, eds., *Public Records of the State of Connecticut*

Rev. Dip. Corr. F. Wharton, ed., *Revolutionary Diplomatic Correspondence*

RPB Brown University Library

Rush, *Autobiography* G. W. Corner, ed., *Autobiography of Benjamin Rush*

Sabine, *Loyalists* L. Sabine, *Biographical Sketches of the Loyalists of the American Revolution*

SCHGM South Carolina Historical and Genealogical Magazine

SCHM South Carolina Historical Magazine

Shaw, *Hist. of Essex and Hudson* W. H. Shaw, *History of Essex and Hudson Counties, New Jersey*

Sh–Sh R. R. Shaw and R. H. Shoemaker, comps., *American Bibliography . . . Imprints, 1801–1829*

Sibley's Harvard Graduates J. L. Sibley and C. K. Shipton, *Biographical Sketches of Those Who Attended Harvard College*

S.P.G. Society for the Propagation of the Gospel in Foreign Parts

Som. Cty. Hist. Quart. Somerset County Historical Quarterly (N.J.)

Sprague, *Annals* W. B. Sprague, *Annals of the American Pulpit*

St. Rec. N.C. W. Clark, ed., *State Records of North Carolina, 1777–1790*

STE C. K. Shipton and J. E. Mooney, *National Index of American Imprints Through 1800: The Short Title Evans*

Stiles, *Itineraries* F. B. Dexter, *Extracts from the Itineraries . . . of Ezra Stiles*

Stiles, *Literary Diary* F. B. Dexter, ed., *The Literary Diary of Ezra Stiles*

Susquehannah Papers J. P. Boyd and R. J. Taylor, eds., *Susquehannah Company Papers*

Thorp, *Eighteen from Princeton* W. Thorp, ed., *Lives of Eighteen from Princeton*

Tyler's Quarterly Tyler's Quarterly Historical and Genealogical Magazine

VHi   Virginia Historical Society

ViU   University of Virginia Library

VMHB   Virginia Magazine of History and Biography

Washington Writings   J. C. Fitzpatrick, ed., *Writings of George Washington . . . 1745–1799*

Webster, *History*   R. Webster, *History of the Presbyterian Church in America to 1760*

Webster, MS Brief Sketches   R. Webster, Brief Sketches of Early Presbyterian Ministers, PPPrHi

Weeks, *Index*   S. B. Weeks, comp. and ed., *Index to the Colonial and State Records of North Carolina*

Wertenbaker, *Princeton*   T. J. Wertenbaker, *Princeton, 1746–1896*

Wheeler, *Ogden Family*   W. O. Wheeler, *The Ogden Family in America*

Wheelock MSS   Microfilm edition of the Papers of Eleazar Wheelock, originals in Dartmouth College Library

Wickes, *Hist. of Medicine N.J.*   S. Wickes, *History of Medicine in New Jersey and Its Medical Men from the Settlement of the Province to A.D. 1800*

WMQ   William and Mary Quarterly

CLASS OF 1748

Enos Ayres, A.B.

Benjamin Chestnut, A.B.

Hugh Henry, A.B.

Israel Read, A.B.

Richard Stockton, A.B.

Daniel Thane, A.B.

Enos Ayres

ENOS AYRES, A.B., Presbyterian clergyman, was probably born in Woodbridge, Middlesex County, New Jersey, about 1723, the son of Joseph Ayres, a moderately well-to-do farmer, most likely by Joseph's second wife, Elizabeth. Since he had two contemporaries of the same name, and also two other contemporaries named *Enoch* Ayres, accounts of his career have been confused.

As a youth Ayres was familiar with the preaching of the great evangelist George Whitefield, for in 1745 he wrote to the New Light theologian Joseph Bellamy from Elizabethtown that Whitefield's "seeming to favour the Moravians causes our ministers to keep aloof from him." He was probably directed toward the new College by his pastor, John Pierson, one of the founding trustees. He was most likely among Jonathan Dickinson's students when the College began operation in Elizabethtown in May 1747. Three months later Ayres was one of the three witnesses to Dickinson's will. After Dickinson's death he moved to Newark to continue his studies under Aaron Burr.

On May 8, 1749, Ayres married Mrs. Martha Gold, a widow from Woodbridge. The following winter he served as a supply pastor at Wallkill, in Orange (then a part of Ulster) County, New York. He was licensed by the Presbytery of New York before May 16, 1750, and ordained in the same year. Ayres's activities between 1750 and 1759 are obscure. Only two references to him have been found from this period: he was a witness to a will made at Hermitage, Ulster County, in 1753, and he attended only one of the annual meetings (in 1754) of the Synod of New York held during this period.

Most likely Ayres was itinerating and holding cottage prayer meetings in the Ulster–Orange County area in these years. They were dangerous ones. The Minis branch of the Delaware Indians was conducting raids in the area; the Wallkill district, already settled by whites, had to be temporarily evacuated. Many of the operations of the Seven Years War took place on the borders of Orange and Ulster Counties.

By the end of the 1750s relative peace had returned to the area. More settlers were arriving from the old Puritan parts of Long Island and from Northern Ireland. On November 28, 1758, Jacob Blackwell of Queens County, New York (father of Robert Blackwell, A.B. 1768), donated for the nominal sum of five shillings, and "for the Love and Affection which I bear unto the Presbyterian Congregation at Blooming Grove," about two and a half acres on which to construct a meetinghouse, cemetery, and school. Ayres organized this Ulster County congregation, most of whom were, or were descended from, migrants from Long Island, in 1759. Two years later he and his wife bought from Jacob Blackwell a farm of about 134 acres in Blooming Grove. For the rest of his life Ayres served as pastor at Blooming Grove and also at the neighboring Bethlehem church. He and Martha had two daughters, Martha and Mary, and accumulated more property. Ayres died between May and July 1764. He is buried in what is now a furnace room beneath the present Congregational Church of Blooming Grove between two of his successors, Samuel Parkhurst (A.B. 1757), and Benoni Bradner (A.B. 1755).

SOURCES: Date of birth: MS Geneal. Notes on pre-Rev. N.J. Families, C. C. Gardner Col., NjR; father's will: 30 *NJA*, 16; MS Ayres Family Geneal. created from variety of sources by Mrs. Constance K. Escher and Mr. John P. Furman, Enos Ayres File, PUA; brief account: Webster, *History*, 214, 586; mentions: Maclean, *History*, I, 115, 116; commencement notice: *Parker's Gaz. and Post-Boy*, Nov. 21, 1748; marriage: MS Ayres Marriage License (copy), Ayres File, PUA; Ayres as witness to will: B. Fernow, *Cal. of Wills . . . at Albany* (1896), 213; pastorates: *Hist. Orange Cty.*, 53-55, and passim; A. E. Corning, *Hist. of the Congregational Church of Blooming Grove* (1929), 3-8; Jacob Blackwell's Deed of Gift, copy of MS, on wall of Congregational church, Blooming Grove., N.Y.; *Rec. Pres. Church*, passim; Ayres's will: *N.Y. Wills*, VI (1897), 353.

Benjamin Chestnut

BENJAMIN CHESTNUT, A.B., A.M. 1751, Presbyterian clergyman, was born in England. His whereabouts before entering the College are unknown, but he was reputed to have been a shoemaker. Chestnut was licensed by the Presbytery of New York in 1748 or 1749. In 1750 he was called to a new Presbyterian church being organized at Timber Creek, or Blackwood (near present Woodbury), Gloucester County, New Jersey. The Reverend Charles Beatty of Neshaminy, Pennsylvania, preached the ordination sermon.

The area had been settled by, among others, a good number of Scotch-Irish. One of them, John Blackwood, was a prime organizer of the church and in 1751 donated for the nominal sum of two shillings sixpence an acre of ground on which to build it. Chestnut accepted the call on May 22, 1751, and was ordained by the Presbytery of New Brunswick on September 3, 1751. He served as pastor at Timber Creek and also part-time at neighboring Penn's Neck and Woodbury from then until 1753. Difficulties arose over the organization of the church and the payment of Chestnut's salary. In 1753 he requested dismissal and received it.

Chestnut then moved to New Brunswick, New Jersey, but soon decided to make his career in Pennsylvania. His movements there over the next ten years are difficult to trace. He apparently served as supply pastor to several churches in Chester and Philadelphia (now Montgomery) Counties, an area that included a large number of Scotch-Irish. Between 1753 and 1763 he was associated in one capacity or another with Presbyterian churches at Charlestown, Lower Providence, Fagg's Manor and Forks of the Delaware, Pennsylvania. In December 1756 Chestnut married Judith Smith, and they had one daughter, Sarah.

In 1763 the Presbytery of Philadelphia dismissed Chestnut, since there seemed no chance of his ever being paid regularly. He kept a school about twenty miles from Philadelphia, and on direction of the synod, visited the southern colonies on a missionary tour in 1765. In 1767 Chestnut's old congregation at Timber Creek joined nearby ones in calling him back to serve them. Though the congregations at Timber Creek, Woodbury, and Longacoming (now Berlin), seem to have spent most of their time squabbling amongst themselves over which was to pay what percent of Chestnut's salary and which was to receive how much of his services, he managed to serve them all until his death on July 21, 1775. He was survived by his second wife, Ruth, and his daughter. A Philadelphia newspaper recorded his death at the time of Boston's interdiction by the British thus: "he was a gentleman of great integrity and undissembled piety; a very considerable divine; a faithful, judicious, experimental preacher of the Gospel of Christ; and possessed of truly patriotic sentiments in his country's cause, a specimen of which appears in his having, among other legacies, bequeathed the sum of £25 to the supply of the distressed poor of Boston." Chestnut also left £25 to the College of New Jersey.

SOURCES: Much material concerning Chestnut is contradictory. Brief accounts: Webster, *History*, 646; Giger, Memoirs, 1; Alexander, *Princeton*, 1; ordination sermon: C. Beatty, *A Sermon Preached in Woodbury, at the Ordination of the Reverend Mr. Chestnut there. . . .* (1752); pastorates: *PMHB*, 9 (1885), 38-44; Blackwood church: *Sesqui-Centennial of the First Presbyterian Church. . . .* (1900), 3-9; obituary: *Penn. Packet*, July 31, 1775; will: 34 *NJA*, 90.

Hugh Henry

HUGH HENRY, A.B., Presbyterian clergyman, was the son of Hugh Henry. He may have been born in Ireland. After graduation he studied theology with the Reverend Samuel Blair at Fagg's Manor, Chester County, Pennsylvania. He was ordained by the New Side Presbytery of New Castle at Rehobeth, Maryland, before September 26, 1751.

Samuel Davies had hopes that he would do great work for the Presbyterians in Maryland. Beginning in 1750, Henry served simultaneously as pastor to several churches at places on inlets to Chesapeake Bay: the Wicomico church at Salisbury, the Rehobeth church, the Buckingham church, the Laurel church, and Manokin church at Princess Anne, Somerset County. After October 18, 1758, he served the Manokin church only. He married Sarah Handy, daughter of Colonel Isaac Handy, "Gent.," and a sister of Isaac Handy (A.B. 1761), with whom he had five children. Henry died, probably in Princess Anne, between November 8, 1762, and March 16, 1763, leaving a substantial estate of £686.

SOURCES: Hugh Henry File, PUA; for very brief accounts: Webster, *History*, 616; Carnahan and Alexander, MS Notes of Distinguished Graduates, NjP; Alexander, *Princeton*, 2; H. R. Ford, *Hist. of the Manokin Pres. Church, Princess Anne, Myd.* (1910), 18-19, 44-47; C. Torrence, *Old Somerset on the Eastern Shore of Myd.* (1935), 254-55; I. M. Page. *Old Buckingham by the Sea on the Eastern Shore of Maryland* (1936), 44-48, 52.

Israel Read

ISRAEL READ, A.B., A.M. 1751, Presbyterian clergyman, was born on June 24, 1718. In May 1747, the Old Side Synod of Philadelphia appointed a committee to examine Read for the ministry "and to give him a certificate if he be approved." He was, apparently, not approved, and must have gone to Elizabethtown or Newark shortly afterward to take his A.B. Read was licensed by the New Side Presbytery of New York almost immediately after graduating. In 1750 he joined the Presbytery of New Brunswick and was ordained pastor of the Presbyterian church at Bound Brook, Somerset County, New Jersey. From 1768 to 1786 Read divided his time between the Bound Brook church and the Presbyterian church in New Brunswick. He married Mary Campbell of New York, who died on January 30, 1770. Two sons and one daughter were living in 1785.

Although Read's life must have been a busy one (he was the first graduate of the College to become a member of the Synod of the Presbyterian church and was a trustee of the College from 1761 to 1793) almost no record of his activities has been found. In 1786 he began to cut down his pastoral responsibilities. On November 25, 1793, he was thrown from his carriage while driving near New Brunswick. Two days later he died of his injuries. His style of life had been modest but comfortable: the inventory of his estate was a little over £304. In his will he divided his silver and other possessions among his three children. An "old negro wench, Jean," was given her freedom; his daughter received a "negro girl named Isabel"; a "Negro man, Toone," was to be kept by his sons.

SOURCES: Israel Read File, PUA; Webster, *History*, 585-86; Giger, Memoirs, 1; Alexander, *Princeton*, 2; for undated marriage license, see: 22 *NJA*, 319; for will, see: 37 *NJA*, 292.

Richard Stockton

RICHARD STOCKTON, A.B., A.M. 1751, lawyer, landowner, and public official, was born in Princeton, New Jersey, on October 1, 1730, the son of Abigail Phillips and her husband, John Stockton, a well-to-do landowner, public official, and early patron of the College. Richard was prepared for college by two years at the Reverend Samuel Finley's academy at West Nottingham, Maryland. From there he was sent by his parents to the new College at Elizabethtown. After graduation Richard stayed in Newark to read law with David Ogden (Yale 1728), the leading lawyer in the province.

Stockton was licensed an attorney in 1754 and a counselor in 1758. Although the law was the most important focus of Stockton's career, nothing is known of the nature of his practice—except that it was extremely successful. Stockton swiftly established a large and lucrative practice not only in New Jersey (where he maintained an office in Newark) but in New York and Philadelphia as well. Over the years he instructed many legal apprentices, among them Joseph Reed (A.B. 1757), Jonathan Dickinson Sergeant (A.B. 1762), William Paterson (A.B. 1763), and a future president of the Continental Congress, Elias Boudinot, husband of Stockton's sister and brother of his wife.

Stockton's marriage to Annis Boudinot of Princeton came in about 1757. At his father's death in that year Stockton inherited some land and the family home in Princeton, along with responsibility for several younger brothers and sisters. Annis and Richard moved into the house, a simple Palladian villa christened by Annis "Morven," after the home of Fingal, mythical king of the Caledonians and hero of James Macpherson's enormously popular fake epic of 1762, the *Poems of Ossian*. The Stocktons enjoyed an extremely close and successful marriage. Annis wrote reams of bad Augustan poetry, Richard discovered a family coat of arms, and both of them filled Morven with fine furniture, pictures, and an extensive library. Over the years they had six children, among them Richard (A.B. 1779), Lucius Horatio (A.B. 1787),

Richard Stockton, A.B. 1748
BY JOHN WOLLASTON

Julia, who married Dr. Benjamin Rush (A.B. 1760), and Mary, who married Andrew Hunter (A.B. 1772).

Stockton was preoccupied with his profession and purely local affairs until the mid-1760s. He served as a trustee of the College from 1757 until his death and as clerk of the board of trustees from 1757 to 1765. In 1764 he was made sergeant at law (an old English title peculiar in America to New Jersey) and saw a change in his affairs. He would never become a public servant, he wrote to Joseph Reed in that year, "till I am convinced that by neglecting my own affairs I am doing more acceptable Service to God and Man." But events of the succeeding months brought a complete change in Stockton's views on public life.

With the passage of the Stamp Act in 1765, Stockton suggested that Americans should sit as members of Parliament. He urged New Jersey's assembly speaker Robert Ogden to be sure to send a delegation to the Stamp Act Congress. In November 1765, he even drew up "A

Draft Petition of New Jersey to the King Against Taxation without Representation," but this was not used by the Assembly.

Steady work had undermined Stockton's health; in 1766 he undertook a trip to Britain. Health restored, he reached London early in August, with a letter of introduction from Governor William Franklin. For a provincial lawyer he met with an astonishing reception in the capital. He presented in person an address from the trustees of the College to George III; he conferred about colonial affairs with the Marquis of Rockingham and Benjamin Franklin. Nor was social life neglected. He had an interview with Lord Chesterfield and was a guest at many country seats, including Rockingham's. He sent seeds and bulbs back to Morven. He even made a special trip to Alexander Pope's famed garden at Twickenham and had a plan of it drawn up. But a more important mission than measuring Pope's garden soon came to hand.

President Samuel Finley died on July 17, 1766, while Stockton must have been at sea. The trustees elected the Reverend John Witherspoon of Paisley, Scotland, as the new president. Stockton was commissioned to travel north to persuade Witherspoon to accept the post. Stockton's Caledonian reception was as warm as his English one had been. He was given the freedom of Edinburgh and tendered a dinner by the Lord Provost and Council. Stockton talked with Witherspoon and campaigned to have the Scottish clergy put heavy pressure on him to accept the American offer. Stockton was unable to persuade Mrs. Witherspoon, a feat subsequently accomplished by Benjamin Rush.

Stockton returned home late in 1767. He and Annis immediately proceeded to reproduce at Morven Pope's garden at Twickenham, right down to a grotto built of souvenirs such as a Roman brick from Dover Castle and a piece of George III's coronation chair. Stockton's trip to Britain had enhanced his status at home. Within a year of his return Governor Franklin made Stockton a member of New Jersey's governor's council.

On February 28, 1774, Governor Franklin nominated Stockton to the province's supreme court. Counted a moderate Whig in the governor's council, in December 1774, Stockton drafted "An Expedient for the Settlement of the American Disputes" to be sent to Lord Dartmouth. His plan suggested that America be independent of Parliament while retaining allegiance to the Crown. Stockton was active on the provincial council as late as November 24, 1775. Elected to the Continental Congress on June 22, 1776, he became a Signer of the Declaration of Independence. At home he was almost elected governor of New Jersey, though the post ultimately went to William Livingston. In Congress Stockton was appointed to several important committees. One of his tasks involved an investigation of American forces in the north. Reporting from Saratoga on October 28, he found that New Jersey soldiers were "marching with cheerfulness, but great part of the men barefooted and barelegged. . . . There is not a single shoe or stocking to be had in this part of the world, or I would ride a hundred miles through the woods and purchase them with my own money."

On November 23, while still in the north, Stockton was appointed to a committee charged with reinforcing Washington and trying to block General Howe. By then the main theater of military operations had shifted to New Jersey, as Washington retreated across the province toward Pennsylvania. General Howe offered an amnesty to all rebels who would sign an oath of allegiance to the king. Many accepted the offer. Princeton was evacuated. Most Whigs headed west across the Delaware to safety. Stockton made the mistake of evacuating his family east, to the Monmouth County home of a friend, John Covenhoven. Betrayed by Loyalists on his second night there, Stockton was made prisoner by the British and taken first to Perth Amboy, then to New York, where he was imprisoned.

Stockton, apparently, was treated so brutally by the British that on January 3, 1777, Congress requested Washington to investigate and protest. But at some time during this period Stockton made his private peace with the British and was released. "I was at Princeton from Saturday s'en night till Wednesday," President Witherspoon wrote to his son David (A.B. 1774) on March 17. "Judge Stockton is not well in health and is much spoken against for his conduct. He signed Howe's Declaration and gave his word of Honor that he would not meddle in the least in American affairs during the war." Stockton kept his word.

Back in Princeton Stockton found his family well but Morven sacked, partially burnt, and the family papers destroyed or dispersed. Stockton picked up the pieces of his life and resumed the practice of law. He even took on new law students. Some time during 1778 he developed cancer of the lip. It was removed in December 1778; the disease continued to spread. After a long period of ever-increasing pain, mitigated only slightly by drugs, Stockton died at Morven on February 28, 1781. He was buried not with his fellow Presbyterians but among his Quaker forebears outside the Stony Brook Meeting House.

SOURCES: No full-scale study of Stockton exists. Except on his renunciation of the American cause, the *DAB* is exemplary. See too: D. D. Egbert, ed., *Princeton Portraits* (1949), 176-78, and 10 *NJA*, 427-30n. The fullest account of Stockton, from which most of the quotations are drawn, is: H. Bill, *A House Called Morven, 1701-*

1954 (1954), 18-51. Stockton in Scotland: L. H. Butterfield, *John Witherspoon Comes to America* (1953); Witherspoon quotation, *LMCC*, II, 243. The Stocktons' marriage date is usually given as 1755. However, since Mrs. Aaron Burr was referring to Annis as "Annis Boudinet" as late as August 1757, it seems probable that the marriage took place after this date. Esther Burr, MS Journal, CtY, entry for August 30, 1757.

Mss: MHi, NjHi, NjP

Daniel Thane

DANIEL THANE, A.B., A.M. 1751, Presbyterian clergyman, was born in Scotland. He may have attended one of the colleges of the University of Aberdeen. In 1742 he sailed for America, most likely as a redemptioner (a person bound to work for a certain number of years in exchange for his passage). Thane was employed for about four years by Charles Clinton at Little Britain, Ulster County, New York, as tutor for Clinton's sons, Alexander (A.B. 1750), Charles, and James. When Alexander set off for the College in 1746 or 1747, Thane accompanied him. Thane probably studied with President Dickinson and tutor Caleb Smith before the College's formal opening. Thane was *Orator Salutatorious* at the College's first commencement. After receiving his degree, a New York newspaper reported, "he in a modest and decent Manner, first apologizing for his Insufficiency, and then having spoken of the Excellency of the liberal Arts and Sciences, and of the numberless Benefits they yield to Mankind in private and social life; addressed himself in becoming Salutations and thanks to his Excellency [Governor Belcher] and the Trustees, the President and whole Assembly: All which being performed in good Latin from his Memory, in a handsome oratorical Manner in the Space of about half an Hour."

After graduation Thane, like his classmate Enos Ayres, acted as a supply preacher at the Wallkill church, Ulster County, New York, and possibly studied with Aaron Burr. On April 8, 1749, Thane married Mary Clowes of Long Island. He was ordained by the Presbytery of New York and installed at the Presbyterian church at Connecticut Farms (now part of Elizabeth), New Jersey, on August 29, 1750. Except for a three-month missionary trip in 1754 to North Carolina and South Carolina, where he preached at the forks of the Broad and Saluda Rivers, Thane remained in New Jersey until 1757. It was probably in this period that the Thanes' only child, Catherine, was born.

With the reunion of the Presbyteries of New York and Philadelphia in 1758, Thane was dismissed and left free to join either the Presbytery of New Castle or that of Lewes. He chose the New Castle Presbytery and was soon installed as pastor of the united congregations of New Castle and Christiana Bridge, New Castle County, Delaware. He also served as pastor of the nearby White Clay Creek church from 1757 to 1763. He kept up his Scots associations by joining the St. Andrew's Society of Philadelphia in 1759.

In 1763 charges of drunkenness were brought against Thane. He may have been seriously ill at the time, for he was cleared by the presbytery "on the ground that the appearances which were against him might easily be accounted for from his disordered state of mind and body." Thane afterward dissolved his connections with his congregations. He may have returned briefly to Ulster County before dying on Staten Island in 1763.

SOURCES: Thane's background and immigration: Daniel Thane File, PUA; E. W. Spaulding, *His Excellency George Clinton* (1938), 6-8; Thane's commencement oration: *Parker's Gaz. and Post-Boy*, Nov. 21, 1748; Thane's marriage and death: *NYGBR*, 50 (1919), 161; pastorates: J. M. Dickson, *The Goodwill Memorial* (1880), 25-26; Hatfield, *Elizabeth*, 639-40; Webster, *History*, 586; *An Historical Catalogue of the St. Andrew's Society of Philadelphia* (1907), 338-39.

CLASS OF 1749

John Brown, A.B.

William Burnet, A.B.

John Hoge, A.B.

Thomas Kennedy, A.B.

John Moffat, A.B.

John Todd, A.B.

Eliezer Whittlesey, A.B.

John Brown

JOHN BROWN, A.B., Presbyterian clergyman, was born in County Limerick, Ireland, the son of Jennett Stevenson and her husband, James Brown, in 1728. In about 1722 Brown's older sister Janet married Archibald Stuart (or Stewart). Stuart, who had engaged in political and religious opposition to the government, fled to Pennsylvania about 1725, leaving his family behind in Ireland. Freed from fear of arrest by an amnesty in 1732, Stuart sent for his family, which included his wife, two children, and Janet Stuart's four-year-old brother, John Brown. In 1738 the family moved south down the Valley of Virginia to what is now Augusta County, Virginia, and settled about midway between present Staunton and the Rockfish Gap. There, on the unsettled frontier, Brown grew to manhood.

The impulse that sent Brown to the College of New Jersey is unknown; possibly he had been converted by Samuel Davies's preaching. Soon after graduation Brown was licensed by the Presbytery of New Castle and sent home to the Valley as a missionary. In August 1753, Brown was called to serve the Timber Ridge and New Providence congregations near what is now Fairfield, Rockbridge County, Virginia, just to the south of his sister's home in Augusta County. Brown was ordained at Fagg's Manor, Pennsylvania, on October 11, 1753. Samuel Davies, about to leave for England on a fund raising tour for the College, preached the ordination sermon, with, he wrote in his diary, "a good deal of inaccuracy and confusion, though with some tender sense of the subject. I have hardly ever thought myself in so solemn a posture as when invoking the God of heaven, with my hand on the head of the candidate. May the Lord be his support under the burden of that office which he has assumed, I doubt not, with very honest and generous intentions!"

Good intentions were hard to carry out on the Virginia frontier in the 1750s. The Seven Years War was beginning, and the area was a scene of major operations. With Indians on the one side, and Anglicans and slightly less pernicious Old Sides on the other, Brown lived a busy life. In 1755 he joined Samuel Davies, Alexander Craighead, Robert Henry (A.B. 1751), and John Wright (A.B. 1752), in petitioning the Synod of New York to establish a new presbytery in Virginia, to be called Hanover, in opposition to the Old Side Presbytery of Donegal. In 1755 he also took the risky step—in the face of Virginia's established Anglican church—of performing two marriage ceremonies. He did not repeat the ceremony until 1781. It was probably around 1755 that

Brown married Margaret Preston, daughter of a prominent Valley family. Visting the Browns in 1775 Philip Fithian (A.B. 1772) found Margaret "a woman of uncommon understanding. . . . Her Ideas are extensive & distinct. She speaks slow—pronounces her Words something on the Scotch Accent—Her Style, or Way of speaking, is something more than eligant & classical; it is peculiarly forceable; as it comes from a Female, & is unexpected.—She was at no Loss in talking of any triffling Incident which has taken place at Princeton." John and Margaret Brown produced two daughters and five sons. Three of the latter achieved considerable eminence in later years (two became United States senators, one United States minister to France).

Constant Indian raids caused considerable tension in the Valley in the 1750s. The Reverend Hugh McAden (A.B. 1753), visiting Brown in the 1750s, recorded in his diary that Brown had set aside a day of fasting and prayer "on account of the wars and many murders committed by the savage Indians on the back inhabitants." The following year Brown was preaching to troops organized to quell the tribes. The see-saw battle between Indians and settlers continued until well into the 1760s.

In about 1764 Brown found time to take over general supervision of a struggling academy, which later evolved into Liberty Hall Academy and finally into Washington and Lee University. He continued in this role until about 1774. In 1767, for reasons now obscure, Brown gave up the pastorate of Timber Ridge, though he continued to serve as pastor at New Providence for several years. The Brown household must have been a happy one: "the Hours always fly like Sun-Beams without either Observation, or sensible Time, when we are at instructive, facetious Mr Brown's," wrote Philip Fithian on a visit in January 1776.

By the 1780s Brown's sons had moved across the mountains to Kentucky. It was perhaps at this time that Brown wrote, "What a Buzzel is amongst People about Kentuck? to hear people speak of it one would think it was a new found Paradise and I doubt not if it is such a place as represented. Ministers will have thin congregations but why need I fear that? Ministers are moveable goods as well as others and stand in need of good land as any do for they are bad farmers." Brown followed his sons to the new paradise in about 1796. He proved to be a passable farmer: in the tax books of Woodford County, Kentucky, for February 10, 1798, he was listed as owning ten slaves and seven horses. In Woodford County Brown continued as a minister in the service of the Pisgah church. He died in 1803 at "Liberty Hall," Frankfort County, the home of his son, Senator John Brown (Class of 1777).

SOURCES: Brown's ancestry and immigration: H. W. Wilson, *The Tinkling Spring, Headwater of Freedom* (1954), 32. For many reasons this seems more accurate an account than that in B. E. Hardin, "Dr. Preston W. Brown, 1775-1826, His Family and Descendents," *Filson Club Hist. Quart.*, 19 (1945), 3-28; Davies quotation: Webster, *History*, 656; Pilcher, *Samuel Davies*, 159; Brown's marriages, McAden quotation, and continuing incursions of Indians: J. A. Waddell, *Annals of Augusta County, Va.* (1886), 85, 176; Kegley, *Va. Frontier*, 289; O. Crenshaw, *General Lee's College* (1960), 6; O. F. Morton, *A Hist. of Rockbridge County, Va.* (1920), 247; Brown on Ky.: F. H. Hart, *The Valley of Virginia in the Amer. Rev.* (1942), 74; Brown's property in 1798: Hardin, above, 22 n7; Fithian's quotations: *Fithian Journal*, II, 141, 169.

William Burnet

WILLIAM BURNET, A.B., A.M. 1752, physician, public official and farmer, was born at Lyon's Farms, between Newark and Elizabethtown, New Jersey, on December 2, 1730, the son of Hannah and Dr. Ichabod Burnet, a prosperous physician prominent in local affairs who had been educated in Edinburgh.

William, as Latin Salutatorian, was the best student in his class. After graduation he studied medicine, first with a Dr. Staats in New York City and then with his father. After completing his studies Burnet set up what became a very successful medical practice in Newark, where except for the years of the Revolution he remained for the rest of his life. On January 23, 1754, Burnet married Mary Camp, with whom he had eleven children, among them Ichabod (A.B. 1775), Jacob (A.B. 1791), and George Whitefield (A.B. 1792). One of the founders of the New Jersey Medical Society, he was chosen president in 1767. He was for many years an elder of the First Presbyterian Church in Newark and was a trustee of the Newark Academy.

In May 1775, Burnet became chairman of the Newark Committee of Safety and shortly thereafter was made chairman of the Essex County Committee of Safety. He was active in the arrest of the royal governor, William Franklin. In 1776 he helped recruit and send several military companies to help in the defense of New York.

Made presiding judge of the Essex County courts, Burnet was busy in prosecuting Loyalist neighbors, including several members of the Anglican branch of the Ogden family. He set up a military hospital in Newark and paid for it out of his own pocket. Sent by New Jersey to the Continental Congress in 1776–1777, he was made physician and surgeon-general of the Eastern District. He was sent to the Continental Congress again in 1780. By July 23 of the following year he was chief physician and surgeon of the military hospital at West Point.

William Burnet, A.B. 1749
ATTRIBUTED TO JOHN TRUMBULL

With the peace Burnet resumed his Newark medical practice and also farmed. At some time after the death of his first wife in 1781 he married Gertrude Gouverneur, widow of Anthony Rutgers, with whom he had three more children. Elected president of the New Jersey Medical Society for a second time in 1786, Burnet revived the old custom of giving the inaugural address in Latin. Burnet died in Newark on October 7, 1791, dividing his considerable estate among his many children. Three years after his death, the New Jersey legislature authorized the manumission of ten of Burnet's slaves, perhaps because they had become too much of a burden on the estate.

SOURCES: The *DAB* sketch of Burnet is full, but can be supplemented by: Joseph P. Bradley, "William Burnet, M.D.," *PMHB*, 3 (1879), 308-14. For will, see: 13 *NJA*, 59; manumissions: *NJHSP*, 12 (1927), 152.

PUBLICATIONS: "Dr. Burnet's Dissertation on the Nature and Importance of our Indefatigable Researches after Medical Knowledge; Together with A Few Observations on the Effects of Opium in the Cure of Dysentery [1787]," in *The Rise, Minutes and Proceedings of the New Jersey Medical Society* (1875).

Mss: PPAmP, PHi, MHi, NjHi, ViU

John Hoge

JOHN HOGE, A.B., Presbyterian clergyman, was the son of Gwenthelen Bowen Davis and her husband John Hoge, who founded the village of Hogestown a few miles east of Carlisle, Pennsylvania. After graduation Hoge applied to the New Side Presbytery of New Castle for licensing, but the presbytery refused, "lest his genius not be fit for the ministry," Hoge persevered and finally received his license on October 10, 1753. He was ordained in 1755 and immediately took up a pastorate at the northern entrance to the Valley of Virginia at Occoquan in Frederick County. Hoge's grandfather, William Hoge, donated land for a church and cemetery, while Hoge became the congregation's organizer and first pastor. Hoge also served as pastor of Presbyterian congregations at nearby places: at Cedar Creek, Frederick County, 1755–1780; at Tuscarora, Frederick County, 1760–1776; and at Back Creek, Berkeley County, 1760–1780.

In the spring of 1775 Philip Fithian (A.B. 1772) visited Hoge and his family at their "well-chosen, rich, & in many ways agreeable Farm," at what was then Stephenburg, Virginia, a few miles south of Frederick. Hoge, for causes unclear, was without a congregation. Fithian found him "a lusty well made Man. . . . He is remarkably chatty, & in some Cases facetious; Has the Reputation, I believe justly, of a sound, well-meaning, Man—I grieve for his present State; he has a large family, no way of supporting it, has been dismiss'd from this Society near three Years, the People in general, it is said without an Exception, are highly enraged at several Parts of his Conduct, they have never invited him to preach, & when he does, they never attend, on his Sermons." Fithian was not able to discover the cause of Hoge's difficulties with the congregation; he did discover that Hoge was jealous of him.

In 1780 Hoge moved northward to Pennsylvania. From that time until his death he served as a minister without charge—a sort of roving missionary—in, successively, the Presbyteries of Carlisle and Huntington in south-central Pennsylvania. When the latter presbytery was organized Hoge served as moderator and delivered the inaugural sermon. He seldom attended church conventions. In 1790 he was living in a household in Northumberland County, Pennsylvania. He died on February 11, 1807.

SOURCES: Most sources confuse Hoge with his nephew, John Hoge (1760-1824), a Penn. congressman. *The Scotch-Irish in America: Proceedings, 9th Congress* (1900), 273-84; Webster, *History*, 662-63; *Fithian Journal*, II, 14, 26-27; W. J. Gibson, *Hist. of the Presbytery of Huntington* (1874), 211-12; *Historical Memorial of the Centennial Anniversary of the Presbytery of Huntington* (1896), 42.

Thomas Kennedy

THOMAS KENNEDY, A.B., has not been identified. His name was spelled "Kenneday" in the minutes of the Board of Trustees. The College's catalogue of 1770 indicates that he had died by that year. The 1773 catalogue indicates that he was thought to have been a clergyman, but this may be a printer's error. No other information seems to be available.

John Moffat

JOHN MOFFAT, A.B., Presbyterian clergyman and schoolmaster, was the son of Margaret and William Moffat, who migrated from Scotland —possibly from Normangill, Lanarkshire—to Woodbridge, Middlesex County, New Jersey, sometime before 1746. Whether Moffat was born in Scotland or New Jersey is unknown. He was possibly inspired to attend college by his pastor, John Pierson, one of the founders and first trustees of the College of New Jersey. Moffat was licensed by the Presbytery of New York on May 30, 1750, and ordained on October 4, 1751. He immediately took up the pastorate of the Goodwill (or Wallkill) church near the present town of Montgomery, Orange (then Ulster) County, New York.

Between the time of his licensure and ordination Moffat married Margaret Little, daughter of John Little, "Gentleman," of "Stonefield," a plantation in New Windsor, Ulster County. Little died in 1752, leaving to Margaret "a negro Winch Rachel" and also leaving to John and Margaret Moffat's as yet unborn oldest son half of his plantation. (The Moffats eventually saw eight children grow to maturity.) Moffat was named executor of the estate.

Moffat served the Goodwill church until some time between 1765 and 1769. During his pastorate a church and parsonage were built. When he retired from the ministry the Reverend John Blair succeeded him. Moffat did not abandon the ministry completely. When Blair left in 1771 Moffat filled in from time to time, performing baptisms and other ceremonies. Moffat's activities after his early retirement from the ministry are not completely clear. The Moffats apparently lived at "Stonefield," Mrs. Moffat's father's place. Since at his death Moffat left, besides his books and a large amount of real estate, substantial quantities of grain, flax and wool, it would appear that he farmed extensively. The large house itself was one-and-a-half stories with a basement.

The Moffat family lived in the basement, and in the upper stories Moffat conducted a classical school, known locally as "Moffat's Academy." Although the school was broken up in the early years of the Revolution, it was operating again in the late 1770s. At the school Moffat educated many of the children of the area, among them Alexander, Charles, George, and DeWitt, the sons of his nearest neighbor, General James Clinton. Clinton, like other parents, paid for his children's education in wheat and corn. Moffat died on March 10, 1787.

SOURCES: R. B. Moffat, *Moffat Genealogies* (1909), 22-44; G. Anjou, *Ulster County, N.Y., Probate Records* (1906), II, 162-63; John Little's will: J. M. Dickson, *The Goodwill Memorial* (1880), 26-27, 32-33; *Hist. Orange Cty.*, 211-12.

Mss: NjP (a few sermons)

John Todd

JOHN TODD, A.B., Presbyterian clergyman, schoolmaster, miller and planter, was born in County Armagh, Ireland, in 1719, the son of Robert Todd and his wife, Ann Smith. In 1737, after his wife's death, Robert Todd and his family migrated to Pennsylvania, where they eventually settled in Lower Providence, Chester County. Young Todd possibly earned his living as a weaver after the family's arrival in America. The decision that sent him to the College of New Jersey is unknown: perhaps there was some connection between the Todd family and William Tennent, who came from the same area of Ireland.

A few months after graduating from the College, on March 7, 1750, Todd presented himself to the Presbytery of New Brunswick for licensing. The presbytery put him through stiff trials and licensed him June 13, 1750. In Virginia, for several years Samuel Davies had been forced to minister alone to scattered and ever-growing congregations of Presbyterians. He had received some assistance from the notorious New Light, James Davenport, and had come close to persuading Jonathan Edwards to join him. Davies constantly urged the synod to send him help. In May 1751, the Presbytery of New Brunswick finally responded by asking Todd to take the assignment. After consideration, Todd accepted, and was ordained June 25, 1751. Davies had ministered to seven separate congregations. Todd—with some opposition from Governor Dinwiddie, who thought that both Davies and Todd were spreading themselves too thin—was finally licensed as a dissenting minister by Williamsburg and took over four of Davies's churches.

Todd was installed at his new church at Gun Spring, Louisa County (near present Richmond), in November 1752. Davies preached the installation sermon. Within a short time Todd proved himself an excellent preacher and an efficient pastor. He became one of Davies's closest advisers and persuaded him to make a fund-raising trip to Britain for the College of New Jersey.

After Davies left Virginia to become president of the College, Todd became the acknowledged leader of Presbyterians in mid-to-western Virginia. Over the years he was in the forefront of the movement to disestablish the Anglican church in Virginia. "The experience of all the Churches Since *Constantine*, shew the absurdity of Establishments," Todd wrote to Thomas Jefferson when the latter sent him a copy of his Bill for Establishing Religious Freedom. "*Virtue and pure religion* do better without earthly emoluments than with. . . . I am also confident that people of all sorts of religion will be the real friends of the State that secures them their rights religious and civil."

Todd was a man of great energy and many interests. He maintained a classical school in his home (the first in the area), and also gave postgraduate training to aspiring ministers. He was active in the establishment of Hampden-Sydney College and helped obtain the charter for Transylvania Seminary in Kentucky, to which he contributed scientific apparatus and part of his library. In 1762 he found time to write an extensive treatise in favor of the use of modern psalms in church services. His political activities were as extensive as his religious. Apparently a well-tempered Whig, late in 1775 he became a member of Louisa County's second Committee of Safety. On December 4, 1775, the committee passed a resolution thanking Todd and another clergyman "for the unwearied application of their abilities in the service of their country, as well as in checking the wild irregular sallies of those who would aim at too much, as in rousing those lethargick wretches, who would timely submit to a deprivation of their rights and liberties, to a proper sense of their danger and duties." In 1777–1778 Todd was both chaplain to and colonel in the Louisa County militia.

Sometime before 1758 Todd married Margaret Thompson, daughter of John Thompson, a merchant of Hanover County. The Todds had nine children. It was perhaps his mercantile connection that inspired Todd to build a mill on the South Anna River. The mill, apparently, prospered greatly; Todd sold considerable amounts of grain to the American armies during the Revolution. Todd died on July 27, 1793, on the way home from delivering a sermon in Albemarle County. For a frontier minister, he had accumulated an astonishing amount of property: several houses and farms, his mill, government stocks, considerable personalty, well over 20,000 acres of land in Kentucky, lands in other parts of Virginia, and upwards of fourteen slaves.

SOURCES: L. B. Todd, "Some Notes on the Todd Family," MS 1966 typescript, PPPr-Hi; Todd genealogy and early career: John Todd File, PUA; "Data Relating to John Todd: Extracts from the New Brunswick Presbytery Minutes," typescript, PPPrHi; Pilcher, *Samuel Davies*, 96-99; Davies, *The Duties, Difficulties and Reward of the Faithful Minister. A Sermon, Preached at the Installation of the Revd. Mr. John Todd . . .* (1754); *Jefferson Papers*, III, 69; C. F. James, *Documentary History of the Struggle for Religious Liberty in Virginia* (1900), 220-40; Todd, *An Humble Attempt towards the Improvement of Psalmody: the Propriety, Necessity and Use, of Evangelical Psalms in Christian Worship. . . .* (1763); M. H. Harris, *Hist. of Louisa County, Va.* (1936), 52, 66, 184; *Va. Gaz.* (Purdie), Dec. 29, 1775, 3; will: *Louisa County Will Book*, III, 528-31, typescript copies in John Todd File, NjP and at PPPr-Hi.

PUBLICATIONS: see STE

Mss: PPPrHi

Eliezer Whittlesey

ELIEZER WHITTLESEY, A.B., Presbyterian clergyman, was born in Wethersfield, Connecticut, on March 25, 1711, the son of Lydia Way and her husband, Jabez Whittlesey. The elder Whittlesey was prominent in both church and civil affairs in the town. At some time Eliezer moved to Salisbury, Connecticut, where his name appears in the church records until 1740. His occupation during this period is unknown. One day in the winter of 1741–1742 Whittlesey appeared at the home of Aaron Burr in Newark, carrying a letter of recommendation from the Reverend Joseph Bellamy, the Connecticut New Light theologian. Thirty years old, he wanted to study with Burr in hopes of becoming a minister. Burr took him in, and shortly reported to Bellamy that Whittlesey "makes good progress in learning." But Burr had typically New Light doubts about the depth of Whittlesey's spiritual convictions. "He was not converted in the way you think necessary," Burr wrote to Bellamy, "and that I have thought so, though now I am in some doubt of it. I have met with others of God's dear people, who don't tell of such *particular* submission as we have insisted on, though the substance of the thing may be found in all."

Whittlesey apparently did not manage to complete his studies with Burr. He was next heard of five years later. On August 3, 1747, the Reverend Samuel Finley reported to Bellamy from his new academy in West Nottingham, Maryland, that that very day Whittlesey was setting off to attend the new college in Elizabethtown after having studied with Finley for an unspecified length of time. "He has made considerable proficiency in learning," Finley wrote. "I have been well pleased with his company and hope he will be useful in the Church."

Whittlesey had little time to be useful to the church after his graduation from the College. He spent the winter after his commencement moving from one lonely log church on the borders of Maryland and Pennsylvania to another. Licensed by the New Side Presbytery of New Castle sometime in that winter, he served as pastor to the scattered congregations of Lower Chanceford, Peach Bottom, and Slate Ridge, all in York County. "I have (by order of Presbytery)," Whittlesey wrote to Joseph Bellamy in May 1750, "spent this winter at Deer Creek and the adjacent congregations, and have chiefly kept close in my study a groaning under and struggling with and fighting against, what you call melancholy though I call it by another name; but be it what it will, it has (as I have often said to myself alone) rendered me as unable to study or preach as I am to create, and so I have spent the greater part of the winter, lamenting myself as being under a most unhappy necessity of wearing away my remaining days in the most painful idleness, scarce able so much as to attempt the performance of any duty whatsoever and if at any time I did attempt. . . . how I have gone out and preached is quite beyond me to describe; now thro the whole, what has been peculiarly distressing and condemning to me is that when I would be out among the people, talking on trifles of no value, I have felt well, and had some use of my reason at times, but as soon as I would enter my study and attempt any of the duties of it, I was still as one void of reason and religion, filled with and carried before every wickedness, before a naughty torrent, which proves it not melancholick but diabolick, as I have often concluded."

Only one thing gave him hope, Whittlesey confided to Bellamy: the reading of Jonathan Edwards's *A Treatise Concerning Religious Affections* (1746). "I chuse his religion before all others, let it turn as it may with me," Whittlesey wrote.

Things did not turn well for Whittlesey. On July 3, 1753, Samuel Finley wrote to Joseph Bellamy thus: "Mr. Whittlesey left my house on a Thursday morning cheerful and in pretty good health, preached next Sabbath at Muddy Creek not designing to continue there longer; on Monday was taken sick with a pleurisy in a cold house and a cold time; continued in pain till Saturday and then gave up the ghost." He had died on December 21, 1752, leaving his watch to Joseph Bellamy and his horse to the Reverend John Rodgers.

SOURCES: Brief account: Webster, *History*, 653-54; parentage and date of birth: *NEHGR*, 20 (1866), 319; C. B. Whittelsey, *Genealogy of the Whittelsey–Whittlesay Family* (1941), 64; quotations: Webster, *History*, 653, and Finley to Bellamy, August 3, 1747; Whittlesey to Bellamy, May 8, 1750; Finley to Bellamy, July 3, 1753; all in Webster/Bellamy Transcripts, PPPrHi.

Mss: NN, PPPrHi (only as noted above)

CLASS OF 1750

Hugh Bay, A.B.

James Beard, A.B.

Alexander Clinton, A.B.

Daniel Farrand, A.B.

Jacobus Frelinghuysen, A.B.

Simeon Mitchell, A.B.

Hugh Bay

HUGH BAY, A.B., lawyer or physician, has proved to be elusive. He is reputed to have been the brother of Andrew Bay, a weaver who emigrated from Ireland and was ordained a Presbyterian clergyman by the Presbytery of New Castle before 1748. Many Hugh Bays were living at the time. Writing to his father in June 1752, Joseph Shippen, Jr. (A.B. 1752), said that Samuel Livermore (A.B. 1752) had entrusted a large sum of money to a Hugh Bay and expected it to be recovered. Shippen added that Bay had received a license to practice law at "York Town"—whether in Pennsylvania or in Virginia is uncertain. What is clear is that two other sources refer to the Reverend Andrew Bay's brother Hugh as a graduate of the College who practiced medicine at Herbert's Cross Roads (now Churchville), near Deer Creek, in Harford County, Maryland. Andrew Bay became pastor there in 1760, had an extremely stormy career, and left in 1767. No further record of Hugh Bay has been found. However, a Maryland census of 1776 lists a "Jennet Bay, Sr.," living in Bush River, Lower Hundred, Harford County. She was 53 years old and had six minors in her household: William Bay (20), Hugh Bay (18), Jennet Bay, Jr. (18), Alexander Bay (12), and Elizabeth and Sarah Bay, both aged 16. Jennet Bay, Sr., may well have been Hugh Bay's widow; the fact that her youngest child was 12 in 1776 suggests that Hugh Bay may have died in the mid-1760s. Note of his death was made in the College's catalogue of 1770.

SOURCES: Two references to Hugh Bay as Harford County physician: Webster, *History*, 573, and W.T.L. Kieffer, *A Brief History of the Presbyterian Church of Churchville, Harford County, Md.* (1886), 19; Shippen letter: Shippen Papers, NjP; census: G. M. Brumbaugh, *Maryland Records* (1967), 122. The Hugh Bay who appears in later Maryland records seems to be the Hugh Bay who was 18 in 1776. No Bay genealogy has been located.

James Beard

JAMES BEARD, A.B., A.M. Yale 1754, lawyer and public official, was born on August 28, 1728, in Stratford, Connecticut, the son of Joanna Walker and her husband, James Beard. After graduation from the College Beard read law and settled in Derby, Connecticut. On October 31, 1754, Beard married Ruth Holbrook, who bore him eight children before her death from smallpox in May 1778. Beard subsequently married, in December 1781, Mrs. Mary Hobart of Guilford, Connecticut. No children appear to have been born of his second marriage.

Beard early achieved prominence in Derby, serving his town as a selectman in 1762, 1765–1766, and from 1777 through 1781. Derby sent Beard as its deputy to the Connecticut General Assembly in 1774–1775, in 1777, in 1779–1780, and again in 1785–1786. He also served as a judge of New Haven County's court of common pleas for many years. In 1783 Derby's Congregational church drew up a new confession of faith that rejected the Half-Way Covenant, which had permitted the baptism of the children of members not in full communion. Beard assisted in drafting the document.

Beard was a prominent local participant in the Revolution, becoming a member of Derby's Committee of Inspection in December 1775. He served in the military as well, being appointed in January 1777 a captain in a state militia unit assigned to assist the Continental army. But in 1786 Beard's public career came to an abrupt end. While a member of the state legislature Beard had been put in control of accounts relating to confiscated Loyalist estates. In 1786 charges were brought against Beard in the legislature that maintained he had misused the funds. The precise circumstances of the case are now obscure, but Beard appears to have ended—perhaps because of fluctuations in currency—by owing the state a considerable sum. In any case, strongly denying any wrong-doing, he resigned from the legislature.

Beard's public difficulties followed him home to Derby. Charges, based upon the proceedings in the legislature, were brought against him in his church. The church prepared a confession for Beard to sign. He refused, and the church excommunicated him: "henceforth we shall exercise no watch over, nor treat him with any respect as a brother until he come to repentance." Beard appears to have moved immediately to Trumbull, Connecticut, where he died in December 1812, without having left any further mark in the public record. When his estate was settled in 1815, $433.51 remained to be divided among his heirs.

SOURCES: Date of birth, parentage, some vital data: Ruth Beard, *A Genealogy of the Descendants of Widow Martha Beard of Milford, Conn.* (1915), 17-18, 15-16; place of birth: Stratford Vital Records, vol. LR5, p. 28, Barbour Col., Conn. State Lib., Hartford; death of first wife: *NEHGR*, 84 (1930), 138; public career: *Rec. State Conn.*, I, VI; public career, church: S. Orcutt, *Hist. of Derby, Conn.* (1880), 175, 186, 188, 204, 283-85, 701, 793, 799; estate: Probate Record File, Conn. State Lib.

Alexander Clinton

ALEXANDER CLINTON, A.B., A.M. 1753, surgeon apothecary, was born at Little Britain, Ulster (now part of Orange) County, New York, the son of Charles Clinton and his wife, Elizabeth Denniston, on April 28, 1732. Clinton's parents, fairly well-to-do minor dissenting gentry, chartered a ship and in company with others migrated from Corbay, County Longford, Ireland, to New York in 1729. Charles Clinton purchased considerable property in the Highlands Precinct, Ulster County, and became an important public figure in the province.

Alexander and his brothers were tutored by Daniel Thane (A.B. 1748), who accompanied his young charge to the College of New Jersey in 1746 or 1747. After graduation Clinton studied medicine in New York with the Scots Dr. Peter Middleton, one of the foremost physicians in the city. It is possible that Clinton witnessed Middleton and Dr. John Bard make one of the first dissections of a human body for purposes of medical instruction in America in about 1752. After finishing his studies Clinton returned to Little Britain, set up shop as an apothecary and began the practice of medicine. "He excelled in everything to which he turned his attention," a contemporary recalled. "He was a good classic scholar, a great physician, a considerable poet, an excellent musician, and understood the use of the broad sword in a superior degree; but what furnished and gave lustre to a truly great character was, that he was a most placid, agreeable, benevolent, friendly being beloved and highly respected by every person who knew him."

Clinton married Mary Kane (or Keen) in November 1757. Not long afterward he contracted smallpox and died at Shawangunk, New York, on March 11, 1758.

SOURCES: Alexander Clinton File, PUA; E. W. Spaulding, *His Excellency George Clinton* (1938), 1-7; D. Hosack, *Memoir of DeWitt Clinton* (1829), 139-40; will: G. Anjou, *Ulster County, N.Y., Probate Records* (1906), II, 160.

Daniel Farrand

DANIEL FARRAND, A.B., A.M. 1753, Yale, 1777, Congregational clergyman, was born in Milford, Fairfield County, Connecticut, in 1722. As a young man he was unusually attached to books, and had an almost photographic memory. He was converted in 1740 or 1741, most likely in the fall of 1740, during George Whitefield's tour of New England. "After many weeks of most painful distress and conviction," an early nineteenth-century memoralist recorded, Farrand "was hopefully brought to bow at the feet of Jesus." Probably quite poor, he studied with the Reverend James Graham in Southbury, Connecticut, and entered Yale College in 1746. In about 1748 Farrand transferred to the

College of New Jersey. He had known President Burr, also from Fair-field, for some time.

After graduation Farrand studied theology. Refusing an offer to succeed to Jonathan Edwards's pulpit in Northampton, Massachusetts, after officiating there for thirty Sundays, in 1752 he was ordained pastor of the Congregational church in South Canaan, Litchfield County, Connecticut, where he remained until his death on May 28, 1803. He married Jerusha Boardman, the youngest daughter of the Reverend Daniel Boardman, Congregational minister at New Milford, Connecticut, on March 25, 1755. The Farrands had nine children.

With a large family and a small salary, Farrand made ends meet by preparing young men from western Connecticut for college. He had New Divinity inclinations but seems to have got on well with members of all Calvinist factions. Possessing a dry but kindly wit, he was often called upon to settle disputes between quarreling groups. He attended over one hundred church conventions, and was instrumental in per-suading Jonathan Edwards to accept the presidency of the College of New Jersey.

SOURCES: Daniel Farrand File, PUA; Sprague, *Annals*, I, 490-92; A. Goodenough, *The Clergy of Litchfield County* (1909), 48-50, 189-90; *Conn. Evangelical Maga-zine*, 4 (1803), 71-74; New Divinity leanings: Stiles, *Literary Diary*, II, 395; Ed-wards's presidency: ibid., III, 4.

PUBLICATIONS: see STE

MSS: PHi

Jacobus Frelinghuysen

JACOBUS [or JAMES] FRELINGHUYSEN, A.B., Dutch Reformed clergyman, was the son of Eva Terhune and her husband, Theodorus Jacobus Frelinghuysen, the Dutch Reformed clergyman who was one of the central figures of the Great Awakening. Jacobus was born most likely at Raritan, Somerset County, New Jersey. It was probably Theodorus's close friendship with the Tennents that sent Jacobus to the College of New Jersey.

By May 10, 1751, Frelinghuysen had accepted calls from Dutch Re-formed churches at Marbletown, Rochester (Ulster County), and Wa-warsing, New York, before he decided to travel, along with his brother Ferdinandus, to the Netherlands in order to be ordained. After suc-cessful examination and "signing the Formulae of Concord, promising to read the Forms of Baptism and the Supper without change, & repudiating the condemned opinions of Rev. Bekker and Prof. Roel," Jacobus and Ferdinandus were ordained by the Classis of Amsterdam on July 3, 1752. Either before or, more likely, after his ordination Jacobus studied in Utrecht.

Jacobus and Ferdinandus sailed for America in April 1753. While at sea both contracted smallpox. Ferdinandus died on June 11 and Jacobus on June 19, 1753. Their deaths led to a successful movement to permit ordination by the Coetus of New York so as to avoid the unnecessary dangers of travel.

SOURCES: James Frelinghuysen File, PUA; *Ecclesiastical Records of the State of New York*, v, 3169, 3255, 3256, 3263-64, 3284, 3375; J. R. Tanis, *Dutch Calvinistic Pietism in the Middle Colonies* (1967), 78, 92-93; C. E. Corwin, *A Manual of the Reformed Church in America* (1922), 334.

Simeon Mitchell

SIMEON MITCHELL, A.B., was an aspirant Presbyterian clergyman. After graduation Mitchell studied with the Reverend Samuel Finley in Maryland. Along with John Wright (A.B. 1751), he was sent south to Virginia at some time in 1752. On May 29, 1753, the Reverend James Davenport reported to Joseph Bellamy that "Mr Simeon Mitchel, a promising youth who was upon trials with Mr Wright & upon the point of Licensure, died of ye smallpox, as perhaps you have heard, last winter."

SOURCES: Samuel Finley to Joseph Bellamy, August 1, 1751; James Davenport to Joseph Bellamy, May 29, 1753; both in Webster/Bellamy Transcripts, PPPrHi.

CLASS OF 1751

Jonathan Badger, A.B.

Samuel Clark, A.B.

Alexander Gordon, A.B.

Robert Henry, A.B.

Samuel MacClintock, A.B.

Henry Martin, A.B.

Benjamin Youngs Prime, A.B.

Robert Ross, A.B.

Nathaniel Scudder, A.B.

David Thurston, A.B.

Jonathan Badger

JONATHAN BADGER, A.B., A.M. 1754, College tutor, was born in Union, Connecticut, on December 4, 1729, the son of Captain Daniel Badger and his wife, Patience Durkee. After graduation Badger served as a tutor in the College from 1752 until late in 1755. He was also perhaps studying for the ministry, for he paid seven shillings for one of Jonathan Edwards's books in 1755. His salary was very small: £10 a quarter. His activities after leaving the College are unknown, but he was in Newark on Sunday, May 19, 1756, when on returning home from church Esther Burr recorded in her Journal that "Mr Badger praied & he is very gifted in prayer." Badger returned to Union, where he died on January 25, 1757.

SOURCES: Parentage and vital data: H. M. Lawson, *Hist. of Union, Conn.* (1893), 68-69; accounts with College: Aaron Burr, MS Account Book, 132, 134, 168; and Esther Burr, MS Journal, May 9, 1756.

Samuel Clark

SAMUEL CLARK, A.B., A.M. Yale 1757, Congregational clergyman, may have been born about 1725, in Newton, Sussex County, New Jersey, the son of Hannah and Thomas Clark. (Several Thomas Clarks with sons named Samuel lived in New Jersey at the time.) After graduation he probably studied theology. On July 14, 1756, he was ordained and settled as pastor of the Kensington Congregational Church in Farmington (now part of Berlin), Connecticut. A bachelor, Clark must have been well-off, for he erected a rather grand house, with bricks and hardware imported from England. The house was finished in 1759, but not until July 1, 1766, did Clark marry. His bride was Jerusha White of Bolton, Massachusetts. Samuel and Jerusha Clark had two children of the same names.

Clark must have been well regarded by his peers. When the Congregationalists and Presbyterians met in their general convention at Elizabethtown, New Jersey, in June 1772, Clark was chosen to deliver the opening sermon. But Clark's days of peace and affluence were numbered. In 1772 his congregation divided (in part for reasons of convenience), and Clark became caught in the middle of quarrels between the two successor churches. Apparently feeling that his finances had been injured by the new arrangement, Clark in 1774 memorialized the Connecticut Assembly to that effect; the assembly refused his petition.

Clark finally accepted the invitation of the Kensington church, with the following proviso: "I do not desire the money of those who do not desire my labors." He added that he wanted no one to be "tyed to me by the mere force of civil law who is unwilling himself to be under such wise and good civil regulations while we are blest with such good civil rulers in this land."

In the meantime, Clark set about attempting to make money in other ways. In 1773 he entered into a silent partnership with a local merchant, Jonathan Heart (Yale 1768), but the venture was not a success. Clark died on November 6, 1775. At the time he was facing dismissal from his pastorate because of suspected Tory sympathies.

SOURCES: Authority for Clark's parentage is a note by W. Hall, *NEHGR*, 38 (1884), 231, which seems tenuous at best. He might also have been the son of Richard Clark (d. 1743), Thomas Clark (d. 1731), or various other N.J. Clarks: 30 *NJA*, 96, and Samuel Clark File, PUA; pastorate: *Kensington Congregational Church: Two Hundreth Anniversary* (1912), 64-84; J. H. Trumbull, *Memorial Hist. of Hartford County, Conn.* (1886), II, 17; D. N. Camp, *Hist. of New Britain with Sketches of Farmington and Berlin, Conn.* (1889), 112-15; Clark's sermon: *N.Y. Gaz.*, Sept. 28, 1778; Clark's petition: *Rec. Col. Conn.*, XIV, 61-63; Dexter, *Yale Biographies*, III, 279-82; dismissal and Tory sympathies: *Fithian Journal*, II, 257n.

Alexander Gordon

ALEXANDER GORDON, A.B., College tutor and missionary, may have been a member of the numerous Freehold, New Jersey, family of that name. After graduation Gordon went to Freehold to study for the ministry, probably with the Reverend William Tennent, Jr., a trustee of the College and minister of Freehold's Presbyterian church. Gordon was, apparently, lonely, for on March 21, 1752, Joseph Shippen (A.B. 1752) wrote to him thus: "I perceive that amid your suitable Convenience for Study, you are destitute of any agreeable Set of Companions." Shippen went on to add that his fellow students eagerly awaited Gordon's return to Newark as a tutor: "their Words declared, but their actions were a bright Emblem of the Joy they felt in hearing such pleasant News."

Gordon did not long remain a tutor in the College. In June 1753, he left to assist Gideon Hawley (Yale 1749) on a missionary trip to the Iroquois Indians in New York. The passage west was arduous. "We assended the steepest and most lofty mountains," Hawley reported. "On their summits we behold the immense wilderness, and mountains piled on mountains. At other times we are in the recesses of a gloomy Valley. We often descend dangerous precipices entangled with logs, rocks and roots." Gordon and his companions reached Oghwaga on the Susquehannah, near present Binghamton, on June 5. There, with the help of the Indians, they repaired an old house as their winter quarters. In September, Gordon and Hawley set out for Stockbridge, Massachusetts. The trip was so rough that Hawley almost died. It apparently killed Gordon, for on March 14, 1754, the trustees of the College appointed George Duffield (A.B. 1752) tutor "in the Room of Mr. Gordon who accepted a mission among the Indians and is now deceased."

SOURCES: Gordons of Freehold: F. R. Symnes, *Hist. of the Old Tennent Church* (1904), 424-25; Joseph Shippen, Jr., to Gordon, March 21, 1752, Shippen Papers, NjP; Hawley and quotation: *Sibley's Harvard Graduates*, XII, 395; MS Trustees' Minutes, I, 38, PUA.

Robert Henry

ROBERT HENRY, A.B., A.M. 1754, Presbyterian clergyman, was born in Scotland, the son of Robert Henry, a native of Campbellton, Argyleshire. William and Samuel, the two brothers of Robert, Jr., migrated to Dublin, where they became well-to-do merchants and shippers. Robert, Jr., went farther west: in about 1740, after graduating from the High School of Edinburgh, he migrated to America.

Henry was licensed by the Presbytery of New York in 1752 and sent to Virginia as a missionary. He was ordained the following year. On February 11, 1754, Henry married Jane Johnston (or Jean Johnson), widow of Thomas Caldwell. The Henrys had seven children, all of whom later migrated to Kentucky. Henry was installed as pastor of two churches in Lunenberg County, Virginia, in 1755: the Cub Creek church (now in Charlotte County) and the Briery church (now in Prince Edward County). The former had a largely Scotch-Irish congregation, while the latter was largely English. John Todd (A.B. 1749) and Samuel Davies preached for four days at Henry's installation.

Aside from a dispute over the introduction of Watts's hymns in his services, Henry's pastorates were uneventful.

Somewhat eccentric, Henry had a strong sense of humor, which some of his fellow ministers found disconcerting. "He required," a contemporary recalled, "grace enough for two common men, to keep him in order; and he had it." Possessed of an extremely colorful preaching style, he was particularly effective with the young and the blacks. The number of black communicants in his churches was said to be over one hundred—the largest in the presbytery. He spent an hour before and an hour after his regular Sunday services instructing them.

In October 1766, the presbytery granted Henry permission to accept a call from churches in Mecklenberg County, North Carolina, if a salary dispute with his Virginia congregations was not resolved to his satisfaction. Henry never took up his North Carolina pastorates, for he died on May 8, 1767, at Cub Creek.

SOURCES: W. H. Eldridge, *Henry Genealogy* (1915), 183-84, and J. F. Henry, *Hist. of the Henry Family* (1900), 3-8; Foote, *Sketches, Va.*, I, 220, II, 49-52; Henry's wife: K. B. Elliott, *Early Wills, 1746-1776, Lunenberg County, Va.* (1967), 146; Webster, *History*, 651-52; E. V. Gaines, *Cub Creek Church and Congregation* (1931), 19-22; H. C. Bradshaw, *Hist. of Prince Edward County, Va.* (1955), 75 (Briery Church); *VMHB*, 63 (1955), 175; J. W. Alexander, *Life of Archibald Alexander* (1854), 157-58.

Samuel MacClintock

SAMUEL MACCLINTOCK, A.B., A.M. 1755, Harvard 1761, D.D. Yale 1791, Congregational clergyman, was born in Medford, Massachusetts, one of the nineteen children of William MacClintock, a well-to-do farmer, on May 1, 1732. William had emigrated from Scotland to Ireland, where he lived through the siege of Londonderry, and thence to America. Samuel prepared for college first at the Medford Grammar School, then with Timothy Minot in Concord, and last with the Scots Reverend Robert Abercrombie at Pelham, Massachusetts. President Burr was so impressed with MacClintock that he asked him to stay on in the College as a tutor. MacClintock instead returned home to spend two years keeping school in Chelsea while he read for the ministry with the Reverend David McGregore of Londonderry, New Hampshire.

In 1754 MacClintock married Mary Montgomery of Portsmouth, New Hampshire. The MacClintocks had fifteen children in the next sixteen years. In 1756 MacClintock accepted a call to serve as pastor of the First Congregational Church in Greenland, New Hampshire. He was ordained on November 3 and spent the rest of his life there. Active in the Seven Years War, MacClintock served as chaplain in Colonel John Goff's New Hampshire regiment for several summers through the fall of Montreal in 1760. MacClintock was the leading citizen of Greenland. Witty, studious without being scholarly, a direct and simple preacher, he became the spokesman for the Congregational clergy of the region.

Though apolitical, MacClintock rushed off to join the American army when the Revolutionary War began and was probably present at the battle of Bunker Hill. "Never did men act with more wisdom, prudence, and fidelity, than they have hitherto done in the great trust committed to them by their country," he wrote on hearing of the Declaration of Independence. The war cost MacClintock dear: three of his sons died in service and his wife followed them to the grave in 1785. He then married Mrs. Elizabeth Fernald Dalling of Portsmouth.

As the spokesman for New Hampshire Congregationalism, in 1790 MacClintock was drawn into controversy with the Reverend John Cosens Ogden (A.B. 1770), Episcopalian pastor of Queen's Chapel, Portsmouth. The first American Episcopalian bishop, Samuel Seabury, had preached Ogden's ordination sermon. MacClintock publicly attacked Seabury's episcopal pretensions; Ogden publicly attacked MacClintock's Calvinist pretensions. The dispute ended with Ogden's dismissal from his church for the sake of peace. Yale was so pleased at having Bishop Seabury attacked that it awarded MacClintock the degree of Doctor of Divinity.

Although he joined in the 1790s witch-hunt against deists and "infidels," in time MacClintock came to be a strong supporter of Thomas Jefferson. He found himself, ironically, holding much the same views as his one-time opponent, John Ogden. "I am sensible that politics are not the business of ministers of religion, in their publick capacity," he wrote at some time after 1800, "and therefore have avoided making this the subject of my public discourses, but . . . I think no one has a better right to speak his mind." MacClintock rehearsed the deaths of his sons during the war, his financial losses, and decided: "if my country might be free and happy, it would be a sufficient compensation." Looking about him he saw the country ruled by a "junto of little tyrants . . . immense fortunes suddenly amassed by iniquitous speculations, and superb palaces erected on the spoils of the widows and fatherless children of men who had shed their blood in their country's cause," and all under the rule of "a proud domineering aristocracy." But things were now changed; Thomas Jefferson was president, "a great man of great, and distinguished abilities is now placed in the chair of government, who all along has shewn himself the friend . . . of the natural rights of man." It was an extraordinary performance for a Congregational minister in New England; but MacClintock did not live to see the end of Jefferson's presidency. After preaching the annual Fast sermon in 1804 he returned home, told his family his work was done, and died four days later, on April 27, 1804.

SOURCES: Most complete source: *Sibley's Harvard Graduates*, XIII, 102-12; quotations: Force, *Am. Arch.* (5 ser.), I, 734, and MacClintock to William Bentley, Bentley MSS (MWA), III, 112, as quoted in *Sibley's*.

PUBLICATIONS: see STE

Mss: MH, MHi, NjP, PHi, MWA

Henry Martin

HENRY MARTIN, A.B., A.M. 1754, Presbyterian clergyman, was licensed by the Presbytery of New York and supplied churches at Maidenhead (now Lawrenceville) and Hopewell, New Jersey, in 1752. Martin was called to churches in Newtown and Salisbury, Bucks County, Pennsylvania, in May 1753. He was ordained and installed as pastor at both places by the Presbytery of Abingdon on April 9, 1754. Within a few years Martin gave up his pastorate at Salisbury because of declining numbers. He remained at Newtown until his death on April 11, 1764. He married Elizabeth Slack.

SOURCES: Webster, *History*, 662; Henry Martin File, PUA.

Benjamin Youngs Prime

BENJAMIN YOUNGS PRIME, A.B., A.M. 1754, A.M. Yale 1761, M.D. Leyden 1764, physician and poet, was born at Huntington, Long Island, New York, December 9, 1733, the only son of Experience Youngs and her husband, Ebenezer Prime (Yale 1718), a Congregational clergyman. "My mother dyed ye 1st of January following," Prime wrote about 1757, "so that I was left motherless in my Infancy, & my life which has been so useless, proved the Death of her that bare me. Thro' the industrious care of my Hon^d Father over me, I was very early taught the first Rudiments both of Religion and Learning. . . . Sometimes about the year 1740, I began ye study of the Languages . . . yet I dont remember any remarkable convictions that I had, till, as near as I can recollect, about the 10th year of my Age, when one Evening, as I was sitting by the Fireside, meditating upon a future State, I had given me such a solemn View of Eternity, such a realizing Sense of the Certainty of future Judgment, & of the importance of fleeing from the Wrath to come, which I was sensible I must eternally suffer if I continued & dy'd in a state of Unregeneracy, that it . . . fill'd my soul with Anxiety and Distress. This Concern continued, as I remember for some Weeks, during which I laid aside my childish Vanities, attended secret prayer steadily, read good Books &c. & made for a while the one thing needfull the main object of my pursuit, but alas! at length the World diverted my Thoughts, my Convictions dy'd away, and I grew secure as ever.

"In July AD. 1748 having gain'd some acquaintance [sic] with the Languages I was sent to the College of New Jersey to be under the

Benjamin Youngs Prime, A.B. 1751
BY JOHN MARE

Care & Tuition of the Revd Mr Aaron Burr, where, tho' (without Vanity) I was industrious enough in my Pursuit of humane Learning, I too much neglected that which is divine, & when I did study Divinity, I like a Theorist studied it more for speculation than practice. In short I was cumber'd about so many things that I neglected the one thing needfull. . . . Many a pathetic Address, many an earnest exhoration has the Revd President given us, that were his Pupils, in the Hall, as well as from the Pulpit, to urge us to a life of practical Piety. But alas! How did I hate Instruction! &c

"After the Commencement in September AD 1751 having taken the Degree of AB, I return'd home to live with my Father, & follow'd my Studies but principally that of Physick. . . . the latter End of March AD 1754 I went to Jamaica to accquaint myself with the Practice of Physick under the Tuition of D^r J[aco]b O[gde]n." Troubled by obscure physical ailments all his life (seemingly closely related to his spiritual anxieties), Prime returned home late in 1754. He lived with his father and cultivated his torments until September 1756, when, on Aaron Burr's request, he returned to the College as a tutor. He spent only one year at Princeton, resigning four days after Burr's death:

> Lamented Burr! how shall I mourn thy end?
> My teacher, guide, my father, and my friend!
> Must I behold thy rev'rend form no more,
> Nor see the smiles thy pleasant features wore?
> No longer sit amongst the list'ning throng,
> Nor hear the heav'nly music of thy tongue? – . . .
> What tongue can tell, how fatal is his fall;
> How great *my* loss, how great the loss to *all*?

Again, Prime returned to his father's house. He remained there until some time between October 1757 and July 1758, when he moved to East Hampton, Long Island, and probably began the practice of medicine. He published the first of his poems—most of which concerned the progress of the Seven Years War—in the same year. For the next five years Prime moved back and forth between East Hampton and his father's home in Huntington, spending most of his time at the latter place.

In June 1763, Prime sailed for England, and took up an internship at Guy's Hospital in London shortly after his arrival. With time out for a tour in France, Prime studied medicine—mainly obstetrics—in London until 1764. He wrote his doctoral dissertation, *De Fluxu Muliebri Menstruo*, that year and dedicated it to his father. On June 12, 1764, Prime registered at the University of Leyden, presented his dissertation, and received the degree of M.D. on July 7, 1764. At about the same time he published in London a collection of twenty of his poems —*The Patriot Muse, or Poems on Some of the Principal Events of the Late War.*

Prime returned to America late in 1764, and shortly set up a medical practice in New York City. It was not a successful practice, for almost no record of him—aside from a few reproachful and hectoring letters from his father—survives for the years 1764 to 1774. But however obscure his professional life, Prime was deeply involved with the great public issues of the day. In 1765–1766, after the passage of the Stamp Act, he published a popular ballad, "An Excellent New Song, for the Sons of Liberty in America." The first two stanzas convey its flavor:

> In Story we're told, How our Fathers of old,
> Brav'd the Rage of the Winds and the Waves,
> And cross'd the Deep o'er, To this desolate Shore,

All because they were loth to be SLAVES: *Brave Boys,*
All because they were loth to be SLAVES.

Yet a strange Scheme of late, Has been form'd in the State,
By a Knot of political Knaves,
Who in secret rejoice, That the Parliament's Voice,
Has condemn'd us by Law to be SLAVES; *Brave Boys,*
Has condemn'd &c.

Thomas Jones, Loyalist historian of New York, thought that "doctor Prime, a most violent, persecuting republican," was one of the authors, along with William Livingston, of the "American Whig" essays that appeared in the New York newspapers in 1768 and 1769.

In 1774 Prime returned to Huntington to marry Mary Wheelwright, the widow of an Anglican clergyman, James Greaton, on December 18. The Primes settled into the family homestead. Their residence there was short. A vehement Whig, Prime (along with many others) was forced to flee to Connecticut for safety from the British on September 1, 1776. Prime, his wife, and year-old son (the first of the Prime's five children) took up residence first in Wethersfield, later in New Haven. Their exile from Long Island lasted for almost seven years. Prime practiced medicine in his usual unsuccessful fashion, made friends with President Stiles of Yale and other Connecticut literati, wrote poetry, complained, and begot children.

At the end of hostilities in 1783 the Primes returned to Long Island. There Prime, tended by three slaves, complained about his deprivations and wrote more poetry. His longest work, *Columbia's Glory, or British Pride Humbled; A Poem on the American Revolution* was published in 1791:

The muse for Britain sings no more,
The British Laurel withers on my brow,
COLUMBIA only is my country now;
To her alone my services belong:
  My head, my heart, my hands,
  My pen, my lyre, my tongue,
COLUMBIA'S int'rest now demands,
Engrosses all my cares and claims my ev'ry song.

On October 31, 1791, five weeks after seeing his poem through the press, Prime died of apoplexy at Huntington.

SOURCES: Above sketch based largely on C. W. Wheelock's exhaustive two-volume biography and a critical edition of Prime's writing, "Dr. Benjamin Youngs Prime (1733–1791): American Poet," (Ph.D. diss., Princeton U., 1967), which corrects many errors in the sketch on Prime in the *DAB*. Quotations are from following works, all reproduced in Wheelock: spiritual and secular autobiography: "Some Remarkable Passages in the Life of B.Y.P.," Prime Family MSS, NjPT; "An Elegy on the Lamented Death of His Excellency Jonathan Belcher, Governor of New Jersey, and The Rev. Aaron Burr, President of Nassau-Hall," ca. 1757, in *The Patriot Muse* . . . (London, 1764), 20; *Columbia's Glory* . . . (New York, 1791), 3; Thomas Jones, *Hist. of N.Y. during the Rev. War* (1879), I, 20; for slaves, see: *U.S. Census of 1790, N.Y.*, 164.

PUBLICATIONS: see text, STE, and Wheelock above

Mss NjPT

Robert Ross

ROBERT ROSS, A.B., A.M. 1754, Yale 1754, Congregational clergyman and author, was born in Ireland in 1726. He was brought to America by his father, probably about 1729. Ross may have taught in the Latin grammar school connected with the College after graduation, for in 1752 he published *A Complete Introduction to the Latin Tongue, Published, for the Use of the Grammar School at Newark*, a revision of a work of President Burr. Ross was ordained pastor of the Congregational church in Stratfield (now Bridgeport), Connecticut, on November 28, 1753, where he remained for almost fifty years. On December 18 Ross married Mrs. Sarah Hawley, a widow. The couple had one daughter, named Sarah.

Ross had a gift for lucid, logical exposition. Over the years he published at least eight editions of his Latin grammar. The fifth edition, in 1770, exhibited something of a burgeoning American consciousness, for with that edition the title of the work was changed to *The American Latin Grammar*. The book was advertised as the one used in the College's grammar school and recommended especially to those "who design to send their children to NEW–JERSEY COLLEGE." Ross also published English grammars and readers. If the publication date of 1785, which scholars have assigned to Ross's *The New American Spelling Book*, is correct, Ross antedated Noah Webster (Yale 1778) by three years in affixing "American" to the title of a textbook designed for a wide circulation. Of an English textbook widely used in America before the Revolution, Ross later declared: "Dilworth's Spelling Book, recommending Subjection to a Foreign Power, has a Tendency to promote Disaffection to the present Government, and must therefore be very improper for the Freeborn Youth of America, since we have become an INDEPENDENT NATION." Among the endorsers of the 1785 volume were many connected with the College, including President Witherspoon, New Jersey's governor, William Livingston, and Samuel Stanhope Smith (A.B. 1769), future president of the College.

Ross was as clear and concrete in writing to Connecticut theologian Joseph Bellamy on abstruse subjects such as freedom of the will and idealism as when writing textbooks. Theologically conservative, he would have no part of the ideas of Bellamy and his followers. Ross went out of his way to preach and write against Separatist and Sandemanian tendencies in Connecticut Congregationalism. His accomplishments and, perhaps, his theological views led Old Side Presbyterians to suggest Ross as a teacher of languages, logic, geography, and composition when they attempted to take control of the College in 1766.

In his politics Ross was a thoroughgoing Whig: "Why should the industrious farmer suffer by heavy taxes, which are not needful for the real expenses and exigencies of government?" he asked his congregation on a thanksgiving day in 1775. "Why should the industrious poor, be squeezed, to support the corruption and luxury of the great, who know no bounds to their pride and grandeur? . . . If the British Parliament had any right to tax us, why did they never set up a plan before? . . . Now we never chose the British Parliament to represent us, and therefore they can have no manner of right to give away our money to the Crown."

Ross lived a busy life. He attended many church meetings, preached often at Yale, and even joined in a now obscure attempt to reform that college in 1784. Ross's first wife died in 1772. He then married Eulilia Bartram of Fairfield, who died in 1785. Ross next married Sarah Merrick of North Branford. He died in Bridgeport on August 29, 1799. Within twenty-four hours his wife died. Nine days later their only surviving son, Merrick Ross, died.

SOURCES: Robert Ross File, PUA; C. R. Palmer, *The Bi-Centennial Celebration of the First Congregational Church and Society of Bridgeport, Conn.* (1895); brief mentions and Dilworth quotation: H. R. Warfel, *Noah Webster, Schoolmaster to America* (1936), 62, 73; theological position: Ross to Joseph Bellamy, Sept. 29, 1755, Webster/Bellamy Transcripts, PPPrHi, and C. C. Goen, *Revivalism and Separatism in New England* (1962), 53, 132-33, 163; Old Side proposal: L. H. Butterfield, *John Witherspoon Comes to America* (1953), 13; Whig quotation: Ross, *A Sermon, in which the Union of the Colonies is Considered and Recommended; and the Sad Consequences of Divisions are Represented* . . . (1776), 9, 11; mentions of Ross's activities are scattered throughout: Stiles, *Literary Diary*, III.

PUBLICATIONS: see STE

Nathaniel Scudder

NATHANIEL SCUDDER, A.B., A.M. 1756, physician and public official, was the son of Abia Rowe and Jacob Scudder, a miller and planter, who moved from Huntington, Long Island, New York, to Freehold, Monmouth County, New Jersey, and eventually settled at "Scudder's Mills," just northeast of Princeton, New Jersey. Scudder's parents moved at about the time of his birth in 1733; it is uncertain at which place he was born.

After graduation Scudder studied medicine and in 1752 married Isabella Anderson, daughter of a well-to-do landowner of Monmouth County. The Scudders had five children, among them John Anderson (A.B. 1775), and Joseph (A.B. 1778). Scudder established a successful medical practice in Freehold and other parts of Monmouth County. In 1760 he inoculated many of the students in Nassau Hall, somewhat to the distress of President Davies. In 1766 he was one of the founding members of the New Jersey Medical Society. Extremely active in church affairs, he was a member of the Tennent church near Freehold and served for a time as one of the ruling elders. He was a trustee of the College from 1778 to 1781.

Scudder was in the forefront of the events leading to the Revolution in Monmouth County. In June and July 1774, he was a member of a Monmouth County committee that drafted resolutions in support of the inhabitants of Boston. On December 10, 1774, he was appointed a member of the county's "committee of Observation and Inspection," formed to whip recalcitrant citizens into line against the British government.

At the outbreak of the war Scudder was commissioned a lieutenant-colonel in the First New Jersey Regiment; he became a full colonel in November 1776. In August 1776, Scudder became a member of New Jersey's Legislative Council, serving on it until November 1, 1777. Early in 1778 Scudder became a member of the Continental Congress, taking his seat on February 9, 1778. He served in Congress until December 1779. Almost immediately, Scudder was appointed to a medical committee. He spent most of his time working on a special committee that supervised the affairs of the quartermaster's departments. Scudder was instrumental in preventing the recall of Arthur Lee from France. But his most important action came in the support he gave within his home state for the ratification of the Articles of Confederation. Along with President Witherspoon, he became a signer of that document.

By October 1779, Scudder felt himself so strapped by the expense of attending Congress that he declared another year there would ruin him and declined renomination. "I say not these things as the least Reflection on my Constituents," he wrote, "or under an Expectation of any further Compensation than my legal Wages for past Service, but sincerely for the Benefit of the State, least *that same* necessity, which now compels my Declination, may soon occasion other faithful Servants to retire from it's Service; when possibly their Places may be filled by ambitious designing Men, or by others, who being Persons of like contracted Fortunes with myself, may not perhaps so fully withstand those powerful lucrative Temptations, which *here* surround us, as I firmly boast *I have* done."

Scudder returned home and on October 10, 1780, was elected to the New Jersey General Assembly from Monmouth County. Although the legitimacy of the election proceedings was challenged, he managed to keep his seat. In the assembly he handled a great deal of routine committee work with his customary ability.

On the night of October 15, 1781, a party of Loyalist refugees from Sandy Hook landed at Shrewsbury, Monmouth County, and marched fifteen miles to Colt's Neck, where they kidnapped six residents. Scudder happened to be in the neighborhood. With a group from Freehold he set out to rescue the captives. Scudder's party caught up with the Loyalists and attacked them. In the ensuing melee Scudder was shot through the head, the only member of the Continental Congress to die in battle. His service there had indeed eaten into his fortune: although he owned eight slaves, the inventory of his estate came only to a little over £809. His classmates did not forget him; Benjamin Prime immediately composed an elegy:

> In med'cine skillful & in warfare brave,
> In council steady, uncorrupt, and wise,
> It was thy happy lot, the means to have,
> To no small rank in each of these to rise.

SOURCES: *DAB* sketch is in error: he was not a delegate to N.J.'s first provincial congress, nor was he a member before 1780 of N.J. legislature, nor was he ever speaker of legislature. Wickes, *Hist. of Medicine N.J.*, 389-94; Samuel Davies to David Cowell, Feb. 15, 1760, PPPrHi, discusses inoculation of students; *Journal of the Proceedings of the Legislative Council of N.J.* [27 Aug. 1776-11 Oct. 1777] (1779); *JCC*, x-xv, passim.; Lee/Deane affair: *Penn. Evening Post*, July 9, 1779; support for Articles of Confed.: *LMCC*, III, 326-28; resignation from Congress: Lundin, *Cockpit of the Revolution*, 303; Scudder's legislative activities: *Votes and Proceedings of the General Assembly of N.J.* [session begin. 24 Oct. 1780], (1780), 7, 8, 46; *et seq.* issues; account of Scudder's death: *N.J. Gaz.*, Oct. 24, 1781; Prime, "On the Death of Dr. Nathaniel Scudder Who was slain in a skirmish with a party of Refugees at Shrewsbury in New Jersey October 16th 1781. An Elegy," in Wheelock, "Prime," I, 194-97 (*q.v.* PRIME '51); slaves, inventory of estate: MS, N.J. State Lib., Trenton.

David Thurston

DAVID THURSTON, A.B. 1751, Congregational clergyman, farmer, was born in Wrentham, Massachusetts, on May 6, 1726, the son of Deborah Pond and her husband Daniel Thurston, a farmer. Thurston was ordained pastor of the West, or Second, Congregational Church of Medway, Massachusetts, on June 23, 1752. Exactly three months earlier he had married a widow, Mrs. Susanna Fairbank. The Thurstons had seven children.

On March 18, 1761, Thurston asked to be dismissed from the Medway church, claiming that he was not receiving enough financial support. The request was refused. Almost eight years later, on February 22, 1769, Thurston again requested dismissal, pleading poor health resulting from the "persecution of constant study and preaching," and, according to a nineteenth-century historian of the church, because of some unexplained "difficulties, supposed to grow out of the revival of 1740, with which he did not sympathize." This time the request was granted. Thurston then turned to farming. Early in 1772 he purchased for £700 a farm in Oxford, Massachusetts. He sold the farm in 1776 and moved first to Auburn, then to Sutton, Massachusetts, where he died on May 5, 1777.

SOURCES: Alexander, *Princeton*, 16; E. O. Jameson, *Hist. of Medway, Mass.* (1886), 123; M. Blake, *A Centurial Hist. of the Mendon Association. . .* (1853), 91-92; G. F. Daniels, *Hist. of the Town of Oxford, Mass.* (1892), 353.

CLASS OF 1752

George Duffield, A.B.

Jeremiah Halsey, A.B.

Samuel Livermore, A.B.

Cornelius Low, A.B.

Nathaniel Whitaker, A.B.

John Wright, A.B.

George Duffield

GEORGE DUFFIELD, A.B., A.M. 1755, D.D. Yale 1785, Presbyterian clergyman, was born on October 7, 1732, in Pequea, Lancaster County, Pennsylvania, the son of George Duffield, a farmer, and his wife Margaret. He may have been prepared for college at Newark, Delaware. After graduation Duffield went back to Pequea to study theology with the Reverend Robert Smith. In 1754 he returned to New Jersey and served as a tutor in the College for the next two years.

On March 8, 1756, Duffield married Elizabeth, daughter of the Reverend Samuel Blair of Fagg's Manor, Pennsylvania; she died in childbirth the following year. Three days after his marriage Duffield was licensed by the New Side Presbytery of New Castle. He preached in the south and in 1759 accepted a call to Presbyterian churches at Carlisle, Big Spring, and Monaghan, Cumberland County, Pennsylvania. On March 5, 1759, Duffield married Margaret Armstrong, daughter of a prominent citizen of the region. The Duffields had four children.

Duffield's ordination by the Presbytery of Donegal had been delayed by a dispute between traditionalist Old Sides and more evangelical New Sides, and did not take place until September 25, 1761. The Carlisle area was a raw frontier region. Presbyterians there not only were split from within but faced constant threats from hostile Indians on their doorsteps. Duffield was a strong supporter of the rights of the white inhabitants of the region and became widely popular. During his years in Carlisle Duffield was twice called by the Second Presbyterian Church in Philadelphia, but the presbytery felt that he would be more useful in Carlisle. His service in the area was interrupted by a two-month missionary tour to the Indians and backwoodsmen on the frontier that he and the Reverend Charles Beatty made at the direction of the synod in 1766.

In 1772 Duffield finally accepted a call to the Third, or Pine Street, Presbyterian Church in Philadelphia. Controversy followed Duffield to Pine Street. The church had been paid for by Philadelphia's Old Side First Presbyterian Church. The pastors of that church, Francis Alison and John Ewing (A.B. 1754), objected strenuously to having the Pine Street Church taken over by an outstanding New Light. After considerable controversy, they lost and Duffield was installed.

Duffield was an early and ardent Whig. During the meetings of the Continental Congress in Philadelphia he became John Adams's favorite "parish Priest." On June 11, 1775, Adams wrote to his wife that he had been that morning "to hear Mr. Duffield, a preacher in this city, whose principles, prayers, and sermons more nearly resemble those of our New England clergy than any that I have heard. His discourse was a kind of exposition on the thirty-fifth chapter of Isaiah. America was the wilderness, and the solitary place, and he said it would be glad, 'rejoice and blossom as the rose.' He labored 'to strengthen the weak hands and confirm the feeble knees.' He 'said to them that were of a fearful heart, Be strong, fear not. Behold, your God will come with vengeance, even God with a recompense; he will come and save you,' 'No lion shall be there, nor any ravenous beast shall go up thereon, but the redeemed shall walk there,' etc. He applied the whole prophecy to this country, and gave us as animating an entertainment as I ever heard. He filled and swelled the bosom of every hearer. . . . the clergy this way are but now beginning to engage in politics, and they engage with a fervor that will produce wonderful effects."

Duffield engaged himself in more than politics. Shortly after Adams heard him preach he became a chaplain in the Pennsylvania militia and spent much of 1776–1777 with the American forces near New York, preaching to the troops. On October 1, 1777, Duffield joined the Anglican Reverend William White as one of the two chaplains to the Continental Congress. ("It pleased Saint Anthony to preach to brutes / To preach to devils best with Duffield suits," was the bitter comment of the Tory satirist Jonathan Odell, A.B. 1754.)

At the peace Duffield preached a widely circulated sermon, which expressed his hopes for the young republic:

Here has our God erected a banner of civil and religious liberty, and prepared an asylum for the poor and oppressed from every part of the earth. Here, if wisdom guides our affairs, shall a happy equality reign, and joyous freedom bless the inhabitants wide and far, from age to age. Here, far removed from the noise and tumult of contending kingdoms and empires—far from the wars of Europe and Asia, and the barbarous African coast—here shall the husbandman enjoy the fruits of his labor; the merchant trade secure of his gain; the mechanic indulge his inventive genius; and the sons of science pursue their delightful employment, till the light of knowledge pervade yonder yet uncultivated western wilds, and form the savage inhabitants into men. Here, also, shall our Jesus go forth conquering and to conquer, and the heathen be given him for an inheritance, and these uttermost parts for a possession.

Duffield played many public roles: among other posts, he served as a trustee of the College from 1777 to 1790, as a manager of the Philadelphia Dispensary, and was elected to the American Philosophical Society in 1779. He was a leader in the postwar reorganization of the American Presbyterian church, and became the first stated clerk of its General Assembly. "An excellent Character," President Stiles of Yale noted in his diary on hearing news of Duffield's death in Philadelphia on February 2, 1790.

SOURCES: Considerable primary material: George Duffield File, PUA; *DAB*, 489-90; Webster, *History*, 672-73; *JPHS*, 33 (1955), 3-22; *DAB* states that Duffield prepared for college at the Academy of Newark; Newark Academy, forerunner of the University of Delaware, did not move there until 1767 (*Delaware Notes*, ser. 9 [1935], 9-42); C. Beatty, *The Journal of a Two Months Tour. . .* (1768); C. F. Adams, ed., *Familiar Letters of John Adams and his Wife Abigail Adams. . .* (1875), 65; preaching to troops: *PMHB*, 8 (1884), 262; *JCC*, VIII, 756; Duffield, *Sermon Preached in the Third Presbyterian Church. . .* (1784), as reprinted in Moore, *Patriot Preachers*, 359-60; E. F. Humphrey, *Nationalism and Religion in America* (1924), 260-62; Stiles, *Literary Diary*, III, 380.

PUBLICATIONS: see STE

Mss: PHi, PPPrHi, NjP

Jeremiah Halsey

JEREMIAH HALSEY, A.B., A.M. 1755, college tutor and Presbyterian clergyman, was born in Morristown, Morris County, New Jersey, in 1733, the son of Abigail Howell and her husband, Silas Halsey, a prosperous hatter. Halsey's whereabouts immediately after graduation are unknown, but he must have been studying for the ministry, for he was licensed by the Presbytery of New Brunswick on October 26, 1757.

Instead of taking up a pastorate after his licensure, Halsey became a tutor in the College. He would serve as a tutor for nine years—longer than anyone else in the eighteenth century. He began by buying the necessary books—a dictionary, a Latin edition of the classical rhetorician Longinus (shortly followed by an English translation of the same), a two-volume Hebrew bible, and Robert Dodsley's *The Preceptor*, with its introduction by Dr. Johnson. After burying Presidents Burr and Edwards, in 1758 Halsey was sent by the trustees to Virginia to persuade Samuel Davies to assume the presidency of the College. Something happened along the way. As John Ewing (A.B. 1754) described it, when Halsey left Princeton he was ready "to use all the arguments he could, in order to persuade Mr. Davies to come with him, but on the Road was either checked by his Conscience, or some other way was convinced, that he could not do it." The upshot was that because of "honest Mr. Halsey's account" of divisions among the trustees,

Davies refused his first call to Princeton. He later accepted, and Halsey served satisfactorily under him and President Finley.

A prejudiced contemporary (John Cosens Ogden, A.B. 1770, an Anglican clergyman) later gave a vivid account of the College in Halsey's years:

> The clergy had reduced it to a regular rule to make ministers out of every class in New-Jersey college. . . . Presidents Burr, Edwards, Davis and Finly [sic] had encouraged Calvinistic conversions. Mr. Halsey and the other tutors, joined with the neighboring clergy, could create these at pleasure. An alarming sermon or two, created a gloom and solicitude which led the susceptible youth to apply for spiritual advice; they were directed to pray, to pray alone, and loud, in the college garret and meadows in the rear of the college. Delirium seized some, fanaticism or deism generally resulted from such disorders. A few became Calvinistic ministers and imbibed the errors of Calvin, Edwards, Hopkins and Bellamy. Very many, now matured by age and reflection, condemn the attempts upon their understandings and the principles taught to them in that college.

From the scant evidence that survives, it appears that Halsey had almost as much influence on the day-to-day operation of the College as Finley. But sometimes Halsey grew weary of his work. "I am to the last Degree uncertain whether to stay here or not, if not, where to go," he wrote in April 1765 to Eleazar Wheelock (Yale 1733), founder of Dartmouth College. "Sometimes one thing preponderates, then another. Divine Direction I much need." It came the following year with President Finley's death, which left Halsey the senior member of such faculty as there was. He thereupon resigned his tutorship. The trustees resolved that "because of the great and important services that have been rendered to this institution by Mr. Jeremiah Halsey, over and above the necessary duties of his office as a tutor of the college," they would award him £60 from the regular commencement fees.

In 1767, shortly after leaving the College, Halsey was ordained by the Presbytery of New Brunswick. An old-fashioned New Light, his preaching soon caused consternation far to the north. In March 1768, Halsey preached a sermon in latitudinarian Boston. As the Reverend Samuel Hopkins reported it, "he greatly disobliged every clergyman in town, except one or two. His theme was that it is impossible for an impenitent to believe on Christ. And one inference was that faith is not the first act of the renewed soul. Dr. [Charles] Chauncey says he is astonished at the man's impudence, that he sho'd being a stranger, presume to preach doctrines which he knew were contrary to the body of the clergy in Boston & do it with so much confidence, bawling &c. Mr. Halsey cares for none of them."

In 1770 Halsey finally found a pulpit. On April 17 he became pastor of the Presbyterian church at Lamington (now Bedminster), Somerset County, New Jersey. In the same year he was elected a trustee of the College, a post he held until his death. In 1772, at the age of almost forty, Halsey finally married; his bride, Mary Henry, was seventeen. His former students were amused. "Yesterday I went to hear Mr Halsey & then too I saw his young & blooming wife," wrote William Paterson (A.B. 1763) to Aaron Burr (A.B. 1772), not long after the event. "The old genn. seems very fond of his rib, & in good sooth leers very wistfully at her, as she trips along his side; some allowance however must be made: he is in the vale of life, love is a new thing to him, & the honey moon is not yet over."

Halsey continued to spend a good deal of his time involved with the affairs of the College. He became clerk of the Board of Trustees in 1772, and in the same year assisted President Witherspoon in running a fund-raising lottery in Delaware. And the students were still aware of Halsey's ideas. In 1774 one was reporting to a recent alumnus that according to Halsey's calculations the millennium was sure to occur in the eighteenth century.

Halsey was a fervent Whig. In 1775, when the Synod of New York and Pennsylvania issued a pastoral letter that dealt with current political difficulties, Halsey was the only clergyman who refused to subscribe to a paragraph that contained a declaration of allegiance to George III. Halsey died before the Revolution was over. On the way to a meeting of the Board of Trustees on September 26, 1780, he was taken ill in Griggstown, New Jersey, and died there on October 2. The owner of one slave, he had lived modestly but comfortably: his estate was inventoried at £605. A Philadelphia newspaper recorded his death thus: "As a Minister of the Gospel he was faithful and assiduous in the service of his Lord; and, as a member of civil society, steady, uniform and zealous in his attachment to the interest of his country; and, from a just sense of American rights, and early discovery of the subversive designs formed against them, was among the first who gave an alarm and awakened the attention of the public to the insidious measures and oppressive views of the British Court."

SOURCES: J. L. Halsey and E. D. Halsey, *Thomas Halsey of Hertfordshire, England* (1895), 60-61; father's will: 34 *NJA*, 220; books: Aaron Burr, MS Account Book, 306, 32; mission to Davies: John Ewing to David Cowell, November 6, 1758, PPPrHi; Halsey as tutor: Ogden, *Friendly Remarks to the People of Conn.* (1799), 20-21;

Halsey to Wheelock, April 2, 1765, Wheelock MSS, NhD; MS Trustees' Minutes, I, entry for Sept. 24, 1766, PUA; Boston sermon: Samuel Hopkins to Joseph Bellamy, April 4, 1769, Webster/Bellamy Transcripts, PPPrHi; Paterson quotation: Mills, *Life at Princeton College*, 130; "Our Older Churches—Lamington," in *The Two Hundredth Anniversary of the Founding of the Lamington Presbyterian Church* (1940), 5-7; millennium: William Bradford to James Madison, August 1, 1774, *Madison Papers*, I, 119; marriage: *Som. Cty. Hist. Quart.*, 7 (1918), 109; allegiance to crown: *Minutes of the Synod of N.Y. and Pa.*, 466-69; account of death: *N.J. Gaz.*, Nov. 22, 1780; estate inventory: MS, N.J. State Lib., Trenton; obituary: *Pa. Packet*, Oct. 14, 1780.

Mss: NhD

Samuel Livermore

SAMUEL LIVERMORE, A.B., A.M. 1755, LL.D. Dartmouth 1792, lawyer and public official, was born at Waltham, Middlesex County, Massachusetts, on May 25, 1732, the son of Hannah Brown and her husband, Samuel Livermore, a farmer, deacon, and selectman. Samuel was the

Samuel Livermore, A.B. 1752
BY JOHN TRUMBULL

first of three Livermore brothers (the others were Isaac and William, both A.B. 1756) to attend the College of New Jersey. Before entering college Samuel taught school in Chelsea for a year and a half. Apparently, Samuel had hoped to go through Harvard in one year. Nathaniel Oliver (Harvard 1733) explained to Governor Belcher of New Jersey that Livermore's "father's circumstances would not permit him being admitted into our College [i.e. Harvard] at the equal Season which was not accepted in its true light by the governors of our College and as he was debar'd a just privlege which we hear is indulged freely at your new Academy" he will go south. "In my esteem," Oliver added, "he might have merited a degree this year as most that were admitted thereto" at Harvard. What Oliver meant, most likely, was that Livermore's father could afford to keep him in college for only one year and that Harvard was demanding a longer residency before granting a degree.

On September 5, 1751, armed with letters of introduction, Livermore set sail for New York. He packed a goodly supply of clothes (though his breeches were constantly in need of repair for the next year) and a small library: his bible, the Latin and Greek testaments, a Latin dictionary and lexicon, John Ward's *The Young Mathematician's Guide* (which spent much of the following year on loan to other students), Patrick Gordon's *Geography Anatomiz'd* and copies of Virgil and Cicero. But neither his wardrobe nor his library were complete. Stopping in New York, Livermore paid £5.11.2 for his college gown. When he arrived in Newark he paid tutor Jonathan Badger (A.B. 1751) 19s.6d. for a Hebrew bible and grammar.

Livermore's year in Newark passed quickly. He roomed at Mrs. Camp's boardinghouse, and, if his account book is to be trusted, subsisted largely on tobacco, limes, and rum. As commencement neared, Livermore looked after the preparation of his own diploma and those of his classmates, Duffield, Halsey, Low, Whitaker and Wright. On September 26, 1752, he recorded that he "paid Mr Burr for my Degree £1.10.0 proc[lamation money,]" and headed back to Massachusetts, bearing letters for alumni in New England.

Though Livermore had gone to college intending to become a minister, back in Chelsea he resumed schoolteaching, while at the same time he began the study of law with Edmund Trowbridge (Harvard, 1728). In June 1756, he was admitted to the Massachusetts bar. However, things looked more promising in the north. In 1757 Livermore moved to Portsmouth, New Hampshire, and was shortly admitted to the New Hampshire bar. On September 23, 1759, Livermore married Jane Browne of Portsmouth, daughter of the Reverend Arthur

Browne, Anglican rector of Queen's Chapel. The Livermores had five children.

As one of the few lawyers in the province, Livermore developed a flourishing practice and became a close friend of Governor Wentworth. It was perhaps this connection that enabled him to become one of the original grantees of Holderness, on what was then the northern New Hampshire frontier, in 1765. Livermore soon owned more than one half of the largely wilderness township.

In 1765, when trouble with Britain was brewing, Livermore withdrew to Londonderry, New Hampshire. The township elected him to the General Assembly in 1768. In 1769 Livermore returned to Portsmouth when Governor Wentworth appointed him judge-advocate of the admiralty court and king's attorney-general of the province. It must have been something of a hot seat politically, for in 1774 Livermore moved back to Londonderry and in 1775 prudently removed himself even farther from the growing conflict by retreating to his lands at Holderness. There he built a mansion, a church, and a mill and presided as a wilderness squire.

Revolution or not, Livermore held the confidence of the various New Hampshire political factions. In 1776 he was elected state attorney-general, and from that year on held one or more state offices. In 1779 and 1780 Livermore was elected to the New Hampshire House of Representatives, and in 1779 the legislature appointed him a representative to the Continental Congress to deal with the dispute between New Hampshire and Vermont over lands west of the Connecticut River. He was elected to Congress in 1785, 1789, and 1791. In 1782 Livermore was appointed chief justice of the superior court of New Hampshire. Livermore belonged to the generation of judges that relied more on equity than formal law and placed little trust in English common law. "Every tub must stand on its own bottom," he would say when a precedent was quoted to him.

In 1788 Livermore was a member of the New Hampshire convention on the ratification of the federal constitution. He has been credited with playing a major role in the state's acceptance of the document. One historian has assigned him a significant voice in phrasing the First Amendment to the Constitution. In 1793 Livermore was elected to the United States Senate, largely because, while a representative, he had voted against the Hamiltonian policies of funding the domestic debt at par and having the federal government assume the state debts. He was elected president of the Senate *pro tempore* twice. Livermore resigned from the Senate because of ill-health on June 12, 1801. William Plumer, the successor to Livermore's Senate seat, described him thus:

"He rose, and continued in office, by the force of talents and the reputation of integrity, and not by the mildness of his temper, or the amenity of his manners. He was a man of strong intellectual powers, of great shrewdness—possessed much wit, and had a vein for severe satire. He reasoned and studied much—he drew from himself more than from books—indeed he was not a great reader—not being fond of books. He had great decision of character—an independence and frankness of mind, which never stooped to please a friend, or avoid an enemy. His passions and prejudices were strong—he was naturally positive and arbitrary—too often imprudent—and too much governed by passion. His principal property was in lands, which were not productive; but he had a competence—his mode of living was neither profuse or sparing. He loved wine, ardent spirits, and a good table, but was not intemperate.

"His last years were gloomy and disconsolate—life had few or no charms for him. He died at Holderness, in May, 1803."

SOURCES: *DAB*; W. Plumer, "Samuel Livermore," in E.E.S. Batchellor, ed., *Early State Papers of N.H.* (1892), XXI, 816-18; C. R. Corning, *Samuel Livermore: Address before the Grafton and Coos Bar Association* (1888); material on year at CNJ including copies of letters in Livermore, MS Account Book, NjP; role in ratification: F. McDonald, *We the People* (1958) 238, 242; election to Senate: J. R. Daniell, *Experiment in Republicanism* (1970), 221; First Amendment: A. P. Stokes, *Church and State in the U.S.* (1964 ed.), 47-48.

MSS: MHi, NhHi, PHi, NjP

Cornelius Low

CORNELIUS LOW, A.B., lawyer and older brother of Nicholas Low (Class of 1757) was, most likely, born in Raritan, Somerset County, New Jersey, the son of Cornelius Low and his wife, Johanna Gouverneur. The father was a prosperous merchant and landowner. Soon after graduation Low sailed for England, and on May 28, 1754, was admitted to the Middle Temple in London as a law student. After completing his studies Low returned to New Jersey, where he became a counsellor-at-law on November 3, 1757. Low set up practice in New Brunswick, New Jersey, possibly in association with Isaac Ogden (Class of 1758). He died in New Brunswick in 1769, probably late in September. He left his two slaves, goods, and house to his wife, Catherine Hudé, and three minor children.

SOURCES: W. H. Benedict, "The First Settlers of New Brunswick," *NJHSP* (3 ser.) 7 (1912), 13, confuses Low's marriage with his father's; Jones, *Inns of Court* (1924), 138; will: MS, N.J. State Library, Trenton.

Nathaniel Whitaker

NATHANIEL WHITAKER, A.B., A.M. 1755, D.D. St. Andrews 1767, D.D. Dartmouth 1780, Presbyterian clergyman, was born at Huntington, Long Island, New York, about 1732, the son of Elizabeth Jarvis and her husband Jonathan Whitaker, a farmer and immigrant from England who had settled first at Salem, Massachusetts, before moving to Long Island. When Whitaker was a boy his family moved to lands it had purchased just west of Elizabethtown, New Jersey. After graduation Whitaker studied theology and was licensed by the Presbytery of New York in 1753. On Sunday, October 26, 1754, Esther Burr recorded in her journal that she "went to a meeting heard one Mr Whittaker a young Preacher, he was brought up at this College, he did better than I expected." In the fall of 1755 Whitaker was installed as pastor of the Presbyterian church at Woodbridge, New Jersey, not far from his family's home. In Woodbridge Whitaker married Sarah Smith; they had eight children.

Nathaniel Whitaker, A.B. 1752

On June 30, 1759, Whitaker was called to the Sixth, or Chelsea, Congregational Church at Norwich, Connecticut, and offered a salary of £100. The church, formed by a New Light secession in 1751, had no building; Whitaker's first services were held in a tavern and he was installed outdoors. Whitaker insisted on a Presbyterian form of church organization; this demand was laid aside by a church council, but Whitaker proceeded as if his demands had been met.

While in Norwich Whitaker became friendly with the Reverend Eleazar Wheelock (Yale 1733), who was operating a charity school for Indians in Lebanon, Connecticut, about twenty miles distant. When Whitaker's father died in 1763 he left a legacy to Wheelock's school, if it should continue; if not, the College of New Jersey was to receive the money for the support of Indian students. (The College eventually got the money.) George Whitefield had visited both Wheelock and Whitaker and suggested that funds could be raised for the school in Britain. "Had I a converted Indian Scholar," Whitefield wrote to Wheelock in 1760, "that could preach and pray in English something might be done." Within a few years Wheelock found his Indian. He was Sampson Occom, a Mohegan educated by Wheelock, then serving as a missionary to other Indians. After careful preparation, Occom and Whitaker—who was chosen more or less by default—were sent abroad in December 1765. Whitefield saw that the doors of influential evangelicals (such as the Earl of Dartmouth and the Countess of Huntington) were opened to them throughout north and south Britain. Occom was an enormously successful public relations device; an Indian Puritan, he preached hundreds of times to thousands and watched the donations pour in. Whitaker managed the tour, which lasted for two years, with considerable business ability, and was awarded the degree of Doctor of Divinity by the University of St. Andrews. The venture was the most successful fund-raising tour conducted by Americans in Britain to that time: Occom and Whitaker grossed more than £12,000. On the basis of this, the governor of New Hampshire granted Wheelock a charter for Dartmouth College. Over the years Wheelock continued to turn to Whitaker for advice, while Dartmouth became more or less the personal property of the Wheelock family and shifted its interest from Indians to the education of whites.

On his return Whitaker remained less than two years at Norwich. In 1769 he received a call to what Ezra Stiles called "a more eminent Chh. in Salem," Massachusetts. Whitaker unceremoniously dumped his Norwich parishioners, who had barely seen him for the past few years, and moved north. Whitaker's call to the Third Church in Salem was

engineered by Timothy Pickering (Harvard 1763), a well-to-do young
lawyer who hoped to use Whitaker as a Calvinist-Presbyterian warning to the liberal Congregational-Harvard clergy. Pickering made a
mistake. "Salem is Salem Still, careless & worldly," Whitaker reported
to Wheelock in 1771. "I never saw a people more void of hon[or] & religion than this," he complained to Wheelock a year later. "Their views
& promises are as rotten wood, & nothing holds them but interest. O
for the outpouring of the Spirit to reform a degenerate covenant
br[e]aking people." Whitaker insisted on the Presbyterian form of
church government and on the repudiation of the Half-Way Covenant
which had permitted the baptism of children of members of the
church not in full communion. Pickering and others disagreed; Whitaker excommunicated Pickering, the church split, and a long and bitter
dispute, in which other clergymen became involved, followed. In 1774
the church burned, and Whitaker reconstructed it on the plan of
Whitefield's Tabernacle in London. Whitaker had the church rebuilt
on his own land and tried to assure that its ownership would be vested
in his successors only so long as they remained "orthodox."

Whitaker had engaged in trade while in Norwich (he was accused
of having cornered the wine and raisin market); in Salem during the
Revolution he started a saltpeter factory. Whitaker was an ardent and
early Whig, almost as intent on persecuting Tories during and after
the Revolution as in winning the war. His bitter sermons against Toryism were reprinted by New England Republicans early in the nineteenth century. On the basis of these sermons one historian has
claimed that Whitaker was "the first orator of American Democracy."

In 1784 a group of Whitaker's parishioners grew dissatisfied with his
Presbyterian form of church organization; after much controversy and
complicated maneuvering, Whitaker found himself without a church.
Within seven months he had moved to a new church on the Kennebec
River in Maine, about thirty miles north of Augusta. However, the following year he withdrew and with twenty-two others founded still another church based on the Presbyterian system at the frontier settlement of Canaan (now Skowhegan), Maine. In January 1785, a church
was organized on the Presbyterian plan, and Whitaker was installed
by the four-member Presbytery of Salem. In Canaan Whitaker acted
as pastor, physician, lawyer, and leading spokesman for the town, and
was a skilled cabinetmaker as well. Within a few years controversy
arose again in a Whitaker congregation. In the spring of 1789 he was
accused, as an extremely prejudiced contemporary put it, of "having
debauched the young women of his congregation under the pretense
of converting them." Actually, only one young woman was involved,

and the legal trials Whitaker subsequently went through may well have been a mask covering deeper conflicts between him and some members of his congregation. Before this trial had gone to court Whitaker had brought charges against various residents for libel; he was eventually acquitted on technical grounds.

In 1789 the inhabitants of Canaan dissolved their contract with Whitaker and reverted to the Congregational form of church organization. On June 9, 1790, William Bentley, the gossipy and unsympathetic minister of Salem's First Church saw Whitaker and noted that the "gracefulness of person, & air of confidence which once distinguished him are lost. He is emaciated, & dressed in a very beggarly manner. . . . The bitter execrations of the people of Maine follow him." Whitaker busied himself with properties in New England, and in about 1792, for unknown reasons, moved south to the vicinity of Hampton, Virginia. He died there, possibly at the home of his son, Dr. William Smith Whitaker, on January 21, 1795.

SOURCES: *DAB*; O. M. Voorhees, "Nathaniel Whitaker, An Old-Time Middlesex County Preacher. Read before the New Brunswick, N.J. Historical Club, February 17, 1910," 30p. transcript, Whitaker File, PUA; *Som. Cty. Hist. Quart.*, (1913), 99-106; Esther Burr, MS Journal, entry for Oct. 26, 1754; long description of Whitaker and church organization: Stiles, *Literary Diary*, I, 38; complete account of British trip reproducing much MS material: L. B. Richardson, ed., *An Indian Preacher in England* (1933); Pickering: *Sibley's Harvard Graduates*, XV, 450; Whitaker to Wheelock, Aug. 17, 1771, and Sept. 29, 1772, Wheelock MSS; Whitaker's sermons, esp.: *An Antidote against Toryism* (1777), reprinted in Moore, *Patriot Preachers* (1860), 187-231; "first orator" and complex discussion of ideology: Heimert, *Religion and the American Mind* (1966), 500-509; L. H. Coburn, *Skohegan on the Kennebec* (1941), I, 339-49; "debauching" quotation: Bentley, *Diaries*, I, 34; Whitaker's appearance: ibid., I, 64.

PUBLICATIONS: STE and also Whitaker, *A Brief Narrative of the Indian Charity-School in Lebanon in Connecticut, New England* (London, 1766).

Mss: MHi, PHi, NhD

John Wright

JOHN WRIGHT, A.B., Presbyterian clergyman, was born in Scotland. He was tutored in Virginia by Samuel Davies before entering the College. In Newark, he became particularly close to President Burr. The summer before graduation Wright visited Jonathan Edwards in Stockbridge, Massachusetts. Edwards found him "a person of very good character for his understanding, prudence and piety."

Wright was licensed by the Presbytery of New Castle in 1752 and ordained in June 1753. He supplied various of Samuel Davies's pulpits in Virginia while Davies was in Britain on a fund-raising tour for the College. Wright was installed as pastor of the Presbyterian church at Farmville, Cumberland County, Virginia, in July 1755. That summer was one of drought, heat, and military defeat for British forces under General Braddock. Wright thought that he saw a spiritual change come over Virginians because of their military reverses. "There seems to be a general concern among all ranks," he wrote. "People generally begin to believe that our judgments are inflicted for our sins! . . . They now believe that the *New Light* clergy and adherents are right." A revival began; it spread quickly among the young, and, particularly, among the blacks. "I could see the Sun of Righteousness shining upon the Negro quarters," Wright recalled a few years later, "in the darkest & stormiest part of our spiritual winter. And when the revival began, it spread more powerfully among the Blacks than the whites, insomuch that they crowded to me in great numbers (solemnly engaged & deeply affected) to know what they should do to be saved." Over the next year or so Wright preached to thousands, black and white, and made many converts. He also found time to distribute religious tracts among the blacks and to lash out against the emotionalism of his rivals, the Baptists.

Late in 1757 Wright was overcome by an undefined malady. "I was obliged to quit preaching altogether, but could not keep silence; at last I fled from my flock, to be out of temptation of preaching, but could not keep away long; and upon my return must preach or sink into melancholy." Two months later, on January 25, 1758, the Presbytery of Hanover ordered Wright to stop preaching, since it only exacerbated his illness. By the following year he was well enough to accompany Samuel Davies to an audience with Virginia's new governor, Francis Fauquier, in order to present a letter assuring him of their loyalty and requesting continuation of their religious liberties.

Wright's recovery was short-lived. At a meeting of the presbytery the following summer, his peers found Wright "guilty of an indecent Piece of Conduct, by taking more spirituous Liquor at this Presbytery than his Constitution would bear at that Time." Wright confessed his error and was reinstated. After this, however, things seemed to go only downhill for him. In the following year, 1760, he was accusing the Reverend Samuel Black of circulating slanderous rumors about him. In April 1761, he accused the Reverend Alexander Miller of doing the same. The matter came to a head in a trial before the presbytery on October 8, 1761. Black admitted making remarks indicating that Wright was guilty of "the horrid Crime of Sodomy." Miller and Black said that it had all been an unfortunate mistake. Black also admitted that he had accused Wright of "Drunkeness, Popery & Racing"—but explained that this too had been merely hearsay and apologized.

Wright, apparently, was not able to pull himself together. On May 18, 1763, the Presbytery of Hanover reported to the Synod of New York that they had suspended John Wright. No further record of him has been found. His death was first noted in the College's catalogue of 1789.

SOURCES: Giger, Memoirs, I; Edwards's quote: Alexander, *Princeton*, 20; John Wright to ———, Aug. 18, 1755, in *Evan. and Lit. Mag.*, IV (1821), 572-73; Foote, *Sketches, Va.*, II, 52-55; Gewehr, *Great Awakening* (1930), 131; for Fauquier: Pilcher, *Samuel Davies*, 168; David Bostwick to Joseph Bellamy, October 9, 1761, enclosing letter of Wright to Bostwick, Webster/Bellamy Transcripts, PPPrHi, reprinted in part in Webster, *History*, 625-27; "Early Minutes of Hanover Presbytery," *VMHB*, 63 (1955), 71, 174, 179, 181, 183-84.

CLASS OF 1753

Daniel Isaac Browne, A.B.

Israel Canfield, A.B.

John Harris, A.B.

Robert Harris, A.B.

John Houston, A.B.

David Jamison, A.B.

Hugh McAden, A.B.

John McKesson, A.B.

Lewis Ogden, A.B.

Nathaniel Potter, A.B.

Nathaniel Sherman, A.B.

Joseph Shippen, Jr., A.B.

Elijah Williams, A.B.

Benjamin Woodruff, A.B.

Joseph Woodruff, A.B.

Daniel Isaac Browne

DANIEL ISAAC BROWNE, A.B., A.M. 1756, A.M. King's 1758, lawyer and public official, was probably born in 1739 or 1740 at Setauket, Long Island, New York, the son of an Anglican clergyman and sometime physician, Isaac Browne (Yale 1729). In 1747 Browne's father became rector of Trinity Church in Newark, New Jersey. It could only have been proximity that led Browne's father to send him to a college for radical dissenters.

Browne was licensed as an attorney in New Jersey in 1760, and set up practice in Hackensack, Bergen County. It was not, apparently, a flourishing practice. In 1786 a neighbor remembered that Browne indeed "had Practice as a Lawyer," but "not so much as some others. Not so clear in speaking. He was much employed in giving advice, tho. has heard him blamed for giving advice which tended to promote suits which often proved unsuccessful, but produced fees to himself." Another neighbor thought that Browne "was not one of the first Lawyers of the Place." Browne himself estimated that his legal practice earned him between £400 and £450 a year.

Browne also held two minor governmental posts. In 1771, he was appointed clerk of the peace and clerk of the court of common pleas for Bergen County. In 1774, Governor William Franklin appointed him surrogate of the Eastern Division of New Jersey. Browne estimated that the former place was worth £50 a year, the latter £30. When the events leading to the Revolution began to take shape, as a placeman Browne found himself in an awkward position. Bergen County was mildly, but predominantly, Loyalist in sentiment. In 1775 a Bergen County "Association" was formed to decide on the position of the County vis-à-vis the troubles with Britain. A radical statement was framed; Browne countered with a "moderate" one, urging people only to comply with the "legal" orders of the Continental Congress, "so that people should not sign a worse," as he later explained. The moderates apparently carried the day, for on September 25, 1775, Browne was appointed president of the Bergen County Committee of Safety. The following summer Browne was a delegate from Bergen County to the New Jersey provincial congress. In a quandary, he asked Governor Tryon of New York what his course should be. Tryon advised him to continue in his role. At the provincial congress in June 1776, Browne found himself consistently voting in the minority against the Whig majority: he voted to support Governor Franklin on several motions and voted against the establishment of a new government and the adoption of a new constitution for New Jersey. By the end of the year he found himself very much out in the cold. He was one of what William Paterson (A.B. 1763) labeled that "Class of Beings called moderate Men," who could be "more hurtful to the Cause than even the most avowed and envenomed Tories."

With the formation of the new revolutionary state government Browne moved from place to place, awaiting the arrival of British troops. In November 1776, he helped recruit a Loyalist foot company of fifty-six men, and was commissioned a major in the Fourth Battalion of the New Jersey Brigade by General Howe in the same month. Browne's health allowed him to serve in the army only until 1778. In 1777 Browne's father had become a refugee in New York and later a chaplain to Loyalist troops. Browne possibly joined his family in New York.

Browne's small New Jersey estate (8 3/4 acres) was confiscated in 1779 and on September 6, 1780, was sold for a little over £204 to one Peter Wilson. In 1783, at the end of the war, Browne, his parents, and his brother Peter accompanied other Loyalists to Nova Scotia, where they settled in Annapolis. In 1784 Browne was granted 500 acres of land in Annapolis and 1,000 acres in Kings County, Nova Scotia. His claims as a Loyalist were heard at Halifax on February 10, 1786. He died sometime between that date and 1800, when his Annapolis County lands reverted to the crown by escheat.

SOURCES: Father: Dexter, *Yale Biographies*, I, 380-82; testimony on Browne's career by himself and others, given at Loyalist claims hearing in 1786: Province of Ontario, *Second Report of the Bureau of Archives* (Toronto, 1905); *WMQ* 18 (1961), 558-71; committee of safety: *N.Y. Gaz. and Weekly Mercury*, Mar. 4, 1776; Browne's voting record at provincial congress: *Journals of the Votes and Proceedings of the Convention of N.J., 10 June 1776-21 Aug. 1776* (1776), 13-15, 31-32, 49-50; "moderate Men" quotation: R. C. Haskett, "William Paterson, Counsellor at Law" (Ph.D. dissertation, Princeton University, 1951), 117; W. S. Stryker, *"The New Jersey Volunteers" (Loyalists) in the Revolutionary War* (1887), 32; W. W. Clayton, *Hist. of Bergen and Passaic Counties, N.J.* (1882) explains sale of estate; land grants and escheat: M. Gilroy, comp., *Loyalists and Land Settlement in Nova Scotia* ("Public Archives of Nova Scotia, Publication No. 4," Halifax, 1937), 30, 63.

Israel Canfield

ISRAEL CANFIELD, A.B., was born in February 1728, the son of Sarah Johnson and her husband Israel Canfield of Morristown, New Jersey. By the 1770s the elder Canfield was a general merchant; what he was doing at the time of Israel's birth is unknown. Israel died less than a year after graduation, on August 2, 1754. He was interred in the Old Burying Ground in Newark, New Jersey.

SOURCES: F. A. Canfield, *A Hist. of Thomas Canfield and of Matthew Canfield with a Genealogy of their Descendents in N.J.* (1897), 64; father's occupation: *MHSP* (3 ser.) 44 (1910-11), 376.

John Harris

JOHN HARRIS, A.B., Presbyterian clergyman, planter, schoolmaster and sometime physician, was born on the Eastern Shore of Maryland on September 29, 1725, the son of immigrants from Wales. He possibly lived for some time in Virginia, for in 1751 he carried north a request to Jonathan Edwards in Stockbridge from Samuel Davies in Virginia to move south. About a year after graduation, on October 12, 1754, Harris was licensed by the New Side Presbytery of New Castle. In 1756 he was ordained pastor of the Presbyterian church at Indian River, near Lewes, Delaware. In the following years he also ministered to the Wicomico church at Salisbury and the Manokin church at Princess Anne, Maryland. While in Maryland he married Elizabeth Handy, a sister of Isaac Handy (A.B. 1761). The couple had at least one son, Handy Harris.

In 1769 Harris was sent south at the direction of the synod to preach in North Carolina. He eventually settled in the Ninety-Six (later the Abbeville) District of western South Carolina. Over the next few years he served as pastor to several churches on the Carolina frontier: at Long Cane, Fort Boone, Bulltown, and Greenville. He joined the Presbytery of Orange in 1774.

Harris became an important figure in the area. He established a plantation on the Little River, ran a school, and acted as a physician. He was a vehement Whig. Elected to the South Carolina provincial congress late in 1775 as a member for the Ninety-Six District, he was appointed to a committee charged with the encouragement of manufactures in the province. He was a member of the provincial congress when it adopted a constitution for the state in March 1776.

During the war Harris ministered to his scattered congregations along the Savannah River, preaching at times with his gun beside him in the pulpit and his ammunition strung about his neck. Most of his slaves were driven off his plantation by Tories during the war. In 1779 Harris resigned his ministry because of ill health, though he was active in the formation of the Presbytery of South Carolina in 1784. Harris died in 1790 or 1791.

SOURCES: Webster, *History*, 669-70; Giger, *Memoirs*, I; G. Howe, *Hist. of the Presbyterian Church in S.C.* (1870-1883), I, 338-42; *Extracts from the Journals of the*

Provincial Congress of South-Carolina (1-20 November, 1775) (1776), 133; son: S. Nottingham, ed., *Wills and Administrations of Accomack County, Va.* (1973), 281-82.

Robert Harris

ROBERT HARRIS, A.B., A.M. 1759, surgeon apothecary, may have come from Lancaster County, Pennsylvania, and perhaps attended Samuel Finley's academy at West Nottingham, Maryland. After graduation Harris studied medicine. On December 12, 1759, identified as Dr. Harris of New Brunswick, New Jersey, he married Hannah Gibb of Amboy, described by a New York newspaper as "a young lady of Beauty and a handsome Fortune and endowed with every Qualification to render the Marriage State agreeable." In 1761 Harris was elected a trustee of the College, a post he held for fifty-four years.

Soon after his marriage Harris moved to Philadelphia, where in 1762 he set up in business with Isaac Smith (A.B. 1755) at the Sign of the Golden Pestle. Harris and Smith advertised that they stocked "a very large and general assortment of fresh drugs, chymical and galenical medicines, apothecaries utensils, furniture for shops, etc. etc." In 1765 Harris's partnership with Smith broke up. In November of the same year he signed the merchants' nonimportation agreement. Harris later entered into two more partnerships, but both foundered.

Although he was a founding member of Philadelphia's College of Physicians, Harris's medical practice appears to have been small and his attention to it desultory. Perhaps his wife's "handsome Fortune" made diligence unnecessary. But Harris was busy with many civic, religious, and other affairs: he was active among Presbyterians; he was an agent for a Philadelphia lottery held for the College of New Jersey; and he was a member of the American Philosophical Society. In 1767 Harris, along with other Philadelphians, purchased land in Nova Scotia and even visited it with his family for a few months.

During the Revolution Harris put his talents to new uses. In February 1776, he suggested to the Committee of Safety that he start a powder works near Chester, Pennsylvania. The committee loaned him £110. The venture apparently was a success, for in June the state paid him £100 for the first shipment of gunpowder. Harris's second venture during the Revolution was not as successful. In 1777 he set up a salt works at Cape May, New Jersey. In 1779 the Pennsylvania authorities confiscated a load of the scarce commodity that Harris was shipping from Cape May via Philadelphia to Trenton. Unbeknownst to the authorities, Harris spirited the salt out of the city. The state ordered him to bring back the salt, supply an equal amount, or face prosecution. Harris did neither. Instead, he stayed out of Pennsylvania. Elected to the New Jersey Assembly from Cape May in 1782, Harris apparently never took his seat, for his name does not appear in the legislature's records.

In 1783 Harris returned to Philadelphia, where he dabbled in literary affairs and pursued an interest in ballooning. He may have had a medical student or two. Harris survived a bout of yellow fever in 1793, and remained a trustee of the College until his death in Philadelphia on January 9, 1815, "after a severe and lingering illness."

SOURCES: Sketch is based mainly, but not completely, on Whitfield J. Bell's extensive unpublished draft (Feb. 9, 1970) sketch of Harris prepared for the Biographical Dictionary of Members of the American Philosophical Society. Quotation on wife: *N.Y. Gaz. or Weekly Post Boy*, Jan. 7, 1760; for advertisement: *Penn. Gaz.*, June 20, 1765.

John Houston

JOHN HOUSTON, A.B., A.M. 1786, Presbyterian clergyman, was born in Londonderry, New Hampshire, the son of Samuel Houston, one of the original proprietors of the town and an immigrant from Ireland, and his wife, Mary, on April 4, 1722. The town was settled in 1719 almost completely by Scotch-Irish followers of the Reverend James Mac-Gregore, who came from Ireland in 1718. MacGregore's son, the Reverend David MacGregore, prepared Houston for college. He was the only boy from Londonderry to attend college before 1774.

After graduation Houston returned home to study theology with MacGregore. He was licensed by the Boston Presbytery on May 14, 1754. In 1756 Matthew Patten of Bedford, New Hampshire, was authorized to negotiate with Houston about becoming the town's pastor. If Houston took the post, he would receive a tract of land set aside for the town's first minister. Houston accepted, and was ordained on September 27, 1757. Shortly thereafter he married Anna Peebles; they had five children.

The inhabitants of Bedford—particularly Matthew Patten and his brother Samuel—seem to have been an extraordinarily contentious lot. And Houston was a remarkably stubborn and stiff-necked man. He got into arguments with neighbors over land and with some members of his congregation over what they considered his autocratic ways. Worst of all, he entered into a long-lasting feud with the influential Patten brothers. Any well-educated minister, Patten wrote to Houston on

May 5, 1761, should "be able to Deliver his sermons on the Sabath days without being obliged to repeat three quarters of his sentances over twice and many of them three times and after getting almost through with a Sentace to Drop it and fall too and Deliver a Sentance forign from the one he broke off and having contracted a habit of useing a sound of *Mnea* many times in his sermon to every word in a sentance and to three quarters or more of all the words he pronounces in a Sermon these things indicate to me that he does not take the pains to Collect and Deliver his sermons that he ought to do and more especially observe that he is capable to Deliver a discourse on any of the other six days of the Week about worldly affairs without a Mnea or be at a loss to find a sentance that is suitable to the subject he is talking about." In his reply Houston loftily refused to take notice of Patten's rebuke. It was a mistake. For the next thirteen years Houston's days were filled with claims and counterclaims about his salary, with lawsuits with the Pattens, and with the almost annual disruption of his congregation.

Houston's poor relations with some of his parishioners were compounded in 1774, when he refused to observe July 14 as a fast day, as demanded by New Hampshire Committees of Correspondence. To make matters worse, he drank tea, which to Whig eyes was sheer subversion. An angry citizen of Bedford sat down and wrote the following lines:

> In Treason, wit or common learning
> he surely is as great a Bungler
> as E'er presumed the word to preach
> his words are naught but common place
> the same thing O'er and O'er repeating
> now comes the Sum of all his Teaching
> to deal damnation to all those
> his vicious ways that dare oppose
> or seek for truth in Sacred letter
> unless the same he do Interpret
> Did you him hear and see his actions
> you scarcely could refrain from laughter
> on Sabbath days when in Desk placed
> he roars like wild boar closely chased
> In B[edfor]d tis he now resides
> The Text Confounds & with gross Lies
> Strives to support the Unjust Acts
> of Parliament that lately pas't
> us and our Children to Enslave

for which the D[ev]l will him have
In church at home and in place every
he shows himself a horrid Tory
Gods Laws & Mans he does pervert
with a most base & vile Intent.

Houston was not a Tory; he seems, instead, to have been that most unfortunate of men, a neutral in a revolutionary situation. Nevertheless, he was the closest to a Tory that Bedford could find. He was subjected to a midnight ride on the "wooden horse," and in 1775 was locked out of his church. He was imprisoned and brought to trials, both civil and religious. Houston finally gave in, and on October 24, 1778, signed a statement to the effect that "within these three or four years past I have spoken several Things Imprudently Respecting the Disputes between great Britain & these several states for which I am heartily sorry & do now Desire to be Reconciled again to the State by taking the oath of fidelity & to govern myself accordingly." Although Houston never preached in Bedford again, he was reinstated by his presbytery and supplied various pulpits in Vermont and New Hampshire.

In the years after the Revolution Houston made his living by farming his lands and occasional preaching. In 1784 the citizens of Bedford elected him hog reeve; in 1785 they elected him pound keeper; in 1786 Princeton awarded him the A.M. Houston died in Bedford on February 3, 1798. "He left," a letter written shortly after his death reads, his sons "Sam'l two, Robert and John $1 each by his will, which they design to break. If they do, it will be more than any man could do in his lifetime."

SOURCES: K. Scott, "John Houston, Tory Minister of Bedford," *JPHS*, 22 (1944), 172-97, an exhaustive article based on extensive archival research, reprinting MS sources quoted above. Parents: *Manchester Hist. Soc. Collections*, 7 (1914), 75; also E. L. Parker, *Hist. of Londonderry, N.H.* (1851), 356.

Mss: NhHi

David Jamison

DAVID JAMISON, A.B., A.M., landowner, was born about 1736, probably in New York City, the son of William Jamison, a lawyer who later became high sheriff of New York City and County. William's father, also David, was a Scotch immigrant who had achieved wealth and success in America as a lawyer, public official and land speculator. A member of the councils of both New York and New Jersey, the elder David had been chief justice of New Jersey from 1711 to 1723. One of the original "Nine Partners" in the vast land grant of that name in Dutchess County, New York, the first David also left lands in other parts of New York and one of the best law libraries in the province.

William Jamison died in New York City in April 1746. "I leave to my son David Jamison," his will reads, "(if he shall incline to the study or be educated in the profession of the law), all my law books, manuscripts, and precedents; but if he be inclined to any other profession, then to Jamison Johns[t]on, son of Mrs. Elizabeth Johns[t]on, widow." David was left the greater part of his father's other property. Elizabeth Johnston was David's widowed aunt, the only sister of his father. She and her children lived in Monmouth County, New Jersey. David probably went there to live after the death of his father. Elizabeth Johnston's brother-in-law was Andrew Johnston, treasurer of the College in 1748–1749 and an early trustee. Most likely it was this family connection that brought David to Newark.

Whether or not David followed his father's hopes by studying law after graduation is unknown. In fact, very little concerning Jamison's career has been discovered. He appears to have settled at New Market, in Piscataway Township, not far from New Brunswick. Jamison apparently spent time in New York City, too, for on January 31, 1756 he witnessed there the will of the well-to-do widow of a former rector of Trinity Church. Jamison also spent time in Newark. When St. John's Lodge, the first Freemasons' organization in New Jersey was founded there in May 1761, Jamison was appointed its first senior warden. On November 6, 1763, he married one Elizabeth Johnston—who does not seem to have been a cousin—in New York City.

Jamison was still living in New Market in 1765 when he and David Johnston, a cousin, petitioned the governor of New York for confirmation of land rights in the Minisink patent in southeastern New York that they had inherited from their grandfather. The land rights were apparently confirmed. On August 1, 1765, Jamison advertised a full share in the Minisink patent for sale in a New York newspaper, advising prospective purchasers to contact either himself at New Market or James Duane, a prominent lawyer and land developer, in New York City. Two years later Jamison, again in association with Duane, advertised a house (not his own) in New York City for sale. No further record of Jamison has been found. He was first listed as dead in the College's catalogue of 1818.

SOURCES: A garbled account of parentage: P. M. Hamlin and C. E. Baker, *Supreme Court of Judicature of the Province of New York, 1691-1704, Biographical Dictio-*

nary, *NYHS Col.*, 70 (1959), 117, n. 37; grandfather: *DAB;* father's will (the anno-
tations are incorrect): *N.Y. Wills*, IV, 159-60; W. A. Whitehead, *Contributions to the
Early Hist. of Perth Amboy* (1856), 71-73; presence in Piscataway in 1756: "Piscataway Earmarks," *GMNJ*, 26 (1951), 17; presence in NYC in 1756: *N.Y. Wills*, VI, 284;
Freemasonry: J. H. Hough, *Origin of Masonry in the State of N.J.* (1870), xii-xiii;
marriage: *New York Marriages* (1860), 212; Minisink rights: *NYHS Col.*, 68 (1935),
198-200; land sales: *N.Y. Gaz.*, Aug. 1, 1765, and *N.Y. Mercury*, Jan. 5, 1767. E. O.
Jameson, in *The Jamesons in America, 1647-1900* (1901), 133, states that David
Jameson, a Virginia merchant who served as lieutenant-governor of that state under
Patrick Henry, attended the College of New Jersey. Other evidence indicates that
the Virginia David was involved in business affairs there throughout 1751–1753 and
thus could not have been a student at the College.

Hugh McAden

HUGH McADEN, A.B., Presbyterian clergyman, was born in Pennsylvania, the son of immigrants from northern Ireland. After graduation
McAden studied divinity with the New Light Reverend John Blair. He
was licensed by the Presbytery of New Castle in 1755 and in June set
off on a missionary trip to North Carolina. On the way he stopped with
John Hoge (A.B. 1749) and John Brown (A.B. 1749). He preached a
sermon to Brown's congregation at Timber Ridge, Virginia, on the occasion of a fast day. News of General Braddock's defeat so disturbed
McAden that he almost returned to Pennsylvania. But he continued
south, and preached among several settlements of Scots Highlanders
in North Carolina. He found their singing execrable and was never
sure whether or not they understood English.

McAden returned north in May 1756, made a report on his tour, and
was ordained by the Presbytery of Newcastle the following year. On
July 18, 1759, McAden joined the Presbytery of Hanover and in the
same year was installed as pastor to congregations in Duplin and New
Hanover counties, North Carolina, the first settled Presbyterian
clergyman in the province. It was probably in these years that he married a Miss Scott of Lunenberg County, Virginia. The McAdens had
seven children.

When the Regulator conflict between seaboard and poor inland inhabitants broke out in North Carolina in the late 1760s McAden joined
with other Presbyterian clergymen in publicly deploring the movement
and in worrying about the effect it might have on the liberties of religious dissenters, since so many Presbyterians were involved. Mc-
Aden's health declined, and in 1769 he moved north to Caswell County.
In 1770 he joined with other clergymen in founding the Presbytery of
Orange, which encompassed all the territory south of Virginia. Mc-

Aden was the pastor of several churches in Caswell County until his death at Red House on January 20, 1781. Shortly thereafter his papers were destroyed in a British raid.

SOURCES: Sprague, *Annals*, III, 264; reprints of sections of now missing 1755–56 diary: Foote, *Sketches, N.C.*, 158-76; D. Meyer, *Highland Scots of N.C.* (1961), 113-15; "Early Minutes of Hanover Presbytery," *VMHB* 3 (1955), 168, 170-75, 178-80; Regulators: W. N. Saunders, ed., *Col. Rec. N.C.* (1890), VII, 813-16, and *NCHR*, 44 (1967), 373-91.

John McKesson

JOHN McKESSON, A.B., A.M. 1760, A.M. King's 1758, lawyer and public official, was born at Fagg's Manor, Chester County, Pennsylvania, on February 20, 1734, the son of Alexander McKesson, a farmer and immigrant from Ireland. After graduation McKesson studied law, probably in New York. His legal practice appears to have been associated closely with John Morin Scott, one of the most prominent lawyers in the city, since their names often appear together as witnesses to the same wills. Scott was the close associate of William Livingston and the younger William Smith, the leaders of the Whig Presbyterian faction in the New York politics of the 1750s and 1760s. Scott was also one of the organizers of the Sons of Liberty in New York. McKesson possibly was involved in these affairs.

McKesson's name appeared in 1769 signed to a broadside letter attacking attempts to establish an Anglican episcopate in America and directed against the "Episcopalian" faction in New York politics. Whether or not he was the author of the piece is uncertain. McKesson remained close to the Whig Presbyterian group in the early 1770s. When a provincial congress met in New York on April 20, 1775, to choose delegates to the Continental Congress, McKesson was appointed its secretary. He was also secretary to the New York Council of Safety, of which John Morin Scott was a member.

McKesson's career was fixed: he was a ubiquitous, reliable, and almost anonymous revolutionary functionary. On July 31, 1776, the New York provincial council appointed him registrar in chancery, a post he held for several years. When the New York Assembly convened on September 1, 1777, he was appointed its first clerk, and held the office until 1794. He was one of the clerks of the New York convention on the ratification of the federal constitution. He held minor legal posts in New York City.

McKesson never married. He lived in Manhattan, attended by two slaves, and, possibly, his sister Maria. He must have been a fairly wealthy man, for immediately after the Revolution he had purchased considerable property that had been confiscated from the Loyalist De-Lancey and Jauncey families. He died intestate of yellow fever on September 7, 1798.

SOURCES: McKesson's name appears on many documents of the period but he remains elusive. W. M. MacBean, *Biog. Register of St. Andrews Society of . . . N.Y.* (1922), 17; John Morin Scott: *DAB*, XVI, 495-96; though McKesson is not mentioned, for the political milieu in which he moved: P.U. Bonomi, *A Factious People* (1971), Ch. VII; McKesson?, "As Civil & Religious Liberty . . . New York, June 16, 1769," printed letter; for unrevealing letters from McKesson: *Clinton Papers* (1889), I, 194-97, 205, 409-12; slaves: *U.S. Census of 1790, N.Y.*, 131; sister: *N.Y. Wills*, XV, 254; land purchases: A. C. Flick, *Loyalism in N.Y. during the Am. Rev.* (1901), 216, 230, 244.

Lewis Ogden

LEWIS OGDEN, A.B., lawyer, was born in Newark, Essex County, New Jersey, in about 1730, the son of Elizabeth Charlotte Thébaut, wife of Uzal Ogden, an iron manufacturer and county judge. After graduation Ogden studied law and was clerk of the prerogative court of New Jersey from 1765 to 1772. He was also involved in his family's iron business, for a newspaper advertisement of 1769 lists him as a Newark agent for the firm's products. In 1761 Ogden became first treasurer and secretary *pro tempore* of the first New Jersey organization of Freemasons, St. John's Lodge in Newark. In 1770 Odgen married Margaret Gouverneur. The Ogdens had four children.

Ogden was involved early in the events leading to the rupture with Great Britain. On July 21, 1774, a general meeting of New Jersey county committees appointed him to a standing Committee of Correspondence for the province. When the provincial congress met early in 1776 Ogden was appointed to one committee after another: he was involved in issuing currency, in communicating with the Pennsylvania Committee of Safety, and in establishing qualifications for voting for and serving in the provincial congress. When the New Jersey convention met from June to August 1776, Ogden was appointed to the committee to draft a constitution for the new state. He also served on committees to confine suspected Loyalists, to keep open communications with New York, to establish armed patrol boats on the Passaic and Hackensack rivers, and to deal with the disposition of the state militia.

Ogden's multifarious activities slacked off suddenly and inexplicably late in 1776. His name does not appear again in public records until

1779, when a Newark town meeting voted him and the Reverend Alexander MacWhorter (A.B. 1757) to a committee to send instructions to the state legislature "as the Occasion may arise."

In 1786 Ogden moved to New York City. There he and Peter Hill of Newark bought five blocks of the old DeLancey farm. Ogden must have been fond of music, for he served as president of New York's St. Cecilia Society from 1790 until the time of his death. He lived comfortably, attended by three slaves. He died intestate on September 18, 1798. His New Jersey property was inventoried at £710.

SOURCES: Wheeler, *Ogden Family*, 93; *N.Y. Gaz. and Weekly Mercury*, Oct. 30, 1769; J. H. Tatsch, *Freemasonry in the Thirteen Colonies* (1929), 51; Committee of Correspondence: *Penn. Journal*, July 27, 1774; *Jour. of the Votes and Proceedings, as well as of the Com. of Safety (Jan. 1776) of the Provincial Congress of New-Jersey (June-Aug. 1776)* (1776), 35, 52, 84, 102, 103; *Records of the Town of Newark, N.J. (1666-1836)*, NJHS Col., 6 (1864), 159; slaves: *U.S. Census of 1790, New York*, 117; intestate: *N.Y. Wills*, xv, 254; inventory of N.J. property: 38 *NJA*, 269.

Nathaniel Potter

NATHANIEL POTTER, A.B., A.M. Harvard 1758, Congregational clergyman and secretary to Major Robert Rogers of the Rangers, was born at Elizabethtown, Essex County, New Jersey, in about 1733, the son of Phebe Bunnell and her husband, Noadiah Potter, Esq., a substantial farmer, miller, and landowner. In college Potter became friendly with Samuel Livermore (A.B. 1752). Livermore borrowed at least £14 from Potter during his year in Newark. On March 20, 1752, the two friends made an expedition to the falls of the Passaic, where they managed to consume almost £2 worth of tobacco, rum, and sugar. After graduation Potter went north to Massachusetts and kept school at Watertown, not far from Chelsea, where Livermore was teaching school and studying law. Potter must have seen much of the Livermore family, for on November 24, 1755, he married Samuel's sister, Hannah. They had one daughter.

Potter was a prepossessing young man. On September 10, 1755, he was called to become pastor of the Congregational church at Brookline, Massachusetts. He was ordained on November 19, five days before his marriage. At first his ministry proceeded smoothly. On January 1, 1758, he preached a powerful sermon on the degeneracy of the times, the threats of the French in the north, and the blood-thirstiness of the Indians. Later in the year he requested leave from the church to "go in the Intended expedition against Canada," but was refused permission. The following year he requested a salary increase but, after complicated bargaining, was dismissed—ostensibly for financial reasons—on June 17, 1759.

President Burr apparently had had long-standing doubts about Potter's character. After visiting the Woodruff family in Elizabethtown in May or June 1756, Esther Burr recorded in her journal that "Mrs Woodruffe tells us that when Mr Potter was at their house last he received Mr Burrs last Letter & was very angry & displeased that Mr Burr Should express a concern for his Carracter & Said he did not want Mr Burr to be concerned for his Carracter but would have him take care of his own & that he had more reason to be concerned for himself than for him or words to the same efect but I think these were the very words."

Burr's concern was well-taken. After his dismissal from the Brookline church Potter assisted briefly at the Old South Church in Boston and then received a call from the First Church of Plymouth. Then news broke of "Parson Potters Affair, with Mrs. Winchester, and other Women." John Adams recorded in his diary that Potter was the "Minister, famous for Learning, oratory, orthodoxy, Piety and Gravity, discovered to have the most debauched and polluted of Minds, to have pursued a series of wanton Intrigues, with one Woman and another, to have got his Maid with Child and all that." Potter declined the call to Plymouth, left his family, and disappeared into the New Hampshire wilderness.

Potter's association with the Livermore family finally came to his rescue. Samuel Livermore had married one of the daughters of the Reverend Arthur Browne of Portsmouth; another Browne daughter had married Major Robert Rogers of the Rangers, the most romantic hero of the Seven Years War. In 1765 Potter, probably through this connection, became Rogers's secretary. It was probably his last connection with the Livermore family, for in 1764 he had visited them long enough to father an illegitimate son by his wife's sister, Anne Livermore, who at the time was betrothed to Nathan Ker (A.B. 1761). Rogers was a colorful, barely literate adventurer. Potter took Rogers's notes and recollections and turned them into two, still fascinating accounts, the *Journals of Major Rogers* and the *Concise Account of North America*. Potter and Rogers traveled to England to have the works published. Rogers was lionized by London society.

Potter returned to America alone. He soon learned that Rogers had been appointed "Governor Commandant of Michilimackinac and its

Dependencies." Potter joined Rogers there, and was soon drawn into his wild schemes. Rogers was deeply in debt. He told Potter that unless the British government would make the Michilimackinac region a separate province with himself as governor, he would go over to the French. Rogers demanded that Potter deliver his proposals to England. Potter refused several times. Then, as Potter testified later, "Rogers . . . took an Indian Spear that was in the room in which this conversation passed, pointing it at Potter, threatening him with instant death if he did not keep this matter secret. Potter seeing his life in danger cried out for help, but was not heard; upon which he fell upon his knees and begged Rogers to spare his life till the next day when they might converse upon the Subject again, and he hoped with mutual satisfaction." Satisfaction was not forthcoming. Potter suffered several more indignities at Rogers's hands. Finally, he fled to Montreal and told his tale to the British authorities. They in turn sent Potter to England to present his evidence to higher authorities. Potter sailed the following summer. He never reached England, but died at sea in August 1768.

SOURCES: *Sibley's Harvard Graduates*, XIII, 346-49; father's will: 32 *NJA,* 256; Samuel Livermore, MS Account Book, NjP; Esther Burr, MS Journal, entry of May/June, 1756; John Adams, *Diary and Autobiography* (1961), I, 183; J. R. Cuneo, *Robert Rogers of the Rangers* (1959), 183, and passim; deposition *re* Rogers: *Doc. Col. Hist. N.Y.*, VII, 990-92.

PUBLICATIONS: see STE

MSS: MHi

Nathaniel Sherman

NATHANIEL SHERMAN, A.B., Congregational clergyman, was born on March 5, 1724, at Stoughton, Massachusetts, the son of Mehitable Wellington and her husband, William Sherman, a former cordwainer who had achieved a modest prosperity as a farmer. By the time Sherman went to college the family was living in New Milford, Connecticut. After graduation Sherman studied theology, possibly, as his younger brother Josiah (A.B. 1754) did, with the Reverend Joseph Bellamy.

On February 18, 1756, Sherman was ordained second pastor of the Congregational church in Bedford, Massachusetts. The congregation had been strongly New Light for some years and had encountered considerable difficulties with its first minister, Nicholas Bowes (Harvard 1725), who was a determined Old Light, announcing publicly that he would refuse to admit George Whitefield to his pulpit. Sherman, apparently, proved acceptable. He married Lydia Merriam, the daughter of one of his deacons, on March 1, 1759. The Shermans had three children.

In 1767 a now obscure controversy between Sherman and some of the members of his congregation concerning the Half-Way Covenant arose. Dismissed on December 17, 1767, Sherman was not long without a pulpit. In 1768 he moved to Connecticut, where his older brother, Roger, was beginning to make a name for himself in public affairs. On May 18, 1768, Sherman was installed as minister of the Congregational church at Mount Carmel, Connecticut, just north of New Haven. President Naphtali Daggett of Yale preached a vehemently New Light sermon at Sherman's installation. The Mount Carmel post was hardly a lucrative one: Sherman received a salary of only £85 a year, plus fifty cords of firewood (twenty-five of them specified to be of walnut).

Sherman was to spend less time at the Mount Carmel church than he had at the Bedford church. At first his new parishioners responded enthusiastically to his preaching. Soon, however, personal and doctrinal wrangling between Sherman and his congregation developed. He was dismissed on October 9, 1771. Sherman remained in Mount Carmel until 1778—doing what is unclear. In 1778 Sherman moved to East Windsor, Connecticut, after selling his house and land in Mount Carmel for £600 and investing the money in government securities. It was a mistake. Sherman had hoped to live on the interest from his bonds, but none was forthcoming. And, in 1782, Congress officially stopped payment on them. In October 1787, Sherman petitioned the Connecticut legislature for aid. It eventually granted him a loan of £30, but insisted on keeping his securities as collateral. By 1788 Sherman was in what he called "a state of decay." His brother Roger helped him frame a new petition to the assembly, which returned £400 of his securities to him. Sherman died in East Windsor on July 18, 1797.

SOURCES: Family background: H. Bond, *Genealogies of the Families & Descendents of the Early Settlers of Watertown, Mass.* (1855), I, 431; F. Jackson, *Hist. of the Early Settlement of Newton, Mass.* (1854), 409; and C. Collier, *Roger Sherman's Conn.* (1971); Nicholas Bowes: *Sibley's Harvard Graduates*, VII, 454-57; wife and children: L. K. Brown, *Wilderness Town, The Story of Bedford, Mass.* (1968), 212; dismissal from Bedford: Giger, Memoirs, I; N. Daggett, *The Great Importance of Speaking in the Most Intelligible Manner in the Christian Churches* (1768); Mt. Carmel salary: Stiles, *Itineraries*, 269; Mt. Carmel dismissal: Stiles, *Literary Diary*, I, 172; Mt. Carmel pastorate: G. S. Dickerman, *Old Mount Carmel Parish* (1925), 89-92.

Joseph Shippen, Jr.

JOSEPH SHIPPEN, JR., A.B., A.M. 1756, soldier, merchant, public official and farmer, was born in Lancaster, Pennsylvania, on October 30, 1732, the son of Sarah Plumley, wife of Edward Shippen, a judge, prosperous merchant, and trustee of the College from 1748 to 1767. Shippen's letters to his father during his student days are one of the few sources for the history of the College in this period and have been used by historians to reconstruct the curriculum of colonial Princeton. Written in French, Latin, and English, and obviously meant as exercises for the parental eye, they dutifully inform his father of the nature of his reading, the progress of his studies, and of President Burr's difficulties in bringing a lecturer on science and apparatus to Newark. To his brother Edward, Shippen was less lofty: "This Village consists of one continual Series of Rustick Actions throughout the year, & can afford only trifling Occurences not worth writing you."

After graduation Shippen probably joined the family business for a

Joseph Shippen, Jr., A.B. 1753
BY JOHN HESSELIUS

few years. Early in the Seven Years War, on April 3, 1756, he was commissioned a captain in the Pennsylvania provincial forces, and by 1758 had risen to the rank of colonel. Shippen saw most of his service in western Pennsylvania and was with General Forbes's expedition when it captured Fort Duquesne from the French in 1758. A busy and competent officer, his duties were largely administrative. His letters to his family concern problems such as sickness among his troops, scarcities of provisions, arms, clothing and blankets, the dilatoriness of the Pennsylvania Assembly, the difficulties of recruiting troops (and of paying them), and such matters.

Leaving the war behind, in spring 1760 Shippen sailed for Europe, bent on both pleasure and business. Aboard the same vessel was a young Pennsylvania painter, Benjamin West, bound for study abroad. Shippen may have encouraged West's ambitions. Shippen returned to America in the fall of 1761 and almost immediately—on January 2, 1762—was appointed clerk of the provincial council of Pennsylvania, an important bureaucratic post in the Penns's proprietary government that he held until 1776. Shippen and his brother Edward were among the younger men advanced by the new governor, John Penn. Over the next decade and a half the Shippens became powerful figures in the Presbyterian-Proprietary faction in Pennsylvania politics. They also acquired large tracts of land in Northumberland County as well as in other parts of the province.

Among the shifting factions of the Pennsylvania politics of the 1760s, the Proprietary party was the more "radical" of the various groups: in 1766, on hearing of the repeal of the Stamp Act, Shippen greeted it as "joyful news." His duties as clerk of the council involved him, among other things, in the affairs of Connecticut settlers in the Wyoming Valley who were trying to wrest control of the area from the Proprietary government.

On February 29, 1768, Shippen married Jane Galloway of "Tulip Hill" in Maryland. The Shippens had a Philadelphia residence and eventually bought "Plumley Farm," an 108-acre estate named for Shippen's mother, near Kennett Square, Chester County. Shippen's activities were not confined to war, business, and government. He was an accomplished writer of occasional verse and had a strong interest, perhaps developed during his college days, in science. Elected to the American Philosophical Society in 1768, he served (along with John Ewing, A.B. 1754) on one of the society's committees formed to observe the transit of Venus in June 1769. And at Plumley Farm, his tombstone records, he "brot. in to use the most approved mode of farming."

Shippen's connections with the Proprietary government brought him only grief in the revolutionary years. He hoped for reconciliation with Britain but on American terms, as the following letter, written in November 1775, makes clear: "We are daily in expectation of receiving News of the further success of the Continental Forces at Montreal & Quebec. I would fain hope these fortunate enterprizes will tend rather to induce the Ministry to bring about an Accomodation, than to irritate the Mother Country & provoke its further Vengence against us. But if the latter should unhappily prove to be the Case, our having possession of Canada, with the Canadians and Indians in our Interest will be of immense advantage to us, as thereby the Ministry will be deprived of the great addition of strength they expected to derive from that Country, and the Forces from Great Britain must necessarily be much divided in their operations next year." Despite Shippen's obvious Whig sentiments, as a Proprietary officeholder he was placed upon parole in a limited area by the new state government in October 1777. The parole was later enlarged to include the whole state; in May 1778, the Supreme Executive Council of Pennsylvania released him from parole completely.

While hardly an active Whig, there was little doubt among Shippen's friends or enemies about where he stood. In 1778, while attending Congress in Philadelphia, Robert Morris, the financier, entrusted the care of his children to the Shippens. Late in the same year the Shippens were reduced to near penury because of the depredations of British troops around Kennett Square.

In the years after the peace Shippen appears to have spent his time as a gentleman farmer, land speculator, and sometime judge. He served as an associate justice in the Chester County courts in the 1790s. After his wife's death in 1801 Shippen married Jane Fishbourne, probably a relative of his first wife. Shippen had inherited land in Lancaster County, and it was probably about this time that he moved there. He served as a judge in the Lancaster County courts. He died on February 10, 1810, and was buried in the graveyard adjoining St. James's Episcopal church in Lancaster.

SOURCES: No full-length sketch of Shippen exists, but see W. U. Hensel, *The Shippen House* (1910), 16-17; remarks on Newark: Shippen to "Neddy" [Edward] Shippen, Feb. 9, 1750, NjP; Shippen's college years are fully reconstructed in F. J. Broderick, "Pulpit, Physics and Politics: The Curriculum of the College of New Jersey, 1746-1794," *WMQ*, 6 (1944), 42-68; service in Seven Years War: *PMHB*, 36 (1912); trip to Europe and Benjamin West: *Pa. Arch.* (2d ser.), 18 (1890), 699, and *Lanc. Co. HSPA*, 29 (1925), 61; appointment as clerk to council: *Pa. Col. Rec.*, 8 (1882); political role: W. S. Hanna, *Benjamin Franklin and Penn. Politics* (1964), 162; landholdings: *Pa. Arch.* (3rd ser.), 25 (1897), and other listings scattered throughout series; Stamp Act: *Lanc. Co. HSPA*, 11 (1907); governmental activities: *Pa. Arch.*, 4 (1853), and *Pa. Col. Rec.*, 9 (1852); wife: *MHM*, 60 (1965), 363-66; transit of

Venus: *PMHB*, 51 (1927), 297; epitaph: *Lanc. Co. HSPA*, 37 (1933), 145; views at beginning of Revolution: *PMHB*, 24 (1900), 386-87; paroles: *Pa. Col. Rec.*, 11 (1852), 269, 490; Morris children: *Lanc. Co. HSPA*, 35 (1930), 130-31; finances during Revolution: ibid., 11 (1907), 18.

Mss: DLC, NjP, PHi, PPAmP

Elijah Williams

ELIJAH WILLIAMS, A.B., A.M. 1760, iron manufacturer, merchant, landowner and public official, was born in Newton, Massachusetts, on November 15, 1732, the son of Colonel Ephraim Williams and his wife Abigail Jones. In 1737, along with three other white families, the Williamses moved to Stockbridge, where they were meant to serve as civilized models for the newly gathered Indian inhabitants. The senior Williams soon became the wealthiest and most important man in the village.

During his years at the College (and afterward) Williams was bombarded with admonitory letters from his father. An extract from one, written from Stockbridge on March 15, 1750, conveys the tone of most: I "intreet and advise and charge you to improve your time to the best advantage from Body & soul. now is your day to work in, dont neglect it. time is flying on Swift wings and the past hour can never be recald: be diligent in your Studyes and I pray God bless and smile on you in them & give you abbility to make a Laudable proficiency in learning; endeavor to excell, coppy after the best patterns: endeavor by your Courteous Carriage and dutifull behavior to win the affections of all about you in and according to the Severall relations in which they stand; especially let the worthy Pressident have all possible Respectfull Regards paid him, and be allways ready to apply to him for Instruction and advice, and thankfull for all you receive: that will Ingage his affections. and. ready assistance which will be of great Service. one word in your favour from him may be by and by of vast and unknown Service to you."

After graduation Williams returned home to Stockbridge, which at the time was more or less a family concern. In 1761 Williams was appointed the first sheriff of Berkshire County, a post he held until about 1776. He did well in Stockbridge. In 1762 he paid Paul Revere £18 for a gold necklace. Perhaps there was no connection, but two years later Williams was sued in the Great Barrington court by one Mary Willson, who claimed that he was the father of her son. She won her case, and Williams paid child support. Williams must have cut a fine figure in the frontier village: a suit for which he paid £12.3s.9d. was composed of "scarlet cloth, shalloon, gold vellum lace, fustian, two pairs of leather pockets and lining for breeches . . . velvett for the collar, and a pair of gold straps." Not long after this purchase Williams married Sophia Partridge of Hatfield, Massachusetts, with whom he had a son.

In about 1763 Williams started an iron forge in Queensborough, just to the west of Stockbridge, and later opened a marble quarry. In 1773 he opened the first store in the area and in 1774 was instrumental in having it chartered as the town of West Stockbridge. Williams became the local magnate: he was the largest landowner in West Stockbridge and employed many laborers. Every inhabitant of the town was in debt to him. He dealt with merchants such as Nathaniel Hazard (A.B. 1764) in Philadelphia and William Imlay (A.B. 1773) in New York. His iron ($£20$ a ton) and potash were sold as far away as London. When a Congregational church was finally formed in West Stockbridge in 1789, Williams was one of its deacons.

The revolutionary years were difficult ones for Williams. As a government official and one of the richest men in the area he was forced by suspicious citizens to make constant declarations of his loyalty to the patriot cause. He was jailed twice during the war, despite carrying around with him a declaration which read: "We the subscribers have at the request of . . . Colonel Williams heard his declaration and being satisfied therewith respecting his political sentiments are of opinion that he ought to be released from his present confinement and . . . restored to the charge of all good people."

After the war Williams quickly regained his former prominence and influence. In about 1802 he moved back to Stockbridge, where he spent the rest of his life. Williams was among the first trustees of Williams College, which was named for his half-brother, Ephraim, who had been killed during the Seven Years War. He died in Stockbridge on June 9, 1815.

SOURCES: Nineteen letters from the senior to the junior Williams are printed in *Scribner's Mag.*, 17 (1895), 247-60; references scattered throughout: E. F. Jones, *Stockbridge, Past and Present* (1854), and S. C. Sedgwick and C. S. Marquand, *Stockbridge, 1739-1938* (1939); also W. C. Spaulding, "Town of West Stockbridge," in *Hist. of Berkshire County, Mass.* (1885), II, 629-30, 634, 641; C. Durfee, *A Hist. of Williams College* (1860), 151; and F. H. Denison, *Mark Hopkins, A Biography* (1935), 5.

Benjamin Woodruff

BENJAMIN WOODRUFF, A.B., A.M. 1756, Presbyterian clergyman and older brother of Joseph (A.B. 1753), was born in Elizabethtown, Essex

County, New Jersey, on December 26, 1732, the son of Elizabeth Ogden and Samuel Woodruff. Samuel was one of the wealthiest and most influential citizens of the town, a merchant engaged in trade with Madiera and the West Indies, mayor, member of the governor's council, and one of the original trustees of the College.

Benjamin grew up with the Brainerds, George Whitefield, and Governor Belcher as familiar visitors to his home. "He has but a middling Genius," President Burr wrote to trustee David Cowell of Trenton in recommending Woodruff as a schoolmaster shortly after his graduaton. "Rather below than above the Common sort. He is a Person of great Industry, of great Integrity and by his good Behaviour he recommends himself to all his Acquaintance. He is a middling good Scholar, writes a pretty good Hand." Whether Woodruff was offered the job or not is unknown. Woodruff studied theology, probably with his Elizabethtown pastor, Elihu Spencer. In 1756 Woodruff married Mary Cross, with whom he had two children.

On March 14, 1759, Woodruff was ordained pastor of the Presbyterian church in Westfield, New Jersey, a post he held until his death. His wife Mary died in 1762. On June 1, 1763, Woodruff married Elizabeth Bryant, with whom he had five children. On his father's death, intestate, in 1768 Woodruff, as eldest son, inherited a considerable estate, which he divided with his mother and two brothers. Aside from revivals in 1764, 1765, 1774, 1785, and 1786, his pastorate was uneventful. He was remembered as being "small in person, dignified and precise in his manners, social in his habits, scrupulously exact and fastidious in his dress, and a fine specimen of what is known as a 'gentleman of the old school.' " He died on April 3, 1803, leaving a considerable amount of land to his wife and two daughters.

SOURCES: Date of birth, name of first wife, from Woodruff's bible in his possession: Mr. Woodruff Wallner to Sec., Princeton University, Oct. 23, 1961, Benjamin Woodruff File, PUA; much primary material on Woodruff and father, including wills: C. N. Woodruff, *Woodruff Chronicles: A Genealogy* (1967), 58-73; Aaron Burr to David Cowell, Nov. 7, 1753, PPPrHi; pastorate: W. K. McKinney, et al., *Commemorative Hist. of the Presbyterian Church in Westfield, N.J., 1728-1928* (1929), 164-68.

Joseph Woodruff

JOSEPH WOODRUFF, A.B., A.M. 1758, merchant and younger brother of Benjamin (A.B. 1753), was born in Elizabethtown, Essex County, New Jersey, in about 1734, the son of Samuel Woodruff and his wife, Elizabeth Ogden. Samuel was one of the wealthiest and most influential citizens of the town. A merchant, he traded with Madiera and the West Indies, was mayor of the town, a member of the governor's council, and one of the original trustees of the College.

After graduation Woodruff joined his father in business. In 1754 he married Anne Hunloke, who died on June 28, 1757. Woodruff died in February 1769. He left a considerable amount of property, including the twelve-room family mansion and four slaves. He was survived by his second wife, Rebecca, and his fifteen-year-old son Hunloke (class of 1772), then a student in the College.

SOURCES: C. N. Woodruf, *Woodruff Chronicles: A Genealogy* (1967), 72-81.

MSS: NjP

CLASS OF 1754

Moses Barrett, A.B.

Benjamin Chapman, A.B.

John Ewing, A.B.

Benjamin Hait, A.B.

Ezra Horton, A.B.

Samuel Kennedy, A.B.

Hugh Knox, A.B.

David Mathews, A.B.

Jonathan Odell, A.B.

Sylvanus Osborn, A.B.

David Purviance, A.B.

William Ramsay, A.B.

James Reeve, A.B.

Benajah Roots, A.B.

Josiah Sherman, A.B.

William Shippen, Jr., A.B.

Thomas Smith, A.B.

William Thomson, A.B.

Noah Wadham[s], A.B.

Moses Barrett

MOSES BARRETT, A.B., schoolmaster and preacher, was probably the Moses Barrett, son of Rachel Buge and Thomas Barrett, born at Chelmsford, Massachusetts, on February 1, 1719. By October 22, 1747, Barrett had moved to Voluntown, Connecticut, where he married Mary Dow on that date. The couple had four children.

On October 24, 1753, Barrett bought property in Lebanon, Connecticut. It was presumably shortly after this that he traveled south to Newark. Whether he actually attended the College or not is unclear. In the manuscript minutes of the Board of Trustees Barrett is listed along with the other regular A.B.s of 1754. However, his name does not appear in President Burr's Account Book. Moreover, in the College's printed catalogues of the eighteenth century Barrett's name is consistently listed with the recipients of honorary A.B.s. Whatever the case, after receiving his A.B., Barrett returned to Connecticut to become first master in a charity school for Indians, the precursor of Dartmouth College, that the Reverend Eleazar Wheelock (Yale 1733) opened on Barrett's Lebanon property in December 1754. On June 28, 1755, Barrett sold his property, which included a "shop and schoolhouse," to Colonel Joshua Moor, who in turn conveyed it to Wheelock. A historian of Dartmouth has suggested that in fact Wheelock had taken over a school established by Barrett, but more information on this point is lacking. In 1756 Wheelock reported to the great evangelist George Whitefield that Barrett had become a minister and was conducting a revival in New Fairfield, Connecticut. No mention of Barrett has been discovered in Connecticut church records. At some time after this Barrett, in an attempt to raise money for missionary work among the Indians, traveled to England, where he died of smallpox in 1762. "My children have lost the guide of their youth and the instructor of their younger Years," Barrett's widow wrote to Eleazar Wheelock in October of that year, "even at that age when they seem most of all to need instruction but I Desire to submit to Divine providence and to be patient under all trials."

SOURCES: Material concerning Barrett is extremely fragmentary. Most extensive source: series of extracts from MS Conn. public records, Moses Barrett File, PUA; geneal.: William Barrett, *Geneal. of the Descendants of Thomas Barrett* (1888), 24; G. C. Marbin, *Barrett Ancestry* (1912), 12; Alexander, *Princeton*, 27; Frederick Chase, *Hist. of Dartmouth College* (1928), 10; Mary Barrett to Eleazar Wheelock, Oct. 8, 1762, Wheelock MSS.

Benjamin Chapman

BENJAMIN CHAPMAN, A.B., A.M. Yale 1761, Congregational clergyman, was from Connecticut. Although his parentage is uncertain, it seems possible that he was born near Haddam, Connecticut, about 1725, the son of Samuel Chapman, who eventually settled in Sharon, Connecticut, and who may have died while his son was a child. It seems clear that Chapman was raised in Litchfield County, Connecticut, perhaps under the tutelage of the Reverend Joseph Bellamy. Chapman and two classmates from Litchfield County, Benajah Roots and Noah Wadhams, entered the College at the same time. A notation that he once borrowed a Hebrew bible from President Burr is the only surviving record of Chapman's college career.

Within two months after graduation Chapman was licensed to preach by the Congregationalists of Litchfield County. On March 17, 1756, he was installed as pastor of the Congregational church at Southington, Connecticut. Joseph Bellamy preached the installation sermon. The Southington church had been split between Old Lights and New Lights; the choice of Chapman, a moderate revivalist, was meant as a compromise between the various factions. Chapman had little use for the abstruse theological debates of Bellamy, Hopkins, and others. "The Lord reigns let the earth rejoyce, Truth will finally prevail and triumph in Spite of Earth and Hell," he once somewhat resignedly wrote to Enoch Green after recounting New England's latest theological controversies. As the years went by Chapman's moderation grew less and less satisfactory to his congregation, which was rent by opposing factions. Chapman was not able to control the various groups and was forced out of his pulpit on September 28, 1774. However, he remained in Southington and continued to preach there and elsewhere for the remainder of his life.

Until the Revolution Chapman possessed an income independent of his earnings as a minister. He owned several slaves and lived in a somewhat more comfortable style than his neighbors. The phrase "to live like Chapman's niggers" was current in Southington a century after his pastorate. But Chapman lost his property during the war. He was reduced to near penury in his later years and was forced to petition the Connecticut legislature for relief, which was granted.

On January 8, 1756, Chapman married Abigail Riggs of Derby, with whom he had eight children. After an attack of smallpox in the 1770s, Abigail gradually sank into insanity, helped along by the constant and apparently vicious bickerings of her husband's former congregation. Despite his misfortunes Chapman's activity never slackened; he was an active preacher throughout his area of the state, especially among the Baptists, and was involved in a revival as late as 1783. He died in Southington on June 22, 1786.

SOURCES: An exhaustive effort to discover Chapman's parentage and a full account of his career: H. R. Timlow, *Ecclesiastical and Other Sketches of Southington, Conn.* (1875), xliii-xliv, 97-107; bible: Aaron Burr, MS Account Book, 10; quotation: Chapman to Enoch Green, November 4, 1770, PHi; brief mentions of Chapman: Stiles, *Literary Diary*, II, 403, 405, and III, 229.

Mss: PHi (1 ALS)

John Ewing

JOHN EWING, A.B., A.M. 1757, D.D. Edinburgh 1773, Presbyterian clergyman, scientist, and college tutor, professor, and official, was born in East Nottingham, Cecil County, Maryland, on June 22, 1732, the son of Alexander Ewing, a farmer who had emigrated from Ireland. Inheriting only £20 from his father, John determined to secure an edu-

John Ewing, A.B. 1754
BY EDWARD D. MARCHANT AFTER PEALE

cation for himself. He attended the academy run by the Reverend
Francis Alison, a leading Presbyterian educator, at New London,
Pennsylvania. After completing his course he spent three years more
at the academy as a tutor in Greek, Latin and mathematics.

In 1754 Ewing went north to Newark to become the chief instructor
in the College's grammar school. He also joined the senior class, receiving his A.B. in less than a year. President Burr and the trustees
thought highly enough of Ewing to employ him as a tutor in the College from 1754 to 1758. Mrs. Burr was less sure; while she thought
Ewing a good preacher, she found him somewhat misogynous. "I have
had a smart combat with Mr Ewing about our Sex," she reported to
a friend, "—he is a man of good parts and lerning but has mean
thoughts of Women—he began the dispute in this Manner, speaking
of Miss [Annis] Boudanot I said she was a sociable friendly creture . . .
but Mr Ewing says—She and the Stocktons are full of talk about
Friendship and Society and Such Stuff—and made up a Mouth as if
much disgusted—I asked him what he would have em talk about
whether he chose they should talk about fashions and dress—he said
things that they understood, he did not think women knew what
Friendship was, they were hardly capable of anything so cool and rational as friendship." Ewing conquered his distrust of women sufficiently to marry, probably in 1759, Hannah Sergeant, daughter of the
College's treasurer, Jonathan Sergeant. Over the years the Ewings had
eleven children.

Before his marriage Ewing returned to his old mentor, Francis Alison, to study theology. In 1752 Alison had left his academy at New
London to take charge of an academy in Philadelphia. When the College of Philadelphia was chartered in 1755 Alison became its vice provost and not long afterward became associate pastor of the Old Side
First Presbyterian Church in Philadelphia as well. Ewing joined him
there and was licensed by the Presbytery of New Castle in 1758 and
ordained in 1759. In 1758, doubtless through Alison's influence, Ewing
was called upon to take over the teaching duties of the Reverend William Smith, Anglican provost of the College of Philadelphia, who was
making a trip to England. Ewing took over Smith's course in moral
philosophy and at the same time was called to serve with Alison as associate pastor. In February 1762, Ewing was appointed professor of
natural philosophy in the college.

Ewing successfully maintained his double role as professor and pastor, and his associations with both the College of Philadelphia and the
First Presbyterian Church, for the rest of his life. As pastor he was a
steady, rational, Old Light, advising his congregation that "this spa-

cious earth on which we live, is but a small province of God's universal empire, one little wheel in the vast machine." He opened his course
at the college by declaring to his students: "There is more in a single
vegetable, than has yet been adequately accounted for by the ablest
philosopher that ever lived." He demanded strict adherence to scientific method, advising his students, "to admit of no solution, but what
appears to be founded on the established principles and properties of
matter, and sufficiently confirmed, by an adequate number of observations and experiments."

Ewing's most important scientific achievements were in the field of
astronomy. Elected to the American Philosophical Society in 1768 (he
later served as one of its vice-presidents), he proposed that the society
set up a special committee to make observations of the transit of Venus
due in 1769, an event which had aroused great interest in the international scientific community. Ewing found a rival in his college's provost, William Smith. Smith proposed that his protégé, David Rittenhouse, make the society's observations. The society ended by setting
up two committees to observe the transit, one including Rittenhouse
to be headed by Smith, the other to be headed by Ewing. Ewing persuaded the Pennsylvania Assembly to contribute funds to erect a
wooden observatory in State House Square, while Rittenhouse's observations were made at nearby Norriton. The work of Ewing and his
committee was successful and more than creditable to American science, even though William Smith managed to communicate the results
of his group to Europe first, thus garnering most of the credit. Over
the years Ewing put his scientific knowledge to practical use, serving
on commissions set up to survey the Massachusetts–New York boundary, the Pennsylvania–Virginia boundary, and others.

Throughout his life Ewing was involved with institutions of higher
education other than the College of Philadelphia. In 1766 he joined
with Francis Alison in an Old Side Presbyterian attempt to gain control of the College of New Jersey. In 1773 he made a trip to England
in order to raise funds for the Newark Academy in Delaware, which
he hoped to raise to collegiate status. While abroad Ewing conferred
with Lord North on the colonial situation, met Dr. Johnson and other
literati, and was accorded a particularly warm reception in Scotland,
where several towns granted him their freedom and the University of
Edinburgh awarded him the D.D.

Unable to raise funds because of the impending conflict, Ewing returned home in 1775. A Whig, like most members of his congregation,
over the next few years he spent his time preaching and trying to hold
the college together. In 1779 the revolutionary state government trans-

formed the College of Philadelphia into a new institution, the University of the State of Pennsylvania, ousting Provost William Smith in the bargain. Ewing was elected first provost of the new institution and moved into Smith's house. In the following years Ewing lived an intensely busy life, teaching, preaching, and overseeing the affairs of his institution. He incurred the intense enmity of one of his parishioners, Dr. Benjamin Rush (A.B. 1760), for his opposition to Rush's efforts to establish what eventually became Dickinson College in Carlisle, Pennsylvania. Despite Rush's attacks, Ewing continued to retain his standing and to increase in influence among the Presbyterians. And among others as well, since when the University of the State of Pennsylvania was reorganized as the University of Pennsylvania in 1791 Ewing continued as provost.

Over the years Ewing played a prominent part in Presbyterian church affairs. During the Revolution and for many years thereafter he was treasurer of the Corporation for Relief of Poor and Distressed Presbyterian Ministers and of the Poor and Distressed Widows and Children of Presbyterian Ministers, one of the earliest American insurance organizations. Responsible for the corporation's investments, Ewing bought and sold lands in many parts of the state. By the mid-1790s the affairs of the corporation, as well as those of the university and his own personal finances, were in a troubled state. In 1797 the senior class at the university numbered only three, the corporation's investments were tied up in the Morris-Nicholson land empire, and Ewing himself was in poor health. On January 5, 1802, the university's trustees resolved that Ewing's health did not permit him to fulfill his duties and stopped his salary, leaving him with a pension. He died on September 8th of that year.

SOURCES: *DAB*; Sprague, *Annals*, III, 216-19; L.E.E. Ewing, *Dr. John Ewing and Some of His Noted Connections* (1924), which reprints letters from Britain; Esther Burr, MS Journal, April 12, 1757, and passim; scientific activities: B. Hindle, *The Pursuit of Science in Rev. Am.* (1956), 146-65, and Hindle, *David Rittenhouse* (1964); both histories of the Univ. of Pa. are disappointingly thin on Ewing: T. H. Montgomery, *A Hist. of the Univ. of Pa.* (1940), and E. P. Cheyney, *Hist. of the Univ. of Pa., 1740-1940* (1940); opposition to Dickinson College: C. C. Sellers, *Dickinson College* (1973), 56-72; Rush quotation: Butterfield, *Rush Letters*, I, 433-34. The quotation *re* "vast machine" is from Ewing, *Sermons*, 16; on scientific study, from Ewing, *Natural Philosophy*, 12-13.

PUBLICATIONS: STE, and: "Proposal for observing the Transit of Venus, June 3, 1769," in *Early Transactions of the Amer. Phil. Soc.* (1969), 40-43; J. P. Wilson, ed., *Sermons, by the Rev. John Ewing, D.D.* (1812); *A Plain Elementary System of Natural Philosophy* (1809).

Mss: MHi, NjP, PHi, PPPrHi

Benjamin Hait

BENJAMIN HAIT, A.B., A.M., 1757, Presbyterian clergyman, was born in Stamford, Connecticut, supposedly on June 13, 1718, the son of Elizabeth Jagger and her husband, Benjamin Hait, a farmer. On March 6, 1744, Hait's father gave him a house, home-lot, and lands in Stamford. Over the next few years (in 1746, 1749, and 1752) Hait gradually sold off his property to his brothers Jonas and Abraham. The proceeds were possibly used to finance his preparatory education and his years in the College.

While at College Hait bought a lottery ticket and a copy of Isaac Watts's essays. He also accompanied Samuel Davies one day on a trip from Newark to New York. "A promising young man," Davies noted. "I had an agreeable conversation with him on original sin, and the influence of the flesh upon the spirit to incline it to sin." Within a month after graduation, on October 25, 1754, Hait was licensed by the Presbytery of New Brunswick and sent to supply at the Forks of the Delaware. He also preached at the Amwell Presbyterian church at Reaville, Hunterdon County, New Jersey. He was ordained and installed at that church on December 4, 1755, and remained there for the next decade.

On April 18, 1756, Hait married Ann (or "Nancy") Smith of Long Island. On their way home to Amwell after their marriage in New York the couple stopped to visit the Burr family in Newark. "They seem to be quite pleased with one another," Esther Burr noted in her journal. "I hope it may hold—tho Nancy's temper is a little out of the common road, but Mr Hait is a very good tempered man." The Haits had seven children.

In May 1765, Hait left the Amwell church, and, perhaps, briefly and informally succeeded John Moffat (A.B. 1749) in the service of the Goodwill Church at Wallkill, New York. In the succeeding winter Hait returned to New Jersey and was installed as pastor of the Presbyterian church at Connecticut Farms (now part of Elizabeth), Essex County.

Active in church affairs, Hait was moderator of the Synod of New York and Philadelphia when it met at Philadelphia in 1775. Hait was a Whig. At some time after 1776 he joined Washington's army encamped at Morristown as a chaplain. During his service he contracted a debilitating fever. On March 4, 1779, Hait made his will; on March 15, he advertised a 210-acre farm he owned in Sussex County for sale; on June 27 he died.

SOURCES: Hait's name was pronounced "Hoit"; one of his sons changed the spelling to "Hoyt." Some doubt about the year of Hait's birth exists. The otherwise generally accurate sketch by D. W. Hoyt, in *A Genealogical Hist. of the Hoyt, Haight, and Hight Families* (1871), 340, states that Hait was the tenth child of a man born in 1697, which makes the 1718 birthdate suspect. College accounts: Aaron Burr, MS Account Book, 10; for Davies quotation, Webster, *History*, 667; J. B. Kugler, *Hist. of the First English Presbyterian Church in Amwell* (1912), 79-82; G. S. Mott, *Hist. of the Presbyterian Church in Flemington, N.J.* (1894), 30-32; and Hatfield, *Elizabeth*, 641; Esther Burr's remark: her MS Journal, April 1756; moderator: *Presbyterian Records*, 462; sale of farm: 3 *NJA*, 168-69; will: 34 *NJA*, 218.

Ezra Horton

EZRA HORTON, A.B., A.M. Yale 1772, Congregational clergyman, was born at Southold, Long Island, on Christmas Day 1733, the son of Anne Goldsmith and James Horton, a moderately well-to-do farmer. In College Horton bought a few books—a Hebrew grammar and bible and a copy of Cicero's *De Oratore*. After graduation Horton studied for the ministry, probably with President Burr. In 1757 he married Mary Hempstead at a ceremony held in Hempstead, Long Island. The Hortons had three children.

On June 14, 1759, Horton was ordained and installed as pastor of the Congregational church at Union, Connecticut. His salary was low— only £67 a year. At the time of Horton's installation there was some sentiment in the parish for the Presbyterian form of church government, but Horton was finally settled on Congregational principles. Horton's pastorate was marked by frequent disciplinary problems with members of his flock. In 1783 several members of the congregation called for Horton's dismissal. A church council was called; he was mildly reproved for the wording of some of his sermons, for using strong words against some of his parishioners, and for not properly examining new applicants for communion. The church, however, insisted upon his dismissal. He resigned on August 6, 1783, and died in Union on January 13, 1789.

SOURCES: Father's will (Horton was left £30): *N.Y. Wills*, VII, 152-53; brief sketch: G. G. Horton, *Horton Genealogy* (1876), 183; college account: Aaron Burr, MS Account Book, 12-13; pastorate: H. M. Lawsen, *Hist. of Union, Conn.* (1893), 67-71.

Samuel Kennedy

SAMUEL KENNEDY, A.B., A.M. 1760, Presbyterian clergyman, physician, and teacher, was born in Scotland in 1720. All authorities agree that he studied at the University of Edinburgh but his name does not appear on the university's lists of graduates. Kennedy's son, Samuel, Jr. (ca. 1744–1803), was also a physician; the careers of the two are almost hopelessly intertangled in the records.

The time and circumstances of Kennedy's emigration to America are unknown. Even more puzzling are the circumstances that led to the conferral of an A.B. on him by the College in 1754. On May 18, 1750, the Presbytery of New Brunswick licensed Kennedy; he was ordained minister of the Presbyterian church at Basking Ridge, Somerset County, New Jersey, on June 25, 1751. The bestowal of an A.B. by the College in 1754 was probably a pro forma affair. The A.M. was conferred on him in course in 1760.

Kennedy ministered to his congregation until his death and often supplied the Amwell and other Presbyterian churches in the area. He also maintained a classical school on his 300-acre farm near Bernard's Town. In it he prepared several students for the College. Not only a minister, teacher, and planter, he augmented his ministerial salary of £110 a year with an extensive medical practice. Elected to the New Jersey Medical Society on May 3, 1768 (his son was admitted the following year), he served for a time as its secretary and regularly attended its meetings until his death. He also prepared candidates for the ministry (although after six months' study with Kennedy, Andrew Kirkpatrick [A.B. 1775] decided against becoming a clergyman). Widely respected for his learning, he had an influential voice in church councils. He preached the funeral sermon of trustee Jeremiah Halsey (A.B. 1752) in November 1780. Kennedy died intestate at Basking Ridge on August 31, 1787.

SOURCES: J. C. Rankin, *Historical Discourse* (1892), 13-16; I. V. Brown, *Memoirs of the Rev. Robert Finley, D.D.* (1819), 229-35; Wickes, *Hist. of Medicine in N.J.* (1875), 22, 24, 28; 24 *NJA*, 407; 25 *NJA*, 350-51; 3 (2 ser.) *NJA*, 322; 5 (2 ser.) *NJA*, 120.

Hugh Knox

HUGH KNOX, A.B., A.M. Yale 1768 D.D. Glasgow, Presbyterian and Dutch Reformed clergyman and sometime physician, was born in Ireland about 1727. "I was bred in a very pure district of the Church of Scotland, of which my father was a faithful minister," he once wrote, neglecting to mention the name either of his father or the district. Knox emigrated to America in 1751, at the age of twenty-four. Handsome, well-mannered, with a good, basic classical education, he apparently applied to the New Side Presbytery of New Castle for licensing shortly after his arrival. The license was refused. Knox then asked the Old Side leader Francis Alison for a teaching position in his academy at New London, Pennsylvania. Alison had no need of an assistant, but recommended Knox instead to the New Side leader, Reverend John Rodgers, pastor of churches at St. George's and Middletown, Delaware. With Rodgers's patronage, Knox founded a successful school at Head of Bohemia, about ten miles from Middletown, and regularly attended Rodgers's church.

Unmarried, Knox spent Saturday afternoons visiting other young men at the local tavern, run by an elder of the church. Because of his admiration for Rodgers and his solemn expression, his companions called him "Parson." One Saturday afternoon, hoping to have some fun, one of his friends said, "Come parson, give us a sermon." Knox refused. The group insisted. Knox finally gave in, and recited from memory the sermon Rodgers had preached the Sunday before. He preached it to such good effect, in fact, that the innkeeper in the next room thought that Rodgers was actually in the tavern. Finished, Knox was shocked at himself: this was profanity. But the imitation of Rodgers had apparently worked an inner transformation: Knox was converted—and ashamed to see Rodgers or his other patrons, he immediately fled Head of Bohemia.

The next time Rodgers met Knox was at the College of New Jersey commencement of 1753. Arriving in Newark for the ceremony, Rodgers was surprised to discover Knox in Burr's house. Knox, it seemed, had applied to Burr for admission to the College. Apologizing profusely to Rodgers, he convinced him of his conversion. Rodgers said nothing of the Delaware affair to Burr, but supported Knox's request for admission.

After graduation Knox studied theology with President Burr. He apparently made rapid progress, for as early as Sunday, February 9, 1755, Esther Burr noted in her journal that she had been "at meeting all day Mr Burr preached in the forenoon, & Mr Knox in the afternoon, a very ingenious good young man." On Thursday evening, July 1, 1755, Knox was ordained by the Presbytery of New York meeting at Morristown. President Burr preached the ordination sermon. Knox's own ordination sermon, *The Dignity and Importance of the Gospel Ministry*, was so admired by the Presbytery that they ordered it printed. ("I think it is an ingenious discourse for a young man," wrote Mrs. Burr.)

The Dutch Protestant Reformed church on the island of Saba, one

of the three Dutch Windward Islands in the Carribean, had requested
a minister from the Presbytery of New York. The Presbytery recommended Knox; within a month of his ordination he had left the mainland to take up his post. Saba, a tiny island only 4.8 miles square, was
populated predominantly by whites in the eighteenth century. In 1781
it consisted of about 150 families engaged in shipbuilding, shoe-
making, fishing, and agriculture. It had one town, called The Bottom.
For the next sixteen years Hugh Knox remained at The Bottom. He
lived in the house of the governor of the island and within a year or so
had married the governor's fourteen-and-a-half-year-old daughter, a
Miss Simmons, with whom he had one son and other children as well.

Knox must have been lonely on Saba, for he carried on an extensive
correspondence with his colleagues on the mainland, only a few items
of which survive. He was not, however, intellectually isolated. He read
widely in current books, thought much, and wrote. His works were
published in America, England, and Scotland. In theology he was a
moderate Calvinist. "The system of the ancient Calvinists," he once
wrote, "is well jointed, and hangs together; but Calvinism, as held by
President [Jonathan] Edwards' admirers, seems to me as different
from it as Arminianism,—a middle thing patched up out of both,—and
ought to be called 'Edwardism.' " He prefaced a 1768 collection of his
sermons with the fashionable ideological concerns of the day: "The
present growth and progress of infidelity," he wrote, "and the great
disingenuity of infidels in repeating old objections, which have been
long ago answered and confuted, and in coining new ones, which have
more of shew than of substance, render the defense of Christianity of
almost perpetual necessity in every corner of the Christian world." Infidels must have been scarce on Saba. And Knox was beginning to feel
his isolation. "I want to be a *hearer* sometimes, as well as a *preacher*,"
he complained to a friend on the mainland in the late 1760s. "I want,
not always to *lead the devotion* in publick and private (which is ever
my lot here) but sometimes to be a fellow worshipper, under the conduct of a holy and skilful leader."

Knox's chance came three years later. He spent September and Oc-
tober, 1771, on the wealthy island of St. Croix, in the Danish West
Indies. He found there, he told a friend, "a number of Scotch, English,
Irish, and North American, Presbyterians . . . who gave me a cordial
and unanimous invitation to come among them." Knox moved to St.
Croix late in the spring of the following year.

His shift came at just about the right time. On the night of Monday,
August 31, 1772, the Caribbean was struck by a hurricane of intense

force. Saba was devastated, and Knox's old church destroyed. The Sunday following the storm Knox preached a powerful sermon to a community meeting on St. Croix:

"O! let the ruins, the multiplied ruins, the dreadful and almost universal desolation of this lately blooming, fertile, flourishing, but now poor, distressed, miserable, helpless Island, bear witness whether the present is not a season of adversity," he cried. "Whether it does not call us to consideration and repentance.— And whether the Lord God of Hosts, who is terrible in majesty and abundant in mercy, is not calling the inhabitants of this and the neighboring Islands, to weeping, and to mourning, to the most speedy and effectual review of their ways, and reformation of their lives and manners, by the voice of alarming judgment?"

The sermon was almost indistinguishable from hundreds that had been given throughout the western world after the great Lisbon earth-quake of 1755. However, it so inspired a pious young clerk in the audi-ence named Alexander Hamilton that he went home and wrote his own moralizing account of the storm. Knox read young Hamilton's effort, was impressed, and saw to it that it was published in the *Royal Dan-ish-American Gazette*. Ever on the outlook for undiscovered talent, Knox and others decided that Hamilton should be sent to the mainland for further education. Equipped with letters of introduction from Knox to the Reverend John Rodgers (by then a trustee of the College), the Livingstons, and others, Hamilton sailed for the continent that fall. He would continue his education at the academy run by Francis Bar-ber (A.B. 1767) in Elizabethtown, New Jersey.

Knox kept in touch with Hamilton over the years. But Hamilton was only one strand in a busy and fruitful life on St. Croix. Knox was a strong supporter of the American Revolution (he urged Hamilton to become its historian), but the continent was far away. When he died on October 9, 1790, the local newspaper described Knox as "Pastor of the Presbyterian Church, and Physician; Eminent in, and an ornament to the former Profession, Judicious and successful in the latter . . . a sincere . . . and firm friend, and an Universal lover of Mankind."

SOURCES: S. Miller, *Memoirs of the Rev. John Rodgers, D.D.* (1813), 96-103; *NJHSP*, 69 (1951), 88-114; B. Mitchell, *Alexander Hamilton: Youth to Maturity, 1755-1788* (1957), 31-35; Sprague, *Annals*, III, 180-86; Webster, *History*, 658-62; study with Burr and ordination: Esther Burr, MS Journal, scattered entries extending from March through August 29, 1755; Saba: J. G. Crane, *Educated to Emigrate: The So-cial Org. of Saba* (1971), 19-21; infidelity quotation: Knox, *Discourses on the Truth of Revealed Religion and other Important Subjects* (1768), I, xi; "hearer" quotation: Knox to Jacob Green, August 29, 1768, PPPrHi; hurricane sermon: Knox, *A Dis-*

course Delivered on the 6th of Sept., 1772 (1772), 16-18; Hamilton's effort: *Hamilton Papers,* 1, 34-38; Knox's obituary appeared in the *Royal Danish Am. Gaz.,* Oct. 13, 1790.

PUBLICATIONS: Works cited above, and *The Probable Sources of Our Savior's Tears Shed at the Tomb of His Friend Lazarus* (1765); *A Funeral Discourse for Mrs. Sarah Heyliger* (1774); *Select Sermons on Interesting Subjects* (1776); *Transitory and Evanescent Nature of all Sublunary Things* (1782).

Mss: PHi, MHi, PPPrHi

David Mathews

DAVID MATHEWS, A.B., A.M. King's 1758, lawyer and public official, was born in the Cornwall precinct of Orange County, New York, the son of Vincent Mathews and his wife, Catalina Abeel. The elder Mathews was a landowner, lawyer, holder of several minor public offices, a member of the New York Assembly from 1739 to 1750, and an Anglican.

On November 9, 1758, Mathews married Sarah Seymour in Trinity Church, New York. The Mathews had nine children. Mathews studied law and was admitted to the bar of Orange County in 1760. At some time in the next few years Mathews and his family moved south, setting up residences in New York City and in Flatbush, Long Island. Mathews began the practice of law in New York and was a charter member of "The Moot," a debating club of New York lawyers that flourished from 1770 to 1774.

On September 29, 1774, Mathews was elected alderman for the East Ward of New York City. He served on various committees over the following year, including one regulating grain brought into the city and another charged with the supervision of the building of New York's new prison, Bridewell. He was reelected to his post in the following September. By fall 1775, political affairs in New York were reaching a crisis. Suspected Loyalists were being proscribed by the provincial congress; effective powers of government had passed out of the hands of the royal government. On October 19, 1775, Governor Tryon fled from the capital and attempted to govern the province from the *Duchess of Gordon,* a British naval vessel anchored in New York harbor. At a meeting of the common council of the city held on February 20, 1776, Mathews produced a letter from Whitehall Hicks, mayor of the city since 1766, resigning that position and also his posts as water bailiff and clerk of the markets. At the same time Mathews produced a commission from Governor Tryon appointing him to all these offices.

On the face of it, being mayor of New York in 1776 would seem to offer little in the way of reward. But Mathews was not long without recompense: on March 7 he was one of several patentees who received a grant of land of 63,000 acres on the east side of Lake Champlain. Mathews had little time to enjoy his new lands. On June 5, 1776, New York's revolutionary congress ordered the arrest of "certain persons, either royal officials, or notoriously disaffected"—Mathews among them. Shortly thereafter Mathews was implicated in the "Hickey Plot," a conspiracy said to have been instigated by Governor Tryon that involved a scheme to assassinate George Washington. Mathews was arrested at his home in Flatbush at 1 a.m. on the morning of June 22. On the following day he was questioned at length in New York about his role in the plot by a committee consisting of Philip Livingston, John Jay, and Gouverneur Morris.

No direct evidence linking Mathews with the plot was discovered. He was, however, sent to Connecticut and placed on parole under a relative of his wife, Colonel Moses Seymour. Miserable in relative confinement, he wrote to his old friend John McKesson (A.B. 1753) thus: "I have made so many fruitless applications lately that I am almost discouraged putting pen to paper again. Is it not very hard Mr. McKesson that the convention will not furnish me with some resolve or certificate to enable me to contradict a most hellish report that has been propagated, and is verily believed throughout this Colony, that I was concerned in a Plot to assassinate General Washington and blow up the Magazine in New York? The Convention well knows that such a report prevails. They also know it is as false as hell is false."

Although the exact circumstances are unclear, late in 1776 Mathews either was released or broke his parole and escaped from Connecticut to return to New York City, which had been occupied by the British in September. There he reassumed his duties as mayor, which were largely nominal, since a military commandant actually governed the city during the war. In the years that followed, Mathews built up an unenviable record. The major Loyalist historians of New York, William Smith and Thomas Jones, disliked each other intensely. Both, however, were agreed on one thing: their detestation of fellow-Loyalist David Mathews, who aside from being mayor also served as assistant judge in the court of police. Jones described Mathews's activities thus:

> David Mathews, Esq., then Mayor of the city, [was] a person low in estimation as a lawyer, profligate, abandoned, and dissipated, indigent, extravagent and voluptuous as himself, and no

method of supplying his wants till this "judicious" appointment. After which, with the assistance of General Howe's "legal" present of the revenues of the City Corporation, and by exercising every kind of villany, extortion, oppression, peculation, and rapine, upon a set of loyal subjects deprived of the benefits of the law, and consequently without redress, he became before the end of the war a man of great property, lived in the style of a gentleman, gave what the military called, "damned good dinners," wallowed in luxury, and rioted upon plunder *illegally* and *unjustly* extorted from his Majesty's loyal subjects within the lines, to whom upon every occasion he behaved with all the haughtly superciliousness of a Turkish Bashaw, or a proud, over-bearing, Highland Scottish Laird.

By 1780 William Smith would declare in his diary: "Mathews is one who on every Contingency must at the end of the War quit the Country. He is offensive to Whig and Tory." The New York Assembly had decided the matter earlier: on October 22, 1779, Mathews was one of 59 persons declared felons. He was attainted, his property was forfeited to the state (he lost 26,774 acres), and he was to be executed if found in the state. When his father made his will in 1783, disposing of extensive properties, he purposely skipped over David (doubtless to avoid the consequences of confiscation) and left David's share of his estate to David's children.

At the peace Mathews and his family emigrated to Nova Scotia. Mathews put in a claim for £2,059 in losses incurred during the Revolution. He was originally allowed £230, but this was dropped when the claim allowances were later revised. He claimed £400 for loss of income and received all of this. In 1784 he received a grant of 700 acres at Cape St. Mary's in Annapolis County. But Mathews had his eyes on higher things. He shortly applied for the position of attorney-general of Nova Scotia.

Mathews did not receive the Nova Scotia post. Faced with a glut of Loyalist office-seekers, in 1784 the British government split the province into three new units—Nova Scotia, New Brunswick, and Cape Breton Island. Scarcely inhabited, the latter province seems to have been created merely to increase the supply of official positions. Mathews was shortly appointed attorney-general of the new province. The post was not a plum from the patronage tree.

The lieutenant governor of Cape Breton (the province was not important enough to have a full governor), Joseph Desbarres, had grandiose plans for his province. He founded the town of Sydney and claimed that it would soon outrank Halifax as an entrepôt of the North Atlantic. Mathews was not only the province's first attorney-general but also a member of the council. Cape Breton was quickly filling up with Loyalist immigrants, troops and disbanded soldiers: many were almost destitute and all were sorely in need of provisions. Mathews and Desbarres came into conflict over the treatment of immigrants, Mathews supporting their claims. Hardly appointed to the council, Mathews resigned on December 11, 1785, protesting that "the council have been called in only to be informed of measures which had already taken place without their previous advice or opinion."

Desbarres resigned in 1787, but not before more conflict with Mathews. In 1787 charges were brought against Mathews (by the Desbarres party, he claimed) to the effect that Mathews was raising discontent, debasing the currency, and had fixed "an advance price on moose meat." Little came of the charges.

Desbarres's successor reappointed Mathews to the council but life on Cape Breton was not easy. In 1790 Mathews was complaining to the royal government of his plight. His salary was too low. He was unable to supplement it with fees because the inhabitants had little need for legal services and no money to pay for them anyway. Worse, he had a large family to feed that for the preceding three months had had no meat but moose.

One historian of Canada has claimed that "the history of Cape Breton is a monotonous tale of petty squabbles among officials." From the scanty remaining records, this would seem to be an accurate description of Mathews's life during the 1790s, though he eventually became president of the council. Mathews, however, found some consolation, for the records of his parish for March 19, 1793 read: "Then baptised W^m a natural son of David Mathews Atty Genl and Mrs. Docla Marshall." Mathews died on July 28, 1800, and was buried in Sydney.

SOURCES: There is no sketch of Mathews, but see Sabine, *Loyalists*, I, 51-52. Father and family background: *Hist. Orange Cty., N.Y.*, 129, 141-42, 202, and *NYHS Col.*, 67 (1934), 226-40, 68 (1935), 77; marriage: *NYGBR*, 69 (1938), 372; "Moot": P. M. Hamlin, *Legal Education in Colonial N.Y.* (1939), 202; political activities in N.Y.: *Minutes of the Common Council of the City of New York, 1675-1776* (1905), VIII, 56, 61, 67, 88, 107, 127; land grant: B. Mason, *The Road to Independence* (1966), 48; Hickey Plot and Mathews's role: C. L. Becker, *Hist. of Political Parties in the Province of N.Y., 1773-1777* (1909), 264-65; M. J. Lamb, *Hist. of the City of N.Y.* (1868), I, 354-55, and R. M. Calhoon, *The Loyalists in Rev. Am., 1760-1781* (1973), 372-73; letter to McKesson and description as mayor: T. Jones, *Hist. N.Y. during Rev. War*, 416-17, 121-22; Smith quotation: H. W. Sabine, ed., *Hist. Memoirs of William Smith (1781-1783)* (1971), 598. Role as mayor and postwar claims, see preceding and also: O. T. Barck, *New York City during the War for Independence* (1931), 40, 43, 53-54; attainder and confiscations: A. O. Flick, *Loyalism in New York during the Am. Rev.* (1902), 33, 204n, 217; father's will: *N.Y. Wills*, XII, 325-26;

request for Nova Scotia attorney generalship and 1790 complaints: M. B. Norton, *The British Americans* (1972), 238; Annapolis land grant: M. Gilroy, comp., *Loyalists and Land Settlement in Nova Scotia* (1937), 17; Desbarres: *DNB*, XIV, 402-403; political conditions on Cape Breton and quotation: A. Shortt and A. G. Doughty, eds., *Canada and Its Provinces* (1914), XIII, 229-32. Other activities on Cape Breton and quotations: the extensive series of transcripts from local records prepared in 1915 by Walter Crowe of Sydney, N.S., for V. Lansing Collins, Secretary of Princeton University, now in the David Mathews File, PUA.

PUBLICATIONS: *Address to the Earl of Carlisle* (1778)

Mss: PHi (1 ALS)

Jonathan Odell

JONATHAN ODELL, A.B., A.M. 1757, Anglican clergyman, physician, man of letters and public official, was born in Newark New Jersey, on September 25, 1737, the son of Temperance Dickinson, a daughter of the College's first president, Jonathan Dickinson, and her husband John Odell, a joiner. By the terms of his father's will, made in 1750,

Jonathan Odell, A.B. 1754

Jonathan was "to be kept to learning till he hath taken his degree at college."

After graduation, in 1755–1756, Odell served as master of the grammar school connected with the College in exchange for two-thirds of the school's profits. After leaving the school he studied medicine and then joined a regiment of the British army, seeing service as a surgeon in the West Indies. At some time during this period Odell decided to become an Anglican clergyman. He traveled to England and, while studying for the ministry, taught for two years at James Elphinston's academy at Kensington. While in England he tried his hand at poetry, writing "A Welcome Home to the Twenty-Third Regiment after the Peace of 1763," and "On Pope's Garden at Twickenham, 1765." Odell made many friends in England, among them Benjamin Franklin, who recommended him to the Anglican Society for the Propagation of the Gospel and to his son, New Jersey Governor William Franklin, as missionary to the Anglican church at Burlington, New Jersey.

Odell was ordained in January 1767 and returned to America later in the year. On July 26 Governor Franklin inducted him as rector of St. Ann's (now St. Mary's) Church in Burlington. Over the next nine years Odell also served at St. Andrew's Church in Mount Holly and across the Delaware in Bristol, Pennsylvania, at St. James's Church. Shortly after his return home, on February 26, 1768, he was elected a member of the American Philosophical Society, for which he translated French treatises on the breeding of silkworms.

On May 6, 1772, Odell married Anne de Cou of Burlington. The Odells had two daughters and a son. The latter was named, after his father's patron, William Franklin Odell. In 1771, in order to supplement his clerical income, Odell resumed the practice of medicine. He was elected to the New Jersey Medical Society in November 1774.

On the eve of the Revolution Odell took an outwardly neutral stance, writing to the secretary of the S.P.G. in 1775 that he thought it the duty of ministers to promote "a spirit of peace and good order among the Members of their Communion." He offered to do anything he could "towards obtaining a recovery and securing the future permanency of that harmony & peace upon just and practicable grounds, which is essential to the happiness & glory of the whole Empire." In October 1775, two of Odell's letters to England were seized and placed in the hands of the provincial congress. The congress found that Odell "disapproves of, and is in principle opposed to, the measures of de-defense adopted by the Continent, to prevent the oppressive designs of the British ministry." But the congress declined to censure him on the ground that he had made no attempt to influence public opinion.

Odell did not long manage to sustain a neutral stance. In 1776 a group of captured British officers (among them John André) was brought to Burlington. As an old army man, Odell became friendly with the officers. He composed a song for them to sing on June 4, the King's birthday, which went in part:

> O'er Britainnia's happy land
> Ruled by George's mild command,
> On this bright auspicious day
> Loyal hearts their tribute pay.
>> Ever sacred be to mirth,
>> The day that gave our Monarch birth! ...
>
> Here we now lament to find,
> Sons of Britain, fierce and blind,
> Drawn from loyal love astray,
> Hail no more this welcome day. ....

The response to Odell's song was swift. On July 20 the Burlington Committee of Safety "parolled" Odell—"a person suspected of being inimical to American liberty"—to within eight miles of the Burlington courthouse. Odell survived peaceably enough until December 11. Then, caught in melee between Hessians and American naval forces, he inadvertently became the quarry of Whig searching parties. After various misadventures Odell took refuge behind the British lines in New York City.

Odell found a warm welcome in New York. He met old friends from the army, acted as chaplain to a regiment of Pennsylvania Loyalists, and translated official papers from the French and Spanish. Recommended to Sir Henry Clinton by his old patron William Franklin, Odell also began work as a Loyalist propagandist. His 1778 and 1779 satires on the Whigs ("The Word of Congress," "The American Times," and others) led the historian Moses Coit Tyler to label Odell "the most powerful and most unrelenting of the Tory satirists." Odell had burned his bridges thoroughly. In October 1778, the Burlington grand jury indicted him for treason; in the following year it confiscated his property.

Odell's most important service to the mother country came in a clandestine capacity. In New York he served as intermediary between General Clinton, Clinton's aide Major John André, and General Benedict Arnold in Arnold's attempt to sell West Point to the British. He also served as assistant secretary to the board of directors of the Associated Loyalists, and on July 1, 1783, became assistant secretary to Sir Guy Carleton, then commander-in-chief of British forces and governor of New York.

When the British evacuated New York in 1783 Odell accompanied Carleton to England, taking along his wife and children. The following year he left England for New Brunswick, Canada, where Colonel Thomas Carleton, brother of his patron, was serving as governor. There Odell became a member of the council and secretary and registrar to the province at a salary of £1,000 a year. When claims for Loyalist losses were being considered Odell waived his, saying that his salary was compensation enough. Odell held his posts until 1812, when his son William Franklin Odell succeeded to them. William held his father's offices for thirty-two years. Odell died at Fredericton, New Brunswick on November 25, 1818. His experience as an exile had not embittered him. In 1810, on their thirty-eighth wedding anniversay, he composed a long poem for his wife, which reads in part:

> Twice nineteen years, dear Nancy, on this day
> Complete their circle, since the smiling May
> Beheld us at the altar kneel and join
> In holy rites and vows, which made thee shine. . . .

> But ah, how soon this dawn of Joy so bright
> Was followed by a dark and stormy night.
> The howling tempest in a fatal hour,
> Drove me, an exile, from our nuptial bower,

> To seek for refuge in the tented field,
> Till democratic Tyranny should yield.
> Thus torn asunder, we, from year to year,
> Endured the alternate strife of Hope and Fear;

> Till, from Suspense deliver'd by Defeat,
> I hither came and found a safe retreat.
> Here joined by thee and thy young youthful train,
> I was o'erpaid for years of toil and pain; . . .

SOURCES: The most thorough account is still M. C. Tyler, *Lit. Hist. of the Am. Rev.* (1900), II, 97-127; also *DAB*; F. B. Rogers, "Dr. Jonathan Odell—Tory Satirist," *Transactions and Studies of the College of Physicians of Philadelphia*, (4 ser.) 24 (1956), 70-75; father's occupation and will: 30 *NJA*, 358; grammar school: Aaron Burr, MS Account Book, 162-63; pastorate, printing MS material: G. M. Hills, *Hist. of the Church in Burlington, N.J.* (1885), 291-322; N. R. Burr, *The Anglican Church in N.J.* (1954), 629-31, 394-95, 497-98; role in Arnold-André affair: C. Van Doren, *Secret Hist. of the Am. Rev.* (1951).

PUBLICATIONS: Nelson Burr, above, 693, gives complete bibliography, but see esp.: W. Sargent, ed., *The Loyalist Poetry of the Rev.* (1857), and Sargent, ed., *The Loyal Verses of Joseph Stansbury and Doctor Jonathan Odell; relating to the Am. Rev.* (1860).

Mss: CaNBA, CaOOA, MHi, NjP, PHi

Sylvanus Osborn

SYLVANUS OSBORN, A.B., A.M. Yale 1757, Congregational clergyman, was born about 1731. In college he managed to lose £1.12s. in a lottery. Part of his college costs were paid for by his classmate Noah Wadhams and by Israel Canfield (A.B. 1753). In 1757 Osborn was installed as first minister of the Congregational church at East Greenwich (now Warren), Litchfield County, Connecticut, where he remained until his death in 1771. Osborn married Abigail Noble of New Milford, Connecticut. After his death she married the Reverend Jeremiah Day (Yale 1756).

SOURCES: For bare facts, see: Sylvanus Osborn File, PUA, and Giger, Memoirs, I; for college accounts, see Aaron Burr, MS Account Book, 14-15.

David Purviance

DAVID PURVIANCE, A.B., aspirant Presbyterian clergyman, was probably the son of Mary and Samuel Purviance, Sr., immigrants from Ireland. The date of the family's emigration to America is unknown, but the elder Purviance became a prosperous Philadelphia merchant and prominent Presbyterian layman. David, apparently, was raised by a maternal uncle. The only record of his stay in the College is a brief notation in President Aaron Burr's Account Book, from which it appears that David spent less than a year at Newark.

Sometime after graduation Purviance was licensed by the Old Side Presbytery of Philadelphia and was sent as a missionary to Delaware. He spent much of his time ministering to the Presbyterian church at Snow Hill. Exposure brought on a lung disorder, and Purviance died suddenly at Snow Hill in the spring or summer of 1757. His sister Mary married Samuel Eakin (A.B. 1763).

SOURCES: For extensive and confused attempts to trace Purviance's parentage and career, see his file, PUA; a brief account of his life, which should be used with caution: I. Spence, *Letters on the Early Hist. of the Presbyterian Church in America addressed to the Late Rev. Robert M. Laird* (1838), 100-105.

William Ramsay

WILLIAM RAMSAY, A.B., A.M. 1765, Presbyterian clergyman and older brother of David (A.B. 1765), physician and historian, and Nathaniel

(A.B. 1767), was born in East Drumore Township, Lancaster County, Pennsylvania, in 1732, the son of Jane Montgomery and her husband, James Ramsay, a farmer and immigrant from Ireland.

Soon after graduation Ramsay was called to the Presbyterian church at Fairfield, in Cumberland County in southern New Jersey. The town had been settled by immigrants from Connecticut late in the seventeenth century and in the 1750s was split into Old Side and New Side factions. To unify the various groups Ramsay was first licensed by the Congregational Association of the eastern district of Fairfield, Connecticut. He returned to New Jersey and joined the New Side Presbytery of Abingdon on May 11, 1756. He was ordained and installed at Fairfield on December 1 of the same year. The Reverend Charles Beatty preached the installation sermon.

Ramsay remained at the Fairfield church for the rest of his life. Apart from a revival in 1765, his pastorship was uneventful; he quickly united the various factions in his congregation. Ramsay died, apparently of typhoid fever, on November 5, 1771. At his funeral his brother-in-law, Jonathan Elmer, pronounced a eulogy: "Few were ever possessed of a more public spirit, or genuine *amor patriae*. He entertained the highest opinion of our excellent constitution, and gloried in the privileges of a Briton, as much as he lamented their prostitution and abuse. As he was an utter enemy to despotism, he was greatly grieved at the arbitrary proceedings of the British Ministry, in attempting to enslave their loyal subjects, by depriving them of their constitutional rights and privileges."

In February 1759, Ramsay married Sarah Seeley. They had five children. On the occasion of the marriage his congregation bought him a farm of 150 acres. Ramsay's estate was inventoried at a little over £602. In his will he appointed his brother, Dr. David Ramsay, guardian of his four surviving sons. Three of the boys were raised by their uncle in Charleston, South Carolina and one (John) attended the College in the 1780s but did not graduate. Ramsay's widow married the Reverend Robert Smith of Pequea, Pennsylvania, the father of Samuel Stanhope Smith (A.B. 1769) and John Blair Smith (A.B. 1773).

SOURCES: Brief accounts of Ramsay (the name was sometimes spelled Ramsey): *Vineland Hist. Mag.*, 26 (1941), 233-42; L.Q.C. Elmer, *Hist. of the Early Settlement and Progress of Cumberland Cty.* (1869), 98-99; and *Bi-Centennial Celebration of the Old Stone Church* (1881), 20-21; installation sermon: C. Beatty, *Double Honour due to the Laborious Gospel Minister* (1757); funeral eulogies: J. Elmer, *A Funeral Eulogium . . . to . . . William Ramsey* (1772), and also Enoch Green, *Slothfulness Reproved . . . A Sermon Occasioned by the death of the Rev. Mr. William Ramsay, M.A.* (1772); Ramsay's will and inventory of estate: 34 *NJA*, 413; account of death: *Pa. Jour.*, Nov. 14, 1771.

James Reeve

JAMES REEVE, A.B., farmer, local magistrate, and sometime preacher, was born at Mattituck, Long Island, in 1733, the son of Mary Hudson and her husband, James Reeve, a prosperous farmer. His purchase of a copy of Cicero's *De Oratore* is the only record of his college career.

A little more than a year after graduation, on October 23, 1755, Reeve married Anne Wines, with whom he had seven children. Reeve apparently returned to the family farm after graduation, for in his father's 1768 will Reeve's brother Selah was left the "privilege of cutting the same meadow twenty-five years next after my decease which his brother James usually cut when he lived on the farm, and also privilege of cutting wood of the same piece of woodland, said son James used to cut on." A local historian thought that Reeve might occasionally have served as a preacher; for much of his life he was associated with the Presbyterian church in Southold.

Reeve was active on the Whig side before the Revolution, and with many others was forced to flee Long Island when it was occupied by the British. A justice of the peace, by 1782 he considered himself to be of sufficient substance to sign himself "James Reeve, Esquire," when he witnessed his mother's will. He died at Mattituck on June 8, 1789.

SOURCES: Cicero: Aaron Burr, MS Account Book, 14; wills of father and of mother: *N.Y. Wills*, x, 150-51, 278; brief references: F. G. Mather, *The Refugees of 1776 from Long Island to Conn.* (1913), 522-23, and C. E. Craven, *Hist. of Mattituck, Long Island, N.Y.* (1906), 140, which is inaccurate.

Benajah Roots

BENAJAH ROOTS, A.B., A.M. Dartmouth 1784, Congregational clergyman, was born at Woodbury, Connecticut, on May 5, 1725, the son of John Roots and his wife, Ruth Hickok. The only record of Roots's college career is a notation that he purchased a Hebrew lexicon for nine shillings.

After graduation Roots studied theology with the Reverend Joseph Bellamy in Bethlehem, Connecticut. Called to the Congregational church in Simsbury, Connecticut, in December 1756 he was ordained and installed there on August 10, 1757. A little over one month later, on September 25, 1757, Roots married Elizabeth Guernsey, with whom he had six children.

Roots's pastorate was, apparently, uneventful until the early 1770s.

In 1770 a protracted controversy, ostensibly concerning the Half-Way Covenant and Roots's views on baptism, erupted between Roots, some of his parishioners, and his ministerial association. "Baptism does no good to the infant without spiritual baptism and baptism of the holy ghost," Roots declared in best New Light fashion. The dispute seems to have been due as much to personality and authority conflicts between Roots and a few of his more prominent parishioners as to doctrinal issues: Roots had excommunicated a prominent member of his congregation without consulting his ministerial association. Though his ministerial peers upheld Roots's views, his congregation dismissed him in 1771.

The following year Roots led a party of prospective Connecticut settlers into the disputed Wyoming Valley, an area in Pennsylvania claimed by the Susquehannah Company, a group of Connecticut land speculators. In a melee that occurred near Sunbury with supporters of the Penn family's claims in the area, Roots was captured and imprisoned. He was released on £1,000 bond only on condition that he leave the province.

Roots returned to Connecticut, sold his land there, and in 1772 along with a group of his Simsbury parishioners migrated to Rutland, Vermont. There Roots bought lands, settled his family, and became minister to a new Congregational church. Though the evidence is unclear it appears that about 1783 Roots again broke with his congregation over the issue of baptism and gathered still another congregation at West Rutland. Roots died in West Rutland on March 15, 1787.

SOURCES: Lexicon: Aaron Burr, MS Account Book, 14; Roots in Simsbury: W. M. Vibert, *Three Centuries of Simsbury, 1670-1970* (1970), 60, and J. H. Trumbull, *Memorial Hist. of Hartford County, Conn., 1633-1884* (1886), II, 352. Roots's intricate Simsbury controversies can be followed in: L. I. Barber, *Record and Documentary Hist. of Simsbury, Conn.* (1931), 278-92; and *The Result of an Ecclesiastical Council Convened on Call of the First Society in Simsbury, February 22, A.D. 1770*, and in Roots, *A Few Brief Remarks, on a Late Publication . . .* (1770). Roots in Pa.: O. J. Harvey, *A Hist. of Wilkes-Barre* (1909-30), II, 736-38; Roots in Vermont: C. K. Williams, *Centennial Celebration of the Settlement of Rutland, Vermont* (1879), 28-29; A. M. Hemenway, *Vermont Hist. Gazetteer* (1868-91), III, 548, 1050, 1060-61, and H. P. Smith and W. S. Rann, eds., *Hist. of Rutland County, Vermont* (1886), 320. The most recent piece on Roots is: Stephan A. Freeman, "Puritans in Rutland Vermont 1770-1818," *Vermont Hist.*, 33 (1965), 342-48.

PUBLICATIONS: see STE

Josiah Sherman

JOSIAH SHERMAN, A.B., A.M. Harvard 1758, Yale 1765, Congregational clergyman and younger brother of Nathaniel (A.B. 1753), was born on

April 29, 1729, at Stoughton, Massachusetts, the son of Mehitable Wellington and her husband, William Sherman, a former cordwainer who had achieved a modest prosperity as a farmer. By the time Sherman went to college the family was living in New Milford, Connecticut. The year before Josiah's graduation, his father served as one of New Milford's delegates to the Connecticut General Assembly.

After graduation Sherman studied theology, first with the Reverend Joseph Bellamy in Bethlehem, Connecticut, and later with the Reverend John Graham in Southbury. In December 1755, Sherman was called to serve as minister to the Congregational church at Woburn, Massachusetts, and was ordained there on January 28, 1756. A year later Sherman married Martha Minot of Concord, with whom he had six children.

Sherman was active in his ministerial association, but difficulties over his salary soon developed with his congregation. On March 27, 1775, he resigned his pastorate. "Their history has been that of a contentious people," a contemporary described Sherman's Woburn congregation. It took them ten years to agree on another pastor.

Sherman moved to Connecticut, where his brother Nathaniel was living in Mt. Carmel and another brother, Roger, was becoming prominent in public affairs. On August 23, 1775, Sherman was installed as pastor of the separatist church in Milford, Connecticut. But greater affairs intervened before Sherman could take up his post. In the summer of 1776 his brother, Roger, signed the Declaration of Independence. In 1777 Sherman himself spent time as chaplain to the Seventh Connecticut Line at Germantown and Valley Forge.

Back in Milford, Sherman was soon embroiled in difficulties with the pastor of the larger Congregational church there, Samuel Wales (Yale 1767). Each congregation was jealous of the other; their respective ministers came to believe that each was plotting against the other. Sherman finally requested dismissal, which was granted on June 21, 1781. He then moved to Stratford, Connecticut.

In June 1781, the town of Goshen, Connecticut, acting on a recommendation of Sherman's old teacher, Joseph Bellamy, invited Sherman to preach with a view to settlement there. After much close bargaining over his salary (£115 a year) Sherman moved to Goshen in the summer of 1782. His ministry began auspiciously enough, with a revival in 1783–1784, but controversy with his congregation soon arose. Sherman published a sermon called *God in No Sense the Author of Sin* . . . (Hartford, 1784); Joseph Bellamy charged that it exhibited Arminian tendencies. Sherman was incensed and had his church withdraw from the Litchfield Consociation. Sherman excommunicated members of his church who did not agree with him and stated of the richest and best-educated member of his congregation that "he has not doctrinal knowledge enough to be regenerated."

In the late 1780s Sherman achieved notice beyond Goshen with the publication of several sermons, among them an attack on the "infidel" doctrines of Ethan Allen, called *A Sermon to Swine* . . . (Litchfield, 1787). But influence abroad did not repair the situation in Goshen. In 1788 the town voted that they wished Sherman "to lay down the work of the ministry in this town." He did so on March 1, 1789.

Sherman and his family moved to Sheffield, Massachusetts. In the summer of 1789 he was called to the Congregational church at Wood-bridge, Connecticut. Sherman accepted, but died in Woodbridge on November 25, 1789, before being formally installed.

SOURCES: *Sibley's Harvard Graduates*, XIII, 488-91, is fairly complete and errs only in stating that Sherman went from Milford, Connecticut, to Princeton: he went from New Milford to Newark. Supplement with: Samuel Sewall, *The History of Woburn* . . . (1868), 350-57, and A. B. Hibbard, *History of the Town of Goshen, Conn.* (1897), 86-89, 306-307. Quotation *re* Woburn congregation: Bentley, *Diaries*, III, 107.

PUBLICATIONS: see STE

William Shippen, Jr.

WILLIAM SHIPPEN, JR., A.B., A.M. 1763, M.D. Edinburgh 1761, physician and early medical educator, older brother of John Shippen (A.B. 1758), was born in Philadelphia on October 21, 1736, the son of William Shippen and his wife Susannah Harrison. The senior Shippen, brother of trustee Edward Shippen and a grandson of the first mayor of Philadelphia, was a prosperous physician who helped architect Robert Smith draw up plans for Nassau Hall.

Shippen was prepared for college at the Reverend Samuel Finley's academy at West Nottingham, Maryland. Chosen salutatorian of his college class, his commencement address so impressed the Reverend George Whitefield (who received an A.M. from the College and preached on the same day) that he urged Shippen to study for the ministry. Instead, Shippen returned home to Philadelphia to study medicine with his father. In the fall of 1758, after a four-year apprenticeship, Shippen's father found money enough to send "Billey" to Britain for further study.

Settled in London by early 1759, Shippen enrolled in the anatomical courses of Dr. William Hunter, soon to be known as the foremost obstetrician in Britain, and walked the wards of St. Thomas's Hospital

William Shippen, Jr., A.B. 1754
BY GILBERT STUART

with Dr. Colin Mackenzie, the famous male midwife. In October 1759, Shippen moved into Hunter's house in the Great Piazza of Covent Garden. He dissected all day with Hunter, attended the doctor's lectures at five, and often talked anatomy with him until bedtime. But London was not all work and study. Shippen saw almost every play starring David Garrick that appeared on the boards. There were weekends in the country, dinners with sometime Governor James Hamilton of Pennsylvania, and, with Benjamin Franklin as guide, visits to the Royal Society and to court to see the royal family. In 1760, courses in London completed, Shippen traveled north to study with, among others, the famed William Cullen at the University of Edinburgh. On September 16, 1761, he was awarded the M.D. when he presented his dissertation, *De Placentae cum Utero nexu.*

While in England Shippen won the friendship of Dr. John Fothergill, Quaker physician, botanist, and patron of young Americans abroad. Together they discussed the possibility of Shippen's inaugurating a series of lectures on anatomy and establishing a medical school on his return to Philadelphia. Early in 1762, after his return to London from Scotland, Shippen made a brief visit to France, inspecting medical facilities there.

Before returning to America Shippen had one more important piece of unfinished business. On April 3, 1762, he married Alice Lee of Virginia in London. The daughter of the late Colonel Thomas Lee of Stratford Hall, Virginia, Alice had expatriated herself to England where some of her brothers (Arthur, Francis Lightfoot, Richard Henry, William, and Thomas Lee) were being educated at Eton and the Inns of Court. William and Alice Shippen would have eight children, only two of whom lived to maturity.

On their return home in 1762 the Shippens moved into the family mansion in Philadelphia, and William began the practice of medicine. Almost immediately Shippen started the most important and significant activity of his life—teaching. In November a series of splendid anatomical drawings and casts arrived from London, the gift of Fothergill. On November 16, Shippen inaugurated his first series of anatomical lectures, utilizing the material sent by Fothergill. As time went on Shippen added lectures on midwifery to his courses, attempting to transform the ancient craft into the modern science of obstetrics. Shippen was, by all accounts, a brilliant teacher. Years afterward Benjamin Rush (A.B. 1760), one of his pupils and later a bitter enemy, wrote that as a teacher Shippen had been "eloquent, luminous, and pleasing." Shippen introduced to Philadelphia the English method of teaching by the dissection of human bodies, and at times found his quarters besieged by angry mobs that suspected him of grave-robbing. As a practicing physician he was gentle and reassuring with his patients and skillful and resourceful in his methods.

While Shippen was abroad another young American, John Morgan of Philadelphia, arrived in England to study medicine. Brilliant, handsome, and on occasion charming, Morgan studied with the Hunters and wrote an outstanding dissertation at the University of Edinburgh. He made Shippen's acquaintance and also became friendly with Fothergill. The three discussed founding a medical school in Philadelphia. Ambitious and energetic, Morgan returned home in 1765, determined to revolutionize the practice of medicine in America and to start a medical school in Philadelphia. Within a few days of his return—and without any consultation with Shippen—Morgan showed his plans for organizing a medical school to the trustees of the College of Philadelphia. On May 3 the trustees unanimously elected him professor of the theory and practice of medicine, the first in British North America. Shippen was first surprised, then irritated, as Morgan proceeded to take full credit for founding the Medical School. On September 17

Shippen announced to the trustees that he too was available for a professorship. They promptly elected him professor of anatomy. In 1766 Morgan repeated his snub of Shippen when he founded the Medical Society of Philadelphia without informing the older man. Morgan's actions laid the base for an extraordinarily bitter feud that would in time involve Benjamin Rush and the Continental Congress.

While hostilities between Britain and America developed, Shippen was active in Philadelphia with his teaching, his medical practice, and his very active social life. A member of the American Philosophical Society, he also served as a trustee of the College of New Jersey from 1765 to 1792.

On October 17, 1775, John Morgan was appointed by Congress to be director general and chief physician of the medical forces of the American army. His job, essentially, was to organize a complete medical service for the Continental Army. It was not an easy one, and Morgan performed as creditably as anyone could under the confused circumstances of 1776. On July 15, 1776, Shippen was appointed director of the hospital of the Flying Camp in New Jersey, designed to serve various militia units from New Jersey, Pennsylvania, and Maryland. Shippen organized the camp with dispatch and sent glowing reports to Congress. In the meantime Director General Morgan was staggering under the casualties from the battles about New York. It made an unhappy contrast in the eyes of congressmen. Morgan came under heavier and heavier criticism. In October 1776, Shippen was appointed director of all the Army hospitals west of the Hudson River. An inevitable conflict of authority with Morgan developed, exacerbated by their longstanding hostilities. On January 9, 1777, Congress summarily dismissed Morgan and on April 11 appointed Shippen to his position.

Shippen's term as director general was to be even less happy than Morgan's. A poorer administrator than Morgan, he faced the same problems: congressional ineptness, lack of supplies, poor organization, and confused logistics. Moreover, he was subjected to a vindictive campaign to discredit him from a new quarter, Dr. Benjamin Rush, a member of the Continental Congress who in April 1777 was appointed surgeon general of the armies of the Middle Department. "We will bring the Shippens down; they are too powerful and have reigned long enough," Rush declared. When not criticizing George Washington's generalship, Rush spent his time attacking Shippen for maladministration. Rush made a series of charges against Shippen, coupled with an attack on his character, to Washington. Washington referred the matter to Congress. Shippen admitted only to having sold six pipes of wine assigned to him as army supplies for his personal profit, declaring somewhat airily that this was common practice. John Witherspoon, then chairman of the congressional committee concerned with the matter, decided that either Shippen or Rush had to go, and forced Rush to resign.

Shippen was by no means in the clear. In June 1779, Congress in effect apologized to John Morgan for his abrupt dismissal by commending his work as director general. Morgan took this as a signal to attack Shippen and enlisted Rush's aid. Washington reluctantly consented to a courtmartial of Shippen, which began in March 1780. Rush gave testimony accusing Shippen of murdering 4,500 troops—then, on second thought, reduced the figure to 1,000. The trial dragged on through June 1780, when the court acquitted Shippen on all charges brought against him but reprimanded him for his speculation in wine. He was dismissed from his post, but in October Congress turned around and reappointed him. Rush was outraged; Morgan launched a vitriolic attack on both Congress and Shippen. On January 3, 1781, Shippen resigned his post for the last time. "I believe no hospitals could have been better administered," George Washington wrote in a testimonial letter. Shippen, Morgan, and Rush all resumed what must have been a somewhat strained colleagueship on the faculty of the Medical School in Philadelphia.

When the University of Pennsylvania was established in 1791 Shippen became its first professor of anatomy, surgery, and midwifery. One of the founders of the College of Physicians of Philadelphia, he served as its president from 1805 to 1808. Although he continued to teach, his last years were spent in a deep depression over the death of his only surviving son. He died on July 11, 1808.

SOURCES: There is no full-scale biography of Shippen, but see: *DAB*; James Thacher, *American Medical Biography* (1828), II, 82-87; and B. C. Corner, *William Shippen, Jr., Pioneer in Am. Educ.* (1951), which reprints Shippen's dissertation and a journal he kept while a student in London. There are full and balanced accounts of Shippen in W. J. Bell, Jr., *John Morgan, Continental Doctor* (1965), and in D. F. Hawke, *Benjamin Rush, Rev. Gadfly* (1971). For intimate glimpses of Shippen by his daughter: E. Ames, ed., *Nancy Shippen, Her Journal Book* (1935); for Shippen's letters to Thomas Jefferson concerning his son, Thomas Lee Shippen: *Jefferson Papers*, XII, XIII.

Mss: PPAmP, PHi, DLC, MHi, DNLM, VHi

Thomas Smith

THOMAS SMITH, A.B., lawyer, older brother of James Smith (A.B. 1757), was born in New York City on March 11, 1734, one of the fourteen children of William Smith, Sr., and his wife Mary Het. In 1715, the father had emigrated from England to New York as a child with his family and shortly thereafter was enrolled at Yale, where he graduated with great distinction in 1719. In 1727 William Smith traveled to England to study at the Inns of Court. On his return to New York he quickly rose to the top of the province's legal profession and acquired a great deal of land. Closely associated with the Presbyterian faction in New York politics, Smith was one of the founding trustees of the College. At about the time Thomas was entering the College in 1751 his father was serving as attorney-general of the province of New York.

After graduation Thomas studied law with his father, who possessed one of the best law libraries in the province. On November 22, 1756, he married Elizabeth Lynsen in the Presbyterian church in New York City. Over the years the couple had eight children.

In the early 1750s Thomas's older brother William, Jr. (Yale 1745), in partnership with William Livingston (Yale 1741), was rapidly establishing himself as one of New York's ablest lawyers and also, with the 1757 publication of his *History of the Province of New York*, as its first historian. He became chief justice in 1763 and in 1767 a member of the governor's council. Both the Smith brothers were noted for their wide learning and their extensive legal practices. As early as 1764 Thomas joined with his brother and others in founding the New York Bar Association in order to raise the quality of the legal profession and, incidentally, to limit access to it. On his father's death in 1769 Thomas inherited considerable property. He and his brother built imposing houses on adjoining estates overlooking the Hudson at Haverstraw, New York. Like William, Thomas, along with his classmate David Mathews and William Livingston, became a charter member of The Moot, a Whiggish debating club of New York lawyers that flourished between 1770 and 1774.

Thomas Smith entered active politics in 1769–1770, when along with his brother, John Morin Scott, and William Livingston, he tried to prevent the indictment of "the American Wilkes," Alexander McDougall, a merchant and pamphleteer, for libel against the New York Assembly. Thomas's precise activities between that time and 1775 cannot be determined; it can safely be assumed that like his brother and associates he was involved with the Whig-Presbyterian faction in the New York politics of the period. Thomas was a member of the "Committee of One Hundred" formed in New York on May 5, 1775, after the news of the battle of Lexington reached the city. For that month the committee, in effect, directed local affairs and organized for war. Later in the summer responsibility for the direction of affairs passed to the provincial congress, of which Smith became a member. On December 4,

1775, Governor Tryon issued an appeal to the colony to take "the sense of its inhabitants, in a constitutional manner," concerning the difficulties with Britain. Thomas was at that point a member of the provincial congress, his brother William still a member of the governor's council. William drew up a peace plan that Thomas was supposed to introduce to the Congress. William's resolutions called for recognition of American rights, but lodged ultimate legislative authority in Parliament. Thomas introduced the resolutions to the provincial congress on December 8. They were defeated on December 13, John Morin Scott playing a leading role in the opposition. Thomas then retired from the Congress.

When New York was occupied by American forces in the summer of 1776 Thomas retired to his estate at Haverstraw. Shortly thereafter his brother William was confined on parole at Livingston Manor by revolutionary leaders suspicious of his loyalties. Thomas communicated often with Governor George Clinton in 1777 and 1778, complaining of the extremely exposed and dangerous position of himself and his family and advising Clinton on British troop movements. In July 1778, William Smith decided to cast his lot with the Loyalists and moved behind the British lines into New York City. There he remained for the rest of the war, building an extensive intelligence network. He remained in communication with Thomas, sometimes writing to him in letters written in lime juice. Although Benedict Arnold and Colonel John André met in Thomas's Haverstraw house to plot Arnold's treason in August and September of 1780, Thomas was not involved, nor do the meetings appear to have compromised his position. In the following year, 1781, although Thomas thought seriously of moving to New Jersey to escape the threat of marauding troops, he took on a new law student at Haverstraw, young Colonel Aaron Burr (A.B. 1772), whom he prepared for admission to the bar in six months of strenuous work.

At the end of 1781 Smith rented the Haverstraw house; his whereabouts for the next two or more years are unknown. When New York was evacuated by the British in 1783 his brother William left too, eventually becoming chief justice of Quebec. The brothers remained in close contact over the years, Thomas managing William's extensive American landholdings. In the late 1780s and early 1790s Thomas's main residence was, apparently, in New York City. On October 16, 1795, Thomas made his will at Haverstraw, leaving his properties there and in New York City, slaves, and a large amount of personal and other real property to his wife and six sons and two daughters. He died sometime between that date and December 11, 1795, when his will was probated.

SOURCES: Basic biographical data and will: *NYGBR*, 67 (1936), ~~306-307~~ *305-306*; early legal career: P. M. Hamlin, *Legal Education in Colonial N.Y.* (1939); Smith's later career has been pieced together from: L.F.S. Upton, *The Loyal Whig: William Smith of N.Y. and Quebec* (1969); L. E. Kimball, "The Smiths of Haverstraw: Some Notes on a Highland Family," *N.Y. Hist.*, 16 (1935), 392-404; T. Jones, *Hist. of N.Y. during the Rev. War* (1879); W.H.W. Sabine, ed., *Hist. Memoirs of William Smith* (1956, 1971); C. Becker, *The Hist. of Political Parties in the Province of N.Y.* (1909); D. R. Dillon, *The N.Y. Triumvirate* (1949); and M. L. Davis, ed., *Memoirs of Aaron Burr* (1836), I, 218-19, 223.

William Thomson

WILLIAM THOMSON, A.B., lawyer, was probably born in Millstone, Somerset County, New Jersey, the son of Mary and Benjamin Thomson, a farmer who served for many years as a justice of the peace and as a judge of the courts of oyer and terminer and of common pleas in that county. The only record of Thomson's student days is a notation that he once purchased a copy of Isaac Watts's "Philosophical Essays" for eleven shillings. After graduation, in 1755–1756, Thomson served as a tutor in the College. He was in Princeton in May 1757, when he borrowed Johann Huebner's *The Historical Companion: being a New Introduction to the Political History of All Nations* (London, 1742) from President Burr.

Thomson was doubtless studying law, for he was admitted to the New Jersey bar as attorney and counsellor on May 11, 1758. A few months later, on November 2, Thomson married Margaret Leslie, daughter of a well-to-do citizen of Perth Amboy, in Anglican St. John's Church there. The couple had at least four children. Thomson and his father were active in local affairs in Somerset County. In 1759 they managed a lottery designed to raise funds for finishing the Presbyterian church in Bound Brook. And in 1764 William acted as agent in Millstone for the sale of tickets in a lottery meant to raise money for the College of New Jersey.

On September 14, 1765, Thomson made his will, leaving his property to his wife and naming his father as one of his executors. He died at some time between that date and October 2, when his will was probated. On September 18, 1766, William's executors advertised in a New York newspaper the sale of all of his real and personal property at Millstone: "The real estate, consisting of a lot of land, containing about 4 acres with a new dwelling-house nearly finished, two stories high and four rooms on a floor. Also a large kitchen joining the said house: It is well improved with out-houses, gardens &c. The personal estate consists of houshold furniture, some law books, and some other valuable books, one negro man, one negro boy about 14 years old, one negro girl about 10 years old, Horses, cattle, farming utensils and sundry other things."

SOURCES: Parentage and relationships, see father's will in: 33 *NJA*, 428; father's career: *Som. Cty. Hist. Quart.*, 8 (1919), 121; Watts and Huebner: Aaron Burr, MS Account Book, 18-19; admission to bar: 25 *NJA*, 112; marriage: *GMNJ*, 5 (1929), 34; lotteries: *N.Y. Mercury*, Sept. 24, 1759, Jan. 9, 1764; will: 33 *NJA*, 429; advertisement: *N.Y. Gaz.*, Sept. 18, 1766.

Noah Wadham[s]

NOAH WADHAM[s], A.B., A.M. Yale 1764, Congregational and Methodist clergyman, was born on May 17, 1726, at Wethersfield, Connecticut, the son of Anne Hurlbert and her husband, Noah Wadham. (In 1773, for reasons unknown, the junior Wadham added an "s" to the end of his name.) In 1736 the family moved to Middletown, Connecticut. After graduation Wadhams studied theology with the Reverend Abel Newell (Yale 1751), newly installed pastor of the Congregational church at Goshen, Connecticut, and Wadhams's junior by four years. In 1757, when a Congregational church was formed at New Preston, Connecticut, Wadhams was ordained and installed as its first minister. On November 8, 1758, Wadhams married Elizabeth Ingersoll of Great Barrington, Massachusetts, with whom he had six children.

In 1768 Wadhams left New Preston to visit some of his former neighbors and parishioners who were attempting to settle the Wyoming Valley of Pennsylvania under the auspices of the Susquehannah Company, an organization of Connecticut land speculators. The settlers asked Wadhams to move from Litchfield County and become their pastor. Wadhams, however, remained in the Wyoming Valley for only a few weeks before returning to New Preston.

In 1773 the Connecticut settlers again requested Wadhams to settle among them. Wadhams replied that he thought that the disputed claims of the Connecticut settlers to the Pennsylvania lands stood a good chance of validation. "I have not forgot the state I see the inhabitants were in, as sheep without a shepherd, when I was with you," he wrote to the settlers. In the fall of 1773 Wadhams moved to the Wyoming Valley, bought one share in the Susquehannah Company for £7, and settled in Plymouth, Pennsylvania. He soon began preaching—but not Congregationalism. In barns, schoolhouses, and homes, he spread the doctrines of Methodism. He took an active role in the public affairs of his newly adopted community, joining the Connecticut settlers in signing petitions pressing their Pennsylvania property rights that were presented to the Continental Congress and to the Connecticut General Assembly in 1783. He must have suffered with his flock, too: after Loyalists and Indians under British direction raided the Wyoming Valley in 1778, massacring many inhabitants, Wadhams claimed £193.6s. damages.

Though many members of his family moved to Pennsylvania in the 1770s and 1780s, Wadhams kept up his Connecticut associations. In fact, when the Continental forces were being demobilized, a distinctly embarrassing incident involving Wadhams occurred: "As Perkins happened to be in want of a Waggon Wheel on his Journey," an observer reported in 1783 to Timothy Pickering (Harvard 1763), the United States quartermaster general, "he was inform'd of a Continental Waggon being at one Noah Wadhams (who is or has been a preacher) in the upper part of New Milford—he went to the Parson's and found, he says an excellent Waggon, taken to pieces and secreted in his barn, he there exchanged one of his wheels leaving the old one with the new Waggon—preachers of the Gospel should learn to be honest."

The possessor of one used wagon wheel, Wadhams may have returned from Pennsylvania to live in Connecticut for a few years, for in the federal census of 1790 he is recorded as a resident of New Milford, Connecticut. On February 19, 1793, Wadhams's wife Elizabeth died in New Preston, Connecticut. Soon afterward he married Mrs. Diana Ross Hageman, a widow, of Kingston, Pennsylvania. Wadhams died at Plymouth, Pennsylvania, on May 22, 1806.

SOURCES: Brief sketch of Wadhams: O. J. Harvey, *A Hist. of Wilkes-Barre* (1909-30), II, 738-40; Bellamy at installation ceremony: Stiles, *Literary Diary*, I, 129; brief references to Wadhams: *Hist. of Luzerne, Lackawanna and Wyoming Counties, Pa.* (1880), 358, 359; and also, *Susquehannah Company Papers*, v, 65-66, 167; VII, 324; X, 379-80; quotation re wagon wheel: Nicholas Gilman to Timothy Pickering, June 24, 1783, Revolutionary War Miscellaneous Numbered Records, #24285 (Manuscript File), National Archives, Washington, D.C.; residence in 1790: *U.S. Census of 1790 Connecticut*, 73.

CLASS OF 1755

Jonathan Baldwin, A.B.

Benoni Bradner, A.B.

Thaddeus Burr, A.B.

Wheeler Case, A.B.

Benjamin Conklin, A.B.

William Crawford, A.B.

John Hanna, A.B.

Gerhardus Leydekker, A.B.

Joseph Montgomery, A.B.

Isaac Smith, A.B.

Smith Stratton, A.B.

Isaac Townsend, A.B.

Jonathan Baldwin

JONATHAN BALDWIN, A.B., A.M. 1758, College steward, merchant, and public official, was born in Newark, New Jersey, on May 22, 1731, the son of Esther and Nathaniel Baldwin. His father apparently took an active interest in the new College of New Jersey, for when he died in 1750 he bequeathed £20 to President Burr. The Baldwins were one of Newark's first families, as were the Sergeants, with whom Jonathan would be closely associated throughout his life.

After graduation, Baldwin became the steward of newly founded King's College in New York City. In 1756, perhaps because of the smallpox epidemic in New York, he returned to Newark to take up the stewardship of his own College. Ironically, the disease seemed to follow him south, but while it ravaged New Jersey until 1758, it did not affect Baldwin. He assumed his duties in time to help move the College to Nassau Hall.

In Princeton Baldwin married Sarah Sergeant, the daughter of the College's treasurer, Jonathan Sergeant. She bore him eight children between 1767 and 1782, including at least one more graduate of Nassau Hall, John (A.B. 1784), who later practiced law in New York City. For a time Baldwin owned and occupied Prospect, a farm adjoining the College. His kinship with Sergeant proved a boon both to his duties as steward and to his personal welfare, for he frequently relied upon his father-in-law to provide ready funds to keep student accounts balanced and to finance his own household. In 1770 he bonded himself to Sergeant for a loan of £1,200, at least part of which was used to pay certain of his debts to the trustees of the College.

The eighteenth-century college steward was the officer chiefly responsible for the physical maintenance of the institution and its students. Baldwin's most time-consuming task was the feeding of young scholars on a limited budget—a job made even more difficult when the trustees decided in 1768 to provide "small beer" for each student. Inevitably, there were complaints about the steward's performance. The most serious came from a neighbor of the College who called himself "Publicola." In early 1767, he publicly charged that Baldwin was so gullible that he allowed farmers and retailers to gouge the College treasury by charging excessive prices for food and was so "easily imposed on" that he could not manage "unfaithful servants who have nothing at heart but their own interests." This mismanagement, said Publicola, was causing the cost of schooling to rise unconscionably, thus negating one of the most attractive aspects of an education at the College of New Jersey. He suggested that the steward pay for all goods in cash to make a better deal, and withdraw himself from "various other branches of business" that interfered with his duties.

Baldwin vehemently denied that he was guilty of any negligence and explained that he used cash as often as possible, but that in order to have more cash on hand he was trying to see to it that students paid their bills promptly. The real financial problem, he said, was that overdue accounts had been tolerated too long. His balance sheets indicate that he did, indeed, try to rationalize the bookkeeping at Nassau Hall; by 1780 most students were paying their tuition and other bills while they were still in Princeton rather than years later. How much credit for this should go to Baldwin is uncertain, but the casual accounting system used earlier by President Burr gave way to a far more efficient procedure during Baldwin's stewardship. He also was active in the lottery of 1764, which was planned to raise up to £3,000 for the College's immediate needs. As to the "other branches of business," Baldwin denied that he was engaged in any that would detract from his work as steward.

Still, he suffered abuse. In 1772, his barn was destroyed by a fire which he suspected had been "wickedly and maliciously set," and he offered a £65 reward for the arrest of the culprit. Less felonious was a protest in 1773 against the low quality butter that Baldwin provided. Some students made an effigy of him from their table spread and "hung it up by the neck in the dining room." One later took the figure to Baldwin's home and returned to report that it did "not sit very easily upon his stomach." It seems that the steward's domestic affairs were also troubled, for one young Irish servant was a frequent runaway, and Baldwin was constantly offering rewards for his recapture.

While steward of the College, Baldwin took part in other activities, including the publication of a collection of sermons by the late President Samuel Davies in 1762. In the same year he contributed generously for the building of the Presbyterian church in Princeton, and in 1769 he was an agent for the new *American Magazine, or General Repository*, edited by Lewis Nicola. A member of the American Philosophical Society, Nicola printed the society's "Transactions" as an addendum to his monthly. As a result, the *American Magazine*, in its nine-month existence, was the foremost journal of American scientific thought in the third quarter of the eighteenth century.

In 1773 Baldwin resigned as steward to devote himself to business and public affairs. He quickly became active in the political ferment that was rampant in the so-called "corridor counties"—Essex, Middlesex, Somerset, and Hunterdon. The radicals of the corridor were New Jersey's leaders in the revolutionary cause. In 1774 and 1775 Baldwin was a member of the Middlesex County Committee of Correspondence and of the Committee of Observation and Inspection of Windsor. When the New Jersey Provincial Congress convened in May 1775, he was one of the eighty-five delegates who attended. His colleagues from Middlesex included his father-in-law and his brother-in-law, Jonathan Dickinson Sergeant (A.B. 1762), as well as Enos Kelsey (A.B. 1760), William Paterson (A.B. 1763), and Frederick Frelinghuysen (A.B. 1770). These men filled many of the most responsible positions in the provincial congress; Baldwin himself was appointed to the New Jersey Committee of Correspondence in 1775.

As a member of the Princeton Council of Safety Baldwin had charge of the town's balls and cartridges; in 1778 Governor Livingston made him responsible for the distribution of such ammunition throughout the state. But his public offices could not protect him from an old nemesis, and he was in trouble over the price of food again in 1778, when he was fined for charging too much for sugar in violation of an Act of 1777. Assuming that he was not trying to rob the population, there are two possible explanations for his misdemeanor: he may have neglected to apply for the required certificate to sell sugar; or he may simply have been testing an unpopular law, which was repealed soon after his offense.

Baldwin remained in Princeton throughout the war, and in 1779 held what may have been one of the town's first "barn sales," advertising livestock, feed, and furniture. In 1781, he again took up the stewardship of the College, but this time his tenure was only one year. Some time after 1782 he moved back to Newark; he may have been the "old man named Baldwin" who in 1803 was claiming the rights to more than 100 acres of land on the basis of an eighty-six-year-old deed. He died in Newark on November 28, 1816.

SOURCES: Hageman, *History*, I, 74, 104, 165, 439; family: Jonathan Baldwin File, PUA; W. H. Shaw, *Hist. of Essex and Hudson Counties, N.J.* (1884), 358-59; Alexander, *Princeton*, 220; father's will: 30 *NJA*, 33; smallpox epidemic in New York and Princeton: David C. Humphrey, "King's College in the City of New York, 1754-1776" (Ph.D. dissertation, Northwestern University, 1968), 59; and Wertenbaker, *Princeton*, 43; Baldwin as steward: MSS, NjP; Maclean, *History*, 303; Publicola letter and Baldwin's response: 25 *NJA*, 269-71, 288-91; arson of barn: 28 *NJA*, 188; notices for return of runaway servant: 26 *NJA*, 578, and 24 *NJA*, 410; CNJ lottery of 1764: 24 *NJA*, 294-96; publication of Davies's sermons: 24 *NJA*, 7; *American Mag.*: L. N. Richardson, *Hist. of Early American Magazines, 1741-1789* (1931), 54, 140, 150-56; F. L. Mott, *Hist. of American Magazines, 1741-1800* (1930), 26n; 26 *NJA*, 348; barn sale: 3 (2 ser.) *NJA*, 146; butter effigy: *Fithian Journal*, I, 433-34; public life: extracts from the *Journal of Proc. of the Prov. Congress of N.J., 1775* (1775), 14282-83; and Hageman, above; "corridor" radicals: J. E. Pomfret, *Colonial New Jersey* (1973), 153-54; "old man" quote: GMNJ, XXII, 39.

Mss: NjP   RAH

Benoni Bradner

BENONI BRADNER, A.B., A.M. 1758, Yale 1758, Presbyterian clergyman, was born in Goshen, New York, in 1733, the last child of the Reverend John Bradner and his wife, Christian Colvill. His maternal grandfather had objected to the marriage of his daughter to a young divinity student. Perhaps because of that, John Bradner emigrated from his native Scotland to America where he was ordained at Cape May, New Jersey, in 1715. He then became the first pastor of the Congregational church at Goshen, where he died shortly before the birth of his youngest son.

At the College, Benoni Bradner prepared himself for the ministry with the usual academic training. Unlike most of his classmates, however, he also undertook to learn French. He paid for his tuition, books, and special lessons in a variety of currencies, ranging from gold to forty pounds of butter. His education for the pulpit was supervised by a Reverend Mr. Graham (probably Chauncey Graham, Yale 1747), and he was ordained in time to preach at his mother's funeral.

In 1760, Bradner assumed his first pastorate at Jamaica, Long Island, where he married Rebecca Bridges on December 20. Their son, John, was born the following autumn. By 1762, the family had moved to Dutchess County, New York, and Bradner became the pastor at Nine Partners. After bearing him three daughters, his wife died there, and Bradner left his church to return to Goshen. The loss of his wife was a severe blow, and he regularly commemorated her death with prayers and fasting. For a decade he served as a supply preacher and teacher in various destitute congregations, taking time from those duties to enlist as a private in the First Regiment of Orange County Militia. Although most sources date his military service from 1778 to 1779, he apparently was active in the regiment as late as 1780.

In June 1786, Bradner assumed the pulpit of the Independent Church of Blooming Grove. Part of the West (of the Hudson) Congregational Association that had seceded from the Presbytery and Synod of New York some years earlier, the Independent Church had a small congregation in 1786, and Bradner worked diligently to increase his flock. The effort was a visible strain on a constitution that was already weak from a life-long malady variously described as consumption or a nervous disorder. A man of erudition, eloquence, and generosity, he was held in high esteem by his congregation. Its affection was manifested when it voted him approximately £400 to compensate him for losses in a fire. And when he reluctantly appealed to the New York legislature for aid because his loans to the public had not been repaid, he was awarded a similar sum.

While at Blooming Grove, he was a founder and trustee of the Morris County Society for Promoting Religion and Learning, and he helped to found the Congregational church at Ridgebury in 1792. His physical infirmity gradually overtook him, however, and he resigned his pastorate in 1802. The pain that racked him in his last years was so profound that his screams could be heard for some distance. On January 29, 1804, he died in his sleep, and was buried next to his predecessors Enos Ayres (A.B. 1748) and Samuel Parkhurst (A.B. 1757) in what is now the furnace room of the Congregational church at Blooming Grove.

SOURCES: A. E. Corning, *History of the Congregational Church of Blooming Grove* (1929), 15-19; parents: Alexander, *Princeton*, 34; Webster, *History*, 351; E. M. Ruttenbur and L. H. Clark, *Hist. of Orange County, N.Y.* (1881), 128; years at CNJ: Aaron Burr, MS Account Book; pastorates: Giger, Memoirs, I; S. W. Eager, *Outline Hist. of Orange County* (1846-47), 548; secession of West Congregational Association: Stiles, *Literary Diary*, III, 442; military service in 1780: Revolutionary War Miscellaneous Numbered Records, #1141 (MS file), National Archives, Washington, D.C.

Mss: Congregational Church, Blooming Grove, New York

RAH

Thaddeus Burr

THADDEUS BURR, A.B., A.M. Yale 1759, landowner and public official, was born at Fairfield, Connecticut, on August 22, 1735, the son of Abigail Sturges and Thaddeus Burr, a wealthy landowner, justice of the peace, and sometime member of the Connecticut General Assembly. A first cousin, once removed, of President Burr, young Thaddeus boarded with the Burr family in Newark until January 12, 1754, when he found other quarters. He purchased many more books than the average student, among them Alexander Pope's translations of the *Iliad* and the *Odyssey* (rather expensive at £3), a translation of Xenophon, a three-volume translation of Cicero, and John Locke's *Essay Concerning Human Understanding*.

On his father's death in the year of his graduation Thaddeus inherited considerable property. On March 22, 1759, he married Eunice Dennie of Fairfield. "Having been blessed with a liberal education and an ample estate," Burr's Congregationalist pastor declared in a funeral oration, "he in the first place sat down to the cultivation of them, and in connection with his amiable consort he enjoyed an almost uninterrupted scene of domestic felicity, and in which he exhibited himself the faithful and tender husband, the kind and indulgent master and

valuable neighbor." The Burr mansion in Fairfield was a center of social life in the northeast; over the years it was visited by Washington,
Franklin, Lafayette, Timothy Dwight, Joel Barlow, by one of Burr's
closest friends, John Hancock (Harvard 1754), and, of course, by
Aaron Burr, Jr. (A.B. 1772). The Burrs often visited Boston; Copley
painted their portraits there.

Burr's public life began in 1766, when he became a member of the
committee of correspondence set up by the Connecticut Sons of Liberty at their convention in Hartford. In 1769 Burr was elected deputy
from Fairfield to the General Assembly, and in 1771 was appointed
sheriff of Fairfield County. He represented Fairfield again in the General Assembly in that year. In 1774 and 1775 Burr was a member of
both town and county committees of correspondence in Fairfield.
Elected to the General Assembly again in 1775, Burr served there with
some interruptions until 1789.

Upon taking his seat in the Assembly in 1775 Burr was appointed to
a committee charged with speeding communications from Boston to
New York. Along with Pierpont Edwards (A.B. 1768) he was assigned
to confer with the provincial congresses of New York and New Jersey
about establishing a common course of action. During the Revolution
Burr served on Connecticut's Committee of Safety, and spent most of
the time gathering provisions for the army. There was time for social
life too. On September 28, 1775, Burr's old friend John Hancock returned from presiding over the Continental Congress in Philadelphia
to marry Dorothy Quincy in the Burr mansion in Fairfield.

Burr did not escape the Revolution unscathed. On July 7, 1779, British troops under the command of Governor Tryon of New York (a
former guest at the Burr mansion) invaded Fairfield. "By the time that
the main body of the enemy had got up to the court house," Mrs. Burr
testified about four weeks later, "instead of the once humane and polite Britons, a pack of the most barberous ruffians came rushing into
the house, and repeatedly accosted me with you Dam *Rebel* where is
your husband, he is a selectmen—at the same time striping me of my
buckles, taring down the curtains of my bed, breaking the frame of my
dressing glass, pulling out the draws of my table and desk; and after
taking what they could find, they then went up stairs and proceeded
in much the same manner. . . . In the midst of this confused state General Tryon came into the house. He behaved with politeness. He demanded the papers. I told him there were none but of very old dates
related to old estates. The general said those are what we want, for we
intend to have the estates—upon which he ordered an officer to take
them to the court house." Tryon did not get the estates, but despite

protestations from Mrs. Burr he got the mansion, which along with all
its contents (and a good part of Fairfield) was burned to the ground.
The Burrs then moved into some rooms above a store in the town.

John Hancock came to the rescue. Visiting the Burrs a few weeks
later he offered to give Burr all the glass necessary if Burr would build
a new house precisely like Hancock's in Boston. Burr accepted, and the
house was built. It must have made a strong impression in Fairfield,
for Hancock owned the grandest mansion in Boston.

Peace brought no relief from public life. Burr continued to serve in
the legislature in the 1780s. In 1786 he was appointed to the very important committee designated to supervise the sale of Connecticut's
western lands in what is now Ohio. In 1790 Burr claimed £1,373 in
losses during the Revolution, and like many others was recompensed
by a large land grant in the Western Reserve. He also invested $3,854
in state securities and $2,761 in continental securities. A delegate to the
Connecticut convention called to consider the new federal constitution
in January, 1788, he voted for its ratification. He also served as a presidential elector for Connecticut in June 1789.

Burr retired from public life in the 1790s, and died in Fairfield on
February 19, 1801. He left £1,000 and his extensive real and personal
property to his wife during her life. Various nieces and nephews were
left £900. His slave Cato was to be freed if Cato wished to be free.

SOURCES: See the extensive and not always accurate sketch of Burr in Charles Burr
Todd, *A General Hist. of the Burr Family* (2nd ed., 1891), 56-66, which also reprints the Reverend Andrew Eliot's funeral sermon, and the wills of both Burr and
his father (140, 156); college expenses: Aaron Burr, MS Account Book, 22; Fairfield
committee of correspondence: F. S. Child, *An Old New England Town* (1895), 102-
103; Sons of Liberty: C. Collier, *Roger Sherman's Connecticut* (1971), 52; Burr's
public career has been reconstructed from references in *Rec. Col. Conn.*, XII-XV, and
Rec. State Conn., I-XIII; Eunice Burr's lengthy testimony is in the latter series, II, 555-
58; holdings in state and national securities, McDonald, *We the People* (1958), 144.

Mss: PHi, MHi

Wheeler Case

WHEELER CASE, A.B., A.M. 1759, Presbyterian clergyman, was probably born in 1735 at Southold, Long Island, New York, the son of
Henry Case by his first wife, Mary Wheeler. In 1740 Henry Case purchased 300 acres of land near Bethlehem, Orange County, New York,
and moved there with his second wife and family. Henry probably
farmed; in 1745 he was also listed as an attorney in Orange County.

Wheeler Case's activities in the years immediately following his graduation from the College have not been discovered, but at some time he studied for the ministry and was licensed by the Presbytery of Suffolk, which embraced much of Long Island. Before 1765 he became pastor of a Presbyterian church in or near Poughkeepsie, Dutchess County, New York. On November 12, 1765, Case was ordained by the Dutchess Presbytery and installed as pastor of the Presbyterian church at Pleasant Valley, New York. From 1769 to 1771 he was apparently dividing his time between the Pleasant Valley church and the one in Poughkeepsie. After 1771 he ministered only to the former.

Case lived on a farm about one mile east of Pleasant Valley. He presumably married, but no record of his wife or children has been found. In 1777 a band of 400 Tories from lower Dutchess County occupied Pleasant Valley, using Case's church as their headquarters. Whigs sent calls for help east to Sharon, Connecticut, which responded with soldiers who drove the Tories off, but not before the church was badly damaged.

The Tory move seems to have been prompted by General Burgoyne's invasion of New York that year from Canada, which also was responsible for Case's one known claim to fame. On June 23, 1777, Burgoyne made a pompous speech to his Indian allies in which he threatened Americans with scalping, among other things. His speech was parodied by Francis Hopkinson in America, by Edmund Burke in England, and by Wheeler Case in Pleasant Valley. In 1778 Case published his parody of Burgoyne, along with other pieces, under the title of *Poems, Occasioned by Several Circumstances and Occurrences in the Present Grand Contest of America for Liberty* (New Haven, 1778). The poems must have been popular, for they were reprinted at Hartford, Chatham, Philadelphia, and Trenton, and were given a second edition in 1788. Their tone is suggested by the following extract:

> The Lord hath founded *Zion*, God the just,
> In him his poor may safely put their trust.
> Tyrants may rage, their thund'ring cannon roar,
> *Howes* and *Burgoynes* may land upon our shore,
> There boast aloud, and tell their titles o'er;
> We fear them not, nor their oppressive laws,
> While Zion's God maintains our righteous cause.
> Oppression drove our fathers to this land,
> They all were guided by Jehovah's hand. . . .
> The wilderness became a fruitful field,
> Which did to them a thousand blessings yield,
> Like to a tree their branches spread abroad,
> They lived in plenty, and enjoy'd their GOD.

British soldiers and Tories stripped Case of much that he possessed. A meeting to restore the church was held at his home in November 1780, but the damage was not repaired until 1805. In 1787 Case began to devote one-third of his time to a Presbyterian church in nearby Charlotte Precinct (later Clinton). He continued as pastor of the church at Pleasant Valley until his death on August 31, 1791.

SOURCES: Parentage: H. E. Case, *A Family Hist. and Geneal. of Henry Case (1715-1767)* (1961), 5; Eager, *Orange County*, 614; pastorates: J. H. Smith, *Hist. of Dutchess County, N.Y.* (1882), I, 312-13, 315-16; F. Hasbrouck, ed., *The Hist. of Dutchess County, N.Y.* (1909), 274-75, 422, 23; the quotation from Case's *Poems* is from a 19th-century reprint of the New Haven, 1778 edition: S. Dodd, ed., *Rev. Memorials, embracing Poems by the Rev. Wheeler Case* (1852), 41-42.

PUBLICATIONS: see STE

Benjamin Conklin

BENJAMIN CONKLIN, A.B., Congregational clergyman, was born in Southold, Long Island, New York, in 1733. The first thirty years of his life are obscure, attendance at Princeton being one of the few identifiable milestones. In November 1763, Conklin became pastor of the Congregational church in Leicester, Massachusetts. Neither a brilliant nor an original preacher, he worked hard at his ministry and was respected by his parishioners; his amiability and easy sense of humor won him their affection. Like most of his congregation, he was an enthusiastic supporter of the movement that led to the American Revolution.

Conklin married a Leicester widow, Mrs. Lucretia Lawton. Before she died in March of 1793, she bore him two sons and a daughter. Mrs. Conklin's sister was the wife of William Henshaw, a selectman of Leicester and a member of a family that was deeply involved in the politics of revolutionary Massachusetts. His kinsman, Joshua Henshaw, who was a leader of the colony's House of Representatives, lived with Conklin for several months in 1774. Conklin's strong advocacy of the Whig cause further endeared him to his flock. Some neighboring congregations reportedly asked their own clergymen to exchange pulpits with Conklin so that the patriot line could receive wider attention. He was not afraid that he would harm a strange parish by preaching in it. "I would preach from Mars' Hill," he once said, "if I could get a chance."

His unabashed sympathy for the Whig cause led to Conklin's membership on the Leicester Committee of Correspondence. Once the new nation was established he and most other citizens of Leicester became hearty partisans of the state government. During Shays' Rebellion in 1786, Conklin wore the white paper fillet of loyalty to Boston in his hat; rebels from more westerly towns occasionally forced him to flee from his home.

Conklin's political activities diminished when order was restored. He joined the board of trustees of Leicester Academy, but his health began to fail. Always a corpulent man, he began to suffer from a painful illness. In 1794 his congregation urged him to retire from active preaching for his own welfare. As a gesture of their affection they granted him £170 and exempted his property from taxation. He retired happily to the large house—one of Leicester's oldest—and grounds that had come to him from his predecessor as pastor. On January 30, 1798, that property passed on to his successor when Conklin died.

SOURCES: E. Washburn, *Hist. Sketches of the Town of Leicester* (1860), 93-95, 331; accounts at CNJ: Aaron Burr, MS Account Book, 24; Henshaw family activity and contacts with Conklin: *NEHGR*, 22 (1868), 108; 23 (1869), 453-54; also: Benjamin Conklin File, PUA; Alexander, *Princeton*, 35-36; Giger, Memoirs, I.

RAH

William Crawford

WILLIAM CRAWFORD, A.B., A.M. Harvard 1761, physician and sometime clergyman, who held neither a medical nor a theological degree, was born in Worcester, Massachusetts, in August 1730. His parents, Robert and Mary Crawford, had settled in Worcester after emigrating from Ireland in 1718. The elder Crawford was Worcester's first trained physician, and he took personal charge of his son's early education. He was so successful that William was given advanced standing at the College of New Jersey.

In 1756, Crawford became an army chaplain in the Worcester area. His duties included preaching to the civilian population as well, for one of his closest acquaintances was the local schoolmaster, John Adams (Harvard 1755), who often went to hear him. Among his posts was Fort Edward, Nova Scotia, where he served with Colonel Frye's regiment in 1757. After returning to Worcester to recuperate from smallpox, he taught school there until 1758. During that time he applied to Harvard for an honorary A.M. Although it granted similar requests from Nathaniel Potter (A.B. 1753) and Nathaniel Sherman (A.B. 1753), the Corporation denied Crawford the degree because he had not yet qualified for an A.M. from his own college. Not until 1761, on his third application, did Crawford received the honorary degree.

Meanwhile he had returned to military life, serving as chaplain to Colonel Abijah Willard's regiment at Fort Edward at the very moment that nearby Fort William Henry was falling to Montcalm. In 1759 he was attached as the chaplain to General Timothy Ruggles's regiment in Amherst's campaign to the west and north, and then served with Wolfe at Quebec. He apparently spent the next three years with the army on the frontier and in Nova Scotia. In 1763 he married Mary Brewer of Westtown and began to look for a permanent home. His in-laws owned land in Maine and it was there he moved with his wife in 1764, when he was appointed justice of the peace for Lincoln County. From Fort Pownall on the Penobscot River he accompanied a surveying expedition to Quebec in June of that year. When he returned from Canada, Crawford served as the post surgeon at Fort Pownall. Since there was no regular chaplain at the fort, Crawford occasionally took the pulpit. But he did not concentrate on his clerical duties; one soldier asserted that he knew "Mr. Crawford's sermon" by heart. Yet the civilians in the area appreciated his services and asked that he be kept on as chaplain and surgeon even after the garrison was reduced in 1767. The request was granted by Governor Bernard; Crawford began to settle his family in Lincoln County. He purchased some 200 acres on the east side of the Penobscot for slightly less than £30 and also acquired a partial interest in the local sawmill. He was appointed justice of the peace by the provincial congress in 1775, but he died on June 15, 1776, too soon to play an active part on either side of the Revolution. His will was terse and to the point. There was to be no extravagant funeral, and his tomb of brick or stone was to be small. This, he directed, "I expect performed." Crawford was survived by five of his six children and by his wife, who removed to Castine, Maine, where she lived to be one hundred years old.

SOURCES: *Sibley's Harvard Graduates*, XIII, 561-63; military career: *Bangor Hist. Mag.*, I (1885-1886), 144-46; *Bangor Weekly Commercial*, Jan. 22, 1897; W. Lincoln, *Hist. of Worcester, Mass.* (1862), 63, 213; relationship with Adams: *Adams Papers*, I, 10, 33, 37; Adams paraphrases a sermon on p. 43; other preaching: *Bangor Hist. Mag.*, II (1886-1887), 87; sermon quotation: *NEHGR*, XIV, 9; survey in Quebec, *Bangor Hist. Mag.*, IV (1888-1889), 142; will: *Bangor Hist. Mag.*, VI (1891), 142.

RAH

John Hanna

JOHN HANNA, A.B., A.M. 1758, Presbyterian clergyman, was born at sea while his parents, Jane Andre and John Hanna, were emigrating from Ireland in 1731. The family first settled in Bucks County, Pennsylvania, and then moved to Chester County. Young John probably began his education at the Log College in Neshaminy, Bucks County. He then taught Latin and Greek and other subjects in the log schoolhouse in Lamington, New Jersey, near the Somerset County home of the Reverend James McCrea.

After graduation from the College of New Jersey, Hanna studied for the ministry with one of the Tennents, probably the Reverend Gilbert Tennent. He may also have taught at the College at the same time. In about 1759 Hanna married Mary McCrea, one of his Lamington pupils and the daughter of his former neighbor in Somerset County. They had thirteen children, among them James (A.B. 1777), John Andre (A.B. 1782), and William (A.B. 1790).

In May 1760 Hanna was licensed by the Presbytery of New Brunswick at Nassau Hall. He settled in Alexandria, Hunterdon County, New Jersey, and was ordained the following year. Partly because of serious economic problems, the churches in Hunterdon County were hard pressed to find ministers. Hanna held the pulpits in Alexandria and Bethlehem and was a regular supply at Greenwich and Kingwood as well. In October 1763 the presbytery relieved him of his duties in Greenwich so that he could divide his time equally among the other three pastorates, which he did for nearly forty years. During his first years in Hunterdon County he supervised informally the education of several young people.

In 1763 Hanna bought 145 acres near Pittstown, where he became one of the most prominent citizens. Ten years later he moved to a house near Everettstown. There his wife died of smallpox in 1780. Along with tending to his farm and his pulpits Hanna was a practicing physician, the first to settle in the Bethlehem area. His extensive practice did not interfere with his duties as a pastor or as an officer of the church, however. In 1764, he served on the commission of the Synod of New York and Philadelphia. Eight years later he was the moderator of the New Brunswick Presbytery's meeting at Trenton. In 1790 he was a commissioner to the General Assembly.

Hanna was reputed to be a stern but loving pastor, who took a fatherly interest in his parishioners. His sympathies were with the American cause during the Revolution, although his firm advocacy of temperance found little response among soldiers and veterans of the war.

As a physician Hanna believed steadfastly in the use of medicines to treat diseases. He was especially confident of his ability to ease and cure dysentery. On December 9, 1801, he died of that disease in Bethlehem. He was buried at the church there and left his possessions to the trustees of his parishes.

SOURCES: *Som. Cty. Hist. Quart.*, 7 (1918), 92-93; H. Race, "Hist. of the Presbyterian Church of Kingwood, Hunterdon County, N.J." *Jerseyman*, 3 (1895-97), 17-18; teaching career: J. P. Snell, *Hist. of Hunterdon and Somerset Counties, N.J.* (1881), and 9 (2 ser.) *NJHSP*, 95; *Som. Cty. Hist. Quart.*, above; career as pastor: Alexander, *Princeton*, 36; *Rec. Pres. Church*, 298, 307, 334, 364; Webster, MS Brief Sketches; 11 (2 ser.) *NJHSP*, 158; *Presbyterian Encyclopedia*, 302; career as physician: *Transactions of the Med. Soc. of N.J.*, *1872*, 169-70; will: 39 *NJA*, 197.

RAH

Gerhardus Leydekker

GERHARDUS [GARRET] LEYDEKKER, A.B., Dutch Reformed clergyman, was born in Hackensack, New Jersey, in April or May 1729, the son of Maritjie Benson and her husband Ryck Leydekker. He was one of at least six contemporary members of the Leydekker family, which had lived in northern New Jersey for three generations, to be called Garret.

Soon after his graduation Leydekker was involved in the debate that had divided the Dutch Church in America since the Great Awakening. The reform wing of the Church was ecumenical and declared its independence from Holland. One of its leaders, John Maritius Goetschius, was Leydekker's first teacher in his preparation for the ministry. Within a few years, however, Leydekker turned for instruction to Johannes Ritzema, probably the most reactionary member of the Conferentie, the party in the Church that opposed innovation and maintained its traditional ties to the Classis of Amsterdam. With Ritzema as his mentor Leydekker became the first and only native American to be licensed by the Conferentie. The Classis usually insisted on performing the ritual itself in Holland, but it granted Leydekker a special dispensation because his poor health prevented him from crossing the Atlantic.

Immediately after he was licensed in 1765, Leydekker supplied the North Branch church in Readington, Hunterdon County, New Jersey. In 1768 co-religionists in nearby English Neighborhood (now Ridgefield) decided to establish their own congregation; at their request the Synod of Dort named Leydekker their first minister. In the spring of 1770, with Ritzema officiating, he was ordained at the new English Neighborhood Church.

Most Conferentie clergymen were prone to neutralism or Loyalism during the Revolution, and Garret Leydekker was the most outspoken Tory of them all. Even in northern New Jersey, where Loyalist sympathies were strong, his insistence on praying for the king in violation of an order from Congress was too much for the local Whigs. In 1776 he was forced to flee to the British lines in New York City for safety.

Perhaps as vengeance for the damage done to his property by mobs, he took with him all papers belonging to his congregation, leaving his parish both preacher-less and record-less. In New York, Leydekker assumed the pulpit of the Old Dutch Church on Garden Street. The congregation was largely Loyalist and was unhappy with its own minister's sympathy for the Revolution. When the British army appropriated his church for use as a temporary hospital in 1779, Leydekker secured the use of St. George's Chapel in Trinity Church to conduct Sunday worship. His years of cooperation with the English and the Anglican clergy were thus repaid.

Toward the end of the war the English peace commissioners employed Leydekker to translate their proclamations into German. In 1782 he drafted a "Petition of American Loyalists to King George III" and presented it to General Sir Guy Carleton, commander-in-chief of the King's forces. In 1783 Leydekker, his wife Elizabeth Coley, and their three sons joined other Loyalists who were evacuated to England.

In January 1784, Leydekker filed a claim with the royal commission for compensation for his New Jersey property. He estimated his estate at 410 acres with a value of £3,175. Of the more than 200 acres that had been seized after the war, nearly half was actually purchased in 1784 by a nephew, also named Garret Leydekker, at a far higher price per acre. The commission awarded Leydekker a lump sum of £1,730, which was proportionately more than most Loyalists who had not borne arms received. By 1788 he was also receiving a £50 annual pension. On June 28, 1794, Leydekker died at his son's home at Pentonville, England. He was buried at the Dutch Church, Austin Friars, London.

SOURCES: John Wolfe Lydekker, MS biography, Garret Leydekker File, PUA; ministry: C. E. Corwin, *A Manual of the Reformed Church in America* (1922), 405; B. C. Taylor, *Annals of the Classis of Bergen* (1857), 251-52; W. W. Clayton, *Hist. of Bergen and Passaic Counties, N.J.* (1882), 249; schism in the Dutch Church and Leydekker's loyalism: R. M. Calhoon, *Loyalists in Rev. Am.* (1965), 364-65; relations with Trinity Church: W. Berrian, *Hist. Sketch of Trinity Church, N.Y.* (1847) 171-72; claims to Royal Commission: R. M. Keesey, *Loyalty and Reprisal* (1957), 110-12, 132, 242; Keesey, *WMQ*, 18 (1961), 559, 574; M. B. Norton, *The British Americans* (1972), 210-13.

PUBLICATIONS: *A Discourse on the Greatness and Praise of the Lord* (1766).

RAH

Joseph Montgomery

JOSEPH MONTGOMERY, A.B., A.M. Yale 1760, College of Philadelphia 1760, Presbyterian clergyman and public official, was the son of John and Martha Montgomery, immigrants from Ireland. He was born on October 3, 1733, in Paxtang Township, Lancaster County, Pennsylvania, and was a tutor at the College during his postgraduate training for the ministry.

Named master of the College's grammar school in 1757, Montgomery held that post until 1759 or 1760, when he was licensed to preach by the Presbytery of Philadelphia. During the next year he preached frequently at the Presbyterian Church of Georgetown, Kent County, Maryland, where he was ordained and settled as the first (and only) permanent pastor by the end of 1761. In about 1767, Montgomery married Elizabeth Reed, a sister of Joseph Reed (A.B. 1757) who later was president of the Supreme Executive Council of Pennsylvania. She bore Montgomery one daughter before she died in Georgetown in March 1769.

Since his congregation was unable to pay him regularly and he had to take on odd jobs to augment his living, Montgomery asked to be dismissed from his pulpit in June 1768. He received permission to leave in March 1769; by June he was established as the minister of the Presbyterian churches in New Castle and Christiana Bridge, Delaware—the first clergyman to be acceptable to both congregations since Daniel Thane (A.B. 1748). In his new post he created a Presbyterian Education Fund to support the training of pious young men for the ministry. By the end of 1769 he had married a local widow, Rachel Boyce, a sister of Dr. Benjamin Rush (A.B. 1760). She brought with her one son from her first marriage and later had two more children with Montgomery. While at New Castle Montgomery prepared his nephew Samuel Eusebius McCorkle (A.B. 1772) to enter the ministry. He also farmed to supplement his income.

Montgomery was an ardent Whig. In July 1775 he preached a sermon on the official day of fasting for the battle of Bunker Hill, in which he declared that American "connections with the parent State must be dissolved." At the beginning of 1776 he became chaplain to a regiment of the Delaware line and, in October 1777, resigned his pulpit to devote his full attention to the army. He moved his family back to Paxtang and became the chaplain of Colonel Robert Elder's battalion. He then transferred to Colonel Smallwood's Maryland Brigade, with which he traveled to Sunbury, Pennsylvania, in early 1780 to aid citizens of the area in their defense against Indian attacks. The situation there was so bleak that in April he personally appealed to his former brother-in-law, President Reed, for relief supplies and militia.

On November 23, 1780, Montgomery was chosen by the Pennsylvania Assembly to represent the state in the Continental Congress. He was reelected one year later. In 1782 he chaired a finance committee and was sent on a special mission to the eastern states to secure their compliance with congressional requisitions. While still in Congress he was chosen to represent Lancaster County in the Pennsylvania Assembly. He left Congress and assumed that post in October 1782.

Montgomery's attention to his pastoral duties declined in direct proportion to his interest in public affairs. Although he helped to draft the synod's official congratulations to the French Minister on the birth of the Dauphin in 1782, the Presbytery of New Castle asked him to clarify his clerical status in October of that year. He never answered the request, and on October 25, 1784, the presbytery dropped his name from its records. Montgomery accepted that decision with equanimity and explained that his health and his public duties required him to give up the pulpit. His name was therefore removed from the synod's rolls in May 1785.

Montgomery was concerned about the dispute between residents of the Wyoming Valley and Connecticut settlers over land titles in the northeast part of the state. In February 1783, the assembly chose him to head a special commission to investigate the problem. His reputation as a fair man calmed the Connecticut claimants, but Montgomery's sense of fairness did not override his loyalty to his own state. After establishing a commission headquarters in Wilkes-Barre, he proclaimed that the land was Pennsylvania's and offered to show generosity and clemency to interlopers who would surrender their claims. That offer was in line with an earlier decision of commissioners agreed upon by the two states in 1782, but it outraged the Connecticut settlers. They rejected it at once. The commissioners therefore divided Wyoming into two administrative districts and arranged for the election of justices of the peace and then returned to Philadelphia to deliver their report.

One of the assembly's current debates concerned the establishment of a new college in Pennsylvania. Benjamin Rush was one of the leading proponents of such an institution. It was to serve as a "nursery for the Presbyterian Church" in place of the College of Philadelphia, which Rush believed had been corrupted in recent years. Montgomery supported the plan. But while Rush wanted the college to be located in Carlisle, Montgomery preferred the new town of Harrisburg, which he and others expected to be the state and perhaps even the national capital. By a narrow margin the assembly chose Carlisle instead of what Rush called the "sickly bank of the Susquehanna." The brothers-in-law were bitterly divided. "No one," complained Rush, could have opposed Carlisle "with more specious and insidious maneuvers" than Montgomery. As a result, Montgomery was dropped from the roster of prospective trustees of what became Dickinson College. He was restored to the list in 1787 and served on the board until he died.

In 1784 Montgomery was part of an assembly commission to study the Susquehanna's navigability and to survey the state's northern boundary. When Dauphin County was created out of a corner of Lancaster in 1785, Montgomery became its first register of deeds and recorder of wills and justice of its court of common pleas.

Within two years he was back in Wilkes-Barre to hear the claims of the contestants in Wyoming, where the struggle had not abated. But Montgomery's membership on the claims commission was violently opposed by the Connecticut claimants, who accused him of "prejudice and Usurpation." Under the pressure of their protests, he resigned from the commission on May 31, 1787.

In June, he patented 206 1/2 acres of land, which he called "Bloomsbury" in Paxton Township, Dauphin County. He occasionally slipped back into clerical garb, as in December 1791 when he preached in Harrisburg to an audience that was unconcerned by the absence of his name from synod rolls. In 1793, he sold his farm and moved into the center of Harrisburg. When he died, on October 14, 1794, his property was divided in accordance with his will among his wife and children, and his two black slaves were set free.

SOURCES: J. M. Forster, *A Study of the Life of the Reverend Joseph Montgomery* (1879); also: W. H. Egle, *Centenary Memorial of the County of Dauphin* (1886), 46-48; Egle, "Joseph Montgomery," *PMHB*, I, 217, II, 424; CNJ: Aaron Burr, MS Account Book, 250, 310; MS Trustees' Minutes, PUA; ministry: Sprague, *Annals*, III, 346; J. D. Hall, *Hist. of the Presbyterian Church in Trenton, N.J.* (1912), 135, 171-72; *Rec. Pres. Church*, 298, 314, 400, 476, 507; military service: Stiles, *Literary Diary*, III, 297, 319; 8 (1 ser.) *Pa. Arch.*, 170; Congress: *Susquehannah Papers*, VII, 99n, 261, 278, 283-84, 286-87, VIII, 55, IX, XXIX, XXII, 83, 139; survey of Susquehanna and Pennsylvania border: 10 (1 ser.) *Pa. Arch.*, 416; Dickinson College controversy: Butterfield, *Rush Letters*, I, 294, 309, 310n3; C. C. Sellers, *Dickinson College* (1973), 61, 483; household: 24 (3 ser.) *Pa. Arch.*, 488; slaves: *U.S. Census of 1790, Pa.*, 87.

RAH

Isaac Smith

ISAAC SMITH, A.B., A.M. 1758, A.M. College of Philadelphia 1762, physician, judge, public official, and banker, was born in Trenton, New Jersey, in 1736. After graduation he remained in Princeton until 1758, serving for at least one year as a tutor in the College. After receiving his A.M. he moved to Philadelphia to study medicine. In 1762, while still a "Student of Physic," he was awarded an honorary A.M. by the College of Philadelphia.

Isaac Smith, A.B. 1755
PASTEL BY JAMES SHARPLES

Smith and Robert Harris (A.B. 1753) formed a partnership and established a "medicinal store" at the Sign of the Golden Pestle in Philadelphia. The partnership was dissolved in 1765, apparently with ill
feeling on both sides, and Smith returned to Trenton to practice medicine. He took with him his wife, Mary Pennington, whom he had married in Philadelphia's First Presbyterian Church on December 1, 1763.
By 1767 Smith was a member of the newly formed New Jersey Medical Society. He was its secretary in 1768 and its president in 1771 and
1772. In the latter year he read a paper before the society dealing with
the diseases of infants. His interest in medicine and the society was
strong throughout his life—he led the society's revival after the Revolution—but as he became more involved in public affairs he gradually
abandoned his practice. He seems to have ignored his election to the
American Philosophical Society in 1768.

    As early as 1764 Smith had joined twenty-six other Presbyterians in
calling on their co-religionists to unite for political purposes. On
April 21, 1768, he assumed his first public office when Governor Wil-

liam Franklin named him to the bench of the Hunterdon County court of pleas. In July 1774 Smith joined other citizens of Hunterdon County to protest Parliament's policy toward the colonies, and the group selected Smith as a member of the convention that would name New Jersey's representatives in the first Continental Congress. At the same time he was appointed to the New Jersey Committee of Correspondence.

Early in the war Smith received a colonel's commission in the New Jersey militia and took command of the first regiment of the Hunterdon County line. Attached to Brigadier General Philemon Dickinson's brigade, his unit was with Washington on the Delaware in December 1776. Smith's own home, like the homes of many prominent Trentonians, was occupied by Hessian officers. New Jersey militiamen organized the logistics of Washington's crossing of the Delaware on Christmas Eve and Smith's unit thereby played a significant part in the battle of Trenton. On January 14, 1777, Washington called Smith and his men back to the New Jersey side of the river to rejoin Dickinson's command.

On February 15, 1777, Smith resigned his commission to accept the New Jersey legislature's appointment as associate justice—then called "second justice"—of the State supreme court. Although he was not a professional lawyer, he held his seat on the court for four seven-year terms. In that capacity, he administered the oath of office to John Jay, the first chief justice of the United States, on December 21, 1790.

In 1788 Smith was elected a trustee of the Trenton Presbyterian church. He was also one of the original proprietors of Trenton Academy, a member of the Trenton Library Company, and a financial backer of the inventor John Fitch. In April 1789 he was among the Trenton city fathers who feted George Washington as the president-elect rode to New York for his inauguration.

Politically, Smith became an ardent Federalist. He was reputed to be a close friend of both Washington and John Adams. On the bench, he took a dim view of dissenters from civil order. During the Whiskey Rebellion in October 1794, Smith was proud of the absence of violence in New Jersey when compared to the situation in Pennsylvania. Nevertheless, he felt constrained to warn a grand jury in Bergen County that "seditious practices and speech" were alive "even in this part of the country." He took a hard line against all such offenders and prodded the grand jury to seek them out and punish them. Toward the end of the century Smith's dedication to social stability led him to be bitterly antagonistic to revolutionary France. He believed that "genuine religion" and morality were the bulwarks of democracy, and he blamed the "anarchy, tyranny, bloodshed, and ferocity" in France on "the infidel, the deist, and the atheist." That "degenerate nation," he told a Gloucester County grand jury, was trying to take advantage of America's "mistaken gratitude for past insitious [sic] favors," and to bring the United States "into bondage." To protect the nation he called for the strict enforcement of laws against "blasphemy and immorality."

In March 1795 Smith was elected as a Federalist to the House of Representatives in the fourth United States Congress. There he spoke predictably enough in favor of Jay's Treaty with England. In September 1795 he was considered for the directorship of the United States Mint. The appointment finally went to Elias Boudinot, but only after Boudinot himself had enthusiastically endorsed Smith's candidacy.

Smith served his single term in Congress while retaining his seat on the New Jersey Supreme Court. In 1800 he was a presidential elector for Adams. The defeat in that election foreshadowed the growth of Republican strength in New Jersey. When his term expired in November 1804, Smith was not reappointed by the state's new administration. Retiring to Trenton, he became the first president of the Trenton Banking Company in 1805.

Smith made his will in August 1804. In it he bequeathed most of his possessions to friends. But he reserved $100 for the Presbyterian church in Trenton on the condition that it keep his family's tombstones in good repair. This was necessary, he pointed out, because he had no descendants. His wife, whom he considered the embodiment of "what a woman OUGHT to be," had died in 1801 after "a long and helpless illness." His three sons had all reached maturity but had died young. On August 29, 1807, Smith died. He was buried in the churchyard in Trenton. At his death, his estate was valued at $2,383.

SOURCES: W. J. Bell, unpublished draft sketch of the "Life of Isaac Smith" (1970), PUA; medical study: 24 *NJA*, 39; marriage and family: 2 (2 ser.) *Pa. Arch.*, 269; Hall, *Hist. Pres. Church Trenton*, 13; S. S. Smith, *Battle of Trenton* (1965), 9, 29; *Washington Writings*, VII, 12; court of pleas: 17 *NJA*, 504; prerevolutionary political activity: 10 *NJA*, 587-88; 29 *NJA*, 415-16, 432; medical practice and New Jersey Medical Society: Wickes, *Hist. of Medicine N.J.*, 398-99; *NJHSP*, 10 (1862), 372; 26 *NJA*, 292; 5 (2 ser.) *NJA*, 312; judicial career: J. Whitehead, *Judicial and Civil Hist. of New Jersey* (1897), I, 402; oath to Jay: F. Monaghan, *John Jay* (1935), 231; Washington in Trenton: Stryker, *Washington's Reception by the People of New Jersey in 1789* (1882), 4; charges to grand juries: STE, 38517; W. R. Fee, *NJHSP*, 50 (1932), 41-42; U.S. Mint Appointment: G. A. Boyd, *Elias Boudinot* (1952), 224; J. J. Boudinot, ed., *Life of Elias Boudinot* (1896), II, 107-108; Congress: E. K. Smith, "Trent-Town's Unknown Hero of 1776," *Mich. Quart. Review* (Summer 1965), 205; will: 40 *NJA*, 309; relations with Washington and Adams: 2 (3 ser.) *Port-Folio*, 35; Hall, above, 147.

PUBLICATIONS: see STE

Mss: PHi, NjP   RAH

Smith Stratton

SMITH STRATTON, A.B., was born near East Hampton, Long Island, New York, in 1727 and baptized in the Congregational church there on July 16 of that year. He was the son of Elizabeth Smith and her husband John Stratton, a weaver and farmer. In College Stratton bought copies of the *Newark Grammar*, Isaac Watts's *Essays*, and other books. He found it necessary to borrow eight shillings from President Burr, which he promptly repaid. Stratton became a member of the Congregational church in East Hampton on a trip home in 1754. A family tradition states that he was a Presbyterian clergyman, but no mention of him has been found in church records. Stratton died at Southold, Long Island, on March 16, 1758.

SOURCES: H. R. Stratton, *A Book of Strattons* (1908), I, 125-26; Aaron Burr, MS Account Book, 28; father's will: *N.Y. Wills*, VII, 60.

Isaac Townsend

ISAAC TOWNSEND, A.B., entered the College on September 26, 1753, bought the usual books, graduated in due course, and was listed as dead in the College's first catalogue, published in 1770. No further information about him has been found. Townsends were numerous in Cape May County, New Jersey, Long Island and Dutchess County, New York, and in Connecticut and Massachusetts. All of the contemporary Isaac Townsends who have been located and who would have been of an age appropriate to attend the College at this time lived beyond 1770, and so are not likely to have been this matriculant. It is possible that the graduate was related to Micah Townsend (A.B. 1766), who came from Oyster Bay, Long Island, but this has not been definitively established.

SOURCES: Entrance to CNJ: Aaron Burr, MS Account Book, 30-31.

CLASS OF 1756

Stephen Camp, A.B.

David Hull, A.B.

Isaac Livermore, A.B.

William Livermore, A.B.

Alexander Martin, A.B.

William Mills, A.B.

Josiah Ogden, A.B.

Joseph Peck, A.B.

Azel Roe, A.B.

Jesse Root, A.B.

Jeffrey Smith, A.B.

Stephen Camp

STEPHEN CAMP, A.B., physician, was born at Newark, New Jersey, in 1739, the son of Nathaniel, a well-to-do citizen of the town (he left an estate valued at over £1,582), who was very active in the affairs of the College. Stephen's mother boarded many students in her house, and William Burnet (A.B. 1749) married Stephen's sister. In College Stephen bought copies of Watts's *Logic* and Plato's *Dialogues* and took special lessons in French.

After graduation Camp studied medicine and then set up practice in Bridgetown (now Rahway), New Jersey. He married Hester Birt, daughter of a British officer. The Camps had two children. Camp was reputed to have been "full of fun and frolic." One of the founders of the New Jersey Medical Society in 1766, he went to only two of its meetings and was expelled for non-attendance in November 1771. Camp died in Rahway on March 19, 1775, leaving three slaves and a substantial estate inventoried at over £1,562.

SOURCES: Wickes, *Hist. of Medicine N.J.*, 193; father's will: 36 *NJA*, 39; college accounts: Aaron Burr, MS Account Book, 30, which contains many references to father; *Proc. N.J. Med. Soc.* (1875), 7-8, 31; will: 34 *NJA*, 82.

David Hull

DAVID HULL, A.B., the ninth child of Elizabeth Burr and her husband Nathaniel Hull, and the nephew of President Aaron Burr, was born in Fairfield, Connecticut, on December 10, 1734. He entered the College on or before September 26, 1753. In Newark he boarded with the mother of Stephen Camp (A.B. 1756) for one year, and then with a Mrs. Sawyer. In the summer of 1755 he moved into the president's own house. In addition to the usual curriculum, Hull was trained in French. He also purchased a scale and dividers in 1754.

Hull was a peripatetic student who made at least three long journeys during his college years. For one of them he rented a horse, but for the others he may well have walked. Between 1753 and 1756 he purchased at least three new pairs of shoes and he frequently visited local cobblers to have his older footwear repaired. President Burr kept a careful record of his young relative's expenses, which totaled more than seventy pounds during his stay at the College. Most of Hull's expenses were handled by Joseph Sherwood, the husband of Burr's sister Jane and another of Hull's uncles.

In October 1754 Hull was attended by a Newark physician, possibly for podiatric trouble. Within two years of his graduation, he was dead.

SOURCES: Aaron Burr, MS Account Book, 32, 33, 148; for relationship of Hull, Burr, Sherwood: E. H. Schenk, *Hist. of Fairfield, Conn.* (1889), I, 360, 382.

RAH

Isaac Livermore

ISAAC LIVERMORE, A.B., A.M. 1759, teacher and preacher, was born in Waltham, Massachusetts, on January 28, 1735, the son of Samuel Livermore, a local official, and his wife Hannah Brown. Isaac was the third of the Livermore brothers to attend the College, the others being Samuel (A.B. 1752) and William of this class. Isaac and William each sent a £5.5s. prepayment on their tuition before traveling south from Waltham to enter the junior class together on June 19, 1755.

After graduation Isaac returned home to Waltham to keep the school there from November 1756 to August 1757 and for part of 1758. Livermore was probably studying for the ministry, for in 1759 he preached briefly to a group at Bath, Maine, that was trying to organize itself either as a Presbyterian or a Congregational church. The people were most contentious and could find no permanent minister. They offered Livermore a salary of £53 6s.8d. per year to settle there, but he refused. In 1755 Livermore's sister Hannah married Nathaniel Potter (A.B. 1753) of New Jersey. At some time after 1759 Isaac returned to New Jersey, perhaps in some association with the Potter family. When Isaac died intestate in Rockaway, Morris County on January 7, 1765, Nathaniel Potter's father, Noadiah, acted as a fellowbondsman for Isaac's estate.

SOURCES: W. E. Thwing, *Livermore Family in America* (1902), 38; Aaron Burr, MS Account Book, 126; J. Sewall, "The Hist. of Bath," *Maine Hist. Society Collections,* 2 (1847), 223; intestate: 33 *NJA*, 254.

William Livermore

WILLIAM LIVERMORE, A.B., A.M. 1759, lawyer and public official, younger brother of Samuel (A.B. 1752) and older brother of Isaac of this class, was born in Waltham, Massachusetts, on October 9, 1737, the son of Samuel Livermore and his wife Hannah Brown. The senior Livermore was a ubiquitous local official, holding over the course of his lifetime almost every position available in the town—town clerk, selectman, deacon of the church, and so forth.

Both William and his brother Isaac entered the junior class of the College on June 19, 1755. After graduation William studied law, possibly with his older brother Samuel, who in 1757 began the practice of law in Portsmouth, New Hampshire. After completing his law studies William moved north to Falmouth (now Portland) in Maine, which in 1760 was split into two counties and doubtless looked promising to a young lawyer. On August 27, 1761, the following notice appeared in a Boston newspaper: "We hear from Falmouth, that last Tuesday Se'nnight died there, of a slow Fever, in the 24th Year of his Age, Mr. William Livermore, Attorney at Law, to whom, just before his Death, was granted a Commission for Register of the Probate of Wills &c for the County of Cumberland."

SOURCES: W. E. Thwing, *Livermore Family in America* (1902), 38; Aaron Burr, MS Account Book, 126; obituary: *Boston News-Letter*, Aug. 27, 1761.

Alexander Martin

ALEXANDER MARTIN, A.B., A.M. 1759, LL.D. 1793, merchant, lawyer, planter, and public official, brother of Thomas (A.B. 1762), was born about 1740 at Lebanon, Hunterdon County, New Jersey, the oldest son of Jane Hunter and her husband, Hugh Martin. The father, born in County Tyrone, migrated from Ireland in the 1720s. In New Jersey Hugh became a moderately prosperous farmer (he left an estate inventoried at £362 and four slaves) and served as a justice of the peace for Hunterdon County.

Martin prepared for college at Francis Alison's academy at New London, Pennsylvania. In College he purchased copies of Watts, Plato, Locke, and also bought one of President Burr's sermons. After graduation Martin traveled south to Cumberland, Virginia, where for a little over a year he tutored the son of one N. Davies and ran a school in the area. Martin then returned home to New Jersey, but soon decided to seek his fortune in the South. He moved to the village of Salisbury, North Carolina, where he established himself as a merchant. He may also have read law, for by 1764 he was a justice of the peace and in 1766 became deputy king's attorney for Rowan County.

Rowan County was a center of activities for the Regulators, poorer backcountry farmers who felt that they were being exploited by law-

Alexander Martin, A.B. 1756

yers and easterners. In 1770 the Regulators attacked Hillsborough, where court was meeting, and whipped many lawyers, Martin among them. Six months later, in March 1771, a mob of Regulators assembled just outside Salisbury as court was about to meet. A repetition of the Hillsborough incident seemed imminent. Martin, however, went to meet with the Regulators and negotiated an agreement promising them lower legal fees and other benefits. Governor Tryon rebuked him soundly for his interference.

These activities did not damage Martin's career. Shortly afterward he moved to Guilford County, which he represented in the North Carolina House of Commons in 1773–1774. He lived not far from the North Carolina Moravian settlement and, although himself an Anglican, over the years became the Moravians' close friend, attending their prayer meetings and looking after their land interests and political affairs. In 1775 Martin was made a judge. At the same time he became deeply involved in the Whig cause, serving as Guilford County's representative to the second and third North Carolina provincial congresses in 1775. Appointed a lieutenant colonel in the Second North Carolina Continental Regiment in 1775, Martin served in several campaigns, culminating in the battle of Germantown in October 1777. There he was arrested for cowardice, court-martialed, and acquitted. Honor preserved, Martin resigned from the army.

Back in Guilford County in 1778, Martin served in the state senate from that year until 1782 and again in 1785 and 1787–1788, acting as speaker in every session except his first. Martin served on several important committees, and when North Carolina's governor was captured by the British late in 1781 Martin became acting governor. He was elected governor in his own right in 1782 and reelected in 1783 and 1784. As governor he sought cooperation with Virginia in securing humane treatment for and peace with the Cherokee and Chickasaw Indians and urged the promotion of commerce, agriculture, manufactures, education, and religious toleration. Martin was elected to Congress in 1786 but resigned the following year. As a member of the North Carolina delegation to the federal convention in 1787 he impressed William Pierce of Georgia as "a Man of Sense, and undoubtedly a . . . good politician, but . . . not formed to Shine in public debate, being no Speaker." Martin left the convention in August without signing the new constitution. Considered a moderate Federalist, he was not elected to North Carolina's ratifying convention, which neither accepted nor rejected the Constitution. Martin was elected governor again for three consecutive terms beginning in 1789. In 1792 he was elected to the United States Senate, where his most conspicuous actions were his constant urging of open sessions, his opposition to Jay's Treaty, and his vote in favor of the Alien and Sedition laws.

Always the conciliator in his home state, Martin cannot easily be categorized as either a Federalist or a Republican. He was simply the leader of one of the four political factions in western North Carolina. The interests closest to Martin's heart appear to have been literary, scientific, and educational. A strong supporter of the University of North Carolina, he served from 1790 to 1793 as the first president of its board of trustees and donated to it a microscope and a telescope. On July 21, 1797, during his Senatorial term, he was elected to the American Philosophical Society. Throughout his life Martin aspired to write poetry. His specialty was the funeral ode. In 1798, while a Senator, he wrote a play called *A New Scene* (it was actually a neoclassical masque) and dedicated it to former President Washington. The first stage direction hints of its quality: "Scene the Last. The GENIUS of America descends in a Purple Robe, on his head a Roman cap, encircled with a

Crimson Tiara, adorned with Sixteen Stars, and crested with the American Eagle; holding in his Right Hand a spear. GENIUS: 'All hail Columbus! . . .' "

At some time before 1790 Martin bought a 400-acre plantation on the Dan River in Rockingham County, which he called "Danbury." It was an extensive establishment, for in 1790 Martin was recorded as owning forty-seven slaves. In 1799, after his failure for reelection to the Senate, he retired to "Danbury," where he remained except for a period of service in the state senate in 1804–1805. Martin died on November 2, 1807. His mother, who lived with him, died six days later. Martin, who never married, left his extensive library and most of his property to his nephews, but he also remembered an illegitimate son named Alexander Strong.

Sources: *DAB*; for considerable geneal. and primary material: Alexander Martin File, PUA, and Martin Family File, PUA; father's will: 33 *NJA*, 273; Alison's academy: *PMHB*, 8 (1884), 46n.; college accounts: Aaron Burr, ms Account Book, 34; tutoring: *WMQ*, 9 (1952), 380; Regulators: S. Powell, et al., *The Regulators in North Carolina . . . 1759-1776* (1971); Moravians: references in A. L. Fries, ed., *Records of the Moravians in N.C.* (1922-69), II-VI; service in Revolution: A. Henderson, *North Carolina, the Old and the New* (1941), I, 345; Pierce quotation: *AHR*, III (1898), 332; political position: McDonald, *We the People*, 33, 34, 78, 86, and D. H. Gilpatrick, *Jeffersonian Democracy in N.C., 1789-1816* (1931), 42-43n., 66-67; UNC; K. B. Battle, *Hist. of the Univ. of N.C.* (1907), I, 13, 133, 826, as corrected by references in R.D.W. Conner. *A Doc. Hist. of the Univ. of N.C., 1776-1799* (1953), I; quotation is from Martin, *A New Scene . . .* (1798), 1; for slaves, see: *U.S. Census of 1790, N.C.*, 169.

Publications: see STE

Mss: MiU-C, NcU

William Mills

William Mills, A.B., A.M. 1759, A.M. Yale 1771, Presbyterian clergyman, was born in Smithtown, Long Island, New York, on March 13, 1739. His parents were Isaac and Hannah Mills of Mills's Pond, Long Island. Following his graduation, he was tutored in theology by Charles Beatty of Neshaminy, Pennsylvania, who later became a trustee of the College. Mills was licensed by the Presbytery of New Brunswick in March 1760 and was ordained by the same body on April 21, 1762, in Flemington, New Jersey.

Soon after his ordination, Mills succeeded Benoni Bradner (A.B. 1755) as pastor of the Presbyterian church in Jamaica, Long Island. During his ministry Jamaica had its first significant revival, probably in 1764. In 1767, Mills received a "pressing" call to take a pulpit in

Philadelphia. He preferred to stay in Jamaica, however, and was supported by his congregation and the Presbytery of Suffolk. After a full hearing the synod agreed that he should remain where he was. That decision was undoubtedly influenced by Mills's success in increasing the church from only thirteen in 1762 to a membership of many more.

Early in his ministry Mills married Mary Reading, the daughter of New Jersey's Lieutenant Governor John Reading. Their daughter Mary, the first of their six children, was born in 1763. Mary Mills later married Robert Halsted (A.B. 1765) and traveled with him on horseback to establish a church in Cincinnati, Ohio. Mills suffered from a chronic disease for which he frequently sought medical treatment in New York City. It was on such a trip that he died on Friday, March 18, 1774. He was interred at his own church in Jamaica on the following Monday. He had accumulated considerable property during his career, for "three improved farms," representing only part of his estate, were offered for sale after his death.

SOURCES: N. S. Prime, *Hist. of Long Island* (1845), 316-17; daughter and son-in-law: Wheeler, *Ogden Family*, 141; also: Giger, Memoirs, I; *Rec. Pres. Church*, 298, 314, 451; B. F. Thompson, *Hist. of Long Island* (1839), 391.

RAH

Josiah Ogden

JOSIAH OGDEN, A.B., probably a law student, was born in February 1739 in Newark, New Jersey, to Gertrude Gouverneur and her husband David Ogden (Yale 1728). His father, an Anglican, was already one of the colony's foremost attorneys.

After graduation Ogden remained at Princeton, perhaps to oversee the education of two of his younger brothers, Isaac (Class of 1758) and Abraham, who was in the grammar school. In March 1757 David Ogden called his sons home to preserve them from the revival that was sweeping Nassau Hall, where scholars were said to "Run wild." Esther Burr thought that young Abraham, at least, might have been "Savingly rought," but she did not speculate on the state of either Josiah or Isaac.

In November 1760, Josiah died intestate in Burlington County, New Jersey. His five surviving brothers went on to distinguished careers. Some of them, like their father, were leading Loyalists during the Revolution. Others were distinguished Whigs.

SOURCES: Wheeler, *Ogden Family*, 67-69; return from Princeton to Newark: Esther Burr, MS Journal, entry for March 1, 1757; will: 32 *NJA*, 239; careers of father and brothers: *DAB*; Dexter, *Yale Biographies*, I, 373-75.

RAH

Joseph Peck

JOSEPH PECK, A.B., was a Congregational and Presbyterian clergyman. The family was widespread in Massachusetts, Connecticut, and New Jersey, and the name "Joseph" was common in each branch. An extensive genealogical search has failed to establish the birthplace or family history of the alumnus. The weight of the evidence suggests an origin in Fairfield County, Connecticut.

Peck entered the College by December 26, 1753, when he was first billed for tuition by President Burr. After graduation he studied for the ministry and was licensed by the Congregationalist Fairfield East Association of Connecticut on May 29, 1758. About 1762 or earlier Peck became pastor of a Presbyterian church at Phillipi (between Fishkill and South Salem), New York. The area had been settled by Congregationalists who had been deeply influenced by the Great Awakening. In 1762 Peck was among the three ministers in the area who organized the Presbytery of Dutchess. He remained at the Phillipi church until June 1769, when he moved a short distance east to become pastor of a Congregational church at New Fairfield, Connecticut. He remained there until 1775, when he resigned his pastorate. No certain further trace of Peck has been discovered. The federal census of 1790 listed twelve men of that name in Connecticut and three in New York. The College first took notice of Peck's death in its catalogue of 1818.

SOURCES: CNJ: Aaron Burr, MS Account Book, 38-39; Alexander, *Princeton*, 39-40; Webster, MS Brief Sketches, PPPrHi; Dutchess Pres.: V. H. Paltsits, "Beginnings of Pres. in Albany," *JPHS*, 5 (1909), 157.

Azel Roe

AZEL ROE, A.B., D.D. Yale 1800, Presbyterian clergyman, was born at Setauket, Long Island, New York, on February 20, 1738, the son of John Roe, "a man of substantial property." He matriculated at the College on September 26, 1753, and purchased the usual books while there—Locke, Watts, Plato, and various textbooks. After graduation Roe studied theology with the College's first tutor, the Reverend Caleb Smith (Yale 1743), at Newark Mountain (now Orange), New Jersey. Licensed by the Presbytery of New York late in 1759 or early in 1760, he was ordained by the same Presbytery, *sine titulo*, in August 1762. He was installed as pastor of the Presbyterian church at Woodbridge,

New Jersey, in 1763. In September of the same year he married Rebecca Foote, widow of his teacher Smith. The Roes had eight children. After Rebecca's death in 1794 Roe married in 1796 Hannah Bostwick, widow of General Alexander McDougall. Roe served as pastor at Woodbridge for fifty-three years and also, until 1793, at the neighboring Presbyterian church in Metuchen.

Roe was an active Whig, so active in fact that he became a target for Tories. One night during the Revolution a group of Tories and British captured Roe at his home and bore him off a prisoner to New York City. On the way there the British officer in charge offered to carry Roe across a stream. "Well, Sir," Roe is reported to have said, "if never before, you can say, after this, that you was once priest-ridden." After his exchange Roe moved his family to Piscataway, New Jersey.

A trustee of the College from 1778 to 1807, Roe served also as a member of the first General Assembly of the Presbyterian Church in 1789 and as moderator of the General Assembly in 1802. He was widely liked and respected in his area. Aside from revivals in the late 1780s his pastorate was uneventful. One day followed the other, much like the one he described in his journal on November 23, 1815: "A fine clear morning. Mrs Roe very unwell, spent ye day at home reading & writing attended one Thursday evening lecture in the evening but few met —owing in some measure to ye sickly season, & perhaps to the too prevailing indifference & backwardness in coming to such religious exercises. How different the attention & engagedness of people in the things of religion now, from what it was this time twelve months! Oh that it might please God, to visit us again with the influence of his Spirit." Five days later Mrs. Roe was dead of typhus. Roe followed her to the grave on December 2.

SOURCES: Azel Roe File, PUA; Sprague, *Annals*, III, 232-35; Aaron Burr, MS Account Book, 68-69; Roe, MS Journal, November 10-24, 1815, PPPrHi; death notices of Roe and wife: *The Centinel of Freedom*, Dec. 21, 1815, 3.

Mss: NjP, PHi, PPPrHi

Jesse Root

JESSE ROOT, A.B., A.M. Yale 1766, LL.D. 1800, lawyer and public official, was born on December 28, 1736, in Coventry, Windham County, Connecticut, the son of Sarah Strong and Ebenezer Root, a migrant from Northampton, Massachusetts. A nineteenth-century memorialist claimed that Root "experienced the renewing influences of the Holy

Jesse Root, A.B. 1756
BY JOSEPH STEWART

Spirit, at four years of age." In College Root purchased the usual books
—Plato, Ward, Watts, Cicero, and Locke, and also a "Scale & Dividers." After graduation Root studied theology with the Reverend Samuel Lockwood (Yale 1745) at Andover, Connecticut. After less than six
months' study he was licensed as a Congregational preacher by the
Hartford South association of Hartford County. During this period—
on May 18, 1758—Root married Mary Banks of Newark, New Jersey.
The Roots had nine children.

In 1759 Root's brother was killed in the Seven Years War, and in the
following year his father died. Changed family circumstances led Root
to seek another occupation. Eliphalet Dyer (Yale 1740) and others suggested that he would make a good lawyer. Root read law and in February 1763 was admitted to the bar in Windham County, and he later
practiced in Hartford.

Root's rise was slow but steady. By November 1771 he was the
colony's lawyer for various tax cases. He served on the board of the
Hartford Grammar School and in 1775 and again in 1776 was a justice

of the peace for Hartford County. In June 1776 he called for the direct election of delegates to the Continental Congress by the people, as the rightful source of all authority. In December 1776 Root was authorized to raise troops in western Connecticut for Washington's army. He was appointed lieutenant colonel of the regiment he raised and later rose to the rank of adjutant general. From May 1778 through 1780 he was a member of his state's Council of Safety, and represented the town of Coventry in the assembly in 1778 and 1779. In December 1778, his state sent him as a delegate to the Continental Congress, where he served on and off until 1782. There the crochety delegate from Delaware, Thomas Rodney (obviously unfamiliar with Connecticut's political style), described Root as "a man that seems to be without passions and therefore has a Capacity to Conceal the most Artful designs under the most specious shew of Candor, and plausible argument, yet his language is so weak and innervate that he seldom succeeds in making much impression on the audience—in short his Talents seem better suted [sic] to some European Court than to a republican assembly." Root had no "artful designs"; one major theme runs through his letters from Congress to the governor of his home state: the weakness of the national government and the ills that flowed from such weakness.

Root was a participant in a legal case, the only one arising under the provisions of Article IX of the Articles of Confederation, which undertook to settle the dispute between Connecticut and Pennsylvania over jurisdiction of the Wyoming territory in Pennsylvania. The trial itself opened in Trenton in November 1782. It was almost a reunion of College of New Jersey alumni. Root was one of the three Connecticut agents; the four Pennsylvania agents included Joseph Reed (A.B. 1757), Jonathan Dickinson Sergeant (A.B. 1762), and William Bradford, Jr. (A.B. 1772). Among the commissioners appointed to judge the case was William Churchill Houston (A.B. 1768). Root made the opening arguments for Connecticut in the long and precedent-making case. But his mind was sometimes elsewhere. On the day before his state was to make its final arguments he underwent a mystical experience: "Friday morning, the happiest I ever beheld. Although I have frequently experienced something like it, I never had my heart so ravished with the beauty of divine things—the excellent glory of God the father—the infinite love, condescension, and mercy of Jesus Christ the Son, towards our ruined race; and his boundless grace towards me, a poor, miserable sinful creature. The view was so transporting, I was scarce able to compose myself to go down to my breakfast, or to conceal the tremor it produced in my nerves. Oh, my Soul! what a blessed foretaste of the joys of heaven, with which thou wilt forever solace thy-

self! Oh! what is the world and all its pleasures to one moment's bliss?"
Connecticut lost the case: Pennsylvania was awarded jurisdiction over
the territory while Connecticut settlers there retained their land rights.

The decision against his state did not harm Root's position at home.
He continued to serve until 1789 (as he had been doing since 1780) as
a member of the upper house of the Connecticut legislature and also
as state's attorney for Hartford County. In 1784 Root was involved in
an unsuccessful attempt to reform the governance of Yale College,
which President Stiles looked upon favorably. A member of the convention called to consider the new federal constitution in January
1788, Root voted for its ratification. In the following year Root was appointed an assistant judge of Connecticut's superior court and in 1798
became chief justice. In that year he published *Reports of Cases Ad-
judged in the Superior Court and Supreme Court of Errors . . . 1789
to . . . 1793*. A second volume followed in 1802.

In 1807 Root retired from the bench and busied himself with local
affairs at his home in Coventry. He served as a presidential elector in
1808, voting, like the other Connecticut electors, for Charles Cotes-
worth Pinckney as president. When a convention was called to write
a constitution for Connecticut in August 1818, Root, as the oldest
member, brought it to order. During the sessions of the convention
Root worked against an independent executive and opposed a bill of
rights, fearing that it might tend to abridge the authority of the people. Root was active in town affairs until a week before his death on
March 29, 1822.

SOURCES: *DAB*; long obituary in *Christian Spectator*, 6 (1824), 389-92, from which
1782 quotation is drawn; college purchases: Aaron Burr, MS Account Book, 40;
Root's political career has been reconstructed largely from: *Rec. Col. Conn.*, XIII-XV,
and *Rec. State Conn.*, I-IV; authority of people: C. Collier, *Roger Sherman's Connecticut* (1971), 133; activities in Continental Congress: *LMCC*, passim and esp. v,
504-505, 547, and for Rodney description, VI, 20; Trenton trial: *WMQ*, 26 (1969),
521-47, and also *Susquehannah Papers*, esp. VI and VII; Yale incident: E. S. Morgan,
The Gentle Puritan: A Life of Ezra Stiles, 1727-1793 (1962), 354-56; role in 1818
convention: R. F. Purcell, *Connecticut in Transition, 1775-1818* (1918), 377-85.

PUBLICATIONS: see text above.

Jeffrey Smith

JEFFREY SMITH, A.B., A.M. 1760, landowner, ironmonger and public
official, was born at Smithtown, Long Island, on March 3, 1734, the son
of Hannah Conkling and her husband, Solomon Smith, a farmer, landowner, and grandson of one of the original patentees of the town. Jef-

frey entered the College at some time before April 26, 1753, when he was charged for tuition for the first time. He bought the necessary texts—Isaac Watts's *Essays*, Patrick Gordon's *Geography*—and in April 1754 borrowed eight shillings from President Burr in order to make a trip home to Long Island.

After graduation Smith returned to Smithtown, where he spent the rest of his life. He was chosen one of the town's tax collectors in 1760 and the following year became a fence viewer and appraiser of damages. In 1767 he was one of the overseers of highways and in 1771 an overseer of the poor, a post to which he was reappointed in every year through 1783. At some time—probably in the early 1760s—Smith married Prudence Smith. The couple had four children—Solomon, Nathaniel, Abraham, and Onee.

The Smiths were a Whig family. Jeffrey's father, Solomon, was elected to the Suffolk County Committee of Correspondence in August 1774. In 1775 the son signed the local association that boycotted British goods and served on a committee to raise Suffolk County's First Regiment, in which he became a major. He became the town's first mayor in the same year. On August 29, 1776, two days after the battle of Long Island had begun, Smith assembled his militiamen in hopes of coming to the aid of the Americans. After some reconnoitering westward, however, he decided that the cause was hopeless, as indeed it was. He advised his men to return to their homes, declaring that he "designed to decline his commission." Given the situation, it was a sensible decision. Smith did not evacuate to Connecticut as did many other Long Islanders during the years of British occupation. He remained in Smithtown in his household, which in 1776 consisted of thirteen persons, including six slaves.

Immediately after the war, in January 1784, Smith was elected a delegate to the New York Assembly from Suffolk County. There he found himself facing difficult problems. The areas of New York state that had not been occupied by the British had been taxed highly during the Revolution. With peace and independence secured, these areas sought to tax heavily the sections of the state that had been occupied by the British. Smith fought vigorously against all such tax measures and also in favor of bills assuring the payment of debts to those who had remained in British-occupied areas during the war. His other important votes came in favor of bills for the gradual elimination of slavery in his state. He served in the assembly until May 1786.

Smith was a large landowner on Long Island. His major interest, however, appears to have been the iron forge he established on the south side of the island, which specialized in the manufacture of anchors for ships. He also owned a store and a gristmill in the area. Whether Smith established these enterprises before or after the Revolution is uncertain, but he put them all up for sale in March 1798, when he probably retired.

Smith remained active in local affairs throughout the late 1780s and 1790s. He was a trustee of the well-known Clinton Academy in East Hampton in the late 1780s, and in 1795 and 1797 served as one of Smithtown's school commissioners. In 1800 the federal census-taker found him living in a household of ten people, which included three slaves. He died at Smithtown in 1812.

SOURCES: Parentage and innumerable references to local activities: W. S. Pelletreau, *Records of the Town of Smithtown . . .* (1898), 476 and passim; F. K. Smith, *The Family of Richard Smith of Smithtown, Long Island* (1967), 172; Aaron Burr, MS Account Book, 64; H. Onderdonk, *Revolutionary Incidents of Suffolk and Kings Counties* (1849), 43, 64; Onderdonk, *Suffolk and Kings Counties in Olden Times* (1866), 26, 28, 31; F. G. Mather, *Refugees of 1776 from Long Island to Connecticut* (1913), 570; *Journal of the Assembly of the State of New York*, title varies, see issues for 7th and 8th Sessions, 1784, 1785, 1786; 1776 census: J. L. Smith, *Hist. of Smithtown* (1961), 14; 1800 census: *NYGBR*, 56 (1925), 11; Smith's will does not appear in: *Surrogate Records at Riverhead, N.Y., 1787-1829* (1905-1918).

CLASS OF 1757

Moses Baldwin, A.B.

Caleb Barnum, A.B.

Nicholas Bayard, A.B.

Noah Benedict, A.B.

John Boyd, A.B.

Abner Brush, A.B.

Caleb Curtis, A.B.

Timothy Edwards, A.B.

Peter Faneuil, A.B.

Elnathan Gregory, A.B.

Thomas Hun

William Kirkpatrick, A.B.

Nicholas Low

Alexander MacWhorter, A.B.

Samuel Parkhurst, A.B.

Joseph Reed, A.B.

Stephen Sayre, A.B.

David Smith, A.B.

James Smith, A.B.

John Strain, A.B.

Samuel Taylor, A.B.

Joseph Treat, A.B.

Abner Wells, A.B.

Henry Wells, A.B.

Moses Baldwin

MOSES BALDWIN, A.B., A.M. 1760, Dartmouth 1791, Presbyterian clergyman, was born in Newark, New Jersey, on November 5, 1732. His father John Baldwin, Jr., a farmer, died before the end of the year. His mother, Lydia Harrison Baldwin, died in the early months of 1737. At her death her estate was valued at £258.08.11.

For two years after his mother's death, Baldwin lived with his uncle, Moses Harrison. He then moved to the home of his great-uncle Moses Ball, who was an associate of Jonathan Sergeant, a trustee of the College. When Ball died in 1747, leaving a small portion of his land to his young relative, Baldwin, as he later wrote, became "an apprentice in search of a trade." At the age of nineteen he turned to religion.

Baldwin entered the College in Newark and moved with it to Princeton. During the revival of February 1757 Esther Burr noted that "one Baldwin of Newark has met with Something yt looks of a Saving nature." Two days after President Burr's death, Baldwin graduated at the head of the first class to complete its education at Nassau Hall. He was ordained as an evangelist in 1759, probably by the Presbytery of Suffolk.

In 1760, while Baldwin was serving as a supply pastor at Southold, Long Island, New York, the town of Palmer, Massachusetts, sent a delegation to fetch him to their church. In March 1761 the citizens of Palmer voted to ask him to settle there. His annual salary was to be £60, and he was also to receive the deed to a 150-acre lot at the price of one pound per acre. It was a high price for the new pastor, but the land was exempted from taxes, and he was given five years to settle the debt. In fact, Baldwin took nearly ten years to pay off his farm and was able to do so only because the town voted to remit the interest. He was installed at Palmer by the Presbytery of Boston on June 17, 1761.

Financial problems plagued Baldwin throughout his long tenure in Palmer. The town voted a £232 addition to his salary for 1778, but in the debased currency of the day that sum was negligible. In the next year he was paid the equivalent of his £60 in grain and meat. It was a necessary expedient but one that Baldwin did not approve. After four more years of haggling over his stipend, he asked to be dismissed in November 1784. That had its effect: the town promptly voted him a £15 annual raise in pay.

Money was not the only cause of tension between Baldwin and his congregation. Palmer had been founded by Irish Presbyterians who subscribed to the conservative Presbyterian platform of the Church of Scotland. Tall and dark, and a flamboyant speaker, Baldwin offended some of his parishioners with his innovations in church ritual. Older worshippers were unhappy with the introduction of Watts's psalms and hymns into the services, and they did not approve of serving the bread and wine of the Lord's Supper in the pews instead of on the traditional long table.

Baldwin managed to control this undercurrent of dissent until January 1810, when he was too old to fight anymore. The town decided to reduce the minister's salary to $100 per year and to use the remaining money to hire an assistant pastor. Although he was hurt by the decision, Baldwin accepted it. He offered his resignation in May 1811, on the condition that he still receive a $100 annual pension and with a request that his property continue to be exempted from taxes. It was a council of the Congregational Church rather than a presbytery that agreed to his dismissal—the only official indication that the church in Palmer had become Congregational. Baldwin died on November 2, 1813, and was buried in the cemetery at Palmer. He was survived by his wife, the former Becca Seymour Lee, and by six of their nine children. *Their daughter Hannah was the mother of Abraham Harrison (A.B. 1797).*

SOURCES: J. H. Temple, *Hist. of Palmer, Mass.* (1889), 217-22; parents' and uncle's will: 30 *NJA*, 32-33; CNJ: Alexander, *Princeton*, 43; T. Alden, *Collections of American Epitaphs* (1814), III, 99-100; "Saving nature" quote: Esther Burr, MS Journal, entry for Feb. 23, 1757; tension with congregation: Giger, Memoirs, I.

PUBLICATIONS: see STE   RAH

Caleb Barnum

CALEB BARNUM, A.B., A.M. 1760, Harvard 1768, Congregational clergyman, was born on June 30, 1737, to Deborah and Thomas Barnum of Danbury, Connecticut, probably in that part of Danbury later set off as the town of Bethel—"a sort of hive of the Barnums," as a nineteenth-century historian called it. Barnum entered the College on December 26, 1753, and proceeded to buy the usual texts. After graduation he studied for the ministry and on May 30, 1759, was licensed to preach by Connecticut's Congregational Fairfield East Association. To the north the Congregational church at Wrentham West (now Franklin), Massachusetts, had gone through thirteen candidates in its search for a minister. Barnum was asked to try out, pleased the congregation, was called to the church and was ordained there on October 28, 1759. He received £133 settlement money and an annual salary of £70. On

Caleb Barnum, A.B. 1757

June 18, 1761, Barnum married Priscilla Rice of Sturbridge. The couple had eight children.

Barnum was well-informed about public affairs. Preaching on a Thanksgiving Day—December 9, 1762—he celebrated the birth of the future George IV: "We may this day with pleasure congratulate each other on the birth of a *Prince*,—one, whom we ought to hope and pray may be raised up for a *scourge* to Popery and a friend to Protestantism." He went on to give thanks for the fall of Havana to the British during the previous August and to outline succinctly the international situation. But Barnum's Wrentham West pastorate did not proceed smoothly. His congregation was divided over the introduction of Isaac Watts's hymnal and would not allow its minister to resolve the matter. When the Baptist clergyman Hezekiah Smith (A.B. 1762) visited him in 1764 Barnum put Smith up in his home, but, as Smith wrote, "genteely excused himself from inviting me into his pulpit to preach, by telling me of the difficulty in his church, and the dangerous consequences he was afraid would ensue." Ecclesiastical councils were not able to resolve the matter and Barnum, over the protests of a majority of his church and parish, was granted a dismission on March 6, 1768. When the church finally agreed on a successor in 1773 it was Nathanael Emmons (Yale 1767), the famous New Divinity theologian.

Barnum was not long without a pulpit. On December 5, 1768, the Congregational church at Taunton, Massachusetts, called him. The church had recently dismissed its minister, John Crocker (Harvard 1738), a leading New Light preacher who had taken to drink. Barnum accepted the Taunton offer and was installed late in January 1769. "I've come, ye dear people of my charge," he told his congregation in his first Sunday sermon, "as an Ambassador of Christ to you, and would now in his name and stead, pray you to be reconciled to God." Whatever their reconciliation to God, not all of his parishioners were reconciled to Barnum. An acrimonious dispute with the most prominent of them, Robert Treat Paine (Harvard 1749), concerning the baptism of Paine's children, marred Barnum's Taunton ministry.

On the whole, however, Barnum's Taunton pastorate appears to have been successful. He seems to have been immune to the New Divinity theology that attracted so many of his fellow alumni. After a dinner in Newport, Rhode Island, with Barnum and Ebenezer Pemberton (A.B. 1765), Ezra Stiles, minister of the Second Congregational Church there, recorded that Barnum did not "coincide with Mr. [Samuel] Hopkins' Sentiments and Peculiarities." Stiles went on to add that he found Barnum "of good person and agreeable Appearance, but I believe not of great Abilities or Improvements; I believe an amiable useful Man."

Barnum proved to be of considerable use on the Whig side during the early stages of the Revolution. He was commissioned chaplain of Walker's Massachusetts regiment on May 3, 1775, and on February 27, 1776, was commissioned chaplain of the 24th and 26th Continentals. After the siege of Boston he marched with the army to New York, and from thence northward on the early stages of the Canadian campaign, pausing to be inoculated for smallpox along the way. Returning south to New York, he was taken sick with a "bilious fever" at Ticonderoga and was discharged on July 24. He reached Pittsfield, Massachusetts, on August 2, and collapsed. "During this season of distress," a resident of Pittsfield reported, "aggravated by diverse moving considerations, he maintained an unclouded serenity of mind, the most exemplary patience, and submission to the will of heaven." At this time Barnum condemned "the practice of enslaving the negroes, and called witness to the purity of his intentions in regard to his own negro servant, and sufficiently justified his past and present intentions toward him." Asked about the Revolution, he replied: "I have no doubts concerning the justice and goodness of that cause, and had I a thousand lives, they should all be willingly laid down in it." However, he had but one life and lost that on August 23, 1776.

SOURCES: Fullest sketch, reprinting parts of sermons from which quotations are drawn: S. H. Emery, *Ministry of Taunton* (1853), II, 1-29; see too: *Sibley's Harvard Graduates*, XIV, 132-34, and for Crocker and Paine, ibid., X, 277-82, XII, 462-82; CNJ: Aaron Burr, MS Account Book, 44; Smith quotation: R. A. Guild, *Chaplain Smith and the Baptists* (1885), 48; Stiles quotation: *Literary Diary*, I, 216; account of death: *Conn. Courant*, Sept. 16, 1776.

MSS: NjP (1 sermon)

Nicholas Bayard

NICHOLAS BAYARD, A.B., merchant, was born in New York City on November 4, 1736, the son of Elizabeth Rynders, a granddaughter of the seventeenth-century merchant-revolutionary Jacob Leisler, and her husband, Nicholas Bayard, an extremely wealthy merchant with heavy interests in sugar-refining. While in college young Nicholas boarded for a time with the Burr family and received special schooling in French. Nicholas was one of many sons of New York merchants to attend the College or the Grammar School in the mid-to-late 1750s.

Bayard probably joined the family business after graduation. On November 4, 1762, he married Catherine Livingston, a daughter of the wealthy merchant Peter Van Brugh Livingston (Yale 1731), a trustee of the College from 1748 to 1761. Eight children were born to the Bayards before Catherine's death after a brief illness on November 2, 1775.

Bayard's father died at his country seat in the Bowery on November 21, 1765, splitting his large estate among his several children. Nicholas inherited the family home, a good deal of prime real estate in New York City, and the right to purchase his father's sugar-refining houses. In the late 1760s Bayard had extensive business relations with the Virgin Islands. He had his agents there sell slaves in order to raise capital for the purchase of sugar which in turn was to be sent to New York for refining. In 1771 Bayard leased the New York City slaughterhouse for a period of eighteen years. This in effect gave him a monopoly on the slaughter of animals within the city, with the exception of the Outward (what is now the Bowery area), where his own residence was located.

Bayard entered the public scene during the 1770 excitement over the arrest of Alexander McDougall, "the American Wilkes," for seditious libel against the New York Assembly. When McDougall was released on bail Bayard and his brother-in-law Philip Livingston (A.B. 1758) acted as McDougall's sureties. In 1775 Bayard was elected an alderman of the city from the Outward. It was hardly an auspicious moment to be taking a seat on the Common Council.

When the New York Provincial Congress met for the first time in 1775 Bayard's father-in-law, Peter Van Brugh Livingston, became its president. In February 1776, the records of the province that had not already been transferred to British ships in New York harbor were hurriedly moved by the Whigs to Bayard's estate. Bayard, recently bereft by the death of his wife and with five children on his hands, already had the house filled with furniture sent out by friends in town for safekeeping. He now found himself saddled with the maintenance of the fifteen soldiers assigned to guard the records. "The expense of supplying the privates with liquor and other necessaries they constantly wanted, was considerable, to say nothing of their plundering," Bayard wrote later in applying for relief to the state. He was awarded £50. Bayard's house remained the repository for the records for four and a half months.

By September 1776, the British had occupied New York City; Bayard declared on October 4 that he had been "deprived of the whole of his estate by the enemy." Because Bayard was related by birth or marriage to most of the New York merchant and landed classes, he saw some of his relatives become Whigs, others Loyalists. Since no record of Bayard's activities during the war years has been discovered, it can be assumed that he sat them out with his children well away from the scene of battle. Bayard's older and wealthier merchant brother, William, was a Loyalist who evacuated the City with the British in 1783, declaring: "God d - - n them, I thought it would come to this. What is to become of me, sir. I am totally ruined, sir. I have not a guinea, sir." (He was awarded £19,397 compensation by the Loyalist Claims Commission.)

Back in New York City in 1784, Nicholas resumed his old position on the New York Common Council. Over the years he was a ubiquitous committee member, serving on committees concerned with the Fourth of July, bulkheads, meadows, bridges, tax collection, drainage, nuisances, firehouses, hackney coaches, slaves, polls, contested elections, and so on. Elected to the New York Assembly from the city in 1787, he voted consistently with his Livingston relatives and the urban, mercantile, Federalist interests in the state. In 1790 he was living comfortably at his estate in a large household of sixteen people, including five slaves. Bayard attended his last Common Council meeting in 1797 and died on March 19 of the following year.

SOURCES: The only other attempt at a sketch of Bayard is a three-sentence paragraph in J. T. Main, *Political Parties before the Constitution* (1973), which concludes (418) that "for a man of such a family he is singularly obscure"; see ibid., 37, 152 for voting record in 1787-88 assembly; vital data and Virgin Islands: Nicholas Bayard MSS, NjR; father's will: *N.Y. Wills*, VI, 428-30; college accounts: Aaron Burr, MS Account Book, 46; marriage: *NYGBR*, 79 (1948), 191; wife's death notice: *N.Y. Gaz. and Weekly Mercury*, Nov. 6, 1775, 3; description of Bowery estate: M. Lamb, *Hist. of the City of New York* (1896), III, 571; McDougall episode: D. R. Dillon, *The New York Triumvirate* (1949), 113; city political career: *Minutes of the Common Council of the City of New York, 1675-1776* (1905), VII, VIII, and *Minutes of the Common Council . . . 1784-1831* (1917), I, II; provincial records: Force, *Am. Arch.*, III, 222, 254; William Bayard: T. J. Wertenbaker, *Father Knickerbocker Rebels* (1948), 253, 266; 1790 household: *U.S. Census of 1790, New York*, 131.

MSS: NHi, NjR

Noah Benedict

NOAH BENEDICT, A.B., A.M. Yale 1760, Congregational clergyman, was born in Danbury, Connecticut on May 25, 1737, the son of Captain Daniel Benedict and his wife, Sarah Hickock. Noah matriculated at the

Noah Benedict, A.B. 1757

College on December 26, 1753. After graduation he studied theology, possibly with the Reverend Joseph Bellamy of Bethlehem, Connecticut, whose funeral sermon he preached in 1790. Bellamy delivered the sermon when Benedict was ordained pastor of the Congregational church at Woodbury, Connecticut, on October 22, 1760.

Benedict's predecessor for sixty-one years at Woodbury was Anthony Stoddard (Harvard 1697), a son of the Reverend Solomon Stoddard (Harvard 1662), a leading proponent of the Half-Way Covenant in New England. Within a few months after his installation, on November 6, 1760, Benedict's congregation rejected the Half-Way Covenant that had permitted the baptism of children of parents not in full communion. The action caused no immediate breach in the congregation because Benedict evidently agreed with the decision. In the fifty-three years of his pastorate Benedict added 272 communicants to his church and baptized 758 persons. The historian of Woodbury portrays Benedict's ministry as one of extraordinary harmony. However, on November 16, 1791, President Ezra Stiles of Yale made the following notation in his Diary: "I have been applied to come & baptize about 200 unbaptized children in Woodbury whose pious & worthy Min[ister] Rev. Mr. Benedict could not conscientiously baptize, because the Parents tho' ready to own the Cov[enan]t & make public Profession of Religion & of good lives, yet were not Communicants, thro' fears & scruples of their preparedness dare not approach the Table of the Lord. Quere. What was Duty?" No record of Stiles's decision has been found.

On February 16, 1763, Benedict married Rhoda Bennet. The Benedicts had at least one son. Rhoda died in 1795; the following year Benedict married Nabby Sheldon of Hartford. He served as a Fellow of Yale College from 1801 to 1812, and died in Woodbury on April 30, 1813.

Sources: W. Cotren, *Hist. of Ancient Woodbury, Conn.* (1854), 301-304; Stiles, *Literary Diary*, III, 434-45.

Publications: see STE

John Boyd

John Boyd, A.B., A.M. 1760, physician and druggist, was born about 1738, perhaps in Pennsylvania. His parentage has not been established. The sparse entries in President Burr's Account Book make it impossible to determine the length of time Boyd spent in the College. He either entered the freshman class on September 26, 1753, and spent four years in the College, or entered as a senior on December 2, 1756, spending less than one year in Princeton.

After graduation Boyd studied medicine. About 1761 nine Presbyterian families from Pennsylvania moved to the rapidly growing city of Baltimore. Boyd was probably among them, for his presence in the city was recorded in that year. He established a medical practice, opened the city's second apothecary shop in 1767, and throughout his life played an active part in the affairs of Baltimore's First Presbyterian Church. It was probably not long after settling in Maryland that Boyd married a woman named Ann, whose last name has not been discovered. If any children were born to the couple, none survived their father.

Boyd's involvement in the politics of his town and province was early and sustained. In October 1770 he was a delegate from Baltimore to an Annapolis convention called to consider the boycott of the importation of British goods; in the same month he received a sharp rebuke from the Maryland legislature for protesting the assembly's removal of the Baltimore elections from that town to Joppa because of smallpox. In May 1774, when Baltimore formed a Committee of Correspondence, Boyd was a member. He was elected to the city's Committee of Safety in September of the following year, serving as clerk to the latter committee. Boyd was extremely active in purely local affairs throughout the war. Peace saw him equally active in working toward various civic improvements. In 1789 he was among the founders of the short-lived Medical Society of Baltimore, which found its attempts to dissect a cadaver thwarted by an angry mob.

Boyd died in Baltimore on February 4, 1790. In his will he directed that his slaves be freed at certain times after his death. Over the years he had acquired a considerable amount of real property in Baltimore County. He had also acquired a very respectable reputation, for a Baltimore newspaper reported his death in the following laudatory lines:

He was eminent in his Profession, and alike distinguished himself by his Skill in relieving, and Humanity in sympathizing with, the Distressed. In domestic Life, he was truly amiable—a Pattern of conjugal Affection—all the social Virtues flourished within his Dwelling. In his Intercourse with the World, his Character was fair and unblemished—no one ever had occasion to question his Veracity, or doubt his unshaken Probity. The last Scene of his well-spent Life was closed in PEACE, nor did the Sweetness and Serenity of his Disposition forsake him in the most trying Hour of Pain and Affliction.

SOURCES: CNJ: Aaron Burr, MS Account Book, 238-39; Baltimore Pres. and church affairs: W. Reynolds, *First Presbyterian Church of Baltimore* (1913), 1, 14-16; *MHM*, 4 (1909), 230; medical career: E. F. Cordell, *Medical Annals of Md.* (1903), 17, 19, 656, 660; political activities: J. T. Scharf, *Hist. of Baltimore City & County* (1881), 730n.; Scharf, *Hist. of Md.* (1879), II, 119-20; 144, 185; *Md. Archives*, XLVIII and LXII, passim; *Cal. Md. State Papers*, numbers 4, 5, passim; medical soc.: T. W. Griffith, *Annals of Baltimore* (1824), 125-27; property holdings and will: MS Md. records, courtesy of Md. Legislative Hist. Project, E. C. Papenfuse and D. W. Jordan, principal investigators; obit.: *Md. Jour. & Baltimore Advertiser*, Feb. 5, 1790.

Abner Brush

ABNER BRUSH, A.B., A.M. 1760, Presbyterian clergyman, was born before 1739 at Huntington, Long Island, New York, the son of Philip Brush, a farmer, probably by his second wife, Rebecca Rogers. Philip's father Thomas moved to a 300-acre farm in Amwell, Hunterdon County, New Jersey, at some time before his death in 1749, when Philip inherited sixty acres of the farm.

Abner studied briefly in the Grammar School before being admitted to the College in 1754. In college he bought the usual books—a Hebrew bible and grammar, and copies of Watts and Locke. After graduation Brush studied theology. He was ordained a Presbyterian clergyman at Brookhaven, Long Island, on June 15, 1758. The Reverend Ebenezer Prime, father of Benjamin Prime (A.B. 1751), preached the ordination sermon. In the fall of 1758 Brush was installed as pastor of the Presbyterian church at Goshen, Orange County, New York. At some time between 1764 and 1766 Brush went to Lattintown, Ulster County, as pastor of the church there. He also supplied the pulpit at the Presbyterian church in New Marlborough until 1772. After that date he seems to have been without a pulpit, although he performed many baptisms in the Hudson River Valley and various towns in central New Jersey between 1772 and 1784. Brush inherited his father's Hunterdon County property, and on a visit to New Jersey in 1769 advertised it for sale before returning to New York state. Brush died in Dutchess County, New York on January 9, 1791. Apparently he never married.

SOURCES: The main source, based on exhaustive research, is: Conklin Mann, "Thomas and Richard Brush of Huntington, Long Island," *NYGBR*, 66 (1935), 369-70; also: M. P. Seese, *A Tower of the Lord in the Land of Goshen . . . First Pres. Church, Goshen, N.Y., 1720-1945* (1945), 18; College accounts: Aaron Burr, MS Account Book, 80-81.

Caleb Curtis

CALEB CURTIS, A.B., A.M. 1760, Congregational clergyman, public official and farmer, was born in Wallingford, Connecticut, on February 3, 1727, the son of Martha Collins and her husband, Joseph Curtis. Caleb entered the College on December 26, 1753, at the age of almost twenty-seven. His activities during the years before have not been discovered. He was probably of slender means, for he was awarded £10.10s. from the College's Fund for Pious Youth on July 29, 1757.

After graduation Curtis studied theology. In January 1761, the inhabitants of Charlton, Worcester County, Massachusetts, completed their new meetinghouse. In May they extended a call to Curtis to settle there as their minister. He accepted and was ordained on October 15. Curtis probably married Charity Coombs at about this time, for the first of their four children was born the following year.

In the summer and fall of 1774, when Worcester County's Committees of Correspondence met in convention, Curtis served as Charlton's representative. When Massachusetts' third provincial congress met at Watertown on May 31, 1775, Curtis again served as Charlton's representative, but not for long. Curtis and Alexander Thayer (A.B. 1765) were the only two clergymen among the delegates. Massachusetts had a long tradition of frowning upon clergymen in political office. A committee of the Congress decided that Curtis and Thayer had no right to sit for their districts. Curtis remedied this defect by requesting dismissal from his pastorate on October 29, 1776. It was granted, but Curtis did not immediately return to public office.

No record of Curtis's activities during the war years or immediately thereafter has been found. He seems not to have appeared on the public scene again until 1787, when he was elected Charlton's representative to the Massachusetts Assembly. In January 1788 Curtis served as one of Worcester County's delegates to the Massachusetts convention called to consider the new federal constitution. Like forty-three of the fifty delegates who came from his county Curtis voted against ratification. After the death of his first wife Curtis married on May 21, 1796, Lucy Putney of Charlton. Much respected, Curtis died at his farm just outside Charlton on March 21, 1802.

SOURCES: Parentage: Caleb Curtis File, PUA; College expenses: Aaron Burr, MS Account Book, 48, 246; pastorate and political posts: E. B. Crane, et al., *Hist. of Worcester County Mass.* (1924), I, 211; J. Nelson, *Worcester County, A Narrative Hist.* (1934), I, 217; W. Lincoln, ed., *Journals of Each Provincial Congress of Mass. in 1774 and 1775* (1838), 314-15; general background of western Massachusetts opposition to ratification: R. J. Taylor, *Western Mass. in the Revolution* (1954), 168-77.

Timothy Edwards

TIMOTHY EDWARDS, A.B., A.M. 1760, merchant and public official, was born in Northampton, Massachusetts, on July 25, 1738, the first son of Sarah Pierpont and Jonathan Edwards, third president of the College. In 1750, when Timothy was twelve, the Edwardses moved to the frontier village of Stockbridge, Massachusetts. In June 1752, Timothy's older sister, Esther, married President Aaron Burr. The following April Timothy traveled south to Newark to live with his sister and brother-in-law and to matriculate at the College. Timothy stayed with the Burrs only a short time; wanting to be independent, he soon moved to other quarters. ("Only to think of it, *No Brother!*," his sister Esther exclaimed. "I expect it will set all the Town a talking, tis a pity.") However, when Timothy was caught up in the revival spirit that swept the College during his senior year Mrs. Burr was delighted. "My Brother is under a great deal of concern amongst the rest," she happily wrote in her journal on February 21, 1757. The following evening she had even better news to record: "Had a good deal of conversation with my

Timothy Edwards, A.B. 1757

Brother and think him in a hopeful way—Mr [William] Tennent Says yt for the World he would not venture to say yt he [Timothy] had not Grace in his Heart now. if yt be so, it will do him no harm to be converted over again."

Timothy would have need of a double conversion over the next few months. In October 1757 President Burr died. Timothy apparently remained in Princeton, reading law and helping his sister, while the College's trustees picked a new president. The presidency was kept in the family. It was announced shortly that Timothy's father would succeed Aaron Burr. Leaving his wife in Stockbridge to pack, Jonathan Edwards arrived in Princeton in February 1758 to take up his new duties. Smallpox was abroad in the area, so Dr. William Shippen traveled up from Philadelphia to inoculate the president, along with Esther Burr and her two children. Within two months both Jonathan Edwards and his daughter were dead. Timothy's mother, Sarah Edwards, journeyed down from Stockbridge to settle the affairs of husband and daughter and to collect her two orphaned grandchildren, Sally and Aaron Burr, Jr. Exhausted, she contracted dysentery; pausing in Philadelphia in October 1758, on the way back to Stockbridge, she too died. At twenty Timothy was left the oldest surviving Edwards son. He was now head of a family that consisted, besides the two Burr children, of six unmarried brothers and sisters between the ages of six and twenty-four. All thought of a legal career gone, Timothy took charge of his brothers and sisters as well as his niece and nephew. He would spend much of the rest of his life assuming responsibilities for members of his family.

On September 25, 1760, Timothy married Rhoda Ogden, daughter of a prominent citizen of Elizabethtown and herself one of twenty-two children. Edwards, his bride and his wards moved to Stockbridge and settled in Jonathan Edwards's house. They soon began to produce children of their own. They would eventually have fifteen.

At the urging of Robert Ogden, Rhoda's father, Timothy moved back to Elizabethtown within two years. He set himself up as a merchant, prospered and acquired sufficient substance to be appointed a justice of the peace for Essex County by Governor William Franklin in 1767 and again in 1768. In their years in Elizabethtown Timothy and Rhoda looked carefully after the welfare of their wards. The Edwards children were educated and married off. Tapping Reeve (A.B. 1763), master of the Latin grammar school in Elizabethtown, acted as tutor to Sally Burr (whom he later married) and prepared Aaron for the College of New Jersey.

In 1771 Rhoda Edwards's health failed. The Edwards home in Elizabethtown was surrounded by salt marshes. There was much malaria.

The Edwardses decided to return to Stockbridge. Back in Berkshire County, which was rapidly moving beyond the frontier stage, Timothy opened Stockbridge's first general store. It prospered to such a degree that he soon purchased a farm of several hundred acres on the Housatonic. At peak times of the year he employed as many as forty to fifty laborers in his various enterprises.

As relations with Britain began to deteriorate, Edwards took the side of the colonies. Along with his brother-in-law, Jahleel Woodbridge (A.B. 1761), he was a delegate to the first Berkshire County convention called to consider British measures in July 1774. The following year he was elected a delegate to the third Massachusetts Provincial Congress. Indeed, the years from 1774 to 1783 were spent largely in one public capacity or another. On the local level Edwards served as a member of the Stockbridge Committee of Safety and Correspondence. On the national level General Washington used Edwards as an agent in dealings with the Indians. He was also elected to the Continental Congress but did not serve because of the press of other duties, which included service on the Massachusetts Council from 1775 to 1780 and as a judge of the probate court of Berkshire County from 1778 to 1787.

Edwards sold a considerable amount of supplies to the American army during the Revolution and suffered financially from doing so. Estimated to be worth £20,000 at the outbreak of the war, he was left holding little more than large amounts of depreciated paper currency at its end. With his depreciated continental currency Edwards purchased even more depreciated Massachusetts securities. Next, he was appointed a Massachusetts representative on the commission formed to settle long-standing boundary disputes between his state and New York. In the final settlement the property rights to a vast tract of land —230,000 acres—in western New York was ceded to Massachusetts, while legal jurisdiction remained with New York. A company was formed to buy the lands. The purchasers paid 1¢ an acre to Massachusetts and 1¢ an acre to the Indians. Edwards became a partner in the company, sold his Massachusetts securities, and reinvested the proceeds in the land company. The speculation was successful: Edwards was saved from bankruptcy, paid his debts, settled some of his sons on the western lands, and was left comfortably enough off to support himself and his family in some style for the rest of his life.

During Edwards's later years, his peace was marred only by the sacking of his store during Shays' Rebellion in 1786–1787. Order was soon restored; Edwards spent the rest of his life settling the affairs of the town and the local Congregational church (of which he became a deacon in 1784) from the back room of his store. Greatly respected and not a little feared, he died in Stockbridge on October 28, 1813.

SOURCES: The fullest account is E. Y. Smith, "The Descendants of William Edwards," *NYGBR*, 73 (1942), 173-89; also scattered references in: Electa F. Jones, *Stockbridge, Past and Present* (1854), S. C. Sedgwick and C. S. Marquand, *Stockbridge, 1739-1939* (1939), and R. J. Taylor, *Western Massachusetts in the Revolution* (1954); removal from Burr's house: Esther Burr to Lucy Edwards, quoted in E. D. Dodds, *Marriage to a Difficult Man* (1971), 177; College revival: Esther Burr, MS Journal, entries for Feb. 21 and 22, 1757; guardianship of Burr children: Edwards to Jonathan Sergeant, Dec. 10, 1759, Gratz Col., PHi; dealings with Indians: Force, *Am. Arch.*, (5 ser.), I, 822-23, 888, 1038.

Mss: MHi, NjP, PHi, CtY

Peter Faneuil

PETER FANEUIL, A.B., A.M. 1760, merchant, was born in Little Cambridge (now Brighton), Massachusetts, in about 1738, the son of Mary Cutler and her husband, Benjamin Faneuil, Sr., a prosperous merchant. One of Peter's grandfathers was the Reverend Timothy Cutler (Harvard 1701), the rector of Yale College whose public conversion to Anglicanism in 1722 sent a seismic shock throughout the New England Calvinist establishment. Peter was baptized in Trinity Church, Boston, of which his grandfather was pastor, in 1738. Peter was the nephew and namesake of the enormously wealthy merchant who gave Faneuil Hall to the city of Boston. In college Peter became the bane of Esther Burr's existence. "You know my dear that P[eter] Funil studies here," Mrs. Burr informed her friend Miss Prince of Boston in January 1755. "Well, he takes it into his head to talk about Suky my Sister that is here [Susannah Edwards, daughter of Jonathan, then fifteen], thus far was hinted to me yesterday & no more, to day I have inquired in to what he has Said, & am glad to find not so much in it as I feared, tho' tis true he has been foolish, yet has not said any thing very bad about her,—I am very Sorry for his dear Mamma['s] sake that he is such a *trifling good-for-nothing Chap*. It looks very doubtful to me whether he will be able to get safe through College."

Peter got through college, but not safely. A year later Esther Burr was reporting that Peter had been rusticated for two weeks in the country under the charge of the once-notorious New Light preacher, James Davenport. ("Indeed he is a very Wicked Boy," she wrote.) Davenport apparently worked a change in Peter. Seeing Peter on a visit to the Davenports a short time later, Mrs. Burr found "a very great alteration in him for the better, he seems under a good deal of concern about his Soul."

Peter's concern with his soul lasted for some time. About three months after the College moved from Newark to Princeton, on Sunday, February 20, 1757, Elihu Spencer, pastor of the Presbyterian church at Newark, preached a sermon at Princeton. "Mr Burr was sent for to the College about dark," Mrs. Burr reported, "& when he came their he found above 20 young men in one room Crying & Begging to know what they Should do to be Saved, & of them under the deepest Sense of their wicked Hearts & need of Christ, Faneuil amongst the rest, & how it will rejoice his good Mother's Heart."

Signs of Peter's conversion proved to be misleading. In May 1757, Mrs. Burr recorded her impressions of the senior class: "O what a Joyfull prospect does it afford a large class goes out into the World & almost all of them we have reason to hope truely Pious—Poor P[eter] F[aneui]l I fear will be ruined . . . he was near the Kingdom of Heaven."

Faneuil came near to ruin, but not for several years thereafter. After graduation he became, like most of his relatives, a merchant. He carried on his business in Montreal. The business failed, possibly in 1768 when his arrival in Boston on the schooner "Rainbow" out of Quebec was recorded. Faneuil then turned to business in the West Indies. His activities during the Revolution have not been discovered. His father (one of the consignees of the famous tea shipment of 1773) and older brother Benjamin, Jr., were both Loyalists who left Massachusetts during the war years. Peter—apparently always in frail health—returned to Brighton to live with his sister, Mary Bethune, in about 1785. He died there on March 20, 1790.

SOURCES: For family background: A. E. Brown, *Faneuil Hall and Faneuil Hall Market, or Peter Faneuil and His Gift* (1900); brief mention: L. M. Sargent, *Dealings with the Dead* (1856), II, 509; college accounts: Aaron Burr, MS Account Book, 52, 54, 55, 120, 278; Esther Burr's remarks: her MS Journal, entries for Jan. 1755; Jan. 9, 1756; Feb. 7, 1757; Feb. 20, 1757; May 1, 1757; arrival in Boston: *Volume of Records Relating to the Early Hist. of Boston* (1900), 306; brief sketches of father and brother: Sabine, *Loyalists*, I, 418; death notice: *Boston Gaz.*, Mar. 22, 1790, 3.

Elnathan Gregory

ELNATHAN GREGORY, A.B., Congregational clergyman, was born about 1734 in Danbury, Connecticut, possibly the son of Mercy Wildman, wife of Ephraim Gregory. Elnathan entered the College on December 26, 1753. He seems to have been the first youth to have been caught up in the revival spirit that swept the College in February and March 1757. "Farther encouragement," Esther Burr recorded in her journal. "Mr. Burr tells me [tha]t yesterday a young Man from Danbury in New [Eng]land one of his Schollars came to talk with him under very pressing concern for his Soul. This morn came again." Two days later Gregory was well on the way to conversion. "The young Man from Danbury (Gregory by Name)," Mrs. Burr wrote, "we have reason to hope had found God—the temper of his mind is very Christian like, he seems to have a great Sense of God & himself, & the Sufficiency of Christ & the Safety of venturying his Soul upon him, & wonders he could ever be affraid to trust his all upon him—the Concern is now become general in College—none of it in Town—Several under very great distress of Soul. O Help me to bless the Lord!"

Gregory's concern with God was lasting. After graduation he studied theology and was licensed by the Congregationalist Fairfield East Association of Connecticut on May 29, 1758. To the west of Danbury, in Carmel, New York, a new Congregational church had been constructed in 1756. In 1760 Gregory became pastor there, though no formal record of his installation has been preserved. He remained as pastor at Carmel until 1773. Gregory's congregation, apparently, was severely torn over the Sandemanian-Separatist controversy raging among Congregationalists in western Connecticut and the adjoining New York counties at the time. In 1774, the year after Gregory left the Carmel church, it changed its allegiance from Congregationalism to Presbyterianism. Gregory probably married during the period of his Carmel pastorate, though his wife's name has not been discovered. Four daughters, and perhaps other children as well, were born to the couple.

It has not been possible to trace with any degree of certainty Gregory's activities after leaving Carmel. He moved to Dutchess County, New York, and was a member of that county's Committee of Safety in 1775. He was reputed to have been a staunch Whig during the Revolution, with a price set upon his head by the British. In 1790 the federal census-taker found Gregory living in Middletown, Ulster County, New York, and he is said to have become a miller. In 1792 Gregory, claiming a little over £31 in damage to property in Danbury when the British burned the town in 1777, was granted a share of lands in the Western Reserve by the Connecticut legislature. At some time after this he returned to Carmel, where some of his children had settled, and died there in 1816.

SOURCES: Parentage, which is conjectural: J. M. Bailey, *Hist. of Danbury, Conn.*, *1684-1896* (1896), 15, 47; for CNJ accounts: Aaron Burr, MS Account Book, 54, 133, 145, 215, 255; Esther Burr quotations: her MS Journal, entries for Feb. 1757; licensing: Alexander, *Princeton*, 45; Carmel pastorate and political views: L. H. Zimm et al., *Southeastern New York* (1946), II, 896, and *Hist. and Geneal. Record, Dutchess and Putnam Counties, N.Y.* (1912), 178; Committee of Safety: F. Hasbrouck, *Hist. of Dutchess County, N.Y.* (1909), 120; marriage, children, miller: Peters Papers, PUA; *U.S. Census of 1790, N.Y.*, 175; property damage: *Rec. State Conn.*, VII, 460.

Thomas Hun

THOMAS HUN, merchant and public official, was born in Albany, New York, and baptized there on February 29, 1736. He was the son of Anna Winne, wife of Johannes Hun, a merchant. Hun, along with his cousin Peter Winne Douw (A.B. 1758) entered the College's grammar school on May 5, 1754, and matriculated in the College about March 26, 1755. He did not graduate but left the College for reasons unknown at some time after March 26, 1756, when he was billed for tuition for the last time (whether or not he paid the bill went unrecorded).

Hun returned to Albany. His early years there are obscure, but he seems gradually to have established himself as a substantial, if fairly minor, merchant. He married Elizabeth Wendell on August 27, 1761. The couple had three children. Through his marriage Hun became brother-in-law to Philip Lansing, another merchant with whom he was closely associated in various land dealings. At some time in his career Hun became a business agent—probably the chief one—for Stephan Van Rensselaer, the patroon, a post in which he was succeeded by his son, Abraham. Hun and Van Rensselaer had been students in the College's grammar school at the same time.

By July 1763, Hun was acting as a fireman for Albany's Third Ward. He became fire master for the Third Ward the following November, and was elected to Albany's Common Council from his ward in September 1764. Albany's firemen made a name for themselves over the next few months. They constituted the core of the membership (twenty out of the original twenty-six) of the Albany Sons of Liberty. They were young men—eighteen of them, like Hun, under thirty-five— "originally formed and led," according to one historian, "by representatives of the older, conservative, property-holding dominant social class in Albany." The Sons of Liberty (among them Stephen Van Rensselaer), formed a mob that sacked postmaster Henry Van Schaack's house in protest against the Stamp Act. In the same year Hun signed a petition of Albany merchants to the Lords of Trade objecting to new restrictions on trade with the Indians.

Hun was not reelected to the Common Council in September 1766. In 1769 he was surveying land disputed between New York and New Hampshire in what is now Vermont. In 1773 he reappeared (after a disputed election) as alderman from Albany's Third Ward. He was immediately appointed to a committee charged with surveying the city and laying out ward divisions. In May 1775, Hun was among the citizens of Albany who contributed money for supplies for the New England troops at Ticonderoga. He served on the Common Council throughout the war years.

After the war Hun was involved in extensive land dealings. He retained his seat on the Common Council and served on various municipal committees—on those establishing a city watch, building a slaughterhouse, and on the committee on burying grounds. He appears to have retired from the Common Council in 1789. In 1794 and again in 1795 Hun was elected to the New York Assembly from Albany County. There he voted for the Federalist candidate for the United States Senate, Rufus King. He served on several committees, the principal one being involved with settling the claims for and against Loyalist refugees and the disposition of their lands. Hun's name does not appear in the public record after 1795. He died at some time after 1800.

SOURCES: A Thomas D. Hun of Albany's First Ward was an exact contemporary of the CNJ alumnus. Parentage, marriage, and children: J. Munsell, *Collections of the Hist. of Albany* (1865-71), IV, 135; attendance at school and College: Aaron Burr, MS Account Book, 92, 131, 145, 189; association with Lansing: *Papers of Sir William Johnson* (1921-65), VII, 365, 396-97, 411; local political activities, etc.: Munsell, above, I, II; and, *Proceedings of the Common Council of the City of Albany* (1907), 374-375; Sons of Liberty: *WMQ*, 4 (1947), 488-98; Lords of Trade: *Doc. Col. Hist. of N.Y.*, 615; surveying: *NYGBR*, 74 (1943), 104; donation to troops: J. Sullivan, ed., *Minutes of the Albany Committee of Correspondence* (1923-25), II, 992, 994; land sale: 3 (2 ser.) *NJA*, 71-72; Assembly: *Journal of the State of New York* (1794), 3, 9, 12, 14, 18, 58, 67, 84; and, *Journal of the Assembly of the State of New York* (1795), 3, 25, 28, 32, 55, 93.

William Kirkpatrick

WILLIAM KIRKPATRICK, A.B., A.M. 1760, Presbyterian minister, was born in 1726, probably abroad. He was unusually old when he entered the College in the junior class on November 27, 1756. Along with his classmate Alexander MacWhorter, Kirkpatrick was taken up as a candidate for the ministry by the Presbytery of New Brunswick in June 1758. His theological training was directed by Joseph Bellamy in Bethlehem, Connecticut, and by Samuel Finley in West Nottingham, Maryland.

Both MacWhorter and Kirkpatrick were licensed by the presbytery on August 15, 1758. Each was assigned a circuit of vacant pulpits in the south. Kirkpatrick's five circuit posts were increased to six by the presbytery in the fall of that year. In February 1759 Kirkpatrick was in Newark, where he found religion at "a low ebb." He may not have been delighted with the situation there, but he was no more eager to settle at any of the three congregations that had called him by that time. The idea of going to "George's Town on Kennebeck River" did not appeal to him because the people were said to be "remarkably contentious, brawling, difficult." His "inclinations," he told Bellamy, led him to some other part of New England.

His "inclinations" and requests from three more congregations notwithstanding, Kirkpatrick was assigned by the synod to serve in Virginia and the Carolinas in 1759. To insure that he and his friend MacWhorter would be welcome there, the synod ordained them on July 4 of that year, somewhat earlier than usual. Although Kirkpatrick accepted a call from the church in Hanover, Virginia, neither he nor MacWhorter traveled south. Instead, the synod agreed to his request that he be allowed to serve as a chaplain with the New Jersey forces in the French and Indian War. Between August and November 1760 Kirkpatrick participated in the capture of Ft. Levy on Ile Royale, was present at the victory at Montreal, and was posted in Albany. By February 1761 he had returned to his civilian duties.

In March 1760 the Presbyterian church in Trenton had called Kirkpatrick to its pulpit. His military service was only the first of many circumstances that disrupted his relationship with that congregation. For seven years Trenton renewed and repeated its calls. And for seven years Kirkpatrick served enthusiastically as its temporary pastor. But he refused to settle there, probably because he and the trustees of the church could not agree on an equitable salary. The result was that Kirkpatrick became a semi-regular itinerant who traveled throughout the middle colonies, Virginia, and Connecticut to preach at a variety of pulpits for short periods of time. No fewer than fifteen separate congregations had called him to settle with them by 1766, but Kirkpatrick was allowed by the presbytery and the synod to make his own decision and he accepted none of the offers. It is likely that he truly wanted to settle in Trenton and hoped that his reticence would lead the church there to increase its salary proposals, and the church councils were willing to indulge him rather than take the time to assign him to a post. Indeed, in 1762 the congregation at Trenton did purchase a house and twenty-eight perches of land as a permanent home for its minister, at a cost of £270, in order to lure Kirkpatrick. It did not work. Nor did Kirkpatrick's election to the board of trustees of the church in Trenton in 1764 seem to make him any more anxious to settle there.

Meanwhile, he was an extremely active member of the synod and the presbytery. In May 1764 he was one of the synod's officers who dispensed money to the College of New Jersey.

In April 1766, by which time some of the faithful in Trenton had grown disgusted with Kirkpatrick's diffidence, the church at Amwell, New Jersey, called him to its pulpit. The presbytery, finally tired of the long controversy, told him to accept the call; after two months of additional temporizing he did so. He was installed at Amwell in August 1766. Nevertheless, he continued to supply the Trenton congregation for brief intervals.

In the next year, Kirkpatrick represented the synod in its contacts with the Consociated Churches of Connecticut to discuss a plan for union in order to counter the rumored establishment of a Diocesan Episcopy in America by the Church of England. He was also elected to the Board of Trustees at Nassau Hall in 1767. In May 1769 he was the moderator of the synod when it met in Philadelphia. Only four months later, on September 8, 1769, Kirkpatrick died in Amwell. He was buried in front of the pulpit of his one permanent church.

His estate, valued at £957.17.2, was left in the care of his widow, Elizabeth, who was to administer it for their three children. She later married Kirkpatrick's successor at Amwell, John Warford (A.B. 1774). Kirkpatrick's one black slave, who reportedly loved his master, remained with the family. Kirkpatrick's pastorate at Amwell was said to have had a lasting and positive effect on the worshipers there, for an Anglican minister posthumously credited him with the congregation's lack of "that rigid severity in their religious notions often-times so peculiar to Dissenters."

After all his difficulties with the Trenton church, Kirkpatrick died without collecting the salary and arrears that were still due him there. His account was perfunctorily settled by the presbytery, undoubtedly with a sigh of relief, in 1776.

SOURCES: J. Hall, *Hist. Pres. Church of Trenton*, 99-117; offices in synod: *Rec. Pres. Church*, 334, 331, 364, 390; study with Finley: Butterfield, *Rush Letters*, II, 1193; study with Bellamy: Glenn P. Anderson, "Joseph Bellamy," (Ph.D. dissertation, Boston University, 1971), 425; will: 33 *NJA*, 235; "rigid severity" quote: H. Race, "Rev. William Frazer's Three Parishes," *PMHB*, 12 (1888), 220.

Mss: PHi, NjP

RAH

Nicholas Low

NICHOLAS LOW, merchant, banker, land-speculator, entrepreneur, public official, and younger brother of Cornelius Low (A.B. 1752), was born at Raritan Landing, near New Brunswick, New Jersey, on March 30, 1739, the son of Johanna Gouverneur and Cornelius Low, a prosperous merchant and landowner. Nicholas entered the College on September 26, 1753, and purchased the usual texts—Lucian, Salmon's *Grammar*, and so forth. His last tuition bill (£3.15) extended through December 29, 1756. The bill was paid, but Nicholas did not take his degree with his class. Instead, he was shortly apprenticed to a prominent New York merchant, Hyman Levy. In May 1760, Nicholas's sister Sally married Hugh Wallace, an immigrant from Ireland who was doing extraordinarily well as a merchant in New York City. Nicholas soon entered into a partnership with the Wallace family and prospered.

As the events leading to the American Revolution took shape Low appears to have taken little or no part in public affairs. In this he was unlike his older brother Isaac. Isaac was a delegate to the Stamp Act Congress in 1765, a leading proponent of the non-importation agreements, and a delegate from New York to the first Continental Congress. Yet Isaac became a Loyalist, remaining in New York when it was occupied by the British late in 1776. Nicholas doubtless faced difficult choices in this period. His business partner, Hugh Wallace, a member of the governor's council, also became a Loyalist. Nicholas ended by taking a course opposite to that both of his brother and Wallace. He threw in his lot with the American cause, left New York City, and appears to have spent most of the war years in Philadelphia. However he kept in touch with Loyalist friends, meeting Isaac Ogden (Class of 1758) in Elizabethtown in May 1780.

At the peace in 1783 Low returned to New York. Over the succeeding years he became one of the city's richest bankers and merchants. He bought confiscated Loyalist property to the tune of $8,250. He was involved in speculation in state securities in sums amounting to tens of thousands of dollars (in 1790 his holdings in South Carolina securities alone amounted to over $54,000). He was one of the directors of the Bank of New York (1784–1792) and was later director of a branch of the Bank of the United States. His one venture into active politics came in 1788, when he was elected a delegate from New York City to the New York convention called to consider ratification of the new federal constitution. Low voted for its adoption. In all these ventures, financial and political, Low was closely associated with Alexander Hamilton. His most sustained involvement with Hamilton involved the Society for Establishing Useful Manufactures. This enterprise, begun in 1791, attempted to set up a planned industrial city specializing in the manufacture of cloth in New Jersey. The new city was named Paterson, after New Jersey Governor William Paterson (A.B. 1763), and involved many of the College's alumni. The expensive and extensive scheme, however, failed.

It was probably in the 1790s that Low married a widow, Alice Fleming. The couple had three children, Cornelius, Nicholas, and Henrietta. In the late 1790s Low's attention turned to the vast tracts of land he had acquired in St. Lawrence, Lewis, and Jefferson counties in upstate New York. Already one of the largest real estate proprietors in New York City, he vigorously encouraged the settlement of his undeveloped lands, which eventually included the sites of the towns of Adams, Watertown, and Lowville. He built a hotel, Sans Souci, on his lands at Ballston, which became a fashionable spa early in the nineteenth century. Apparently not disillusioned by his Paterson experience, Low built a cotton factory at Ballston after the passage of the Embargo Acts. Unfortunately this venture fared little better for Low than the New Jersey one.

When New York City seemed threatened by British invasion in 1814, Low, then seventy-five, joined the New York Hussars as a captain. Always an Episcopalian, he seems to have taken no active part in church affairs. Hard of hearing and almost blind, Low died at his home at 400 Broadway on November 16, 1826.

SOURCES: Sketches of Low and brother Isaac in *DAB*; attendance at CNJ: Aaron Burr, MS Account Book, 58, 135, 217; sister's marriage: *N.Y. Mercury*, May 12, 1760; Wallace family: Sabine, *Loyalists*, II, 392-93; presence in Philadelphia: *Clinton Papers*, V, 195; Ogden meeting: W.H.W. Sabine, ed., *William Smith's Hist. Memoirs, 1778-1783*, 267; Bank of N.Y.: H. W. Domett, *A Hist. of the Bank of New York* (1884); association with Hamilton, banking and speculation: *Hamilton Papers*, III-XV; S.C. securities: *WMQ*, 19 (1962), 36; Paterson venture: J. C. Davis, *Essays in the Earlier Hist. of Am. Corporations* (1917), 349-503; political activities: McDonald, *We the People*, 302, 309n; J. T. Main, *Political Parties before the Constitution* (1973), 421; A. F. Young, *Democratic-Republicans of New York* (1967), 71, 191, 219n., 218, 238; NYC activities: *Minutes, NYC Common Council* (1917), II-XIX; development of N.Y. lands, marriage, children and later years: F. B. Hough, *Hist. of Lewis County* (1860), 135-37; death: *N.Y. Evening Post*, Nov. 16, 1826.

Mss: NjR, MiD.

Alexander MacWhorter

ALEXANDER MACWHORTER, A.B., A.M. 1760, D.D. Yale 1776, Presbyterian clergyman, was born on July 15, 1734, in New Castle, Delaware. He was the son of Jane and Hugh MacWhorter, a prosperous farmer who had been a linen merchant in County Armagh, Ireland. About 1730 the family moved to America at the urging of their oldest son, Alexander, a divinity student at the University of Edinburgh. After Alexander died in Scotland his parents gave his name to their eleventh and youngest child.

During his early life this second Alexander MacWhorter was greatly influenced by the teaching of his pious father and the preaching of the Reverend John Rodgers, later a trustee of the College. When his father died in 1748, MacWhorter went with his mother to North Carolina, where three of his older brothers and sisters were already living. There his interest in religion was aroused by the Reverend John Brown (A.B. 1749) of Virginia. MacWhorter returned to Delaware to

Alexander MacWhorter, A.B. 1757
BY JOHN SINGLETON COPLEY

study at the Newark Academy. Then, much concerned with the welfare of his soul, he went to West Nottingham, Maryland, to study with Samuel Finley. In July 1756, after two years with Finley, MacWhorter entered the junior class at the College.

After graduation in 1757 MacWhorter studied theology in Freehold, New Jersey with trustee William Tennent, Jr. In August 1758 he was licensed to preach by the Presbytery of New Brunswick. In October he married Mary Cummings, the daughter of the high sheriff of Monmouth County, a relative by marriage of the Tennents, and a niece of Samuel Blair (A.B. 1760). The couple had five children, including Alexander Cummings McWhorter (A.B. 1784) who changed the spelling of the family name. At its session in May 1759, the new Synod of New York and Philadelphia appointed MacWhorter and his classmate William Kirkpatrick to preach in various pulpits in Virginia and North Carolina; MacWhorter was ordained for the task in Cranbury, New Jersey, on July 4, 1759. Meanwhile, however, he had preached one sermon at the Old First Presbyterian Church in Newark, New Jersey. The congregation was so impressed with his ability that it begged the presbytery to release him from his mission to the south and allow him to settle at Newark. The synod passively accepted the *fait accompli*. MacWhorter immediately plunged into a bitter controversy with the "Mountain Society" (later the First Presbyterian Church of Orange) and the local Anglican church over title to the land claimed by the Old First Church of Newark. The dispute was partly theological, but the basic issue was the question of which congregation would own the property.

In May 1764 the synod resurrected MacWhorter's missionary assignment in the south and sent him and Elihu Spencer to organize and regulate congregations in North Carolina. They managed to establish several new churches before MacWhorter was stricken with a serious lung disease that ended his mission. While in North Carolina, MacWhorter heard of the first six of major revivals that occurred in his church in Newark during his lifetime.

In 1766 MacWhorter went to Boston to try to regain his health. His wife's brother, Alexander Cumming, had been the minister of the Old South Church in Boston until his death in 1763. After MacWhorter's visit, the congregation at the Old South Church asked him to settle as their minister. He declined and returned to his duties in Newark. Later in 1766, two of the churches he helped to found in North Carolina also asked him to settle with them. This time the synod intervened to prevent the move. MacWhorter's prominence as a preacher and a statesman of the church was well-established by this time. He was the clerk of the synod in 1766 and its moderator in 1770. In 1772 he became a trustee of the College.

MacWhorter was one of the most prominent Presbyterian support-ers of the Revolution. In June 1775, when George Washington passed through Newark, he visited for some time with MacWhorter, with whom he became friendly. Later that year Joseph Hewes of North Carolina succeeded in persuading his colleagues in the Continental Congress that two Presbyterian ministers should be sent to convince the highlanders and former Regulators in his province to join the Rev-olution. On the recommendation of George Duffield (A.B. 1752), Hewes selected Spencer and MacWhorter for the job, for which each would be paid $40. Loyalist sympathies in western North Carolina were too strong even for two such skillful ministers to change them. Neverthe-less, MacWhorter was honored with a doctorate of divinity from Yale when he returned in 1776. In March, he was elected by a Newark town meeting to serve on a committee to advise local legislators.

In November 1776 MacWhorter had to flee from his home as Corn-wallis's troops marched through Newark. The parsonage of the Old First Church was ransacked by redcoats who were searching for the minister, and MacWhorter sent a detailed account of the depredations of British troops in Newark to fellow clergymen and to members of the Continental Congress. After leaving his family in a safe place, Mac-Whorter attached himself to the retreating Continental forces as a sort of general chaplain. While the Americans crossed the Delaware from New Jersey into Pennsylvania on December 7, he set up a temporary altar to preach a sermon. It may have been unique in the annals of Presbyterian oratory, for although at least 200 camp-following women were among the thousands who heard him, MacWhorter never re-ferred to the sinfulness of his audience. All of his condemnation was reserved for the "Papist Highland barbarians"—actually the Presby-terian Scots whose bagpipes could be heard close behind the fleeing Continentals. At Penn's Shore, Pennsylvania, General Washington asked MacWhorter to participate in the council of war that planned the Christmas attack on the Hessians and the subsequent battle of Trenton.

In 1777 MacWhorter joined the artillery brigade of General Henry Knox as chaplain and served with it at White Plains. In July 1778 when his wife was critically injured by a bolt of lightning, he left the army to care for her in Newark. Constantly in danger from British forces eager to arrest him, MacWhorter had to keep an armed sentry at his doorway. He and his friend Elisha Boudinot appealed for greater mili-tia protection of Newark. On October 12, 1778, Washington asked

MacWhorter to visit two condemned spies and counterfeiters from whom the Americans had been unable to obtain any information. The General wanted MacWhorter to prepare the captives for the next world and suggested that in the course of his ministrations he might obtain important military intelligence. MacWhorter cooperated fully.

In March 1779 the trustees of MacWhorter's church were forced to pay their minister from the proceeds of the sale of firewood since the parish financial situation was desperate. That, combined with the perils to his life in Newark, convinced MacWhorter to leave the town. After receiving a call from the church in Charlotte, Mecklenburg County, North Carolina, that included an offer of the presidency of the local academy, once called Queen's Museum, he obtained a dismission from his post and took his family south in October. Mecklenburg County was a bastion of revolutionary zeal, and MacWhorter would have found a congenial home there had it not been for the invasion by British troops in early 1780. By May, Charlotte had been sacked. Mac-Whorter blamed the citizens of the area for their foolish defense of the city. When the American forces suffered another defeat at Camden, South Carolina, the minister lost hope. With his family he fled northward, finally stopping in Abington, Pennsylvania. He preached there for the winter and in early 1781 visited his old church in Newark, which was still without a minister. The congregation resolved to call him back and he moved to Newark in April. Although he was never formally reinstated, he regarded the Old First Church as his pulpit and the congregation regarded him as their pastor until he died. In 1783 he rejected an appeal from Washington Academy in Maryland to assume its presidency.

MacWhorter was instrumental in the creation of the synod's plan for union with the Consociated Churches of Connecticut in 1767; in 1785 he helped to arrange fraternal contacts between the synod and the Dutch and Associated Reformed Churches. In 1788 he was a member of the first General Assembly of the Presbyterian Church of the United States, which he helped to create. And he served with John Witherspoon on a committee to formulate the "Book of Discipline and Government" and to revise the Westminster Directory of Worship for the church. When the General Assembly was incorporated by Pennsylvania in 1799, MacWhorter was one of the assembly's original trustees.

MacWhorter was also extremely active in municipal affairs. In November 1791, he helped lead a drive to raise funds for the rebuilding of the Newark Academy. He had founded and directed that school personally in order to supplement his income until 1786, when his congregation offered to raise his salary to £300 per year if he would spend less time with the students. After a serious fire in 1797, he was instrumental in obtaining modern fire fighting equipment for the city. When the College of New Jersey suffered heavy damage in a fire in 1802, MacWhorter went to England to collect money for repairs, and his efforts produced $7,000.

Meanwhile, he had won an important personal victory on a matter of theology in his own congregation, which, after 1791, sat in a brand new church for which MacWhorter had broken ground. Like many New Lights, he had long opposed the Half-Way Covenant that allowed the children of congregation members to be baptized regardless of whether their parents were full members of the church. As early as 1764, he had written a thorough indictment of the practice in a letter to Bellamy. In March 1794 he managed to win over the majority of his congregation to his point of view and the Half-Way Covenant was void in Newark.

In November 1789 MacWhorter appealed personally to Alexander Hamilton to hire his son-in-law as a clerk in the new Treasury Department. Yet, in spite of his long association with Washington, he grew suspicious of the Federalist administration. In a sermon in February 1795, he echoed Jeffersonian-Republican caveats against "despotism" and aganist the exaltation of any man or set of men. "The Constitution," he proclaimed, "is made to be changed as circumstances demand." Nevertheless, in December 1799, he preached a sermon on the death of Washington in which he compared the late president to Cicero, Pliny, and Moses and praised him as a great Christian. MacWhorter's fellow Masons in St. John's Lodge of Newark thanked him officially for his words.

In 1800, MacWhorter gained an assistant minister to tend to the Old First Church. The senior pastor was severely injured in a fall at the end of 1806 and within three months both his wife and son died. On April 9, 1807, MacWhorter made out a will that divided his estate between his two surviving children. He died on July 20 and was buried in the graveyard of the Old First Church. He was remembered as an excellent classical scholar and a man of great common sense, if not genius.

SOURCES: *DAB*, XII, 175; D. L. Pierson, *Narratives of Newark* (1917), 180-255 passim; J. F. Stearns, *Historical Discourses Relating to the First Presbyterian Church of Newark* (1853), 216-61; Sprague, *Annals*, III, 208-15; J. Atkinson, *Hist. of Newark, N.J.* (1878), 83-133; wife's family: W. S. Ray, *The Mecklenburg Signers and Their Neighbors* (1946), 506; CNJ: Aaron Burr, MS Account Book, 200, 253; 1764 mission to N.C.: *Col. Rec. N.C.*, V, 1215, 1224; synod offices, and reputation: Stiles, *Literary Diary*, II, 397-98; III, 431, 526; Washington in Newark: *Hist. of the City of Newark, N.J.* (1913), I, 274; 1775 mission to N.C.: P. Davidson, *Propaganda and the*

Am. Rev. (1941), 199-200; D. Meyer, *The Highland Scots of N.C., 1732-1776* (1961), 144; *LMCC*, I, 296, 300; description of British depredations in Newark: 1 (2 ser.) *NJA*, 350-53; crossings of the Delaware: H. Fast, *The Crossing* (1971), 28-29, 109; Washington's instructions on condemned spies: Washington's *Writings*, XIII, 71-72; moves to and from N.C. in 1779-80, see: E. Marting, "Alexander MacWhorter's Southern Adversities," *JPHS*, 26 (1948), 11-18; views on Half-Way Covenant: MacWhorter to Bellamy, April 16, 1764, Webster/Bellamy Transcripts, PPPrHi; appeal to Hamilton: *Hamilton Papers*, V, 506; Antifederalist sermon, see: *Hist. of the City of Newark*, above, I, 449; sermon on Washington: A. MacWhorter, *Funeral Sermon . . . December 27, 1799 . . . for General Washington* (1800); Masonry: J. H. Hough, *Origin of Masonry in the State of N.J.* (1870), 86; will: 11 *NJA*, 227; change in spelling of family name: *NJHSP* (1 ser.), x, 52-53.

Mss: PPPrHi

PUBLICATIONS: see STE, Sh-Sh 4576, 4577, 8827, 12971

RAH

Samuel Parkhurst

SAMUEL PARKHURST, A.B., A.M. 1760, Presbyterian clergyman, the son of Samuel Parkhurst and Esther Baldwin Parkhurst, was born in Essex County, New Jersey, in 1737. At the age of fourteen he entered the grammar school of the College of New Jersey, where he studied for two and one-half years. His financial accounts for those years were settled in October 1755, at approximately the same time that he entered the College.

After graduation Parkhurst prepared for the ministry and was licensed by the Presbytery of New Brunswick in April 1761. Following his ordination one year later, he became the pastor of both the Florida and Warwick Presbyterian churches in Orange County, New York. There he met Renaltje (or Renlike) DuBois, and a license for their marriage was issued in early 1764. She bore him two children: a son, Nathaniel, and a daughter, Mary.

While he still held the pulpits at Florida and Warwick, Parkhurst was a supply preacher at the Congregational Church of Blooming Grove. After only six months there, he was stricken ill. On March 11, 1768, he died intestate, leaving all three churches without a minister. He was buried next to his predecessor at Blooming Grove, Enos Ayres (A.B. 1748). One of their successors, Benoni Bradner (A.B. 1755), was laid to rest beside them twenty-six years later.

SOURCES: A. E. Corning, *Hist. of the Congregational Church of Blooming Grove* (1929), 12; Alexander, *Princeton*, 34; Webster, *History*, 351; S. W. Eager, *Outline Hist. of Orange County* (1846-47), 523; years at CNJ and grammar school: Aaron Burr, MS Account Book; will: *N.Y. Wills*, VII, 466.

RAH

Joseph Reed

JOSEPH REED, A.B., A.M. 1760, A.M. College of Philadelphia 1766, law-
yer, soldier and public official, was born in Trenton, New Jersey, on
August 27, 1741, the first son of Theodosia Bowes and her husband,
Andrew Reed, a merchant. His paternal grandfather Joseph had emi-
grated to America from Northern Ireland in 1671. In 1750 Andrew
Reed moved to Philadelphia, where, in 1751, he entered his son in the
Philadelphia Academy. Joseph attended this school until 1753, when
the family moved back to Trenton following the death of his mother.
Upon returning to New Jersey Andrew Reed entered his son, now
twelve years old, at the College. At Newark he boarded with a Mr.
Baldwin and a Mr. Beach, purchased the usual books, and bought a
copy of one of President Burr's sermons. Joseph Reed's connections
with the College remained close, especially during the later years of
his life, when he served as a trustee (1780–1785) and accompanied
President Witherspoon to Europe on an unsuccessful fund-raising mission in 1784.

Joseph Reed, A.B. 1757

After graduation Reed continued to reside in Princeton, studying law under Richard Stockton (A.B. 1748). In 1763 he received a license from Governor William Franklin to practice law in New Jersey and traveled to England to study at the Inns of Court. On his return to America in 1765 he established a law practice in Trenton and engaged in mercantile and real estate business. In 1770 he returned to England, where on May 22 he married Esther De Berdt, daughter of Dennys De Berdt, London merchant and colonial agent for Massachusetts. Before her death, she and Reed had at least six children, including Joseph (A.B. 1792), Dennis De Berdt (Class of 1797), and George Washington (A.B. 1798). On his return from England in 1770, Reed transferred his residence and legal business to Philadelphia.

Reed entered public life in 1767, when he was appointed deputy secretary of New Jersey. He held this office until 1769. His characteristic political stance of conciliation and moderation, early apparent in a 1766 essay urging a closer union between Britain and the American colonies, was manifest in his 1773–1775 correspondence with Lord Dartmouth, in which he attempted to provide the British Secretary with accurate information regarding colonial attitudes toward imperial policy. By the late stages of the colonial controversy with Great Britain Reed had become active in the patriot cause, although he remained hopeful of reconciliation with England until early 1777. He served on the Philadelphia Committee of Correspondence (1774–1776), in the first and second Pennsylvania Provincial Conventions (1774 and 1775, being president of the latter), on the Pennsylvania Committee of Safety (1775–1776), and in the Pennsylvania Assembly (1776). Although Reed had no previous military experience, he was appointed lieutenant colonel of the Philadelphia militia in 1775. Shortly thereafter he became military secretary to George Washington, serving the Continental commander-in-chief as secretary and adviser until October 1775. In June 1776 he was appointed adjutant general of the Continental army, a position he held until early 1777. During his military career, Reed participated in the siege of Boston, the New York campaign of 1776, and the New Jersey and Pennsylvania campaigns of 1776–1777. In 1777 he was offered command of the Continental cavalry, but declined the appointment.

Joseph Reed's political activity remained extensive during the early years of the war. Although he refused appointment as chief justice of Pennsylvania, he was elected by that state as a delegate to the Continental Congress in 1777. Before his resignation from Congress in October 1778, Reed was active in the committee on army affairs. In 1778 he was approached by George Johnstone of the Carlisle peace commission with an offer that Reed construed as a bribe to win him over to the cause of reconciliation with Great Britain. He rejected this offer, later publishing an account of the incident in *Remarks on Governor Johnstone's Speech* . . . (Philadelphia, 1779).

In 1778 Joseph Reed became actively involved in Pennsylvania state politics again. At this time the patriots of that state were deeply divided politically. The Constitutionalists, who held a majority in the assembly, defended the Pennsylvania Constitution of 1776 as a bulwark of the patriot interest in the state, while the Anticonstitutionalists attacked the frame of government as ultra-democratic, unstable, and subject to legislative tyranny. Although Reed had expressed dissatisfaction with several sections of that constitution in his letter declining the office of chief justice, Constitutionalist leaders fixed upon him as a compromise candidate for the presidency of the Supreme Executive Council, the highest executive office in the state. Genuinely afraid that partisan strife might lead to the collapse of the patriot cause in Pennsylvania, Reed negotiated with the Anticonstitutional faction, apparently receiving assurances from opposition leaders that they would work for a reduction of party strife in return for his promise not to thwart their efforts to call a new state convention to alter the constitution. In December 1778 the Supreme Executive Council and the General Assembly by a joint vote elected Reed, who had previously been chosen a member of the council by Philadelphia County, president of that body. He was reelected in 1779 and 1780. In a letter to Jared Ingersoll he explained his decision to accept the office. "I was unanimously elected to the Presidency of the State," he wrote, "A Station equally unlooked for & undesired by me, but the unhappy Division of our State upon Matters of Government had thrown us into such Disorder that the Step appeared necessary to cement the Coalition of Parties which had taken Place just before."

Reed's hope of uniting Pennsylvania's Whigs politically was frustrated in the years that followed. The problems facing the state during his administration, 1778–1781, were enormous. The material burdens of the war, problems of military organization, the existence of a large body of Loyalists and non-jurors in Pennsylvania, inflation, and the constant derangement of the state's finances guaranteed a continuation of factional strife, which took the form of partisan battles over the state constitution, the economy, the treatment of Loyalists and non-jurors, and the legal status of the College of Philadelphia. Reed, who had initially conceived his role as a conciliator of parties, increasingly became identified with the Constitutionalists, although he disagreed with other leaders of that faction on matters of public finance. He came gradually to perceive the activities of the Anticonstitutionalists as a threat to the security and well-being of the state and to the patriot cause. Despite the continuation of partisan rivalry, Reed's years in office were notable for several attempts to reorganize the state's military and financial structure, the abolition of slavery by the assembly following the council's recommendation, the prosecution of Benedict Arnold for corruption in office while military commander in Philadelphia, and a general invigoration of the war effort.

As Reed became identified with the Constitutionalist party and the political status quo in Pennsylvania, he was subjected to severe attacks by members of the Anticonstitutionalist faction on the grounds of political opportunism and treasonous activities during the war. The continuation of these attacks after his retirement from office demonstrates the extent to which Reed himself became an ideological and political symbol. His attitude toward this vilification was generally stoical, but a trace of bitterness sometimes crept into his correspondence. "I have never given Occasion to the personal Enmity which some Gentlemen have expressed toward me," he wrote to an unknown correspondent on November 11, 1779, "unless accepting a Station full of Trouble & Difficulty unattended by any Profit can be accounted one." One of these controversies was revived several times during the nineteenth century, most notably when George Bancroft repeated earlier accusations that Reed had gone over to the enemy at one point during the early stages of the war. However, this argument was disposed of in 1876 by William S. Stryker, who demonstrated that Bancroft had confused Joseph Reed with Colonel Charles Read.

Reed retired as president of the Supreme Executive Council in 1781, having served the constitutional limit of three consecutive terms. During the next few years he successfully revived his legal business in Philadelphia, but this period of his life was marred by poor health and reverses in his real estate concerns. He did, however, find more time to participate in the affairs of the Second Presbyterian Church and the American Philosophical Society, to which he had been elected in 1768. He also served as a trustee of the University of the State of Pennsylvania (1782–1785). During the last years of his life, his public activity was restricted to service on the commission to argue Pennsylvania's claims against those of Connecticut in the Wyoming land controversy (1782). He was elected once again to Congress in 1784, but was unable to serve because of his poor health. Reed died in Philadelphia at the age of 43 on March 5, 1785.

SOURCES: John Roche's fine modern biography, *Joseph Reed* (1957), is a rich source of fact and analysis. William B. Reed, *Life and Correspondence of Joseph Reed*

(1847), contains many valuable letters and a reprint of the 1766 essay. Brief sketch: best of many is in *DAB*. College career: Aaron Burr, MS Account Book, 66, 122. Geneal. data: Joseph Reed Folder, PUA. Letter to Ingersoll, Dec. 15, 1778, MS, Joseph Reed Papers, Vol. 5, NHi. Letter to unknown correspondent: MS, Peter Force Papers, Series IX, Box 27, DLC.

PUBLICATIONS: see Evans #10400, also STE

Mss: NHi, DLC, P   DMA

Stephen Sayre

STEPHEN SAYRE, A.B., A.M. 1760, Harvard 1766, merchant, banker, diplomat, public official, landowner, adventurer, was born in Southampton, Long Island, New York, on June 12, 1736, the tenth child of Hannah Howell and John Sayre, a prosperous farmer. He entered the College on September 23, 1756. Two years after graduation Sayre formed a company of volunteers in the New York militia, but after receiving a bounty of £1,452 for asembling the men, he abandoned military life

Stephen Sayre, A.B. 1757

without ever seeing battle. By 1762 he was a merchant in New York City, and in that capacity he undertook the first of the many intrigues that filled his life. He was hired by Pennsylvania to collect information on Connecticut's plans for the disputed Wyoming Valley settlements. That mission completed, he took ship for London to report on colonial commerce before the Board of Trade.

In England Sayre's view of British colonial policy became quickly and permanently jaundiced. He joined the so-called Artillery Row cabal, young men who frequented the home of the merchant Dennys De Berdt, an agent for Massachusetts in Britain. The group included Sayre's classmate Joseph Reed as well as Arthur Lee, Samuel Powel, and John Morgan. Sayre adopted London as his home, though he returned to America in 1764 and 1766 on business. He was forever on the lookout for some arrangement that would guarantee his prosperity while he lived in England, and he counted on his extraordinary physical attractiveness and charm to ingratiate himself with wealthy women, the De Berdt family, and influential Britons whose patronage he readily accepted but never trusted. He counted Charles Townshend and General Oglethorpe among such patrons.

Sayre had an unhappy faculty for competing with men whose enmity would later do him harm. As a leader of the Artillery Row circle, he was among the most prominent critics of Benjamin Franklin, whose agencies were coveted by De Berdt and his associates. When De Berdt died in 1770 Sayre inherited the De Berdt firm in London, and thereby earned the jealousy of Reed and Lee. As opponents of British policy toward America the Artillery Row circle was naturally drawn to the radicalism of John Wilkes, whose uninhibited life-style also attracted the adventurous young men. Sayre became one of the most ardent Whigs in London. His diatribes against competing colonial agents reserved special venom for those men who were notorious opponents of Wilkes. Sayre's radicalism was noted by kindred spirits in the colonies, and he was the Whig candidate for the post of agent for New York in 1769 and for Massachusetts in 1770. He obtained neither agency.

By 1770 Sayre had been drawn into British politics. He joined the Society of Supporters of the Bill of Rights and gained entry into the pro-Whig livery of London by joining one of the lesser guilds. When Wilkes became Lord Mayor of London in 1773 he supported Sayre and Arthur Lee's brother William for the joint shrievalty.

A prerequisite for being Sheriff of London was that the candidate possess at least £15,000. Sayre had managed to rescue his personal fortune from the collapse of De Berdt's firm by establishing a banking house on Oxford Street, which managed to stay solvent for a few years, partly because its notes were circulated throughout the city by Sayre's paramours. Shortly after his election he began a long affair with the famous actress Sophia Baddeley. Their house in Cleveland Row became a gathering place for antigovernment Englishmen and Americans.

The crisis in the colonies tended to unite the disparate Americans in England. By 1774 Sayre was helping to defend Benjamin Franklin in the litigation over publication of the Hutchinson-Oliver letters. The sheriff was also among the leading opponents of the Coercive Acts. In that cause he had the support of Lord Chatham, who relied on Sayre for advice and information about colonial affairs and who supported the American in an abortive stand for Parliament in 1774.

In February 1775 Sayre finally married the rich woman for whom he had been searching—a London heiress, Elizabeth Noel. The wedding took place shortly before Mrs. Baddeley gave birth to Sayre's illegitimate son. Sayre continued to profess his love for the actress, swearing that he detested his wife and had married her only for her money. The bank on Oxford Street was beginning to fail, and the shrievalty and Mrs. Baddeley's affections had proved great strains on his finances.

By October the former sheriff was in prison on a charge of high treason. A young American officer in the King's Guard, Ensign Richardson, testified that Sayre was plotting to seize the Tower of London, kidnap the king, and turn the government over to London's Whigs. Eager to silence its flamboyant critic, some of whose inflammatory letters had already been seized as proof that he was plotting to incite rebellion, the government did not bother to investigate Richardson's incredible story. Sayre spent five days in the Tower before he was released for lack of evidence. London's Whigs ballyhooed the affair as an example of governmental stupidity. The official who had directed Sayre's arrest was dismissed and Sayre, wrote Horace Walpole, was "at liberty, instead of being, as he ought to be, in Bedlam." Claiming £30,000 damages, Sayre sued for false arrest. He was represented by the same law firm that had defended Wilkes in the case of the *North Briton No. 45*. The verdict was for the plaintiff, but the award, only £1,000, was never paid.

His bank and his affair with Mrs. Baddeley having collapsed, Sayre was clapped into debtor's prison. This final indignity confirmed him as a dedicated Anglophobe. He emerged from prison in 1777 ready to serve America's cause as a diplomatic agent. Except for a few months in 1777, when he accompanied Arthur Lee on a mission to Berlin, he was never an official representative of the United States. Yet he never disabused anyone of the impression that he was acting in an official capacity and for the next several years engaged in a variety of intrigues that brought him into contact with the monarchs or first ministers of most European powers. His questionable status led his fellow countrymen to distrust him and foreign statesmen to deal with him cautiously. His true role may never be known. It is certain that he participated in the earliest discussions of the League of Armed Neutrality that was proclaimed in 1780. Under various aliases he traveled across Europe to promote his special plans against England. He hoped to convert the West Indies into an entrepôt for supplies for the United States. He devised a plan for a new warship that many experts agreed would revolutionize naval warfare. He did his best to slander and discredit Britain's representatives in every capital. When he went to St. Petersburg it was with the intention of seducing Catherine the Great so that she would support the American cause. He was hated by Englishmen, and other American representatives eventually stopped answering his letters. He described himself to Franklin as a "modern Don Quixote," and like the Don he schemed incessantly to no avail.

Back to America after the war, Sayre continued to make powerful enemies. He joined Chancellor Robert Livingston in a plan to create a bank of the state of New York in competition with Alexander Hamilton's proposal for a Bank of North America. In New York Sayre became a close friend and patron of the South American revolutionary Francisco de Miranda. Never satisfied with mundane business affairs, Sayre returned to Europe in 1785 with a letter from congressional leaders who wanted Thomas Jefferson to appoint him to the upcoming American mission to the Barbary States. Jefferson was sympathetic, but the post was already filled. After a brief stay in Spain, Sayre took another alias and returned to London. When his identity was discovered in the spring of 1787 a still-bitter British government sent him to debtor's prison again. Released eighteen months later, he opened another bank in London.

Sayre's first wife died in November 1789. Shortly thereafter he moved to revolutionary France, where he established a snuff factory and married another wealthy heiress, Elizabeth Dorone. His revolutionary sympathies were so obvious that officials in Paris commissioned him as a spy and sent him back to London. The mission failed when the American representatives in England refused to provide him with the necessary immunity.

After several more futile attempts to obtain employment from the

United States government Sayre returned to America to join the opposition to Jay's Treaty. Much of the rest of his life was occupied with appeals to Congress for payment for his wartime services, which he ultimately claimed had cost him £93,700. The government adamantly refused to pay him for anything more than his two months in Berlin. In 1793 he bought Point Breeze, an estate near Bordentown, New Jersey. In 1816 he sold it to Joseph Bonaparte. But he could not be content with farming even in his old age. He still dreamed the dreams of Don Quixote; he still could find no one to listen to his plans. On September 27, 1818, Sayre died at the home of his one legitimate child, a son by his first wife, near Brandon, Virginia.

SOURCES: Sibley's Harvard Graduates, XIV, 204-15; and DAB; and J. P. Boyd, "The Remarkable Adventures of Stephen Sayre," Princeton Library Chronicle, II (November 1940), 51-64; father's will: N.Y. Wills, VII, 67-68; military career: NYHS Col., XXIV, 200, 542-43; Wyoming Valley: Susquehannah Papers, II, 52-55; London: W. B. Reed: Life of Joseph Reed (1847), I, 27; and Life of Esther De Berdt (1853), 83-88, 122-26; V. W. Crane, ed., Benjamin Franklin's Letters to the Press (1950), 126; M. G. Kammen, A Rope of Sand (1968), 150, 291-92; J. F. Roche, Joseph Reed (1957), 25, 28; WMQ, 17 (1961), 233-34; H. A. Cushing, ed., Writings of Samuel Adams (1906) II, 66, 68; WMQ, 20 (1963), 373-95; B. Bailyn, Pamphlets of the Am. Rev. (1965), I, 60-85; W. L. Sachse, The Colonial American in Britain (1956), 130-31, 152-53; F. Wharton, ed., Revolutionary Diplomatic Correspondence (1889), I, 519, 614; R. W. Postgate, That Devil Wilkes (1929), 214-15, 218; D. M. Clark, British Opinion in the Am. Rev. (1930), 165; J. Bigelow, ed., Life of Benjamin Franklin (1875), II, 153; Elizabeth Steele (pseud.), Memoirs of Mrs. Sophia Baddeley (1787), VI, passim; MHSP, 56 (3 ser.), 1922-1923, 95, 107-10, 112, 114-16; C. Van Doren, Benjamin Franklin (1937), 444-46; C. R. Ritcheson, British Politics and the Am. Rev. (1954), 52, 163n, 170, 182, 224; F.A. Mumby, George III and the Am. Rev. (1923), 346; B. Williams, Life of William Pitt (1916), I, 329; II, 301; B. Donoghue, British Politics and the Am. Rev. (1964), 150, 183; B. Tunstall, William Pitt (1938), 448-50; J. Sparks, ed., Writings of George Washington (1834), III, 186; Ezra Stiles, Literary Diary, I, 657; MHSP, 7 (2 ser.), 1891, 358; P. Cunningham, ed., Letters of Horace Walpole (1891), VI, 277; R. Gore-Browne, Chancellor Thurlow (1953), 92-93; J. Hampden, An Eighteenth Century Journal (1940), 234, 293-94; G. Nobbe, The North Briton (1939), 228-29, 231-33; H. Bleakley, Life of John Wilkes (1917), 91-92; diplomatic career and issues: I. DeMadariaga, Britain, Russia, and the Armed Neutrality of 1780 (1962), 73; Wharton, ed., above, I, 615-19, III, 107-08; A. Johnson, Swedish Contributions to American Freedom (1953), I, 558; A. B. Benson, Sweden and the Am. Rev. (1926), 42; LMCC, IV, 361-62, VIII, 198; D. M. Griffiths, "American Diplomacy in Russia, 1780-1783," WMQ, 27 (1970), 384-89; 3rd Earl of Malmesbury, Diaries and Correspondence of James Harris (1845), I, 283; C. F. Adams, ed., Works of John Adams (1852), VII, 468, VIII, 317-18; WMQ, 16 (1959), 337; Deane Papers, NYHS Col., III, 276; postwar activities: T. M. Banta, Sayre Family (1901), 93; Hamilton Papers, III, 507-08, 521, XIX, 294; Jefferson Papers, VIII, 425, IX, 85, XI, 366, XVII, 421; W. S. Robertson, Life of Miranda (1929), I, 42, 44, 86, 88, 90, 296, 321; J. F. Thorning, Miranda (1952), 108; C. F. Adams, ed., Memoirs of John Quincy Adams (1874), I, 463; James Madison, Report of the Secretary of State on the Memorial of Stephen Sayre (1805); Richmond Enquirer, Feb. 28, 1806.

PUBLICATIONS: See STE

RAH

David Smith

DAVID SMITH, A.B., A.M. 1760, entered the College as a senior on November 22, 1756. The only other fact discovered about Smith is that found in a sketch of Edward Rutledge, a Signer of the Declaration of Independence, by David Ramsay (A.B. 1765) in his *History of South Carolina*. Ramsay wrote that Rutledge "received his classical education in Charlestown under David Smith, A.M. of New-Jersey College, who was an able instructor in the learned languages." Since Rutledge was born in 1749, Smith must have moved to South Carolina not long after receiving his A.M. The only other reference to a David Smith found in South Carolina records of this period indicates participation in a law suit in 1771. Smith may well have left South Carolina after the 1760s. If so, he is impossible to distinguish from the scores of men of that name in North America. His death was first indicated in the College's catalogue of 1827.

SOURCES: Aaron Burr, MS Account Book, 234; David Ramsay, *Hist. of S.C.* (1809), II, 519-20; *Records of the Court of Chancery of S.C.* (1950), 585-86.

James Smith

JAMES SMITH, A.B., M.D. Leyden 1764, physician, medical educator, and man of letters, was born in New York City on February 12, 1738, one of the fourteen children of Mary Het and her husband William Smith, Sr. The senior Smith was a prominent and prosperous New York lawyer and one of the founding trustees of the College. James was the second of his sons to attend the College, the other being Thomas (A.B. 1754).

James was enrolled by his father at the Academy of Philadelphia in 1752. The date he entered the College of New Jersey is unknown, as are his expenses in College, since President Burr scrambled together the accounts of both James and his older brother, Thomas. When a revival swept the College in February 1757, James was deeply affected. "Lawyer Smiths Son is in great Horrer," Esther Burr wrote in her journal on February 22. The following day she reported that "Mr. Tennent & Burr think there is no doubt but God has got possession of Smiths Heart altho' as yet hasn't found comfort, but I imagine Conversion and comfort to be two distinct things." Relief came the next day: "Smith has found comfort," Mrs. Burr recorded.

In 1759 Smith set off for England in pursuit of a medical education.

James Smith, A.B. 1757

There his course of study was supervised by Dr. John Fothergill, Quaker physician, botanist, and patron of young Americans abroad. Smith became a special pupil of Dr. William Hunter, soon to be known as Britain's foremost obstetrician; he lodged in London with Hunter and Hunter's brother John, a great teacher of anatomy. At the same time he "entered perpetual Physicians pupil" at St. Thomas's and Guy's hospitals. After finishing his work in London, Smith studied at the universities of Edinburgh and Paris, and received the M.D. from the University of Leyden in 1764 on the presentation of his dissertation, *De febribus intermittentibus.* At home others were keeping a close watch on young Americans studying abroad. In 1765 Ebenezer Hazard (A.B. 1762) forwarded Smith's dissertation, along with that of Benjamin Prime (A.B. 1751) to Benjamin Rush (A.B. 1760), then a medical student in Philadelphia. "I admire the sentiments, the good sense, and the truly classic style of Dr. Prime's," Rush commented, "but in justice to Dr. Smith (inter nos) I say he has published nothing new upon the subject. I can trace many of his very expressions in Vanswieten and Huxham very near word for word. But his would have been excusable, nay commendable, had he not marred the beauty of them by his Latin. His very paper of errata wants an erratum."

Rush notwithstanding, on his return home about 1767 Smith became lecturer in chemistry and then professor of chemistry and materia medica at King's College. Smith held the post until 1770. Either at some time during this period, or just before his return to America, Smith married one Mrs. Atkinson, a widow. John Adams described her as "a Lady, a most perfect Antithesis to beauty in the face and to Elegance in Person. She was however infinitely too good for him, for she had some property in the West Indies, enough I suppose to afford them a bare Subsistance, and she was what is much more, a discreet, virtuous and worthy Woman." With Mrs. Smith's prospects and recommendations from New York Governor Sir Henry Moore (formerly governor of Jamaica and a friend of James's brother William, a member of the New York Council), the Smiths set out to seek their fortune in the Caribbean. Smith remained in Jamaica for at least four years. Then, because of what he described as "three different attacks of the Nervous Cholic and Yellow Fever," he decided to return to England. Over the next several years, according to his own account, he lived in Surrey.

Smith's role in the American Revolution is difficult to determine; he may have acted as an agent of the Earl of Shelburne, a foe of the American war and leader of one of the two main opposition factions to Lord North's ministry. In April 1778, James appeared in France with his family. There he approached the American commissioners to the court of Louis XVI, Benjamin Franklin, Arthur Lee, Silas Deane, and John Adams. Smith made a vivid impression on Adams: "The Dr. had received a good Education in Letters, I know not where, and was a tollerable Writer. . . . This Man was supposed to come over from England, either to solicit some Employment, or to embarrass and perplex the American Ministers, or to be a Spy both upon the Americans and the French. Which of the three was his Errand, or whether either of them I know not. When he first arrived in Paris he visited Franklin and brought him some English Newspapers containing a Number of Pieces upon Liberty which he said he had written. Franklin told me that he read them and found them to contain some good common place principles of Liberty and that they were moderately well written, but of very little value or consequence." Smith's goals are as unfathomable today as they were to John Adams. What is clear is that through conversations and letters Smith managed to irritate and alienate all the American commissioners and accomplish nothing for himself, for America, for the British ministry, or for the British opposition.

On November 21, 1778, James's brother William, then a declared Loyalist living in New York City, wrote in lime juice on a scrap of paper to their Whig brother Thomas the following cryptic note: "Say not a Word of this. James is out [of France]. Supposed to be employed by Opposition. He was to leave his Family in France and land in South Carolina, and advance North in the Winter. Be Careful. Opposition is divided." The American commissioners would not grant Smith a passport to America; instead, he returned to England.

Back in London Smith once more plunged into the fringes of political activity. In the mid-1780s the Loyalist historian Thomas Jones, who disliked all members of the Smith family, described James as "a person of strict republican principles, a professed enemy to monarchy, a hater of Episcopacy, and of a most turbulent, factious, seditious disposition . . . he carried on a constant correspondence with the rebels in America, advising them never to submit, but to contend to the last; and upon every occasion haranguing the mobs in London in favor of the 'rights of mankind' and the 'liberties of the people.' " A 1784 English pamphlet (which reads as if it might have been composed by Thomas Jones) attacking James's brother William described James as "the more famous Doctor [Smith] who harangued upon a Tub (as a then Violent American) for the Mob to burn Lord [Chief Justice] Mansfield's House in Bloomsbury Square." All these references refer to the anti-Catholic Gordon Riots of 1780. Just what Smith's role in them was is unclear. At the time the riots were attributed to the machinations of Shelburne and the British opposition. The Privy Council apprehended James as "the Catiline of the conspiracy and the secret agent of Dr. Franklin to burn the city"—or at least so Smith wrote to John Jay in America. No evidence was found, and Smith was never brought to trial. He appears to have spent the rest of the war years in Brussels.

In January 1784, William Smith, then a Loyalist exile in London, reported to his wife that James had come from France to discuss with him the possibility of James's returning to America to live. But a serious illness intervened, and Smith was delayed until the end of the year. In January 1785, Smith decided to return to America. Before leaving England he addressed a letter to the Earl of Shelburne. In it Smith wrote that he had "never interfered here in condemning the late War but from Apprehension of its injuring the common Welfare of the united Empire and persuaded as I am that your Lordship was animated by the same Motive I shall certainly endeavor in America to second every Measure tending to close the late Wounds & to co operate with your Lordship in so useful and benevolent a Design[.]" Smith also had an interview with Shelburne in which he tried—apparently successfully—to advance his brother William's interests.

Smith finally returned to America at some time after 1785. He did not appear on the public scene again until the presidency of his old acquaintance, John Adams; this time he emerged as a target of the Sedition Laws. In 1798 Smith, along with the Irish Republican editor John Daly Burk, became owner of the *Time Piece*, a New York newspaper originally edited by Philip Freneau (A.B. 1772). During the anti-French hysteria of July 1798, Smith was arrested for libel against President Adams, while Burk was charged with sedition and libel. Members of his family provided bail for Smith. He claimed that his was a repetition of the famous case of the printer John Peter Zenger. But no trial emerged from the incident. Instead, Smith was soon charging that Burk had defaulted on payments due to him for the original purchase of the paper.

Smith's later years appear to have been spent in relative peace. Aside from supplying pamphleteers with material to attack John Adams, he lived quietly in New York. In 1806 he published an interesting treatise condemning both the expiring aristocratic order and the approaching democratic one. He served as a trustee of New York's College of Physicians and Surgeons from 1807 to 1811. His death on February 12, 1812, was the occasion for flowery and uninformative obituaries in New York newspapers.

Sources: The main source for the early years is the autobiographical fragments in Smith, *A Concise Economical Plan of the Family Medical Institution for Administering Advice and Medicines; to Families and Individuals, Possessing Small Fortunes and Moderate Incomes: Upon Liberal, Safe, Honorable and Easy Terms* ([1798?]), 4-11; Philadelphia Academy: T. H. Montgomery, *A Hist. of the Univ. of Pa.* (1900), 550; Princeton revival: Esther Burr, ms Journal, entries for Feb. 22, 23, and 24, 1757; Rush's comments: *Rush Letters*, I, 21; Adams's comments on wife and French encounter: Adams, *Adams Papers*, IV, 74-76; attempts to visit America: I. M. Hays, ed., *Calendar of the Papers of Benjamin Franklin* (1908), I, 482-532, 540, IV, 7, 491; lime juice note: W.H.W. Sabine, ed., *Hist. Memoirs of William Smith 1778-1783* (1971), 80; Jones's description: Thomas Jones, *Hist. of New York during the Rev. War* (1879), I, 20; "Tub" quotation: L.F.S. Upton, ed., *Diary and Selected Papers of Chief Justice William Smith, 1784-1793* (1963), I, 116, and for Shelburne letter, I, 180-83; "Catiline" quotation: Smith to John Jay, Brussels, Sept. 12, 1780, John Jay Papers, quoted in R. B. Morris, *The Peacemakers* (1965), 85; *Time Piece* affair: J. J. Shulim, "John Daly Burk: Irish Revolutionist and American Patriot," *APS Trans.*, n.s., 54 (1964), 22-32; also: James M. Smith, *Freedom's Fetters* (1956), 204-20; comparison with Zenger case: *Time Piece*, #134, July 23, 1798, p. 3; pamphlet: Smith, *The Commonwealth's-Man: in a Series of Letters, Addressed to the Citizens of New-York* (1806); among obituaries: *N.Y. Columbian*, Feb. 14, 1812.

Publications: See above and STE

John Strain

JOHN STRAIN, A.B., Presbyterian clergyman, was born in 1728 or 1729. No record of his life before he entered the College as a charity scholar in September 1752 has been found. The cost of his education was borne by the institution's Fund for Pious Youth.

After graduation Strain served as the usher of the grammar school at Princeton. He then studied theology with the Reverend Samuel Finley in West Nottingham, Maryland. On May 29, 1759, Strain was licensed to preach by the Presbytery of New Castle. Two years later he was ordained and installed as the pastor at Chanceford and Slate Ridge congregations in York County, Pennsylvania. In 1763, Strain's churches were included in the New Side Presbytery of Donegal. Worshippers who withdrew from nearby Old Side churches joined his flock.

Outside of the pulpit Strain was a dour and solemn figure who was reputed to have almost no sense of humor, an image doubtlessly exaggerated by his extreme nearsightedness. But when he preached he electrified his listeners. He was said to be the equal of George Whitefield in eloquence; and his parishioners were either spellbound by his oratory or so offended that they had to leave his church. He was so well respected that when Gilbert Tennent died Strain was called to succeed him at Philadelphia's Second Presbyterian Church. He declined the invitation because he preferred to stay in York County. On May 21, 1774, Strain died in Slate Ridge. He was buried in the cemetery there. Benjamin Rush (A.B. 1760), who rarely had a kind word for anyone, described Strain as a "great man" whose exertions in behalf of the church caused his untimely death.

SOURCES: CNJ: Aaron Burr, MS Account Book, 245; training with Finley: Giger, Memoirs, I; *Rush Letters*, II, 1193-94; Sprague, *Annals*, III, 215-16; *Centennial Memorial of Presbytery of Carlisle* (1889), II, 45-46; Webster, MS Brief Sketches, PPPr-Hi; C. Hodge, *Constitutional Hist. of the Pres. Church* (1840), II, 379; also: Alexander, *Princeton*, 50; death: *Pa. Gaz.*, June 1, 1774.

RAH

Samuel Taylor

SAMUEL TAYLOR, A.B., A.M. Yale 1765, has not been identified. He entered the College on December 26, 1753, bought the usual books, paid his tuition bills on time, and graduated in due course. The only other certain fact discovered about Taylor is that he was listed as the recipient of a Yale A.M. in Princeton's catalogue of 1770, which suggests

—but only suggests—that he may have been a professional man and a resident of Connecticut. However, an exhaustive search of Connecticut manuscript records and twenty-four Taylor family genealogies has not established a connection between the many contemporary men of this name and the College's alumnus. Taylor's death was never noted in any of the College's catalogues.

SOURCES: CNJ: Aaron Burr, MS Account Book, 74.

Joseph Treat

JOSEPH TREAT, A.B., A.M. 1760, Presbyterian clergyman, was baptized in Abingdon (now Abington), Pennsylvania, on April 21, 1734. His mother, Mary Thomas, was the first wife of Richard Treat (Yale 1725) a trustee of the College of New Jersey and a zealous New Light Presbyterian revivalist who preached at Abingdon from 1731 until his death in 1778.

Treat entered the College on September 25, 1753. In his senior year he was one of the scholars most profoundly affected by the revival at Nassau Hall. Esther Burr called his conversion "very clear and remarkable," and it encouraged her to believe that God was "about to revive Religion in general." After graduation Treat served as a tutor in the College until 1760, when he was licensed by the Presbytery of New Brunswick. He supplied the pulpit of the Presbyterian church in Elizabeth, New Jersey twenty-five times between 1760 and 1762. There he came into contact with the family of Samuel Woodruff, Elizabeth's mayor, member of the provincial council, and a trustee of the College. In 1761 or 1762, Treat married Elizabeth Bryant, Woodruff's widowed daughter and the sister of Benjamin and Joseph Woodruff (both A.B. 1753).

In October 1762 Treat was sent to New York City's First Presbyterian Church to assist the aging Reverend David Bostwick. When Bostwick died in November 1763 Treat assumed the full leadership of the congregation. One year later the Reverend John Rodgers of St. George's, Delaware was appointed as Treat's assistant. Together they supervised the construction of a new brick building to house their congregation. John Adams, visiting New York in 1774, noted that both men were good extemporaneous speakers.

Treat's four children were born in New York City between 1766 and 1774. During those years the minister took on some of the responsibilities—and benefits—of managing part of the considerable estate of his wife's family. Joseph Woodruff bequeathed £500 to his sister in 1769, and his death left the family mansion in Elizabeth unoccupied. Treat served as one of the agents for the rental of the property. He was also a casual friend and correspondent of Ezra Stiles, to whom he reported in 1769 that the Jewish community in New York was "greatly disappointed" that the Messiah had not come in 1768 as had been predicted. In September 1770 Stiles heard that the Presbyterian congregation in New York had given Treat £150 and a house worth more than £600. Rodgers received only £250 in cash.

The Revolution disrupted Treat's settled life in New York. Like most presbyterian clergymen he fled the city as the British army entered it in 1776. On May 8 he was commissioned as chaplain of Colonel William Malcom's regiment in General John Morin Scott's brigade. In August his appointment was renewed and extended to include Colonel Lasher's battalion. During that summer he purchased one of the Woodruff family homes in Elizabeth from his wife's uncle. For £420 he received the house on a large lot adjoining the property of Elias Boudinot, as well as another tract of land in Elizabeth. Apparently he began to preach at various New Jersey pulpits, such as Lower Bethlehem and Greenwich, toward the end of the war.

Rodgers returned to New York in 1783 but Treat did not go back until the next year. The delay may have been costly, for the congregation had made up its mind that it needed only one minister and that Rodgers was to be the one. In a curt message to the Presbytery of New York on July 1, 1784, the members of the First Presbyterian Church asked that Treat be dismissed from their pulpit.

It is possible that that decision was based on recent lapses in Treat's behavior. In 1782 the Presbytery of New York had reported that the "moral character" of one of its members, then living "in the bounds of the Presbytery of New Brunswick," was "under some implications." Treat had apparently behaved badly while at the New Jersey quarters of General William Maxwell in 1781. The synod ordered an investigation. In 1783 Treat was dismissed by the Presbytery of New York. Ostensibly, that action was taken so that he could join the Presbytery of New Brunswick in whose territory he was living and preaching. But Treat never joined the New Brunswick Presbytery. In 1786 the synod demanded an explanation but, before it could get one, Treat died. His will, probated in February 1787, named his wife and two sons as heirs to an estate that was estimated to be worth £865. Apparently his wife's inheritances were all kept in her name.

SOURCES: J. H. Treat, *The Treat Family* (1893), 253; father: Dexter, *Yale Biographies*, I, 319-20; CNJ: Aaron Burr, MS Account Book, 78; and Esther Burr, MS Journal, entry for Feb. 21, 1757; supply in Elizabeth: Hatfield, *Elizabeth*, 513; ministry: Sprague, *Annals*, III, 132; and Giger, Memoirs, I; and Nevins, *Encyclopedia*, 948; military career: Force, *Am. Arch.* (5 ser.), I, 1542; and *New York Rev. War Papers* (1868), I, 317; Woodruff family connections: C. N. Woodruff, *Woodruff Chronicles* (1967), I, 58, 62-68, 76, 80, 87-88; and 33 *NJA*, 487; Adam's opinion: *Adams Papers*, II, 104; relations with Stiles: Stiles, *Literary Diary*, I, 17, 191; dismissal from Presbytery of New York: *Rec. Pres. Church*, 495, 507, 517, 529; and Webster, MS Brief Sketches; and Thomas Jones, *Hist. of New York during the Rev. War* (1897), II, 395-96; will: 36 *NJA*, 233.

RAH

Abner Wells

ABNER WELLS, A.B., merchant, was born in Southold, Long Island, New York, on November 13, 1737. He was the son of Katherina Penny, the second wife of Henry Wells. Another Henry Wells of this class was the son of Abner's half-brother Obadiah, who became Abner's guardian when their father died. Both Abner and the younger Henry entered the College on September 26, 1753.

In 1757 Obadiah heard that the revival that was sweeping Nassau Hall had managed to make "sincere converts" of fourteen seniors, including Abner. He was so pleased that he planned to send both his son and his half-brother to study theology with Joseph Bellamy in Connecticut. Henry was sent, but Abner apparently did not go. On December 10, 1758, he married Mary Case of Southold. All of their eight children were born there.

In the summer of 1775 Abner Wells declared his loyalty to the Continental Congress as an Associator in nearby Brookhaven, Long Island. He probably saw military service during the Revolution, for he is identified as a "captain" on his tombstone. Before 1789 he moved his family to the town of Chemung (later Newtown, later Wellsburg), Montgomery (later Tioga) County, New York. On September 7, 1791, he received a patent for 420 acres. Most of the town of Ashland was later built on this property. He opened Newtown's first store, and his family was always active in community affairs. His son Henry was to become a local judge, the county sheriff, and a member of the state assembly. Wells died intestate on September 21, 1797. He was buried in Newtown beside his wife.

SOURCES: Abner Wells File, PUA; C. Hayes, *William Wells of Southold and his Descendants* (1878), 195-96; CNJ: Aaron Burr, MS Account Book, 75; religious conversion: Giger, Memoirs, I; Brookhaven Association: New York State, *Calendar of Hist. Manuscripts Relating to the War of Revolution* (1868), I, 64.

RAH

Henry Wells

HENRY WELLS, A.B., A.M. Yale 1760, M.D. Dartmouth 1804, physician and municipal official, was the grandson of one of the founders of Southold, Long Island, New York. He was born June 14, 1742, in Connecticut Farms (now Union), Essex County, New Jersey. His parents, Mary Conkling and Obadiah Wells, had moved from New York City in about 1739 when the elder Wells joined a group of speculators in purchasing Connecticut Farms. Although he was primarily a painter and glazier, Obadiah Wells was involved in land speculation throughout his life. He returned his family to New York City in 1745 or 1746.

Henry Wells entered the College on September 26, 1753, accompanying his father's half-brother Abner of this class who was only five years his senior. Even before they graduated when Henry was only fifteen, Obadiah was laying plans to send both of them to Bethlehem, Connecticut, to study theology with Joseph Bellamy. It seems that Abner did not go, but Henry was sent to Connecticut immediately after graduation, and between 1757 and 1760 he spent occasional weeks in Bellamy's care. His chief interest, however, was medicine, and he spent far more time with a Dr. Hull (probably Titus Hull) of Bethlehem than with Bellamy.

In 1761, after receiving an honorary A.M. from Yale, Wells returned to New York City to continue his medical studies. He may have opened an apothecary shop in partnership with his father in 1763. In May 1764 Wells married Hannah Stout. Their first two children were born in New York. In July 1766 Henry and Obadiah Wells received patents from New York's Governor Sir Henry Moore for land in territory whose ownership was the cause of bitter dispute between New York and New Hampshire. Later to become Vermont, the area was called Cumberland County by the government of New York. Traveling by sloop along inland waterways, both generations of the Wells family moved north in 1766 to settle at Brattleboro.

Henry Wells's patent was to a farm of nearly 1,000 acres. On it he built a capacious house that stayed in his family until the mid-nineteenth-century. Because the dispute with New Hampshire was far from solved, it was necessary to establish a strong local government in Brattleboro as quickly as possible. The New Hampshiremen posed a serious physical, as well as political, threat to the town. From the outset, Henry Wells played a prominent role. He was Brattleboro's first physician, and thus one of its early leaders. Town meetings were held in his house until 1772. In 1768, he became the first town clerk as well

as overseer of highways and overseer of the poor. In 1769 he was instrumental in securing the town's first permanent minister for the Presbyterian church, and he signed the church covenant in 1770. He served
as the equivalent of tax collector during those years, was chosen as a
trustee (roughly, selectman) in 1771, and was moderator of the town
meeting in 1781.

The antagonism between the Green Mountain Boys and the New
Yorkers seemed to drive the citizens of Brattleboro toward Loyalism
during the Revolution. Certainly they were less flamboyant Whigs
than were their New Hampshire neighbors. Henry signed a petition
to the king in behalf of New York's claim to the territory during the
war. And his father served on the local Committee of Safety.

In Brattleboro Henry and Hannah Wells had seven more children.
The doctor also supervised the medical education of Lemuel Dicker-
son, who eventually joined Wells in practice. He soon became more
popular than his mentor, and in 1781 Wells moved his wife and eight
surviving children to Montague, Massachusetts.

In his new home Wells concentrated completely on practicing medicine. He quickly acquired a reputation as one of New England's best
diagnosticians and was in demand for consultations from Boston to
Albany. In 1785 he was elected to the Massachusetts Medical Society,
which he served for most of the rest of his life. Broad chested, with a
tendency to corpulence, Wells was said to bear a physical resemblance
to Benjamin Franklin. His dress was simple, almost in the Quaker fashion, and included a broad-brimmed hat. He was known for his genial
and reassuring bedside manner. He developed a relatively successful
treatment for hydrophobia, but its long-term efficacy is questionable
because it was based on mercury compounds. In 1802, when the small
town of Greenfield, Massachusetts, was crippled by a typhus epidemic
after an early summer flood, Wells was a tireless and diligent worker
in treating the victims. In 1804 Dartmouth College rewarded the doctor for his services by conferring an honorary M.D.

Wells was not a wealthy man in his later years. Most of his income
was spent on his large family, which included twelve surviving children. Four of them were deaf mutes. One was apparently insane. He
personally trained his son Richard to become a physician. Although
Henry suffered *Angina pectoris*, he refused to abandon his regular
two-mile rides through the country until just before his death on August 24, 1814. He was buried beside his wife, who had died one year
earlier, and his father in Montague's old burial ground. His estate
was divided among his children. Richard received his instruments

and papers—an extensive collection of manuscripts that was destroyed by a maniac in Richard's office in Canadaigua, New York, in 1838.

SOURCES: C. W. Hayes, *William Wells of Southold and his Descendants* (1878), 90-105; father: Hayes, above, 76-78; CNJ: Aaron Burr, MS Account Book, 76; study with Bellamy: Glenn P. Anderson, "Joseph Bellamy" (Ph.D. dissertation, Boston University, 1971), 440-41; career in Brattleboro: M. R. Cabot, ed., *Annals of Brattleboro* (1921), 36, 52, 57, 69, 73, 108, 196; A. M. Hemenway, ed., *Vermont Hist. Gazeteer* (1891), V, 22, 23, 57, 191; medical career: S. W. Williams, *American Medical Biography* (1845), 610-13; epidemic: F. M. Thompson, *Hist. of Greenfield, Mass.* (1904), 998-99.

RAH

CLASS OF 1758

John Borkuloe, A.B.

Peter Winne Douw, A.B.

William Hanna

John Johnston, A.B.

Jacob Ker, A.B.

Peter R. Livingston

Philip Peter Livingston, A.B.

Philip Philip Livingston, A.B.

John Milner, A.B.

Isaac Ogden

James Paterson, A.B.

Ralph Pomeroy, A.B.

John Shippen, A.B.

Jasper Smith, A.B.

Thomas Smith, A.B.

Dirck Ten Broeck

John Van Brugh Tennent, A.B.

William Tennent, Jr., A.B.

Joseph Tichenor, A.B.

Jeremiah Van Rensselaer, A.B.

William Whitwell, A.B.

Jesse Williams, A.B.

John Borkuloe

JOHN [JOHANNES] BORKULOE [BORKULO], A.B., farmer, was probably the son of Harmanus Borkuloe and his wife Sarah Terhune of the Narrows, Brooklyn, New York. He was baptized in the Dutch Church of Flatbush on September 1, 1734. The Borkuloe family, whose name was spelled with absolutely no consistency, was extensive. It included at least one branch in Kingston, New Jersey, and many members were named John or Johannes. The Princeton alumnus apparently returned to Brooklyn to help manage his father's farm after graduation, and he was actively farming in 1760. By 1766, however, when Harmanus Borkuloe's property was divided among his children, John was not listed among the surviving divisees. He was listed as dead in the College's catalogue of 1770 and probably died unmarried.

SOURCES: *NYGBR*, 84 (1953), 206.   RAH

Peter Winne Douw

PETER WINNE DOUW, A.B., merchant and public official, was born in Albany, New York, and baptized there on November 2, 1735. He was the son of Lyntie Winne and Abraham Douw, a merchant. Peter's father died in 1749. It seems probable that Johannes Hun, Peter's uncle, assumed guardianship of the boy, for both Peter and his cousin Thomas Hun (A.B. 1757) entered the College's grammar school on the same day, May 5, 1754. Peter appears to have matriculated in the College itself about a year later, on May 26, 1755. While in College he bought volumes of Horace, Plato, and Livy.

After graduation Douw returned to Albany, where by 1759 he was of sufficient substance to be occupying a pew in the Dutch Reformed church. Douw married Ryckie Van Schaick in Albany on July 21, 1762. The couple had four children. The exact nature of Douw's business interests has not been discovered, but some bills for goods Douw sold to Sir William Johnson, superintendent for Indian affairs, suggest that he dealt in materials such as nails, glass, white lead, fabrics, fruit trees, and so forth.

Douw embarked on a public career in November 1775, when he was appointed a fire master for Albany's Second Ward. The Albany fire company had provided the core membership of the Sons of Liberty in the 1760s and was a Whig stronghold. In January 1778, Douw was elected to Albany's Committee of Correspondence. In September of that year Douw was elected an assistant to the Common Council. Douw served on the council as assistant and later alderman until 1787. The good burgher, Douw served over the years on committees such as those dealing with dock repairs, repairing the public cage, and erecting a pillory. In 1790 Douw was recorded as the owner of three slaves. His house and store were destroyed in the fire that swept Albany in 1793, but he appears to have escaped unharmed. He died on March 27, 1801.

SOURCES: Parentage, marriage and children: J. Munsell, *Collections of the Hist. of Albany* (1865-71), IV, 118; school and College: Aaron Burr, MS Account Book, 94, 96, 97, 131, 145, 215, 281; political activities, etc.: Munsell, above, I, II; Johnson bill: *Papers of Sir William Johnson*, VII, 373; Committee of Correspondence: J. Sullivan, ed., *Minutes of the Albany Committee of Correspondence* (1923-25), I, 895, 907-63; slaves: *U.S. Census of 1790*, N.Y., 13. Another Peter Douw of Albany (d. 1775) was contemporary with the CNJ alumnus.

William Hanna

WILLIAM HANNA, A.B. King's 1759, A.M. 1765, Yale 1768, Presbyterian and Anglican clergyman, lawyer, was born in Litchfield, Connecticut, about 1738. Hanna studied for several years at Samuel Finley's academy in West Nottingham, Maryland. In 1755–1756 he taught Latin there and began to teach Greek. In the fall of 1756 Hanna moved to Robert Smith's academy at Pequea, Pennsylvania, where he assisted Smith in teaching Latin and Greek until the end of the following winter. On April 17, 1757, Hanna was admitted to the College of New Jersey's junior class. He did not, however, take the A.B. at Princeton. As tutor John Ewing (A.B. 1754) explained in 1759, while at the College Hanna "behaved himself soberly . . . & applyed himself diligently to his Studies and had passed one Examination for a Degree with the approbation of the Trustees & would have been admitted to the Honours of the College had he attended at the Commencement last; For he left the College only for a Season by Permission of the authority of it, & was as well qualified to stand a second Examination as any one of his Class who were all admitted without Exception. So that the only reason of his not geting [sic] a Degree was his absence he was free of all College Censure." Hanna did not return to Princeton for commencement in 1759. He presented himself instead at King's College in New York City, which awarded him the A.B. in that year.

After receiving his degree Hanna traveled north to Litchfield County, Connecticut. By 1760 he was a communicant of the Reverend Jonathan Lee's church at Salisbury. On May 28 of that year he was licensed to preach by the Congregational Association of Litchfield County. He then traveled south to within the bounds of the Presbytery of New Castle. A complex series of personal, theological and ecclesiastical disputes involving Hanna, Samuel Finley, the New Light theologian Joseph Bellamy, and others ensued. "Mr Hannah came to our Presby-[tery]," Finley reported to Bellamy in October 1761, "with credentials from your Association & out of respect to you, we employed him in our vacancies for some months, but at our next general meeting I was obliged to inform ye Presbytery of many unministerial, not to say unchristian things, on account of which they refused to employ him any more; we could not give him any testimonial but such as implied as his charracter was not fair." Whatever had happened, Hanna managed to persuade the Old Side faction of the Synod of Philadelphia to assign him to a new Presbyterian church that was being gathered in Albany, New York. On October 6, 1761, before taking up his Albany post, Hanna obtained a license to marry Hanna Lawrence.

Hanna served as pastor of the Albany church for about five years. In 1767, because of a dispersal of some of his congregation and the resulting reduction in his salary, he decided to give up the ministry in favor of the law. Hanna and the remaining members of his congregation parted amicably enough, the congregation testifying that Hanna "Mentained an unblemished Moral and Religious character during his incumbancy." Hanna practiced law in Schenectady until 1771. In May of that year Sir William Johnson, superintendent of Indian affairs in New York, reported to Samuel Auchmuty, rector of New York's Anglican Trinity Church, that Hanna wished to become an Anglican clergyman and asked Auchmuty to investigate Hanna. Auchmuty reported that Hanna's "moral character formerly was very good; but since he has commenced Lawyer it is altered. Many dirty things are reported of him, which if true, must greatly hurt him." Auchmuty recommended that Hanna secure the patronage of Maryland's proprietor, Lord Baltimore, "who can provide for him at a distance from his old Friends the Dissenters, who will be watching every opportunity to prejudice him, and render abortive any usefulness he may attempt to be of. I am very certain it will never do for him to think of settling in these parts."

Hanna went to England before seeking a pulpit in the south. He was ordained a priest in the Church of England at Fulham Palace, London, on June 14, 1772. He also, he wrote to Sir William Johnson, equipped himself with letters of recommendation from persons in London to influential Virginians such as Lord Fairfax and Colonel George Washington. Hanna returned to America and took up a rectorship in Culpepper County, Virginia, in 1772. He seems to have remained there until 1775, when he became rector of Christ Church parish, Kent Island, Kent County, Maryland, where he stayed until 1777. For part of that year he served as curate at St. Anne's parish, Anne Arundel County, and in 1777–1778 as curate at St. Margaret's Church, Westminster parish, also in Anne Arundel County. After 1777 he seems to have lived for most of the time in Annapolis, officiating from time to time at Westminster parish.

Hanna's first wife, Hanna Hanna, died at some time before 1778, for on February 3 of that year he married Sarah Turner in Anne Arundel County. Hanna's constant movements in these years were probably due to the exigencies of war and the consequent disruption of the Anglican clergy. Hanna was one of the few Anglican clergymen to take the oaths of the allegiance to the revolutionary government. He appears to have served—or at least to have requested to serve—as a chaplain in Colonel William Richardson's Maryland regiment in 1777. Shortly after the end of the war, on January 26, 1784, he was appointed coroner for Anne Arundel County. He died at some time between that date and March 12, 1785, when the county appointed a new coroner because of his death. His widow advertised the sale of their house and modest possessions in an Annapolis newspaper on March 25.

SOURCES: Many basic documents on Hanna to 1772, including Ewing testimony, Johnson and Auchmuty letters, etc., are printed in *Doc. Col. Hist. N.Y.*, IV, 236, 279-81, 284, 296-98, 307; see also V. H. Paltsits, "The Beginnings of Presbyterianism in Albany," *JPHS*, 5 (1909), 159-61; entrance to College: Aaron Burr, MS Account Book, 272, 281; David Bostwick to Joseph Bellamy, August 21, 1761, and Samuel Finley to Joseph Bellamy, Oct., 1761, both in Webster/Bellamy Transcripts, PPPrHi; marriage: *New York Marriages*, 168; and G. M. Brumbaugh, *Maryland Records* (1967), 441; Maryland clerical career: *MHM*, 10 (1915), 143, and N. W. Rightmyer, *Maryland's Established Church* (1956), 136, 139, 187; wartime activities: *Calendar of Maryland State Papers* (1953), 162, and *Archives of Maryland*, XLV, 317, XLVII, 71, XLVIII, 515, LXXI, 25; advertisement: *Maryland Gaz.*, March 31, 1785.

John Johnston

JOHN JOHNSTON, A.B., merchant and public official, was born in 1737, probably in Perth Amboy, New Jersey, the first child of Andrew Johnston and his wife, Catharine Van Cortlandt. The father was a prosperous merchant who conducted business in New York City and in Perth Amboy. He had inherited proprietary rights in East Jersey and was for a time president of the Board of Proprietors. A member of the

New Jersey Assembly, the father served for a time as its speaker. He was an early trustee of the College and acted as its treasurer in 1748–1749. At his death in 1762 he was a member of the provincial council.

John entered the College's grammar school on May 10, 1753, and matriculated in the College itself in September 1755. After graduation Johnston returned to Perth Amboy, where he entered business with Peter Barberie, a brother-in-law. One of his major assets appears to have been land, some of which he inherited from his father, for he was listed as one of the principals in many land sales of the late 1760s. Johnson married Isabella Hooper of Trenton on January 30, 1768. The couple had eleven children and were communicants of Anglican St. Peter's Church in Perth Amboy. In the 1780s and 1790s Johnston was a vestryman and warden of the church.

On November 16, 1763, Johnston was elected to the New Jersey Assembly from Perth Amboy. Most of his committee assignments involved such relatively routine matters as the overseeing of public accounts and arranging for meeting rooms for the council. However, he made strenuous efforts over the years to assure that the Middlesex County gaol was built in Perth Amboy. Johnston's most important work in the assembly came in November 1765, when he was appointed to a committee charged with pressing for the repeal of the Stamp Act. In the June session of the following year he was one of four members of a committee responsible for composing an address to the king. Johnston retired from the assembly in June 1767; his seat from Perth Amboy was then occupied by a cousin, John Lewis Johnston.

Johnston was not left without public employment, however. In 1767 and in 1773 he was serving on committees of the Board of Proprietors of East Jersey concerned with the governor's house in Perth Amboy. In 1767 he was also a member of the Perth Amboy Common Council.

Johnston was a member of the Middlesex County Committee of Correspondence in 1774. But the Revolution must have presented him with unpleasant choices. Two of his cousins, John Lewis Johnston and Heathcote Johnston, his business partner, John Barberie, and his brother-in-law, Stephen Skinner, all became Loyalists. Johnston himself appears to have been a neutral. He survived the war and was a regular attendant at the first meetings of the East Jersey Proprietors held after the Revolution in April and September 1784. He served as town assessor for Perth Amboy in 1788 and as collector of the port of Perth Amboy from 1786 to 1789. After that date he appears to have retired, except for some involvement in church affairs. Johnston fell ill in 1810 and made his will, leaving everything to his wife. He died in Perth Amboy on January 15, 1820.

SOURCES: The name was sometimes spelled Johnstone, and is often misprinted as Johnson; parentage, marriage, children and church affairs: W. N. Jones, *Hist. of St. Peter's Church in Perth Amboy, N.J.* (1924), 312, 86; and also: W. A. Whitehead, *Contributions to the Early Hist. of Perth Amboy* (1856), 72-73; school and College: Aaron Burr, MS Account Book, 82, 133, 215, 251; father's will: 33 *NJA*, 223; Board of Proprietors: *NJHSP* (n.s.), 15 (1930), 471, 475, 476; Assembly: N.J. Journals, *Votes and Proceedings of the General Assembly*, 1763-67 inclusive, place of publication varies; Common Council: *NJHSP* (3 ser.), 5 (1906-1907), 164-65; Loyalist relatives and associates: E. A. Jones, *Loyalists of New Jersey* (1927), 107, 197; references to land sales are scattered throughout 24 and 26 *NJA*; postwar activities: R. P. McCormick, *Experiment in Independence . . . 1781-1789* (1950), 138n, and W. C. McGinnis, *Hist. of Perth Amboy, N.J. 1651-1962* (1958-62), I, 41, II, 36, IV, 56; MS Will, N.J. State Lib., Trenton.

Jacob Ker

JACOB KER, A.B., A.M. 1761, Presbyterian clergyman, was born at Freehold, Monmouth County, New Jersey, on October 31, 1738, the son of Catherine Mattison and her husband, Samuel Ker, a well-to-do citizen of the town. He was probably prepared for College by his pastor William Tennent, a trustee of the College. Ker entered College in the junior class in the fall of 1756.

After graduating Ker served as a tutor in the College from 1760 to 1762. In 1763 he was licensed by the Presbytery of New Brunswick and in the following year was ordained. Shortly thereafter Ker joined the Presbytery of Lewes and was installed as pastor of three different Presbyterian churches in Maryland. He served the Manokin church at Princess Anne, Somerset County, from 1764 to 1795; the Wicomico church at Salisbury from 1764 to 1795 and the Rehobeth church in Somerset County from 1764 to 1779. The various congregations split Ker's time and salary among themselves; he was the first minister they had had since the death of Hugh Henry (A.B. 1748). Shortly after his installation at the Manokin church, Ker married Esther Wilson, a sister of one of his well-to-do parishioners. The Kers had three children before Esther's death in 1778. Their daughter Margaret married John Collins (A.B. 1789). After Esther's death in 1778 Ker married Jane Winsor.

Like most of his parishioners, Ker was a staunch Whig. He was held in high regard by his various congregations and by others in the area as well. He served as one of the trustees of Somerset County's Washington Academy. Ker died at Manokin on July 29, 1795.

SOURCES: F. R. Symmes, *Hist. of the Old Tennent Church* (1904), 390, 43-44; Aaron Burr, MS Account Book, 228, 251, 255; Giger, Memoirs, I; Alexander, *Princeton*, 52; H. P. Ford, *Hist. of the Manokin Pres. Church* (1910), 7-8, 18-19, 35, 50-52; R. B. Clark, Jr., "Washington Academy, Somerset Cty., Md.," *MHM*, 44 (1949), 203.

Peter R. Livingston

PETER R. LIVINGSTON, A.M. Harvard 1779, merchant, landowner, soldier, public official, was the second son of Robert Livingston, third lord of New York's immense Livingston Manor, and his wife, Maria Thong. Peter was born at the Manor on April 27, 1737. In 1754 he joined his older brother Philip at Harvard. There his attention to wine, women, and song earned him several reprimands from the faculty. Late in 1755 Philip fell ill and, accompanied by Peter, he returned to the Manor. Peter's sights must have been raised by his stay in Cambridge, for he soon became bored: "I am quite weary of living in the country and am almost become a Priest for want of exercise and diversion," he wrote to a friend in May 1756. "I would not live another year here." He did not have to. His older brother died at about this time, making Peter the potential fourth lord of Livingston Manor. It was decided shortly that his education should be completed. He was sent to the College of New Jersey, where, by June 1756, he was installed in President Burr's house. "I am now at Newark College where I intend to get as much knowledge as possibly I can," he wrote. "I have determined to mind nothing but my studies and stick closely to them while I am here." Peter's sticking qualities were never pronounced. He did not receive his A.B., although he later hoodwinked Harvard into awarding him an A.M. by falsely claiming that he already possessed one from Princeton.

Peter left Princeton and in 1758 married a distant cousin, Margaret Livingston. He established a dry goods store in New York City but his primary source of income was his investment in a number of armed ships which regularly broke the British blockade to engage in illegal trade with the French West Indies. In 1763 he was elected to the St. Andrew's Society, and as a trustee of the English Presbyterian Church in New York he was instrumental in raising funds to build the city's famous Brick Presbyterian Church.

In 1761 Livingston assumed the Manor's seat in the New York Assembly when his uncle William was too busy to take it. During the furor over the Stamp Act he was a leader of the opposition to British policies. The Livingstons led the incongruous combination of country landlords and popular leaders of the city that constituted the assembly's anti-British faction in opposition to the DeLancey party, comprised primarily of wealthy merchants. Peter R. Livingston was one of the most consistent Whigs in the legislature. As the assembly came under DeLancey control during the 1760s Livingston went to drastic lengths to maintain his family's political leverage. Against his own father's better judgment he joined New York City's Society of Dissenters and exploited religious divisions by appealing to the population of New York City, the great majority of whom were Dissenters, to resist the Anglican DeLanceys. In 1769 he and his Whig associates literally drummed up votes on the wharves and in the taverns and incited an armed mob to intimidate voters during the provincial election. Their efforts were to no avail. Even Philip Van Brugh Livingston, speaker of the assembly, failed to win reelection. Peter R. Livingston was one of the few to survive the vote. According to a family custom, he relinquished his seat to his cousin, the former speaker, in order to keep the leader of the family party in the assembly.

During his seven years in the assembly Livingston's personal financial situation had grown perilous. At the end of the French and Indian War, his lucrative trade with the enemy had also ended. By 1771 he had to borrow £15,000 from his father to pay his debts. If Peter's politics sometimes appalled his father and brothers, his lack of business acumen and financial profligacy left them aghast. In 1771 Peter's father, in order to protect the family fortune, took the extraordinary step of breaking the entail on 160,000 acre Livingston Manor. This meant that Peter and his brothers would now inherit more or less equally.

Livingston now sought provincial office from the royal government, and when he was refused he grew even more resentful of British rule. In 1774 he was among the leaders of the Whig group who supported the anti-British agitator Alexander McDougall. In the same year he assumed the assembly seat of another uncle, Robert R. Livingston, whom that body had refused to seat. Although Peter R. Livingston was not denied the seat, his participation in Whig mobs had by then earned him the hatred of the legislature's conservatives.

Days after the assembly adjourned in April 1775 the news of Lexington and Concord arrived. Livingston took part in the seizure of a British sloop off New York and in the raid on city hall that netted weapons for the rebels. He had been among the first to sign the Association against British imports proclaimed by the Continental Congress and was a leader in the city's welcomes for Samuel Adams and John Hancock, and for George Washington on his way to take command of the Continental army in 1775. It was his money that bought the liquor with which yet another mob ennerved itself to attack the home and press of a Loyalist printer. On October 20, 1775, Livingston was commissioned as a colonel in the New York militia with command of a regiment from the Manor which became the Tenth Albany. But his civil duties prevented him from ever seeing battle. In 1776 and 1777 he was president of the provincial congress, and he occasionally chaired the Committee of Public Safety although his attendance at its meetings was rare.

Livingston's financial plight was not helped by the war. As the British army seemed to be winning its battle to recapture New York he began to doubt the wisdom of the American cause. His frequent support of mob violence notwithstanding, he distrusted the people and was suspicious of the democratic tendencies of the Revolution. His close association with his Loyalist brother-in-law William Smith, who lived at the Manor between 1776 and 1778, undoubtedly influenced his own growing conservatism. His relationship with his father and brothers was strained since he did everything he could to avoid appearing responsible for what was happening in New York. He abstained from voting on the Declaration of Independence in 1776 and was the only member of the provincial congress to vote against the state constitution in 1777 even though he had been president of the convention that drafted it. His previous republicanism was enough for his Loyalist tenants to plan to kill him should the British capture the Manor—a fate he escaped by fleeing to Boston for a few months. Yet he was so negligent in raising the Manor's army quota and in supporting the Revolution in general that the leaders of the Committee of Public Safety berated him publicly.

Livingston was back in the assembly by 1780 but played a conspicuously minor role. He had inherited only the manor house, the income from fifty farms, and a few minor pieces of property. Plagued with debts during his last ten years, he almost never left the Manor lest a creditor spot him. (He was not, however, left without help, for he owned thirteen slaves in 1790.) The bulk of the huge estate was divided among Peter's brothers. It was only by dint of tradition that Livingston was considered the fourth lord of the Manor. He died on November 13, 1794, survived by his wife and eight of their eleven children, *including Peter William Livingston (A.B. 1786).*

SOURCES: Sketch, which contains Livingston's quotations and crucial account of 1771 breaking of entail: P. J. Gordon, "Livingstons of N.Y., 1675-1860" (Ph.D. diss., Columbia U., 1959), 295-303; less reliable: *Sibley's Harvard Graduates*, XIV, 183-90; E. B. Livingston, *Livingstons of Livingston Manor* (1910), 175, 181-82, 183, 192-93, 253 n4, 527-28, 558; G. Dangerfield, *Chancellor Robert R. Livingston* (1960), 23, 39-40, 69, 75, 193, 249-50; political activity: P. U. Bonomi, *A Factious People (1971)*, 232, 238, 246, 253-54, 264-65, 273-77; relations with Smith: L.F.S. Upton, *Loyal Whig* (1969), 107, 114, 199; and D. R. Dillon, *New York Triumvirate* (1949), 145, 149; and W. H. Sabine, ed., *Hist. Memoirs of William Smith* (1971), 103, 592, 596; Loyalist view of republicanism: T. Jones, *Hist. of New York During the Rev. War* (1897), I, passim; slaves: *U.S. Census of 1790, N.Y.*, 70.

Mss: Museum of the City of New York, NHi   RAH

Philip Peter Livingston

PHILIP PETER LIVINGSTON, A.B., A.M. 1773, King's 1763, lawyer, public official and businessman, cousin of his classmates Philip Philip Livingston and Peter R. Livingston and brother of William Alexander Livingston (Class of 1776), was born in New York City on November 3, 1740, the eldest son of Mary Alexander and Peter Van Brugh Livingston (Yale 1731). The father, who served as a trustee of the College from 1748 to 1761, was a very wealthy merchant and landowner and one of the leaders of the Whig-Presbyterian faction in New York politics during the 1760s and early 1770s.

After graduation Livingston studied law and was licensed to practice in New Jersey on November 13, 1761, and in New York effective in March 1762. But Livingston's legal education was not completed. In 1762 he traveled to London to study at the Inns of Court. He was shortly established in a "pleasant Sett of Chambers" in the Middle Temple. "My mornings," he wrote home, "are generally engaged in Study, which as they are very long I am told is sufficient time to be applied in Reading, for I seldom dine till four O'Clock and then with a Sett of Gentlemen, at the Turks Head Coffee House in the Strand in whose acquaintance I think myself very happy." The only drawback to his London stay, Livingston wrote to his uncle William Alexander, self-styled "Earl of Stirling," was the cost, which he estimated at £450 per year—"the Rent of Chambers being high, the Expences of Servant, Cloaths, & other et cetera's, so many, & so great, that it is absolutely impossible for an American, who has never lived in London, to have an idea of it."

The duration of Livingston's stay at the Inns of Court has not been discovered, but it proved worthwhile. He made good use of his family's British contacts. He hobnobbed with what he described as "Gentlemen of considerable fortunes," among them members of the Penn family. And in 1764 a new contact appeared from the island of Jamaica, where the Livingstons had extensive holdings. In 1764 the governor of that island, Henry Moore, resigned and returned to England to be knighted. Sir Henry was appointed governor of New York in November 1765, and not long afterward made Livingston his secretary. Livingston may well have made Moore's acquaintance while in London, though this is uncertain. It was a potentially lucrative and influential post. Throughout his tenure in New York Moore consistently favored the political faction with which the Livingstons were closely connected.

In January 1769, Moore dissolved the New York Assembly and

called for new elections. In the ensuing campaign Livingston, according to one contemporary, "openly canvassed and made promises in the name of the Governor, threatened some with the vengeance of his Excellency, abused members, and coaxed, flattered, and endeavoured to cajole others." But Livingston's powerful position dissolved suddenly in September 1769, when Sir Henry died. The lieutenant governor, Cadwallader Colden, always aloof from the various New York political factions, almost immediately appointed his son David to Livingston's post. Livingston was left with the satisfaction, if such it was, of being named one of the executors of Sir Henry's estate.

Livingston appears to have returned to England late in 1769. He and his family still possessed considerable leverage in the network of official patronage, for in 1770 Livingston was made secretary to the newly appointed governor of the province of West Florida, Peter Chester. (Livingston was actually a deputy of the official provincial secretary, James McPherson, who remained in England. McPherson got the salary granted by Parliament, Livingston the fees collected in Florida.)

Settled in Florida, Governor Chester made Livingston a member of the council and receiver-general of the province. On the southern frontier Livingston exhibited the same genius for land acquisition that had distinguished his family in the northeast for almost a century. He assisted Chester in dealings with the Creek, Choctaw, and Chickasaw Indians, and was well-rewarded for his efforts. In the summer of 1772 he bought for 248 Spanish dollars 2,950 acres of land that had been granted to five officers six weeks before. Livingston himself may have arranged the grant. In August of the same year he purchased from Governor Chester for 326 Spanish dollars 6,050 acres of land that the governor had granted to himself shortly before. On July 10, 1773, he saw that a tract of 25,000 acres in the western part of the province was reserved for his father and associates. "The banks of the Mississippi are settling very fast and every planter in great spirits," Livingston wrote to a friend on November 19, 1775. "I am so much convinced of the advantages to accrue from the planting business that I have established a young brother on a settlement with about 20 working hands." (The brother was probably youthful William Alexander Livingston, who left the College about this time without receiving his degree.)

The outbreak of Revolution to the north placed the secretary to the royal governor in a difficult position; back in New York Livingston's father and other relatives were among the leading revolutionaries. In 1778 Livingston delegated all the offices he held in West Florida to another man. It was a timely move, for in the following spring 136

"Gentlemen, Freeholders and Principal Inhabitants" of West Florida petitioned the king charging Governor Chester and Livingston with misappropriation of funds and other serious irregularities.

Chester replied that the petitioners were, in fact, "far from being what they so stile themselves the Principal Inhabitants of the said Province and that many of them are persons of very inferior Rank and indeed scarce known there." He defended his "late Secretary Philip Livingston Junior as if he was a disaffected Person from the unfortunate Circumstance of some part of his Family in America having been so far mislead to have joined in the Rebellion," declaring that "a Division in Families there is not uncommon and this Respondent is certain that his said Secretary is as Loyal and faithful a subject as any that his Majesty has in the said province." "Loyal and faithful" or not, Livingston seems to have disappeared quickly from the province. His whereabouts during the later revolutionary years have not been discovered. He may have been in continental Europe.

With the peace Livingston returned to New York, where he resumed his primary occupation—acquiring land and money. In 1784 and 1785 he bought £5,080 worth of confiscated Loyalist properties, much of it from the former holdings of the Delancey and Philipse families. He invested heavily in state securities. He also entered politics. A delegate from Westchester County to the New York convention called in 1788 to consider the new federal constitution, he voted for its adoption. In 1789 Livingston was elected to the New York State Senate. There his primary interest was in ensuring the incorporation of the Bank of New York. Founded in 1784, it still lacked a charter. When the Bank of the United States was established, Livingston became first president of its New York branch. His other business activities included a directorship of the Northern New York Canal Company. He was also among the earliest investors in "The Society for Establishing Useful Manufactures," New Jersey's first business corporation, which with the leadership of Alexander Hamilton tried to establish a planned industrial community at Paterson.

On October 20, 1790, two weeks before his fiftieth birthday, Livingston married Cornelia Van Horne in a Presbyterian ceremony in New York City. The couple had two sons, Peter Van Brugh and Charles Ludlow. In his later years Livingston was occupied with his business affairs, New York's St. Andrew's Society, and Columbia University, which he served as a trustee from 1797 to 1806. A nineteenth-century memorialist described Livingston as "not an orator, but an excellent business member, and highly respected for his strict integrity, sound judgement, general information, and good sense. From his high breeding and courtly manners, he early acquired the soubriquet of 'Gentle-man Phil.' " A remark of a contemporary rings truer: "Philip Living-ston is a great, rough, rapid mortal. There is no holding any conversation with him." He died in 1810.

SOURCES: In his *Princeton College During the 18th Century* (1872), 52-53, S. D. Alexander confused Livingston with his cousin and classmate Peter R. Livingston; Philip Peter has been absent from the University's records since that time. How-ever, his name appears in President Burr's MS Account Book, 110-11, in the Col-lege's catalogues of 1770 and 1773, and when he was awarded the A.M. in 1773, he was identified with unusual precision as: "The Hon. *Philip Livingston*, Esq.; one of his Majesty's Council, in West-Florida, an Alumnus of this College, A.M." (*Pa. Gaz.*, Oct. 13, 1773). Geneal.: E. B. Livingston, *Livingstons of Livingston Manor* (1910), 549; father: *DAB*; legal licensing, etc.: P.M. Hamlin, *Legal Ed. in Colonial N.Y.* (1939), 30, 32 n28; Livingston to Wm. Alexander, Oct. 25, 1762, in *NJHS Col.*, 2 (1847), 67; quotation about N.Y. Assembly: T. Jones, *Hist. N.Y. during Rev. War* (1879), I, 19; background N.Y. politics in 1760s: P. U. Bonomi, *A Factious People* (1971), 229-78; West Florida secretaryship: Cecil Johnson, *British West Florida, 1763-1783* (1943), 22, 130, 213-14, 227-28; Indian negotiations: *Pubs. of the Miss. Hist. Soc.*, 5 (1925), 108, 134-35; "banks of Miss." quotation: Livingston to A. V. Fraser, Nov. 19, 1775, MS, NHi, as quoted in P. J. Gordon, "The Livingstons of N.Y. 1675-1860: Kinship and Class" (Ph.D. Dissert., Columbia U., 1959), 230 (see also 219, 243); Chester quotation: *Louisiana Hist. Quart.*, 22 (1939), 31-32; purchases of Loyalist lands: *NYGBR*, 60 (1929), 165; A. C. Flick, *Loyalism in N.Y. during the Am. Rev.* (1901), 230, 239; H. B. Yoshpe, *Disposition of Loyalist Estates in the Southern District of N.Y.* (1939), 29n, 32, 58; 1788 property: F. McDonald, *We the People* (1958), 302; constit. convention: J. Elliot, *Debates on the Fed. Constit.* (1901), II, 207, 412-13; Senate, banking, and business activities: H. W. Domett, *A Hist. of the Bank of N.Y.* (3rd ed., n.d.), 31, 33-34, 138; J. S. Davis, *Essays in the Earlier History of Am. Corporations* (1917), 371, 392-95; marriage and children: *NYGBR*, 12 (1881), 140, 13, 15; "no orator" quotation: *NJHS Col.*, 2 (1847), 67n.; "rough, rapid," quotation: E. W. Spaulding, *N.Y. in the Critical Period* (1932), 246.

MSS: NHi

Philip Philip Livingston

PHILIP PHILIP LIVINGSTON, A.B., merchant, was born on May 1, 1741, in Albany, New York, the eldest son of Philip Livingston, a merchant and philanthropist, and his wife, Christina Ten Broeck. He entered the College, where he studied French as well as the more traditional sub-jects, on September 26, 1754.

Within a few years after graduation Livingston moved to Jamaica in the West Indies, where his family owned property. There were many Livingstons in Jamaica during the 1760s, and as his older rela-tives died young Philip inherited portions of their estates and added them to his own. On June 29, 1768, he married Sarah Johnson, the daughter of a British merchant, in the Half-Way-Tree Church in St. Andrew's Parish, Jamaica. Late in that year he also entered politics.

Philip Philip Livingston, A.B. 1758

Livingston was a member of the Jamaica House of Assembly, rep-resenting Portland Parish, in 1768, 1770, and 1776–1781. As such he participated in the intense political struggle between the lower house and the royal governors of the island. The assembly was generally op-posed to British colonial policies that not only limited its own privi-leges and imposed taxes on Jamaicans but also restricted the crucial trade between the West Indies and the northern colonies. Although the assembly successfully refused to meet the financial demands of the Board of Trade and managed to limit the power of the governor, it never pursued its radicalism to the point of rebellion. Livingston therefore remained a British subject until the end of the Revolution, even though his father was one of the Signers of the Declaration of Independence.

Philip Philip and Sarah Livingston had ten children. Most of them were born in Jamaica, but the fourth was born in New York in 1774 while the family was visiting the province. By 1785 Livingston re-moved to his home state for good, and it was there that his last child was born. Livingston died on November 2, 1787, less than three months before his youngest daughter was baptized in the Dutch Reformed Church in New York City. In his will he directed that part of his Jamaican property was to be sold in order to provide seven of his surviving children with £4,000 each. The bulk of his estate was left to his eldest son.

SOURCES: Vital data: E. B. Livingston, *Livingstons of Livingston Manor* (1910), 224, 551, 560-61; CNJ: Aaron Burr, MS Account Book, 110; family property in Jamaica: R. Pares, *Yankees and Creoles* (1956), 3; other Livingstons in Jamaica: *N.Y. Post-Boy*, Aug. 6, 1771; and *N.Y. Wills*, VI, 423, VIII, 180; marriage: F. Cundall, *Historic Jamaica* (1915), 206; membership in assembly: Philip Livingston File, PUA; politics in Jamaica: G. Metcalf, *Royal Government and Political Conflict in Jamaica* (1965), 167-221; and G. W. Bridges, *Annals of Jamaica* (1828), II, 158-59; presence in New York in 1785: *NYGBR*, 90 (1959), 115; last child's baptism: *NYGBR*, 30 (1899), 217; will: P. J. Gordon, "Livingstons of N.Y., 1675-1860 " (Ph.D. Diss., Columbia U., 1959), 229.

RAH

John Milner

JOHN MILNER, A.B., Anglican clergyman, was born in Westchester County, New York, in 1738, the son of Nathaniel Milner. John entered the College's grammar school on October 7, 1753. There he bought and studied a spelling book and a copy of Ovid's *Metamorphoses* before moving on to the College. After graduation Milner traveled to England to study for the priesthood. He was ordained by the bishop of London on February 25, 1761, and named as a missionary for the Society for the Propagation of the Gospel to the province of New York.

After a stormy voyage that took three months, Milner landed in New York City on May 13, 1761. On June 12 he was installed as rector of St. Peter's Church in Westchester. His parish also included Eastchester, Yonkers, and Pelham. His vestry bought him a glebe of 200 acres, on which a house was to be built. In June 1762, Milner wrote to the S.P.G. in London that he had baptized 114 persons and doubled the number of his congregation to forty communicants. Over the next three years Milner's congregation continued to increase. He had difficulty building a parsonage and outbuildings, which he estimated would cost at least £300, but said that the parish had promised to reimburse him. He was wrong. He put £200 of his own money in the buildings but the vestry was slow in repaying him. On September 10, 1765, he resigned his rectorship. "I leave the churches that I found decaying, flourishing," he reported to London. "I should never desire to leave them if I thought I could be of any further service to them, but alas I fear not. My character has been traduced in such a manner that I can only vindicate it among the few friends that know me best. I hope God who Knows all things will deliver me from all my enemies."

The exact circumstances surrounding Milner's resignation are not clear. Milner claimed that an "enemy" had made "it impossible for me in any court of justice [to] obtain the satisfaction that my injuries required." Concerning the affair, the Reverend Myles Cooper, president of King's College, simply reported to the S.P.G. that "there are in all Countries persons enough to be found, who are glad to give disagreeable Intelligence on any subject."

Milner soon found a new post. In February 1766, he became rector of Newport parish in Isle of Wight County, Virginia. There, he wrote the S.P.G., "the Church is established in reality, and some certain provision made for the clergy." The "provision" was, in fact, uncertain: Milner was paid in tobacco, the value of which fluctuated with the market. Whatever his finances, Milner managed to accumulate a considerable library, consisting of many volumes of sermons, theology, poetry, history, reference works and periodicals. But Milner's Virginia ministry proceeded no more smoothly than had his New York one. The vestry of Milner's church, a successor to his post reported, "forced Him to resign July 1770, to escape trial on charges of immoral conduct." The "immoralities" were not specified. Milner probably died some time between his resignation and April 23, 1772, when a Newport merchant advertised for the return of books from Milner's library, which had been stored in a neighbor's cellar.

SOURCES: Final dismissal and other information: John Milner File, PUA; school and college expenses: Aaron Burr, MS Account Book, 86-87; Westchester pastorate: R. Bolton, *Hist. of the Several Towns, Manors, and Patents . . . of Westchester* (1881), II, 365-67; quotations from S.P.G. correspondence: Records of the S.P.G. Letter Series B, vol. 3 (1701-86), numbers 280, 281, 283, 284, 285, 287, 291, 371 (microfilm, NjP); Virginia pastorate: W. Meade, *Old Churches, Ministers, and Families of Virginia* (1900), I, 304, and "Isle of Wight Records," *WMQ* (1 ser.), 17 (1899), 210; library: *Va. Gaz.* (Purdie and Dixon), April 23, 1772, 2.

Isaac Ogden

ISAAC OGDEN, A.B. King's 1758, lawyer and public official, younger brother of Josiah (A.B. 1756), was born in Newark, New Jersey, on January 23, 1741, the son of Gertrude Gouverneur and her husband, David Ogden (Yale 1728), one of the province's foremost lawyers and an Anglican. Isaac entered the College along with his brother Josiah on September 26, 1753. In February and March 1757 a religious revival swept Nassau Hall. Isaac's father was so disturbed by the students' emotional upheavals that he withdrew Isaac from the College and his younger son, Abraham, from the grammar school. Isaac was shortly enrolled at King's College in New York City, which awarded him the A.B. in its first graduating class in 1758.

After commencement Ogden studied law, most likely with his father. He established a successful practice in Newark, practiced also in the admiralty court of New York, and served as clerk of New Jersey's highest court, of which his father was a justice. It was probably in the 1760s that Ogden married Mary Browne, a sister of Daniel Isaac Browne (A.B. 1753). The couple had three children before Mary's death on March 15, 1772. Ogden later married Sarah Hanson of Livingston Manor, sister of a British army officer. He had six children by his second marriage.

After the passage of the Boston Port Bill, Ogden, in June 1774, was one of the leaders in calling for a Newark meeting to consider American responses. At first Ogden seemed to be a violent Whig, who "harangued the mob in public places in order to keep up their spirits." Elected to the New Jersey Provincial Congress which met in May 1775, Ogden's position soon shifted. In August he resigned from the congress because of its inability to stop violent actions. By April 1777 Ogden was in jail, accused of high treason by the New Jersey state government. Alexander Hamilton wrote to Governor William Livingston that "Ogden in particular is one of the most barefaced, impudent fellows, that ever came under my observation. He openly acknowledged himself a subject of the King of Great Britain and flatly refused to give any satisfaction to some questions." The Ogden family, in fact, was badly split by the Revolution: Isaac, his father, and his younger brother Nicholas became extremely active Loyalists, while his two younger brothers, Abraham and Samuel, were Whigs.

The circumstances surrounding Ogden's release from jail have not been discovered, but by July 1779 he was behind the British lines in New York City. There he appears to have acted as an intelligence-gatherer, slipping into New Jersey from time to time to see other members of his family. When the British evacuated New York City in 1783 Ogden and his immediate family accompanied them to England. In England Ogden claimed £2,927 in losses before the Loyalist Claims Commission. He was allowed £660, and £240 per year for the loss of his professional income during the war. In 1788 Ogden was appointed a judge of the admiralty court of Quebec and moved there. It was not, at first, a comfortable post; in 1789 Ogden was accused by Canadians of furnishing "a recent distinguished visitor, Prince William Henry, with information false and injurious to their religion and clergy, and their laws." Under Lord Dorchester Ogden was appointed a puisne judge of the Court of King's Bench of Montreal, where he moved with his family. He served there until 1818, when because of a painful illness he went to England for a series of operations. He died at Taunton, Somerset, on September 10, 1824.

SOURCES: Brief sketches: Wheeler, *Ogden Family*, 101-102; J. Bloomer, "King's College Alumni, Class of 1758," *Columbia Univ. Quart.*, 9 (1907), 478-79; E. A. Jones, *Loyalists of N.J.* (1927), 161-63; father: Dexter, *Yale Biographies*, I, 373-75; attendance at CNJ: Aaron Burr, MS Account Book, 60, 145, 215; removal from CNJ: Esther Burr, MS Journal, entry for March 1, 1757; 1774 Newark meeting: *NJHSP* (2 ser.), 4 (1877), 190; treason and imprisonment: *Minutes of the Council of Safety of the State of New Jersey* (1872), I, 74; Hamilton letter: *Hamilton Papers*, I, 243; for N.Y. activities during Rev. see references scattered throughout: W.H.W. Sabine, ed., *Hist. Memoirs of William Smith, 1778-1783* (1971); "information false" quotation: H. M. Neatby, *Quebec, The Revolutionary Age* (1966), 262.

James Paterson

JAMES PATERSON, A.B., was listed as dead in the College's first catalogue, published in 1770. The only James Paterson discovered to have died at about that time was the James "Patterson" who died intestate in Freehold, Monmouth County, New Jersey in 1769, leaving a widow named Catherine and a brother named Peter.

SOURCES: Estate: 33 *NJA*, 321.

Ralph Pomeroy

RALPH POMEROY, A.B., A.M. Dartmouth 1786, lawyer, merchant, and public official, was born in Hebron, Connecticut, in 1737, the son of Benjamin Pomeroy (Yale 1733) and his wife Abigail Wheelock, a sister of Eleazar Wheelock (Yale 1733), the founder of Dartmouth College. The father, a Congregational clergyman extremely active in the Great Awakening, served as an army chaplain in the Seven Years War and was one of the founding trustees of Dartmouth. A contemporary described him as "an excellent scholar, an exemplary gentleman, and a most thundering preacher of the new-light order."

Ralph entered the College in the junior class on December 9, 1756. After graduation he taught for about a year at the Indian charity school run by his Uncle Eleazar at Lebanon, Connecticut. Late in 1759 Pomeroy decided to study for the ministry with Samuel Finley, future

Ralph Pomeroy, A.B. 1758
ATTRIBUTED TO WILLIAM JOHNSTON

president of the College, at West Nottingham, Maryland. "I arrived at Mr Finleys the 17th of Nov^m," Pomeroy reported to Wheelock, "was very agreeably surprised, to find my Jorneys end, at a small Logg-House, the only House in sight in the midst of a very pleasant Plantation, and that the school House of Nottingham, a seat so famous for Learning, was built with Loggs and Clay. –In Mr Finley I find all I could expect in a tender Father, a sincere freind [sic], and Faithful Instructor." Pomeroy remained with Finley until October 1760, when, short of funds and uncertain about his calling to the ministry, he moved to Princess Anne, Somerset County, Maryland, and opened a school. Finally deciding against a clerical career, he returned to Connecticut, where he appears to have established himself in business in Hartford by January 1764. He read law as well and was admitted to the bar in Hartford in 1768. Two years later, on January 31, 1770, Pomeroy married Eunice Belden, the widow of William Gardiner of Hartford. The couple do not seem to have had any children.

Pomeroy was involved in many activities. He handled a good deal of legal business for Dartmouth College. In 1773, when a group of

Connecticut officer veterans of the Seven Years War founded a "company of military adventurers" to exploit lands in West Florida, Pomeroy became clerk to the company and a member of its standing committee. Pomeroy, apparently restless, planned to leave Connecticut at about his time, writing thus to his uncle in January 1774: "I must take the Liberty to Mention to you my Intentions of leaving this Country as Soon as I can find a Place where my services can be usefull and necessary to myself and friends which I am fully convinced is not the Case at Present." But circumstances soon considerably expanded Pomeroy's opportunities to be useful. As the Revolution entered its military phase, he took an active part on the Whig side. As early as 1776 he was supplying American troops with stockings. On February 8, 1777, he became paymaster to Colonel Wyllys's Third Connecticut Regiment, and was appointed a second lieutenant on June 1, 1778. Eventually he rose to the rank of major. During the war his most important role was as deputy quartermaster general for Connecticut, a post that involved him in complicated procurement and supply activities. In 1783 he was appointed a justice of the peace for Hartford County, a post he held until 1798, and in 1784 was elected an alderman of the city. In 1789 he was appointed comptroller of public accounts for the state of Connecticut, succeeding Oliver Wolcott, Jr. In the late 1780s Pomeroy was involved with Jesse Root (A.B. 1756), Oliver Ellsworth (A.B. 1766), and others in starting a broadcloth manufacturing plant in Hartford. George Washington wore a suit made of the stuff at his first presidential inauguration.

In 1790 Pomeroy was living in Hartford in a large household of eleven people, which included two slaves. Outside of his business affairs and public offices Pomeroy's major interest appears to have been Freemasonry. He became a Mason as early as 1765, and was a Master from 1782 to 1789. When Connecticut's Grand Lodge was organized in 1789 Pomeroy was elected Grand Senior Warden of the organization. In 1792 Pomeroy joined with "The Nocturnal Society of the Stelligeri"— many of whom, such as Pierpont Edwards (A.B. 1768) and David Daggett (Yale 1783), were Freemasons—in an attempt to lessen clerical representation on the Yale corporation. Pomeroy died suddenly in Hebron, Connecticut, on March 19, 1819. A Connecticut newspaper described him as "an active and able officer in the army of the revolutionary war; and to the close of that eventful period, he was employed in various departments of trust, the duties of which he discharged with zeal and fidelity."

SOURCES: Father: Dexter, *Yale Biographies*, I, 485-88, and Sprague, *Annals*, I, 394-97; Pomeroy to Wheelock, Jan. 1, 1760, June 31, 1761, and Jan. 2, 1774, Wheelock MSS;

Indian school and establishment in Hartford: D. McClure and E. Parish, *Memoirs of the Rev. Eleazar Wheelock, D.D.* (1811), 208, 238; Hartford bar: J. H. Trumbull, *Memorial Hist. of Hartford County* (1886), I, 122; marriage: *NEHGR*, 37 (1883), 35; West Florida venture: *Va. Gaz.* (Rind's), Dec. 16, 1773; also C. Johnson, *British West Florida* (1943); Pomeroy's public career has been reconstructed from: *Rec. State Conn.*, I-VIII, and C. W. Burpee, *Hist. of Hartford County* (1928), I, 219, 225; there are inconsequential references to Pomeroy's multifarious activities as quartermaster and as comptroller scattered throughout the published papers of Washington, Jefferson, Hamilton and others; 1790 household: *U.S. Census of 1790, Conn.*, 46; Freemasonry: J. H. Tasch, *Freemasonry in the Thirteen Colonies* (1929), 184-85, and J. R. Case, *Freemasonry in Conn.: XIII. Elective Officers 1783-1853*, offprint from *Proc.* of 1967 Grand Lodge of Connecticut, Ralph Pomeroy File, PUA; membership in Stelligeri: Stiles, *Literary Diary*, III, 451; death notice: *Conn. Courant*, Mar. 30, 1819.

Mss: NhD

John Shippen

JOHN SHIPPEN, A.B., M.D. Rheims, physician, was the son of Susannah Harrison and her husband William Shippen, a prominent Philadelphia physician who was closely associated with the College. "Jackey" was born in Philadelphia on March 20, 1741. At the age of ten he was enrolled by his father in the Academy of Philadelphia and on April 18, 1753, he entered the grammar school of the College of New Jersey. During his years at the grammar school he was an occasional boarder in the home of President Burr.

On September 26, 1755, Shippen entered the College. The College's religious revival of February 1757, which Esther Burr called "not a noisy distress but a deep concern, not a flight of fancy," affected Shippen profoundly. On a visit to Princeton his father was delighted to find young Jackey "under great concern for his soul."

After graduation Shippen returned to Philadelphia. Like his brother William, Jr. (A.B. 1754), he studied medicine under his father's supervision. He continued those studies during the 1760s at the University of Rheims, France, one of several European degree mills that attracted American medical students in the eighteenth century. After receiving his M.D. he returned to America at the end of the decade, a time when recent research on electricity was generating widespread popular interest in scientific lectures. Shippen made his contribution with an illustrated lecture on fossils that he gave in Philadelphia on April 5, 1770. In the summer of that year he went to Baltimore, Maryland, to set up a medical practice. Shortly thereafter he was stricken with a "bilious fever." He lingered for several days, but died on November 26, 1770.

SOURCES: Birth and baptism: *Pa. Geneal. Mag.*, 19 (1952-1954), 303; grammar school and CNJ: Aaron Burr, MS Account Book, 86, 87, 168; revival: Esther Burr, MS Journal, entry for Feb. 22, 1757; American medical students in Europe: W. J. Bell, "Philadelphia Medical Students in Europe, 1750-1800," *PMHB*, 67 (1943), 1-29; scientific lectures: *PMHB*, 1 (1877), 109 and R. P. Stearns, *Science in the British Colonies in America* (1970), 511; obituary: *Pa. Chronicle*, Dec. 3, 1770; short sketch: R. S. Klein, "The Shippen Family" (Ph.D. Diss., Rutgers U., 1971), 223-24.

RAH

Jasper Smith

JASPER SMITH, A.B., A.M. 1765, lawyer, was born at Maidenhead (now Lawrenceville), New Jersey, the son of Jasper Smith, a prosperous farmer, and his wife Kezia, whose maiden name was Smith. Young Jasper entered the College's grammar school on October 1, 1753. He bought a Greek history, a spelling book, an English grammar, and began the study of Cicero. He moved up to the College the following year. Many years later, in his will, which is in part an autobiography, Smith described his life thus: "Whereas my Father designing to give me a public Education died Sudenly in the year 1754 about the time I had entered College then at Newark he did not make any Will and I not being the Oldest Son none of his Real estate (by Law) fell to me but only a Dividend of his Moveable estate with which by the great prudent management of my most excellent Mother Aided by her Oldest Son I was Carried through the College then held at Princeton where I took my first degree in 1758 and then had to Study the Law five years According to the Rule of the Supreme Court before I could be admitted & Licensed to Practice tho by favour I was admitted a few Months Sooner."

After licensing in 1763 Smith was commissioned a surrogate of the prerogative court of New Jersey in that year, and moved to Flemington, New Jersey, where he began the practice of law. "On entering on this business (my patrimony expended) I used the utmost industry & diligence to obtain an estate by every honest exertion in this in a few Months I was engaged in as much business as I could attend to and might have had more if I could have attended more Courts[.] In a little more than two years being in business I Married a most excellent Woman [Eleanor (Ryerson) Gouverneur, a widow, on October 25, 1765] & had one Child by her which died in about three weeks of Age & my wife in about thirteen Months after our Marriage[.] Between one & two years after that I married another wife [Theodotia Reid, on November 27, 1767] by whom I have not had any children. She was a very weakly and infirm constitution & after a Number of years died since which I have married my present Wife [Anne Peck, on January 3, 1811] and as by the blessing of divine providence I have gathered an estate beyond what my friends & even myself expected considering the Losses I have met with and very little with either of my Wives, altho they were of very credible families and as I have now for Several years past Left off practising in Law business having a Sufficient estate to live on the income without Lessening the principal & unless some adverse fortune may happen to me perhaps my estate may remain of Nearly the Same Value as long as I may live."

About the only things that Smith forgot to include in his will were his service as a delegate from Hunterdon County to the Provincial Congress of New Jersey in May 1775 and his membership on the Amwell Committee of Safety in 1776. After his retirement, he returned to Maidenhead to live. In his will (his property was inventoried at $16,590.52 1/2) he disposed of his estate in an extraordinarily detailed fashion. He left bequests to his wife and many relatives, $400 to the College for the education of youths for the ministry, and his home farm to the Presbyterian church at Maidenhead. He died there on October 5, 1813, and was buried in the town's Upper Cemetery.

Sources: Sketch: L. D. Cook, "Jasper Smith, Esq., of Lawrenceville," *GMNJ*, 46 (1971), 31-32; will is in Hunterdon County Will Book #2, 320-27; xerox copy in Jasper Smith File, PUA, sections reprinted in 41 *NJA*, 344-45; also F. W. Gnichtel, "Jasper Smith's Peculiar Will," *NJHSP*, 53 (1937), 89-95; College accounts: Aaron Burr, MS Account Book, 90, 281; marriages: 22 *NJA*, 351; political action: J. P. Snell, *Hist. of Hunterdon and Somerset Counties* (1881), 204, which conflates the CNJ graduate with two other Jasper Smiths. *GMNJ* 46 (1971), 54-55.

Thomas Smith

Thomas Smith, A.B., A.M. 1763, Presbyterian clergyman, was born in 1737. He began his studies in Newark on May 21, 1753, probably in the College's grammar school. His parentage and place of birth are uncertain.

Smith matriculated in the College itself on March 26, 1755. After graduation he studied theology and was then licensed by the Suffolk Presbytery. In 1761 he transferred to the Presbytery of New Brunswick, which ordered him to supply at the Presbyterian church in Cranbury, New Jersey. He was ordained and installed there on October 19, 1762. Plagued by a chronic disease that sapped his strength, Smith tended to avoid the less essential duties of his office. He rarely attended meetings of the synod except when they were held in Cranbury. And he kept absolutely no records for his church. He was, recalled his successor, a pious man but at the "opposite point of exactness" in his bookkeeping. His contract at Cranbury called for him to preach occasionally at the nearby church in what was to become Dutch Neck, New Jersey. However, there is no indication that he upheld his part of that bargain.

Yet in his ministry Smith was respected and successful. From a typically parsimonious congregation he managed to extract agreement for an assessment on pews with which he financed the construction of a new church building. Completed in 1788, the structure cost £1,247. In the same year Smith nagged his congregation into increasing his salary from £60 to £100 annually. It took half a century for the congregation at Cranbury to give its minister another raise. Smith also managed to increase the membership of his church by fifty souls during his tenure.

On December 23, 1789, Smith was attending a prayer meeting at the home of a parishioner when he suddenly collapsed into his chair. Within two hours he was dead. He was buried in the churchyard at Cranbury. His wife and one daughter survived him.

SOURCES: J. G. Symmes, *Hist. Sketch of the First Pres. Church of Cranbury, N.J.* (1869), 11-15; CNJ: Aaron Burr, MS Account Book, 88, 131, 215, 283; ministry: *GMNJ*, 27 (1952), 49; Alexander, *Princeton*, 53-54; and *Rec. Pres. Church*; year of birth: tombstone, First Presbyterian Church, Cranbury, N.J.

RAH

Dirck Ten Broeck

DIRCK TEN BROECK, merchant and public official, was born in Albany, New York, and baptized in the Dutch Reformed church there on July 26, 1738. He was the twelfth and youngest child of Grietja (Margaret) Cuyler and Dirck Ten Broeck, a prominent merchant and fur-trader who served as a commissioner of Indian affairs and held many Albany public offices. Since young Dirck had at least three contemporary cousins of the same name, some prominent, his career is difficult to reconstruct. Dirck's father died in 1752, leaving the bulk of his considerable property to Dirck and his older brother, Abraham. Along with a cousin named Johannes, Dirck entered the College's grammar school on June 23, 1755. He matriculated in the College at some time between that date and March 26, 1756, "when," President Burr recorded in his Account Book, "he left College."

Back in Albany Dirck probably joined his brother in business. Throughout his life he was overshadowed—and probably assisted—by

Abraham (1734–1810), a leading Whig political figure who married a daughter of Stephen Van Rensselaer, the patroon. The career of neither brother was hurt by the fact that two of their older sisters married members of the wealthy and powerful Livingston family. On November 25, 1761, Dirck himself married Ann Douw, a cousin of Peter Winne Douw (A.B. 1758) and Thomas Hun (Class of 1757). Shortly thereafter Ten Broeck joined Albany's fire company, a group of the younger members of Albany's elite that provided the core membership of the city's Sons of Liberty in the 1760s. During the Revolution, Ten Broeck served as lieutenant colonel of Albany's First Regiment and took part in municipal affairs. Ten Broeck's most significant service during the Revolution was in his role as Continental loan officer for the state of New York, which involved him in constant activities to raise money for the war effort. Ten Broeck fell ill late in 1779, and in October of that year resigned his office. He died on May 29, 1780. In his will he left his property to his wife. He was not, apparently, survived by any children.

Sources: Family and vital data: *NYGBR*, 20 (1889), 128; father's will: *N.Y. Wills*, VII, 159-61; attendance at College: Aaron Burr, MS Account Book, 136-37; brother Abraham: *DAB*; fire company and Sons of Liberty: *WMQ*, 4 (1947), 490-91; militia and loan office: *Cal. of Historical Manuscripts* (Albany, 1868), I, 169, 323, II, 349; and, *Clinton Papers*, II, 289-90, 349, III, 73, 228, IV, 374, V, 173, 216; will: *N.Y. Wills*, IX, 198-99.

John Van Brugh Tennent

John Van Brugh Tennent, A.B., A.M. 1763, M.D. Leyden 1764, physician, was born in Freehold, New Jersey, in 1737, the oldest son of Catherine Van Brugh and William Tennent II, pastor of the Presbyterian church there, a trustee of the College from 1746 to 1777, and one of President Burr's closest confidants. John and his brother, William III, of this class were escorted to Newark by their father on December 10, 1754. They lived with the Burr family for a month before finding other quarters in Mrs. Collins's boardinghouse. Both boys appear to have spent a few months in the grammar school before being admitted to the College.

At some time after graduation, Tennent traveled to Britain to study medicine. In London by 1763, he attended the lectures of Dr. William Hunter, the great obstetrician, as did several other alumni of the College. In the winter of 1763–1764 Tennent traveled north to the University of Edinburgh, where he took Dr. William Cullen's course in chemistry. Later in 1764 he presented his dissertation at the University of

Leyden and was awarded the M.D. on June 21. He dedicated it to William Alexander ("Lord Stirling"), to President Samuel Finley, and to Dr. John Redman of Philadelphia (which suggests that he may have studied with Redman before leaving for Europe). The dissertation itself, *De Insitione variolorum*, concerned new methods of inoculation and claimed that in the American colonies only nineteen of the 8,000 persons inoculated to that time had died. (Tennent did not give details on the nineteen, the deaths of two of whom—Jonathan Edwards and Esther Edwards Burr—he may have witnessed himself while an undergraduate.)

Tennent returned to England and on February 23, 1765, was proposed as a Fellow of the Royal Society by, among others, the famous physicians Mark Akenside and John Fothergill. He was elected on June 20, 1765, the only alumnus of the College to become a Fellow during the colonial period.

On his return to America Tennent, along with James Smith (A.B. 1757), became in 1767 one of the founding members of the medical faculty of King's College in New York City, being appointed professor of midwifery. Tennent's promising career was cut short not long afterward when he fell ill, probably of tuberculosis. In an effort to recover his health he traveled to the West Indies. Once there he contracted yellow fever and died in 1770.

SOURCES: M. A. Tennent, *Light in Darkness, the Story of William Tennent, Sr.* (1971), 107-108; H. A. Kelly and W. L. Burrage, *Dic. of Am. Med. Biog.* (1928), 1193-94; arrival at College: Esther Burr, MS Journal, entry for December 10, 1754; college expenses: Aaron Burr, MS Account Book, 118-19, 156; study with Hunter: H. Speert, *Sloane Hospital Chronicle* (1963), 9; study in Edinburgh: *APS Proc.*, 94 (1950), 281; Leyden: E. Peacock, *Index to English Speaking Students . . . at Leyden University* (1883), 97; dissertation: M. Kraus, *Atlantic Civilization* (1949), 211; R. P. Stearns, "Colonial Fellows of the Royal Society of London, 1661-1788," *Notes and Records of the Royal Society of London*, 8 (1951), 224-25, confuses the CNJ alumnus with a Dr. John Tennent of Virginia (d. 1748), but corrects himself in his *Science in the British Colonies of America* (1970), 290n; founding of King's College medical faculty: B. Stookey, *Hist. of Colonial Medical Education* (1962), 47-52.

PUBLICATIONS: *De Insitione variolorum* (Leyden, 1764)

MSS: NNNAM

William Tennent, Jr.

WILLIAM TENNENT, JR. (III), A.B., A.M. 1761, Harvard 1763, Presbyterian clergyman, was born at Freehold, New Jersey, in 1740, the son of Catherine Van Brugh and William Tennent, Jr. (II), Presbyterian pastor there and a trustee of the College. Both William and his older

brother John Van Brugh of this class were delivered to the Burr household in Newark by their father on December 10, 1754. William appears to have spent some time in the grammar school before entering
the College.

After graduation Tennent studied theology and on July 29, 1761,
was licensed by the Presbytery of New Brunswick. The presbytery assigned Tennent six months' missionary work in the presbyteries of
Hanover and Lewes in the south, but he apparently never went. Instead, he was ordained in 1762 and preached as a supply at the English
Presbyterian church in New York City. There he met and soon wished
to marry Susanne Vergereau, daughter of a well-to-do family of Huguenot descent and a cousin of future trustee Elias Boudinot. Susanne's mother had certain doubts about Tennent's occupation and
prospects. "There are above fifty large vacant places," William reas-
sured Susanne, "who cry incessantly for supplies and are almost at
choice. The uncertainty of being *here* or *there* will depend much upon
the reception I meet with from you, or *rather I hope* from your dear
Mama." Mama consented and William and Susanne married. They had
five children, among them Charles (A.B. 1793).

Tennent finally settled at the First Congregational Church in Norwalk, Connecticut, where he was installed as assistant pastor to the
aged Moses Dickinson (Yale 1717) in November 1765. Tennent made
a provision concerning his status before accepting the Norwalk call
that caused his prospective parishioners some consternation. He insisted on retaining his membership in the New Brunswick Presbytery
while being in communion with the Congregational Consociation of
the Western District of Fairfield County. The Norwalk congregation
at first agreed—until it heard that the presbytery was setting the date
for Tennent's installation. Suspecting that they were about to be drawn
into the Presbyterian form of ecclesiastical organization, they objected.
Tennent was finally installed according to the Congregational system,
while retaining his connections with the presbytery.

Settled in Norwalk, Tennent quickly became an effective and extremely popular pastor and preacher. His reputation spread throughout New England, and beyond. On November 17, 1771, the Independent Church in Charleston, South Carolina, voted to call Tennent
there. The Norwalk church did not wish to release him. However, as
President Ezra Stiles of Yale described the situation on March 13, 1772,
"Mr. Tennant some way or other autocratically disengaged himself
from his pastoral Charge, in order to accept a more lucrative [£1,400
Carolina currency, about 1,000 Spanish guineas] and honorable One
in Carolina. On 29th Feb. last he with his Wife and Family sailed for

Charlestown . . . And now Mr. Tennant a Jersey Presbyterian . . . will probably presbyterianize this Church."

Tennent did not "presbyterianize" the Charleston church. However, he was extremely successful in his ministerial role. His influence soon extended throughout the city and province. "I find the non-episcopal Interest here egregiously neglected in this province," he was writing to Ezra Stiles by August 1774. "We have but three professedly congregational Churches, all now under my direction. I am building a second large house of Worship in this place which will easily be filled if I get a Colleague to my mind. The illiberality of the scotch presbytereans in this Country has bro't that Denomination into Contempt. I do not join them tho moderately presbyterean in sentiment. The Episcopalians here are highly enraged at your tory Clergy who are desirous of espiscopal principalities, and many of the first in the province do declare to me that they will turn Dissenters in a Body if the Parliament offers to send Bishops over. The Spirit of constitutional Freedom runs too high here to admit of any Check at present."

In the same year Tennent preached a powerful jeremiad to his congregation that touched on current controversies. "The Question facing Americans," he told his parishioners, "is of no less Magnitude than whether we shall continue to enjoy the Privileges of Men and *Britons*, or whether we shall be reduced to a State of the most abject Slavery." The sermon was printed in Philadelphia and, apparently, widely circulated. At the same time Tennent was writing anonymous letters to Charleston's newspaper urging that women respond to the Boston Port Act by not drinking tea, that "East-India poison."

In January 1775, Tennent was elected from Charleston to South Carolina's first provincial congress. He and Colonel William Henry Drayton were shortly appointed to make a tour of the back country with the object of combating Loyalist sentiment and raising support for the Whig cause. Tennent and Drayton left on August 2, 1775. For several weeks Tennent harangued, threatened, inspired and organized the back-countrymen, sending to Charleston letters warning of the "hellish plots" of Tories to organize the Indians to massacre the whites.

Elected to the second Provincial Congress, Tennent served on several important committees, including those concerned with the manufacture of saltpeter and gunpowder. He even attempted—unsuccessfully—to make the latter himself. Elected to the South Carolina Assembly in September 1776, Tennent took up a new cause—the disestablishment of the Anglican church. As the spokesman for all organized Dissenters in the province, on January 11, 1777, Tennent delivered a powerful speech in favor of religious equality to the Assembly. "Let us all have equal privileges or nothing," he cried. "EQUALITY OR NOTHING! ought to be our motto. In short, every plan of establishment must operate as a plan of injustice and oppression; and therefore, Sir, I am utterly against all establishments in this State." When a new constitution for South Carolina was written in 1778, the Anglican church was disestablished (and clergymen were barred from sitting in the assembly). But Tennent was not there to taste his victory.

On March 8, 1777, Tennent's father died in New Jersey. In April William traveled north to settle his estate. He collected his mother, his sister, and his father's belongings and in August set out for South Carolina. He never reached Charleston, but died in the High Hills of Santee. His death came as a severe shock not only to his parishioners but to many other Carolinians as well.

SOURCES: Clifford Shipton's sketch, in *Sibley's Harvard Graduates*, XIV, 338-45, is excellent, but can be supplemented by Sprague, *Annals*, III, 242-45, and by G. N. Edwards, *Hist. of the Independent or Congregational Church of Charleston, S.C.* (1947), 30-51, and by W. M. Dabney and M. Dargan, *William Henry Drayton and the Am. Rev.* (1962), 93-106; arrival at College: Esther Burr, MS Journal, entry for December 10, 1754; college expenses: Aaron Burr, MS Account Book, 118-19, 156; licensing and failure to make missionary trip: Webster, MS Brief Sketches, Book I, PPPrHi; letter to Susanne: *SCHM*, 61 (1960), 134; Stiles on Norwalk post: Stiles, *Literary Diary*, I, 218; 1774 letter to Stiles: Stiles, *Itineraries*, 576; slavery quotation: Tennent, *An Address, Occasioned by the Late Invasion of the Liberties of the American Colonies by the British Parliament* (1774), 6; important discussion of religious equality speech: W. G. McLoughlin, "Role of Religion in the Am. Rev.," in S. G. Kurtz and J. H. Hutson, eds., *Essays on the Am. Rev.* (1973), 216-17; father's will: 34 *NJA*, 519; among public notices of death, see esp.: "On the Death of the Rev. Mr. Tennent," *S.C. & Am. General Gaz.*, Sept. 5, 1777; among eulogies see esp.: H. Alison (A.B. 1762), *The Faithful Servant of Christ Honored* (1777); will: C. T. Moore, comp., *Abstracts of the Wills of the State of S.C., 1760-1784* (1969), 263.

PUBLICATIONS: STE, and also: N. B. Jones, ed., "Writings of the Reverend William Tennent, 1740-1777," *SCHM*, 61 (1960), 129-45, 189-209, which prints a considerable amount of MS material; also "Fragments of a Journal . . . Describing his Journey, in 1775, to Upper South Carolina," in R. W. Gibbs, *Documentary Hist. of the Am. Rev. . . . in S.C.* (1855-57), I, 225-39; speech on disestablishment was reprinted as an appendix to: D. Ramsay, *Hist. of the Independent or Congregational Church in Charleston, S.C.* (1815).

MSS: PHi

Joseph Tichenor

JOSEPH TICHENOR, A.B., probably was a farmer. The family was widespread in northern New Jersey in the eighteenth century and the name Joseph was popular in every generation. (Four different men of the name served as New Jersey privates in the American forces during the Revolution.) Among several possibilities, it seems likely that the College's alumnus was the son of Elizabeth and Joseph Tichenor of Morristown, Morris County, New Jersey. The father, a shoemaker, died in 1750, leaving young Joseph fifty-six acres of land. Joseph and a brother and a sister, over fourteen years of age but still minors, chose Thomas Woodruff of Elizabethtown as their guardian. Woodruff himself died in 1754.

On June 10, 1754, Tichenor entered the College's grammar school, matriculating in the College in January 1755. In college Tichenor bought the usual books and fell ill for a time, for President Burr credited him with 5s.6d. for missing French lessons because of sickness. Tichenor must have been quite poor, for in January 1757 President Burr himself paid Tichenor's bills.

No further certain record of the College's alumnus has been discovered. However, since all the various men named Joseph Tichenor located were farmers, it seems likely that the graduate was among them. Tichenor was listed as living in all the College's catalogues published through 1827, which may simply mean that news of his death was a long time reaching Princeton.

SOURCES: Possible father's will: 30 *NJA*, 482 (also MS, N.J. State Lib., Trenton); guardian: 32 *NJA*, 325; attendance at CNJ: Aaron Burr, MS Account Book, 104-105, 281.

Jeremiah Van Rensselaer

JEREMIAH VAN RENSSELAER, A.B., was born on August 27, 1738, at Fort Crailo, Greenbush, the eastern manor of Rensselaerwyck, traditionally a home of the cadet branch of the family, in Albany County, New York. Jeremiah's mother was Engeltie Livingston (not of the main branch of the Livingston family); his father, Johannes, was a wealthy landowner. Jeremiah was their first child. He entered the College's grammar school on June 4, 1754. The records of his expenses in Newark and later in Princeton are confused with those of two or three other Van Rensselaers (among them Stephen, the future patroon) who were attending the grammar school in these years. However, it is clear that Jeremiah laid out the sum of £3 for a ten-volume set of "the best edition of Livy" on June 15, 1757.

After graduation Jeremiah probably moved back to his father's estate. Van Rensselaer received a license to marry Judith Bayard, a sister of Nicholas Bayard (A.B. 1757), on July 3, 1760. The couple had only one surviving child, John Jeremiah. In 1764, on a visit to Charleston, South Carolina Van Rensselaer contracted yellow fever and died

Jeremiah Van Rensselaer, A.B. 1758

shortly thereafter. He had made no will. His father, who died in 1783, made careful provisions in his will to protect the estate of young John Jeremiah.

SOURCES: Princeton's General Catalogue of 1906, the most authoritative listing of the University's alumni, unaccountably assigns to Van Rensselaer the career of a distant cousin, also named Jeremiah (1740-1810). However, the College's first catalogue, published in 1770, lists him as deceased, as does the catalogue of 1773. Genealogy: J. B. Holgate, *American Genealogy* (1848), 44; full account of Fort Crailo: H. D. Eberlein, *Manors and Historic Homes of the Hudson Valley* (1924); mother: E. B. Livingston, *The Livingstons of Livingston Manor* (1910), 562; birthdate: *Munsell's Col. on the Hist. of Albany* (1867), II, 425; attendance at CNJ: Aaron Burr, MS Account Book, 102-103; marriage license: *New York Marriages*, 425; intestate: *N.Y. Wills*, VIII, 371; father's will: *N.Y. Wills*, XII, 87-90; place and year of death: courtesy of Cornelia Van Rensselaer Strong.

William Whitwell

WILLIAM WHITWELL, A.B., A.M. 1762, Harvard, 1762, Congregational clergyman, was born in Boston, Massachusetts on December 27, 1737,

William Whitwell, A.B. 1758

the son of Rebecca Keen and William Whitwell, a whalebone cutter
and a deacon of Boston's Old South Church. Young William entered
Harvard College when he was sixteen and a half. He did well in Cambridge until the winter of his junior year. Then, the Harvard faculty
"Voted, That notwithstanding Whitwell's Excuse which he pleads, for
not reciting, and attending, Morning, Viz. The Testimony of his Dr.
(John Perkins of Boston) that he can't bear the Morning Air &c yet he
shall not be excus'd from the above parts of his Duty, nor from reciting
the Greek, tho' he pleads his Eyes cannot bear it."

Whitwell gave up his room at Harvard on March 9, 1757, and
headed south for the more salubrious air of Princeton, where he entered the College of New Jersey's junior class on April 8. Whitwell's
only purchase while at the College appears to have been a rather expensive wig (perhaps meant to protect his head from the morning air),
which he bought from one Plum and paid for in installments.

After graduation Whitwell returned to Boston, joined the Old South
Church, and began preaching in various Massachusetts pulpits, among
them Marblehead. The people there liked him and asked their minis-

ter, Thomas Barnard (Harvard 1700), to investigate. Barnard reported that Whitwell was "a serious, good man, of good learning, and of sound principles." On January 17, 1762, the church at Marblehead called Whitwell to be assistant pastor to Barnard. Whitwell accepted, and was ordained and installed on August 25 at a salary of £104 legal tender during Barnard's lifetime and £100 sterling thereafter.

On September 6, 1762, shortly after his ordination, Whitwell married Prudence Hancock of Tisbury. The couple had four children. Their daughter Elizabeth married Ebenezer Pemberton (A.B. 1765) and their son William married a daughter of Isaac Story (A.B. 1768). Prudence died in Marblehead in February 1773. On June 17th of that year Whitwell married Mrs. Rebecca Parker of Sandwich, with whom he had two more children.

Whitwell was a successful pastor in Marblehead and widely respected in his area. "That most amiable of men," William Bentley, the Unitarian minister at Salem, called him. Whitwell and his congregation were fervent Whigs. When Marblehead held a meeting to denounce the tax on tea on December 7, 1773, Whitwell opened it with a prayer. When the town held a meeting to form a Committee of Correspondence on May 23, 1774, he closed it with prayer. When Marblehead formed an artillery company in May 1775, Whitwell sent it off to war with a sermon and returned home to begin the manufacture of saltpeter.

Marblehead was hard hit by the war. But by 1781 things were beginning to return to normal. Whitwell was busy in the affairs of the town (he was elected to the school board in March) and of his church when he died suddenly on November 8.

SOURCES: Shipton's sketch, in *Sibley's Harvard Graduates*, XIV, 367-69, is accurate except for Whitwell's children, for whom see: *Vital Records of Marblehead, Mass.* (1903), II, 548; CNJ expenses: Aaron Burr, MS Account Book, 268-69.
457;
PUBLICATIONS: see STE

Mss: MHi, PHi

Jesse Williams

JESSE WILLIAMS, A.B., physician and public official, was born in Mansfield, Connecticut, on June 26, 1737, the son of Captain William Williams and his wife Experience, who had migrated from Northampton, Massachusetts. Jesse received his preparatory education at the Reverend Eleazar Wheelock's school in Lebanon, Connecticut. He entered the College on September 26, 1754. After graduation Williams studied medicine and then returned to Mansfield, where he succeeded to the practice of Dr. Jonathan Fuller. On April 11, 1771, Williams married Mary Storrs. The couple had eight children.

In 1770 Williams became a justice of the peace for Windham County. The Revolution brought little change to Williams's life. He was again appointed a justice of the peace for Windham County at the war's end in 1783 and held the post until 1799. He also served as Mansfield's representative in the Connecticut Assembly in 1780–1781, 1788–1793, and for the last time in 1798. His only remotely notable action came in 1792, when he acted as Mansfield's agent in petitioning the legislature to allow the town to conduct a lottery in order to raise £300 to build a bridge.

About 1800 Williams began a quiet campaign to overcome local opposition to smallpox inoculation. He ran a smallpox hospital where he inoculated thirty persons successfully, which swung local opinion in favor of the practice. Highly respected in the area, Williams died in Mansfield on December 4, 1815.

SOURCES: Parentage and date of birth: H. Bond, *Genealogies of the Families and Descendants of the Early Settlers of Watertown* (1855), 655; sketch: J. R. Cole, *Hist. of Tolland County, Conn.* (1888), 187-88; College: Aaron Burr, MS Account Book, 114-15; public career: *Rec. State Conn.*, III, IX.

CLASS OF 1759

James Anderson, A.B.

James Caldwell, A.B.

Jabez Campfield, A.B.

John Carmichael, A.B.

John Clark, A.B.

James Hunt, A.B.

John Huntington, A.B.

Philip Johnston

James Lesley, A.B.

Walter Livingston

James Lyon, A.B.

Samuel Nivins, A.B.

Ebenezer Noyes, A.B.

Joshua Noyes, A.B.

Nathaniel Noyes, A.B.

Thomas Pierce, A.B.

Thomas Reynolds, A.B.

Henry Sherburne, A.B.

Samuel Spencer, A.B.

Jacob Van Buskirk

Barnet Wait, A.B.

James Anderson

JAMES ANDERSON, A.B., Presbyterian clergyman, was born about 1739. He may have come from Chester County, Pennsylvania, but the name was so common in the eighteenth century that it is impossible to distinguish the College's James from scores of contemporaries of the same name. Anderson entered the College's junior class in November 1756. He should have graduated in September 1758, but for reasons now unknown his graduation was delayed until September 1759. At some time during the following years Anderson studied for the ministry and was licensed by the Second Presbytery of Philadelphia in 1766. Shortly thereafter the presbytery sent Anderson to do missionary work near present Pittsburgh. He served as a supply preacher at several churches on the frontier over the next few years, among them the church of John Brown (A.B. 1749) in Rockbridge County, Virginia. In 1770 Anderson settled at a church of his own when he was installed as first permanent pastor of the Presbyterian church at Middletown, Delaware County, Pennsylvania. He may have been the James Anderson who married a Margaret Francis of Chester County on July 29, 1774. In 1780 Anderson was taxed for 120 acres, three horses, three cattle, and one servant. He attended his last presbytery meeting in 1789 and died on September 22, 1795. The following inscription was placed on his tombstone:

> Modest thro' life, an humble path he trod,
> And passed his days in service of his God;
> To guilty men he preached redeeming grace,
> Till death's unsparing scythe cut short his race;
> Called by his glorious Master to the skies,
> He now enjoys, we hope, the immortal prize.

SOURCES: Possibility of Chester County origin: Anderson File, PUA; attendance at College: Aaron Burr, MS Account Book, 230-31; licensing and missionary work: Webster, MS Brief Sketches; pastorate and epitaph: W. T. Kruse, "Curious Records of an Old Church," *Proc. of the Delaware County Historial Society*, 2 (1902), 15; possible marriage: *Pa. Arch.* (2 ser.), 2 (1876), 17; taxes, *Pa. Arch.* (3 ser.), 12 (1897), 290.

James Caldwell

JAMES CALDWELL, A.B., A.M. 1762, Presbyterian clergyman and Army chaplain and quartermaster, was born on April 17, 1734, at Cub Creek, Charlotte County, Virginia, the son of John Caldwell and his wife

Margaret Phillips, immigrants from County Antrim, Ireland. The Caldwells left Ireland about 1727, settling first in Lancaster County, Pennsylvania, before moving to Virginia, where they farmed, early in 1730. In James's youth the College's future president Samuel Davies was active in the area, and the Caldwells doubtless came under his influence. The pastor of James's church at the time he entered College was Robert Henry (A.B. 1751); he was prepared for College at the school run by the Reverend John Todd (A.B. 1749) in Louisa County.

Caldwell studied theology with President Davies after graduation. He was licensed by the Presbytery of New Brunswick on July 29, 1760, and ordained by the presbytery on the following September 17. The synod then ordered Caldwell to act as a supply preacher at various churches in the Carolinas. He had preached in the Presbyterian church in Elizabethtown, New Jersey, before his ordination. He impressed the congregation there, received a call to serve as its pastor, and accepted it. On his return from the Carolinas he was transferred from the Presbytery of New Brunswick to that of New York and installed at the Elizabethtown church in March 1762 at a salary of £160 per year. In March of the following year Caldwell married Hannah Ogden of Newark. The couple had ten children.

As pastor in Elizabethtown, Caldwell tried to move his congregation away from adherence to the Half-Way Covenant, which permitted the baptism of children of members not in full communion. It was perhaps this that led to the resignation of all but one of the church's Board of Trustees in December 1765. However, the retired trustees remained within the congregation, an extraordinarily distinguished one that included at one time or another future New Jersey Governor William Livingston, Francis Barber (A.B. 1767), and College trustee Elias Boudinot, who served as president of the church's new Board of Trustees.

In the 1760s Caldwell was in frequent communication with the Connecticut theologian Joseph Bellamy on church and theological matters, keeping Bellamy informed of efforts to make the theologian Samuel Hopkins a professor in the College. Caldwell's connections with the College were close throughout his life. In 1769 he accompanied President Witherspoon on a successful fund-raising tour to the south. On his return he was elected a trustee of the College. He became clerk of the Board of Trustees in 1772, serving until his death, and also acted as treasurer of the College from 1777 to 1779.

While Caldwell was on his tour of the south in 1769 a praying society was begun in the Elizabethtown church. Caldwell encouraged its efforts on his return. In 1771 fifty converts were added to the church, and in 1772, sixty. In fact, the church seems to have been in a continuous state of revival right up to the time of the Revolution. (By 1776 there were 345 pewholders or subscribers in the church.) Caldwell and his congregation were conspicuous Whigs—at least forty members of the congregation became commissioned officers in the American forces during the Revolution.

In May 1776, Caldwell, as chaplain, accompanied Colonel Elias Dayton's brigade—composed mainly of his parishioners—to relieve the American forces in the north. Caldwell returned home early in the fall but was soon forced to flee with his family before the British, who were advancing across New Jersey. The Caldwells took refuge in the Jersey mountains near New Providence. There Caldwell kept General Washington and other officers constantly informed about British troop movements in the region. He also began raising supplies for the American forces. He was appointed assistant commissary general early in 1777, a post in which he served until his death. He retained the pastorship of his Elizabethtown congregation, preaching when he could.

In 1778 Caldwell moved to Springfield, New Jersey, and in 1780 to Connecticut Farms (now Union), where his family was installed in the parsonage of the Reverend Benjamin Hait (A.B. 1754), who had died a few months before. In June 1780, British troops sacked the town, and in the melee Hannah Caldwell was shot to death by a British soldier as she stood at a window of her home. Chosen a member of the New Jersey Council in the fall of the following year, Caldwell continued his various duties until November 24, 1781. On that day he went to Elizabethtown Point to meet a young lady, Beulah Murray, who was traveling from New York by boat. In a now obscure altercation with a possibly drunken American sentry concerning a package he was carrying, Caldwell was shot and killed. The soldier was tried and executed for murder.

Both Hannah and James Caldwell were transformed into secular martyrs to the American Revolution and symbols of American nationality in the decades after their deaths. Popular woodcuts depicting Hannah's death were printed as late as the middle of the nineteenth century. Monuments were erected to James and he was the subject of innumerable poems, which have continued to be written almost to this day. The most frequently repeated—and unverifiable—anecdote about Caldwell concerns his actions on June 23, 1780, during an action at Springfield, New Jersey. Retreating before the British, the American troops ran out of paper with which to ram powder and balls into their muskets. Caldwell, so the story goes, jumped on his horse, rode to the village church, filled his arms with Isaac Watts's hymn books, and rode back to the troops exclaiming, "Now put Watts into them, boys!"

Caldwell's estate was inventoried at £970. Of his nine surviving children, one, John Edwards Caldwell, was taken to France by Lafayette and educated at the marquis's expense. Another, Elias Boudinot Caldwell, was adopted by the man he was named for and graduated from the College in 1796.

SOURCES: Many sketches of Caldwell, most emphasizing his revolutionary phase, exist: *DAB*; Sprague, *Annals*, III, 222-28; Hatfield, *Elizabeth*, 513-36; *JPHS*, 6 (1911-12), 260-66; W. H. Shaw, *Hist. of Essex and Hudson Counties, N.J.* (1884), I, 42-44, prints poem about Caldwell by Bret Harte; parentage: E. V. Gaines, *Cub Creek Church and Congregation* (1931), 9-13; Foote, *Sketches, Va.*, 102-05; Half-Way Covenant, etc.: Caldwell to Bellamy, April 10, 1766, and March 13, 1767, Webster/Bellamy Transcripts, PPPrHi; account of congregation by a contemporary, see 1774 anonymous letter printed in: N. Murray, *Notes, Historical and Biographical, concerning Elizabethtown* (1884), 143-49; role in Revolution: Force, *Am. Arch.* (5 ser.), III, 1095, 1167, 1189; also *NJHSP*, 60 (1942), 249-53; references to wartime activities scattered throughout: Washington, *Writings*, VI-XXVI; documents relating to Caldwell's death: J. F. Folsom, "Manuscript Light on Chaplain James Caldwell's Death," *NJHSP*, I (1916), 1-12; woodcut depicting Hannah's death: *NJHSP*, 71 (1953), 108; will: 35 *NJA*, 69; poems and accounts of memorials: James Caldwell File, PUA.

Mss: NjHi; NjP; PHi; CtHC; MdAn

Jabez Campfield

JABEZ CAMPFIELD, A.B., A.M. 1762, M.D. Queen's 1792, physician and public official, was born in Newark, New Jersey, on December 24, 1737, the son of Mehetabel Foster and Benjamin Camfield (Jabez later added a "p" to the name), a farmer and tax assessor in Newark. The father died the following year, leaving his sword and land to infant Jabez. Some time later Jabez's mother married Dr. William Hunter of Newark. When Hunter died in 1754 Jabez, although still a minor, was named one of the executors of his estate.

Campfield entered the College's grammar school on May 15, 1755. There he studied mathematics and Greek, Latin, and Hebrew grammar. He appears to have spent about a year and a half in the school before matriculating in the College in September 1756. After graduation Campfield studied medicine with Dr. William Burnet (A.B. 1749) in Newark. Education completed, Campfield began the practice of medicine in Morristown, New Jersey. He married Sarah Ward on April 28, 1765. The couple had one son, Dr. William Campfield (A.B. 1784).

On December 3, 1776, Campfield was appointed surgeon of Colonel Jacob Ford's New Jersey Regiment, and on January 1, 1777, became surgeon of Colonel Spencer's Additional Continental Regiment, serving with it until June, 1780, when he moved to Colonel Matthias Og-

den's Light Infantry Regiment. Early in 1781 he became surgeon of the
Second Continental Dragoons, serving under his old teacher, Dr. William Burnet. He remained with the unit until the end of the war.

Campfield accompanied Sheldon's regiment on General Sullivan's
1779 expedition against the Iroquois in western New York. The campaign severely undermined the structure of Iroquois civilization, and
Campfield kept a detailed journal of its progress. Watching the burning of one Indian village after another, he sometimes grew depressed.
"I very heartily wish these rusticks may be reduced to reason, by the
approach of this army," he wrote on August 12, 1779, "without their
suffering the extremes of war; there is something so cruel, in destroy-
ing the habitations of any people (however mean they may be, being
their all) that I might say the prospect hurts my feelings."

Mustered out of the army at Danbury, Connecticut, on June 15,
1783, Campfield returned to Morristown and resumed his medical
practice in a somewhat desultory fashion, He took on some medical
students, but as the years passed he devoted himself more and more
to civic pursuits, finally turning his practice over to his son in 1792.
Campfield's activities and interests ranged widely. He served as a surrogate for Morris County from 1784 to 1804. He was an early member
of the New Jersey branch of the Society of the Cincinnati. He was an
incorporator of the Medical Society of New Jersey. In 1791 he was one
of the founders and first president of the Morris Academy. In the same
year he founded the Morris County Society for the Promotion of Agriculture and Domestic Manufactures (later the Morristown Library).
He became its librarian in 1812.

In his later years Campfield fell into financial difficulties. Applying
for a government pension in 1818, he declared that "bodily infirmities
occasioned him to lay aside the practice of Physic as many as twenty
years ago, and from loosing its revenues and from misfortunes neither
feigned nor necessary to relate, this Deponent, who is in the eighty-
first year of his age, is now in reduced circumstances and desires and
needs assistance from his country for support." The pension was
granted. Campfield died in Morristown on May 20, 1821, and was
buried in the cemetery of the First Presbyterian Church there. "No
stone marks his grave," a nineteenth-century memorialist wrote. "He
was an infidel, and used to remark that he would as lief have his 'body
after death put out under one of the trees of his place, as buried at
all.' "

SOURCES: Parentage: F. A. Canfield, *Hist. of Thomas Canfield and of Matthew Camfield* (1897), 65-66; father's will: 30 *NJA*, 83; mother's remarriage: *NEHGR*, 12
(1858), 28; stepfather's will: 31 *NJA*, 330; grammar school and college: Aaron Burr,

MS Account Book, 98, 100-101; study with Burnet, *NJHSP* (3 ser.), 10 (1915), 113-14; Sullivan's expedition: "Diary of Dr. Jabez Campfield, Surgeon in 'Spencer's Regiment,'" *NJHSP* (2 ser.), 3 (1872-74), 115-36; Morris Academy and Library: *A Hist. of Morris County, N.J.* (1914), I, 230, 233; N.J. Medical Society: *Proc. N.J. Med. Soc.* (1875), 87-88; Cincinnati: *Society of the Cincinnati in the State of N.J.* (1898), 47, 66; pension: Jabez Campfield Application, August 17, 1818, Revolutionary War Pension and Bounty-Land Warrant Application File, National Archives, Washington, D.C.; infidel quotation: Wickes, *Hist. of Medicine N.J.*, 195.

John Carmichael

JOHN CARMICHAEL, A.B., A.M. 1762, Presbyterian clergyman, was born in Tarbert, Argyleshire, Scotland, on October 17, 1728. He was the oldest son of Donald Carmichael and his wife Elizabeth Alexander, who migrated to America in 1737. In the course of the journey young Carmichael almost drowned when he was washed overboard. His father established a home first in New York and then in Hackensack, New Jersey. Religious differences with the Dutch Reformed population there led to another move to Ward Session, New Jersey, on the outskirts of Newark. There the Carmichael family joined the congregation of Aaron Burr. On September 25, 1755, Carmichael entered the College. Part of his tuition was paid for by the Fund for Pious Youth.

Carmichael's interest in evangelism made him particularly hopeful that the appointment of Jonathan Edwards as president of the College would lift the "heavy gloom and nocturnal darkness" that had descended over Nassau Hall after the death of Burr. It was not Edwards, however, but his successor, Samuel Davies, who presided at the College at the commencement in September 1759. Even after his graduation Carmichael remained at Princeton to study theology under Davies's supervision. He was licensed by the Presbytery of New Brunswick on May 8, 1760. He then supplied at various pulpits, including the church at Forks of Brandywine (Brandywine Manor) in Chester County, Pennsylvania. The congregation there called him permanently in 1760, and on April 21, 1761, he was ordained at Brandywine by the Presbytery of New Castle. He lived on a farm in nearby East Caln.

Carmichael was a peripatetic minister who frequently assisted colleagues at other churches and traveled into the Pennsylvania wilderness as a missionary. He also led a vigorous campaign to raise the money for a new church building for his own congregation. By the late 1760s, however, his overriding interest was in resisting British rule in the colonies. He wrote articles for Pennsylvania newspapers in which he called for loyalty to the king but opposition to the policies of the government in London. He quickly gained a reputation as an ardent Whig. In June 1775 he preached to a company of the Chester County militia on the legality of a war for self-defense. The sermon was published and widely circulated. Later in that same year he visited Philadelphia to preach to the members of the first Continental Congress and to entreat them to take firm action. His text for one such sermon was "Trust in the Lord and do good."

His sermons at Brandywine were so persuasive that most of the men in his congregation joined the Continental army. He and a neighboring minister visited the Pennsylvania troops at the battle of Long Island, and he was a frequent visitor to Washington's distressed army at Valley Forge. He literally stripped his own household, and called on his congregation to do the same, in order to provide the army with supplies. General Washington personally thanked him for those efforts. Carmichael took special pains to transcribe an account by one of his parishioners of the life of an American prisoner of war in New York in 1776.

Carmichael's patriotism was so well-known that the English were said to have offered a bounty for his capture. His political beliefs cost him a large legacy from an uncle in Scotland and some property around Albany, New York, the title to which was stolen by a Tory lawyer. He did not suffer excessively, however. Between 1767 and 1781 Carmichael owned more than 200 acres of land in East Caln.

On May 8, 1761, Carmichael married Phebe Cram, a widowed daughter of Jonathan Dickinson, the College's first president. She died in 1772 after bearing him three children. Carmichael's second wife, Catherine Mustard, whom he married in 1773, died after the birth of their only child in 1774. On April 24, 1775, Carmichael married a third time. His last bride was Sally Blair of Fagg's Manor, Pennsylvania, the daughter of Reverend Samuel Blair, a trustee of the College. She bore him three more children.

In October 1785 Carmichael traveled to Pequea to assist in the opening ceremonies for a new church. Already ill, he was caught in a cold rainstorm as he returned home. He developed pneumonia. After carefully putting his affairs in order and warning his congregation that he would not be with them long, he died on November 15, 1785. He was buried in the upper graveyard in Brandywine. In his will he divided his land, which included his farm, 100 more acres in the area, and fourteen acres in Newark, among his family.

SOURCES: Sprague, *Annals*, III, 228-32; J. McClune, *Hist. of the Pres. Church in the Forks of Brandywine, Chester County, Pa.* (1885), 244-47; J. S. Futhey and G. Cope, *Hist. of Chester County, Pa.* (1881), 493-94; CNJ: Aaron Burr, MS Account Book, 158, 245; political and military activities: Butterfield, *Adams Papers*, II, 220; *NJHSP*, 78 (1960), 122; and *PMHB*, 28, 377; property: 11 (3 ser.) *Pa. Arch.*, 367, 587, 778 and 12 (3 ser.) *Pa. Arch.*, 61, 428, 567, 689.

PUBLICATIONS: see STE   RAH

John Clark

JOHN CLARK, A.B., Presbyterian clergyman, was born in 1718, probably in New Jersey. He was thus the oldest student in the College during his time there. He joined the Presbytery of New Brunswick on November 30, 1759. After licensing him on May 9, 1760, the presbytery sent him to supply the churches at Tehicken, Allenstown, and Mt. Bethel (Hunter's Settlement), Pennsylvania. In October 1760 both the Tehicken and Allenstown churches asked him to serve as their permanent minister. He considered the calls but did not accept either of them. On April 29, 1761, he was ordained as an evangelist in the church in Bethlehem, New Jersey, and was immediately sent to supply at Oxford, New Jersey, and then at Smithfield and the Forks of the Delaware, Pennsylvania.

On August 13, 1761, Clark was dismissed by the New Brunswick Presbytery so that he could accept a call from the congregation at the Forks of the Delaware. He was installed in the Settlement Church there by the Presbytery of Philadelphia on October 13, 1762. Unfortunately, he was not the unanimous choice of the congregation and by 1766 both the dissenters, who accused him of misrepresentation, and Clark himself were asking the presbytery to release him. The question was set aside for the moment but by late 1767 it could no longer be ignored. On November 4, Clark was dismissed on the excuse that his health was poor. He promptly moved to the jurisdiction of the Presbytery of New Castle where he supplied at various churches. One of them, the Bethel Church of Upper Node Forest in Baltimore County, Maryland, called him to its pulpit on December 27, 1769. He was installed there ten months later at a salary of £80.2.6 per year—a two shilling raise over his previous one. While in Maryland he also served the Centre Church near Bethel on the Pennsylvania border. During the years before the Revolution Clark was an active member of citizens' committees in Harford County, Maryland. He took the oath of fidelity to the United States on March 24, 1778.

Clark resigned from his full-time duties on April 25, 1775, once again claiming that his health was poor. But he remained in the area as a supply preacher for several years. In 1781 he visited western Pennsylvania where he preached at the East and West Peter's Creek churches in Allegheny County. He so impressed his listeners that they asked him to serve as their permanent minister. He accepted the call and was dismissed from the New Castle Presbytery on August 14, 1782. By March 1783 he was one of the five original members of the new Presbytery of Redstone. There he changed the names of his two churches to avoid confusion. He named them Lebanon and Bethel after his former parishes in the east. Ten years later, Clark joined the same band of pioneer ministers as one of the five members of the newly created Ohio Presbytery.

His advanced age and his habit of wearing a peruke made Clark a venerable figure. He quickly became known as "Father Clark" and "the Nestor of Redstone." His colleagues in the new presbytery were all Princeton alumni: John McMillan (A.B. 1773), Joseph Smith (A.B. 1764), James Power (A.B. 1766), and Thaddeus Dodd (A.B. 1773). Together they undertook to bring education to the frontier. Clark was one of the original trustees of the Washington Academy, established by McMillan in 1787. Clark and the others also took pious young men into their homes to tutor them.

In 1787 Clark led a religious revival that swept the Redstone district. Seven years later he was one of the few people in the area to speak against the Whiskey Rebellion. On June 14, 1794, when 500 armed men gathered at Couch's Fort near the Bethel church, Clark pleaded with them not to destroy the estate of the government agent General John Neville. In spite of his reputation he failed to dissuade the mob from one of the most sensational acts of violence of the entire insurrection.

Age and poor health made Clark give up his duties at the Lebanon church in 1788. He continued at Bethel until 1794. He and his wife Margaret had no children of their own but they adopted a young war orphan, William Jones, in 1779. When Clark died on July 13, 1797, his estate was divided between his wife and Jones. A lump sum of $1,600 from that estate was intended by Clark as a gift to the new Jefferson College in Washington County, Pennsylvania. It was duly passed on to the college when Margaret died in 1807. At her death the family's two black slaves, whose choir singing was famous throughout the area, were freed in accordance with the terms of her husband's will.

Sources: "Historical Narrative of the Bethel Presbyterian Church," MS c548.3, PPPr-Hi; Penn-Germania, I (1912), 639-40; W. F. Hamilton et al., Hist. of the Presbytery of Washington (1889), 396-97; D. R. Guthrie, John McMillan (1952), 104-107;

D. M. Bennett, *Life and Work of Reverend John McMillan* (1935), 294; J. C. Clyde, *Hist. of Allen Township Presbyterian Church* (1876), 156-57; *JPHS*, 10 (1919-1920), 76-77; and W. W. McKinney, *Early Pittsburgh Presbyterianism* (1938), 58-59; H.T.W. Coleman, *Banners in the Wilderness* (1956), 15, 23.

RAH

James Hunt

JAMES HUNT, A.B., A.M. 1763, Presbyterian clergyman and school-master, was born in 1731 in Hanover County, Virginia. His father, James Hunt, was apparently a prosperous farmer who was a very active elder in the Presbyterian church. The senior Hunt frequently attended meetings of the Hanover Presbytery with Samuel Davies, who was a major influence on young James's life. It was Davies's associate John Todd (A.B. 1749) who prepared the boy for college, and it was Davies himself who urged Hunt to go to New Jersey to complete his education. By the time Hunt graduated from the College, Davies was its president.

After graduation Hunt studied theology under the supervision of the Presbytery of New Brunswick, which licensed him in 1760 and ordained him in 1761. Among the churches he supplied after his ordination was one in the northern neck of Virginia. In April 1761 the congregation there tentatively called him to be its permanent minister, but a faction of the congregation soon had second thoughts. By August several respected members of the church decided that Hunt did "not seem fit" for their church. The young minister refused to accept the call unless it was unanimous, and so he withdrew his name from consideration.

In October 1761 Hunt obtained a dismission from the Presbytery of New Brunswick and was unanimously accepted into the Hanover Presbytery. He was appointed to supply at his own discretion. After a tour of churches in Lancaster and Northumberland Counties, Virginia, and in North Carolina he was called by the congregations in Rowan and Anson Counties, North Carolina. He declined both calls because he expected to move to Pennsylvania. In October 1764 he asked to be dismissed from the Hanover Presbytery. Instead of Pennsylvania, however, he moved to Maryland, where he first settled in Cecil County. There he was a neighbor and associate of the Reverend Samuel Finley of West Nottingham.

Hunt's inclination to teach was undoubtedly fostered by Davies's life-long interest in classical schools. Hunt established a secondary school on the Octorara Creek, only a few miles from Finley's academy. In 1766 Luther Martin (A.B. 1766) left Princeton in the hope of becoming Hunt's assistant at the school. The post was already filled, but Hunt saw to it that Martin found a suitable teaching position elsewhere.

By 1773 Hunt had moved to Bladensburgh, Maryland, where he was the senior pastor of the Presbyterian church and where he established another school. He removed the school to Montgomery County in 1783. While serving as the pastor of the Old Bethesda Church near Rockville he conducted classes on his extensive farm, "Tusculum." Some of the boys were boarded in their teacher's one-story rustic mansion. The Tusculum Academy flourished for a few years, and Hunt gained a widespread reputation as an excellent teacher. Among his favorite pupils was William Wirt, future prosecutor of Aaron Burr (A.B. 1772), three-term attorney general of the United States, and litterateur.

For a tuition of £6 per year (board was an additional £15), Hunt's students were instructed in Latin and Greek, arithmetic, geography, geometry, surveying, navigation, and other arts and sciences. The school's strongest attribute was Hunt's library, where the boys had free rein. It included a variety of books, from Smollett's *Peregrine Pickle*, to old English dramas, to Guy of Warwick, to Pope and Addison, to Horne's *Elements of Criticism*. The preceptor himself, in his customary suit of black velvet, would often read to the students from his personal favorites such as Flavius Josephus, the historian of the Jews. Hunt also possessed a pair of globes and a telescope, which he used to teach the rudiments of astronomy. And he delighted in entertaining and instructing his pupils and neighbors with his electrical machine. One of Hunt's special interests was rhetoric. He regularly marched his young wards four miles to the county courthouse to hear lawyers' arguments. The experience made a deep impression on the students, who established a moot court of their own at Tusculum. It was a turning point in the lives of Wirt and of Hunt's own son, William Pitt Hunt (A.B. 1786), both of whom made the law their careers.

While he lived in Cecil County Hunt had married Mrs. Ruth Hall, the widow of a local physician. She was at least four years older than her second husband. She had had six children during her first marriage, and she had two sons by Hunt.

Hunt's health may have been failing by 1785 when he made out his will. It included a special provision for the education of his younger son William. The Tusculum Academy, although it had become one of the most notable secondary schools in the middle states, was disbanded in 1787. Hunt died on June 2, 1793.

SOURCES: Giger, Memoirs, I; father's role in church: W. E. Rachal, ed., "Early Min-
utes of the Hanover Presbytery," VMHB, 63 (1955), 59; Davies and Northern Neck:
Foote, Sketches, Va., 221, 366; Hanover Presbytery: Rachal, above, 183, 185; Finley:
Butterfield, Rush Letters, 1193-94; school on the Octorara: P. A. Clarkson and R. S.
Jett, Luther Martin of Maryland (1970), 18-19; and MHM, 44 (1951), 51-52; Tus-
culum Academy: B. C. Steiner, Hist. of Education in Maryland (1894), 37; and J. P.
Kennedy, Memoirs of the Life of William Wirt (1849), I, 41-48; and W. Wirt, Let-
ters of a British Spy (1970 ed.), 19-28; and R. B. Farquhar, Historic Montgomery
County, Md. (1952), 34, 56, 204; and Christian Observer, June 14, 1893, 2; wife and
family: J. H. Pleasants, WMQ (1 ser.), 22 (1913-14), 135-39; reference to will:
James Hunt File, PUA.

                                                        RAH

John Huntington

JOHN HUNTINGTON, A.B., A.M. 1762, Harvard 1763, Presbyterian
clergyman, was born on August 1, 1736, in Norwich, Connecticut. He
was the eldest of the seven sons of Civil Tracy, first wife of the brewer
John Huntington. Young John entered the sophomore class of the College on September 26, 1755, as a charity fund scholar.

After graduation Huntington studied for the ministry. In 1761 he
went to Lebanon, Connecticut to teach at Eleazar Wheelock's Indian
Charity School. Among Huntington's acquaintances in Lebanon were
Samson Occom, the Mohegan minister, and Reverend Nathaniel Whitaker (A.B. 1752), a friend of Wheelock. While at the Indian School
Huntington was a visiting preacher at several churches, and even returned to Princeton to preach at the College. President Finley was favorably impressed by Huntington. "His preaching," Finley reported
to Wheelock in October 1762, "was very acceptable at College & not
less so in Philadelphia—for my Part I am highly pleased with him, &
have raised Expectations from him. Pray, endeavor to prevent his being buried in a Corner, among a handful of People, when he wou'd suit
a large & populous place." Huntington was not buried in a corner. On
May 23, 1763, one faction of the Congregational church in Salem,
Massachusetts, created itself the Third Church of Salem and unanimously called Huntington as its minister. Although he was a Presbyterian, he accepted the call and was ordained and installed in Salem
on September 23, 1763. His salary was set at £100 "lawful currency"
per year plus a £200 settlement allowance.

Huntington's immediate task in his new post was to try to bring
peace to a community that had been bitterly divided over theological
issues for several years. He successfully reduced tensions and won the
respect of all parties to the dispute. Huntington avoided a confronta-

tion with his own flock over the issue of ministerial authority and, by skirting that issue, persuaded his congregation that Presbyterianism was not as evil as they had feared.

Huntington's health deteriorated rapidly in Massachusetts. Long a victim of consumption, he decided to take a recuperative voyage in early 1766. It was no help. On May 29, 1766, only a few days after his return, he died in Salem. He had never married. The community's affection for him was demonstrated by the collection and publication of his sermons by a group of fellow clergymen. In a gesture of respect for him the Third Church accepted Presbyterianism. For their new preacher they called Huntington's former associate Nathaniel Whitaker, who had preached to them occasionally in 1765. But he was not as tactful as his predecessor. He demanded greater authority within the church and so managed to undo Huntington's peace-making. By 1784, when Whitaker was dismissed, Salem was once again embroiled in theological controversy.

SOURCES: *Sibley's Harvard Graduates*, XIV, 443-44; Alexander, *Princeton*, 59; family: M. E. Perkins, *Old Houses of the Ancient Town of Norwich* (1895), 182; and E. B. Huntington, *Geneal. Memoirs of the Huntington Family* (1863), 101-102; CNJ: Aaron Burr, MS Account Book, 129, 234; Indian School: J. D. McCallum, *Eleazar Wheelock* (1939), 64; Finley to Wheelock, Oct. 26, 1762, Wheelock MSS; Whitaker: L. B. Richardson, *An Indian Preacher in England* (1933), 80, 365; Salem: J. B. Felt, *Annals of Salem* (1849), II, 601-605, 619.

PUBLICATIONS: see STE   RAH

Philip Johnston

PHILIP JOHNSTON [JOHNSON], soldier, was born on August 27, 1741, in his father's house in Sidney, near Bethlehem, Hunterdon County, New Jersey. He was the son of Mary Casier, the second wife of Judge Samuel Johnston. As the chief magistrate of his district, Judge Johnston was one of the wealthiest and most prominent citizens of West Jersey. He owned an extensive tract of land, on which he built the area's largest and stateliest mansion. The house was surrounded by a wall for security against marauding Minisink Indians. In times of trouble with the Indians the Johnston home became a refuge for many of the family's neighbors. Judge Johnston conducted his weekly court sessions on Mondays in his own hallway and regularly hosted gatherings of colonial artists, writers, and wits. He was a generous contributor to charities, his favorite being the Bethlehem Presbyterian church.

Philip Johnston entered the College on November 26, 1755, and remained until April 1757. He then abandoned his studies to join the New Jersey militia in the French and Indian War. He was with Colonel Peter Schuyler's troops in the assault on Quebec and distinguished himself for bravery. At the end of the war Johnston went to Pennsylvania to assist his brother-in-law, Colonel Charles Stewart, the deputy surveyor of lands in that colony. By April 1767 he was back in New Jersey to marry Rachel Martin. She bore him three daughters, one of whom was the mother of John Scudder (A.B. 1811).

In June 1776, when the Continental Congress called upon New Jersey to supply 3,300 men to reinforce New York City, Johnston was instrumental in organizing the required forces. His popularity brought men from Hunterdon and Somerset counties into the ranks. As a lieutenant colonel, Johnston was second in command of Colonel Stephen Hunt's First New Jersey Regiment, which was attached to the commands of Generals Nathaniel Heard and Nathanael Greene. Hunt resigned because of disability on July 12, 1776, and on August 1 the New Jersey State Convention promoted Johnston to the colonelcy. His unit consisted of three companies from Somerset and five from Hunterton: a total of 22 officers and 269 enlisted men.

In August Heard's brigade was transferred to the command of Major General John Sullivan charged with a critical part in the defense of Brooklyn Heights in the battle of Long Island. On August 24, Johnston's regiment was located at New Utrecht in modern Brooklyn. When the British attacked on the twenty-seventh, the Americans were completely surrounded. Johnston directed his men in precise fusillades against Colonel Dorp's Hessians on the right and center of the line at Flatbush Pass. Enough time was bought to allow hundreds of men to withdraw and Johnston was acclaimed by his superiors for his courage and firmness. But the praise was posthumous. On his thirty-fifth birthday, August 27, 1776, Johnston was mortally wounded by Hessian musket fire.

SOURCES: W. S. Stryker, "Colonel Philip Johnson," *NJHSP* (2 ser.), IV, 187-89; father and famiy home: J. P. Snell, *Hist. of Hunterdon and Somerset Counties, N.J.* (1881), 203; J. W. Lequear, *Traditions of Hunterdon* (1957), 129-30; CNJ: Aaron Burr, MS Account Book, 160-61; marriage: 22 *NJA*, 573; work with Stewart: *Fithian Journal*, II, 229n; organization of New Jersey militia in defense of New York: G. S. Mott, *Hist. of the Pres. Church in Flemington, N.J.* (1876), 17; *Memoirs of the Long Island Historical Society*, 3 (1878), 112, 130, 132; Force, *Am. Arch.* (4 ser.), VI, 1657; battle of Long Island: *Memoirs of L.I. Hist. Soc.*, 2 (1869), 208; T. C. Amory, *Military Service and Public Life of Major General John Sullivan* (1868), 24-27; *PMHB*, XVI, 400; obituary: 1 *NJA*, 186.

RAH

James Lesley

JAMES LESLEY, A.B., a schoolmaster, was probably born in Scotland about 1720. While Lesley himself consistently spelled his name "Lesley," Presidents Burr, Finley—and almost everyone else—just as consistently spelled it "Leslie." This has led to some confusion in the College's records. Lesley's whereabouts before emigrating to America have not been discovered, but his acquaintance with the London merchant Dennys De Berdt suggests that he may have spent some time in England. The circumstances that brought Lesley to the College are not known, but he entered the sophomore class on November 23, 1756, at the age of about thirty-six. On July 29 of the following year the committee that controlled the Fund for Pious Youth (meant to support prospective clergymen) agreed to contribute £13 to cover some of Lesley's college expenses.

After graduation Lesley probably studied for the ministry with the College's future president, Samuel Finley. On August 1, 1762, he became a master in the charity school for Indians maintained by Eleazar Wheelock (Yale 1733) in Lebanon, Connecticut. "I hope Mr Leslie, since he will not preach ye Gospel, will at least as[s]ist you in this important undertaking," Finley, by then president of the College, wrote to Wheelock in September 1762. Lesley, however, apparently did not find Wheelock's school to his liking. "Keep Mr. Leslie on if you can," Finley advised Wheelock. "Never mind his Whimpers; tell him, I have known many a Maggot got into his Brain, and get out again."

Maggots notwithstanding, Lesley kept the Indian school until September 17, 1763, except for a break of about three months during which he kept the parish school in Lebanon. Then, perhaps because of disagreements with Wheelock, he decided to quit. "I am sorry to hear Leslie is going to leave you," President Finley wrote from Princeton. "I am heartily angry at Him, every time I think of it as are all His Friends here. Tell him so: tell it to him with an Emphasis. What odd Whim has got into his Brain? Has he thoughts of a Wife?" Whatever Lesley's thoughts of a wife (he seems never to have married), his main goal was apparently to establish his independence, for on leaving Connecticut he went to New York City and set himself up as a private schoolmaster. For two years Wheelock pleaded with Lesley to return: "set your own price," Wheelock wrote. Lesley's refusal was adamant.

Lesley remained in New York City for most of the rest of his life. He seems to have left a strong impression on his students, for as late as 1775 one of the Indians he had taught in his brief stay in Connecticut was visiting him in New York. Lesley was active in the affairs of New York's First Presbyterian Church. As with most private schoolmasters of the period, little record of his work survives. A brief notation in an account book indicates that for nine months in 1771 he tutored Catherine Beekman, daughter of a wealthy New York merchant, and charged £3.1s.6d. for it. Lesley died in New York City on April 23, 1792. He must have saved his shillings with traditional Scottish care, for in his will he disposed of substantial sums to a brother, a sister, and his church. But his final bequest sums up his debt to the College and the main concerns of his life:

> I give all the residue of my estate to the Trustees of the College of New Jersey, called Nassau Hall, and to their successors, to be constantly kept at interest by the said Trustees; the interest so arising shall be appropriated to the education of poor and pious youth of the Presbyterian Denomination for the work of the Gospel Ministry, and to no other purpose; if at any time the said interest should be more than sufficient to pay for the education of such youth, in that case the surplus to be given to a Missionary to preach the Gospel to the Frontier Inhabitants of the United States if the General Assembly of the Presbyterian Church shall judge it necessary.

The College husbanded Lesley's legacy well. By June 1975, Lesley's bequest was worth more than $50,000 and in the preceding year had provided over $8,600 in income for Princeton.

SOURCES: Most information from Eleazar Wheelock MSS; Scottish origin and De Berdt connection: E. W. to De Berdt, Dec. 18, 1762; entrance to CNJ, Fund for Pious Youth: Aaron Burr, MS Account Book, 242, 246; Lebanon, "maggot," and "wife": Finley to E. W., Oct. 26, Sept. 30, 1762, Sept. 22, 1763; to NYC: Lesley to Finley, Oct. 20, 1763; plea and refusal: E. W. to Lesley, Mar. 19, 1765; Lesley to E. W., June 8, 1765; First Presbyterian Church: Lesley File, PUA; Indian Student: J. D. McCallum, *Letters of Eleazar Wheelock's Indians* (1932), 186; Catherine Beekman: P. L. White, *Beekmans of N.Y.* (1956), 483; will: *N.Y. Wills*, XIV, 201-202. *Narrative of the State of the Indian Charity School.*

Walter Livingston

WALTER LIVINGSTON, attorney, merchant, speculator, soldier, public official, was the son of Robert Livingston, the third lord of Livingston Manor, New York, and his wife, Maria Thong. He was born on the Manor on November 27, 1740. On May 23, 1756, he joined his cousin Philip P. Livingston (A.B. 1758) as a student at the College. In Septem-

Walter Livingston, Class of 1759

ber of that year Walter's older brother, Peter R. Livingston (Class of 1758) also entered the College.

Walter Livingston withdrew from the College, gave up his pew in the Albany, New York Reformed Protestant Dutch Church, and left America to enter Cambridge University in England, where he was admitted as a pensioner in Peterhouse College in August 1759. In 1761 he became a Fellow Commoner of Peterhouse and at the same time was admitted to the Middle Temple along with his younger brother, Robert. After completing his legal education he returned to assist his father in administering Livingston Manor.

In 1766 the yeomen of New York rose up against the owners of the great estates in the Dutchess County Rebellion. Only the action of Walter Livingston, heading a band of forty armed men, prevented the destruction of the manor house and saved the family. In 1769 Livingston married Cornelia Schuyler and took her to his estate, which he called Teviotdale, in Columbia County, New York. His extensive land-holdings also included at least one tract in New Jersey.

Livingston was basically a conservative man who distrusted the people and whose energies were always devoted to securing the welfare of his class, his family, and himself. Like his brother Peter he was a reluctant participant in public affairs, yet he acknowledged his responsibility as a member of the ruling elite. He was appointed a judge for Albany County in 1774, and in April 1775 he and Peter were chosen by the Albany city and county committee as deputies to the first provincial convention, which was to recommend measures to restore harmonious relations with London while preserving American rights. In May, Livingston became a member of New York's first elected provincial congress.

In July 1775 Livingston was named commissary of stores and provisions for the Department of New York by the provincial congress. At the same time the Continental Congress appointed him deputy commissary general for the Northern Department of the colonies. The latter appointment came through the good offices of his wife's uncle, Major General Philip Schuyler, who commanded the Northern Department. But the department was crippled by factionalism. General Horatio Gates shared a portion of Schuyler's command, and the two men spent as much time taking care of their own careers as they did fighting the British. Both had supporters and opponents in Congress; and Schuyler, because of his family ties to the rich New York manors, earned the special hatred of New Englanders. Very quickly, the office of the deputy commissary general became the focus of the Schuyler-Gates feud. Schuyler successfully defended Livingston's authority against a minor challenge in August 1775, but in the spring of 1776 the controversy deepened. Supported by Gates, Joseph Trumbull arrived in New York claiming to be the new deputy commissary general and insisting that Livingston obey his orders. Livingston refused. Trumbull gained support from General Washington and the leaders of the anti-Schuyler forces in Congress: Samuel Adams, Elbridge Gerry, and William Williams. Livingston was promptly blamed for the chaotic military situation in New England, New York, and Canada. He was accused in Congress of mismanagement and cupidity and Trumbull's appointment was given congressional approval. Livingston had had enough by September 1776, when he resigned.

Of the three reasons for Livingston's resignation, his conflict with Trumbull was the least important. Considerably more influential were the charges of peculation that were to be investigated by Congress. Livingston unabashedly claimed a right, while a servant of the public during the day, to "work at night" for his own advantage. Still, he claimed a personal loss between $30,000 and $50,000, for $18,000 of which he was indemnified by Trumbull. Less than a month before he surrendered his office, Livingston was lobbying with his own friends in Congress to support his and Schuyler's plan for letting contracts. By early 1777 he was in partnership with one John Barker Church, also known as John Carter, who was selling rum to the Continental army. And Livingston's old enemies in Congress were warning Trumbull that a "mercenary party" in Albany would try to cheat the commissary general on the price of supplies.

The third, and equally important reason for Livingston's resignation was his skepticism about the American cause. Always a cautious patriot, he opposed the "levelling tendencies" of the Revolution. He later explained to his brother-in-law, William Smith, that the Declaration of Independence was so radical that it prompted him to resign his commission. He aimed to be as inconspicuous as possible and hoped for a reconciliation with Great Britain. He wanted to accept General Howe's amnesty for those rebels who would abandon the fight and go home. Yet he resented popular rumors that his family was trying to come to terms with the English. As British forces marched deep into New York in 1777, Livingston packed two carts and was ready to flee with his family from the approaching army and his own Loyalist tenants.

To balance the election of George Clinton, who had defeated Philip Schuyler for the governorship in 1777, the New York Assembly chose Livingston as its speaker in the same year. He was contemptuous of the legislature, which he felt was too heavily influenced by the masses, and he contemplated various ruses to avoid being present at its sessions. Yet he did attend and also served as chairman of the state's Committee of Safety, because he feared that by shirking his duties he would endanger his position and even his life. Unable to decide whether to offend the Americans or the British, he chose to protect himself against the more immediate danger by supporting the Revolution.

Livingston remained a strong supporter of the Schuyler faction in New York, but he was more concerned with finances than with politics. Like his father he obtained contracts to supply the Continental army and managed to reap 700% profits on the sale of pork. In 1781 he was a major stockholder in Sands, Livingston and Company when the firm obtained a contract to supply the "Moving Army." His close associates in that enterprise included William Duer. From the outset, this speculative venture was suspected by Livingston's opponents in Congress and the army. Disputes were inevitable, and in November 1785 the company appealed to Congress for payment for its services. The issue dragged on into the next decade.

Meanwhile, Livingston had returned to politics when the war ended. On November 27, 1784, he was elected to represent New York in the Continental Congress, which he attended in December 1784 and the first four months of 1785. At the same time, he was one of the original agents for his state in its dispute with Massachusetts over western lands. That question, too, went unresolved for several years, and Livingston withdrew from the deliberations in early 1785. While in Congress Livingston was also a regent of the State University of New York. In 1785 he, Arthur Lee, and Samuel Osgood were appointed by Congress as the Confederation's Board of the Treasury. They were not the first men to be nominated, but they were the first three to accept. No one was optimistic that the commissioners would be able to restore order to the confused national finances, and their official correspondence was full of lamentations over the uncooperative attitudes of the states. Yet this first Department of the Treasury, relying heavily on ideas from Hamilton and Jefferson, managed to formulate plans for a national currency and mint and to finance the Miami Purchase in Ohio in 1788.

In September 1789 Livingston and his colleagues turned their records over to Secretary Hamilton's assistant, William Duer, whose selection by Hamilton proved to be a serious error. Duer had no intention of divorcing himself from private speculation. Nor did Livingston, who imprudently countersigned a fortune's worth of Duer's notes. In 1791, after Livingston failed to win a seat on the board of the Bank of the United States, he and Duer tried to establish a state bank. At the same time they did all they could to depress the securities market in order to raise the relative value of their own stocks. The result was a speculative bubble and a political debacle, for the state bank competed with Hamilton's national bank scheme. Coincidentally, the factions of the Livingston party in New York were reuniting as Antifederalists. Walter Livingston was considered for a time as the running mate for Governor Clinton, even though Clinton's opponent was to be John Jay, a Livingston in-law. Then Duer's financial bubble burst. The state assembly vetoed the bank plan in January 1792, and Duer was imprisoned in March. Livingston, responsible for more than $800,000 of Duer's debts, fled his law office in New York City to hide at Teviotdale. Congress immediately called for an investigation of the Treasury Department, beginning with the years of Livingston's service there. Even Hamilton's reputation was tainted by the affair.

Desperate to keep his estate, Livingston managed to convey its title to two of his kinsmen so that it could not be seized. He finally obtained permission from the state's chancery court, over which his cousin Robert R. Livingston presided, to sell some of Duer's landholdings in order to recoup a part of his losses. Although their political relationship was shattered, Livingston obtained Hamilton's promise to serve as his counsel after the secretary of the treasury returned to practice law in New York. By the time of his death in New York City on May 14, 1797, Livingston's estate was almost unencumbered. His widow and at least six children were left financially secure after his death. His ten slaves remained in the family.

SOURCES: No single account of Livingston's life is available. Vital data: *Appleton's Amer. Biog.*, III, 743-44; family: E. B. Livingston, *Livingstons of Livingston Manor* (1910), 545; CNJ: Aaron Burr, MS Account Book, 184; Church: J. Munsell, *Collections on the Hist. of Albany* (1865), 78; education in England: Jones, *Inns of Court*, 133-34; Dutchess County Rebellion: P. U. Bonomi, *A Factious People* (1971), 223; G. Dangerfield, *Chancellor Robert R. Livingston of New York* (1960), 19-20; land in New Jersey: *GMNJ*, 26 (1951), 79; participation in New York politics in 1774 and 1775: J. Munsell, *Annals of Albany* (1856), 217-18; Jones, above; Livingston, above, 203-204; Schuyler-Gates controversy and contest for deputy commissary general: D. Higgenbotham, *War of American Independence* (1971), 189; B. J. Lossing, *Life and Times of Philip Schuyler* (1883), 363, 372-74; B. Tuckerman, *Life of General Philip Schuyler* (1903), 104, 140; Force, *Am. Arch.* (4 ser.), V, 777, 813; (5 ser.), I, 193, II, 213, 221, 453; *Washington's Writings*, IV, 503, V, 223-24, 224n, 257, 357; *LMCC*, I, 408, 478, 498, 504, II, 35-36, 84-85; attitude on duties, accusations of malfeasance, congressional investigation, and claim of financial losses as deputy commissary general: R. A. East, *Business Enterprise in the Am. Rev. Era* (1938), 103-105; Force, above (5 ser.), I, 451, 824, II, 1336, 1339; *LMCC*, II, 85n, 204; distrust of democracy and loss of faith in Rev.: Dangerfield, above, 97-98; W. H. Sabine, ed., *Historical Memoirs of William Smith* (1958), 62, 107-108, 128, 131-32, 167, 187, 189, 191-92, 295-96, 361; Committee of Safety and New York Assembly: *NYGBR*, 60 (1929), 334; 62 (1931), 15; D. R. Dillon, *New York Triumvirate* (1949), 154; Sabine, ed., above, 168, 170, 188, 203, 211, 227, 229, 257, 297, 343-44, 398; A. F. Young, *Democratic Republicans of New York* (1967), 27; continuing support of Schuyler: M. H. Bush, *Revolutionary Enigma* (1969), 136-37; army contracts: Young, above, 28, East, above, 116-19, 121, 124-25; *Washington's Writings*, XXIV, 53; *Hamilton Papers*, VIII, 138-41; *LMCC*, VII, 272, 443; New York–Massachusetts border dispute: *Hamilton Papers*, III, 702-703; *LMCC*, VII, 14; Dangerfield, above, 204-205; R. Ernst, *Rufus King* (1968), 46, 51-52; *St. Rec. N.C.*, XXII, 632-33; Board of the Treasury: *LMCC*, VII, 623n, VIII, 14, 16, 92, 98; *Jefferson Papers*, VII, 158-60, VIII, 499, IX, 479-81; *St. Rec. N.C.*, XVII, 538-40, 546-51, 558-62, 597, 606, XVIII, 578, XX, 639, XXI, 556; B. W. Bond, Jr., ed., *Correspondence of John Cleeves Symmes* (1926), 31-32; *NEHGR*, 27 (1873), 214; J. Sparks, ed., *Writings of George Washington* (1837-1839), X, 11n; *Hamilton Papers*, III, 622, V, 233-34, 338-39; state bank, Livingston family politics in 1790s, and Duer's speculation problems: *Hamilton Papers*, III, 634n, 9-10, VIII, 247 n2, XI, 186-90, XIII, 220, 222, XV, 200-203; XVI, 585; East, above, 298; Young, above, 222-23, 284, 298-99; Dangerfield, above, 251-52, 280-82; Hamilton's legal assistance: *Hamilton Papers*, XVII, 205-206, 294; Livingston's descendants and slaves: *U.S. Census of 1790, N.Y.*, 72.

Mss: CtHi, DLC, MHi, MdHi, NHi, NjHi, PHi.   RAH

James Lyon

JAMES LYON, A.B., A.M. 1762, Presbyterian clergyman and psalmodist, was the son of Zophar and Mary Lyon of Newark, New Jersey. He was born on July 1, 1735, and was left fatherless at the age of nine. His uncle Isaac Lyon and John Crane of Newark were appointed as his guardians. On July 6, 1754, Lyon entered the grammar school of the College. He enrolled in the College itself in the spring of 1757. During his senior year copies of his original ode, "Louisberg Taken," were advertised for sale in the *New American Magazine*. He also composed the music for two odes, one to "Peace" and one to "Science," which were sung at his commencement exercises in September 1759. The words to both were written by President Davies.

In 1760 Lyon devoted himself to music. In Philadelphia he collected hymns and wrote a few of them himself. Under the title *Urania*, the hymns were published by Henry Dawkins in 1761. They represent one of the first musical collections published by a native American. Along with Francis Hopkinson, later a signer of the Declaration of Independence, Lyon was a father of American hymnology. *Urania* sold for ten shillings per copy and went through four editions. Of the 159 copies sold by subscription, fifty went to officers and students at the College. Lyon's collection was the first music ever used in a chapel service at Princeton.

When he received his A.M. in September 1762, Lyon delivered the English oration in behalf of his fellow postgraduates. At the same exercises the students sang a "Musical Entertainment" called "The Military Glory of Great Britain," a hymn to the Empire. The lyrics were the work of Hopkinson; the music was by Lyon. In 1763 a tract on the *Lawfulness, Excellency, and Advantages of Instrumental Musick in the Public Worship of God*, in which the Presbyterian Church was urged to relax its restrictions on such music, was published in Philadelphia. It, too, was probably from Lyon's pen.

In May 1762 Lyon was taken up by the Presbytery of New Brunswick, which licensed him in 1763 and ordained him on December 5, 1764. He was immediately appointed to supply for ten months or longer, at his discretion, at the Presbyterian churches in Pinctou and Truro, Nova Scotia. Although provisions were made for his settlement at Truro, he decided to live in Onslow (Cobequid), equidistant from his two churches. He was installed on May 15, 1765, and retained both pulpits for six years.

In April 1765 Lyon accompanied Anthony Wayne and others on a survey expedition along the Bay of Fundy and the Minas Basin. In October, on the basis of that survey, he received a grant of one-eighth of the land then under title to the Philadelphia Company. His property was on the present site of Pictou. But his financial situation was insecure. He received no stated salary from his congregations but may have earned approximately £50 annually. He stayed at his post only because he hoped for better days in the future. The hard life on Nova Scotia required all the Dissenting churches in the province to co-operate, and Lyon worked very closely with the large Congregationalist population. In 1770 he participated in the first Presbyterian ordination in Nova Scotia.

As early as May 1768 Lyon had begun to complain to the synod about his hand-to-mouth existence. On a visit to Boston in 1771 he met a member of the Congregational church in Machias, Maine. The congregation was currently seeking a minister, and Lyon eagerly applied and was accepted. A call came for him in the spring of 1772. His salary was to be £84 per year, plus a £100 settlement allowance. To his new post he took his wife, the former Martha Holden of Cape May, New Jersey, and the first three of their nine children. Lyon and his wife had been married on February 18, 1768. She brought with her some substantial bequests of land. With only two brief interruptions Lyon preached at Machias, at both the East Falls and West Falls settlement churches, until he died.

Lyon retained his passion for music, but as the Revolution approached his attention was drawn to political matters. As a student at Princeton he had composed hymns to the British crown. But he became an ardent Whig in the years before 1775. He was a forceful, energetic man; and as the only minister within a radius of 100 miles he quickly became a secular leader. His church, originally an old barn and after 1772 a plain meetinghouse that had cost $220, was also the gathering place for the Machias Committee of Public Safety and other political groups.

During the first years of the war Lyon did everything he could to convince the Massachusetts legislature, and then the Continental Congress, of the urgency of capturing Nova Scotia for the United States. He deluged the Massachusetts General Court with letters on the general subject of the importance of the eastern lands. By August 1776 he was thoroughly disgusted with that body. He condemned it for failing to provide the money and supplies needed not only to take Nova Scotia but even to defend Maine. And he demanded the region's independence of Massachusetts if Boston was not ready to do more. Lyon himself participated in an abortive attack on Fort Cumberland, Nova Scotia, led by Jonathan Eddy in November and December 1775. Although he originally thought that a few hundred men would be enough to capture Nova Scotia, by December 1776 he had to admit that five or six thousand would be needed. But his enthusiasm for the project never waned, and he was always ready to lead the expedition himself if necessary. He warned Massachusetts that if it did not act another state might grab Nova Scotia for itself; to Congress and General Washington he wrote of the danger of European conquest of the peninsula. But Nova Scotia, and Lyon's considerable property on it, remained British. Lyon's military service after 1775 was confined to defending Machias.

Part of Lyon's anger at Boston was due to the miserable economic conditions in Maine during the war. Supplies were almost nonexistent. Lyon received no salary during the conflict, and he often had to feed his family with the clams that he dug from the shore. To relieve a critical shortage of salt he operated a sea-water distillery on an island off Machiasport, ever since called Salt Island. When hostilities ended, he was given his overdue wages and his congregation voted to raise his annual salary to £86. A permanent church was built for him in 1782. He remained a village leader and Machias's delegates to deliberative assemblies regularly consulted him on matters of policy.

A vigorous man, Lyon enjoyed good health throughout these years. His only infirmity was color blindness. After the death of his wife he married a second time on November 24, 1793. His new bride was Sarah Skillen of Boston. A new marriage may have done what years of hardship could not do. Lyon died on June 12, 1794 in Machias.

SOURCES: *DAB*; S. E. Lyon, *Lyon Memorial* (1907), 241-43; CNJ: Aaron Burr, MS Account Book, 104, 251, 253; musical activities: Collins, *Princeton*, 172-73; *PMHB*, 69 (1945), 112; and 74 (1950), 107; *N.Y. Mercury*, Oct. 1, 1759; 20 *NJA*, 383; 25 *NJA*, 492-93; O.G.T. Sonneck, *Francis Hopkinson . . . and James Lyon* (1905); A.M. oration: 24 *NJA*, 88; Nova Scotia: *PMHB*, 51 (1927), 277, 280; Stiles, *Literary Diary*, I, 137, 263; *MHSP* (2 ser.), IV, 70; I. F. Mackinnon, *Settlements and Churches in Nova Scotia* (1930), 61, 79; W. P. Bell, *"Foreign Protestants" and the Settlement of Nova Scotia* (1961), 599; first wife's inheritance: 33 *NJA*, 249, 322; Machias: G. J. Varney, *A Gazeteer of Maine* (1881), 347; *Fithian Journal*, I, 158 and 158n; plan to attack Nova Scotia: W. R. Bird, *A Century at Chignecto* (1928), 217-25; Force, *Am. Arch.* (4 ser.), IV, 460-61, 1182-83, VI, 484-85; (5 ser.), I, 1280-83, III, 1435-36.

PUBLICATIONS: see STE   RAH

Samuel Nivins

SAMUEL NIVINS/NEVINS, A.B., A.M. 1762, has not been identified in an extensive search. He was not the prominent Connecticut citizen (1749–1815) of that name. He may have been the Samuel Nivens who acquired 300 acres of land in Cumberland County, Pennsylvania, in June 1762 and of whom no further certain trace has been found. The alumnus was first listed as dead in the College's catalogue of 1804.

SOURCES: *Pa. Arch.* (3 ser.), 24 (1897), 737.

Ebenezer Noyes

EBENEZER NOYES, A.B., physician, was born on January 6, 1739. Like his kinsmen Joshua Noyes and Nathaniel Noyes of the same class, he was a native of Newbury, Massachusetts. His parents, Abigail Toppan and Daniel Noyes, were prosperous enough to own four slaves.

Both Joshua and Ebenezer Noyes attended Harvard for three quarters before joining Nathaniel at the College of New Jersey in November 1756. After graduation Ebenezer apprenticed himself to a physician and by 1762 was practicing medicine in Dover, New Hampshire. On November 29, 1764, he married Hannah Chase, a neighbor from Newbury. Their only child, Abigail, was baptized in Dover on March 9, 1766.

Noyes's reputation as a physician was on the rise when he died suddenly on August 3, 1767. He was remembered by patients and friends as having been "extremely useful in his medical capacity."

SOURCES: *Sibley's Harvard Graduates*, XIV, 470; D. H. Hurd, *Hist. of Rockingham and Strafford Counties, N.H.* (1882), 846; CNJ: Aaron Burr, MS Account Book, 210; baptism of daughter: *NEHGR*, XLI, 28; obituary: *N.H. Gaz.*, Aug. 7, 1767, 2.

RAH

Joshua Noyes

JOSHUA NOYES, A.B., A.M. 1762, educator and Presbyterian clergyman, was born in Newbury, Massachusetts, on April 15, 1739. The Newbury area was home to a great many members of the Noyes family, some of whom married members of the Hale clan. Joshua apparently was the son of Sarah Hale and Joshua Noyes. Two relatives, Nathaniel and Ebenezer Noyes, probably Joshua's cousins, were also members of the same class.

Joshua Noyes attended Harvard College for three quarters before enrolling in the College of New Jersey on November 20, 1756. He entered the clergy soon after graduation and was called to the church in Kingston, New Hampshire. But he declined the call. Although he occasionally supplied vacant pulpits, he devoted his life to teaching. In April 1760 he became the master of a private school in Byfield, Massachusetts. The school opened in the home of Samuel Adams and had twenty original pupils. Noyes was to receive a sum of £10 from the ten trustees (including himself) for three months' service as master. By 1765 he was also teaching in nearby Rowley, Massachusetts. Both of these towns were close to his native village of Newbury, which he served as a selectman during the 1760s. In March 1770 he signed the Newbury nonimportation agreement against British goods. He died at Byfield on September 3, 1773, after eight days of suffering with a violent fever.

SOURCES: *Sibley's Harvard Graduates*, XIV, 471; Alexander, *Princeton*, 61; parentage: *Vital Records of Newbury, Mass.* (1911), I, 363; CNJ: Aaron Burr, MS Account Book, 210; late preaching: D. H. Hurd, *Hist. of Rockingham and Strafford Counties, N.H.* (1882), 372; school at Byfield and political activities: "Joshua Coffin Papers," *Essex Institute Historical Collections*, 35 (1899), 156, 157, 158-60; school at Rowley: T. Gage, *Hist. of Rowley* (1840), 396; obituary: *Boston News-Letter*, Sept. 23, 1773.

RAH

Nathaniel Noyes

NATHANIEL NOYES, A.B., A.M. 1762, Congregational clergyman, was born in Newbury, Massachusetts, on August 12, 1735, the first of the ten children of Sarah Mighill and her husband, Parker Noyes. The elder Noyes was a prominent and prosperous citizen of Newbury and one of the first deacons of the Presbyterian church, which was built on property formerly owned by him. His landholdings in the town were extensive, and he was later instrumental in the creation of a new community, Newburyport, from a section of Newbury. His preference for New Light divinity undoubtedly explains the attendance of three members of his family at the College instead of nearby Harvard.

Nathaniel Noyes probably entered the grammar school of the College of New Jersey in September 1755. He matriculated in the College one year later along with his cousins Ebenezer and Joshua Noyes of the same class. After graduation he studied for the ministry with Presbyterian theologians, perhaps including President Davies, and he began preaching in 1760. Among his early pulpits was one in Springfield Parish (Fourth Parish), Dover, Massachusetts.

Despite his Presbyterian training, Noyes was ordained as a Congregational minister at the Congregational church in South Hampton, New Hampshire, on February 23, 1763. He remained there for nearly thirty-eight years. Although he devoted much of his time to serving the poor in New England, neither his outside duties nor illness ever kept him from preaching a Sunday sermon. In 1792 he published a tract in defense of infant baptism. He retired on December 8, 1800, and moved back to Newbury. There he continued to preach at the First Church until he died on December 11, 1810.

Noyes married Sarah Hale, a widow from Newbury, on November 12, 1765. They had three children before she died in 1773. Their eldest son, Nathaniel, was a carpenter who won the contract to build Dartmouth College. On February 8, 1774, Noyes remarried. His second wife was a distant cousin, Sarah Noyes, also from Newbury. She, too, bore him three children. Three of his offspring survived their father.

SOURCES: Birth, marriages and family: *Vital Records of Newbury, Mass.* (1911), I, 366, II, 360; father: J. J. Currier, *Hist. of Newburyport, Mass.* (1906), 13, 16; Currier, *"Ould Newbury"* (1896), 133, 459-60, 518, 545; *Essex Institute Historical Collections*, 21 (1885), 217; 67 (1931), 407; CNJ: Aaron Burr, MS Account Book, 138, 215; H. E. Noyes and H. E. Noyes, *Noyes Descendants* (1904), II, 209, 211, 212; Dover: F. Smith, *Hist. of Dover, Mass.* (1897), 54; ordination and South Hampton: *NEHGR*, 52 (1898), 431; D. H. Hurd, *Hist. of Rockingham and Strafford Counties, N.H.* (1882), 520; ministry in Newbury: Currier, *Hist. of Newbury, Mass.* (1902), 344.

PUBLICATIONS: see STE   RAH

Thomas Pierce

THOMAS PIERCE, A.B., A.M. 1762, Presbyterian clergyman, was born in Newbury, Massachusetts, on October 11, 1737, the son of Abigail and Thomas Pierce. Young Thomas matriculated at the College on September 20, 1755. During his years there he purchased copies of the standard textbooks, such as Thomas Salmon's compendium, *A New Geographical and Historical Grammar*, and Robert Dodsley's *The Preceptor*, with its introduction by Dr. Johnson.

After graduation Pierce studied theology. In 1759 the Congregational parson at Scarborough, Maine, William Tompson (Harvard 1718) had died. Although Tompson had joined other members of the Congregational Eastern Association of York County in denouncing itinerant New Light preachers, he with "much of uneasiness," permitted George Whitefield to preach three times from his pulpit. Some theological dissension apparently existed within the parish, for only after several other candidates had proved unsatisfactory did the Scarborough congregation settle in 1762 on Thomas Pierce as their new minister. Pierce accepted the call, but only upon the condition that the church assume the Presbyterian form of ecclesiastical organization. The congregation agreed, and Pierce was ordained by the Presbyterians in his home town of Newbury.

Settled in Scarborough, in 1762 Pierce married Anne Haskell. Pierce built his bride a fine two-story house. The couple had two sons. Pierce died in Scarborough on January 26, 1775, and was buried beside his predecessor. His parishioners then abandoned the Presbyterian form of church organization and resumed the Congregational one.

SOURCES: Parentage: *Vital Records of Newbury, Mass.* (1911), I, 388; College purchases: Aaron Burr, MS Account Book, 140-41; Tompson: *Sibley's Harvard Graduates*, VI, 284-86; pastorate: W. S. Southgate, "The Hist. of Scarborough from 1633 to 1783," *Collections of the Maine Historical Society*, III (1853), 160-61; marriage and house: Thomas Pierce File, PUA.

Thomas Reynolds

THOMAS REYNOLDS, A.B., mill and plantation owner, soldier and public official, was born in Bridgeton, now Mount Holly, Burlington County, New Jersey. His father, Patrick Reynolds, was a carpenter who had migrated to America from Ireland. Patrick was one of four partners who founded the settlement of New Mills, once called Hampton Hanover and now Pemberton, in 1752. It was he who actually built the grist and sawmills for which the settlement was named. The establishment of New Mills was the first step in the development of the Pemberton area as an industrial center, and the elder Reynolds's one-quarter share of the mills and land made the family rich. When he died in September 1757, Patrick Reynolds left an estate valued at almost £1,500, along with extensive land holdings and several houses, to his five daughters and Thomas.

Even while he was a student in the College, Thomas Reynolds served as co-executor of his father's estate. He helped in selling off some of the land in 1757 and in renting one of the large brick houses as a store. A few months before commencement in 1759 Reynolds obtained a license to marry Elizabeth Budd, the daughter of one of the other partners in New Mills. After graduation he apparently returned to the settlement to take personal charge of the family property and business. His prominence in the community led to his appointment as a justice of the peace for Burlington County by Governor William Franklin in August 1767.

Elizabeth Reynolds, who had given birth to two daughters during her marriage, died probably in 1768. On January 4, 1769, in an Anglican ceremony in Mount Holly, Thomas Reynolds married Mary Bryan, a widow and the daughter of John and Ann Ritchie of Perth Amboy. The new Mrs. Reynolds inherited a very large tract of land from her mother and added it to Reynolds's substantial holdings.

Reynolds was an early supporter of the Revolution. When the Burlington County Militia was organized in 1776 he was made a lieutenant colonel in its Second Regiment. He was also a member of the New Jersey Committee of Correspondence, and as a delegate to the provincial congress in June and July 1776 he voted to arrest Governor Franklin and to call a general assembly. Such a notorious rebel was an obvious target for British troops when they entered New Jersey, and Reynolds was said to have escaped arrest temporarily by hiding himself in a cabin near his mills. In December 1776 he was less fortunate and the British captured him in his home only two days before Christmas. With many other American prisoners of war, he was confined on the prison ship *Old Jersey* in Wallabout Bay off New York City. Conditions on the ship were deplorable. In the *Jersey's* three and one half years as a prison ship, thousands of Americans died aboard her from starvation, overcrowding, heat, cold, beatings, suffocation, or absolute filth.

In January 1778, in an effort to improve the lot of prisoners of war on both sides, Major General James Robertson, the British commissary general for New York, granted privileges to some American prisoners, including Reynolds, who was released on parole. According to the terms of his release, Reynolds returned to confinement in January 1779, shortly before he and most other prisoners of war in New York were set free. During his first year in captivity he had been promoted to full colonel in the New Jersey militia, and he was again on active duty with the Second Regiment in early 1780. When Congress asked for more men to fill the New Jersey line in February of that year, Reynolds was appointed by the state legislature as the muster-master of Burlington County. His salary was to be $200 for each recruit he procured, plus a $16 allowance per man to pay for supplies. Recruiting efforts across the state were generally successful.

On March 22, 1781, a court-martial in Trenton considered charges that Reynolds had failed to execute the sentence of another court-martial that he had convened himself. Found guilty, he was fined £15 lawful state money. On December 18, 1782, Reynolds finally resigned his commission and returned to his home and mills. He apparently devoted the rest of his life to his private affairs. He died in January 1803, leaving an estate valued at $9,129.70.

SOURCES: Father: E. M. Woodward and J. F. Hageman, *Hist. of Burlington and Mercer Counties, N.J.* (1883), 394; George DeCou, *Historic Rancocas* (1949), 72; father's will: 32 *NJA*, 266; disposition of father's estate: 20 *NJA*, 143; 29 *NJA*, 256; first marriage: 22 *NJA*, 321; appointment as justice of the peace: 17 *NJA*, 455; second marriage: J. E. Stillwell, *Historical and Genealogical Miscellany* (1970), II, 68; Woodward and Hageman, above, 394; service on Committee of Correspondence and in provincial congress and escape from arrest: DeCou, above, 74; DeCou, *Burlington* (1945), 143; arrest and conditions on the *Old Jersey*: F. B. Heitman, *Officers and Men of the Continental Army* (1914), 464; D. Dandridge, *American Prisoners of the Rev.* (1911), 481, 125-27, 192-200, 146-53, 432-45; G. A. Boyd, *Elias Boudinot* (1952), 89; General Robertson and Reynolds's parole: 2 (2 ser.) *NJA*, 11-13; Dandridge, above 40-41; return to confinement: 3 (2 ser.) *NJA*, 23; promotion to colonel and recruiting in N.J. in 1780: W. S. Stryker, *Official Register of the Officers and Men of New Jersey in the Rev. War* (1872), 354, 46-47; court-martial: 5 (2 ser.) *NJA*, 248; will: 39 *NJA*, 368.

RAH

Henry Sherburne

HENRY SHERBURNE, A.B., merchant, was born in Portsmouth, New Hampshire, in September 1741. His father, Henry Sherburne, was one of Portsmouth's leading citizens. The son of a colonial chief justice and nephew of a governor, the elder Henry was himself a selectman, a member of the provincial council and of the Albany Congress, and a judge. The senior Sherburne and his wife Sarah Warner produced thirteen children, of whom young Henry was the eldest to reach maturity. The Sherburnes were an Anglican family but the judge, who graduated from Harvard in 1728, was inspired by the Great Awakening. He became a friend of revivalists such as John and Daniel Rogers and a friend of the Reverend Samuel MacClintock (A.B. 1751). His political activities also brought him into contact with Governor Jonathan Belcher of Massachusetts. The religious society that met regularly in his home was strongly tinged with dissent.

The younger Henry Sherburne may have been prepared for college in Boston, which was his point of departure for Newark in 1756. He enrolled in the College on May 20 of that year. During his time at the College he managed to accumulate a sizable debt—to fellow students and to the school itself. In 1757 Philip Livingston contributed nearly £29 to reduce Sherburne's bill. But the young man continued to borrow money for books, college dues, furniture, butter, and even to paint his room. He graduated still owing the College more than £40, and there is no record that the bill was ever paid.

Sherburne returned to Portsmouth, where he apparently joined his father's business. He became an avowed opponent of British policies and during the Revolution he served with General William Whipple under Gates at Saratoga. He signed the New Hampshire Association against the importation of British goods in August 1776. In 1777 Sherburne was one of the Portsmouth patriots who asked the New Hampshire Committee of Safety to expel all Loyalists from the state before the "well affected populace" took the matter into its own hands. He was also interested in the defense of the district of Maine against British operations. He was a leader of the Portsmouth "Committee for Supplying Soldier Familys &c" in 1780, but that was his most responsible position.

His business apparently failed and his propensity for debt had not abated. He was the genuine black sheep of the family. One of his sisters married a prominent Boston attorney, John Wendell (Harvard 1750), who was a close associate of many leaders of the Revolution and the new nation. Another sister was the wife of Woodbury Langdon, a member of Congress and a justice of the New Hampshire supreme court. A brother died a heroic death at Germantown in 1777. Henry never married, and although he is said to have maintained pretensions to importance he was reduced to poverty. In 1790 he petitioned both houses of the New Hampshire legislature for relief. But when he died in 1825 it may have been in the Portsmouth almshouse.

SOURCES: Father: *Sibley's Harvard Graduates*, VIII, 490-95; C. A. Brewster, *Rambles About Portsmouth* (1869), 46; Alexander, *Princeton*, 61; CNJ: Aaron Burr, MS Account Book, 174, 175, 266-67; activity during Rev.: *NEGHR*, 58 (1904), 232; *New Hampshire State Papers*, 13 (1884), 273, 285; 16 (1887), 803; 17 (1889), 138-39; 30 (1910), 118; brothers and sisters: *NEGHR*, 22 (1868), 357; 36 (1882), 249-50; 58 (1904), 233; petitions to legislature: *New Hampshire State Papers*, 21 (1892), 648, 692; 22 (1893), 11, 51.

                                                                        RAH

Samuel Spencer

SAMUEL SPENCER, A.B., LL.D. 1784, lawyer, soldier, public official, was born in East Haddam, Connecticut, on January 21, 1734. His mother was Jerusha Brainerd, the sister of David Brainerd whose expulsion from Yale in 1745 was cited by Aaron Burr as the proximate cause of the founding of the College. Another of her brothers was John Brainerd (A.M. 1749), who succeeded David as a missionary to the Indians and was a trustee of the College between 1750 and 1780. She was the first wife of Samuel Spencer, Sr., the oldest brother of Elihu Spencer, another trustee of the College.

Family ties and New Light religious convictions mandated that young Samuel be a student at the College, and he entered on September 25, 1755. For some of his time in Princeton he lived with President Burr.

After graduating, Spencer went south, finally settling in Anson County, North Carolina, where he began to practice law. On October 16, 1765, he was appointed deputy clerk of the court of pleas for Anson

County. It was a position that provided great opportunities for personal advancement and profit, and Spencer set out to exploit his chances for both. After marrying Phillipa (Sybil) Pegues of South Carolina in 1766, he was appointed by the royal government to see that cattle from his wife's home province were not crossing the border. On November 3, 1766, Spencer was elected as a delegate from Anson County to the North Carolina Assembly. He initiated legislation on matters of taxation, road construction, and local boundaries, but his primary interest was in matters dealing with the colony's judicial and penal systems. He was instrumental, for example, in creating inferior courts of pleas and quarter sessions in some counties.

It was in his capacity as a militia officer and as clerk of the court that Spencer reported to Governor William Tryon on a Regulator uprising in April 1768. The settlers on the western frontier of the colony, long resentful of the tidewater oligarchy, were protesting against new tax levies and abuses in the conduct of local government. When some of them momentarily seized the courthouse in Anson County, there was grave risk of bloodshed, but the protestors were persuaded in time to disperse. As trouble continued in Anson and other counties, Colonel Spencer was among the officers present at a council of war held at Hillsborough in September 1768. He also was in the field on the governor's side when the conflict reached its climax at the battle of Alamance in May 1771. Meanwhile, he had continued to build his legal practice.

Spencer's loyalty to the royal government dissolved as colonial relations with England worsened. In August 1774 he represented Anson County in the first provincial congress, called to discuss ways of maintaining American freedoms. At its meeting in New Bern the congress voted to boycott British goods and created committees of correspondence. Spencer was a member of the committee for Anson County. He spoke for the boycott throughout his district. In the summer of 1775 the royal governor resigned his post and fled, and the provincial congress became the government of North Carolina. At a meeting in August it assigned executive and judicial authority to a cumbersome political structure topped by a thirteen-member provincial council that was given a veto over actions by the local committees of safety. Spencer was one of the original members of the council, whose primary function was to supervise North Carolina's part in the war. He was also a member of the state's committee to try to win the Loyalist Highlanders over to the Revolution. It was a problem recognized in Philadelphia as well, for the Continental Congress sent two Presbyterian clerics to North Carolina to preach the American cause. The two ministers were Spencer's uncle Elihu and Alexander MacWhorter (A.B. 1757).

In March 1776 Spencer resigned his colonelcy in order to concentrate on political affairs. The following month he was chosen by the assembly to sit on the committee that would prepare the first state constitution. By early 1777 he was district judge; and after the assembly created a judicial system in the autumn of that year, Spencer was one of the first men elected to sit on the bench of the state's superior court. In January 1779 he obtained a large land grant in Anson County. His salary for sitting on the bench in 1780 was £20,000 in the vastly inflated state currency of the day. Still, he claimed that he was suffering from monetary depreciation and frequently appealed to the legislature for an appropriate adjustment in his pay.

In 1784 Spencer received an honorary doctorate of laws from the College and became a trustee of Salisbury Academy in North Carolina. He was also involved in a bitter political quarrel. He and two colleagues on the superior court were less radical than their neighbors in the western counties but considerably more radical than the state bar, which was dominated by tidewater attorneys. Under several *noms de plume* Spencer participated in an intense pamphlet war that culminated in 1786 and 1787 when the court declared an act of the assembly unconstitutional. This early application of the doctrine of judicial review was challenged by legislators who joined forces with Spencer's opponents in the bar to bring charges of misconduct against the "radical" judges. After months of hearings, which two of the accused jurists attended, the assembly cleared Spencer and his colleagues of all charges.

In July 1788 Spencer was a major participant in the state convention at Hillsborough that debated adopting the federal constitution. While he was dissatisfied with the Confederation and favored a stronger union, Spencer was suspicious of an excessively powerful central government. He was jealous of states' rights and, along with David Caldwell (A.B. 1761), led the Antifederalist forces at Hillsborough. He resented federal powers of taxation, wanted to restrict the jurisdiction of federal courts, and suggested an advisory council for the president. But his most intense objections were to the powers of Congress to regulate elections and to the absence of a bill of rights. His skillful arguments helped win the day, and the Hillsborough convention refused to accept the constitution. Spencer was less successful in a second convention at Fayetteville in 1789. The Antifederalists were unable to muster enough votes to make him president of the meeting, and the Federalists were never again challenged seriously. The Fayetteville convention ratified the constitution but not until Spencer and others were put on a committee to draft proposals for a bill of rights.

Ratification did not end Spencer's political battles. In 1789 he became a member of the board of trustees of the new University of North Carolina, but he had to survive a bitter fight with Federalist members to gain his seat. In 1790 he was recommended to Thomas Jefferson by prominent Antifederalists for appointment to a federal judgeship that he never received. Between court sessions in April 1793, Judge Spencer sat in the piazza of his house in Anson County, a red cap on his head. As he dozed there and nodded, a large turkey in the yard took the motion of the cap as a challenge. He charged at Spencer, throwing him to the floor, and attacked him. Spencer suffered a wound on the hand that became infected. On April 20, 1793 he died of erisipelas and shock. He left a huge estate: more than 5,000 acres of land in five counties and eighteen slaves. His heirs were his widow, his son, and his daughter.

SOURCES: Parents and their families: D. Brainerd, *Ancestry of Thomas Chalmers Brainerd* (1948), 74; *NEGBR*, 2 (1857), 276; L. A. Brainard, *Genealogy of the Brainerd-Brainard Family* (1908), II, pt. 7, 69; Wertenbaker, *Princeton*, 17-18; CNJ: Aaron Burr, MS Account Book, 253; marriage: *SCHGM*, 38 (1937), 104; public service before 1768: *Col. Rec. N.C.*, VII, passim; Regulator uprising: *Col. Rec. N.C.*, VII, 722-28, 807-808, 842; VIII, 593, 601-608; M. D. Haywood, *Governor William Tryon* (1903), 92-93, 119; legal practice in Tryon County: C. W. Griffin, *Hist. of Old Tryon and Rutherford Counties, N.C.* (1937), 8; first provincial congress: *Col. Rec. N.C.*, IX, xxxi, 1033; promotion of boycott: *Col. Rec. N.C.*, X, 119, 125, 127; provincial council: A. Henderson, *North Carolina* (1941), 301-302; J. H. Wheeler, *Historical Sketches of North Carolina* (1851), II, 24-25; *Col. Rec. N.C.*, X. 214; persuasion of the Highlanders: *Col. Rec. N.C.*, X, 173; D. Meyer, *Highland Scots in N.C.* (1957), 144; resignation of colonelcy: *Col. Rec. N.C.*, X, 472; state constitution: *Col. Rec. N.C.*, X, 515; district and superior courts: Henderson, above, 326; *St. Rec. N.C.*, XI, 481, 825, XII, 104, 232; A. Nevins, *American States During and After the Rev.* (1927), 364; land grant in 1779: *St. Rec. N.C.*, XIII, 545-46; salary: *St. Rec. N.C.*, XVII, 156, 702-703, XIX and XX, passim; LL.D. and Salisbury Academy: *NCHR*, 3 (1926), 371; *St. Rec. N.C.*, XXIV, 690; MS CNJ Trustees' Minutes, I; controversy with lawyers and charges of misconduct: *St. Rec. N.C.*, XVI, 879, 965; XVIII, vi-viii, 421-25, 477-83; H. T. Lefler, ed., *North Carolina Hist. Told by Contemporaries* (1936), 125, 127; Henderson, above, 489-91, 577, 594; R.D.W. Conner, *North Carolina* (1929), I, 395; L. I. Trenholme, *Ratification of the Federal Constitution in N.C.* (1932), 154 and n; Hillsborough convention: Henderson, above, 326; H. G. Conner, "The Convention of 1788-89," *North Carolina Booklet*, 4 (1904), 12, 18-20, 184-185; *WMQ*, 12 (1955), 26; J. T. Main, *Antifederalists* (1961), 150, 181, 243; Trenholme, above, 168-69, 173-74, 179-80; *NCHR*, 17 (1940), 293; *NCHR*, 25 (1948), 455; Fayetteville convention: Trenholme, above, 233, 237, 239; H. G. Conner, above, 195-97; Henderson, above, 410; *NCHR*, 27 (1950), 437, 440; also: J. Eliot, *Debates in the Several Conventions, on the Adoption of the Federal Constitution* (1861), IV; university trusteeship: R.D.W. Conner, ed., *Documentary Hist. of the Univ. of N.C.* (1953), I, 33-34 and 34n; federal judgeship: *Jefferson Papers*, XVI, 476; death: *Fayetteville Gaz.*, April 30, 1793; estate: *NCHR*, 27 (1950), 290; Trenholme, above, 158; *U.S. Census of 1790, N.C.*, 36.

Mss: NjP, NcHi   RAH

Jacob Van Buskirk

JACOB VAN BUSKIRK, Lutheran clergyman, was born in Hackensack, Bergen County, New Jersey, on February 11, 1739, the son of Jacobus Van Buskirk and his wife, Jannetje Schutz or Schultz. A small Lutheran community, closely connected with the one of New York City, had existed in Bergen County for some time. The father was extremely active in the affairs of the congregation. Before attending the College, young Van Buskirk studied with John Albert Weygandt, who was pastor of Lutheran Holy Trinity Church in New York City from 1750 to 1762. The length of time Jacob spent at the College is not certain. His name was first inscribed in President Burr's account book in May 1756. The only other record of his attendance is the notation of his payment of a bill for £1.12s. on September 29 of that year. After leaving the College Van Buskirk studied with Ludolph Henry Schrenck, pastor of several small Lutheran congregations in Hunterdon and Somerset counties, New Jersey.

On December 3, 1759, the Reverend Henry Melchior Muhlenberg, the organizer of the Lutheran Church in America, made the following entry in his journal: "Captain Jacobus van Buschkerk conferred with me in regard to his twenty-two-year old son who has been dedicated to theology." Carefully noting that young Van Buskirk had studied with Weygandt, at "the English Presbyterian College," and with Schrenck, Muhlenberg continued: "Since it is evident that the young man has a chaste temperament and a disposition toward true Christianity, I promised to take him in charge and labor with him as best I could by God's grace and blessing."

For the next four years Van Buskirk remained with Muhlenberg. He accompanied the older man on his incessant travels in the middle colonies as Muhlenberg tried to bring order and support to the rapidly growing number of Lutheran immigrants. Under Muhlenberg's direction, Van Buskirk diligently struggled through works such as Luther's *Erklärung uber die Evangelischen Texte auf Sonn- und Festtage*. By 1761 he was acting as a catechist in Muhlenberg's school.

On October 12, 1763, Van Buskirk was ordained by the Lutheran ministerium at New Hanover, Montgomery County, Pennsylvania, and settled as pastor of the Lutheran church there. New Hanover had other attractions as well; on March 15, 1764, Van Buskirk married Maria Hollebach or Hollenbach, the daughter of one of the elders of his congregation. The couple had at least three sons and four daughters. Van Buskirk's New Hanover pastorate was successful—in fact, so successful that he was shortly lured away to a pulpit in Germantown, Pennsylvania. On November 24, 1765, the Lutheran congregation in Germantown was presented with the following description of Van Buskirk:

> There is a young preacher in New Hannover who was examined and ordained. . . . He understands English, Dutch and German; has a small family; leads an honourable, sober and quiet life; is humble to both high and low; has a fine, clear, and pleasing voice; loves to visit the sick, knows how to gather a congregation together; and is friendly toward everybody. He is the man who has already preached here several times.

The congregation voted to invite Van Buskirk to settle, offering a yearly salary of £60 Pennsylvania currency plus the free use of the parsonage. Van Buskirk accepted. His Germantown pastorate was as successful as his earlier one had been. During his stay there he also ministered to several other Lutheran congregations in the area.

To the north, in the area about what is now Lehigh, Pennsylvania, many small Lutheran communities were expanding rapidly. In 1769 the ministerium directed Van Buskirk to move there and organize new churches. The delegates from Germantown protested strongly, declaring that because of Van Buskirk's work "their congregation is quiet and growing after all the depressing controversies through which it has passed." However, late in 1769 Van Buskirk moved his family to Lehigh, where he ministered to many churches in the area until the 1790s. Visiting Van Buskirk in May 1770, Muhlenberg made a notation in his journal that serves as an accurate index of Van Buskirk's entire career:

> For many years the poor people have been led astray and plagued by bad preachers, poor pastorage, and the wicked lives of their pastors. At present they are united and content with Mr. Buskerk, one of our United co-workers . . . they praise Pastor Buskirk for the special gift which he possesses of attracting the children and dealing with them in a kindly way. . . . Mr. Buskirk is trying with love and wisdom to persuade the parents to put a stop to the great wedding feasts, to have the weddings celebrated with only a few witnesses, and to have them give the amount expended to the young couples as a start in their marriage estate.

Van Buskirk visited various Army camps during the Revolution, but appears to have taken little part in public affairs. He did, however, serve in 1786 as one of many charter trustees of an academy that later became Franklin and Marshall College. Fairly prosperous, he built and operated a tannery and was recorded by the federal censustaker in 1790 as the owner of one slave. About 1793 Van Buskirk moved to the neighborhood of Gwynedd, Montgomery County, Pennsylvania, where he served several Lutheran churches. He was a strong sup-porter of President Adams, and during Fries' Rebellion in 1798 a bullet pierced a window of his home, though no one was injured. Van Bus-kirk died suddenly while mounting his horse to go to church on Au-gust 5, 1800, and was buried in St. Peter's Church in Gwynedd.

SOURCES: Attendance at CNJ: Aaron Burr, MS Account Book, 210-11; most informa-tion and all quotations drawn from: T. G. Tappert and J. W. Doberstein, trans. *Jour. of Henry Melchior Muhlenberg* (1942-58), I-III; N.J. Lutherans: *Bergen County Hist. Soc. Papers & Proc.*, 11 (1915-16), 92-108; A. Mathews and A. N. Hunger-ford, *Hist. of the Counties of Lehigh and Carbon* (1884), 332, 496; H. M. Jenkins, *Hist. Collections Relating to Gwynedd* (1897 ed.), 377; J. H. Dubbs, *Hist of Franklin and Marshall College* (1903), 26; *U.S. Census of 1790, Pa.*, 176; full listing of all churches served: Weis, *Colonial Clergy of Middle Colonies* (1957), 332; parentage: information kindly furnished by Dr. George E. McCracken.

Barnet Wait

BARNET WAIT, A.B., has not been identified with complete certainty. The family was widespread in eighteenth-century New England, with its heaviest concentration in Massachusetts. The name Barnet was not uncommon among them. The Barnet Wait most likely to have attended the College was the one who was probably born not long before 1743 in Shrewsbury, Massachusetts, to Jason and Mercy Wait, who origin-ally came from Marblehead. A family genealogist states that this Bar-net Wait served as a surgeon at the battle of Bunker Hill. Although no mention of Wait has been found in recent accounts of the engagement, record does exist of a Barnet Wait who served as a surgeon in Colonel Ephraim Doolittle's 24th Massachusetts regiment for one month and twenty-five days, beginning on April 27, 1775. No further information concerning the alumnus has been discovered. He was first listed as dead in the College's catalogue of 1797.

SOURCES: J. C. Wait, *Genealogical Hist. of the Wait(e) Families of New England* (1904), 136; mil. service: *Mass. Soldiers & Sailors of the Rev. War* (1907), XVI, 391; see too: A. E. Cudworth, *Hist. with Genealogical Sketches of Londonderry* (1936), 192-93.

CLASS OF 1760

Joseph Alexander, A.B.

John Archer, A.B.

Samuel Blair, A.B.

William Burnet Browne

Richard Crouch Graham

Enoch Green, A.B.

Alexander Huston, A.B.

Enos Kelsey, A.B.

Ammi Ruhamah Robbins

Benjamin Rush, A.B.

John Slemmons, A.B.

Jonathan Bayard Smith, A.B.

Josiah Thatcher, A.B.

Amos Thompson, A.B.

Johannes Martinus Van
    Harlingen

Henry Wynkoop

Joseph Alexander

JOSEPH ALEXANDER, A.B., A.M. 1763, D.D. 1807 South Carolina College, Presbyterian clergyman and educator, was born in Cecil County, Maryland, in 1730, the son of Catherine Wallis and her husband Theophilus Alexander.

Alexander prepared for the College at Nottingham Academy in Maryland. If, as academy head Samuel Finley wrote to acting Princeton President Jacob Green in 1759, he was being sent off "somewhat rusted in ye classicks," Alexander must have compensated for his deficiencies while at the College. For in 1767, the year of his licensing by the New Castle Presbytery, he founded a classical school at Sugar Creek, Mecklenburg County, North Carolina, whose Presbyterian church he served as pastor. Having spent the previous two years at various settlements throughout North and South Carolina preaching and teaching, Alexander had already acquired considerable experience in both realms. It was at Sugar Creek, however, that he earned the reputation for excellence in preaching and teaching alike that he enjoyed for the rest of his life.

Though "of small stature and lame," Alexander, who was ordained in 1768, was "an uncommonly animated and popular" speaker whose personal conduct, it was often remarked, consistently mirrored the precepts he taught his flock and his students. Moreover, he was inspiring as well as forceful. At Sugar Creek alone he guided into the ministry, the law, and medicine some fifty young men who otherwise would probably not have achieved professional status.

So influential, in fact, was Alexander that in 1770 Mecklenburg County Presbyterians founded a college at Charlotte in order to expand the educational system he had begun. They hoped that Queen's College, to which Alexander was appointed a tutor, would keep their sons and their money at home and away from distant "Nassau Hall." Despite its name, Queen's College's charter failed to win approval from the royal government. Yet it opened and remained open until the British occupation of Charlotte a decade later. Alexander himself stayed at Queen's until about 1773, when he moved permanently to South Carolina to become pastor of the Indian Creek Presbyterian Church in Newberry County. The next year he left for Bullock's Creek Church in York County, where he served until "a want of interest and harmony among his people" prompted his retirement in 1801. At Bullock's Creek he established another classical school and may have taught young Andrew Jackson for a short time. It is likely that he was also associated with Mount Zion College in Winnsborough County.

Alexander's endeavors in education if not in religion once more proved successful. In 1797 he was honored by having named after him a proposed new college, Alexandria, which would have been located in Pinckneyville near his home if it had ever materialized. In 1807 he was honored again when he received one of the earliest honorary degrees conferred by the College of South Carolina. A collection of his sermons was published in the same year.

Alexander strengthened his ties to the College of New Jersey in marrying Martha Davies, a daughter of Princeton President Samuel Davies. Alexander named one of his ten children Samuel Davies Alexander. *He was an uncle of Joseph McKnitt, Sr (AB. 1792)*

An enthusiastic supporter of the Revolution, Alexander enlisted in the Charleston Volunteer Militia in October 1775. Though his actual military record has not been discovered, he was apparently driven "into exile from his peaceful abode" at some point in the conflict. He returned to Bullock's Creek, however, and died there on July 30, 1809.

SOURCES: Vital data: Joseph Alexander File, PUA; and also: Alexander, *Princeton*, 63-64; Giger, Memoirs, I; and *SCHGM*, 33 (1932), 144-45; Finley letter: *PMHB*, 70 (1946), 85; ministerial and educational activities in N.C.: Foote, *Sketches, N.C.*, 193-94, 513-14; Charles Lee Smith, *Hist. of Education in N.C.* (1888), 32-35; *WMQ*, 2 (1945), 380-81, 392-93; *NCHR*, 28 (1951), 4-7; *NCHR*, 32 (1955), 21; *NCHR*, 46 (1969), 123, 125; physical characteristics and speaking ability: G. Howe, *Hist. of the Presbyterian Church in S.C.* (1883), I, 603; C. Meriwether, *Hist. of Higher Education in S.C.* (1889), 217-18, 226; will abstract: G. L. Summer, Sr., *Newberry County, S.C. Hist. and Geneal.* (1950), 311.

PUBLICATIONS: *Eight Sermons on Important Subjects* (1807).

HS

John Archer

JOHN ARCHER, A.B., A.M. 1763, M.B. College of Philadelphia 1768, physician, medical educator, soldier, and public official, was born on May 5, 1741, the first child of Elizabeth Stevenson and Thomas Archer. The father, an immigrant from Ireland, settled first near Brinckley's Mills, Cecil County, Maryland, where John was born. There the elder Archer worked as an agent for the local ironworks. About 1750 the family moved near to Churchville, Harford (then part of Baltimore) County, where the father became a planter and storekeeper. John prepared for the College at Samuel Finley's academy at West Nottingham, Maryland.

Archer returned to Maryland after graduation, and by 1762 was teaching school in Baltimore. He was also studying for the ministry, for on August 30, 1764, he presented himself to the Presbytery of New Castle for preliminary examination leading to licensing. He apparently passed these tests, but was less successful with the second phase of his examination, which came on December 6, 1764. "The Pb'y proceeded to hear the exegesis given to Mr. Archer," the group recorded on that date, "& further examined him on Logick, & asked him some questions on Divinity; & on the whole, unanimously judge that though we would gladly encourage youths who offer themselves for the sacred ministry yet think Mr. Archer through the whole course of his tryals discovers such a want of knowledge in divinity & the other particulars he has been examined on, as well as such an incapacity to communicate his ideas on any subject, yt we cannot encourage him to prosecute his tryals for the Gospel ministry any further."

Archer next turned his ambitions toward medicine. In 1765 he enrolled with the newly constituted Medical Faculty of the College of Philadelphia. He received his degree from the institution on June 21, 1768, becoming the first person to be granted a medical diploma in what is now the United States. On October 18, 1766, while pursuing his medical studies, Archer married Catharine Harris, a sister of Dr. Robert Harris (A.B. 1753). The couple had ten children, among then Stevenson Archer (A.B. 1805). In April 1767, before receiving his medical degree, Archer began to establish a practice in New Castle County, Delaware, from where he commuted to Philadelphia to attend medical lectures. Archer kept careful account books. In his two years in Delaware he attended 212 families and for his services received about $1,000, almost three-fourths of it in cash, the rest in rent, produce, and labor. One third of his patients paid him nothing. In July 1769, Archer returned to Harford County, Maryland, where he established a new practice and remained for the rest of his life.

Archer was an early and a leading Whig. In November 1774, he was chosen a member of Harford County's Committee of Safety and served on several subsequent committees through August 1776. In December 1774, Archer became a captain in his county's first militia company, formed largely of his patients. He drilled the men himself, issuing commands through a megaphone because of a weak voice caused by a chronic throat disorder. He became a major in one of the local militia battalions in January 1776, the same month in which he served as a delegate to his state's constitutional convention. The following year he was appointed one of the commissioners of the peace (they constituted the county court) for Harford County, a position he held for thirteen years. Archer saw active military service in 1779, when he acted as volunteer aide-de-camp to General Anthony Wayne in the successful assault on Stony Point, New York. He bore George Washington's dispatches announcing the morale-boosting victory to Congress. Archer's "zeal, activity and spirit are conspicuous upon every occasion," Washington wrote in recommending him to Congress. He retired from active military service, probably because of illness, late in 1779.

At the end of the war in 1783 Archer was living on his plantation of 450 acres at Spesutia Upper Hundred, Harford County. In that year his property was assessed at £926.15, which included eight slaves, four of whom were "old and infirm." About 1785 Archer renamed his house "Medical Hall" and undertook a new career as a medical educator. Beginning with his sons (five out of six became physicians), over the next twenty-five years he trained at least fifty young men as physicians while maintaining his own extensive practice. His students formed their own medical society—the county's first—and delivered formal papers on their medical experiments and observations. In 1799 Archer was one of the founding members of the Medical and Chirurgical Faculty of Maryland (the state's medical society) and served it as an examiner. His one original contribution to medicine was the introduction of *Polygala senega* (seneka snakeroot) as a remedy for croup.

Archer had an active political career. He was a presidential elector in 1797 on the Jeffersonian ticket and served in the United States House of Representatives from 1801 to 1807. A large man of imposing presence, he made no speeches while in Congress, doubtless because of his throat disability. He voted the straight Republican party line on most issues. Archer's health failed shortly after he left Congress. He died at his home on September 28, 1810. In his will he left his 750-acre plantation to his wife in trust for their surviving children and ordered that his slaves (he had owned seven in 1790) be freed upon reaching certain ages.

SOURCES: *DAB*; two long sketches, printing much MS material are: *Bulletin of the Johns Hopkins Hospital*, 10 (1899), 141-47, and *Baltimore Sun*, March 23, 1930, 14-15; Washington quotation and army service: Washington, *Writings*, XV, 443n, 452; 1783 property: *Harford County 1783 Maryland Tax List* (1970), 42; 1790 slaves: *U.S. Census of 1790, Maryland*, 74; for students, see: *Bul. Johns Hopkins Hosp.*, 13 (1902), 181-88; for political career, see: *MHM*, 61 (1966), 218, 227; *Annals of Congress*, 1801-1807.

Mss: MdHi; VHi

Samuel Blair

SAMUEL BLAIR, A.B., A.M. 1763, Harvard, 1767, D.D. University of Pennsylvania 1790, Presbyterian and Congregational clergyman and

Samuel Blair, A.B. 1760

army chaplain, was born in 1741 at Fagg's Manor, Chester County, Pennsylvania, a son of Frances Van Hook and her husband, Samuel Blair. The father, one of the founding trustees of the College, emigrated from Ireland while a youth, was educated at the Log College and became a Presbyterian clergyman. He also ran an academy at which he prepared several youths for the College before his death in 1751. He was described as having been "grave and solemn, yet cheerful, pleasant, and witty."

At his commencement Blair took the positive in a public debate with his classmate Benjamin Rush on the proposition that "the Elegancy of an Oration much consists in the Words being consonant to the Sense." Blair, a Philadelphia newspaper reported, "acquitted himself with universal Applause, in the elegant Composition and Delivery of his Defense; and his opponent answered him with Humour and Pertinency." Blair stayed on in Princeton after graduation to study theology. He and an unidentifiable undergraduate composed *An Oration Pronounced at Nassau-Hall, January 14, 1761, on Occasion of the Death of His Late Majesty King George II*. The opening paragraph conveys its tone:

When majesty itself is clad in the Livery of Sorrow; and the Throne, admist the solemn Emblems of Mourning, forgets her wonted Splendors:—When Europe mingles in one general Concert of Lamentation; and when GEORGE the second forsakes our British World;—what Wonder is *Nassau-Hall*, fond to unite in the sympathizing Chorus, should, this day, drop a filial Tear.

The College authorities thought so highly of the piece that they saw that it was published. The trustees too admired Blair. Appointed a tutor in 1761, he served in the post until 1764. It fell to Blair to write the first official historical account of the College, *An Account of the College of New Jersey*, which was published in 1764. The *Account*, as much a promotional brochure as a history, lucidly described the founding of the College, playing down its Presbyterian connections, and gave a description of the College's tuition, discipline, curriculum, library, and future needs.

Handsome and of commanding presence, despite his weak voice, Blair quickly became popular among Presbyterians for his carefully composed and moving sermons. He was ordained by the Presbytery of New Castle in 1764, and by November 1765, Benjamin Rush (a member of Philadelphia's Second Presbyterian Church) was writing to Ebenezer Hazard (A.B. 1762) that "our congregation is now met and deliberating on the expediency of presenting a call to Saml. Blair, who has preached among us for some time with general approbation." The Philadelphians were not fast enough. On October 14, 1765, Boston's Old South Church asked Blair and two other candidates to try out for the post of junior pastor to Joseph Sewell (Harvard 1707). Blair accepted and traveled north; on May 5, 1766, the members of the church unanimously chose him as Sewell's colleague. He was formally installed on November 9, 1766. Between the time of his election and his installation, Blair returned south to collect his belongings. His return trip to Boston was made by sea. During it he was shipwrecked, lost all his possessions, and may have had his health seriously damaged by the experience.

Samuel Finley, the College's fifth president, had died in July 1766. The trustees first elected John Witherspoon of Paisley, Scotland, to the office, but Witherspoon declined. In October 1767 the trustees elected Blair to the post at a salary of £200 per year, while at the same time his uncle, John Blair, was appointed professor of Divinity and Moral Philosophy. The trustees' hasty election of Blair was made in order to stave off an Old Side Presbyterian attempt to gain control of the College. Blair was obviously an attractive candidate, but his choice doubt-less was not hurt by his marriage on September 24, 1767, to Susannah Shippen, daughter of the Philadelphia physician William Shippen, Sr., long a friend of the College. Susannah's uncle Edward Shippen was a trustee of the College at the time, as was her brother William Shippen, Jr. (A.B. 1753). Blair's age (not yet twenty-six) caused some adverse comments on the move. But when word came that Witherspoon might accept the call if asked again, Blair gracefully stepped aside.

Blair fitted easily into Boston society. Since he was a Boston minister he automatically became an Overseer of Harvard, which awarded him the A.M. in 1767. Blair fell ill in the summer of 1769 and traveled to Philadelphia to recuperate. While he was still there the Old South's senior minister, Sewell, died. The church's congregation wished to re-tain the Half-Way Covenant, which permitted the baptism of children of parents not in full communion. Blair felt that at least one parent should be a full church member. Blair and the congregation could not come to an agreement on the issue, and he resigned on October 10 without returning to Boston. A certain coolness existed between both parties for a time, but in 1771, while Blair was visiting Boston, the Old South presented him with a handsome testimonial to his services.

After his resignation Blair settled in Pennsylvania. He and his wife moved into an imposing mansion in Germantown, now known as the Blair-Shippen House. Fellow clergymen urged Blair to pursue his pro-fession once again, but in 1771 he advertised instead that he planned to open an extremely expensive private school. The outcome of the venture, if any, is unknown. By 1773 President Stiles of Yale was re-cording in his diary rumors that Blair was about to convert to the Church of England and travel to London to be ordained a priest. Whatever the truth of the story, on April 24, 1773, Josiah Quincy, Jr. (Harvard 1763), visiting in Philadelphia, noted in his journal that Blair had attended services at Anglican St. Peter's church that day. But at the same time Blair was helping the Presbyterians to establish a church of their own in Germantown; the congregation's services were held in his own home until a building was ready. Whatever his flirta-tion with Anglicanism, little came of it.

The Boston Port Bill brought Blair back into the pulpit. Readmitted to the Synod of Philadelphia in 1774, he preached in several churches against the "late tyrannical, cruel and vindictive statute of the British Parliament." Blair shortly joined the American armies as a chaplain, and spent most of the war years moving with them from place to place, now Massachusetts, now Pennsylvania, preaching to the troops and dunning the Pennsylvania government for back pay and for clothing for himself and his servant. Blair fell ill during the winter of 1780–1781 and retired from active service. On May 12, 1781, Susannah Blair gave birth to the last of the couple's five children.

The war over, Blair resumed his role as a leading citizen of Germantown. In July 1787 he shocked orthodox Calvinists with a welcome from the pulpit to the doctrine of universal salvation—a decided shift from his earlier rejection of the Half-Way Covenant. His classmate Benjamin Rush was overjoyed, but the Presbytery of Philadelphia ordered an investigation and censured Blair. However, by 1790 Blair was preaching from Presbyterian pulpits again. In the same year the University of Pennsylvania awarded him the D.D.

When the federal capital moved to Philadelphia in 1790, Blair requested of his old commander, General Knox, that he be appointed a chaplain to Congress: "Tho the emoluments are comparatively inconsiderable, they may in several respects be essentially serviceable to me; the appointment, should it take place, will be respectable; its duties may be punctually attended to without injury to my health; and their intention will precisely accord with my professional character." Blair got the appointment and acted as chaplain to the House of Representatives for two years.

Blair obviously never fulfilled his early promise. Princeton University Library possesses many of his papers: sermons, letters, copybooks and the like. From the fragmentary remaining evidence one can conjecture that his career was blighted to a degree by chronic, recurrent, and incapacitating depressions. Blair's later years were devoted largely to Germantown's Presbyterian church and to his own complicated but minor business dealings. From time to time he delivered and had printed sermons—including one of 1798 in support of the policies of President John Adams. Blair died in Germantown on September 24, 1818.

SOURCES: Father: *DAB*; sketches: *DAB*; *Sibley's Harvard Graduates*, XIV, 556-63, from which congressional chaplaincy quotation is drawn; Sprague, *Annals*, III, 268-69; commencement debate: *Pa. Journal*, Oct. 2, 1760; Rush 1765 comment and later observation: Butterfield, *Rush Letters*, 20, 433; correct marriage date (elsewhere given as 1764, 1769); Susannah Shippen Blair Family Bible, MS, NjP; Princeton presidency: esp. L. H. Butterfield, *John Witherspoon Comes to America* (1953); Old South pastorate: H. A. Hill, *History of the Old South Church* (1890), II; Stiles remark: *Literary Diary*, I, 371; Quincy observation: *MHSP* (3 ser.), 49 (1915-16), 471; army activities: scattered references throughout: *Pa. Arch.* (2nd and 5th ser.); 1790 preaching: *MHSP* (1 ser.), 17 (1879-80), 206.

PUBLICATIONS: see STE

MSS: NjP, PHi

William Burnet Browne

WILLIAM BURNET BROWNE, landowner, planter, and public official, was born in Salem, Massachusetts, on October 7, 1738. His father, William Browne (Harvard 1727), was the richest merchant in Salem, an extensive landowner, and a public official. The family was Salem's wealthiest and most distinguished. Young William's mother, Mary Burnet, was a daughter of William Burnet, governor at one time of New York, New Jersey, and Massachusetts, son of Gilbert Burnet, bishop of Salisbury and godson of King William III. Young William, the eldest of eight children, was raised at "Folly Hill," the grandest mansion in Salem. His father was much given to theological speculation and controversy, which perhaps explains why William was sent to the new College of New Jersey rather than to his father's alma mater.

William entered the College's grammar school on September 24, 1755. There he bought copies of the Newark *Grammar*, Isaac Watts's Psalms, a Latin Erasmus, Guthrie's translation of Cicero, and other books. In the six months between his entrance and March 24, 1756, he ran up one of the highest bills of any student on whom President Burr kept records—a total of £41.4s.10d., at a time when the annual salary of a college tutor was £40. Between the time Browne arrived in Newark and the time he left Princeton he spent money on items such as the following: £1.2s. for having shirts made; £2 for special tutoring by John Ewing (A.B. 1754); £4.7s.1d. for having special closets and shelves built into his room; £3.16s for furnishing his room; and £2.4s. for painting his room. His largest expenditure was for a horse, which he bought for £12.1s. on March 21, 1756. On the same day he paid £4.2s. for a saddle and bridle and £2.5s. for thirty bushels of oats. The horse was costly to keep, especially on February 22, 1757, when President Burr had to pay £4.16s.6d. "for redeeming his Mare yt he [Browne] had foolishly exchang'd." The date on which Browne entered the College is unknown, but that he entered it is certain, for he bought College texts and was charged for "tuition" rather than "schooling." On May 26, 1757, President Burr recorded that Browne was "sent to Boston, not returned." His last steward's bill was rendered as of June 29, 1757.

Browne's removal from the College may have been caused by troubles at home in Salem. During 1756 every member of his family fell ill. His brothers Thomas and Francis and his sister Sarah all died in October and November of that year. The Brownes, in fact, seem to have been a short-lived family. Of the original eight children only William and his sister Mary were living when their father died on April 27,

1763. William inherited not only his mother's substantial New York landholdings but his father's substantial estate as well. He also came into possession of his father's extensive library, the family mansion, portraits, Gobelin tapestries, plate, and so on.

In 1764 Browne married Judith Walker Carter, a daughter of Charles Carter of "Cleve," King George's County, Virginia. One student of Virginia's history has declared that "it was the custom for an outsider who married a Virginia lady to settle in the colony and become a Virginian." This custom Browne eventually followed, but not for some years. Known as "Virginia Billy" to Salem's townspeople, after his marriage Browne lived in the Salem mansion and served as a warden and vestryman of Salem's Anglican St. Peter's Church in 1766 and 1767. In the latter year William sold the Salem mansion to his enormously wealthy first cousin, also William Browne (Harvard 1755), later a prominent Loyalist and governor of the Bermudas.

William and Judith Browne moved to Virginia in 1767. There they purchased "Elsing Green," a plantation in King William County with a magnificent mansion house overlooking the Pamunkey River. The precise extent of the establishment is now indeterminable, but in the early 1780s Browne was being taxed in King William County for the ownership of seventy-five slaves and 1,000 acres. Browne must have retained some land in New England, for in 1771 he sold 7,000 acres in Tolland County, Connecticut to Abijah Willard and Samuel Ward.

After his removal south Browne sank almost without trace into the life of the Virginia country gentry. His name appears in no contemporary Virginia newspapers, and the only mention of him found in the public record is a notice that he served as a justice of the peace for his county in 1771. Browne died at Elsing Green on May 6, 1784. Browne had three daughters: Mary, who married Herbert Claiborne (their eldest son changed his name to William Burnet Browne); Elizabeth Carter, who married John Bassett; and Judith Carter, who married Robert Lewis, a nephew of George Washington.

SOURCES: Family: *Sibley's Harvard Graduates*, VIII, 120-24; XIII, 551-60; Salem family home and portions of father's will: E. D. Hines, "Browne Hill in History," *Essex Institute Historical Collections*, 32 (1896), 201-38; College expenses: Aaron Burr, MS Account Book, 152-53, 262-63, 290-91; marriage, children, move to Virginia and Elsing Green: *VMHB*, 32 (1924), 3; Virginia lady quotation: M. Talpalar, *Sociology of Colonial Virginia* (1960), 217; Salem church: *Essex Institute Historical Collections*, 80 (1944), 337; appearance of Elsing Green: E. H. Ryland, *King William County, Va.* (1955), 87; slaves: A. B. Fothergill and J. M. Nangle, *Virginia Tax Payers* (1966), 17; King William acreage: *WMQ* (2 ser.), 6 (1929), 326; Conn. land sale: *Adams Papers*, II, 24; JP: *Bulletin of the Virginia State Library*, 14 (1921), 110, 111.

Richard Crouch Graham

RICHARD CROUCH GRAHAM, A.B. Yale 1760, Congregational clergyman, was born in Southbury, Connecticut, on March 11, 1739. He was the youngest son of John Graham, Southbury's Congregational minister, by his second wife, Abigail Chauncy.

Richard Crouch Graham entered the College on September 15, 1753, but withdrew before completing his education. In September 1756 he enrolled at Yale, where his half-brother, John Graham, had graduated in 1740 and his brother, Chauncy Graham in 1747. Graham's father was an ardent supporter of Yale College and occasionally traveled to England and Scotland to obtain books and money for the school in New Haven.

In 1761 Graham married Molly Lee of Lyme, Connecticut, the sister-in-law of Moses Baldwin (A.B. 1757). On May 25, 1762, Graham was licensed to preach by the Litchfield South Association. Among the churches he supplied was the Congregational meetinghouse in Pelham, Hampshire County, Massachusetts, which had been without a permanent minister since 1754. In early 1763 the Hampshire County grand jury prosecuted the town for negligence in not having secured a pastor, and the town meeting hastily approved a call for Graham. Although twenty-one members of the church objected to his appointment, Graham was ordained and installed at Pelham on July 6, 1763. He was granted £100 for accepting the call and a salary of £60 per year. That sum was to be raised, in triennial increments, to £80 annually. The town also built a new house for Graham, and his land was taxed at a rate of half a penny per acre.

His income was not enough to keep Graham, his wife, and his four children solvent. He fell into debt, was sued, and his possessions were attached. Under intense emotional strain he died on February 25, 1771. His burial in Pelham's Old Burial Ground cost the town £1.18.5. In April 1772 the town meeting called upon his widow to "supply" the pulpit for four sabbaths, which probably meant that she was expected to pay the salary of a temporary preacher.

SOURCES: C. O. Parmenter, *Hist. of Pelham, Mass.* (1898), 62, 116-18, 123-24, 469; Dexter, *Yale Biographies*, II, 655; father: W. C. Fowler, *Memorials of the Chaunceys* (1850), 228-31; W. Cothren, *Hist. of Ancient Woodbury, Conn.* (1854), I, 546-47; marriage: E. E. Salisbury and E. McC. Salisbury, *Family Histories and Genealogies* (1892), III, 56; licensing: General Association of Congregational Church in Conn., *Contributions to the Ecclesiastical Hist. of Conn.* (1861), 318; Pelham: L. E. Wikander, et al., *Hampshire Hist.* (1964), 192.

RAH

Enoch Green

ENOCH GREEN, A.B., A.M. 1763, Presbyterian clergyman, was born in Ewing Township, near Trenton, New Jersey, about 1734, the son of Lydia Armitage and William Green, a farmer and elder of Trenton's Presbyterian church. In College Green kept careful records of his theological studies, noting in short essays his responses to questions such as: "How does it appear consistent with the Justice & Goodness of God to Suffer evil Spirits to roam through the World doing Mischief & Tempting Men to Sin?"; "What are the principal Ingredients of heavenly Happiness?"; and "What is the Difference between the Law of the Gospel, or, between the Covenant of Grace and the Covenant of Works?" At his commencement, a Pennsylvania newspaper reported, Green delivered "a well-composed valedictory Oration in English."

After graduation Green studied theology, first with the Baptist Reverend Isaac Eaton in Hopewell, New Jersey, then with Samuel Finley after the latter assumed the College's presidency. He was licensed by the Presbytery of New Brunswick on December 29, 1761. Even before then, on June 21, 1761, he had received detailed instructions from the Reverend John Brainerd, a trustee of the College, on where he was to preach on the south Jersey shore: Tom's River, Good Luck, Great Egg Harbor, Cape May, Little Egg Harbor as well as other places. He was ordained on October 1, 1762, by the Presbytery of New Brunswick, which sent him on a missionary trip to Virginia.

In 1763 the Presbyterian churches at Maidenhead (now Lawrenceville) and Hopewell, New Jersey, asked Green to serve as their supply preacher and the following year asked him to settle as their permanent pastor. The presbytery advised Green not to accept the position unless the two churches could resolve a long-standing dispute with each other. This they were unable to do, and in 1766 Green was called by the Presbyterian church at Deerfield, Cumberland County, New Jersey. He accepted and was installed there on June 9, 1767.

Shortly after taking up the Deerfield pastorate Green opened a Latin grammar school in his home. Over the years he prepared many youths for the College, among them Philip Vickers Fithian (A.B. 1772) and Samuel Leake (A.B. 1774). On June 7, 1770, Green married Mary Beatty, a daughter of the Reverend Charles Beatty of Neshaminy, Pennsylvania. Green prepared Mary's brother, Charles Clinton Beatty (A.B. 1775), for the College. The couple had three children. Letters of his former students indicate that Green inspired considerable respect and affection as a teacher. Visiting the Greens on April 29, 1774, Philip Fithian (who married a sister of Mrs. Green) found Green "vastly sensible, very intelligible, dry, witty, satirical, yet good and exceedingly agreeable."

At the outbreak of the Revolution, Green was elected chaplain to a battalion of the Continental army (which one has not been discovered). An undated sermon he delivered to his unit still survives in the Princeton University Library. It is a straight-forward exhortation to battle, in which Green justified opposition to the king by recounting the history of the English civil war of the 1640s. He defended the justice of the American cause and assured the battalion that it would account itself bravely. He held up the men of Boston as examples for inspiration and emulation. It was sad to see British blood shed by British hands, he said, but liberty was an American birthright. The American cause would triumph, he thought, because of the distance of England and because in the past, "the Whigs have always gained ye Day."

Shortly thereafter Green fell ill. He made his will on September 9, 1775, and on the next day wrote the following letter to his father:

> I am now reduced very weak and low, and do soon expect to leave this World[;] My Wife a disconsolate Widow and two Fatherless Children, whom I commend to Divine Providence and Your Care.
>
> I have disposed of what little Estate I have to my wife for her Support and the support and maintenance of my Children: and as you have informed me that you have and intend Given me by Will some Real Estate, I am persuaded that the same regard you have for me will be retained for my Children and induce you to Dispose of the said Real Estate to my Son William after my Decease. And I do earnestly request that you would Consider and Provide for my Widow and Children in such a manner as you think best seeing I hav'nt it in my Power in my present Circumstances to make that Provision for them that the tenderness Esteem and Gratitude I owe and bear to my beloved Wife and the affection and regard I have for my Dear Children require. I have requested the Rev.d Mr Fithian to take the Charge of the Education of Billy in Case he inclines and you think best he should have a liberal Education.
>
> My Dear Father, Mother, & all my Friends have my last Prayers for the Protection of a kind Providence, Who I hope will be a stay and stake to you in your advanced years a Husband & Father to my expected Widow & poor Fatherless Children. Adieu.

The letter was somewhat premature, for Green recovered enough to join his battalion near New York and to father a third child. But his health had been weakened. He was struck with "camp fever" and returned home to die on December 2, 1776. His brother-in-law Fithian had died of the same malady on October 8, 1776. When Green's father died in 1786, his will followed the requests of his son's 1775 letter. Neither of Green's sons attended the College, but a grandson, Charles Beatty Green, graduated in 1824. Green's personal estate was inventoried at £657. A listing of all his possessions conveys some sense of the lifestyle of a provincial clergyman of his generation:

	£	S
Horse Bridle Saddle and wearing apparel	62	3
Cash Silver Watch Buckles and Buttons	43	6:3
Plate £10. 1 Clock 36£ with sundries makes	[?]5.	15.
Beds Bedding Meal Yarn and Sundries	147	15
Waggons Horses and a Riding Chair	65	
Negro man £50 a Wench and 2 Children £100	150	
Cattle Corn Grain growing and sundries	20.	16.
Outstanding debts	16	10
5 lb of Wooling Yarn and a Rugg	2	0
A Library of Books and Sundrys	54:	15

SOURCES: Brief sketch: F. D. Andrews, *A Biog. Sketch of Enoch Green* (1933); geneal. data: Enoch Green folder, PUA; "Theological Responses, begun Novem[r] 18th 1759 at Nassau-Hall," MS, NjP; commencement oration: *Pa. Journal*, Oct. 2, 1760; study with Eaton: Butterfield, *Rush Letters*, I, 4; study with Finley (inferential): Rush to Green, April 12, 1762, MS, NjP; Brainerd instructions: *Presbyterian Mag.*, 2 (1852), 471; Fithian quotation: *Journal*, I, 160; battle sermon and letter to father: MSS, NjP; father's will: 35 *NJA*, 166-67; Green's will: 34 *NJA*, 210-11; estate inventory: MS, N.J. State Lib., Trenton.

PUBLICATIONS: STE

MSS: NjP; NjR; PHi

Alexander Huston

ALEXANDER HUSTON, A.B., Presbyterian clergyman, was born in Dublin, Ireland. No information concerning either his parentage or the circumstances of his emigration to America has been discovered. He may have been prepared for the College at Samuel Finley's academy at West Nottingham, Maryland.

Huston was licensed by the Presbytery of Lewes on April 12, 1763. For the next year and a half he acted as a supply preacher at various Presbyterian churches in Delaware and Maryland: at Murtherkill, Three Runs, Wicomico, Princess Anne, Rehoboth, Broad Creek, Nanticoke, and Queen Anne's. On October 9, 1764, Huston was ordained pastor of the churches at Murtherkill and Three Runs, Kent County, Delaware. Huston married Ann ("Nancy") Fullerton on January 23, 1766. The couple had four children.

Huston was a staunch Whig. During the Revolution his farm near Double Run (now Magnolia, Delaware) was raided by the British. In the nineteenth century a story was still current that during the Revolution Huston would often pray "that the Lord would send plenty of powder and ball" to the Continental army. In addition to his double pastorate Huston preached frequently at St. Johnston, Delaware, and taught school in Milford, Delaware. Huston made his will on December 31, 1784, leaving his property to his wife and three surviving children, John, Samuel and Ann. He died on January 3, 1785, and was buried in the vault of the Double Run church.

SOURCES: The name was sometimes spelled "Houston"; for vital data see extensive correspondence in Alexander Huston File, PUA; revolutionary anecdote: J. Ledrum, *A Hist. of the Rise of Methodism in America* (1859), 217; will abstract: *Calendar of Kent County, Delaware, Probate Records, 1680-1800* (1944), 371.

Enos Kelsey

ENOS KELSEY, A.B., A.M. 1801, merchant and public official, was born in Killingworth, Connecticut, on January 16, 1733, the son of Matthias Kelsey. About 1740 the family moved to Salisbury, in the northwest corner of the colony, where the father was a deacon in the local Congregational church.

Kelsey entered the College on June 3, 1757. It was probably shortly after his graduation that he married Elizabeth Davenport, a sister of John Davenport (A.B. 1769) and daughter of the Reverend James Davenport, the once-notorious New Light evangelist who was a warm friend of the College. Not long thereafter Kelsey set up business as a general merchant in Princeton. His two-story brick shop was on Nassau Street, approximately across from the present Chancellor Green. Kelsey was active in Presbyterian affairs, acting in 1772 as a New Jersey agent for a lottery designed to raise funds for Presbyterian churches in New York.

Kelsey's political career began on July 4, 1774, when he attended a Somerset County meeting that passed eight resolutions supporting the beleaguered inhabitants of Boston, calling for the New Jersey Assembly to support them, and recommending a general nonimportation agreement among other things. The final resolution appointed a committee to meet when necessary to correspond with other county committees, and to join them in electing proper representatives to a proposed Continental Congress. Kelsey, along with President Witherspoon, Jonathan Dickinson Sergeant (A.B. 1762), and Frederick Frelinghuysen (A.B. 1770), was one of the nine men on the committee. By 1776 Kelsey was serving as a Somerset County justice of the peace and as a judge in the court of common pleas. In May of that year he was elected to the New Jersey Provincial Congress.

For the following year or so Kelsey was preoccupied with raising supplies for the Continental army. A receipt of his that still survives in the University Library shows that in order to deliver eighty-one barrels of flour to the army Kelsey had to negotiate with seven different individuals. At the same time Kelsey continued his judicial activities, serving as a justice in Somerset County's court of quarter sessions.

On June 16, 1779, the New Jersey Council appointed Kelsey state clothier. The post would not be a happy one for Kelsey. Accountable for £300,000 in state funds, his main responsibility was in clothing state troops. By May 1780 officers of various New Jersey army units were complaining bitterly to a committee of the state legislature about Kelsey's performance. "It is necessary to inform the House," the committee reported, "that a Number of Vests and Breeches were produced to the Committee, which were evidently too small for the most minute Person . . . and which the Officers declared were left after providing the smallest Men, and even Boys with those Articles; some Shirts were also shewn to the Committee, which had been delivered to the Men, much too small for them, by Reason whereof they were greatly worn out, tho' but seldom used."

A committee was appointed to investigate the matter. Though Kelsey was not formally reprimanded, he was apparently forced to resign his post, being replaced by Israel Morris in June 1780. A short time later Kelsey advertised for sale his house "in the healthy and agreeable village of Princeton," describing it as "perfectly agreeable either for a merchant or private gentleman." Whether Kelsey actually moved away from Princeton or not has not been discovered. No mention of him appears in the public record for the next decade and a half. By 1796, however, his reputation seems to have been restored, for in that year he was appointed treasurer of the College. He held the post for the next fourteen years, serving with apparent satisfaction to all. Such fragmentary receipts and accounts of his that survive show him to have been somewhat more businesslike in the handling of the affairs of the College than his predecessors.

Kelsey made his will in October 1810. A codicil provided that if his wife predeceased him half of his estate would go to his brother-in-law, John Davenport, one-quarter to the College, and another quarter to Princeton's Presbyterian church. Kelsey died in Princeton on June 26, 1811. The inventory of his estate came to $4,690. Since his wife lived for many years thereafter, the provisions of the codicil never went into effect.

SOURCES: Substantially inaccurate sketch: J. F. Hageman, *History*, I, 71-73; geneal.: E. A. Claypool and A. Clizbee, *A Genealogy of the Descendants of William Kelsey* (1947), I, 217; College entrance: Aaron Burr, MS Account Book, 276; Presbyterian churches: *N.Y. Jour.*, Feb. 6, 1772; 1774 committee: *Pa. Jour.*, July 20, 1774; Prov. Congr. and JP: *Som. Cty. Hist. Quart.*, 8 (1919), 36; flour: MS receipt, Aug. 5, 1777, NjP; N.J. Clothier and investigation: *Votes and Proc. of the General Assembly of the State of N.J.* (1780), 180, 190, 208-11; see too: L. Lundin, *Cockpit of the Rev.* (1940), 435; house sale ad.: *N.J. Gaz.*, Nov. 8, 1780; treasurer: MS Trustees' Minutes, I, PUA; many misc. receipts: Maclean Papers, PUA; will: MS, N.J. State Lib., Trenton.

Mss: only as noted above.

Ammi Ruhamah Robbins

AMMI RUHAMAH ROBBINS, A.B. Yale 1760, A.M. 1763, Congregational clergyman, was born in Branford, Connecticut, on August 25, 1740. He was the son of Hannah Foote and the Reverend Philemon Robbins (Harvard 1729), a well-known New Light clergyman and associate of George Whitefield, Eleazar Wheelock, Joseph Bellamy, and Aaron Burr. The senior Robbins was a leader of the Great Awakening in Connecticut, at one time having been censured and temporarily deprived of his pulpit by the conservative New Haven Consociation.

After being prepared at home, Ammi Robbins entered the College in the fall of 1756. It was his father's respect for President Burr that brought him to New Jersey, and after Burr died in 1757 young Robbins left Princeton and enrolled at Yale. For a few months after graduation he was a teacher in Plymouth, Massachusetts, where his brother, Chandler Robbins (Yale 1756), had just begun his career as a prominent New Light minister. After studying theology under Bellamy, as Chandler had done before him, Ammi Robbins was licensed to preach by the New Haven East Association on May 26, 1761. The Litchfield Association immediately recommended him to the new church in Norfolk, Connecticut. He supplied the pulpit there until September, when the congregation asked him to settle as its permanent pastor. The members of the church offered him the land that had been set aside for their first minister and a salary of £62.10s. annually for

Ammi Ruhamah Robbins, Class of 1760
BY REUBEN MOULTHROP

the first two years. After that time, his wages would be raised by £70 per year. Robbins accepted the call and was ordained by the Litchfield Consocation on October 28, 1761. His church, which was not completely finished until 1770, was a fifty-by-fifty-foot meetinghouse with galleries. His congregation numbered thirty-eight.

In 1762 Robbins visited Plymouth to marry Elizabeth LeBaron, a direct descendant of Governor William Bradford and the daughter of a Huguenot physician, on May 13. The couple had thirteen children. A short, dark, muscular man, Robbins was constantly active. His strong voice kept his listeners enthralled. A dedicated New Light like his father, he led at least four major revivals in Norfolk. During his years in Norfolk Robbins prepared almost 200 young men, some of whom lived in his house, to enter college. Most of his earlier students went on to attend either Dartmouth or Yale.

The congregation in Norfolk was frequently in financial difficulty, and to ease the situation in 1767 Robbins agreed to accept his salary in kind. Between 1779 and 1783 he also voluntarily sacrificed £14 of his wages per year. In 1776 he joined Colonel Burrell's regiment of Litchfield County militia, which was on its way to reinforce Benedict Arnold's forces, as a chaplain. Robbins left home in mid-March and traveled throughout the Northern Department, comforting the sick and wounded and preaching to troops on the line. He suffered severe attacks of dysentery during his months with the army and had to make two brief visits home in order to recuperate. His diary, which he kept throughout his life, contains a detailed account of his military service. He left his regiment in October 1776, and his commission expired the following January.

After the Revolution Robbins took occasional leaves from his church to do missionary work in Vermont, New Hampshire, and northern New York and to represent the Litchfield General Association at meetings of the Presbyterian General Assembly. An associate of Jonathan Edwards, Jr. (A.B. 1765), he also took a prominent role in the Second Great Awakening in Connecticut. He preached a total of more than 6,500 sermons, of which several were published at the request of his listeners. Besides his congregation, his most regular audience after 1796 was the Western Star Lodge of Masons in Norfolk.

Robbins's church was one of Connecticut's largest and most prosperous, numbering 549 people by 1813. Robbins's reputation for piety and kindness (he was said to agree with Bellamy in most things but to prefer the cheerier parts of the New Testament) was a major reason for the early success of Williams College, of which he was a trustee between 1794 and 1810. His own students in Norfolk were sent to Williams after 1793, as was his son Thomas whom Robbins withdrew from Yale.

In 1810, Robbins's health began to fail. He preached his half-century sermon in October 1811, but rheumatism forced him to seek assistance for most of his duties. He stopped taking pupils in 1810 or 1811, and in May 1813 he preached his last sermon. Suffering from facial cancer, he died on October 31, 1813. He was buried in Norfolk, and his funeral was the first ceremony performed in the town's new church. His grandchildren converted his home into a full-time school as a monument to his memory.

SOURCES: Dexter, *Yale Biographies*, II, 670-73; A. Goodenough, *Clergy of Litchfield County* (1909), 50-53; C. Durfee, *Williams Biographical Annals* (1871), 54; *Appleton's Amer. Biog.*, 270; J. Eldridge, *Hist. of Norfolk* (1900), passim.; parents: R. L. Bushman, *From Puritan to Yankee* (1967), 211; *NEHGR*, 9 (1855), 194; 38 (1884), 365-70; marriage: First Church of Plymouth, Mass., *Plymouth Church Records* (1923), 493; *NEHGR*, 9 (1855), 194; army: F. B. Heitman, *Officers of the Continental Army* (1893), 347; *PMHB*, 59 (1935), 342-46; *Min. of Conn. in Rev.*, 53-55; ministry: C. R. Keller, *Second Great Awakening in Connecticut* (1942), 1, 40, 50-

51; General Association of Congregational Churches in Connecticut, *Contributions to Ecclesiastical Hist. of Conn.* (1861), 165, 324; Stiles, *Literary Diary*, III, 121, 354, 355; I. N. Tarbox, ed., *Diary of Thomas Robbins, D.D.* (1886), I, 140; Williams College: *NEHGR*, 38 (1884), 365-70; personal characteristics: A. Robbins, . . . *Church Records* . . . (1910), 73-74; ill health, death, and epitaph: Tarbox, ed., above, 428, 449, 569; J. W. Barber, *Conn. Historical Collections* (1836), 482-83.

PUBLICATIONS: see STE; Sh-Sh #s 23823, 26630

Mss: CtHi; PHi; PPPrHi (Webster/Bellamy Transcripts).

RAH

Benjamin Rush

BENJAMIN RUSH, A.B., A.M. 1763, M.D. Edinburgh 1768, LL.D. Yale 1812, physician, public official and man of letters, was born on January 4, 1746, in Byberry Township, just outside Philadelphia, a son of Susanna Hall Harvey by her second husband, John Rush, a gunsmith and farmer. The father died when Rush was five years old, and when

Benjamin Rush, A.B. 1760
BY EDWARD SAVAGE

he was eight his mother sent him to the academy in West Nottingham, Maryland, conducted by her sister's husband, Samuel Finley, later fifth president of the College. Although Rush had been baptized into his father's Anglican church, his mother was an evangelical Presbyterian, and at Nottingham Academy Rush came under the full influence of the spirit of the Great Awakening, of which Finley, who was something of a surrogate father to the boy, had been a major leader.

Rush joined the College's junior class in his fifteenth year, in the spring of 1759. In August of that year Samuel Davies entered on his brief tenure as president. "He was truly dignified, but at the same time affable and even familiar in his intercourse with his pupils," Rush wrote of Davies many years later. "He introduced several new subjects of instruction into the College, and gave to the old branches of education a new and popular complexion. It was my happy lot to attract a good deal of his attention. I discovered some talents for poetry, composition and public speaking, to each of which he was very partial." At his commencement in 1760, a Philadelphia newspaper reported, "Mr. *Benjamin Rush* arose, and in a very sprightly entertaining Manner, delivered an ingenious *English* Harrangue in Praise of Oratory." It was an activity to which Rush would devote a good deal of his energy in later years. In his commencement address, President Davies exhorted Rush and the other students to go into "publick life with a new heart and a new spirit . . . the new birth is the beginning of all genuine religion and virtue."

Rush's heart was ever new, but he graduated with a troubled spirit, undecided on the choice of a career. President Davies asked him what profession he intended to follow. Rush replied that he had been advised to read law. But before taking up his studies, he visited his uncle and mentor, Samuel Finley, at Nottingham. "Just before I took leave of him on my return home," Rush later recalled, "he called me to the end of the piazza before his door, and asked me whether I had chosen a profession. I told him I had, and that I expected to begin the study of the law as soon as I returned to Philadelphia. He said the practice of the law was full of temptations and advised me by no means to think of it, but to study physic. 'But before you determine on any thing (said he), set apart a day for fasting and prayer, and ask God to direct you in your choice of a profession.' I am sorry to say I neglected the latter part of this excellent advice, but yielded to the former, and accordingly obtained from Mr. Davies, whom I saw afterwards in Philadelphia, a letter of recommendation to Dr. John Redman to become his pupil."

At the time Redman, a trustee of the College, was Philadelphia's leading physician. Rush served as his apprentice from February 1761 to July 1766, gradually overcoming his repugnance toward surgery and diligently reading through the works of medical giants such as Sydenham, Boerhaave, and Van Swieten. When President Samuel Finley fell ill in Philadelphia in 1766 Rush attended him in his last days and performed the sad office of closing his eyes.

Rush was a diligent apprentice—he claimed that he missed only eleven days' work in the six years he spent with Redman. But when Dr. William Shippen (A.B. 1754) and Dr. John Morgan returned to Philadelphia from their medical studies in Britain, Rush found time to attend their lectures and was doubtless inspired to study abroad himself. His mother—widowed again, operating a grocery store, and educating Benjamin's younger brother Jacob (A.B. 1765)—somehow scraped together money enough to send Rush off to study at the University of Edinburgh. He arrived in England in August 1766 and was enrolled at the University by November.

In 1800 Rush declared that "the two years I spent in Edinburgh I consider as the most important in their influence upon my character and conduct of any period of my life." He fell in love, entered upon an extremely active social life, and, most important, studied with some of the most eminent medical men of the age, chief among them John Black and William Cullen. From Black, Rush learned chemistry, which he planned to teach in Philadelphia's new medical school. From Cullen he learned everything—from his bedside manner to his theory of medicine.

In February 1767, Rush had a visitor from Princeton, the New Jersey lawyer and trustee of the College, Richard Stockton (A.B. 1748). Stockton had been sent to try to persuade the well-known evangelical clergyman, John Witherspoon of Paisley, to accept the presidency of the College. Witherspoon himself was half-persuaded, but Mrs. Witherspoon would not leave home and friends to face a long ocean voyage to a strange land. Rush took it upon himself to provide Nassau Hall with a successor to President Finley. He exhorted Witherspoon: "Let not the college with her last breath proclaim you as the cause of her dissolution. . . . I cannot express it—my heart bleeds within me— O Nassau Hall, Nassau Hall!" He badgered, cajoled, and finally won Mrs. Witherspoon's grudging consent to move to the colonies.

In the spring of 1768 Rush submitted his dissertation, *De Coctione Ciborum in Ventriculo* ("On the Digestion of Food in the Stomach"), to the University and received his M.D. Rush's time in the Scots capital had inspired him with hopes for his homeland: "Methinks I see the place of my nativity becoming the Edinburgh of America," he wrote to John Morgan. But before returning to America Rush traveled south to spend about five months in London. He duly pursued further medical studies, attending the lectures of the famed anatomist Dr. William Hunter, and walked the wards of St. Thomas's and Middlesex hospitals. But there was more to London than study. Befriended by Benjamin Franklin, Rush was soon meeting Benjamin West, Joshua Reynolds, John Wilkes, and other notables. He dined with Oliver Goldsmith and Dr. Johnson and discussed politics with the Whig historian Catherine Macaulay. After a brief trip to France, he returned to London. From thence he sailed for America, arriving on July 14, 1769.

Although in later years Rush characteristically overemphasized his early career difficulties, in fact he met with almost instant professional success. On August 1, 1769, the College of Philadelphia's trustees elected him the institution's first professor of chemistry. He swiftly built up a substantial practice—largely among the poor—took on apprentices, and was shortly possessed of a substantial income. A man of startling and unflagging energy, he was elected to the American Philosophical Society and found time to publish his chemistry lectures (the first such text in America) as *A Syllabus of a Course of Lectures on Chemistry* in 1770. A crusader against the use of hard liquor throughout his life, in 1772 Rush published *Sermons to Gentlemen upon Temperance and Exercise*, one of the first tracts of its kind. The following year he published an important essay condemning slavery (although he owned a slave for many years), and in 1774 and in 1803 helped to found Pennsylvania societies devoted to abolition.

Rush had opposed the Stamp Act in 1765, and his years in the mother country had only strengthened his commitment to republican principles. In about 1773 he became intimate with a somewhat obscure group of Philadelphians who agitated for independence from Britain. During the meeting of the First Continental Congress in Philadelphia in 1774 he widened his circle of acquaintances to include natives of other provinces, particularly a delegate from Massachusetts, John Adams, who became a life-long friend. While Rush kept an eye on politics, he paid even closer attention to his ever-growing practice among Philadelphia's artisans (blacksmiths, shopkeepers, hatters, and the like) and to his apprentices and students. But when the Second Continental Congress met in 1775 Rush became increasingly involved with the members, retailing the latest gossip from group to group. One Philadelphia acquaintance was Thomas Paine, a recent immigrant from England. Both men agreed that Americans needed to be persuaded of the necessity of independence from Britain. Rush suggested that Paine write a pamphlet on the subject. Paine did, showing it to Rush at every stage. Paine wanted to call the piece "Plain Truth"; Rush, who found a printer for it, suggested its ultimate name, *Common Sense*.

Two days after the publication of *Common Sense*, on January 11, 1776, Rush was married in Princeton to sixteen-year-old Julia Stockton, daughter of Richard Stockton. President Witherspoon performed the ceremony at the bride's home, Morven. Thirteen children were born to the couple. It was an extremely affectionate union. During Julia Rush's almost annual visits to her family in Princeton, Rush would bombard her with letters complaining of her absence. Rush's ties with Princeton remained strong throughout his life. When Congress considered leaving Philadelphia in 1779, Rush wrote to a friend that "some of the members talk of purchasing a few square miles of territory near Princetown and erecting public offices and buildings of all kinds for their accommodation upon it. A more central, healthy, and plentiful spot I believe cannot be found on the continent." And, when Congress fled in 1783 from Philadelphia to Princeton, Rush, whose wife had inherited about 250 acres in Princeton on her father's death in 1781, wrote thus to a congressional friend:

> Cities contain the combustible matter of vice; villages are less capable of infection by you. Should Congress conclude finally to settle at Princeton, I shall cheerfully convey to them one half of a 20-acre lot in the heart of the town and an 100 acres of woodland within two miles of the same. The College would make an excellent place for your offices. The wisest thing the trustees of it could do would be to sell it to the public. The revenue arising from the price of it would maintain two or three professors, while the boys might be boarded with more advantage to their morals and manners in private houses.

The College, of course, was not sold, and Rush later sent three of his sons to Princeton: John, who boarded in a private house from 1790 to 1792 and did not graduate; Richard (A.B. 1797), American minister to France and Great Britain, secretary of the treasury and attorney-general of the United States; and James (A.B. 1805), founder of Philadelphia's Ridgeway Library.

Rush's marriage did not interfere with his revolutionary activities. In 1775–1776 he served as surgeon to Pennsylvania's gunboat fleet, and in June 1776, he became a member of Pennsylvania's provincial congress, which in turn sent him to the Continental Congress. He thus became—along with his father-in-law, Richard Stockton—a signer of the Declaration of Independence. In 1776 Rush's political associates wrote a constitution for the new state. Rush, who had swallowed whole John Adams's notions about the necessity for a government finely balanced between democratic, aristocratic, and monarchical elements, objected violently to Pennsylvania's new constitution, which vested most power in a "democratical" unicameral legislature. Rush was highly impetuous and not given to keeping his opinions to himself. His views became known, and he was not returned to Congress. The issue, in fact, would dominate Pennsylvania politics until a new constitution was adopted in 1790. It was the source of unending fulminations by Rush against the group that supported the document of 1776.

Rush had a talent for making friends, but a genius for making enemies. John Adams and Thomas Jefferson became his warm admirers. In his old age Rush persuaded the once bitter political antagonists to bury their ancient differences. The ensuing extensive exchange of letters between Adams and Jefferson resulted in the greatest correspondence of the young republic. But during the revolutionary years it was Rush's capacity for invoking animosity that was most in evidence. Congress appointed Rush physician general of the Middle Department on July 1, 1777. The organization of medical services and provision for the American armies were in a somewhat chaotic state. Rush performed bravely and ably in his post, but grew more and more disturbed by the wretched condition of wounded or sick American soldiers. He soon launched an attack on the capabilities—and ultimately, the character —of Dr. William Shippen (q.v.), director-general of the army's medical services. The attack degenerated into a personal vendetta by Rush against Shippen. The matter was ultimately referred to a congressional committee chaired by John Witherspoon. Witherspoon decided that either Shippen or Rush must go, and it was Rush who went.

The Shippen imbroglio was compounded by Rush's attitude toward George Washington. Distressed by the American forces' poor military showing, in January 1778 Rush criticized the commander-in-chief's leadership in an unsigned letter to Patrick Henry, governor of Virginia. Rush had miscalculated. Henry forwarded the letter to Washington, who immediately recognized Rush's handwriting. Washington was furious. In later years Rush was a leader in the drive for the adoption of the federal constitution and a member of the Pennsylvania convention that ratified it. His approval of Washington as president was somewhat grudging.

Over the years Rush moved from Presbyterianism to Episcopalianism to Universalism, and ended as a fervent, if not strictly denominational, Christian. He brought the moral fervor he had acquired from Presidents Finley and Davies to the problems of the young nation, and was possessed by a compelling vision of America as a model Christian republic. He was an inveterate and prolific propagandist for a number of humanitarian reforms—abolition, temperance, humane treatment for the insane, education for women, and public education in general. His campaign to establish a national university did not succeed, but his drive to found Dickinson College in Carlisle, Pennsylvania, reached fruition in 1783.

Rush's greatest impact on his age came through his role as a medical educator. In 1780 he began to lecture at the new University of the State of Pennsylvania and in 1783 became a staff member of the Philadelphia Hospital, America's first. After the State University was merged with the old College of Philadelphia as the University of Pennsylvania in 1791, Rush gradually assumed various professorial chairs. In 1787 he was among the founders of the Philadelphia College of Physicians. Over the years he instructed at least 3,000 students in medicine. They in turn spread his doctrines and methods throughout the United States and extended his influence long beyond his lifetime.

Rush's medical system was an extension of the ideas of his old professor, William Cullen, and those of a fellow student at Edinburgh, John Brown. Essentially, Rush reduced all types of disease to one, described by a medical historian as "a state of excessive excitability or spasm in the Blood vessels." The main treatment prescribed by Rush was bleeding or purging to relieve the "excitability." Rush was willing to remove as much as four-fifths of a patient's blood. Such ministrations were disputed at the time, but were well within the bounds of respectable eighteenth-century medical theory and practice. Rush heroically remained in Philadelphia throughout the yellow fever epidemics of the 1790s to bleed and purge scores of victims of the disease. The rate of recovery among his patients was not high.

By the early 1800s Rush had become something of an American institution. His students and his writings on a variety of subjects had spread his name to many parts of the western world. In 1805 the King of Prussia sent him a coronation medal; in 1807 he received a gold medal from the Queen of Etruria; in 1811 the Czar of Russia presented him with a diamond ring. And, not long after Rush died in Philadelphia on April 19, 1813, John Adams wrote thus to Thomas Jefferson: "I lament with you the loss of Rush. I know of no Character living or dead, who has done more real good in America."

Sources: Rush (hereafter BR) has spawned a scholarly industry. The best brief bibliographical introduction is Douglas Sloan, *The Scottish Enlightenment and the American College Ideal* (1971), 372-78. Sloan's essay on BR in the same volume is a fine introduction; among many sketches, Richard Shryock's in the *DAB* still repays reading. The best biography to date is D. F. Hawke, *BR, Revolutionary Gadfly* (1971), which carries his life only to 1790. Among other studies which may be consulted are: H. F. Good, *BR and His Services to Am. Education* (1918); N. Goodman, *BR: Physician and Citizen* (1934); W. and F. Neilson, *Verdict for the Doctor* (1958); C. Binger, *Revolutionary Doctor* (1966); and D. J. D'Elia, *BR: Philosopher of the Am. Rev., APS Trans.*, 64 (1974). BR's papers have been the objects of some of the best historical editing of recent times. See: G. W. Corner, ed., *The Autobiography of BR* (1948); L. H. Butterfield, ed., *Letters of BR* (1951), 2 v.; Butterfield, ed., *John Witherspoon Comes to America* (1953); and J. A. Schutz and D. Adair, eds., *The Spur of Fame: Dialogues of John Adams and BR* (1966). All quotations in the above sketch are drawn from these works. For an extensive collection of representations of Rush, see: R. E. Jones, "Portraits of BR, M.D., by his contemporaries," *Antiques*, 108 (1975), 94-113.

PUBLICATIONS: See bibliographies in above works. Some of BR's writings are available in D. Runes, ed., *Selected Writings of BR* (1947).

Mss: See L. H. Butterfield, "A Survey of the BR Papers," *PMHB*, 70 (1946), 78-111.

John Slemmons

JOHN SLEMMONS, A.B., A.M. 1763, Presbyterian clergyman, was born in Chester County, Pennsylvania, in 1734, one of the ten children of Thomas Slemmons, an immigrant from County Antrim, Ireland. In the year of John's birth, his father received a grant of 134 acres of land in Lancaster County, where John was probably raised.

After graduation Slemmons studied theology. On May 11, 1763, he was licensed by the Presbytery of Donegal in central Pennsylvania. He preached at many churches in York County and neighboring areas over the next two years and received calls to settle as permanent pastor of congregations at Lower Marsh Creek, Tom's Creek, and Piney Creek. Slemmons finally accepted the·call of the first of these churches and was ordained and installed there on October 30, 1765. The following year Slemmons married Sarah Dean, daughter of a Presbyterian clergyman who lived near his father's home. The couple had thirteen children.

Slemmons remained with the Marsh Creek church until December 1774. In 1776 he succeeded John Strain (A.B. 1757) as pastor of churches at Slate Ridge and Lower Chanceford, York County. Slemmons was fairly prosperous. In 1782 he was taxed in York County for the ownership of 230 acres of land, three slaves, five horses, and seven cattle. The federal census of 1790 recorded him as the head of a household consisting of nine whites and seven slaves. About 1783 Slemmons gave up his Slate Ridge pastorship because of ill health, although he continued at the Lower Chanceford church for another four years. He died on July 10, 1814, and was interred in the Piney Creek burying ground.

SOURCES: The name was sometimes spelled Slemons; vital data: MS Genealogical Notes on the Slemmons Family, MdHi; biographical sketches: W. C. Carter and A. J. Glossbrenner, *Hist. of York County* (1834), 48-50; W. Simonton, *Historical Sketch of the Presbyterian Churches of Emmittsburg and Piney Creek* (1876), 45-47; Webster, MS Brief Sketches, PPPrHi; taxes: *Pa. Arch.* (3 ser.), 21 (1897), 138, 283, 386, 583, 819; 1790 household: *U.S. Census of 1790, Pa.*, 272.

Mss: PHi

Jonathan Bayard Smith

JONATHAN BAYARD SMITH, A.B., A.M. 1763, merchant and public official, was born in Philadelphia on February 21, 1742, the second son of Mary Harrison and Samuel Smith, a prosperous and prominent merchant and a founding trustee of Philadelphia's Second Presbyterian Church. Jonathan entered the Academy of Philadelphia in 1751 and matriculated in the College of New Jersey on April 10, 1757. As the highest ranking scholar in his class, Smith, a Philadelphia newspaper reported, opened the exercises at his commencement with a "handsome salutatory Oration in *Latin*." After graduation Smith apparently stayed on in Princeton for postgraduate study. "The fair sex are numerous, but . . . we bookworms say . . . they are dangerous creatures," he wrote to his classmate Enoch Green. College, he added, was "a place replete with every valuable." Determined to remain "ignorant" of city life, he explained to Green that he was busy exploring the "depths" of science.

Deep or shallow, Smith's explorations were limited, for he soon returned to Philadelphia and joined his family in business. His interest in science did not desert him; he was elected to the American Philosophical Society in April 1768. Nor did he lose touch with his fellow alumni. Edinburgh was full of Smith's friends, his classmate Benjamin Rush wrote him from Scotland in 1767: " 'Mr. Jonathan Smith of Philadelphia' is my favorite toast when an old friend is called for." In 1765 Smith married Susannah Bayard, daughter of Colonel Peter Bayard. To comply with certain provisions of his father-in-law's will Smith later assumed "Bayard" as his middle name. The Smiths had one son, Samuel Harrison Smith, who became editor of the Washington *National Intelligencer.*

Smith was one of the early younger leaders of the Whig-Presbyterian party in Pennsylvania in the 1770s. He was at the center of scores of the affairs of his city, state and nation during the revolution-

[handwritten marginal notes:] also John Rhea Smith, Susan Bayard Smith, Mary Ann Smith and children of a second wife — Anne Caroline and Jonathan / Jonathan Bayard Smith Collection in Library of Congress (Peter Force mss. Collection)

ary years. He was a member of the provincial conference of June 1774, secretary to the Pennsylvania Convention of January 1775 and to the conference of June 1776, which overthrew the Penns' proprietary government. Although not a member of the Pennsylvania convention that drew up a new constitution for the state in July 1776, Smith, along with Joseph Reed (A.B. 1757), Jonathan Dickinson Sergeant (A.B. 1762), and John Ewing (A.B. 1754), later became one of the leaders of the Constitutionalist party in Pennsylvania politics. Elected to the Continental Congress in February 1777, Smith resigned in September in order to join the Philadelphia militia (in which he rose to the rank of lieutenant-colonel) in the defense of the city against the British. Reelected to Congress in December 1777, over the following year he served on the Board of War. In constant communication with his state government about supplies, troop enlistments, morale and similar matters, Smith apparently worked to the point where his health was impaired. He served as prothonotary of the court of common pleas for the county and city of Philadelphia from 1777 to 1788 and as a justice of the court from July 1778.

After the peace Smith was among the innermost group of Constitutionalists who directed the affairs of Pennsylvania. Long interested in education, he served as a trustee of the College of New Jersey from 1779 to 1807. When the old charter of the College of Philadelphia was abrogated in 1779 he became a trustee of the newly constituted University of the State of Pennsylvania. When that institution was amalgamated with the remnants of the College in 1791, becoming the University of Pennsylvania, he continued as a trustee, serving until 1812.

Like most of the Constitutionalists in Philadelphia, Smith was a strong opponent of the federal constitution. He was a leader of Philadelphia's Sons of St. Tammany, one of the bulwarks of Constitutionalist power in the state. Although the Federalist, anti-Constitutionalist party came to power in Pennsylvania in the late 1780s and wrote a new constitution for the state, Smith was not long without office. He served as an alderman of Philadelphia from 1792 to 1794, and as auditor-general of his state under Governor Thomas Mifflin in 1794. A leading Freemason, he acted as grand master of the Pennsylvania branch of that organization. He remained active within the Democratic-Republican party through the early years of the nineteenth century.

On January 17, 1812, William Findley, an old Pennsylvania Republican leader, wrote to a friend that Smith, though the man most qualified to write a history of Revolutionary Pennsylvania, had "given up all design of writing the History . . . [and] of even writing Letters or corresponding with his most intimate friends." Smith died on June 16 of that year. Closely involved with the affairs of Philadelphia's Second Presbyterian Church throughout his life, he was buried in its church-yard.

SOURCES: Sketch: *DAB*; CNJ: Aaron Burr, MS Account Book, 274; commencement: *Pa. Gaz.*, Oct. 9, 1760; Smith to Enoch Green, n.d. (torn), MS, NjP; wife: *Am. Ancestry*, 9 (1894), 47; son: *DAB*; Rush: Butterfield, *Rush Letters*, 43; Revolutionary and political careers must be pieced together from: T. Thayer, *Pa. Politics and the Growth of Democracy* (1953), 184, 190; S. W. Higgenbotham, *Keystone in the Democratic Arch* (1952); R. M. Baumann, "Democratic-Republicans of Philadelphia: The Origins, 1776-1797" (Ph.D. diss., Pa. State Univ., 1970), 22, 78, 86, 183; references throughout: *Pa. Arch.* (ser. 1, 3, 5, and 6); Force, *Am. Arch.* (sers. 4 and 5); *Minutes of the Supreme Executive Council of Pa.* (1852), II, XII, *LMCC*, II-III; *PMHB*, 17 (1893), 473; 21 (1897), 500-501; 24 (1900), 27-28; 26 (1902), 339, 345, 450; Findley quotation from *ibid.*, 8 (1884), 345.

Mss: NjP, PHi.

Josiah Thatcher

JOSIAH THATCHER [THACHER], A.B., A.M. Yale 1765, Congregational clergyman and public official, was the ninth of the thirteen children of Abigail Hibbard and Peter Thatcher of Lebanon, Connecticut. He was born on July 8, 1733.

After graduating from the College, Thatcher entered the ministry and moved to Massachusetts where he supplied at pulpits in Bedford and in several churches in Maine. In October 1766, he preached at the Congregational church in Gorham, Maine, which had been without a settled minister since Solomon Lombard (Harvard 1723) had resigned to enter politics in 1765. In October 1767 the churches in Gorham and Bedford both called Thatcher, but because of poor communication Bedford's offer did not reach him until he had accepted the other call and been ordained. The congregation at Gorham offered him a settlement bonus of £100 plus an annual salary of £80.

Thatcher's ministry went well enough until 1773 when the growing number of Baptists, Quakers, and Shakers in Gorham refused to pay the tax upon which his salary depended. Thatcher filed suit for his wages and the controversy turned ugly. He was occasionally prevented from preaching by groups of his opponents, and in November 1780 the town meeting voted that he should quit his pulpit. To make their point the citizens boarded the doors of the Congregational meetinghouse. But Thatcher would not resign and led his followers into the locked church through the roof. Unable to force him to stop preaching without breaking the law, the town meeting took another tack. After months of polite negotiations, Thatcher agreed to accept a lump sum of £307 in exchange for his resignation. He obtained a dismission from his duties in April 1781.

As his predecessor had, Thatcher went from pulpit to politics in Gorham. By 1783 he was the local justice of the peace. In May of that year he was chosen by the Massachusetts general court to help manage a lottery to raise money for the town of Fryburgh to clear a log jam from the Saco River in York County, Maine. At about the same time Thatcher was elected to represent Gorham in the Massachusetts House of Representatives. In 1784 he was named a justice of the Cumberland County court of common pleas and in 1785 was chosen for the first time to represent the county in the Massachusetts Senate. Until his death on Christmas Day, 1799, Thatcher remained on the bench in Cumberland County and also served a total of twelve years in the Massachusetts legislature—five in the House and seven in the Senate. His legislative responsibilities included the adjudication of several land claims, at least one major survey of unappropriated land in Maine, and a study of ways to save the coastal fisheries. In spite of his earlier troubles in Gorham he was elected to the Senate in May 1789 by 500 of the 717 votes cast.

When not tending to his official duties, Thatcher spent his time tending to his fruit orchard, said to be the best in Cumberland County. He also owned a large stone house that must have had few windows, for he cut heart-shaped holes in its sides so that light could shine out to show passers-by that there was someone at home. When he died his estate passed to his wife, Apphia, and the three of their ten children who survived him.

SOURCES: J. Pierce, *Hist. of the Town of Gorham, Me.* (1862), 66-68, 210-11, 228-29; H. D. McLellan, *Hist. of Gorham, Me.* (1903), 376-77, 292; Alexander, *Princeton*, 67; family: *NEHGR*, XIV, 12; Fryburgh lottery: Maine Historical Society, *Collections* (2 ser.), XX, 319; service in legislature: Maine Historical Society, *Collections* (2 ser.), XXI, 11-14, 341-42, 356, 435; XXII, 97, 110-12, 162, 204, 207, 317, 355.

RAH

Amos Thompson

AMOS THOMPSON, A.B., A.M. 1763, Presbyterian clergyman, was born in New Haven, Connecticut, on August 7, 1731, the third of the seven children of Sarah Alling and Amos Thompson. In February 1738 the senior Thompson purchased property in the new town of Goshen, Connecticut, and moved his family into a small log house there. In

1741 he was elected town clerk and treasurer and was a deacon of the local Presbyterian church. He retained those posts until 1750, when he sold his house and left Goshen.

After graduating from the College, the younger Amos Thompson entered the ministry. He was licensed by the Presbytery of New Brunswick in 1761. After his ordination by the same body in 1764 he decided to travel to Newport, Rhode Island, to dissuade the Reverend Samuel Hopkins, a disciple of Jonathan Edwards, from his extreme Calvinist religious opinions. Instead, Thompson came away from Newport completely converted to Hopkinsian theology. His fervent espousal of that brand of New Light Presbyterianism made his own ministry one of constant controversy.

In May 1764 the New Brunswick Presbytery sent Thompson to supply in Loudoun County, Virginia. He also served temporarily at pulpits in Virginia in 1765. Although his own preaching caused a furor among his listeners he did not shrink from other disputes. Like Samuel Davies, he was one of the first Presbyterian ministers to stay in northern Virginia, where the Baptists had been the only dissenting sect. His reputation for combativeness made him an ally of beleaguered Baptist clergymen who were frequently abused by mobs from established churches. One such minister, David Thomas, called on Thompson for help when he was threatened with assault if he dared to preach again at a certain church. The Presbyterian, who loved adventure, happily traveled thirty miles to preach at the contested pulpit. He faced an armed mob, which his large and muscular stature quieted rather quickly. After his sermon he warned the ruffians not to molest Thomas again, and then he physically disarmed the burly leader of the group. Thomas was thereafter free to preach when he chose.

A witty, jovial, and cheerful giant, Thompson enjoyed the challenge of preaching in Virginia and decided to settle there. He established churches at Kittocktin and Gum Spring in Loudoun County and supplied pulpits at Elk Branch, Culpepper, and Alexandria. In 1768 he married Jane Evans of Maryland and joined the Donegal Presbytery, which then had jurisdiction over western and northern Virginia. Of the eighteen ministers from Pennsylvania and Virginia in that Presbytery by 1775, fifteen were graduates of the College.

In September 1766, Thompson paid £315.12s. for 505 acres of land in Loudon County. Four years later he bought another 350 acres for £100 and began to build a mill on that tract. But he left Loudon County in 1776 to join the Continental army as a chaplain in Colonel Hugh Stephenson's Maryland and Virginia Rifle Regiment. The unit was created by Congress in June and Thompson's commission, offered in July, was approved on September 7. Before going to New York to join the regiment at Fort Washington, Thompson made out a will in which he provided that his seven slaves were to be emancipated upon his wife's death. The profit from the sale of his mill land was to go to the College for the education of pious young men.

In New York Thompson encountered Nicholas Cresswell, a young Englishman with whom he had argued politics in Virginia. Cresswell was trying to escape his parole and flee to the British forces on Long Island but the chaplain suspected his plan and warned against it. Cresswell was forced to submit to "this puritan Priest for fear of worse consequences" and dolefully returned to Virginia. Although Thompson's regiment, now under the command of Lieutenant Colonel Moses Rawley of Maryland, was decimated at Fort Washington, Thompson remained in the army, possibly accompanying some of the remnant of the unit to Fort Pitt. He was back in Virginia at least twice during the war to tend to sales of his land, as in December 1777 when he sold his 350 acres and mill for £1,500.

Between 1782 and 1794, Thompson was living in Connecticut as the minister of the Second Church in Canaan. He continued to acquire land, and in a second will in November 1787 he gave his property in Canaan and New Marlborough, Massachusetts, to his wife. At her death, the proceeds from that property were to go to Yale College. For the College of New Jersey he reserved the proceeds from his land in Pittsylvania County, Virginia, provided that the trustees delivered a bond they held against him. He also provided for the ultimate emancipation of his five slaves, although most of them would be bound for long terms before they were free.

In February 1789, Thompson was licensed to perform marriages in Virginia under a 1783 law that gave that right to dissenters for a £500 bond. By 1794 he was back in Loudon County and in 1799 he joined the Presbytery of Winchester. At the age of seventy he still traveled many miles on horseback to acquire or clarify titles to more land. Such journeys were slowed considerably by his habit of alighting to kindle the pipe in his mouth. In 1803 he bought 392 acres at a cost of £970; and in May 1804 he sold four and one-half acres, called Thompson's Mill, for £700. His third and last will bequeathed all of his property to his wife and made provisions for his nieces and nephews since he had no children of his own. At his widow's death, the proceeds from his property were to go to Yale—there was no provision for the College of New Jersey. All of his slaves were to be freed when he died, some to be taught a trade and two to be paid fair wages as his widow's servants.

Thompson died suddenly on September 8, 1804. He was buried in the churchyard in Leesburg. In addition to his land, his personal property was valued at $1,386 at his death, including a library worth $100, livestock worth $550, and a liquor case and brandy, which he may have used against the chill of Virginia winters, worth $4.

SOURCES: *Loudoun Times-Courier*, Aug. 27 and Sept. 3, 1964; J. D. Graham, *Planting of the Pres. Church in Northern Virginia* (1904), 70-71, 79, 82, 85-87, 98, 103; Alexander, *Princeton*, 68-69; parentage and father's life: W. B. Thompson, *Thompson Lineage* (1911), 46; A. B. Hibbard, *Hist. of the Town of Goshen, Conn.* (1897), 39-78, 531; early years in Virginia: *Rec. Pres. Church*, 339; L. P. Little, *Imprisoned Preachers and Religious Liberty in Va.* (1938), 44; defense of Thomas and late travels to secure land: J. W. Alexander, *Life of Archibald Alexander* (1854), 228, 229; Donegal Presbytery: *Fithian Journal*, II, 5, 33-34n; commission as chaplain: Force, *Am. Arch.* (5 ser.), II, 1333; wills: Loudon County Will Book "G," 296, 316, 319; Cresswell: *Journal of Nicholas Cresswell* (1924), 227-28; the fate of Stephenson's Regiment: F. A. Berg, *Encyclopedia of Continental Army Units* (1972), 120, 104-105, 64; H. B. Carrington, *Battles of the Am. Rev.*: (1876), 248-51; ministry in Connecticut after the Rev.: Giger, Memoirs, I; Stiles, *Literary Diary*, III, 203, 291; presence in Connecticut in 1790: U.S. Census of 1790, Connecticut, 61.

Mss: PPPrHi   RAH

Johannes Martinus Van Harlingen

JOHANNES MARTINUS VAN HARLINGEN, Dutch Reformed clergyman, was born in Somerset County, New Jersey, in 1724, the son of Maria Bussing (Businck) and Johannes Martinus Van Harlingen, a prosperous farmer. The father, a native of Westbroeck in the province of Utrecht, the Netherlands, emigrated to America about 1703. In 1744 he inherited the lordship and manor of Old Beyerland in the Netherlands. He sold his European lands in 1767. In his will he divided his property equally among his children, with the exception of an extra £25 left to the younger Johannes as the eldest son.

Van Harlingen entered the College on September 29, 1756. The only record of his stay there is President Burr's notation of his purchase of a lexicon and a copy of Lucian. He paid for the books on December 24, 1756. Whether or not he remained in the College after that date cannot be discovered. Van Harlingen traveled to the Netherlands and on January 15, 1761, requested a preparatory examination for the ministry by the Classis of Amsterdam. The request was granted, and on April 6, 1761, Van Harlingen preached a sermon on Hebrews 1:3, 8. After subsequent examination he was ordained on May 4, 1761. On his return to America in 1762 Van Harlingen became minister to the Dutch Reformed Church near Princeton at what is now Harlingen in Montgomery Township, Somerset County, New Jersey. Shortly thereafter he took on an additional post, becoming pastor of the Dutch Reformed Church at nearby Neshanic. It was probably at about this time that Van Harlingen married Sarah Stryker, with whom he had two children. After Sarah's death he married Elizabeth Van Deusen, with whom he had three more children.

Van Harlingen's activities were not limited to Somerset County. When emigrants from Somerset and Bergen counties settled Conewago in Adams County, Pennsylvania, in the late 1760s, Van Harlingen helped them organize a church and made several trips west to baptize their children. When the community broke up in 1780 Van Harlingen memorialized Congress on their behalf asking for a grant of land in Kentucky. And, when a charter was granted late in 1766 to a new New Jersey college to be called Queen's, Van Harlingen was among the original trustees. In 1771 he served as one of the temporary governors of Queen's while a search for a president was being conducted.

No record of Van Harlingen's activities during the Revolution has been discovered, but his brother Ernestus suffered £626.9.11 in losses from British attacks on his property in 1776–1777. In 1779 classes of peripatetic Queen's College, perhaps at Johannes's suggestion, were held in Ernestus's house.

Van Harlingen's ministries proceeded uneventfully in the years following the Revolution. He continued to deliver his sermons to his two congregations in Dutch, as he had always done. But a feeling arose among his parishioners that English-language services were needed. In 1794 William Richmond Smith (A.B. 1773) joined Van Harlingen as associate pastor charged with delivering English sermons. Van Harlingen died on December 23 of the following year. He had made no will. His estate, which included four slaves, was inventoried at £579.

SOURCES: Van Harlingen's record is sometimes confused with that of his nephew, John M. Van Harlingen (1761-1813), also a Dutch Reformed clergyman of Somerset County; brief sketches: C. C. Hoagland, *Gleanings for the Hist. of the Protestant Reformed Dutch Church of Harlingen, Somerset County, N.J.* (1847), 9; and, C. E. Corwin, *A Manual of the Reformed Church in America, 1628-1922* (rev. ed., 1922), 551-52; and A. Messler, *Forty Years at Raritan* (1873), 260-61; family: *GMNJ*, 2 (1926), 90; father's will: 34 *NJA*, 544; attendance at College: Aaron Burr, MS Account Book, 244; Pa. activities: *Som. Cty. Hist. Quart.*, 4 (1915), 163, 166; connections with Queen's College: W.H.S. Demarest, *A Hist. of Rutgers College, 1766-1924* (1924); brother's losses: *Som. Cty. Hist. Quart.*, 1 (1912), 285; property: estate inventory, MS, N.J. State Lib., Trenton.

Mss: Harlingen Reformed Church, Montgomery Township, N. J.

Henry Wynkoop

HENRY WYNKOOP, farmer, jurist, public official, was the only son of Ann Kuypers and Nicholas Wynkoop, a prosperous farmer in Bucks County, Pennsylvania. He was born on his father's estate, "Vredens Hoff" near Newtown on March 2, 1737. The 153-acre farm and its elegant stone mansion were inherited by Henry when Nicholas died in 1759.

Although he had been prepared at home to attend the College, Wynkoop did not graduate with his class, possibly because of his father's death. He returned to Pennsylvania to tend the farm but quickly became involved in local politics. In 1760 he was elected to the colony's provincial assembly. Soon after his reelection in 1761 he married Susannah Wanshaer of Essex County, New Jersey. Between 1762 and 1764 Wynkoop served on local grand juries and on the assembly's committee of accounts. In 1764 he was named a justice of the peace for Bucks County. For the next six years he served alternately in that position and as an associate judge of the county court.

Henry Wynkoop, Class of 1760

In July 1774 Wynkoop was one of the members of the Bucks County Committee of Safety named by the group to attend the first provincial conference in Philadelphia, which recommended an association to boycott British goods. In December Wynkoop was elected to the county Committee of Observation that enforced the association called for by the first Continental Congress. He was the treasurer and as such collected money for the relief of Boston. In 1775, Wynkoop was again a delegate from Bucks County to the provincial conference. When the Committee of Observation, of which he was clerk as well as treasurer in 1775, endorsed a plan for the organization of local militias in May of that year, Wynkoop enlisted as a private in one of the companies. Although he was addressed later as "Major," he neither held a commission nor actually served in the militia at any rank. He continued, instead, to hold various posts of responsibility in civilian revolutionary groups.

After delivering more than £75 to John Adams for Boston in August 1775, Wynkoop was asked by the Bucks County government to raise money for the manufacture of arms for the militia. As a member of the Committee of Observation he reported in September 1775 that the number of Associators was only slightly higher than the number of non-Associators and expressed his frustration that more people were not joining the boycott. He was especially perplexed about the local Quakers, who refused to take either side. By mid-1776 he was a delegate to another provincial conference and was also in charge of collecting arms to be sent to Philadelphia. This final conference granted the franchise to free, adult, male Associators and called for a provincial convention to draft a constitution. Although too busy to be a member of the convention, Wynkoop was a judge to decide the election of delegates from Bucks County. After the Declaration of Independence was signed, Wynkoop represented his county on the state Committee of Safety at a salary of eight shillings per day. In September 1776 as a justice of the peace for the entire state, he presided at the opening of the reorganized Bucks County courts.

By that time, Wynkoop was so prominent a rebel that British forces, advancing through New Jersey, were eager to arrest him. Although he managed to evade capture, his wife was drowned when she fled their house at night and fell into an open well. After the battle of Trenton in December 1776, General Washington personally asked Wynkoop to provide shelter for two British prisoners and an American officer who had been wounded. The American was James Monroe, who stayed with Wynkoop for nine weeks and was later said to have fallen in love with Christina, the eldest of Wynkoop's seven children.

In 1777 Wynkoop married Maria Cummings and continued to serve on state and local courts. At the end of 1778 he was appointed by the state assembly as a commissioner to settle the accounts of county lieutenants, and he also served temporarily on a committee created by the Continental Congress to study available food supplies for the army. In March 1779 he was elected to fill a vacancy in the Continental Congress itself. He attended congressional sessions religiously and retained his judicial post in Bucks County, although he was forced to resign as county treasurer. In Congress he was a member of the treasury board. By 1780, as political factions began to congeal into parties, Wynkoop was clearly siding with the more conservative group in Congress. Arthur Lee saw Wynkoop's reelection in November 1780 as proof that "Toryism" had triumphed in Pennsylvania. Lee had good reason to resent Wynkoop's presence, for, although the Pennsylvanian was not entrenched in any political camp, he was a supporter of Silas Deane, and hence an opponent of Lee. One of Wynkoop's close associates in Congress was Alexander Hamilton.

Wynkoop was reelected in 1781 and 1782. Never a particularly active member he took a forward position on very few issues, such as when he supported a plan to back a French attack on Bermuda. He seems to have been preoccupied with state business and was especially distressed at the low value of Pennsylvania's credit in 1780. After completing his third term in the Continental Congress he took a seat on the state's supreme tribunal, the high court of appeals and errors, to which he had been named by President Joseph Reed (A.B. 1757) in 1781. At the same time he served as the presiding judge of the Bucks County courts. Afer his second wife died in 1781 Wynkoop married for a third time. His bride in 1782 was Sarah Newkirk of Pittsgrove, New Jersey. She bore him one child.

In 1787, Wynkoop was an ardent supporter of the constitution. He was a member of Pennsylvania's ratifying convention in November of that year. On March 1, 1789, an avowed Federalist, he was elected to the first United States Congress. Before taking his seat he resigned his judgeships and his position as an elder of the Presbyterian church in Northampton and Southampton.

Three questions dominated the Congress at its original meeting. The first concerned the titles by which national officers were to be addressed. Unlike many other Federalists, Wynkoop dismissed titles as "European feathers." A colleague from Pennsylvania, Frederick Muhlenberg, took to calling Wynkoop "His Highness of the Lower House" —a jocular reference to Wynkoop's fervency on the issue as well as his six-foot, four-inch frame. Muhlenberg once said that if all future presidents were sure to be as tall as Washington or Wynkoop he would not object to calling the Chief Executive "Your Highness." But he thought it would be foolish when applied to shorter men. Ultimately, the Congress rejected all titles.

The second question of major importance was the permanent location of the national capital. Like almost every other member of Congress, Wynkoop hoped that the seat of government would be in his own state. But there were divisions among Pennsylvanians on the matter. At this first congressional session in New York, Wynkoop shared a room with his state's anti-Federalist Senator, William Maclay, who supported a new city on the Susquehanna, which later became Harrisburg, as the capital. Wynkoop preferred a site further east. The difference became an emotional chasm between the roommates. By September 1789 Maclay decided that Wynkoop was among the most "useless" members of Congress. He resented Wynkoop's readiness to vote in line with the Federalist members from Philadelphia and decided that Wynkoop had no mind of his own. "Well it is for him," Maclay growled to his journal, "that he is not a woman and handsome, or every fellow would debauch him."

The question of locating the capital was soon complicated by the third issue, that of federal assumption of state debts. Most Pennsylvanians who supported assumption owned state securities and thus had vested interests in the matter. Wynkoop was the exception. He supported assumption but held no bonds. Gradually, assumption became more important than building the capital in Pennsylvania, and Wynkoop agreed to a southern demand for a capital on the Potomac in exchange for southern votes for assumption. Maclay, who opposed assumption, muttered that it was as fruitful to discuss the topic with Wynkoop as with a "mute camel, or . . . a dead horse." Maclay notwithstanding, the "Compromise of 1790" passed with Wynkoop's support.

In 1791 the Federalists in Pennsylvania failed to organize themselves. As a result, Wynkoop and his old ally Muhlenberg contested for the same seat in the House. Wynkoop lost that race and another one in 1792. After the first defeat he was appointed by the governor of Pennsylvania to be an associate judge of Bucks County. And as a farmer he assisted his friend Hamilton in trying to estimate the total value of cultivated land in the United States in 1791.

In 1813 Wynkoop's third wife died and in the same year the county court was transferred to Doylestown. The old judge retired to spend his last years concentrating on his orchards and cider press. He died on March 26, 1816, and was buried in Richboro. His estate, which in 1779 had totaled more than 600 acres and a gristmill and had since been increased, went to his only surviving son. His slaves, of whom there were nine in 1790, were set free when he died but chose to remain with the family.

Sources: Bucks County Historical Society, *Papers*, 3 (1909), 158-59, 197-217; J. M. Beatty, Jr., ed., "The Letters of Judge Henry Wynkoop," *PMHB*, 38 (1914), 39-64, 183-205; *PMHB*, 54 (1930), 157; *PMHB*, 11 (1887), 273-74; provincial assembly: *Pa. Arch.* (8 ser.), vi, 5366; activities in 1774-75: *Pa. Arch.* (2 ser.), i, 551; *PMHB*, 15 (1891), 257-65, 275-79; state Committee of Safety: Force, *Am. Arch.* (5 ser.), ii, 9; Monroe's recuperation: S. G. Brown, ed., *Autobiography of James Monroe* (1959), 26; congressional supply study: *LMCC*, iii, 490n; resignation as county treasurer: *PMHB*, 3 (1879), 439; Continental Congress: *LMCC*, iv, lxii, 395, vi, 1; Silas Deane controversy and Arthur Lee: H. J. Henderson, "Congressional Factionalism and the Attempt to Recall Benjamin Franklin," *WMQ*, 27 (1970), 253-54; *LMCC*, v, 439n; *WMQ*, 24 (1967), 33n; plan to attack Bermuda: *LMCC*, vi, 422-24; concern about state credit: *Pa. Arch.* (1 ser.), viii, 557; high court of appeals and errors: B. A. Konkle, *George Bryan and the Constitution of Pennsylvania* (1922), 254; Pennsylvania Convention of 1787: J. B. McMaster and F. D. Stone, eds., *Pennsylvania and the Federal Constitution* (1888), 299; H. M. Tinkcom, *Republicans and Federalists in Pennsylvania* (1950), 24; election to Congress: Tinkcom, above; *Jefferson Papers*, xiv, 395, 473; question of titles: E. S. Maclay, ed., *Journal of William Maclay* (1890), 33; Compromise of 1790: *WMQ*, 28 (1971), 637-38; Maclay, above, 168, 174, 190, 228, 245-56; *Jefferson Papers*, xvii, 169; Tinkcom, above, 28; defeats for Congress: Tinkcom, above, 47, 65-66; Hamilton's land survey in 1791: *Hamilton Papers*, ix, 35-37, 123-27; slaves: *U.S. Census of 1790, Pennsylvania*, 47.

Mss: Bucks County Historical Society

RAH

CLASS OF 1761

David Caldwell, A.B.

David Gillespie, A.B.

Isaac Handy, A.B.

Thomas Henderson, A.B.

William Jauncey, A.B.

Nathan Ker, A.B.

John Lefferty, A.B.

Thomas McCracken, A.B.

Benjamin McDowell

David Rice, A.B.

John Rosbrugh, A.B.

Samuel Sloan, A.B.

James Hamden Thomson, A.B.

Lawrence Van Derveer, A.B.

Jahleel Woodbridge, A.B.

David Caldwell

DAVID CALDWELL, A.B., D.D. University of North Carolina 1810, carpenter, Presbyterian clergyman, schoolmaster, public official and sometime physician, was born in Lancaster County, Pennsylvania, on March 22, 1725, the eldest of the four sons of Ann Stewart and Andrew Caldwell, a farmer and immigrant from Ireland. When Caldwell was seventeen his father apprenticed him to a carpenter. After reaching journeyman status at the age of twenty-one Caldwell followed his craft for four more years. Then, at the age of twenty-five, he underwent a religious conversion and determined to become a clergyman. He studied at the Reverend Robert Smith's academy at Pequea, Pennsylvania, and later taught at the school. The date at which Caldwell went to Princeton is not known. A fellow student, John Hulbert (A.B. 1762), recalled Caldwell as an "inveterate student;—it was his practice, while in College, to study at a window, with the sash raised, until a late hour, then cross his arms on the table, lay his head on them, and sleep in that position until morning."

After graduation Caldwell taught school for a year in Cape May, New Jersey, before returning to Princeton to study theology with President Finley. He may have taught in the College's grammar school during this period. Licensed by the Presbytery of New Brunswick on June 8, 1763, he was ordered to spend a year as a missionary to North Carolina. Before leaving for the south Caldwell preached in many New Jersey churches, as he did on his return home. It was probably on his trip south that Caldwell met Rachel Craighead, daughter of Alexander Craighead a Presbyterian clergyman of Mecklenberg County, North Carolina, and sister of Thomas Craighead (A.B. 1775). On July 6, 1765, shortly after his return home, Caldwell was ordained by the Presbytery of New Brunswick. In 1766 he returned to North Carolina to marry Rachel. The couple had at least eleven children.

In 1767 Caldwell accepted a call to serve as joint pastor to two Presbyterian churches in what was to become Guilford County, North Carolina, where many of his boyhood neighbors from Lancaster County had settled. One church, at Buffalo (near Greensboro), had a largely Scotch congregation and was Old Side in sentiment; the other, at Alamance, was mainly Scotch-Irish and New Side. In March 1768 Caldwell was installed at his new churches in a ceremony presided over by the Reverend Hugh McAden (A.B. 1753). Despite the differing outlooks of his two congregations, Caldwell managed to satisfy each of them.

Caldwell's two churches together paid him only a small salary. In order to augment his income he opened an academy near his home. Over the years he educated hundreds of youths, including at least fifty clergymen and the future governors of five states. Most of the students boarded with families in the area, but Caldwell occasionally took a boy into his own home. Some of his early students went on to the College of New Jersey; later ones were more likely to attend the University of North Carolina. When Liberty Hall Academy in Charlotte was chartered in 1777, Caldwell, like several other alumni of the College, became a trustee. Aside from his duties as minister and schoolmaster Caldwell also acted as a physician in his area. He was no quack. Early in his pastorate he began studying medical books he had requested from Philadelphia. Later a young Philadelphia physician, a relative of his wife, practiced in the district. Caldwell learned everything he could from the young man and after his death acquired his medical library.

When the Regulator movement—a protest by poorer backcountry farmers against lawyers and officeholders—began to develop in the late 1760s Caldwell joined other Presbyterian ministers in assuring Governor Tryon of Presbyterian loyalty. At the same time Caldwell and other divines urged the insurgents—"especially of the younger sort"—to resort to legal means for redress of their grievances and to obey "those powers whom God has ordained." Just before the Regulators met government troops in the battle of Alamance in May 1771, Caldwell, with no success, acted as mediator between the Regulators and Governor Tryon. After the defeat of the Regulators Caldwell was among those signing petitions for their pardon.

In these years Caldwell was active in church affairs. In 1770 he was among those who successfully petitioned for the establishment of the Presbytery of Orange, which embraced the area south of Virginia. In 1774 he traveled north to attend meetings of the Synod of New York and Philadelphia.

As events leading to the Revolution took shape, Caldwell's earlier reverence toward the "powers whom God has ordained" shifted. In about 1774 or 1775 he rallied his congregations to the revolutionary cause in a stirring sermon which traced the history of British civil liberty. "Attempts have been often made, since the reformation," he admonished his listeners, "to introduce popery and slavery into the British nation; but they were always resolutely and successfully withstood . . . our forefathers, or many of them, sacrificed at Londonderry and Enniskillen, their lives, that they might hand down to us the fair inheritance of liberty and the protestant religion; and in the whole course of their conduct in the support and defense of their rights, they have set us an example which ought not to be disregarded. . . . We have therefore come to that trying period in our history in which it is manifest that the Americans must either stoop under a load of the vilest slavery, or resist their imperious and haughty oppressors."

In October 1776 Caldwell was elected from Guilford County to North Carolina's fifth provincial congress, called to draw up a constitution for the new state. Caldwell has been credited by many with authorship of the section of the constitution that made active clergymen ineligible for the Senate, House of Commons, and Council of State, and for the section that barred atheists, non-Protestants, and "those whose religious views were incompatible with freedom" from holding public office.

Caldwell's actions during the war years are difficult to trace. The British supposedly put a price of £200 on his head, and he was often in hiding. Part of his time was spent as unofficial chaplain and surgeon to various American army units. His home was occupied by the British and his papers and library were destroyed.

With peace Caldwell resumed his several occupations. Between fifty and sixty students a year attended his academy. He was prosperous; by 1790 he owned 791 acres of land and eight slaves. He retained the trust of his neighbors, who in 1788 elected him a delegate to the North Carolina convention called to consider ratification of the federal constitution. Caldwell vigorously opposed its adoption. He objected strongly to the phrase "we the people," declaring that the Constitution's framers were representatives of state legislatures and derived no power from "the people." He deplored many provisions in the document and decried its lack of a religious test for officeholders. He feared that Jews and pagans might be drawn to the United States, claiming that even those who did not practice Christianity knew that it was the religion best suited to make good members of society. The delegates must have shared some of Caldwell's views, for the convention did not ratify the constitution.

Caldwell welcomed the second Great Awakening in 1800. He tried to introduce Isaac Watts's hymns into one of his churches, but the congregation preferred to continue the old Scotch custom of singing psalms. Although the University of North Carolina never offered Caldwell its presidency, as has often been stated, it did award him the D.D. Caldwell's later years were shadowed by the insanity of three of the eight of his surviving children. But he remained active. In 1811 the father of John Morehead, a future governor of North Carolina, delivered the youth to Caldwell to be educated. "We found," Morehead remembered, "a few hundred yards from the house . . . an exceedingly old gentleman, bowed down by some eighty-six or seven winters, enveloped in large cape made of bear skin, with a net worsted cap on his head, (for the evening was cool,) and supporting himself with a cane not much shorter than his own body." Caldwell took on Morehead's education and prepared him for the University of North Carolina. Morehead was not Caldwell's last pupil. He continued to preach to his congregations until 1820, when he retired permanently to his plantation. He died on August 25, 1824, a few months short of his one-hundredth birthday.

SOURCES: E. W. Caruthers, *A Sketch of the Life and Character of the Rev. David Caldwell, D.D.* (1842), is a rambling collection of fact and dubious anecdote; brief sketches: *DAB*; Foote, *Sketches, N.C.*; Sprague, *Annals*, III, 263-67 (from which Morehead quotation is drawn); A. L. Brooks, "David Caldwell and His Log College," *NCHR*, 28 (1951), 399-407; Hulbert quotation: *Princeton Standard*, Nov. 2, 1859; N.C. churches: *Col. Rec. N.C.*, V, 1218; Regulator involvement: *Col. Rec. N.C.*, VII, 813-16; W. S. Powell, *Regulators in N.C.* (1971), xxiv; *Col. Rec. N.C.*, X, 950; academy: *WMQ*, 2 (1945), 379-80; Orange Presbytery: *NCHR*, 44 (1967), 381; *Presbyterian Records*, 450; 1776 Congress and constitution: *WMQ*, 5 (1948), 59, and *ibid.*, 24 (1967), 575; sermon quotations: Caldwell, "The Character and Doom of the Sluggard," reprinted in Caruthers, above, 279, 280, 283; 1790 property: *NCHR*, 27 (1950), 297; federal constitution: *WMQ*, 12 (1955), 14, 17, and: J. Eliot, *Debates in the Several State Conventions on the Adoption of the Federal Constitution* (2nd ed., 1861), IV, iv, 9, 15-16, 23, 25, 26, 62-63, 65, 187, 199; 1800 revival and hymns: *NCHR*, 43 (1966), 20, 410-11.

PUBLICATIONS: Caldwell's two surviving sermons are reprinted in Caruthers, above.

David Gillespie

DAVID GILLESPIE, A.B., has not been identified with absolute assurance. The only certain facts concerning the alumnus are that he was listed as living in the College's catalogue of 1770 and as dead in the catalogue of 1773. However, there seems no reason to doubt that he was the David Gillespie, a schoolmaster, who in June 1768 served as witness to a will in Charleston, South Carolina, together with the Reverend Hugh Alison (A.B. 1762). On May 14, 1770, listed in a Charleston newspaper as "Mr. David Gillespie, A.B.," he married Mary, widow of Captain James Rogers. The only further information available is that Gillespie died, apparently without having made a will, in Charleston during the second week of January 1772.

SOURCES: Will witness: T. Moore, *Abstracts of the Wills of the State of S.C.* (1969), 138; occupation: *SCHGM*, 17 (1916), 48; marriage: A. S. Salley, Jr., *Marriage Notices in the S.C. Gaz.* (1904), 16; *SCHGM*, 11 (1910), 93; death: *SCHGM*, 10 (1909), 167.

Isaac Handy

ISAAC HANDY, A.B., lawyer and planter, was born on December 19, 1743, probably at "Pemberton Hall" in what is now Wicomico County, Maryland, one of the several plantations owned by his family. He was the fourth son of Colonel Isaac Handy, an influential and wealthy planter, and his wife Anne Dashiell. Among young Isaac's brothers-in-law was the Reverend Hugh Henry (A.B. 1748), pastor at nearby Presbyterian churches. When Isaac's father made his will in 1760, he appointed Henry one of the guardians of the youth. It may have been Henry's influence that directed Handy to the College.

On his father's death in November 1762 young Handy inherited an indeterminable amount of land, some funds in England, four slaves, and, the father specified, "my troopers saddle and bridel and silver hafted sword." Once back in Maryland Handy studied law. He married Esther Winder, daughter of Captain William Winder, a well-to-do planter and elder of the Wicomico Presbyterian church. The couple had two children, Margaret Winder Handy and Richard Henry Handy.

If the contents of Handy's law library are any indication, he was learned in his profession. His legal collection included all the standard law books of the day. He must have been a busy lawyer, too: after his death on July 14, 1772, his widow listed approximately 140 individuals who owed money to his estate. The estate, which was inventoried at £826.15, included thirteen slaves. After her remarriage Handy's widow had a supplemental inventory of his library drawn up. The appraisers carefully itemized each book. Apparently Handy had never thrown anything away, for the inventory includes many of the books he must have purchased while a student in the College—among others, "Tennents Sermons," "Salmon's Modern Gazeteer," "Martin's Grammar," "Locke on Human Understanding," and "Doddridge's Rise and Progress of Religion."

SOURCES: Handy had a first cousin of the same name who was mentioned in his father's will. The cousin died at about the same time as the CNJ alumnus, and care must be taken to distinguish one from the other in the records. Geneal. and vital data: Alexander, *Princeton*, 71, and Isaac Handy File, PUA; father's will: *Maryland Wills*, XXXI, 77-78; Pemberton Hall and family lands: S. Earle and P. G. Skirven, *Maryland's Colonial Eastern Shore* (1916), 185-86; children and date of death:

Handy Family Bible, in 1975 in possession of William R. Bishop, Jr. (Class of 1939), to whom we are indebted for this and other information; estate inventories: MSS, Hall of Records, Annapolis, Md.

Thomas Henderson

THOMAS HENDERSON, A.B., A.M. 1764, physician, public official and soldier, was born on August 15, 1743, just outside Freehold in Monmouth County, New Jersey, the fourth son and seventh child of Ann Stevens and her husband, John Henderson, a farmer and elder of trustee William Tennent's Presbyterian church. After graduating from the College Henderson studied medicine with Dr. Nathaniel Scudder (A.B. 1757). He then established his own practice, eventually settling back in Freehold. Henderson was a member of the New Jersey Medical Society, organized in 1766. However, he never attended its meetings and was dropped from its rolls in 1772, though he eventually served as the society's secretary in 1787-1788.

On September 23, 1767, Henderson married Mary Hendricks. She died of tuberculosis the following year, and Henderson himself contracted the disease. In search of a cure he traveled south, probably to Cuba. He recovered sufficiently to return to his medical practice. Henderson did not remarry until 1778. On January 26 of that year he wed Rachel Burrowes. The couple had seven daughters. Henderson was an active member of William Tennent's Presbyterian congregation at Freehold, serving in time as a trustee and elder of the church. He was particularly close to Tennent, acting as his personal physician and after Tennent's death contributing to a memoir of him.

As difficulties with Britain developed, Henderson placed himself firmly in the Whig camp. On December 10, 1774, he became a member of Freehold's Committee of Observation and Inspection. In August 1775 he was a lieutenant in the First Company of Minute Men of Monmouth County. Later in the year he was elected major and then a lieutenant-colonel in the county's First Regiment. He later became a lieutenant-colonel in Colonel David Forman's battalion, General Heard's brigade. Present at the battle of Long Island, Henderson met another alumnus of the College: "Col. Henderson civilly invited me to lodge with him," the Reverend Philip Vickers Fithian (A.B. 1772) reported from Jamaica, Long Island, in July 1776. "Here I have a good Bed & a sensible Companion. And have good Reason to believe, he is a hearty Friend to sound Religion."

Henderson was back in Freehold by 1778, where he married for the second time in January. In June 1778 General Sir Henry Clinton started to march across New Jersey from Philadelphia in order to consolidate the British forces in New York City. The British arrived at Freehold on June 26. The following day they burned Henderson's house. By that time he had joined Washington's army. That Henderson took part in the ensuing battle of Monmouth is certain, but his role is unclear. A strong local tradition contends that Henderson was the "countryman" who brought Washington news of General Charles Lee's "retreat."

Elected to the Continental Congress in November 1779, Henderson never took his seat. He served in the New Jersey Assembly from 1780 to 1784 and on a local Monmouth County Committee of Retaliation (a quasi-vigilante group formed to harass suspected Loyalists) after July 1, 1780. Henderson also served as a surrogate of Monmouth County in 1776, a judge of common pleas in 1783 and 1799, and as master of Chancery in 1790.

A presidential elector in 1792, Henderson in 1793 was elected to the New Jersey Council; as vice-president of the council he served as acting governor while Governor Howell was away helping to put down the Whiskey Rebellion in Pennsylvania. A member of the Pennsylvania-New Jersey boundary commission, in 1795 Henderson was elected to Congress, where he served until 1797. Put forward as a "local son," Henderson was a moderate Federalist. He came out in favor of strengthening the army and navy, hard money, and for a revenue tariff. "I have a stronger attachment to my own Country than to all the nations upon earth," said Henderson in supporting Jay's Treaty, adding that he did not care if he were "charged with undue favoritism to Great Britain and want of friendship to the Republic of France," since in his "opinion under existing circumstances, the persons representing nine-tenths of the property of this State are in favor of the measure." He urged his fellow Federalists to be moderate in their tax and military programs.

Henderson was not reelected to Congress; his only later public post was as a member of the New Jersey Council in 1812–1813. In 1817 he was one of the founders of the Monmouth County Bible Society. Henderson died in Freehold on December 15, 1824. In his extremely detailed will he directed that "my aged Slaves Robert and Violet . . . be provided for as humanity would require." He left a considerable amount of real estate and his personal property was inventoried at $14,646.71.

SOURCES: Sketches: *DAB*; Wickes, *Hist. of Medicine in N.J.* (1879), 279-82; and: D. H. Fischer, *The Revolution of American Conservatism* (1965), 324; N.J. Medical Society: S. Wickes, *Proc. N.J. Med. Soc.* (1875), 15, 32, 53, 54; war record, burning of house, etc., see: widow's MS Pension Application, August, 1838, National Archives, Washington, D.C.; Fithian quotation: *Fithian Journal*, II, 192; Committee of Retaliation: Lundin, *Cockpit of the Revolution*, 291; election to Congress: R. P. Mc-Cormick, *Experiment in Independence* (1950), 290; Jay's Treaty quotation: *Annals of Congress*, V, 1170; will: MS, N.J. State Lib., Trenton.

PUBLICATIONS: Henderson is reputed to have been the main author of *Memoirs of the Life of the Rev. William Tennent* (1807).

Mss: NjP, PHi

William Jauncey

WILLIAM JAUNCEY, A.B., merchant, was the son of Maria Smith and her husband, Captain James Jauncey, and the brother of James Jauncey, Jr. (A.B. 1763). He was born on December 17, 1744, on an estate in what is now Greenwich Village which his father purchased soon after retiring from the sea and moving from Bermuda to New York City in 1743. By the time of William's birth the father was one of the wealthiest merchants in New York. He owned several privateers during the French and Indian War, was a founder of the New York Chamber of Commerce, and sat on the board of the Wall Street Presbyterian Church, where his children were baptized. James Jauncey, Sr., was a leader of the futile attempt to coax Joseph Bellamy to settle as pastor of the Wall Street Church; and in the course of that effort he became a close personal friend of the Connecticut minister and theologian. He was also a member of the New York Assembly and was a strong supporter of movements to redress colonial grievances within the Empire. But as the Revolution approached his loyalism to the British crown put him in the center of the political turmoil in the city.

After graduating from the College, William joined his father's business in New York. He was far less active in political affairs than his father and brother James, both of whom were at the fore of the conservative faction. Nevertheless, when General Washington ordered that the Jaunceys be expelled from New York in 1776, William was arrested as well. In August all three men were sent to Middletown, Connecticut. Within days of William's thirty-second birthday, the Connecticut Committee of Safety allowed them to return home on parole.

After the death in August 1777 of James, Jr., whose marital ties to prominent Britons made him the most conspicuous Loyalist in the family, there was a temporary respite from persecution for the Jaunceys. In December of that year James, Sr., was named by the governor of New York to serve on a committee for the relief of the poor. In October 1779, however, the state government ordered the banishment of the elder Jauncey to England and the forfeiture of his extensive estates. William and his youngest brother John (King's 1774) petitioned the legislature to repeal their father's banishment and allow him to return from exile in England but they were not successful until April 1790, two months after James Jauncey, Sr., had died in London.

The old merchant and sea captain had managed to transfer most of his personal property to England before his deportation. Although much of his land in New York was sold in 1784 for a total price of £8,435, his fortune was largely intact when he died. He bequeathed the bulk of his money to his children, and William received some £60,000 in his father's will. Since he had retained most of his own property in New York his inheritance made him one of the richest men in the city.

He was also active in municipal affairs. He served as a governor of the city hospital from 1797 until 1802, was a member of the Public School Society, and was a trustee of the Society for the Promotion of Religion and Learning. In November 1799, the city's Common Council chose him as an assessor for the second ward but he declined to serve because a fracture in his leg had made him lame. In addition to his mercantile affairs, Jauncey was also a landlord. In December 1819, one of his properties was cited as a public nuisance because its privy had not been emptied.

Jauncey never married. He lavished his affection and considerable wealth on his brother John's daughter, Jane Mary Thorn, and her children. In his will he bequeathed several thousands of pounds sterling to the Thorn family provided that the two oldest sons should legally change their name to Jauncey. (They did.) He died in New York City on September 19, 1828.

SOURCES: *NYGBR*, 26 (1895), 185-86; *ibid.*, 96 (1965), 90-91, 93; J. O. Brown, *Jaunceys of New York* (1876), 17-21; arrest as Loyalist: Sabine, *Loyalists*, II, 536; election as assessor and citation of property as public nuisance: *N.Y. Com. Council Mins.*, II, 583; x, 653; family estate in Greenwich Village: V. D. Harrington, *N.Y. Merchant on the Eve of the Rev.* (1935), 23; sale of father's confiscated property: A. C. Flick, *Loyalism in N.Y. During the Am. Rev.* (1901), 242-62.

RAH

Nathan Ker

NATHAN KER, A.B., Presbyterian clergyman, was born in Freehold, New Jersey, on September 7, 1736, the son of William Ker, a prominent citizen of the town, by William's second wife, Catherine Loofbourow. Nathan was probably prepared for the College by his pastor, the Reverend William Tennent II, a trustee. A year after his graduation Ker was licensed by the Presbytery of New Brunswick. Ordination followed on July 15, 1763, when Ker was installed as pastor of the Presbyterian church at Springfield (part of Elizabeth), New Jersey.

On November 8, 1764, Ker married Anne Livermore, a sister of Isaac (A.B. 1756), Samuel (A.B. 1752), and William (A.B. 1756) Livermore. The marriage began badly. On May 28, 1765, Ker presented the following petition to the New Jersey Assembly: "Very soon after [Ker's marriage] all his prospects of future Ease and Comfort at once vanished, by discovering Reasons to suspect, that his said Wife was then and had been in pregnant Circumstances at the Time of their Intermarriage." He stated that Anne had admitted that she had been made pregnant by her brother-in-law, the Reverend Nathaniel Potter (A.B. 1753), after she had agreed to marry Ker. "She was afterwards," Ker's petition continued, "in *February* last delivered of her spurious issue [Oliver Livermore Ker, A.B. 1784], which, with the Mother, the unhappy Petitioner is reduced to the Necessity of supporting by the Laws of the Land, to his great Hardship and intolerable Grievance; and praying such Relief in the Premises, as the Nature of the Case may suggest."

1785

A second petition from several ministers supporting Ker and requesting that the marriage be dissolved was presented on the same date. The assembly ordered a second reading of Ker's petition on the following day, at which time Ker presented a certificate from his wife declaring that she had, as required by law, agreed to the publication of the story. The assembly deferred action on the petition to the next week. But on June 7, 1765, the House received a letter from Ker informing it that when he returned home he had "found the poor Lady mentioned in his Petition, mourning bitterly her unhappy Fortune; he making to her Proposals of Separation, she told him, that if they must separate altho' to her it was like Death, she would leave the Terms to him; and that upon the Whole, her Behaviour was such as excited his tenderest Compassion, especially when he considered what an artful Man seduced her; and her Posture, her Looks and Entreaties were such, as renders him incapable of proceeding; and praying leave to withdraw his Petition." The assembly granted the withdrawal. The couple went on to have five children together.

By the following year Ker had settled in Goshen, Orange County, New York, as pastor of the Presbyterian church. He was a fervent Whig during the Revolution. According to one story he loaned the government $8,000; his only repayment was a cast-off army mare he called "Old Liberty." The war touched Ker and his congregation directly. In July 1779, the Mohawk leader Joseph Brant raided the nearby Minisink area. Ker joined the militias from several places in pursuit of the Indians and Tories. The result, Ker wrote to Governor George Clinton, was "not less than 15 or 16 widows by this affair in this Congregation."

Ker was an influential figure in his region and beyond. Appointed to the New York State Board of Regents in 1787, he was also one of the incorporators and the librarian of Goshen's widely known Farmers' Hall Academy, where young Noah Webster (Yale 1778) taught briefly. Despite a congregation that numbered only 130 in 1792 and a salary— usually in arrears—of £100 a year, Ker was apparently fairly well-to-do. He farmed and in 1790 was recorded as the owner of five slaves. He was active in church affairs, publishing a sermon and presiding at the first meeting of the Presbytery of Hudson held in November 1795. Ker died in Goshen on December 14, 1804. His will was short. He left everything to his "well-belov'd wife, Anne Ker, without any conditions whatever," except that a female slave named Dean was to be freed in five years and Dean's son Alex was to be freed when he was twenty-eight.

SOURCES: Parentage: W. W. Armstrom, *Kerr Clan of New Jersey* (1931), 7; an unreliable sketch is: J. T. Headly, *Chaplains and Clergy of the Rev.* (1864), 365-71; a more reliable one, which includes will, is: M. P. Seese, *A Tower of the Lord in the Land of Goshen* (1945), 20, 26-29; divorce petition: *N.J. Gen. Assembly* [May 21–June 20, 1765] (1765), 20, 22; Brant incident: *Clinton Papers*, v, 162-66; size of congregation: Stiles, *Literary Diary*, III, 476; 1790 slaves: *U.S. Census of 1790, New York*, 139.

PUBLICATIONS: "God's Sovereignty in Conferring Means and Grace," in *American Preacher . . .* (1793), IV, 366-91.

John Lefferty

JOHN LEFFERTY, A.B., A.M. 1764, lawyer, was born about 1741, the fourth child and second son of Mary and Bryan Lefferty. The Leffertys settled in Pluckemin, Somerset County, New Jersey, at some time before 1749. John's birthplace has not been discovered. The father was a prominent citizen of the area. A merchant until 1760, he oversaw the running of many lotteries, became a justice of the peace, a judge of the court of common pleas and of the court of oyer and terminer.

After graduation Lefferty read law and, along with his older brother Bryan, was admitted to practice in Hunterdon County in 1767. It was probably at about this time that Lefferty married Elizabeth Johns, daughter of Timothy Johns, Presbyterian minister in Morristown and a trustee of the College from 1748 to 1788. Elizabeth died in her twen-

ty-sixth year, on April 29, 1772. On December 20, 1773, Lefferty advertised his six-room stone house and lands in Pluckemin, Somerset County, for sale in a New York newspaper. He died on December 2, 1776.
He was interred next to his wife in the Lamington burying-ground.
The value of his estate, which included many law books, came to
£279.15.2.

SOURCES: The name was spelled variously Lafferty, Lefferty, Leferty, etc.; parentage:
NJHS Col., 9 (1916), 150-51; father: *Som. Cty. Hist. Quart.*, 8 (1919), 37; and 20
NJA, 437; admission to bar: J. P. Snell, *Hist. of Hunterdon and Somerset Counties*
(1881), 206, 644; wife, year of birth and date of death: *Som. Cty. Hist. Quart.*, 3
(1914), 132; newspaper advertisement: *N.Y. Gaz.*, Dec. 20, 1773; will and inventory: MS, N.J. State Lib., Trenton.

Thomas McCracken

THOMAS MCCRACKEN, A.B., was a Presbyterian clergyman. Neither his
parentage nor his place of origin have been discovered. After graduation McCracken studied for the ministry. By 1763 he had moved to
Delaware, where on October 12 of that year he presented himself to
the Presbytery of Lewes meeting at Dover as a candidate for the ministry. Licensed to preach on May 9, 1765, he was finally ordained on
October 2, 1767. In May 1768 the Presbyterian congregations at Vi-
enna and Fishing Creek in Dorchester County, Maryland, requested
McCracken to settle there as their pastor. It took McCracken almost
two years to assent to the call, but he had apparently accepted by
June 13, 1770, when he bought 85½ acres of land in Dorchester
County. His career was suddenly cut short by his death on December 9, 1770. Although his estate was modest, it included a few luxury
items, such as a library, an old riding-chair, some Delft ware, and
twenty-two sheets of gilt-edged writing paper. McCracken was survived by his wife, Nancy, and an infant son, Thomas.

SOURCES: All information above kindly furnished by Dr. George E. McCracken
(Princeton, 1926). Drawn from MS Minutes of the Pres. of Lewes, PPPrHi; and MS
sources at Hall of Records, Annapolis, Md. See too: Alexander, *Princeton*, 72; Giger,
Memoirs, I.

Benjamin McDowell

BENJAMIN MCDOWELL, D.D. Edinburgh 1789, Presbyterian clergyman, was born in Bedminster, Somerset County, New Jersey, on
Christmas day, 1739. His parents, Margaret Irving (Irvine) and Ephraim McDowell, were zealous Presbyterians from Connor, County An-

trim, Ireland. Benjamin and his brothers and sisters were raised on a 400-acre farm in what is now Lamington, New Jersey, which his father purchased between 1746 and 1750. The McDowell children and those of their neighbor, Reverend James McCrea, were educated under the direction of John Hanna (A.B. 1755) in a log school house on the farm. Thus trained in Latin, Greek, and other rudimentary subjects, Benjamin entered the College in Princeton. He withdrew before graduating in order to enter the University of Glasgow, Scotland, where he was in residence in 1761 and where he probably received £30 bequeathed to him by his father in 1762.

Although his parents were devoted to the "reform presbyterian" church of the Scottish theologian John MacMillan, McDowell preferred the traditional dogma of the established church in Scotland. The influence of the Great Awakening on Princeton may thus have provoked him to abandon the College for Glasgow. Apparently, he did not receive a degree from his second university, either, but he was licensed by the Presbytery of Glasgow in July 1766. After supplying pulpits in Glasgow he went to Ireland to visit relatives in County Antrim and to preach in local churches. While there he was called to settle with the congregation in Ballykelly, County Londonderry, where he was ordained by the Route Presbytery on September 3, 1766. In his twelve years in Ballykelly he emerged as a leading spokesman for Old Light theology and even contemplated leading a secession of conservative ministers from the church in order to preserve their orthodoxy. His published defenses of conservative doctrine were major contributions to the theological debate.

In June 1777 McDowell preached at the Capel Street Meeting House (the Scots Church), now Mary's Abbey, in Dublin. In 1778 the Synod of Ulster installed him as the permanent pastor there. The congregation, decimated by the doctrinal schism, consisted of only six families when he took charge, but McDowell quickly became a leader of Dublin's Presbyterian community. With diligent evangelism he expanded his congregation until, by 1818, it was the largest Presbyterian church in Dublin, numbering 2,000 members and requiring several ministers. He never abandoned his defense of Old Light Presbyterianism, but he cooperated with New Light leaders after 1783 in negotiating with the government on the public status of the church. In 1786 he was the moderator of the General Synod, and in 1788 he was one of the synod's inspectors in west and southwest Ireland. Meanwhile, he established a charity school at Mary's Abbey that was supported exclusively by donations from his parishioners. On January 22, 1789, he was awarded a Doctorate of Divinity by the University of Edinburgh.

McDowell's efforts in behalf of his church took their toll. His health was precarious after 1789. He spent the summer of 1790 visiting friends in Londonderry, and between 1791 and 1798 he made occasional trips to revolutionary France. Although the journeys were supposed to be vacations, he found the chaos in France so traumatic that he conducted prayer meetings while there. His sympathies, in political as well as theological matters, were strongly conservative. Back in Dublin he was a prominent opponent of the so-called United Irishmen, the movement inspired by the French Revolution to call for the creation of an independent Irish republic. In 1813 McDowell was forced by ill health to retire from the pulpit, and on September 13, 1824, he died in Dublin. He was buried there and a marble commemorative tablet was erected at his church. He was survived by his wife and children.

SOURCES: *DNB*; J. Horner, *Destination of Man after Death: A Sermon, Occasioned by the Death of the Late Benjamin M'Dowell, D.D.* (1825), 16-25, 30-32; J. S. Reid, *Hist. of the Pres. Church in Ireland* (1853), 445-46; parents: Hatfield, *Elizabeth*, 667; *Som. Cty. Hist. Quart.*, 5 (1916), 280; 7 (1918), 52; father's will: 33 *NJA*, 267; Lamington School: *NJSHP* (2 ser.), IX, 95; studies in Glasgow: W. I. Addison, ed., *Matriculation Albums of the Univ. of Glasgow* (1913); United Irishmen: S. D. Alexander, *Hist. of the Pres. Church in Ireland* (1860), 355; service in Ballykelly: W. D. Killen, *Hist. of the Congregations of the Pres. Church in Ireland* (1886), 37.

PUBLICATIONS: *The Requiring Subscription . . . defended; in answer to "The Catholic Christian" . . . in a Letter to the Rev. J-n C-n* (1770); *A Second Letter to the Rev. J-n C-n* (1771); *Observations on Theophilus and Philander* (1772); *A Vindication of the Westminster Confession . . . from two late Writers* (1774); *Letters of Importance . . . to the . . . Synod of Ulster, &c. With an Appendix . . . By Pistophilus Philecclesia* (1775); *The Doctrine of Salvation by Grace* (1777); *A Letter to the Ministers of the Synod of Ulster, by Amicus* (1807); *The Nature of the Presbyterian Form of Church Government* (1808); separate sermons, 1783 and 1799; parts of ordination service for John Baird, 1812.

RAH

David Rice

DAVID RICE, A.B., Presbyterian clergyman, was born in Hanover County, Virginia on December 29, 1733, the son of David Rice, an Anglican farmer of modest means. The son converted to Presbyterianism when he was about twenty, having been influenced by the preaching of Samuel Davies and the teaching of the Reverend John Todd (A.B. 1749) and the Reverend James Waddel. When Davies became president of the College in 1759, Rice traveled north with him and entered the College's junior class with the intention of becoming a minister. He had to work his way through college. Only the financial support which President Davies found for him enabled him to escape damaging his health. Part of the aid came from Richard Stockton (A.B. 1748). It allowed Rice to purchase new clothes, his old ones having become so embarrassingly shabby that he had contemplated leaving Princeton. Stockton refused repayment from Rice, but Rice may have been expressing his gratitude in the "animated English oration on Benevolence" that he delivered at his commencement.

After graduation Rice returned home and resumed his studies with John Todd. Licensed by the Presbytery of Hanover in November 1762, he then preached in various pulpits in southern Virginia and northern North Carolina. On a visit to Pennsylvania he married by prior arrangement Mary Blair, daughter of the Reverend Samuel Blair of Fagg's Manor and a sister of Samuel Blair (A.B. 1760). The couple had eleven children. Shortly after his marriage Rice accepted a pastorate in Hanover County, Virginia, and was ordained in December 1763. Rice replaced Samuel Davies, who had served several local congregations before his departure for Princeton. Although a popular and respected pastor, Rice left Hanover in 1768 rather than try to resolve a dispute between two of the most important elders of his congregation. The dispute had originated during Davies's tenure and apparently had little to do with Rice's work.

From 1768 to 1770 Rice supplied other Virginia pulpits, finally accepting a call from three congregations in mountainous, sparsely settled Bedford County: Hat Creek, Concord, and the Peaks of Otter. He lived in Bedford County for thirteen years and once again proved a successful preacher, often attracting members of other denominations to his services. He remained active in the affairs of the Presbytery of Hanover, particularly in its efforts to bring about the separation of church and state in officially Anglican Virginia. Rice also devoted his efforts to higher education in Virginia, collecting subscriptions in 1774 for Liberty Hall Academy (later Washington and Lee University), and serving as a founder and charter trustee of Hampden-Sidney College.

In May 1775 Rice helped establish Bedford County's Committee of Safety. He preached often in favor of the Revolution, arguing in one sermon that "the grounds of the Americans' struggle and the reason of our opposition to the claims of the British Parliament are very just and important. It is nothing less than a fundamental subversion of the Civil Constitution of the Colonies and the substitution of arbitrary despotic power in the room of a free government that we oppose. . . . Where the very being of the constitution is struck at, resistance is justified by the laws of God and the dictates of common sense."

In October 1783, Rice and his family moved to Mercer County, Kentucky, where he gained his greatest prominence. Years earlier he had contemplated moving west but had hesitated out of fear of conflict over land purchases: "I saw that the spirit of speculation was flowing in such a torrent that it would bear down every weak obstacle that stood in its way. . . . I knew the make of my own mind . . . could not enjoy the happiness of life if engaged in disputes and law-suits." He changed his mind only after receiving a request, signed by three hundred persons, to take charge of three struggling congregations at Danville, Cane-Run, and the Forks of Dick's River. As the state's first permanent Presbyterian minister, Rice became known as the "father of Kentucky Presbyterianism"—or, more affectionately, as "Father Rice."

Rice's new parishioners, as he himself acknowledged, were not particularly religious, and he preached his entire first year without once administering the sacraments. Many Saturdays were spent "in catechizing such as felt an interest in religious matters." The modest revival that his flock experienced in the early 1790s reflected a decade of intensive effort and barely compensated Rice for the many moments of depression he had endured. Both his failure to sustain the revival through the mid-1790s and the toll on his health spurred Rice's resignation from his pulpits in 1798. A third factor was a bitter dispute between Rice and some of his parishioners over his salary.

In Kentucky Rice participated actively in the affairs of the Presbytery of Transylvania, being elected its moderator in October 1786. Despite his own revivalist work, Rice remained an Old Side and condemned Kentucky's New Side crusaders for their theological and emotional excesses—for what he termed their Arminianism, Arianism, Universalism, Deism, and Atheism, as well as the jerking, rolling, barking and dancing attendant at camp-meetings. He termed New Side ministers "men of sound principles and some information but deficient in the spirit of the Gospel." In *An Essay on Baptism* (1789) Rice pleaded with the "plain Christian" to avoid "blind attendance on Gospel ordinances"—in this case, wholesale baptisms of persons of dubious religious convictions. A plan he devised to regulate camp meetings was debated by his presbytery but was ultimately rejected.

As in Virginia, in Kentucky Rice helped found schools. From 1784 to the end of his life he conducted the first Latin grammar school in the state in his home. He served as chairman of the board of trustees of the Transylvania Seminary from 1783 to 1787, and in 1794 helped found the Kentucky Academy following the appointment of a Baptist to the Seminary faculty. When the Baptist resigned in 1796 the academy and seminary merged to form Transylvania University, which Rice, along with Caleb Wallace (A.B. 1770), served as a trustee.

Rice was an outspoken critic of slavery. In a 1792 sermon, *Slavery Inconsistent with Justice and Good Policy*, he condemned it on both economic and moral grounds—economically, because slaves would inevitably revolt against their oppressors and destroy their oppressors' property; morally, because slaves were as much creatures of God as their masters and so were entitled to the very liberties on which the American government was based. "The Slavery of the Negroes," he concluded, "began in iniquity: a curse has attended it, and a curse will follow it. National vices will be punished with national calamities. Let us avoid these vices, that we may avoid the punishment which they deserve." In 1792 he was elected to Kentucky's constitutional convention, where the article he proposed for the gradual emancipation of slaves was rejected. In 1794, however, he successfully pressured the Transylvania Presbytery into ordering all member slaveholders to educate their slaves for the "enjoyment of freedom." And in 1797 he saw that the Presbytery pronounced slavery "a moral evil."

In 1798 Rice moved to Green County, Kentucky, where he spent the rest of his life, preaching occasionally in vacant local pulpits. In 1805, at the request of the Presbyterian General Assembly, he traveled throughout Kentucky and Ohio to assess religious conditions. Upon his return home he composed two *Epistles* to Kentucky Presbyterians repeating his earlier criticisms of revivalism.

Described by contemporaries as "tall and slender, . . . quiet in his movements, and even at the age of seventy . . . remarkabl[y] alert," Rice was widely respected not for brilliance but for sound judgment, industry, seriousness and devotion. His later years were marred by poverty and ill health. Confined to his home in 1812, he continued to preach and write from his bed. He died of influenza on June 18, 1816.

SOURCES: Sketches: *DAB*; Sprague, *Annals*, III, 246-49; R. H. Bishop. *An Outline of the Hist. of the Church in the State of Ky.* (1824); R. Davidson, *Hist. of Presby. Church in the State of Ky.* (1847); Stockton: Alexander, *Princeton*, 72-73; Hanover Co. pastorate: W. M. Gewehr, *Great Awakening in Va.* (1930), 101; Foote, *Sketches, Va.* (1850); *VMHB*, 6 (1898), 176; 12 (1904), 417-21; 13 (1905), 40-45; ed. work in Va.: *WMQ*, 2 (1945), 368; Rev. sermon quotation: E. W. Thompson, *Presbyterians in the South* (1963), I, 93-94; Com. of Safety: *WMQ* (1 ser.), 5 (1896), 253; *Va. Gaz.* (Pinckney), June 8, 1775; separation ch. and state: *Jefferson Papers*, VI, 55-60; Ky. Presbys.: above and: W. W. Sweet, *Religion on the Am. Frontier* (1936), II, 30-31; N. H. Sonne, *Liberal Ky.* (1939), 16-18; R. Peter, *Transylvania University* (1896).

PUBLICATIONS: see text, STE and Sh-Sh 4980.   HS

John Rosbrugh

JOHN ROSBRUGH, A.B., Presbyterian clergyman, was born in 1714, probably in Northern Ireland, to recent immigrants from Scotland. In the early 1730s, John and his brother came to Dansville in what is now Steuben County, New York. There in 1733 he married his first wife Sarah, who later died in childbirth. Nothing more is known of Rosbrugh until he appeared at the College. His education was partially financed through a fund established by President Samuel Davies to assist "poor and pious youth" of Calvinistic principles. After graduation Rosbrugh studied theology with John Blair at Fagg's Manor, Pennsylvania, and after passing with difficulty his examinations, he was licensed by the Presbytery of New Brunswick on August 11, 1764. Called by the Greenwich, Oxford and Mansfield Churches of Warren County, New Jersey, he was ordained by the presbytery on December 11, 1764. This assignment proved very taxing on the energies of a middle-aged man: he had to ride five to ten miles each Sabbath. Furthermore, the congregations unexpectedly began to lose their members and were unable to support a minister. When Rosbrugh asked to be dismissed, he was released from his duties in April 1769.

In 1766 Rosbrugh married Jean Ralston, the daughter of a prosperous elder of the Presbyterian church in Allen Township, Pennsylvania. When his in-laws exerted their influence, Rosbrugh was called by that congregation. But because the church was located outside Rosbrugh's presbytery, it was not until after the synod removed the jurisdiction of the congregation from the Presbytery of New Brunswick that Rosbrugh was at last ordained on October 13, 1772. Later he served as moderator of a meeting of the Synod of Philadelphia in May 1774 and of his own presbytery in 1776.

Together with others in the area and his brother-in-law James Ralston, who served in the Continental Congress, Rosbrugh backed the war for independence. When in 1776 George Washington asked for aid to stop the British invaders, Rosbrugh read the message from the pulpit and preached a sermon on the text of "Curse ye Meroz . . . because they came not to the help of the Lord against the Mighty." Despite his advanced age of sixty some years, Rosbrugh joined the 3rd Battalion of the Northampton County Militia. After receiving his commission as chaplain on December 26, 1776, he wrote to his wife in Allen Township that "the important crisis draws near, which I trust may direct the question to whether the Americans shall be slaves or free men." Shortly thereafter he told her that the battalion was going to attack the enemy, an event that reinforced an impending sense of death: "this may be the last you shall ever receive from your husband," he wrote. In the march toward the battle of Princeton, Rosbrugh became separated from his company. Captured by a group of Hessians, he was killed and his body stripped of its possessions. A Philadelphia newspaper reported that on the night of January 2, 1777, the Hessians bayoneted Rosbrugh "whilst he implored mercy and begging his life at their hands." A straggler buried the abandoned body. Rosbrugh's grave was never identified.

Almost immediately a legend began to grow concerning the "Clerical Martyr of the Revolution." On January 4, 1777, Benjamin Rush wrote to Richard Henry Lee that the "savages murdered a clergyman . . . in cold blood after he surrendered himself and begged for mercy. His name was Rosborough." His fame reached its peak on January 23, 1917, at the First Presbyterian Church in Trenton, when a large marble monument to Rosbrugh's memory was dedicated. Despite such contemporary and later attention, Rosbrugh's death left his widow and their five children in difficult circumstances. Whatever may have been the size of his estate, it seems to have been seriously reduced by inflation. Mrs. Rosbrugh's repeated appeals for assistance were without avail until 1789, when she received £156 due to her husband in back pay.

SOURCES: Family, education, church career, sermons, will, letters to wife, military career, Mrs. Rosbrugh's difficulties: J. C. Clyde, *Rosbrugh, A Tale of the Revolution* (1880), 3-61; church career: F. G. Bulgin, "Clerical Martyr of the Revolution," *Scotch Irish of Northampton County, Pa.* (1926), I, 208-212; expectations of death: Sprague, *Annals*, III, 255-56; account of death: *Philadelphia Evening Post*, Apr. 29, 1777; Rush letter: Butterfield, *Rush Letters*, 128; 1917 memorial service: First Presbyterian Church of Trenton, Pamphlet, John Rosbrugh File, PUA.

LLM

Samuel Sloan

SAMUEL SLOAN, A.B., Anglican clergyman, schoolmaster and planter, was born in Somerset County, New Jersey, about 1740, the son of Mary Shields and her husband, William Sloan. Samuel's parents emigrated from Ireland to New Jersey about the time of Samuel's birth and purchased a farm near Lamington. The father had become a commissioner of highways by the time of his death in 1758.

After graduation Sloan studied theology. He traveled to England and on December 22, 1765, was ordained an Anglican priest in the Chapel Royal, St. James's Palace, London. Shortly thereafter Sloan returned to America. On June 27, 1766, he was appointed curate of St. Paul's parish, Kent County, Maryland, where he remained until December 5, 1767, when he became rector of Worcester parish in Worcester County. About two years later, on November 20, 1769,

Sloan was inducted as rector of Coventry parish, which included parts of Somerset and Worcester counties. The church itself was located in Rehoboth. It was probably in these years that Sloan married. His wife's first name was Elizabeth; the couple had at least one daughter.

In 1770 Sloan became a trustee of the Eden school, formed by a consolidation of the free schools of Somerset and Worcester counties. In 1776 financial support for the Maryland Anglican clergy was cut off. Sloan then opened an academy on his plantation, though he continued to minister informally to Coventry parish until 1783 or 1785.

Sloan's role in the Revolution is difficult to determine. A recent history of the Maryland Episcopal church suggests that he was a "Patriot." However, oral tradition implies otherwise. In 1919 Mr. Gordon Atkinson, who had grown up on what had been Sloan's plantation, recounted the following anecdote: "When my father came into possession of the farm on the [Pocomoke] River there was two very old negro women that were left as charges of [the] Sloan family. They called themselves Lucy & Amis Sloan and seemed very proud to have been the servants of the Sloan family. Lucy was a woman of some natural intelligence and as a boy becoming interested in the history of our Country, she told me things as a girl she remembered of the Revolutionary war—stories of British officers in Red coats being feasted by the Parson—coming up the Pocomoke river in barges filled with soldiers who were fed on corn bred [sic], pork and vegetables, while the officers were served with fowl, ham and the best that was in the farm —also liberally supplied with brandy & rum. She said her old Masse Sloan had barrels of Brandy and Rum brought to him from the West Indies in his vessels. . . . She also told me that the Parson was not averse to indulging the practice of the time smuggling. She also told that many people came to the plantation to buy sugar, Rum & Brandy. Also that he always gave his negro men rum when they pleased him." Since this letter was written shortly before the passage of the Volstead Act, certain emphases may be suspect—but it does have a ring of authenticity.

After the war Sloan took no part in Maryland church affairs, but continued to run his academy until not long before his death on November 16, 1807. He left a considerable amount of property and his slaves to his wife and daughter.

SOURCES: Parentage: *Som. Cty. Hist. Quart.*, 7 (1918), 276-77; clerical career: *MHM*, 26 (1931), 354, 356, 360; J. T. Scharf, *Hist. of Myd.* (1879), 512, 513n.; N. W. Rightmyer, *Maryland's Established Church* (1956), 119; see also extensive correspondence in Samuel Sloan File, PUA, which contains letter of Gordon Atkinson to John S. McMaster, March 8, 1919, from which quotation is drawn.

James Hamden Thomson

JAMES HAMDEN THOMSON, A.B., A.M. 1764, college tutor, schoolmaster, and sometime Presbyterian preacher, was born in either Abington or nearby South Bridgewater, Massachusetts. He was the son of Archibald Thomson and his wife, who emigrated from Ulster to Massachusetts about 1724. The father was a weaver; a local historian has credited him with constructing the first spinning foot-wheel made in New England.

Thomson remained in Princeton after graduation. He must have impressed President Finley favorably, for on September 29, 1762, the trustees unanimously elected him a tutor in the College, a post that he retained until September 28, 1770. One student, Ralph Wheelock (Class of 1765), found Thomson less than congenial as a tutor. He complained to his father, Eleazar Wheelock, founder of Dartmouth College, that Thomson's "Temper is too rough & austere." "I grant it seems to be naturally on that order," President Finley explained to the elder Wheelock, "but as he is, I trust, closely & honestly exercised unto godliness of late, so I think he has got a proportionable victory over his Temper. He is of a strong masculine genius & a good scholar."

While serving as tutor Thomson also preached from time to time in neighboring pulpits. The Presbyterian church at Trenton was so taken with him that in 1767 it tried to secure him as its permanent pastor, but, as the church recorded, "Mr. Thompson's connections with the College of New Jersey as a tutor so embarrass him that it appears inexpedient to lay him under any positive appointment, but only recommend to him to supply as much as he can at these places, at discretion." By 1770, earning £75 per year, Thomson was the senior tutor in the College. In September of that year he and the junior tutor, Joseph Periam (A.B. 1762), resigned their posts. The trustees presented them with handsome testimonials.

At some time thereafter Thomson decided to seek his fortune in the south. By 1773 he was established in Charleston, South Carolina. In August of that year a Philadelphia newspaper named Thomson and William Tennent, Jr. (A.B. 1758), pastor of Charleston's Independent Church, as Charleston agents for a newly founded "American Society for Promoting Religious Knowledge among the Poor in the British Colonies." By the following February at the latest, Thomson was established as the proprietor of a private school in St. Philip's and St. Michael's Parish, Charleston, an occupation he followed with only a few interruptions for the remainder of his life. Thomson was active in the affairs of the Independent Church; in 1775 he served with Dr. David

Ramsay (A.B. 1765) and Richard Hutson (A.B. 1765) on a committee charged with revising the church's constitution. On January 21 of that year Thomson married Elizabeth Martha Trezevant, sister of John Timothy Trezevant (A.B. 1775). The couple had three daughters.

During the early years of the Revolution Thomson kept his school open. But in 1780 Charleston was placed under siege by British forces commanded by Lord Cornwallis. On April 8 David Ramsay reported that "Mr. Thompson has long since given up. Education is at a stand. The path of glory does not lead through the sequestered vale of literature; but, through the noisy din of war." Thomson's path of glory led, in fact, to imprisonment in St. Augustine, Florida.

After Charleston capitulated to the British on May 12, 1780, the conquerors began to round up civilian Whig leaders on the excuse that they had violated their paroles. Thomson was arrested on August 30. Along with many other Charleston notables, including David Ramsay and Richard Hutson, Thomson was placed aboard the transport *Fidelity* in Charleston harbor. From there he was shipped to St. Augustine for internment. Thomson must have gone into exile well-equipped, for on October 31 he was robbed of a striped silk gown, two handkerchiefs, two pen knives, a memo book, and a pair of shoes and buckles. In captivity Thomson acted as chaplain to his fellow prisoners until November 12. In July 1781 Thomson was released. He and his family found refuge in Philadelphia.

Early in August 1782 Thomson and his family left Philadelphia by schooner bound for Edenton, North Carolina, on the first leg of the trip home. Charleston was not evacuated by the British until December 14, 1782. Where Thomson spent the intervening months has not been discovered. Once back in the city Thomson reopened his school, which over the years became known as "one of the best classical seminaries in the United States." Thomson's wife died at some time before 1790, for in that year the federal census taker found him living in Charleston in a household composed of himself, one other free person, and four slaves. On September 22, 1793, he married Elizabeth Young of Goose Creek, South Carolina. He died in Charleston on March 3, 1795.

SOURCES: The name was sometimes spelled Thompson; parentage: E. C. Mitchell, *Hist. of Bridgewater, Mass.* (reprint ed., 1897), 329-30; Finley to Wheelock, Sept. 9, 1763, Wheelock MSS; tutorship and testimonial: MS CNJ Trustees' Minutes, I, 97, 176; Trenton church: J. Hall, *Hist. of the Presbyterian Church in Trenton, N.J.* (2nd ed., 1912), 124; 1773 presence in Charleston: *Pa. Packet*, Aug. 9, 1773; 1774 school: *SCHGM*, 39 (1938), 89; Charleston church: G. N. Edwards, *A Hist. of the Independent or Congregational Church of Charleston, S.C.* (1947), 42, 44; marriage: A. S. Salley, ed., *Marriage Notices in the South-Carolina and American General Gaz.* (1914), 22; David Ramsay to Benjamin Rush, April 8, 1780, in: R. L. Brunhouse, ed., *David Ramsay, 1749-1815*, APS Trans., n.s., 55 (1965), 66; early years of

Revolution: C. Meriwether, *Hist. of Higher Education in S.C.* (1889), 226; arrest: E. McGrady, *Hist. of S.C. in the Revolution,* 1775-1780 (1901; reprinted 1969), 723-74; St. Augustine and return: *SCHGM,* 33 (1932), 7, 16, 23, 81, 83; ibid., 34 (1933), 31, 82, 206; and also: James Hamden Thomson File, PUA.

Lawrence Van Derveer

LAWRENCE VAN DERVEER, A.B., physician, was born near Raritan, Somerset County, New Jersey, on April 28, 1741, the son of Femmetje Strycker and her husband Jacob Van Derveer, a very prosperous farmer who served as justice of several Somerset county courts in the years from 1749 to 1774.

After graduation Van Derveer studied medicine and then began practice in Hillsborough Township, Somerset County. He lived at a place called "Roycefield," somewhere in the vicinity of Harlingen and Neshanic. Johannes Martinus Van Harlingen (Class of 1760) was joint pastor of the Dutch Reformed churches at both places, and over the years Van Derveer was a communicant in each. Like Van Harlingen, Van Derveer became a trustee of Queen's College in New Brunswick,

Lawrence Van Derveer, A.B. 1761

serving in the post from 1782 to 1815. Van Derveer married Maria
Schenck about 1769. The couple had three children. After the death
of his first wife in 1777, Van Derveer married Maria Onderdonk. Six
children were born of this marriage.

In 1766 Van Derveer was among the founding members of the New
Jersey Medical Society, the first organization of its kind in the colonies.
Like many other members his presence at meetings was infrequent,
and he was often threatened with dismissal for non-attendance. His
most active participation in the society came in the 1780s, when he delivered dissertations on "the nature, uses and modes of preparation of
the Chyle" and on nutrition. Van Derveer also invented a remedy for
the prevention and cure of hydrophobia. He was reputed to have
treated successfully over 400 cases with his cure. The remedy involved
the use of *Scutellaria laterifloria* (scullcap, a form of mint), and came
under attack early in the nineteenth century.

During the Revolution, on January 28, 1777, Van Derveer was captured by a party of Hessian soldiers disguised as Americans. He was
imprisoned in British-occupied New Brunswick and then in the Sugar
House prison in New York City. American General Philemon Dickinson tried to exchange Van Derveer for a British prisoner, but was refused by Lord Cornwallis. Van Derveer was finally released, for by
August of the following year he was advertising in no uncertain terms
for the owner of a "remarkably dull and lazy" large sorrel mare that
had strayed onto his lands to "come, prove his property, pay charges,
and take her away."

When Van Derveer's father died in 1777 he left a large estate to be
divided among his many children. Lawrence inherited the plantation
of 430 acres that he lived upon in Hillsborough Township and also 300
acres in Virginia. He seems to have moved to his Virginia property for
a brief time, for in 1790 he was among the trustees of a lottery designed to raise funds to build a Presbyterian church in Shepardstown,
Berkeley County, Virginia.

Van Derveer was noted for benevolence locally. His New Jersey
medical practice was large and lucrative. When he died in Hillsborough on December 8, 1815, the inventory of his personal property
came to $25,180.31 1/2. In his will he left to one son a farm of 160
acres, his medical shop and books; to another son a farm of 160 acres;
to a third son, who was insane, $4,000 if he should recover; to a daugh-
ter a cupboard and $5,500; and to his grandchildren another $5,500.
He also freed one of his slaves.

SOURCES: Brief sketch: Wickes, *Hist. of Medicine* (1879), 427-29; family: *NYGBR*,
(1937), 202-205; father and father's will: *Som. Cty. Hist. Quart.*, 8 (1919), 121;
34 *NJA*, 539; *Catalogue . . . of Rutgers College* (1909), 7; *Proc. N.J. Med. Soc.*,

7, 45, 46; capture: *Va. Gaz.* (Dixon & Hunter), March 7, 1777; mare: *N.J. Gaz.*, Aug. 19, 1778; Va. residence: Hening, *Statutes*, VIII, 174; will: MS, N.J. State Lib., Trenton.

Jahleel Woodbridge

JAHLEEL WOODBRIDGE, A.B., farmer and public official, was born in Springfield, Massachusetts, in 1738, the son of Elizabeth Merrick Barnard and Joseph Woodbridge. The father, a farmer, was a member of a distinguished family that before Jahleel's birth had fallen into comparatively straitened circumstances. Woodbridge's parents moved to Stockbridge, Massachusetts, when he was about one year old. They had sufficient capital to be among those who bought much of Berkshire County from the Indians. It was a rude frontier life, and Woodbridge, like Jonathan Edwards, Jr. (A.B. 1765), and Pierpont Edwards (A.B. 1768), grew up in what was largely an Indian village, speaking their language as well as English. It was also a profitable and healthy life. "This salubrious air makes barren women bring forth men," a neighbor of the Woodbridges wrote to a friend in the east. "Look at Colonel Ephraim Williams in Stockbridge and Joseph Woodbridge. They started poor and now they are exceedingly well off."

By the spring of 1756, in fact, the Woodbridges were prosperous enough to send young Jahleel down to the College of New Jersey's grammar school. Woodbridge bought copies of Terence and Sallust and seems to have matriculated in the College in the fall of 1756. Although his course was interrupted by the deaths of Presidents Burr and Edwards, he must have studied diligently for at his commencement he "agreeably entertained the Audience" with an English oration on the "Blessings of Peace."

The Seven Years War was drawing to a close, and Woodbridge returned home to a frontier that, for the first time in years, was relatively peaceful. Woodbridge originally hoped to be a lawyer, but once back in Stockbridge he found himself saddled by his fellow townspeople with one responsibility after another. In 1764 he became a lieutenant in the Berkshire County militia and in the same year he married Lucy Edwards, a daughter of his old pastor at Stockbridge's Congregational church, Jonathan Edwards. Although Lucy was two years older than Jahleel, and at twenty-eight almost a spinster, the couple went on to have nine children before her death in 1786. At some later time Woodbridge married Mrs. Hannah Robbins Keep.

In Stockbridge Woodbridge farmed, served as a selectman, and was appointed a justice of the peace. Along with his brother-in-law, Timothy Edwards, Woodbridge was a delegate to the first Berkshire

County convention called to consider British measures in July 1774. The following year he and Edwards were elected delegates to the third Massachusetts Provincial Congress. Both men were charged with handling the funds due to the Stockbridge Indians who had joined the American army, since, as the Congress ordered, the Indians, "in their more serious hours, being sensible of their want or prudence in disposing of their money, are desirous that this Congress, in their wisdom, would devise some method to prevent their getting too much strong drink."

Much of Woodbridge's life seems to have been spent in a sort of junior partnership with Timothy Edwards. Between them they managed most of the affairs of Stockbridge—town, church, and Indians When Edwards was made Massachusetts boundary commissioner he employed Woodbridge. Woodbridge served as a judge of the court of common pleas in Berkshire County from 1781 to 1795. When Edwards retired as judge of the county's probate court in 1787, Woodbridge succeeded to the post, serving until 1795. Woodbridge, however, served in the Massachusetts Senate without Edwards from 1780 to 1784.

As a judge and local nabob Woodbridge was a prime target for the insurgents during Shays' Rebellion in 1787. During the rebellion a mob asked four judges to sign a paper that they would not sit "until the Constitution of Government Shall be revised or a new one made." Woodbridge was the only judge to refuse to sign, declaring that "he would resign his commission first." In the early hours of the morning of February 27, 1787, little Timothy Woodbridge, sleeping with his recently widowed father, awoke to find the room filled with soldiers waving green hemlock boughs, the symbol of rebellion, over the bed. The Shaysites plundered the farmhouse of the "aristocratic" Judge Woodbridge and carried him off to Great Barrington as a prisoner. Although a rescue party was made up, the judge managed to persuade his captors to release him and met his would-be saviours on the way home. Woodbridge continued to serve as judge and as community patriarch until a year before his death on August 13, 1796.

SOURCES: The most complete account is Elizur Y. Smith, "The Descendants of William Edwards," *NYGBR*, 72 (1941), 326-31; scattered references throughout: E. P. Jones, *Stockbridge, Past and Present* (1854), and S. C. Sedgwick and C. S. Marquand, *Stockbridge, 1739-1939* (1939); family background: M. K. Talcott, *NEHGR*, 32 (1878), 295, and *Sibley's Harvard Graduates*, IV, 217-18; CNJ accounts: Aaron Burr, MS Account Book, 200-201; commencement oration: *Pa. Journal*, October 8, 1761; Indian quotation: William Lincoln, ed., *Journal of each Provincial Congress of Massachusetts in 1774 and 1775* (1838), 453; Shays' Rebellion: R. J. Taylor, *Western Massachusetts in the Rev.* (1954), 144.

CLASS OF 1762

Hugh Alison, A.B.

Isaac Allen, A.B.

Absalom Bainbridge, A.B.

Ebenezer Davenport, A.B.

Edmund Davis, A.B.

Edward Gantt, A.B.

John Harris, A.B.

Ebenezer Hazard, A.B.

John Hulbert, A.B.

Nehemiah Ludlum, A.B.

John McCrea, A.B.

James Manning, A.B.

Nathaniel Manning, A.B.

Thomas Martin, A.B.

John Dyer Mercier, A.B.

—— Morrow

Francis Peppard, A.B.

Joseph Periam, A.B.

Thomas Ruston, A.B.

Jonathan Dickinson Sergeant, A.B.

Dickinson Shepherd

Hezekiah Smith, A.B.

Caleb White, A.B.

Jacob Woolley

Hugh Alison

HUGH ALISON, A.B., Presbyterian clergyman and schoolmaster, was born in Pennsylvania in 1740 or 1742, the son of Rachel and Hector Alison. The father was a Presbyterian minister who after seeing service in the Seven Years War moved to South Carolina in the mid-1760s where he continued his ministry and also established himself as a planter, accumulating 2,450 acres of land.

After graduation Alison joined his family in South Carolina and was soon installed as pastor of the Presbyterian church at Williamsburg. He served there until 1766. In 1768 Alison became pastor of a Presbyterian congregation on James Island just south of Charleston harbor, a post he held almost to the time of his death. He also served briefly as pastor of a church at Salem, Sumter District, from 1769 to 1770. On January 11 of the latter year Alison married Dorothea Smiser. The couple had two children, Jacob Hyleman and Regina.

Alison's home on James Island was only forty-five minutes from Charleston by boat. In addition to his pastoral duties on the island, Alison found time in 1770 to teach school in St. Andrew's Parish, an activity he probably moved to the island after that date. Alison became well-known in the area. Writing to Benjamin Rush (A.B. 1760) in 1774, Charleston's Dr. David Ramsay (A.B. 1765) called Alison "a worthy son of our college, and a sensible man." Alison early opposed British measures against the American colonies. In October 1769 he preached an interesting sermon, later published, in support of South Carolina's nonimportation resolutions. Called *Spiritual Liberty*, the sermon was as much concerned with the secular as with the sacred. "Liberty," Alison declared, "is an inestimable treasure; the delight and passion of mankind. It is the source of almost all human felicity; the parent of virtue, pleasure, plenty and security." Slavery was the opposite of liberty: it meant living at another man's mercy, often in the fear of death. In many "heroick souls," however, the love of liberty was greater than the love of life, Alison told his parishioners, who presumably knew intimately the nature of slavery. "People must be deceived or frightened before they will become slaves," Alison went on. The British ministry was trying to do just that to the colonists. But Americans would thwart English plans by means of the nonimportation resolutions. "May divine providence smile upon their attempts, and grant the desired success. . . . The nature and design of these resolutions you cannot be ignorant of. They are necessary, practicable, and judiciously calculated to promote the end in view."

Alison remained on James Island over the next few years. When William Tennent (A.B. 1758), pastor of Charleston's Independent Church, died in 1777 Alison was called upon to preach a memorial sermon. Tennent, said Alison in words that may have reflected his own conception of his role as minister and citizen, "never entertained his audience with scholastic niceties or subtle questions . . . but . . . with the plain uncontroverted truths of the everlasting gospel." Alison went on to praise Tennent's "honest, disinterested, yet flaming zeal for his country's good." Alison would soon prove his own zeal. With his family he fled James Island just before the British occupied it about January 31, 1780. He took refuge in Charleston, where he died of tuberculosis at some time during the following year.

SOURCES: Genealogy and data on father: Hugh Alison File, PUA; brief mentions: Alexander, *Princeton*, 76; G. Howe, *Hist. of Presbyterian Church in S.C.*, I, 321; marriage: *SCHGM*, XI, 92; Ramsay to Rush, July 29, 1774, in: R. L. Brunhouse, ed., *David Ramsay, 1749-1815*, APS Trans., n.s., 55 (1965), 52; Alison, *Spiritual Liberty* (1769); Tennent sermon: Alison, *The Faithful Servant of Christ Honoured and Rewarded* (1777); occupation of James Island: R. Lamb, *An Original and Authentic Journal of Occurrences During the Late Am. War* (1809), 293.

PUBLICATIONS: STE

Isaac Allen

ISSAC ALLEN, A.B., A.M. 1765, lawyer, soldier and public official, was born about 1741 in Trenton, New Jersey, the second son of Naomi Watson and John Allen. The father, a prosperous saddler like his father before him, was commissioned high sheriff of Hunterdon County in 1752, serving until about 1762. An Anglican, he was a vestryman of St. Michael's Church in Trenton from 1754 to 1763.

As the best orator in his class Isaac gave the English valedictory oration at his commencement, closing the ceremonies, a Philadelphia newspaper reported, "with graceful ease and propriety." He then returned to Trenton, studied law, and was admitted to practice. It was probably a successful practice, for his name appears as witness to many wills and as agent for many land sales in the 1760s. On December 20, 1769, Allen married in Philadelphia's Christ Church Sarah Campbell, daughter of Thomas Campbell, a well-to-do merchant. The couple had five daughters and one son. Their life in Trenton seems to have been a prosperous, peaceful and successful one, marred only by the destruction of their home by fire in 1772. Allen managed a New Jersey lottery and subscribed to an edition of his province's laws. Like his father, he was active in the affairs of St. Michael's Church, serving as warden from 1770 to 1776 and as vestryman from 1771 to 1775.

When the British occupied Trenton in December 1776 Allen and his family declared their allegiance to the crown. On December 3 Allen joined the British army at New Brunswick and was shortly commissioned an officer in the Sixth Battalion New Jersey Volunteers (Loyalists). Allen's military service over the next few years would be extensive. Appointed commander of the Third Battalion New Jersey Loyalists in 1779, he later served as lieutenant-colonel in the Second Battalion. Allen was engaged in several minor clashes with Whig forces in New Jersey in 1777, but his main service came in the southern theater.

Late in 1778 Allen and his troops sailed to Georgia. There he served under Colonel Archibald Campbell in the successful British siege of Savannah. With the capitulation of the city, much of Georgia came under British control almost until the end of the war. Allen served in other southern campaigns, among them the successful siege of Charleston in 1780. After the fall of the city, Allen was made acting commander of a new British outpost at Ninety-Six, designed to secure the Carolina backcountry. Building a fort was sometimes dispiriting work for the erstwhile lawyer. "The King's work like Church work goes on Slow," Allen wrote on December 29, 1780. "The poor naked Blacks can do but little in the cold weather." Allen and his New Jersey Loyalists were involved in several skirmishes with rebels in the area.

Allen soon returned to Charleston. In February 1782, discussing a meeting called to raise the question of exchanging prisoners, one Whig Carolinian wrote to another that "Colo Allen was the Person who met our Commissary & he very candidly told him the British in his Opinion had nothing farther to do in America, but that they had had no Accounts from England for a considerable time past. I think from every Thing which we hear they dislike their Situation exceedingly, & wish to be gone." The wish was soon granted. The British and Loyalists evacuated Charleston in December, Allen acting as commandant during the process.

Allen's loyalty cost him dearly. He had owned considerable property in Pennsylvania before the war. It was confiscated by the revolutionary state government. In New Jersey, Hunterdon and Monmouth counties did the same with his properties there. His Hunterdon county estate brought £5,076 in probably inflated currency when it was sold by the government in 1779. In 1787 Allen claimed £2,400 in losses before the Loyalist Claims Commission, which granted him £925. But by then he had put New Jersey far behind him.

Along with other Loyalist army officers, on March 14, 1783, Allen signed an address to the crown requesting lands in the remaining British provinces in North America as well as other benefits. The Lands were eventually granted, and much of the province of New Brunswick, Canada, was settled by American refugees—officers, men, and their families. Even before New York was evacuated in 1783 Sir Guy Carleton, British commander-in-chief there, sent Allen off to survey lands in Nova Scotia. On July 14, 1784 Allen and the 2nd New Jersey Volunteers were granted a block of 38,450 acres in the newly created province of New Brunswick. Allen was also appointed to the governing council and made second puisne judge of the province's supreme court. He soon exchanged his original grant and obtained 2,000 acres of land seven miles from the new capital, Frederickton, along with a nearby island of 220 acres. The area contained an Indian settlement called "Auk-pacque." There Allen built a house and raised his family. He was a member of the innermost circle of American refugees who succeeded in creating in this backwater of empire an extraordinarily suspicious and reactionary society, safe from what Governor Carleton called "the American spirit of innovation." Allen continued in his official duties until his death on October 12, 1806. His only son John, born in 1784, became a local judge. His grandson, Sir John Campbell Allen, became chief justice of the province.

SOURCES: Sketches: A. A. Stockton, ed., *Judges of New Brunswick and Their Times* (1907), 59-60; *NJHSP*, n.s., 11 (1926), 80-81; Sabine, *Loyalists*, I, 159; family and geneal.: *GMNJ*, 18 (1943), 27; commencement: *Pa. Gaz.*, Sept. 30, 1762; marriage: *Pa. Arch.* (2 ser.), 8 (1878), 5; lottery: *Pa. Gaz.*, Dec. 8, 1773; law books: *Pa. Gaz.*, Aug. 17, 1774; church involvement: H. Schuyler, *A Hist. of St. Michael's Church, Trenton* (1926), 47; fire: *N.Y. Jour.*, Feb. 20, 1772; allegiance to crown and mil. record: W. S. Stryker, *"The N.J. Volunteers" (Loyalists)* (1887), 28; Ninety-Six and quotations: *SCHM*, 72 (1971), 1-14; prisoner exchange quotation: *SCHGM*, 27 (1926), 7; confiscation of property, etc.: *N.J. Gaz.*: Aug. 19 and 26, Nov. 18, 1778, and Mar. 23, 1780; Loyalist claims: *Second Report of the Bureau of Archives for the Province of Ontario* (1904), 248; survey and settlement in Nova Scotia/New Brunswick: E. C. Wright, *Loyalists of New Brunswick* (1955), and *Canada and Its Provinces* (1914), XIII, 154-79; Carleton quotation: ibid., 162.

Absalom Bainbridge

ABSALOM BAINBRIDGE, A.B., A.M. 1765, physician, was born in Maidenhead (now Lawrenceville), New Jersey on February 3, 1743, the eleventh and youngest child of Abigail White and Edmund Bainbridge, a prosperous farmer. On November 28, 1756, President Burr noted in his Account Book that one "Bembridge" had entered the College's Latin

Absalom Bainbridge, A.B. 1762
ATTRIBUTED TO JAMES SHARPLES

grammar school. It may well have been a misspelling of young Absalom's name.

After graduation Bainbridge studied medicine, probably by apprenticing himself to an established physician. He appears to have begun
his practice working out of his parents' 400-acre farm in Maidenhead.
On January 20, 1768, Bainbridge married Mary Taylor, the only
daughter of John Taylor, a well-to-do citizen of Perth Amboy who
served as high sheriff of Monmouth County. Fourteen children, seven
of whom died in infancy, were born to the couple.

Bainbridge's father died in 1770. Absalom was left the Maidenhead
farm, slaves, and responsibility for his mother's welfare. *She died the same year.* His medical
practice, apparently, flourished. He was elected to the New Jersey
Medical Society on November 10, 1767, became its secretary in 1771
and served as president in 1773. *On April 1, 1773* ~~In about 1772~~ Bainbridge moved into
Princeton and rented a house on what is now Nassau Street from Rob-
ert Stockton. Called "Bainbridge House" today, the building is the
home of the Princeton Historical Society. It is named after one of the
doctor's sons, Commodore William Bainbridge of the U.S. Navy.

As events leading to the Revolution unfolded, friends apparently expected that Bainbridge would take the Whig side. On July 16, 1776, an advertisement was run in the *Pennsylvania Journal* requesting the populace to donate old sheets and linens to, among others, Dr. William Shippen (A.B. 1753), Dr. David Cowell (A.B. 1763), and to Bainbridge so that "bandages made of this linen may be used in dressing and curing the wounds of their own fathers, husbands, brethren or sons."

If Bainbridge received any linens they were probably used for curing British rather than American troops, for he became a Loyalist. His decision may have been due to simple circumstance or, perhaps, to the influence of his wife's strongly Loyalist family. Bainbridge's actions late in 1776 were described succinctly years later by West Hyde, a British army officer present in Princeton just before the battle of that name:

> I do hereby certify that being ordered, with the command of a Detachment of the Guards, to Prince Town in New Jersey in the month of Decr 1776, I made previous enquiry concerning the Disposition of the Principal Inhabitants & was informed that Dr Bainbridge was a Person well-affected to Government—I accordingly applied to Him on my arrival, and during the Short Time I continued in that Command (a few days only) I received every possible assistance from Him & such Intelligence as was of material Consequence to His Majesty's Service in the Situation the Affairs of that country were, at that time.
>
> I cannot express more fully the opinion I had of the advantages derived from His Information, than by mentioning that when the Detachment under my Command was recalled, I thought it my Duty to acquaint the Officer who was to succeed me in the command at that place, with the Service I had received from Dr. Bainbridge.

Bainbridge enlisted in the British Forces the first week of December 1776. When the British evacuated Princeton early in January 1777 Bainbridge went with them. In 1778 he was appointed surgeon to the Third New Jersey Volunteers (Loyalists), but apparently saw little active service. He lived instead with his family in Flatbush, Long Island. During the war his New Jersey property was confiscated and sold by the revolutionary state government. When peace came in 1783 Bainbridge did not, like so many other Loyalists, emigrate from the United States. Instead, in 1785 he traveled to England to present his claims for losses before the Loyalist Claims Commission. Bainbridge, supported by several witnesses, estimated that his confiscated property had been worth £5,965.6.3. He also estimated that he had lost £2,500 in income over

the nine-and-a-half years since control of the property had passed out
of his hands. The commission compensated Bainbridge with £2,250 for
the loss of his property and with £140 a year for the loss of his income
during the war.

His suit successfully pursued, Bainbridge returned to the United
States, where he lived in Flatbush and followed his profession. By 1790
he had moved to New York City, where the federal census taker recorded him as the head of a large household of eleven people, which
included three slaves. He died in New York on June 24, 1807, and was
buried in Trinity churchyard. Several of Bainbridge's grandsons attended Nassau Hall, among them John Maclean (A.B. 1816), president
of the College from 1854 to 1868.

SOURCES: The author is indebted to Dr. George E. McCracken (A.B. Princeton 1926),
for furnishing him with many copies of manuscripts relating to Bainbridge (father's
will, Loyalist depositions, etc.) now in the Public Record Office, London. Permission to use these documents is gratefully acknowledged. Brief sketch and Loyalist
in-laws: E. A. Jones, Loyalists of N.J. (1927), 15-16, 213-17; grammar school: Aaron
Burr, MS Account Book, 226-27; Wickes, Proc. N.J. Med. Soc., 20, 22, 31, 34, 39; surgeon: W. S. Stryker, "The N.J. Volunteers" (Loyalists) in the Rev. War (1887), 39;
quotation: copy of MS deposition by Maj. Gen. West Hyde, dated Sept. 29, 1785,
P.R.O., London; U.S. Census of 1790, N.Y., 118.

Ebenezer Davenport

EBENEZER DAVENPORT, A.B., Congregational clergyman, was born in
Stamford, Fairfield County, Connecticut, on March 15, 1732, one of the
fourteen children of Sarah Bishop and John Davenport. The father
was a grandson of one of the founders of the New Haven colony and
the older brother of James Davenport (Yale 1732), one of the most
prominent preachers of the Great Awakening and a warm friend of the
College.

The circumstances that brought Davenport to the College at a comparatively advanced age have not been discovered. Once there, however, he did poorly. "I understand that the Degredation of two of our
Candidates for Batchelors Degree[s] last Summer particularly that of
Davenport has made a great Noise in your Parts," College tutor Jeremiah Halsey (A.B. 1752) wrote to Davenport's uncle Eleazar Wheelock, the founder of Dartmouth College, on February 12, 1762. Halsey
explained that the award of a degree to Davenport, "notoriously deficient" in some of his studies, would have seriously weakened "the
Credit of the Institution." "Every Body compassionated Davenports
Case," Halsey went on. "He is now returned to College and I hope, if

his Health be spared, will appear worthy [of] the Honours of College at next public Examination." Davenport's health was spared for a time; he received his degree within the next few months.

Almost immediately after graduation, in 1763, Davenport became pastor of the First Congregational Church in Greenwich, Connecticut, not far from his birthplace in Stamford. Accounts differ as to whether his ministry extended to 1769 or to 1773. In any case, Davenport, who apparently never married, died on January 18, 1773. He was buried in Greenwich's Old Sound Beach Cemetery.

SOURCES: Parentage: A. B. Davenport, *A History of the Davenport Family* (1851), 238-39; Halsey to Wheelock, Feb. 12, 1762, Wheelock MSS; ministry: L. Bacon, ed., *Contributions to the Ecclesiastical Hist. of Conn.* (1861), 395; S. P. Mead, *Ye Historie of Ye Town of Greenwich* (1911), 404; date of death: C. R. Hale, comp., [Conn.] *Cemetery Inscriptions*, vol. 60, p. 311, typescript, Conn. State Lib., Hartford.

Edmund Davis

EDMUND DAVIS, A.B., was a schoolmaster. His name was also spelled "Davies." His parentage has not been discovered; he was not a close relation of President Samuel Davies. Immediately after Davis's graduation President Samuel Finley appointed him master of the grammar school connected with Nassau Hall. Finley, apparently, was not sufficiently satisfied with Davis to keep him on in the post after a year. However, he thought highly enough of Davis to recommend him to Eleazar Wheelock (Yale 1733) as an instructor in Wheelock's school for Indians at Lebanon, Connecticut. "Sir Davies, ye Master of my Grammar School, thinks to leave me in ye Fall," Finley informed Wheelock in August 1763. "He is a good scholar, a faithful Instructor, & I trust a pious young man; nor has he Fault unless you reckon a natural somewhat austere mode not very ingratiating w[i]th youth to be one. But he is truly excellent in my view, & his good sense corrects those natural Foibles."

Wheelock appears to have agreed to hire Davis. But Davis seems never to have reached Connecticut, for on April 2, 1765, tutor Jeremiah Halsey (A.B. 1752) wrote to Wheelock as follows: "You have heard before this I suppose of the Death of Sir Davies. He died some Time in the winter past, much regretted by all that knew Him. . . . I think the church of God has suffered a very considerable loss." Davis's death was indicated in the College's catalogue of 1770.

SOURCES: Finley to Wheelock, Aug. 19, 1763; Sept. 30, 1763; and May 26, 1764; Halsey to Wheelock, Apr. 2, 1765; all in Wheelock MSS.

Edward Gantt

EDWARD GANTT, A.B., M.D. Leyden 1767, physician and planter, was born about 1741 in Prince George's County, Maryland, the second son of Rachel Smith and her husband Thomas Gantt, a planter and member of an influential family with extensive landholdings in both Calvert and Prince Georges counties. There were many physicians in Gantt's family, and after graduation from the College he traveled to Britain to study medicine. In London by September 29, 1764, Gantt made plans for the future: "I shall set out for Edinburgh tomorrow or the next Day," he wrote to a friend at home, "there to spend three of four Years, after which I shall return to Maryland to finish my Days. . . . Maryland I find is the place that best pleases me. You need not engage any of the Girls to wait for me, as I am pretty well convinced I shall die an old Batchelor. Money I will never marry for, and one without Money I think won'e suit my Circumstances, therefore I find it bids fair for the single life."

Enrolled at the University of Edinburgh shortly thereafter, during the academic year 1764-1765 Gantt took Dr. William Cullen's course in chemistry, Dr. Alexander Munro's course in anatomy and surgery, and Dr. John Hope's course in materia medica. In 1765-1766 he remained in Edinburgh in order to pursue further studies in chemistry with Cullen. In the following year Gantt traveled to the Netherlands, where he presented his thesis, *De variolis*, to the University of Leyden, which awarded him an M.D. on April 17, 1767.

Back in Maryland, probably by late 1767, Gantt's early resolutions concerning bachelorhood faltered. In June 1768 he was married in Somerset County to Ann Stroughton Sloss. The couple had one son, William Stouton Gantt, and perhaps other children as well. Gantt's cousin, Anglican Reverend Thomas John Claggett (A.B. 1764), performed the ceremony.

The Gantt family was deeply involved on the Whig side during the Revolution. Edward's older brother Thomas served in various Maryland conventions in 1774-1776, and either Edward, or more likely a relative of the same name, served as a Calvert County representative to Maryland provincial conventions held in 1774, 1775, and 1776. By 1788 Gantt had settled at "Park Hall," a plantation in Prince Georges County that he inherited from his father in 1785. It must have been an extensive establishment, for in 1790 the federal census-taker recorded him as living in a household that consisted of eleven whites and twenty-three slaves. In 1791 Gantt sold "Park Hall," and moved to Berkeley County, Virginia, with his family. He continued the practice of medi-

cine, for in the late 1790s, when Dr. Benjamin Waterhouse sent vac-
cines to Thomas Jefferson for distribution to physicians, Gantt found
that his had arrived in an inactive state and refused to "take." In about
1808 Gantt moved westward once again, this time to Kentucky. It was
there that he died in 1837.

SOURCES: Genealogy, wife's name, moves: courtesy of Md. Legislative Hist. Project,
E. C. Papenfuse and D. W. Jordan, principal investigators; 1764 letter quotation,
marriage date: G. B. Utley, *Life and Times of Thomas John Claggett* (1913), 7-8,
18; family status: D. C. Skaggs, *Roots of Maryland Democracy* (1973), 94; study in
Edinburgh: W. J. Bell, Jr., "Some Am. Students of . . . Dr. William Cullen," *APSP*,
94 (1950), 280; Leyden: E. Peacock, *Index to English Speaking Students . . . at Leyden Univ.* (1883), 39; Md. conventions: *MHM*, 60 (1965), 312; ibid., 44 (1949), 89;
1790 household: *U.S. Census of 1790, Md.*, 94; vaccine: *NEQ*, 9 (1936), 526.

John Harris

JOHN HARRIS, A.B., bore a name that was common in every colony in
North America and has proved impossible to identify. The only certain
facts known about the graduate are that he was listed as living in the
College's catalogue of 1800 and as dead in the next catalogue, published in 1804.

Ebenezer Hazard

EBENEZER HAZARD, A.B., A.M. 1765, public official, historical editor,
and businessman, was born in Philadelphia on January 15, 1745, the
son of Samuel Hazard and his wife Catherine Clarkson. The father, a
well-to-do merchant, served as a trustee of the College from 1748 to
1757. The father entered Ebenezer in the Academy of Philadelphia in
1751, and although he died when his son was fourteen, the family was
affluent enough to see that Ebenezer received further preparation for
College at the academy run by his uncle, Samuel Finley, at West Nottingham, Maryland.

After graduation Hazard went to work for another uncle, Nathaniel
Hazard, a New York City merchant. "This, my dear Ebenezer, is our
forming time," Hazard's old schoolmate Benjamin Rush (A.B. 1760),
then a medical apprentice in Philadelphia, wrote to him in 1765. It was
indeed. In that year Hazard moved into the household of Garrat Noel,
a New York bookseller, and began to learn the trade. Rush assured
him that he would soon be a rich man, "if you persevere in your usual

Ebenezer Hazard, A.B. 1762

spirited manner of living and acting." But to become a rich man Hazard needed capital. By August 1766, he was dunning the College's trustees for £150–£200 due his father's estate for expenses incurred while the father had served as a trustee. He also set in motion a long series of ultimately futile attempts to gain control of lands in Pennsylvania that his father had made ambiguous arrangements with the Connecticut Assembly to colonize during the 1750s. By whatever means, by 1770 Hazard had become a junior partner in the firm of Noel and Hazard. He mastered the crafts of printing and publishing thoroughly and in 1770–1771 made a trip to England on business matters.

Soon after his return to America, Hazard was drawn into the events leading to the Revolution. Communications between the colonies were a crucial element in welding together the revolutionary forces. The confidentiality of the royal mail service was suspect by the Whigs—and with reason. On May 1, 1775, New York's Committee of Correspondence authorized Hazard to take over and reorganize the postal service, particularly the routes between New York and New England. Hazard performed his duties in an exemplary fashion, employing new riders, making sure that New England newspapers reached the hands of Whig New Yorkers, and reporting important events to General Horatio Gates and others. (Describing New York's reception of the Declaration of Independence in a letter to Gates on July 12, 1776, Hazard wrote: "The King of England's . . . statue here has been pulled down to make musket ball of, so that his troops will probably have melted Majesty fired at them.")

Shortly before the British occupied New York City in September 1776, the committee ordered Hazard to move the post office to Dobbs' Ferry. He did so, and was then ordered to remain with the headquarters of the American army. Plagued by inflated costs and the necessity of running after the army, Hazard complained to Congress of the difficulties of his situation. It was improved when Congress appointed him surveyor of the post roads on January 6, 1777. Hazard immediately set off for New England. From there he reorganized the postal service in the area between Portland, Maine, and Philadelphia. Successful in the north, he then proceeded to put the system covering the area between Philadelphia and Savannah in order. Communications were crucial, and not only for military reasons. "The speedy and frequent communication of intelligence is really of great consequence," Thomas Jefferson wrote to John Adams in 1777. "So many falsehoods have been propagated that nothing is believed unless coming from Congress or camp. Our people, merely for want of intelligence which they may rely on, are become lethargic and insensible of the state they are in." Although complaints abounded, Hazard performed more than creditably throughout the war in maintaining communications between the new states. On January 28, 1782, Hazard was appointed postmaster-general of the United States by Congress.

Taking up his new post, Hazard settled in Philadelphia. On September 11, 1783, he married Abigail Arthur of Shrewsbury, New Jersey. The first of the couple's four children was born the following May. "Mrs. H. continues remarkably well for the time, and the young gentleman thrives cleverly," Hazard reported to a friend. "We intend to call him *Samuel*, which was my father's name. If he discovers as good an *ear* as he does a *voice*, I think he will be fit for a professor of vocal music, should he live." Samuel lived, and attended the College from 1797 to 1799, though he did not take his degree. Reflecting the major preoccupation of his father's life, Samuel eventually became a distinguished editor of historical documents.

Despite Hazard's achievements with the postal service, his reputation rests on his accomplishments as a collector and editor of documents relating to the history of early America. During his days as a bookseller in the 1760s, he began to collect rare pamphlets that eventually totaled 150 bound volumes. (One hundred sixteen of these volumes are now in the Library of Congress.) After the death of his uncle, President Samuel Finley, he launched an abortive project to publish Finley's sermons. In 1772 or 1773 he began to copy legal documents relating to trade as they affected the colonies, with an aim to publication. As the work progressed Hazard's knowledge of colonial archives became clearer and deeper. He discovered that valuable records had been destroyed and that others were casually stored. He decided to design a publication that would include far more than laws relating to trade—charters for explorations, various royal grants, and other documents. "I wish to be the means of saving from oblivion many important papers which without something like this collection will infallibly be lost," he wrote to Jonathan Trumbull (Harvard 1727). "[Some papers] are intimately connected with the liberties of the people; others will furnish some future historian with valuable materials. The time will doubtless come when early periods of American history will be eagerly inquired into, and it is the duty of every generation to hand to its successor the necessary means of acquiring such knowledge, in order to prevent their groping in the dark, and perplexing themselves in the labyrinths of error."

Receiving encouragement from Trumbull, Thomas Jefferson, and others, in August 1774 Hazard published the prospectus for his proposed five-volume "American State Papers." It is, in a way, an historical "declaration of independence":

> This Collection will begin with the Grant from *Henry* 7th, to *John Cabot*, and his Sons for making Discoveries; and will include every important public Paper (such as Royal Grants, Charters, Acts of Parliament, &c. &c.) relating to America, of which either the original, or authentic Copies can be procured, down to the present Time. The History of the STAMP-ACT, and other Acts of the British Parliament for raising a Revenue among us by internal Taxation;—Resolves of the American Assemblies;—Votes of Town Meetings;—and such political Pamphlets and other fugitive Pieces as are properly connected with the general Design, and are worthy of Preservation, will also be included.

During the 1770s Hazard planned two other large-scale projects: an "American Chronology" and an American geography. He eventually gave up both ideas, but generously contributed much of the material he had gathered for the latter to his relative Jedidiah Morse (Yale 1783), who published the first American geography in 1784. Hazard's wartime activities made the completion of his historical projects next to impossible. However, he spent every moment he could spare from official duties in copying documents during his far-ranging trips for the post office. He became a close friend of the New Hampshire historian and founder of the Massachusetts Historical Society, Jeremy Belknap (Harvard 1762). Their friendship resulted in a voluminous correspondence, extraordinarily revealing of the lives and hopes of early American men of letters. In 1784 Hazard saw the first volume of Belknap's history of New Hampshire through the press in Philadelphia. In 1778 Hazard petitioned Congress to support his publication proposals: "gratitude to heaven and to our virtuous fathers, justice to ourselves, and a becoming regard to posterity strongly urge us to an improvement of it before time and accident deprive us of the means." Congress approved Hazard's plans, offering every support but money.

Hazard's appointment as postmaster general in 1782 and subsequent marriage ended his travels and transcribing of documents. His term as head of the mails has generally been accounted successful, given the circumstances of the time—fluctuating currency, the general ineffectiveness of the national government during the Confederation period, competition from private carriers, and other causes. However, by the late 1780s congressmen were complaining that their mail sometimes took as much as forty days to reach them and the phrase "to hazard a letter" had passed into common usage. The mails became involved in political controversy and were made the subject of congressional investigation. ("Taking advantage of Congressional prerogative," Hazard wrote to Belknap some years later, "a fool can ask more questions in a day than a wise man can answer in a month. . . . I would almost as soon be a Virginia negro as a public officer under such a master.") When the new constitution took effect in 1789 Hazard was not reappointed to his post. President Washington gave the office to a friend without bothering to notify Hazard of his dismissal.

Hazard picked up a few minor jobs in New York, where he was then living. In 1790 he moved back to Philadelphia and revived his "American State Papers" project. Subscriptions seemed promising. The first volume of *Historical Collections consisting of the State Papers and other Authentic Documents intended as materials for a History of the United States* was published in Philadelphia in 1792, the second volume in 1794. The first volume contained documents concerning the discovery and early years of American colonization; the second was devoted completely to the records of the New England Confederation. Before publishing his volumes, Hazard sent manuscript copies to Secretary of State Thomas Jefferson for advance comment. In what Julian

Boyd has described as a "timeless philosophy for archivists, curators of historical manuscripts, and editors of historical documents," Jefferson replied as follows:

> I return you the two volumes of records, with thanks for the opportunity of looking into them. They are curious monuments of the infancy of our country. I learn with great satisfaction that you are about committing to press the valuable historical and state-papers you have been so long collecting. Time and accident are committing daily havoc on the originals deposited in our public offices. The late war has done the work of centuries in this business. The lost cannot be recovered; but let us save what remains: not by vaults and locks which fence them from the public eye and use, in consigning them to the waste of time, but by such a multiplication of copies, as shall place them beyond the reach of accident.

Jefferson's endorsement notwithstanding, so few copies of either volume were sold that the project was abandoned. But Hazard had set a standard for American historical editing; his volumes remained a mainstay for American historians well into the nineteenth century.

In the meantime, Hazard began the construction of a fine three-story brick mansion house in Philadelphia. In 1792 he became first secretary of the Insurance Company of North America, one of the earliest American ventures of this nature. A superb administrator, Hazard skillfully guided the company, which dealt mainly with marine insurance, through the troubled waters caused by the wars of the French Revolution, holding his position until retirement in 1800. Marquis James, a historian of the company, claimed that "unlike so many of his acquaintances, Hazard . . . brought his large personal fortune through the upsetting times without impairment." During the yellow fever epidemic of 1793, Hazard, though a victim of the disease, was shrewd enough to discontinue the murderous treatments administered by his onetime schoolmate, Benjamin Rush. (Characteristically, Rush claimed credit for Hazard's subsequent recovery.)

Hazard was as active during his retirement as during his prime. The list of his civic involvements over the years is remarkable. A Presbyterian, during the Confederation years he had campaigned actively against slavery within his denomination. He took up the cause of Indian welfare and published on the Indians' behalf. He was a manager of the Schuylkill Canal Company, the Philadelphia Dispensary, the Philadelphia Guardians of the Poor, and the Presbyterian Board of Missions. Elected first corresponding member of the Massachusetts

Historical Society, he was also a member of the American Philosophical Society and the New-York Historical Society and a fellow of the American Academy of Natural Science. Besides his other activities, in his later years he also helped his old friend Charles Thomson, secretary to Congress under the Confederation, in translating the New Testament from the Greek. He died in Philadelphia on June 13, 1817.

SOURCES: Best account: Fred Shelly, "Ebenezer Hazard: America's First Historical Editor," *WMQ*, 12 (1955), 44-73; full biog.: R. E. Blodgett, "Ebenezer Hazard, the Post Office, the Insurance Company of North America, and the Editing of Historical Documents" (Ph.D. diss., Univ. of Colorado, 1971); see too: *DAB*, and T. R. Hazard, *Recollections of Olden Times* (1879), 238-47; early and later rel. with Rush: *Rush Letters*; bill to CNJ trustees: ALS, Aug. 16, 1768, NjP; Pa. lands: Force, *Am. Arch.* (4 ser.), I, 861-67; six ALS, beginning 1772, NjP; *Susquehannah Papers*, I, V, VI, VII; "melted majesty" quotation: Force, *Am. Arch.* (5 ser.), I, 227-28; Jefferson on mails: *Jefferson Papers*, II, 19; Samuel quotation: Hazard to Belknap, June 5, 1784, *MHS Col.* (5 ser.), II, 351; Samuel: *DAB*; postal career: *Mag. Am. Hist.*, 13 (1885); Force, *Am. Arch.* (5 ser.), III, 270, 548, 679, 681; *WMQ*, 20 (1963), 555-73; W. E. Fuller, *The American Mail* (1972), 33-41; State Papers prospectus: *Jefferson Papers*, I, 144-49; estimates as editor: J. S. Bassett, *Middle Group of Am. Historians* (1937); L. J. Cappon, "Am. Hist. Editors before Jared Sparks," *WMQ*, 30 (1973); rel. with Belknap: *NEQ*, 2 (1929), 183-98; congr. invests.: *MHS Col.* (5 ser.), III, 323; Jefferson on archives and Boyd comment: *Jefferson Papers*, XIX, 287-88; M. James, *Biography of A Business* (1942), 11-71.

PUBLICATIONS: See text. Many of Hazard's letters have been printed in *The Belknap Papers*, published as *MHS Col.* (5 ser.), II-III; (6 ser.), IV. His important travel diary has been published as follows: F. Shelly, ed., "Ebenezer Hazard in Pa., 1777," *PMHB*, 81 (1957); Shelly, ed., "Ebenezer Hazard's Travels through Maryland in 1777," *MHM*, 46 (1951); Shelly, ed., "The Journal of Ebenezer Hazard in Virginia, 1777," *VMHB*, 62 (1954); H. B. Johnston, ed., "The Journal of Ebenezer Hazard in North Carolina, 1777 and 1778," *NCHR*, 36 (1959); H. R. Merrens, ed., "A View of Coastal South Carolina in 1778: The Journal of Ebenezer Hazard," *SCHM*, 73 (1972).

Mss: DLC, MHi, NjP, PHi, PPAmP

John Hulbert

JOHN HULBERT, A.B., physician, was born in the Roxbury section of Woodbury, Connecticut, on November 9, 1732, the son of Sarah Castle and her husband, Nathan Hulbert, a farmer. "I resided with my Parents until sometime after I was of Age," Hulbert later recalled, "and followed the Agricultural Business. My parents discovered my solicitude to acquire Useful Knowledge particularly in transcribing the Connecticut Lawbook, carrying into the field and committing it to memory, in so much that I began to pettifog; when they proposed giving me a Chance for the Bar, or a Liberal Education; without a moment's hesitation I preferred the latter; and told my Parents, Brothers and Sisters, that if I might have a Liberal Education, I would ask no further share in the estate, which at that time was very large. I was accordingly put under the tuition of the Parson of the Parish, the Rev. Mr. [Thomas] Canfield [Yale 1739], a very able and Judicious Instructor. But my parents soon after removing from thence to Sharon, I was put under the Instruction of the Rev. Cotton Mather Smith [Yale 1751], where I continued not long, before I was removed to Cannan [Canaan], under the tuition of the Rev. Daniel Farren [Farrand, A.B. 1750], where I finished my preparatory studies. From him took my Recommendation to a Mr. [Jacob] Green, then vice-president of Nassau Hall in New Jersey; entered College in the fall of the year, A.D. 1758. My progress with the Class was very easy and delightful! But in the College there was such opposition and Insurrection that it rendered a college life very disagreeable, especially as there was at that time a sore Division between the Collegians, and the Town's People and the Young People of the vicinity. However, these Causes of Infilicity were not of long continuance; the latter being removed by a happy Coalition of Parties!

"At the Spring Vacation of my Sophomore Year I determined to spend my Time at College in the study of Electricity. Doct. Benjamin Franklin had, previous to this Time, sent from Europe a present to the College of a very Elegant Electrical Apparatus*; and there was not anyone in the College, neither Student nor Governor, (safe one Colwell [possibly James Caldwell, A.B. 1759], a Sir), that knew enough about it as to shock a person. I applied to the eldest Tutor, Mr. Jeremiah Halsey [A.B. 1752], for the privilege of the Apparatus and Room during the Vacation; and on taking an Inventory of the Appendages belonging to the Apparatus and becoming responsible for them, I obtained his Guarantee to them, until the Government and Trustees should come together after the expiration of the Vacation. By Intense application, with the assistance of Franklin's letters on that subject, and the knowledge I obtained by attending an evening Lecture of Messrs. Lockwood and Kennersly of Philadelphia in Disguise! I had carried the Experiments to such a pitch, as to excite general attention not only in Town, and the vicinity, but New York and Philadelphia!

* Although President Burr and Franklin corresponded on scientific and other matters there is no record of Franklin's gift of an electrical apparatus to the College. Franklin did send a machine to Governor Jonathan Belcher in 1751, but it arrived broken. President Burr used another machine to shock Belcher for palsy, and eventually procured one for the College. By 1759–1760 it was doubtless College lore that the machine had come from Franklin himself. See: Maclean, *History*, I, 141-42; *Franklin Papers*, IV, 216, 255.

"When the Students came together after the expiration of the Vacation, the Juniors and Seniors claimed a prior Right! and Especially the Sir, Mr. Colwell! It arose to that height, that it would have produced an Act of the greatest personal Violence on my part, but for the Timely intervention of the Steward! It was, however, amicably settled on that Day. And I kept the possession of the Room and Apparatus as 'V. et Armis,' until the Government and Trustees met. They then gave the sole command of the Room and Apparatus, to admit or exclude from the Room at pleasure (the Government of the College excepted) During my residence in College."

After graduation Hulbert studied medicine and before 1770 moved to Alford, Berkshire County, Massachusetts, where he bought sixteen acres of land and began to establish a medical practice. When the town was incorporated in 1773, Hulbert was elected town clerk and selectman. By May 1, 1775, Hulbert felt securely enough established to marry Mercy Hamlin. Eleven children were born to the couple, among them John Whitefield Hulbert, who became a United States congressman from Massachusetts.

When Revolution came to western Massachusetts Hulbert served on the local Committee of Correspondence and on the Committee of Safety. A grandson claimed that at one time during the Revolution Hulbert commanded a militia unit that defeated a party of Tories, but no official record of the incident has been discovered.

In the 1780s Hulbert served his county as a justice of the peace. During Shays' Rebellion in 1787 he took what was an unusual course for a college-educated professional man: he sided with the insurgents. Indicted by a local grand jury for high treason, Hulbert fled, an action that those who petitioned the Massachusetts legislature for his removal as a justice of the peace claimed "could have originated only in a consciousness of guilt." But the citizens of Alford must have trusted Hulbert, for they elected him as their delegate to the Massachusetts House of Representatives in 1788. In the same year he served as a delegate to the Massachusetts convention called to consider the new federal constitution. He voted against its adoption. Nothing concrete has been discovered of Hulbert's activities after 1788 except that in 1790 he was living in Alford in a large household of eleven people. He died there on June 7, 1815.

SOURCES: Autobiographical fragment first appeared in *N.Y. Spectator*, Aug. 2, 1815; quotation taken from reprint with additional notes by grandson in *Princeton Standard*, Nov. 2, 1859; brief sketch: *Hist. Berkshire County, Mass.* (1885), I, 364, 189; Shaysite: R. J. Taylor, *Western Mass. in Rev.* (1954), 148; treason: *Resolves of the General Court of the Commonwealth of Mass., begun May 30, 1787* (1787), 33-34; and ibid., 1788 ed. for House of Rep.; antiratification: J. Eliot, *Debates in State Conventions* (1905), II, 181; *U.S. Census 1790, Mass.*, 24.

Nehemiah Ludlum

NEHEMIAH LUDLUM, A.B., physician, was the son of Phebe and Nehemiah Ludlum of Jamaica, Long Island. The younger Nehemiah was probably born there in 1739. The father, a farmer, fell ill in 1750. "I leave to my wife Phebe," he declared in his will, "the use of all lands, meadows, dwelling house, and all the rest of my movable estate, so long as she remains my widow, or until my son Nehemiah shall be of age, for her support and to bring up my children. I leave to my son Nehemiah my dwelling house, orchard, and all lands (except as above). and he shall pay to my two daughters £25 each." Nehemiah may have been the "Ludlam" whose entrance to the College's grammar school President Burr recorded on May 13, 1755.

After graduating Ludlum studied medicine. He settled in Cranbury, New Jersey, and began to establish a practice. On May 3, 1768, the New Jersey Medical Society, meeting in Princeton, examined Ludlum and admitted him to membership. Shortly thereafter he fell ill. Styling himself a "student in physick" Ludlum made his will in October 1, 1768, and died on October 20. His tombstone dignified him with the title "Doctor." He left £100 to a nephew and the rest of his property to a brother-in-law.

SOURCES: Father's will: *N.Y. Wills*, IV, 273-74; Aaron Burr, MS Account Book, 120; S. Wickes, *Proc. N.J. Med. Soc.* (1875), 22; will: 33 *NJA*, 262.

John McCrea

JOHN McCREA, A.B., A.M. 1774, farmer, soldier and lawyer, was born in 1742 at Lamington, Somerset County, New Jersey, the first of 13 children born to Mary Graham and James McCrea. The father, a descendant of a prominent Scots Presbyterian family in Delaware, attended the Log College at Neshaminy, Pennsylvania. He was ordained in 1741 and became the founder and first pastor of the Presbyterian church in Lamington. Upon his death in 1769, James McCrea left £110 to John; and of his seven sons, two became Loyalists and five Whigs during the Revolution. After John's graduation from the College, he moved to Albany, New York, along with two of his brothers who settled nearby. There he studied law and in 1764 married Eva Beekman; over the next six years they had three children. Growing tired of a legal career, in 1768 McCrea bought a sizable piece of land in Northumberland, Saratoga County, New York, and with the aid of one slave began a prosperous farm.

With the coming of the Revolution McCrea supported the Whig cause. In addition to acting as the chairman for the Committee of Safety in Saratoga County, he served, at a salary of £1 a day, as a colonel in the Saratoga County militia. McCrea at this time became indirectly involved in one of the area's most memorable Revolutionary War incidents. For at least five years after their father's death, his sister, the beautiful Jane McCrea, lived with his family in Northumberland. She fell in love with David Jones, a neighbor who had become an officer in the British army. When her betrothed sent a troop of Indians from Burgoyne's army to escort his twenty-four-year old fiancée to their planned marriage, one of the warrior chiefs killed and scalped her. The next day, July 27, 1777, her brother John buried Jane's body and moved his family from the isolated Northumberland farm to the protection of Albany. Jane McCrea's death—implying that the.English enemy was capable of stealing native girls and leaving them at the mercy of savages—became a rallying cry for the Whig cause in New York. "More than any other incident of the campaign," writes a prominent military historian, Jane McCrea's martyrdom "fanned the hatred" against the British. Shortly thereafter Colonel John McCrea helped repulse these same British troops at the battle of Saratoga. In retaliation Tory refugees burned the house and livestock on McCrea's abandoned farm in Northumberland. Compounding the misfortunes of the war, his wife Eva died while he was still at the front.

Following his discharge McCrea moved to Salem, a Scots-Irish settlement in Charlotte, later Washington, County where he became one of the town's first property holders. There on November 27, 1783, he married Elinor McNaughton in a Presbyterian ceremony. The couple had four children. Noted for his regular attendance at religious services, McCrea was one of the area's leading attorneys, serving as the county clerk from 1780 to 1797. In addition, with the creation of the New York Board of Regents, McCrea served in 1784 as one of the two representatives from Washington County. After a twenty-year stay in Salem, McCrea once again moved his family to a farm; this one in Lisbon, Lawrence County, New York. At the end of a life of service, prosperous husbandry, and geographic mobility, John McCrea died in Lisbon on May 31, 1806. His wife Elinor subsequently remarried Canuth Brisbin, but upon the latter's death in 1835, she petitioned the U.S. House of Representatives for McCrea's revolutionary war pension. Claiming her right as the wife of a veteran officer, and as a destitute woman of seventy-four, she received for the first time on November 4, 1839, a small annual sum from the federal government.

SOURCES: Family: A. B. Honeyman, *Som. Cty. Hist. Quart.*, 7 (1918), 190-93; father's will: 33 *NJA*, 266; first wife, Albany, Salem, and Lisbon residence, Northumberland farm and its destruction: *NJHSP*, 1 (1850-51), 165-67; Jane McCrea episode: *NJHSP* (2 ser.), IX (1886), 95-100; effect of martyrdom on military campaign: D. Higginbotham, *The War of American Independence* (1971), 191; N.Y. Bd. of Regents: D. Murray, *Historical and Statistical Record of the University of the State of N.Y.* (1885), 5, 43, 65; Revolutionary War service, second marriage, church attendance, Elinor's pension: Nella Brisbin's MS Pension Application, Rev. War Pension and Bounty Land Warrant Application Files (Additional), National Archives, Washington, D.C.

LLM

James Manning

JAMES MANNING, A.B., A.M. 1765, D.D. 1786, University of Pennsylvania, 1785, Baptist clergyman, public official and first president of Rhode Island College (later Brown University) was born at Piscataway, Middlesex County, New Jersey, on October 22, 1738, one of the

James Manning, A.B. 1762
BY COSMO ALEXANDER

seven children of Grace FitzRandolph and James Manning, a prosperous farmer. In 1756 the Reverend Isaac Eaton had founded an academy in Hopewell, New Jersey, the first Baptist institution of its kind in the colonies. There several youths were prepared for the College, Manning among them. While in Hopewell he underwent a religious conversion, made a public proclamation of his faith, and was baptized.

Manning entered the College in fall 1758. He did extremely well at Princeton, graduating at the head of his class. A Pennsylvania newspaper reported that he opened the commencement exercises in September 1762 with "an elegant Salutatory oration in Latin." The listeners were doubtless impressed not only by the oration but by the orator: Manning was noted all his life for the power of his voice and his presence was imposing. Over six feet tall, he was muscular and athletic while a youth.

Shortly after his graduation, on December 1, 1762, Manning was licensed as a trial minister by the Scotch Plains, New Jersey, Baptist church, of which he was already a member. Full licensing came on February 6 of the following year. On March 23 Manning married Margaret Stites of Elizabethtown, with whom he had corresponded on religious matters while an undergraduate. Almost four weeks later, on April 19 Manning was formally ordained as a Baptist minister. He received a call to settle as assistant pastor of the Baptist church in Charleston, South Carolina. But Manning declined the offer.

Great changes had occurred in Manning's denomination since the beginning of the Great Awakening a generation earlier. Baptist churches were among the chief beneficiaries of the revivals of the 1740s and early 1750s. As qualification for the ministry Baptists put heaviest stress on the necessity for religious conversion rather than familiarity with the higher learning. Indeed, many Baptists entertained a justified suspicion of existing American colleges and their ministerial products. But not all Baptists did. As their number increased in the 1750s a feeling grew in the Philadelphia Association, the oldest American Baptist union, that provisions for formal ministerial education should be encouraged. Isaac Eaton's Hopewell academy was one result of this concern. Its success in training ministers for the denomination led to a movement in the early 1760s to found a Baptist college. James Manning became the chief instrument of this impulse.

In the year after his ordination Manning made a tour of the American colonies to familiarize himself with the state of religion. In July 1763, along with Morgan Edwards, a leading Baptist clergyman, he landed in Newport, Rhode Island. The colony contained the heaviest concentration of Baptists in New England. The minister of Newport's

Second Congregational Church, Ezra Stiles, along with others in that cultivated and wealthy seaport, had long wished to found a college in the colony. The interests of the Baptists and other Rhode Islanders coalesced. The learned and urbane Stiles was shortly commissioned to draw up a draft charter for a new college.

Manning and his middle colony associates had naïvely plunged into uncharted waters. Baptists within Rhode Island were divided among themselves, rival political factions existed in the colony, and wealthy Newport was engaged in fierce commercial competition with growing Providence. Stiles produced an extremely liberal charter for Rhode Island College within a month of Manning's visit. Presented to the Rhode Island legislature in August, it aroused a storm of opposition among Rhode Island Baptists, who felt that the plan gave almost equal strength on the college's governing boards to Congregationalists and other non-Baptists. The charter was rewritten to assure Baptist control and became law in October 1765.

In the meantime, in 1764, Manning became minister of a Baptist church at Warren, Rhode Island, about ten miles from Providence, and opened a Latin grammar school. In September 1765 he was elected president and professor of languages in Rhode Island College. Classes began in Warren with one student in that year. Five new students were enrolled in 1766, four in 1767, eight in 1768, and eleven in 1769. Increased numbers meant assistance was needed, and in 1767 Manning called David Howell (A.B. 1766) from Princeton to serve as the college's first tutor.

While friends of the college—among them Manning's Princeton classmate, Hezekiah Smith—solicited support throughout the colonies and in Britain, a battle was fought out between various Rhode Island towns, all wishing to be the college's permanent location. The choice eventually narrowed to either Providence or Newport. Although Newport offered more financial inducement, Providence was finally chosen, probably because of the strength of the Baptist community there, Manning's close ties with it, and the influence of the Brown family. Faculty and students moved from Warren to Providence in May 1770 and into the handsome new college building, which was modeled on Nassau Hall, beginning in the fall of 1771. Manning shortly took on an additional post, becoming pastor of Providence's Baptist church, the oldest Baptist congregation in the colonies.

More than the architectual plan of Rhode Island College was borrowed from the College of New Jersey. Not only did its president and first tutor come from Princeton, but Manning also used the College of New Jersey's student laws for his own college. Manning appears too to have borrowed for Rhode Island the curriculum he had become familiar with while an undergraduate at Princeton. Isaac Watts's *Logic* was the basic text on that subject in Princeton; Manning used it in Providence. Longinus was the most popular rhetorical guide and model at New Jersey; he retained the same position in Rhode Island. During Samuel Davies's brief tenure as president of the College of New Jersey, he introduced elaborate commencement exercises. These, too, Manning transferred to Rhode Island.

Rhode Island College was a success, thanks largely to Manning. In 1779, Ezra Stiles, by then president of Yale and still smarting from the success of the Baptists and Providence, described Manning thus: "He is of good natural Parts indifferently improved with a superficial general Knowledge of the Languages & Sciences. But he studies too little to make any Thing great. He loves figure and Splendor, English Orations & Dramatic Entertainments at Commencements. However by the assistance of Mr Ho[well] he makes some good Scholars. He is for close Communion, and very biggotted."

From the point of view of Stiles, a very liberal Congregationalist, Manning might indeed have seemed "biggotted." He opposed infant baptism and favored church membership limited to those who had experienced religious conversion. But as president of Rhode Island College he retained the loyalties of the simpler rural Baptists of New England and gradually won their support for a college-educated ministry. And he accomplished even more outside his college presidency. While pastor in Warren he formed the Warren Association, the first organization of Baptist congregations in New England. The association attracted more and more churches over the years; it succeeded in bringing a degree of unity and harmony to New England Baptists, and gave the once-despised and persecuted denomination a strong lever to influence the civil authorities.

During the Revolution Rhode Island College was used successively as a barracks for American soldiers and as a hospital for French troops. Considerable damage was done to the college building. Manning himself disliked war, but acted as an agent for Rhode Island in dealings with Connecticut in these years. After the war his main energies were devoted to the often extremely discouraging task of restoring the college's plant. In 1786 he was, apparently by default, sent as Rhode Island's delegate to Congress. There he complained about the lack of salary from his home state, the impotence of the national government, and continued his efforts to secure payment from the government for the damages done to the college. (The matter was not settled until after his death.) A strong supporter of the federal constitution, he lobbied vigorously for its passage both in Rhode Island and Massachusetts.

Although Manning inherited a slave named Zip on his father's death in 1767 and owned another named Cato in 1769, he sold both, helped pass Rhode Island's gradual emancipation law in 1784, and joined a Providence society dedicated to the discouragement of the slave trade. Shortly before his death he helped draft a plan to provide free schools for his state.

Manning presided over his last and largest (twenty-two graduates) commencement in 1790. He was, apparently, not feeling well and requested the college corporation to begin a search for a new president. In April 1791 he resigned his Providence pastorate.

Manning weighed upwards of 300 pounds in his later years. While at family prayers on July 24, 1791, he was stricken with apoplexy and died five days later. Shortly thereafter a fellow-Rhode Islander informed Dr. Benjamin Rush (A.B. 1760) "that Revd. Dr. Manning 'had died of his knife and fork,' that is of eating too much." Manning's old detractor, President Stiles of Yale, took a longer view. Manning "was ambitious & haughty, intriguing & avaritious," Stiles noted in his diary, but then added, "of Integrity however, & I believe a Man of Virtue & Religion."

SOURCES: *DAB*; Sprague, *Annals*, VI, 89-97; full accounts in: R. A. Guild, *Early Hist. of Brown University, including the Life, Times, and Correspondence of President Manning* (1897); W. C. Bronson, *Hist. of Brown University* (1914); supplement with: W. G. McLoughlin, *New England Dissent* (1971), I, 491-512; commencement oration: *Pa. Gaz.*, October 21, 1762; Stiles quotations: *Literary Diary*, II, 339; III, 425; Zip: 33 *NJA*, 270; Cont. Congr.: *LMCC*, VIII; Rush, *Autobiography*, 206.

Mss: RPB

Nathaniel Manning

NATHANIEL MANNING, A.B., A.M. 1765, physician and Anglican clergyman, cousin of his classmate James Manning, was born at Piscataway, Middlesex County, New Jersey, on August 19, 1738, the son of Nathaniel Manning, a farmer, and Mary Harris, his second wife. Young Nathaniel entered the College's grammar school on November 26, 1756. The date on which he matriculated in the College is not known. After graduation Manning went to Pennsylvania, where he studied with the newly constituted Medical Faculty of the College of Philadelphia. Manning did not stay in Philadelphia to take his M.B. with the Medical Faculty's first graduating class in 1768, but returned to New Jersey, perhaps in 1766 when he inherited twenty acres of land from his father. Manning began his medical practice in Metuchen. In 1767 he presented testimonials from the Philadelphia Medical Faculty to the New Jersey Medical Society and was admitted to membership.

Manning practised in Metuchen for about five years. It may have been during this period that he married Mary Hite, by whom he had one son, Jacob Hite Manning. On May 14, 1771, Manning requested the New Jersey Medical Society to issue him a certificate attesting to his character as a physician, since he was about to leave the province. The society granted the request. Manning then traveled to England. On March 15, 1772 he was ordained a priest of the Church of England in the Chapel Royal, St. James's Palace, London. He returned to America immediately, and was present at a meeting of the New Jersey Medical Society held in New Brunswick on May 12, 1772. Shortly thereafter Manning moved to Hampshire County, Virginia, where he became first rector of Hampshire parish, a post he occupied for the rest of his life. Manning probably died in January 1777, for his will was probated in Hampshire County on February 11 of that year.

SOURCES: Parentage: *O. M. Manette, First Settlers of Ye Plantations of Piscataway and Woodbridge* (1930); grammar school: Aaron Burr, MS Account Book, 236-37; medical career: Wickes, *Hist. Medicine N.J.*, 321, and: *Proc. N.J. Med. Soc.* (1879), 17, 30, 32; father's will: 33 *NJA*, 270; ordination: *AASP*, 83 (1973), 139; parish: *WMQ* (1 ser.), 5 (1897), 201; marriage and will: Nathaniel Manning File, PUA.

Thomas Martin

THOMAS MARTIN, A.B., Anglican clergyman and teacher, younger brother of Alexander (A.B. 1756), was born at Lebanon, Hunterdon County, New Jersey, the third son of Jane Hunter and her husband Hugh Martin, an immigrant from Ireland who had achieved a modest prosperity as a farmer and local prominence as a justice of the peace.

Thomas's father died in 1761, while Thomas was still at college. His father's will provided that Thomas's education be financed through the sale of the father's real estate. Thomas's activities immediately after graduation are unknown. On June 14, 1767, he was ordained a deacon in the Church of England in the Chapel Royal, St. James's Palace, London. Ordination to the priesthood followed on June 24, 1767. On July 8 Martin received the King's Bounty (money for passage to America) and set out for home.

Back in America Martin became rector of the Brick Church, St. Thomas's Parish, in Orange County, Virginia. Among Martin's parishioners was James Madison, a well-to-do planter. Madison had several children and needed a teacher for them. The unmarried Martin moved into Madison's plantation, Montpelier, and added tutoring to his parish duties. The oldest Madison boy, James, Jr. (A.B. 1771), had just finished his course of study with a Virginia schoolmaster. Martin completed young James's preparatory education, but the question of the choice of a college for James was undecided. Most Virginia youths of his time went to the College of William and Mary. But in the 1760s that College had fallen upon unstable and contentious times. Madison was worried too about the effect of Williamsburg's climate on one raised in the mountains. Moreover the Madisons, though Anglicans, were not strong supporters of the episcopacy advocated at William and Mary. Martin and his older brother Alexander, already an assistant king's attorney in North Carolina, persuaded the Madisons that the best place for James's further education would be their own alma mater, the College of New Jersey.

In June or early July of 1769 Martin, accompanied by his brother Alexander, who was making a trip home to visit their family, took young Madison north to Princeton. Martin's pupil would do well at the College. "Your kind Advice & friendly cautions," Madison wrote to Martin not long after they parted, "are a favour that shall always be gratefully remembered, & I must beg leave to assure you that my happiness, which you and your brother so ardently wish for, will be greatly augmented by both your enjoyments of the like blessing."

Martin continued on from Princeton to his widowed mother's home in Hunterdon County. There he and his family decided that all should seek their fortunes in the South. Martin, his mother, and his sister returned to Orange County. There they set up housekeeping in the Brick Church's glebe house. The family reunion was a short one; Martin died early in 1770, only a few months after returning to Virginia.

Sources: Genealogical and other data in Martin Family Folder, PUA; for father's will, see: 33 *NJA* (1 ser.), 273; Irving Brant, *James Madison: The Virginia Revolutionist* (Indianapolis, 1941), 66-71, 82-83; Ralph Ketchum, *James Madison, A Biography* (New York, 1971), 21-25; on William and Mary in the 1760s, see: R. P. Thomson, "The Reform of the College of William and Mary, 1763-1780," *APS Proc.*, 115 (1971), 187-213; Madison to Martin, August 10, 1769, *Madison Papers*, I, 42.

John Dyer Mercier

JOHN DYER MERCIER, A.B., merchant and public official, was the third child and first son of Ann Bradford, daughter of the well-known printer William Bradford, and her husband, William Mercier, a prosperous ship's captain and sometime local official of New York City.

Not long after the Peace of Paris in 1763, Mercier traveled to the city of Quebec, where he established himself as a merchant. He was made coroner of the city and struck up a friendship with a frequent visitor from New Haven, Connecticut, Benedict Arnold, then a merchant-apothecary who owned a sloop that regularly voyaged from Quebec to Barbadoes. Mercier did not forget Princeton, serving in 1774 as Quebec agent for a Delaware lottery designed to raise $15,000 for the College and for the Presbyterian congregations in Princeton and New Castle, Delaware.

Like most of the British and American merchant community of Quebec, Mercier was doubtlessly shocked by the passage in 1774 of the Quebec Act, which in its effort to protect the French majority must have seemed to deny many traditional British liberties to the inhabitants of that province. When revolution broke out in the colonies to the south, Mercier soon found himself in a hopelessly compromised situation. In the fall of 1775, Benedict Arnold, by now an officer in the American army, led an invasion of Canada. On October 3 Arnold wrote several letters to his commanding officer, General Philip Schuyler, and sent them to Mercier in Quebec to be forwarded to Schuyler. Arnold also sent a letter to Mercier telling him of his approach and requesting all available military intelligence concerning Quebec. The Indian bearer of Arnold's letters turned them over to the British authorities. Shortly thereafter the following report from Quebec was received in England:

> On *Saturday*, the 28th of *October*, Mr. *John Dyer Mercier*, as he was going into the upper Town, was laid hold of by the Town Sergeant, and conducted to the main guard and there confined, and his papers were seized and examined merely by the order of the Lieutenant-Governour, without any crime or accusation alleged against him, and at daybreak the next morning he was put on board the *Hunter*, sloop-of-war. This was very alarming to the citizens of *Quebeck*, who thereupon had a meeting, and appointed three of their number to wait on the Lieutenant-Governour, to know the causes of so remarkable a step. He made answer, "that he had sufficient reasons for what he had done, which he would communicate when and to whom he should think proper."

No evidence connecting Mercier with the American invaders was brought forward, nor has the exact resolution of his predicament been discovered. But Mercier's sympathies lay with the American side during the Revolution. At some time after his imprisonment he made his way south. On May 22, 1779, the Continental Congress's Committee on the Treasury nominated Mercier to serve as one of its commissioners of accounts. The appointment may have come through the influence of Mercier's relative, William Bradford, who had served as printer to Congress. Mercier was but one of the many merchants who were called upon to manage the financial affairs of the new government. He served in his post at least until 1785, apparently to the satisfaction of all. In 1784 he was listed as a member of the 8th Company, 4th Battalion of the Philadelphia militia, and in the same year he acquired 400 acres of land in Pennsylvania's Westmoreland County.

Mercier's name does not appear in the *Journals* of the Continental Congress after 1785, nor was he listed in the federal census of 1790. But he was probably living in New York in 1797 when his father made his will. The father left Mercier "my negro boy, Charles," family pictures, and a great deal of silver. Mercier lived thereafter in what a nineteenth-century antiquarian described as a "beautiful home" at Hallett's Cove, Long Island. Mercier apparently never married. His extensive property was supposed by contemporaries to be destined after his death for a nephew. However, when Mercier died at an undiscovered date, it was found that he had made no will, and the nephew received nothing.

SOURCES: In Princeton's normally authoritative *General Catalogue 1746-1906* Mercier's name is misprinted as "Mercer" and his is assigned the career of a member of the prominent Virginia Mercer family. However, in the College's eighteenth-century sources, his name is consistently given as Mercier. Ancestry, parentage, some vital data: H. L. Butler, *Tales of Our Kinfolk* (1919), 150 and chart in back; *NYGBR*, 45 (1914), 361-65; Arnold: W. M. Wallace, *Traitorous Hero* (1954), 26, 67, 73; lottery: *N.Y. Gaz.*, Mar. 31, 1774; Quebec merchants: D. G. Creighton, *Commercial Empire of the St. Lawrence* (1937); Quebec quotation: Force, *Am. Arch.* (4 ser.), III, 1418-19; activities with Treasury: *JCC*, XIV-XXIX, passim; militia and land: *Pa. Arch.* (6 ser.), III, 1102; ibid. (3 ser.), XXVI, 468.

———— Morrow

MORROW was the only undergraduate of the period mentioned by name in the minutes of the College's Board of Trustees as having done anything other than receive a degree. Unfortunately, they neglected to mention his Christian name. On September 30, 1761, the clerk to the Board made the following notation:

It appearing to the Trustees, that Morrow a Student of the College is greatly in Arrear for his tuition. It is ordered that the Arrears be fully discharged to the Steward of the College before the Expiration of the ensuing Vacancy, or in Default the P[upil?] Morrow to be dismissed from the College.

This undergraduate was presumably the same youth whose entry to the College's grammar school on December 29, 1756, President Burr recorded with the bare notation: "Morrow entered School." Persons named Morrow were widespread in eighteenth-century America, particularly in Pennsylvania, Virginia, and the Carolinas. The College's student possibly had a connection with the Joseph Morrow of Princeton who advertised a large house for sale in 1756 and who in 1762, after moving to New York City, put a Princeton warehouse on the market.

SOURCES: MS Trustees' Minutes, I; Aaron Burr, MS Account Book, 244-45; 19 *NJA*, 430; 20 *NJA*, 107.

Francis Peppard

FRANCIS PEPPARD, A.B., Presbytrian clergyman, was born in Dublin, Ireland, in 1725, the son of William Peppard. Francis immigrated to America in 1743 and settled at Basking Ridge, Somerset County, New Jersey. Dissatisfaction over his early training apparently prompted his departure from Ireland, but the sources are unclear on whether he had been preparing for the Anglican ministry or the Catholic priesthood. In either case, when he began religious training anew at least a decade later it was for the Presbyterian ministry.

Peppard's belated career choice was almost certainly influenced by three major developments in his life between his arrival in 1743 and his entrance into the College sometime in 1761: first, his warm acceptance into the Basking Ridge Presbyterian church, where he soon became an active and popular member; second, his close relationship to the church's long-time pastor, Samuel Kennedy (A.B. 1754), who probably not only tutored him in preparation for the College but also converted him in the course of the several revivals he led; and third, the death of his young wife of eight years, Susan McCollum of Basking Ridge, in 1760, leaving him with four small children. His occupation during these years has not been discovered. That he had won wide community respect is indicated by his becoming a freeholder of Bridgewater Township, Somerset County, in 1753.

Licensed at Basking Ridge by the Presbytery of New Brunswick on April 24, 1764, Peppard was ordained by the Presbytery of New York on October 16, 1764. A month after being licensed Peppard married Phebe Whitaker of Mine Brook, New Jersey; she would care for his motherless four children, who had remained with the McCollum family during Peppard's stay at the College. A niece of Nathaniel Whitaker (A.B. 1752), she bore Peppard nine children.

Despite his late start at the age of thirty-nine, Peppard enjoyed a varied thirty-year ministerial career. After declining a call to Nova Scotia at the outset, he occupied pulpits at Mendham, Morris County, New Jersey, 1764–1769; Bethlehem, Cornwall, Newburgh, and New Windsor, all in Orange County, New York, 1763–1773; Upper and Lower Hardwick, Warren County, New Jersey, 1773–1783; and Allen and Lower Bethel, Northampton County, Pennsylvania, 1783–1795. At New Windsor, at Upper Hardwick, and at Lower Hardwick, Peppard was the church's first pastor and so bore unusually heavy responsibilities. At New Windsor Peppard had George Whitefield, then on his final tour of the colonies, preach to his congregants.

With his "rich Irish brogue" and with "all the zeal of a convert," Peppard nevertheless was an impressive speaker in his own right, adding many members to his churches through the years. His ministries were not, however, without friction. At Mendham his introduction of hymn books and of singing by note aroused the opposition of conservative parishioners; at Allen his condemnation of a nearby religious academy aroused the opposition of, among others, the son of Peppard's predecessor at Allen, the Reverend John Rosbrugh (A.B. 1761). In addition, Peppard several times became embroiled in disputes over salary and, perhaps more importantly, congregational discipline. The latter was attributed later to the "distractions" of the Revolution, which Peppard strongly supported.

In March 1795, at the age of seventy, Peppard returned to the church at Lower Hardwick, where he had earlier spent the happiest period of his life. There he remained until he died on March 29, 1797. His property, inventoried a month later, came to £170.16.6 in personalty plus extensive landholdings. His son Isaac, to whom Peppard willed £50, "1/2 of wearing apparel," and "divinity books" in preparation for the ministry, died less than a year after his father.

SOURCES: Vital data: Francis Peppard File, PUA; O. M. Voorhees, "Rev. Francis Peppard," MS (1926), PUA; E. W. Clarke, "Rev. Francis Peppard," MS PPPrHi; J. C. Clyde, *Hist. of the Allen Township Presbyterian Church* (1876), 164-66; freeholdership: *GMNJ*, 17 (1942), 90; will: 37 *NJA*, 281.

HS

Joseph Periam

JOSEPH PERIAM, A.B., A.M. 1765, college tutor, schoolmaster, Presbyterian clergyman and soldier, was born in 1742. His father, also Joseph, probably migrated from England to America with the great revivalist George Whitefield about 1740. Before leaving Britain the senior Periam had caused a stir in Wesleyan circles during the 1730s. A young clerk to an attorney, he underwent a religious conversion, caused in part by reading Whitefield's sermons on spiritual rebirth. His subsequent conduct so disturbed his friends that they committed him to a madhouse: "(1) Because he fasted for near a fortnight. (2) Because he prayed so as to be heard several stories high. (3) Because he had sold his clothes and given them to the poor." Although the elder Periam died about 1746, he seems to have communicated something of his enthusiasm to his son.

While in the College young Joseph was a diligent student. A commonplace book he kept as an undergraduate (one of the few to survive from this period) shows that he took a delight in music, perhaps under the inspiration of President Davies. He tried his hand at religious verse, as in the following excerpts from a poem called "The Day of Judgement; An Ode Attempted in English Sapphick," which shows the mark of close attention to the sermons of President Jonathan Edwards.

> Hark! the shrill outcries of the guilty wretches, lively
> > Bright Horror, amazing anguish, stear through their
> > Eyelids, while the living Worm lies gnawing within them . . . .
> Hoopless [sic] immortals, how they scream and shiver, while
> > Devils push them to the pit wide yawning hideous and
> > gloomy to receive them Headlong down to the Centre
> Stop, here, my Fancy, away ye horrid doleful Ideas ideas [sic],
> > come arise to Jesus here he is Godlike and the Saints
> > around him, throned yet adoring.

Periam had a less intense side; at his commencement he delivered an English oration on "Politeness" that, a newspaper reported, "gave universal satisfaction for the justness of its sentiments, the elegance of the composition, and the propriety with which it was delivered."

In 1764–1765 Periam served as master in the College's grammar school. The following year he was appointed a tutor in the College itself and also served as clerk to the Board of Trustees. In October 1766 Periam advertised in New York and Philadelphia newspapers that he would open a unique school, limited to six boys, in Princeton on November 10. "The mode of teaching," he explained, "will be somewhat new, and perhaps, has never been before practiced, in America at least." Periam promised that he would teach his students as much Latin in one year as was normally taught in four, thus saving students three years' schooling and parents £140 cash. The results of his experiment have not been discovered. Periam remained in Princeton, and was still regarded well enough by the College authorities to be reappointed as tutor in mathematics for 1768–1769, President Witherspoon's first year in Princeton. Periam resigned his tutorship in 1769 and received a testimonial from the trustees regarding his work.

In July 1769, Periam succeeded Tapping Reeve (A.B. 1763) as master of the Latin grammar school associated with the Presbyterian church in Elizabethtown. The Visitors of the school ambitiously promised that Periam would teach not only "what hath been heretofore taught in the school," but also mathematics, penmanship, composition, elocution, geography, and "such of our protestant Catechisms as may be most agreeable to their [the students'] parents or governors." Perhaps the last had some effect on Periam himself. In April 1772 Jedidiah Chapman (Yale 1762), minister of the Presbyterian church at Newark Mountain (now Orange), New Jersey, recommended Periam to the Connecticut New Divinity theologian Joseph Bellamy, his former teacher. Periam, wrote Chapman, was "a very ingenious young gentleman. I trust a truly pious and humble Christian, one whom I greatly love and esteem, a steady zealous friend to truth,—he comes with a design to spend some time in the study of divinity with you."

How long Periam studied with Bellamy is uncertain. Late in 1773 he was back in Elizabethtown, sponsored by James Caldwell (A.B. 1759), minister of the Presbyterian church there. Almost immediately, Periam caused a major theological scandal. While studying with Bellamy he had, apparently, been deeply influenced by the unorthodox theological ideas of the Reverend Stephen West (Yale 1755), successor to Jonathan Edwards's pulpit in Stockbridge. Periam gave a sermon at Caldwell's church. An enormous uproar followed. Caldwell was appalled: "I was his friend. He had long been dear to me. I was active in introducing him to the Presbytery. We were intimate. Yet I never expected from him what I heard." Caldwell consulted widely with others and then condemned Periam's errors in a public sermon. "You," Caldwell told Bellamy, "say he is a Berkleyan in philosophy. This is hardly just. That good mistaken man believed in the existence of a spiritual world and I believe it would have brot him to his senses, had he seen that it would follow from his doctrine that Jehovah was only an Idea and that what we call the souls of men are but Ideas of an Infinite Idea. Making uncertain philosophy the rule of interpreting divine truths, has always been fatal to Christianity."

Fatal to Christianity or not, philosophy was fatal to Joseph Periam's ministerial career in the New Jersey–New York area. The Presbytery of New York licensed him in 1774, but withdrew the license the following year. In the meantime Periam went north to the town of Alford in Berkshire County, Massachusetts. There, not far from Stockbridge and Stephen West, he tried to gather a congregation. However, he disagreed with his prospective parishioners and retired to Connecticut. Early in 1775 President Ezra Stiles of Yale heard from Joseph Bellamy that Periam had become "gay and merry as a Greek, and mightily carried away with learning to sing, and talks about going into Trade. Dr. Bellamy writes that he has turned out either a high Sandimanian [an arcane theological aberration of the time] or is crazy and distracted. Alas! the poor unhappy Gentleman is smitten in the Intellect! He is full of Ingenuity, Learning, Virtue and Instability and carries the seeds of a flighty and variable Frenzy in his animal Constitution, which will be ever and anon Breaking out, & defeat the Usefulness of perhaps one of the finest Geniuses in America."

The Revolution saved Periam and put his talents to use. In November 1776 he was appointed quartermaster in the First Battalion of the New Jersey Brigade. He served until 1778, when in June he once again took up the post of master of the Latin grammar school in Elizabethtown. It was probably at about this time that he married a widow of the town, Mrs. Elizabeth Ogden Woodruff. A daughter was born to the couple.

Life was not yet settled for Periam. On March 23, 1780, while he was visiting in Paramus, New Jersey, a party of British and foreign troops made a surprise raid. In the confusion Periam was wounded by the Americans and captured by the British. He was exchanged and recovered sufficiently to make his will on March 29. By September he felt well enough to advertise that "Mr. Periam intends, God willing, to open his school at Elizabethtown on Monday the second day of October." But on Sunday morning, October 8, 1780, he died. His only son was born six months later.

SOURCES: Some vital data: Wheeler, *Ogden Family*, 77, 127; father: L. Tyerman, *The Life and Times of the Rev. John Wesley* (1872), I, 247; poem: MS Musick and Commonplace Book, 1760, NjP; commencement address: *Pa. Gaz.*, Oct. 21, 1762; Princeton school: *N.Y. Gaz.*, Oct. 9, 1766, and *Pa. Jour.*, Oct. 16, 1766; Elizabethtown academy: *N.Y. Gaz.*, July 24, 1769; Chapman and West: Dexter, *Yale Biographies*, II, 388-94, 737-39; Chapman and Caldwell letters to Bellamy, dated respectively April 1772 and December 29, 1773: Webster/Bellamy Transcripts, PPPrHi; Stiles's quotation: Stiles, *Literary Diary*, I, 516; account of Paramus incident: *N.Y. Packet*, Mar. 30, 1780; will: 35 NJA, 304; Elizabethtown school: *N.J. Jour.*, Sept. 20, 1780; notice of death (the date on Periam's tombstone is incorrect): *N.J. Jour.*, Oct. 11, 1780.

Mss: NjP

Thomas Ruston

THOMAS RUSTON, A.B., M.D. Edinburgh 1765, physician and businessman, was born at Fagg's Manor, Chester County, Pennsylvania, about

1740, one of the thirteen children of Mary Brown and Job Ruston. The father, born at Berwick on the border between England and Scotland, settled in Chester County in 1739. Reputed to be "a man of considerable wealth," over the years he purchased 905 acres of land in the county, upon which he built a mill and several houses. Both the father and his father before him held a substantial but indeterminable interest in iron works at Principio and Kingsbury in Maryland and at Accokeek in Virginia. The father was a prominent and active member of the Presbyterian church at Fagg's Manor.

Thomas was prepared for college at Samuel Finley's academy at West Nottingham, Maryland. Among his schoolmates there were Benjamin Rush (A.B. 1760), Ebenezer Hazard (A.B. 1762), and Joseph Alexander (A.B. 1760). On April 26, 1759, Finley sent Ruston and Alexander off to Princeton, writing to the College's acting president, Enoch Green, that they "have read the common . . . Latin & Greek Classics used in my school, Longinus excepted; also Logic, Arithmetic, Geography, some Geometry, Part of Ontology, & Natural Philosophy, in a more cursory manner, as far as Opticks in *Martin's* Order. They have both behaved themselves regularly & agreeably; their Geniuses, not mean, nor their inclination to study languid." While Alexander received his degree in little more than a year, Ruston apparently took the complete College course.

After graduation Ruston served a brief medical apprenticeship in Philadelphia. However he soon decided to study medicine in Britain. His old mentor Samuel Finley, by then president of the College, was encouraging: "When you return, I trust that divine Providence will mete out ye Bounds of your Habitation. I would rejoice if Princeton might suit you. We have not one good Physician all around us. If it be not too healthy a place it will do." On June 4, 1763, Ruston set sail for London, landing on July 13.

"London at first seamed [sic] confined, stired up, dirty and disagreeable," Ruston wrote in his diary shortly after his arrival. "But good Company amply makes amends for all these things." Equipped with letters of recommendation, Ruston quickly introduced himself about the city. Under the guidance of Dr. John Fothergill, Quaker physician, philanthropist, and friend to young Americans abroad, he made arrangements to walk the wards of St. Thomas's Hospital. But he spent even more time in tours of the countryside. He visited Oxford, Bath and many of the great country houses: among others, the Temple family's Stowe, the Hoares's Stourhead, Blenheim ("there are several Representations of our Saviour and his Apostles which savour much of Popery . . . the Furniture is Old and wants Repairing"), and Windsor ("a Stately Grand Old Gothic Pile of Building. . . . The Paintings are excessively fine, but every thing is Antient").

In October Ruston left London for Edinburgh. There he matriculated in the university's medical department. Over the next two years he studied with the city's famed array of medical teachers—Cullen, Monro, Whytt, Hope, and Rutherford. Admitted to the prestigious Medical Society in April 1764, the following year he presented his dissertation, *De Febribus bilious putridis*, and received the M.D. Two years later he published in London yet another medical treatise, *An Essay on Inoculation*, which was reprinted in Philadelphia in the same year.

"Judge of the Gay world upon modish Principles," President Finley had advised Ruston before his trip abroad, "& it will appear Great & Glorious; but—upon the Principles of pure Religion and Sound Reason, & it will appear lighter than vanity. Let but the Eye be fixed on Eternal and Substantial Realities." It was to no avail; the "gay world" captivated Ruston, and his eye became fixed on very substantial realities indeed. While in London he had become acquainted with Stephen Sayre (A.B. 1757), an accomplished fortune-hunter. Perhaps with Sayre as his model, after receiving his medical degree Ruston did not fulfill President Finley's hopes and return to Princeton. Instead he stayed on in England to search for a rich heiress to marry. His father, apparently, did not approve. Ruston claimed that in London he was sure to meet wealthy girls. As far as his support was concerned, he pointed out to his father, £500 would amount to very little "out of the fortune of a girl who has ten thousand."

It took some time, but Ruston eventually found his heiress. Late in 1771 or early in 1772 he married Mary Fisher, the niece of a governor of the Bank of England and only child of William Fisher, who appears to have been a prosperous broker. The marriage was a substantial affair: Sir William Browne, lately president of London's College of Physicians, composed a poem celebrating the event. Three children— Thomas, Mary, and Charlotte—were born to the couple. After his marriage Ruston abandoned medicine for business, writing to his father that he was no longer to be addressed as "Dr." "I dare say he will make more money and with more ease of mind," an acquaintance informed his old schoolmate, Dr. Benjamin Rush.

Ruston's English residence did not weaken his ties to America. As the events leading to the Revolution unfolded, he kept his friends at home well-informed about affairs in Britain. "Your letters to me have been singularly useful and interesting, and therefore they have constantly been published in our newspapers," Benjamin Rush wrote to him from Philadelphia in October 1775. In the latter part of 1777 Ruston moved from London to what he later described as "an old mansion" in Devonshire near Exeter. Not long afterward, he moved to Bedford Circus in Exeter itself and resumed the practice of medicine, being appointed physician to the Devon and Exeter Hospital. His removal to the provinces indicated a loss of interest neither in America nor in business. George Washington later described Ruston as "a warm friend of the American cause during the contest with Great Britain." In Exeter he wrote essays on American finance and on banks, which he forwarded to Benjamin Franklin in Paris. Franklin thought highly enough of them to see that they were translated into French and also put Ruston in touch with congressmen concerned with the subjects, particularly Robert Morris, the financier. In 1784 Ruston published anonymously in London a pamphlet, *Remarks on Lord Sheffield's Observations on the Commerce of the United States*, in which he strongly urged the continued involvement of Great Britain in trade with America, pointing out that it had seemed valuable enough to fight a war over.

In January 1784, Ruston's father signed his will. Ruston was left a considerable amount of property, but only on the condition that he return to America. Ruston resigned his position with the Devon and Exeter Hospital, and in the following year (during which his father died) went to Paris to confer with Franklin and Jefferson in preparation for a return to America. After an absence of twenty-two years, Ruston arrived back in Pennsylvania in 1785. Accompanying him were his wife, children, and his father-in-law.

Ruston built an imposing three-story brick mansion house on a large plot at the corner of Eighth and Chestnut Streets in Philadelphia and entertained widely. Among his dinner guests was George Washington, whom he visited for two days at Mt. Vernon in 1787. Elected to the American Philosophical Society in 1787, he played an active role in its affairs. With the support of Washington and Franklin, he tried to revive his family's old interest in the Principio Ironworks in Maryland. In October 1787, he was elected to Pennsylvania's Council of Censors from Chester County in a contest confused by the recent division of the county. (Whether he ever took his seat is unclear.) On his father-in-law's death in 1789 Ruston's wife inherited a fortune that Benjamin Rush later estimated at 40,000 guineas. By 1795 Ruston was so familiar a figure on the Pennsylvania scene that in describing the English political leader Charles James Fox one Philadelphian would write: "When you think of him, figure to yourself a short fat man—in person & gate not unlike Dr Ruston."

Ruston, apparently, did not practice medicine after his return to America. One of his only two late forays in that field came during the yellow fever epidemic of 1793. Safely removed from the contagion at his Chester County farm, he urged in the press the "mild" cure for the disease in direct opposition to the bleedings and purgings prescribed by his old schoolmate, Dr. Benjamin Rush. Rush never forgave him, inscribing an unreliable and vitriolic account of Ruston in his commonplace book.

Ruston's principal occupation after his return to America was business—the promotion of various credit and banking plans, and land speculation. Closely involved with Robert Morris in these ventures, he met the same fate as Morris—failure and imprisonment for debt. Between 1793 and 1796 Ruston accumulated substantial tracts of land in Maine and at least 9,990 acres of land in Pennsylvania's Northampton and Northumberland counties. A large proportion of the Pennsylvania lands was acquired in the names of his wife and children. When Robert Morris's affairs collapsed, Ruston's went with them. His misfortune was complicated by a simultaneous adverse legal judgment concerning the execution of his father's will, an affair that had dragged on for years. "My old friend Dr. Ruston is now expiating his avarice and rapacity in the new jail," Benjamin Rush wrote in September 1796. "His debts it is said amount to 200,000 dollars. He settled the principal part of his productive estate upon his wife and children before he contracted those debts."

Ruston's wife died in August 1797. He appears to have been released from jail at about this time, or perhaps during the following year, when the Chestnut Street mansion was sold by the sheriff. The only account discovered of Ruston's later years comes from one of his bitterest enemies, Rush. Rush claimed that after his release Ruston made a fool of himself trying to repair his fortune by pursuing rich widows and that he died in 1804 "of laudanum." Whatever the cause, in the year of his death Ruston published in New York and Philadelphia a pamphlet called *A Collection of Facts Interspersed with Observations on the Nature, Causes and Cure of Yellow Fever* that was strongly critical of Rush's treatment of the disease.

SOURCES: Genealogy and some vital data: *PMHB*, 2 (1878), 116; ibid., 8 (1884), 111; J. S. Futhey and G. Cope, *Hist. of Chester County, Pa.* (1881), 50, 100, 199, 251, 312-13, 717-18; partial reconstruction of career: L. H. Butterfield, "The Milliner's Mission in 1775," *WMQ*, 8 (1951), 200-201; Finley to Green, Apr. 26, 1759, MS, Gratz Col., PHi; later letters of Finley, copies of Edinburgh diploma, Browne poem, etc., all in Ruston, MS Diary, 1762-65, DLC (copy too at PHi); studies at Edinburgh: *APS Proc.*, 94 (1950), 281; Ruston to Job Ruston, Feb. 4, 1767, July 4, 1768, and Feb. 5, 1772, MSS, DLC; "ease of mind" quotation: Richard Huck to B. Rush, Feb. 3,

1772, in D. F. Hawke, *Benjamin Rush* (1971), 91-92; for relations with Rush, see references scattered throughout: Butterfield, *Rush Letters*, and Rush, *Autobiography*; residence in Exeter: *APS Trans.*, 2 (1786), 231-35; Washington quotation: Washington, *Writings*, xxx, 59; corresp. with Franklin: J. Bigelow, ed., *Works of B. Franklin* (1904), VIII, 308-10; I. M. Hays, *Calendar of the Papers of B. Franklin* (1908), II, 476; Washington and Mt. Vernon: *PMHB*, 19 (1895), 182, 195; Principio claim: *Votes and Proc. of the [Maryland] House of Delegates, Nov. Session, 1788* (1788); Council of Censors: *Minutes of the Supreme Executive Council of Pa.*, (1853), XVI, 201-202; *Pa. Arch.* (1 ser.), XI, 623-33; ibid. (6 ser.), II, 149; comparison with Fox: Samuel Bayard to William Bradford, June, 1795, *PMHB*, 40 (1910), 305; Maine landholdings: *MHSP* (3 ser.), LVI, 69; Pa. landholdings: references scattered throughout: *Pa. Arch.* (3 ser.), XXV and XXVI; origin of Rush's antagonism: J. H. Powell, *Bring Out Your Dead* (1949), 222-24; litigation over father's estate: Ruston's Executors *v.* Ruston, 2 U.S., 243; deaths of father-in-law and wife: W. W. Bronson, *Inscriptions in St. Peter's Church Yard, Philadelphia* (1879), 427.

PUBLICATIONS: see text

MSS: DLC, NHi, PHi, PPC

Jonathan Dickinson Sergeant

JONATHAN DICKINSON SERGEANT, A.B., A.M. 1765, A.B. College of Philadelphia 1763, A.M. 1771, lawyer and public official, was born in Newark, New Jersey in 1746, the first son of Jonathan Sergeant, treasurer of the College from 1750 to 1777, by his second wife, Abigail Dickinson, a daughter of the College's first president, Jonathan Dickinson. Young Jonathan entered the College's grammar school on November 11, 1755, and thus studied under four presidents—Burr, Edwards, Davies, and Finley. After graduation Sergeant remained in Princeton to study law with Richard Stockton (A.B. 1748), finding time to join the newly established Well-Meaning Club, forerunner of the Cliosophic Society. While still a law student he was also a member of the Sons of Liberty and took part in the controversy over the Stamp Act.

Sergeant began his law practice in Princeton, apparently with considerable success. By 1774 his brother-in-law John Ewing (A.B. 1754), then in London, was suggesting to Sergeant that he ask Lord Dartmouth to make Sergeant a member of the Governor's Council of New Jersey. But Sergeant was occupied with other matters. In 1774 he was one of the defense lawyers in the Cumberland County tea case, and in the same year served as clerk of New Jersey's first provincial congress, to which his father was also a delegate. Passing through Princeton on his way to a meeting of the Continental Congress John Adams made a special point of meeting Sergeant. "We sent a card to Mr. Serjeant a Lawyer," Adams recorded in his diary. "He is a young Gentleman of about 25 perhaps. Very sociable. He gave us much Light concerning

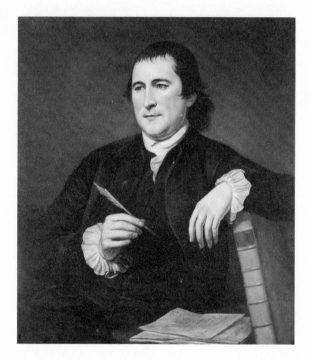

Jonathan Dickinson Sergeant, A.B. 1762
BY CHARLES WILLSON PEALE

the Characters of the Delegates from N. York, Philadelphia, Virginia
&c. and Concerning the Characters of the Principal Lawyers, in all
these Provinces." Whig Jerseymen recognized early and valued highly
Sergeant's talents and dedication to the revolutionary cause: in 1774
and 1775 he served on the Somerset County and Princeton Committees
of Correspondence and as a member of the second provincial congress.
Elected secretary of the Congress, he resigned to serve briefly as
treasurer.

Sergeant found time on March 14, 1775, to marry Margaret Spencer,
daughter of Elihu Spencer, pastor of Trenton's Presbyterian church
and a trustee of the College. The couple had eight children, among
them John (A.B. 1795), twins, Henry and Thomas (both A.B. 1798), and
Elihu Spencer (A.B. 1804). Sergeant built a fine house for his bride
near the present site of the Nassau Club.

Elected to the Continental Congress in February 1776, Sergeant resigned in June in order to remain in the New Jersey Provincial Congress. Appointed almost immediately to a committee charged with

writing a constitution for the new state, within forty-eight hours Sergeant produced a document that endured as the basic law of New Jersey until 1844. He was reelected to the Continental Congress in November 1776. In December Hessians, after sacking his father's home, burned Sergeant's new house. Homeless, he moved to the Philadelphia residence of his brother-in-law, John Ewing.

On February 6, 1777, Sergeant attempted to resign from Congress. "The loss of my house by fire is the least of my misfortunes," he wrote to Speaker John Hart, "as my attention to politics during these unhappy times has at once superseded my business and prevented the collecting of my accounts till the greater part of my debtors, it is to be feared, are either ruined or not to be found. For these reasons I find it necessary to apply myself to some business for the support of my family." Sergeant promised to serve until another delegate could be found to replace him and ended by serving in Congress until November. His wish to resign was doubtless compounded by the death early in 1777 of his father, who had contracted smallpox from the troops in and around Princeton.

In Congress Sergeant was busy with many affairs, one of the chief among them being nagging criticisms of the inadequacies of the commander-in-chief, George Washington. "Thousands of lives and millions of Property are yearly sacrificed to the insufficiency of our Commander-in-Chief," he wrote to Sam Adams on November 20, 1777. "Two battles he has lost for us by such Blunders as might have disgraced a Soldier of three months standing, and yet we are so attached to this Man that I fear we shall rather sink with him than throw him off our Shoulders." But by the time he wrote to Adams, Sergeant was involved in other concerns. On July 28, 1777, he was appointed attorney general of Pennsylvania, though he was not formally commissioned until November 1.

As attorney general, Sergeant, like his brother-in-law Ewing, Joseph Reed (A.B. 1757), and Jonathan Bayard Smith (A.B. 1760), was one of the leaders of the Constitutionalist party, the dominant political group in Pennsylvania for much of the late 1770s and 1780s. His vigorous implementation of Constitutionalist party programs on committees, in public addresses and in the courts led him to be called "Skunk Sergeant"; the party itself soon came to be called the "Skunk Association" by its opponents. Sergeant also prosecuted (some said persecuted) suspected Loyalists and even received a physical beating at the hands of army contractors whose accounts he was investigating.

Sergeant resigned as attorney general on November 20, 1780, writing that "the Office I have held is fatiguing especially as there is very little Reward to Compensate the Labour." (At his appointment his salary had been set at £2,000 Pennsylvania currency.) Sergeant then devoted himself to private practice. Between 1780 and 1783 he pleaded more cases before the Pennsylvania Supreme Court than almost any other lawyer. Occasionally he was appointed to represent his state in important cases. The most significant of these was the precedent-making 1782 dispute between Pennsylvania and Connecticut over lands in the disputed Wyoming Valley, in which several alumni were involved on both sides. For his services in this case alone Sergeant received a fee of £250 plus £73 in expenses, which suggests that his abilities were highly regarded. Part of his fee was invested in Pennsylvania land.

Sergeant remained active in politics throughout the 1780s. One of the leading opponents of the Bank of North America, he presented the case against its establishment to the Pennsylvania legislature. He was also one of the main opponents of the adoption of the federal constitution in his state. Always interested in literature and science, Sergeant served as a trustee of the University of Pennsylvania and in January 1784 was elected to the American Philosophical Society. After the death of his wife in 1787 Sergeant married on December 20, 1788, a woman just half his age, Elizabeth Rittenhouse, daughter of the famed David Rittenhouse. The ceremony was performed by John Ewing in Philadelphia's First Presbyterian Church. Sergeant himself was a member of the Second Presbyterian Church. Three children were born of his second marriage.

Sergeant was a strong supporter of the French Revolution. He was a member of the committee of correspondence set up by the nascent Democratic-Republican party in Pennsylvania in 1792. Extremely active in ministering to the sick during the yellow fever epidemic that struck Philadelphia in 1793, Sergeant himself succumbed to the disease on October 8. "You certainly never felt the terrorism excited by [Citizen] Genet, in 1793," John Adams wrote to Thomas Jefferson twenty years later, "when ten thousand people in the streets of Philadelphia, day after day, threatened to drag Washington out of his house, and effect a revolution in the government, or compel it to declare war in favor of the French revolution and against England . . . nothing but the yellow fever, which removed Dr. [James] Hutchinson and Jonathan Dickinson Sergeant from this world, could have saved the United States from a fatal revolution of government." While Adams may have exaggerated Sergeant's "radicalism," the letter gives a good indication of the significance with which Sergeant's contemporaries viewed him.

SOURCES: Sketches: *PMHB*, 2 (1878), 438-42; D. D. Egbert, *Princeton Portraits* (1949), 244-46; *DAB*; Hageman, *History*, I, 65-69; Ewing offer: L.E.L. Ewing, *Dr. John Ewing* (1924), 22; early revolutionary activities: Butterfield, *Adams Papers*,

II, 113; *Minutes of the Prov. Congr. and the Council of Safety of the State of N.J.* (1879), 253, 445; L. R. Gerlach, "Revolution or Independence? N.J., 1760-1776" (Ph.D. diss., Rutgers Univ., 1968), 610 and passim; N.J. constit.: C. R. Erdman, *The N.J. Constit. of 1776* (1929), and J. P. Boyd, ed., *Fundamental Laws and Constits. of N.J.* (1964), esp. 22-31; Cont. Congr.: *LMCC*, I-II; resignation letter: Hageman, above, I, 68; Washington letter in: B. Knollenberg, *Washington and the Rev.* (1968), 194; Constitutionalist party and politics: R. M. Baumann, "Democratic-Republicans of Philadelphia: The Origins, 1776-1797" (Ph.D. diss., Pa. State U., 1970), 22, 24, 78; Butterfield, *Rush Letters*, 291-92; Loyalists: *PMHB*, 41 (1917), 159-66; beating: ibid., 36 (1912), 73-75, 78; attorney general salary: ibid., 2 (1878), 440; resignation letter: *Pa. Arch.* (1 ser.), 8 (1853), 612-13; SC cases and Bank of N.A.: B. A. Konkle, *George Bryan and the Constit. of Pa.* (1922), 228, 233-34, 254, 273; Wyoming land case: *WMQ*, 26 (1969), 521-47 and sketch of Jesse Root; fee: *Pa. Arch.* (1 ser.), 9 (1854), 738; Bank of N.A.: *PMHB*, 66 (1877), 13; second wife: B. Hindle, *David Rittenhouse* (1964), 304-305; 1790s politics: E. P. Link, *Democratic-Republican Societies* (1942), 80, 170; yellow fever: *WMQ*, 29 (1972), 578; Adams to Jefferson, June 30, 1813, in C. F. Adams, Jr., ed., *Works of John Adams* (1856), X, 47.

Mss: MHi, P, PHi

Dickinson Shepherd

DICKINSON SHEPHERD was born in 1737. The only record the College possesses of him is his gravestone, which at some time in the past was removed from the Princeton Cemetery. It is now in the University Archives in Firestone Library. It reads:

In Memory
of
Dickinson Shepherd
Student of Nassau Hall
who died
Jan 26, 1761
aged 24 year

An extensive genealogical search has not established Shepherd's parentage or place of origin. In 1712 one "Dickison Sheppard" was an elder in the Baptist church at Cape May, New Jersey, but no relation between him and the College's undergraduate has been established.

SOURCES: L. T. Stevens, *Hist. of Cape May, N.J.* (1897), 70.

Hezekiah Smith

HEZEKIAH SMITH, A.B., A.M. Rhode Island College 1769 and D.D. 1797, A.M. Yale 1772, Baptist clergyman, was born in Hempstead, Long Island, New York, on April 21, 1737, the son of Peter Smith and his wife, Rebecca Nicols. When Hezekiah was a child, his family moved to Hanover, Morris County, New Jersey, where he came under the influence of the Reverend John Gano, pastor of Morristown's Baptist church. He was baptized by Gano on February 26, 1756. With his pastor's support Smith defied his father and enrolled in an academy at Hopewell, New Jersey, to prepare for the ministry. Conducted by the Reverend Isaac Eaton, the academy was the first Baptist institution of its kind in the colonies and sent several of its graduates to the College.

Smith entered the College as a sophomore on September 29, 1759. After graduation he began a fifteen-month, 4,000 mile tour of the South, both to regain his health, which had been impaired by his studies, and to acquire experience preaching. The tour culminated in Charleston, South Carolina, on September 20, 1763, with Smith's ordination by the city's Baptist Association. He then acted as a supply preacher to the Cashaway church and other congregations in the Pedee River vicinity.

Early in 1764 Smith traveled north to Rhode Island. There he assisted the Reverend James Manning, a classmate both at Hopewell and Princeton and a close friend, in establishing Rhode Island College, later renamed Brown University. Smith's assistance took the form of a number of fund-raising missions in the South, the most extensive and most profitable of them being in the winter of 1769–1770. For his efforts Smith was made a Fellow of the Rhode Island College Corporation in 1765 and served in the post for the rest of his life.

Smith early won an outstanding reputation as a pulpit orator. After preaching in the Congregational church at Haverhill, Massachusetts, in the summer of 1764 he was invited to become its pastor. When he made known his Baptist affiliation, the invitation was withdrawn, but the town's New Lights promised to form a separate Baptist church, with the result that Smith was installed as its pastor on November 12, 1766. He would serve in the post for forty-two years. In 1767 Smith was among the founders of the Warren Association, the first organization of Baptist congregations in New England. He served on the association's grievance committee from its establishment in 1769, as the Association's moderator in 1769, and as its clerk in 1774. He consistently argued for the separation of church and state, and he composed and signed many petitions and gave many speeches on behalf of that cause. In 1779 he opposed a provision in a new state constitution that promised to continue the Congregationalist establishment. Smith continued his missionary tours long after settling at Haverhill, and so became involved in many controversies with the Baptists' leading opponents.

In May 1775 Smith obtained an extended leave of absence from his congregation and became chaplain of General Nixon's Massachusetts Regiment. On January 1, 1776, he became chaplain of the Fourth Continental Regiment; on January 1, 1777 he took a similar position with the Sixth Massachusetts Regiment; and on August 18, 1778, he became brigade chaplain. He retained this post until he resigned on October 13, 1780. Known throughout the Continental army as "Chaplain Smith," he won wide respect from many, including George Washington, for his bravery, fortitude, and compassion.

After the war Smith returned to Haverhill and reopened the private school he had established just before hostilities began. He also joined the local school committee. In time he became one of the town's most prominent and wealthy citizens. Indicative of his success was the chaise he used for his many travels. His ministry did not win the approbation even of all Baptists. Elias Smith, an itinerant Baptist minister (and eventual schismatic leader of the "New Christian" sect) who preached at Haverhill in 1792 observed that the church had too much sense of respectability and indeed had "more form than spirit." In 1794 Smith was elected a trustee of the Warren Association's newly formed Baptist Education Society, created to assist aspiring young Baptist ministers to obtain a college education.

In the forty-second year of his Haverhill ministry Smith suffered a stroke and died a week later, on January 22, 1805. Dismissed by one contemporary, a Jeffersonian and a Unitarian, as "a man of little learning, small pulpit talents, and no dawn of Genius," Smith was praised by another as "a man of commanding presence, large and well proportioned, inspiring respect by his dignity, and winning affection by his affability and grace." He had married Hephzibah Kimball of Rowley, Massachusetts, on June 27, 1771. Of their six children three sons and a daughter reached adulthood.

SOURCES: R. A. Guild, *Chaplain Smith and the Baptists* (1885); Sprague, *Annals*, VI, 97-103; *DAB*; *GMNJ*, 85 (1954), 85-88; Gano: A. M. Sherman, *Historic Morristown* (1905), 80-82; R.I. College: Guild, *Manning and Brown Univ.* (1864); W. C. Bronson, *Hist. of Brown Univ.* (1914); Haverhill pastorate: I. Backus, *Hist. of New England* (1871), II, 137-38; *MHSP* (2 ser.), 16 (1902), 303, 348; Warren Assoc., missionary tours, etc.: W. G. McLoughlin, *New England Dissent* (1971), I-II, passim.

PUBLICATIONS: STE HS

Caleb White

CALEB WHITE, A.B., was born in Brookline, Massachusetts, on March 10, 1741, the third child and second son of Sarah Aspinwall and Benjamin White, a farmer. The father served as a selectman of the town for several years. After graduation from the College White returned to Massachusetts. On May 14, 1767, he married a second cousin, Elizabeth Craft, daughter of a well-to-do cordwainer of Roxbury. A daughter was born to the couple on September 15, 1768. At about this time White, described as "a young man of unusual promise," was stricken with an undefined "fever," which left him insane. He died in Roxbury on December 16, 1770.

SOURCES: Parentage and marriage: *NEHGR*, 52 (1898), 425; father-in-law: F. S. Drake, *The Town of Roxbury* (1878), 342-43; daughter: *Vital Records of Brookline, Mass.* (1929), 70; fever and insanity: Caleb White File, PUA; death: *Boston News-Letter*, Dec. 20, 1770.

Jacob Woolley

JACOB WOOLLEY, a Delaware Indian, was born in 1743 or 1744, perhaps in the settlement of Christian Indians ministered to by John Brainerd at Cranbury, New Jersey. How Woolley acquired his English name has not been discovered, but a fairly large family of Quaker Woolleys had been present in Monmouth County for some time. Along with another Delaware youth, Woolley was sent by Brainerd to a new Indian charity school, forerunner of Dartmouth College, opened by the Reverend Eleazar Wheelock at Lebanon, Connecticut. The first pupils in the school, the youths began their studies on December 18, 1754.

Woolley entered the College in May 1759, the only Indian known to have attended before 1768. He appears to have been unhappy in Princeton. "I like College as well as ever," he wrote to Wheelock from Nassau Hall on December 14, 1761, "only I think it is too much Confinement: because I want to travel some where or other & get acquainted with Mankind. For I don't see, as I am likely ever to learn anything else, but the Languages & Sciences." The following year tutor Jeremiah Halsey (A.B. 1752) wrote to Wheelock from the College that "we find ourselves obliged to send Jacob Woolley back to you again. He has loitered away so much time this Year, that had he been examined for his standing this Fall, we should have been obliged to degrade him." Halsey lamented the money and time that had been spent on Woolley but said that unless Woolley reformed there was little chance of his ever catching up with his class. He concluded, however, that Woolley was capable of teaching one of the "inferior Classes" in Wheelock's school.

Woolley's conduct did not improve when he returned to Connecticut. He had, apparently, fallen in love with a young woman while in Princeton. Enforced separation did not improve Woolley's disposition.

On July 25, 1763, he signed the following "confession," which is worth quoting at some length:

> I Jacob Woolley acknowledge I have been scandalously guilty of several gross Breaches of the Law of God. Particularly, I have been scandalously guilty of drinking strong Drink to Excess; And of being in a very sinful Passion of Anger, which I shewed by a very boisterous Behaviour, doubling & swinging my Fists, stamping with my Feet, and many violent Motions & Gestures of Body, attempting to throw the Bed and Bed Cloathes out of the Chamber Window; And also by very vile & prophane Language, daring God Almighty to damn me if I were guilty according to what had been reported of me (when at the same Time the Report was true) and frequently challenging of God to it, saying I did not care if I was damned, threatening Vengeance upon the Boy who had reported what he had of me, saying I would be revenged if I were damned for it. And thus I persisted in Imprecations of Damnation upon my self, and blasphemous Treatment of the Sacred Name, against the much repeated and most forcible and kind & urgent Entreaties of M.ʳ Wheelock and M.ʳ Lessly, in Opposition to whose Entreaties to spare and desist from my irreverent and abusive Use and Treatment of the Sacred Name, I increased it with the more Fury & Violence; And also in attempting to go away with [out] Leave or Advice from M.ʳ Wheelock, under whose Conduct Providence has placed me, and pursuing that Design in a very tumultuous Manner, which was aggravated by his Circumstance, that it was on Saturday Evening, Time observed as Holy by Mʳ Wheelock and Family, who were kept in a Ruffle till late in the Night; And also by many undutiful, proud, and ungrateful Expressions toward Mʳ Wheelock.
>
> And all this has been greatly aggravated by the peculiar Obligations I am under to God & Man, by whose Goodness & their Charity I have been so distinguished from all my Nation.

Later in the year Wheelock wrote to President Finley requesting that Woolley be granted his degree, since after his outburst he had returned to his studies. "My hopes are much revived that God will yet make him an Instrument of much Glory to his great Name," Wheelock told Finley. Though Finley seemed amenable to the request, the degree was never granted.

Woolley eventually left Wheelock's charge. On January 20, 1764, the Reverend Joseph Fish (Harvard 1728) of North Stonington, Connecticut, reported to Wheelock that he had met Woolley on the road to

Norwich and had later delivered some letters from Wheelock to Woolley at a nearby Indian settlement. "I found Jacob at his Old Quarters
. . . engag'd in no Business; nor can I learn, e'en from his own Mouth
that he pursues any; except getting a little Fire wood for yᵉ Family
where he eats," Fish wrote. Fish talked with Woolley and tried to persuade him to return to Wheelock and his studies. Woolley replied only
with a "yes" or a "no," and wept. "I cannot tell any further than heretofore," Fish concluded, "what a Character he maintains among yᵉ Indians—his Clothing is much on the decline, and doing nothing to earn
more, (as I told him) he will Soon be naked; with wʰ if Hunger joins
its Force, he may possibly think of his Fathers [i.e., Wheelock's]
house." Nothing more has been discovered of Woolley.

Woolley's case was not unique. Wheelock seems to have had a notable lack of success with his Indians. As Sir William Johnson, superintendent of Indian affairs, observed, Indians "brought up under the
Care of Dissenting Ministers become a Gloomy race & lose their Abilities for hunting &ca spend their time in Idleness & hang[in]g upon the
Inhabit[ant]s. for a Wretched subsistence hav[in]g lost those Qualities
w[hic]h render them usefull to us with[ou]t acquir[in]g any others in
their place."

SOURCES: Background of Cranbury Delawares: C. W. Weslager, *The Delaware Indians, A History* (1972), 261-81; all letters drawn from J. D. McCallum, *The Letters of Eleazar Wheelock's Indians* (1932), 249-62; Johnson quotation: ibid., 21; see
too: Wheelock, *Narrative of the Original Design . . . of the Indian Charity School*
(1763), 33; Fish: *Sibley's Harvard Graduates*, VIII, 417-26.

CLASS OF 1763

James Boyd, A.B.

John Close, A.B.

Robert Cooper, A.B.

David Cowell, A.B.

John Craighead, A.B.

Samuel Eakin, A.B.

Ezekiel Emerson, A.B.

Noah Hart, A.B.

James Jauncey, Jr., A.B.

John Lathrop, A.B.

Joseph Lyon, A.B.

Obadiah Noble, A.B.

William Paterson, A.B.

Tapping Reeve, A.B.

John Simpson, A.B.

William Mackay Tennent, A.B.

James Watt, A.B.

Simon Williams, A.B.

Joseph Worth, A.B.

James Boyd

JAMES BOYD, A.B., Presbyterian clergyman, was born in 1743 at Pequea, Lancaster County, Pennsylvania, to very religious emigrants from northern Ireland. There Boyd was prepared for college by the Reverend Robert Smith. After graduation, Boyd studied theology and received his license from the New Castle Presbytery on July 31, 1766. On the death of Henry Smith, the minister of the combined churches of Newton and Bensalem, Bucks County, Pennsylvania, the congregations unanimously called Boyd to fill the vacancy. There in October 1769 he was ordained by the Presbytery of Philadelphia. Shortly thereafter, he married a woman named Jane, whose last name has not been discovered. In 1774 she gave birth to the first of their eight children. During Boyd's stay in Newton, he carefully increased his material possessions. In 1779 he owned an 80-acre farm, one dwelling place and the labors of an indentured servant; sixteen years later, his taxable property included 173 acres, 3 dwellings, 5 slaves, 4 horses, and 7 cows.

A similar foresight characterized his revolutionary war activities. In 1775, before public opinion had solidified, a local account lists him among Newton's fourteen "non-associators" refusing to "bear arms" against crown officials. Yet he later became known as a "zealous" Whig who used his church to house British prisoners of war. Boyd thus survived the war with his prestige and ambition intact. He served as a trustee of Princeton from 1780 to 1800, while performing the same office for Dickinson College from 1783 to 1787. In local affairs Boyd not only helped establish Newton's library company, but in 1798 acted as the principal teacher at the Bucks County Academy, a "first rate" boarding school. Throughout these years Boyd was apparently a Jeffersonian democrat, for in 1796 he served as an elector for the party in Chester County, Pennsylvania. When Boyd died on February 6, 1814, his parishioners buried him in the Newton churchyard. Over his grave, they erected four massive pillars, surmounted by a marble slab. Engraved on the side is a simple epitaph, proclaiming that James Boyd was "for 45 years and upwards the beloved pastor of our church."

SOURCES: Family background and other materials: James Boyd File, PUA; church career, tombstone, rev. activities: J. L. Vallandigham, *Hist. of Presbytery of New Castle* (1889), 14; *Bucks County Hist. Soc. Papers*, 3 (1909), 390; indentured servant: *PMHB*, 34 (1910), 225; property: *Pa. Arch.* (3 ser.), 13 (1897), 48-49, 537; non-associator, teaching career: E. R. Barnsley, *Historic Newton* (1934), 64, 87; library activities: *Bucks County Hist. Soc. Papers*, 3 (1909), 322; Dickinson: C. C. Sellers, *Dickinson College* (1973), 482; elector: B. Fay, *Early Party Machinery in the U.S.* (1936), 139.

LLM

John Close

JOHN CLOSE, A.B., A.M. 1766, Presbyterian clergyman, was born on September 15, 1737, in either Greenwich, Fairfield County, Connecticut, or North Salem, Westchester County, New York, to Deborah Brush and Solomon Close. The father was a third-generation New Englander and owner of a 326-acre farm. He helped establish the first Presbyterian church in North Salem, where he was an elder and acted as a trustee of the town's academy. At the College John Close was apparently well regarded, for upon his graduation President Finley recommended him as a teacher in Eleazar Wheelock's Indian school. He is "of good parts and not a mean scholar," wrote Finley, "and of good behavior." Instead Close returned to New York and received a license from the Dutchess Presbytery in 1763. He then began three years of missionary work in North and South Carolina. Although he was ordained by the Presbytery of Suffolk in 1767, Close did not immediately occupy his own pulpit. Rather, for the next six years he assisted the Reverend Ebenezer Prime in the church at Huntington, Long Island, while also working within the administrative framework of the presbytery. He served on committees to arbitrate disputes among local congregations, to acquire money for the propagation of the gospel among the poor, and to gather information for ecclesiastical reform. Sometime during this period, he married Mary Wicks of Huntington, Long Island. They had three children.

Two years after receiving an honorary master's degree from Yale, Close was called as minister to the Bethlehem Church in North Windsor, Orange County, New York, in 1773. Here he became an active participant in the Revolutionary War. In 1776 he signed an associators oath at Cornwall to raise arms and resist the crown. Shortly thereafter, he joined the New York militia, serving as a chaplain under the command of Colonel John Hathorn until at least 1779. Upon being discharged from the army, Close returned to his congregation, which in the meantime had moved to Cornwall, Orange County. There he lived an apparently prosperous life, as evidenced by his ownership of three slaves, before moving to a Dutch Reformed parish at Waterford, Saratoga County, New York in 1796.

In the following years Close published several sermons that treated the basis for an ideal social order. One of these explained how a state without an ecclesiastical establishment could bind its citizens to religious purposes. Similar to the theological system of Samuel Hopkins, Close wrote that "love" was the force that afforded its devotees a celestial certainty and allowed God's will to be known across denominations. Unlike divisive faith, love gave intelligent men the ability to lay the foundations of "rational happiness," while distinguishing "devils" from the saved. Finding its goals in advancing the general good, love could banish all disorder from "families, nations, states and the world." Just as men of good conduct "beat down their evil inclinations with the gavel of mortification," so "vice" and "polluters" would flee the community. The result was a nation where charity and the rights of property were honored; where the followers of "universal, superior laws" needed no external, state powers to do the right. "Hence arises the order, proportion and beauty of the stupendous fabric of the moral world." Culminating a life of spreading the new word, Close retired from the pulpit in 1804. When he died on April 9, 1813, he was buried in Waterford, New York.

SOURCES: Family background: S. P. Mead, *Ye Historic Town of Greenwich* (1911), 524, 526; R. Bolton, *Hist. of the County of Westchester* (1905), I, 73, 760, II, 717; Finley's comments: Finley to Wheelock, Sept. 30, 1763, *Letters of Eleazar Wheelock's Indians*, ed. J. D. McCallum (1939), 258; church and revolutionary activities: *Rec. Pres. Church* (1841), 365-92, 400-16, 424-37, 450-71; E. M. Ruttenber and L. H Clark, *Hist. of Orange County, N.Y.* (1881), 304, 757, 767; love sermon: J. Close, *A Discourse on the Superior Excellencies of Love* (1800), 1-12; slave ownership: *U.S. Census of 1790, N.Y.*, 180.

LLM

Robert Cooper

ROBERT COOPER, A.B., D.D. Dickinson 1792, Presbyterian clergyman and farmer, was born in Northern Ireland about 1732. The father died when Robert was nine years old, and his mother then emigrated to Lancaster, Lancaster County, Pennsylvania. There Robert learned the plough-making trade, earning enough money to attend the College. After graduation Cooper studied theology with the Reverend John Roan of Carlisle, Pennsylvania, and married Mary Crawford on April 7, 1764. Receiving his license from the Donegal Presbytery on February 22, 1765, Cooper was asked to supply pulpits on the western frontier, but when Indian attacks began, he was relieved from the assignment. During these years, Cooper became known as a popular preacher, despite his "thin, sparse" appearance and "melancholy disposition." Several congregations asked him to be their minister, but he eventually accepted a call from the parish in Middle Spring, Cumberland County, Pennsylvania, at an annual salary of £100, and was ordained by the Presbytery of Carlisle on November 21, 1765. At Middle Spring he raised his four children and became a prosperous farmer. Over the next twenty years he increased his land holdings from 48

acres to 270 and acquired one of the best private libraries in the area
through the aid of President Witherspoon. Cooper also tutored students for the ministry and carried on an extensive correspondence
with fellow ministers, sprinkling his letters with Latin verses. Clearly
he was recognized as an important figure among Presbyterians, for in
May 1776 he served as moderator of the Synod of New York and
Philadelphia.

Like the majority of his neighbors, Cooper was a zealous Whig. He
not only urged the men in his parish to enlist, but on December 24,
1776 he became a chaplain in the Cumberland County militia. In the
service he gave a notable sermon, entitled "Courage in a Good Cause."
Asking which army was the righteous one, the one that God favored,
Cooper preached, then, that the current rebellion was morally justified. The troops were called upon to fight tyrants who had subverted
the British constitution. An unjust Parliament had sought to make
"slaves" of the unrepresented colonists, taxing them for the support of
"court luxury." The subsequent "civil war" imposed great obligations
on the army to become a true instrument of God's will. The soldiers
were to make their lives a "watch and warfare" against "temptations
from without and corruption from within." Just as they voluntarily
submitted to their officers, so in their voyage through life they must rid
themselves of lustful thoughts and tendencies to debauchery. Through
their victory over sin, they might be able to transcend the fall of Adam
and initiate on American soil a peaceful Eden. Cooper saw action in
the battles of Long Island and Trenton, and later recalled that he had
"marched and countermarched through the Jerseys on foot, so long as
I was able."

Upon Cooper's discharge on January 27, 1777, after only a month's
service, he returned to his parish and resumed numerous administrative duties within the church and in civic life. With his friend and
classmate, John Craighead, Cooper temporarily opposed Benjamin
Rush's plans for Dickinson College. Yet for an unknown reason he
changed his mind and became a warm supporter of the college and
one of the forty trustees serving between 1783 and 1805. In later years
Rush referred to Cooper as a "pious and learned member of the
Board." Despite his success and that of the nation, in 1803 Cooper saw
decay throughout the land, a country filled with "atheistic and an-
archic" influences, so fully embodied in the French Revolution. There
the passion to discard religion had led to a degeneracy far worse than
any "monarchy or hierarchy." Now America faced the same danger.
He even asserted that the writers of the constitution had made a mistake when they separated church from state. But he saw the hope of

salvation for the country in the revivals sweeping over the South and West. Although he feared the false enthusiasms of the Shakers and Methodists, he believed that, through religious revivals, men's behavior would become once again like "a well adjusted machine, all parts duly proportional." During his later years, Cooper suffered from what contemporaries thought was an "inveterate depression," a malady that forced his retirement from the pulpit. Alternating between incapacitation and spurts of activity, Cooper continued his missionary work on the frontier. When he died on April 5, 1805, he was buried in the Middle Spring churchyard.

SOURCES: Family background and church career: Sprague, *Annals*, III, 270-72; *JPHS*, 10 (1919-1920), 61; Nevin, *Churches of the Valley* (1852), 29-33; *Presbyterian Records*, 385, 412, 459, 463, 492-502, 511, 543; marriage and hand holdings: *Pa. Arch.* (2 ser.), II, 66; (3 ser.), XX, 58, 171, 256, 306, 393, 432, 541, 588, 724, writing style: *PMHB*, 24 (1900), 261; army career and sermon: J. J. Pomeroy, *Historical Discourse: Middle Spring Presbyterian Church* (1877), 9-11; "Courage in a Good Cause," given on Aug. 31, 1775, printed in *Shippensburg News* (July 7, 1877), 1; Dickinson College episode: C. C. Sellers, *Dickinson College* (1973), 56-58, 65, 482; Rush comment: *PMHB*, 74 (1950), 452-53; declension sermon: *Signs of the Times* (1803), 1-15; library and death: *Centennial Memorial of the Presbytery of Carlisle* (1889), II, 46.

PUBLICATIONS: see above   LLM

David Cowell

DAVID COWELL, A.B., A.M. 1766, M.B. College of Philadelphia 1768, physician, was born in 1740, probably in Dorchester, Massachusetts, the first son of Sarah and Ebenezer Cowell. The father, a substantial landowner and a smith working largely on guns, swords, locks, and surveyor's instruments, moved to New Jersey about 1761 following the death of his brother David (Harvard 1732), first minister of the Presbyterian church in Trenton, a trustee of the College, and its acting president between the death of President Jonathan Edwards and the arrival of President Davies. In his will the uncle left $20 per year for three years to his namesake, young David, so that the youth could complete his education in the College.

After graduation Cowell studied medicine at the newly constituted Medical Faculty of the College of Philadelphia, receiving his diploma in its first graduating class. Education completed, Cowell settled first in Northampton, Bucks County, Pennsylvania. In 1767 his father conveyed to him over 500 acres of land in Sussex County, New Jersey, and in 1768 two houses in Trenton and more acreage as well. David probably moved from Pennsylvania to Trenton at about this time. He lived on Pennington Road there with his younger brother, Ebenezer, Jr. (A.B. 1766). In 1776–1778 Cowell served as a physician and surgeon with the American army, but no official record of his service has been discovered. His father was one of the leading Whigs in Trenton.

In 1780 Cowell found himself in a bitter public controversy involving his slave, Adam. On January 12 he advertised "to be sold or exchanged for a suitable Negro Boy of about 16 years of age, a sober, healthy, able bodied Negro Man of about 32 years of age, who has had the small-pox, and understands all kinds of farming business, and the care and management of horses, equal to any in the Country." But Adam did not wish to be sold or exchanged, and challenged Cowell's right to do so. On February 2 he ran the following announcement in a newspaper:

> Whereas David Cowell had advertised in the New-Jersey Gazette, "a Negro man to be sold or exchanged for a suitable Negro boy." –As he has no legal right to any such Negro man, nor pretentions to claim any but myself, that I know of, duty to the publick (without any desire to expose his conduct) requires me to inform them, that I have a solemn engagement for my freedom for the consideration therein mentioned, written and executed by his own hand, which he has often attempted, and still persists in endeavouring to violate, although I have very sufficient proof that the said consideration is fully paid him: Therefore this is to caution and warn all persons from buying, exchanging, bargaining, or any way being concerned in an assignment for me, as I have fulfilled my part of the aforesaid agreement, and expect that freedom, justice and protection which I am entitled to by the laws of the state, altho' I am a Negro.
>
> ADAM.

Cowell replied that Adam had received no promises, either oral or written. Adam instead, Cowell claimed, "has proved very unfaithful by a course of disobedience, and attempting last summer to get to New-York, which occasioned me great expense in gaol fees, money paid the guards, and riding more than two hundred miles after him." Cowell claimed that the whole affair was being instigated by two men who wished to employ Adam. Adam—or his supporters—replied the following week in terms Cowell doubtless found somewhat disturbing:

> I might be justified in exposing his [Cowell's] conduct by open design, when perhaps attempting to violate his solemn engagement with me would appear the least exceptionable part of his

character. But I will forbear, only observing, that if a person should become notorious for having defrauded his father, robbed his brothers and sisters of their patrimony, and by venality and debauchery, render his person as nauseous as his character is contemptible, an exposition would avail no more than the repeated curses of an injured country on that Doctor by whose negligence and misconduct numbers of brave soldiers have been sent to eternity, at a time when their services here were most necessary.

Cowell, as later litigation shows, was in fact estranged from his father and some of his brothers and sisters. In his reply, Cowell did not mention his family but stoutly defended his military record and condemned the "unfaithful disobedient negro." The affair was still unsettled at the time of Cowell's death on December 17, 1783. Suffering from quinsy, he made his will shortly before that date. He left "my negro man Adam, and the whole affar [sic] to the Presbyterian Congregation." He also left £100 to the College, £100 to the Trenton grammar school, and £100 to the Congress of the United States if it should settle permanently in Lamberton, New Jersey. The inventory of Cowell's personal property came to £1,162.5.4. His medical shop and books were left to his brother, John, who subsequently took over his Trenton practice. Cowell's family engaged in considerable litigation over his will, which was not resolved until 1795.

SOURCES: Brief sketches of family and father: W. Nelson, *N.J. Biographical and Genealogical Notes* (1916), 79-80; J. Hall, *Hist. of Presbyterian Church in Trenton, N.J.* (2d ed., 1912), 177-78; uncle's will: 33 *NJA*, 94; Adam affair: *N.J. Gaz.*, Jan. 12, Feb. 2, Mar. 1, Mar. 8, 1780; parts of will and subsequent litigation are abstracted in: 35 *NJA*, 97-98, but see original MS, State Lib., Trenton.

John Craighead

JOHN CRAIGHEAD, Presbyterian clergyman, was born near Carlisle, Pennsylvania in 1742, the son of John Craighead, a farmer, and his wife Rachel Rand. Young John's grandfather, the Reverend Thomas Craighead, was an Irish minister who had migrated to New England in 1714, moved to Delaware, and thence to Pennsylvania, where he assumed the pastorate of the Pequea Church, Lancaster County, in 1733. He was dismissed from Pequea in 1736 because of an unseemly family quarrel. He had denied admission to communion to his wife, and she, together with their son John, had refused to live with him. This affair had delayed the presbytery's permission for acceptance of a call to Rocky Spring Church, and after clearance was given, another son, Reverend Alexander Craighead, had refused to preside at the father's installation. Presumably, the younger John was born with a heavy responsibility for redeeming the family name.

Despite his repeated spells of melancholia, John Craighead's career indicated that these hopes were not misplaced. Almost immediately after graduation, he studied theology with Dr. Robert Smith of Pequea, Pennsylvania, and was ordained at the Rocky Spring church in April 13, 1768. In addition to his ministerial duties, Craighead farmed successfully. The owner of a small thirty-acre farm in 1772, over the next twenty-four years he increased his property holdings to include 300 acres, seven horses, and eight cows. He also merged his worldly and spiritual activities with a deep antagonism to British rule. At the beginning of the Revolution, he so aroused his congregation to a patriotic fervor that most of the able-bodied males joined the Pennsylvania volunteers. Until he was wounded in 1780 at Hanging Rock, he alternately acted as chaplain and comrade in arms to his men. Rising from the rank of private in 1776 to captain by 1780, he served at the battles of Brandywine and Long Island. Both before and after the war, he attained a position of some stature in the church. Along with his classmate and friend Robert Cooper, his most conspicuous act lay in opposing Benjamin Rush's (A.B. 1760) plans for a new college in Pennsylvania. Apparently John feared that Dickinson College might rival Princeton as a training ground for ministers.

In 1788 at the age of 46, John married Jean Lamb. No children were born to the couple. Early in 1799, the presbytery relieved John of his ministerial duties because of poor health and "mental derangement." He died eleven days later. A "zealous and faithful servant of Jesus Christ" reads the simple epitaph on his gravestone in Rocky Spring.

Sources: Family background: *PMHB*, 24 (1900), 24-26, 38; career, mental condition and gravestone: A. Nevin, *Men of Mark* (1876), 67-68; land holdings, military career and marriage: *Pa. Arch.* (3 ser.), 19 (1897), 675; 20 (1897), 66, 190, 325, 452, 603; (5 ser.), 6 (1906), 316; (6 ser.), 5 (1906), 174; (2 ser.), 8 (1897), 569; Dickinson College: Butterfield, *Rush Letters*, 301, and D. F. Hawke, *Benjamin Rush*, 287-90.

LLM

Samuel Eakin

SAMUEL EAKIN, A.B., A.M., 1766, Presbyterian clergyman, was born in Pencader, Delaware, in 1745. Licensed by the Lewes Presbytery on May 18, 1768, he was ordained by the Second Philadelphia Presbytery on August 3 of the following year. He served the Third Presbyterian Church of Philadelphia until May 21, 1771, when he was suspended by the Philadelphia Synod.

The synod charged Eakin with deserting his pastoral duties, committing "gross immoralities," with twice failing to appear before the synod to defend himself, and with suborning witnesses to appear on his behalf instead. The initial charges were instigated by the Reverend John Ewing (A.B. 1754) of the First Presbyterian Church in Philadelphia, who had been feuding with Eakin for some time. When finally interrogated by the synod, Eakin confessed to all the charges and declared himself "unfeignedly sorry and deeply penitent."

Following a year's suspension, Eakin was placed on probation for a year under the supervision of the New Castle Presbytery. On May 21, 1773, he was restored to his full ministerial status by the synod. Indeed, the synod was so impressed by his apparent reformation that it appointed him a supply preacher to Philadelphia's First Presbyterian Church.

By late 1773 or early 1774 Eakin had become the first minister of the Presbyterian Church at Penn's Neck, Salem County, New Jersey (not to be confused with the Penns Neck near Princeton). He remained there until 1776, when he returned home to Pencader as minister of its Presbyterian church. The conflict between his ardent revolutionary patriotism and the equally ardent Toryism of his parishioners had prompted his departure from Penn's Neck. His departure cut short his service as a militia chaplain for Salem County, though he may have assumed a similar position in Pencader. In both states Eakin attended as many military drills as possible, never shirking an opportunity to rouse the troops to the cause of the Revolution. Given his contemporary reputation as America's most eloquent preacher, save for George Whitefield, this may have been a fairly easy assignment.

Either because his own health was failing or because the health of his congregation—whether spiritual or financial—was failing, Eakin resigned his Pencader post in 1780, staying on as a supply preacher until his death, at Pencader, on August 29, 1783. He was survived by his wife, Mary Purviance of Philadelphia, a sister of David Purviance (A.B. 1761), and by their two daughters and two of their four sons.

1754

SOURCES: Vital data: Samuel Eakin File, PUA; Alexander, *Princeton*, 84; Giger, Memoirs, 1; Webster, Brief Sketches, Bk. 2; *Appleton's Amer. Biog.*, 11, 288; H. Welbon, *Hist. Pencader Pres. Church* (1936), 22-23; F. R. Brace, *Brief Sketches of N.J. Chaplains in the Continental Army* (1909), 13; Heitman, *Hist. Register of Officers of the Continental Army* (1893); J. W. Barber and H. Howe, *Hist. Col. of State of New Jersey* (1846), 429-430; suspension and reinstatement: *Rec. Pres. Church*, 413-414, 418, 428, 440, 503; will: *A Calendar of Delaware Wills* (1969), 100.

HS

Ezekiel Emerson

EZEKIEL EMERSON, A.B. Presbyterian clergyman, was born in Ux-
bridge, Worcester County, Massachusetts, on March 8, 1732, the son
of John and Mary Emerson. Just before entering the College, Ezekiel
married on March 27, 1760, Catherine Dorr, the daughter of the Reverend Joseph Dorr (Harvard 1711) of Mendon, Worcester County,
Massachuestts. Emerson's married state seems to have been unique
among undergraduates of this period. Faced with a similar undergraduate some years later, President Wheelock of Dartmouth was uncertain how to act. A correspondent of Wheelock's recalled Emerson's
case: "I knew one in Massachusetts who never went to studying till
after he was married & had two Children, who after Two years private
instruction was admitted Junior at the Jersey College, & his circumstances never known to the public till after he was a graduate, at
which time he had a wife and Four Children; & tho' made public then,
yet I never heard the College reproach'd on that account." The Emer-
sons eventually had nine children.

After graduation Emerson was called to be pastor of a church in
Georgetown, Lincoln County, Maine, a seaport village devoted to fishing and farming. Prior to his arrival the community had been divided
into three autonomous townships, and the parish had not been able to
agree on a regular minister for ten years. The most immediate reason
was the friction between Congregationalists and Presbyterians. On
July 1, 1765, the Scottish inhabitants formed a new church and ordained Emerson, a powerful preacher who was convinced that in "religion there is a right way and a wrong way, and I know I am right."
Two days later the remainder of the inhabitants joined their brethren,
and Emerson was once again ordained according to Congregationalist
practice.

As Georgetown's first settled minister, Emerson gained much of his
following through his highly emotional style of preaching. Within a
year the church membership increased from 37 to 100. Nearby settlements also felt his enthusiasm and credited him with the formation of
new churches. In later years the minister described the nature of his
commitments. First, "evangelistic" clergymen were the descendants of
the apostles and emissaries of Christ. As men who had been "reborn,"
they were called upon to convert the world. Dedicated to the calling,
they did not look for honors, riches or acclaim, rather they expected
to "suffer with our Lord" in the promise of future glory. Commending
"themselves to everyman's conscience in the fight of God," the preach-

er set forth in as "lively colors as possible," the torments of Hell for men in revolt against God.

With the coming of the Revolution, Georgetown backed the Whig cause. No direct evidence exists concerning Emerson's own political activities, but it is reasonable to assume that the minister, like the community he served, supported the cause of independence. When the British blockaded the Maine coast and bombarded nearby towns, Emerson moved inland to Norridgewock early in 1778. There he stayed for five years and helped found the town's Presbyterian church. Returning to Georgetown in 1783, he continued to hold the loyalty of his congregation. In 1805, Emerson retired because of illness and mental derangement; he died in Phillipsburg, Lincoln County, Maine, on November 1, 1815.

SOURCES: Family history and Rev. War conditions: *NEHGR*, 3 (1849), 303, 312-13; quotation: Isaac Foster to Eleazar Wheelock, Aug. 3, 1778, Wheelock MSS; Georgetown problems; C. M. Clark, *Hist. of the Congregational Church in Maine* (1940), 130-31; W. D. Williamson, *Hist. of Maine* (1832), II, 89; nature of a minister: E. Emerson, *A Sermon Delivered at New Castle, October 4, 1797* (1798), 3-18; Maine in Rev.: M. J. Smith, *Hist. of Maine* (1949), 203-209, 235-36.

PUBLICATIONS: see above and STE   LLM

Noah Hart

NOAH HART, A.B., physician, was born in Hopewell, Hunterdon County, New Jersey, in 1742 or 1743, the son of Jemina Woolsey and her husband, Ralph Hart. Noah may have been the Hart who entered the College's grammar school on April 25, 1757.

On August 17, 1764, a marriage bond was issued to Noah and to Rachel McKnight, a daughter of the Reverend Charles McKnight of the New Brunswick Presbytery and sister of Dr. Charles McKnight (A.B. 1771). The couple had one child, a daughter.

After his graduation and his marriage Hart studied medicine—first in Philadelphia, then in London, and finally in 1765–1766 under William Cullen at the University of Edinburgh, where he took courses in chemistry, anatomy, surgery, and obstetrics. Hart did not receive a medical degree from Edinburgh. He presumably returned to Hopewell sometime before 1772, for in March of that year he was elected town clerk of Hopewell Township, a post to which he was reelected in 1773. Furthermore, in November 1772 he was appointed commissioner of the peace for Hunterdon County.

Hart remained in Hunterdon County for the rest of his life. The *New Jersey Gazette* of May 9, 1781, which carried a Trenton post office advertisement for an unclaimed letter addressed to him, listed his home as "near Pennington." The March 12, 1782, edition of the *Gazette* carried an advertisement placed by Hart himself, who may have been planning to move. The advertisement announced his desire to sell for cash a plantation of 54 1/4 acres in Cranberry Town, Middlesex County, and "an assortment" of medicines and medical equipment. Of the last two items he noted that "tho' the quantities are small, the variety would make a great addition to a medical shop." Noah apparently had inherited the plantation in 1781 upon the death of his father-in-law, Charles McKnight, whose will he helped execute. His own father died that same year, leaving Noah a bequest of £5. As the son of his father's first wife, he was excluded from the bulk of his father's estate, which went to the second wife and her children.

Whatever plans Noah may have had for a move were short-lived. He died at age forty on September 16, 1783. His wife remarried soon afterward.

SOURCES: Vital data: Noah Hart File, PUA; J. V. Murray, *Hart Family of New Jersey* (1964), printed chart, PPPrHi; H. L. Cooley, *Genealogy of the Early Settlers in Trenton and Ewing* (1883); Aaron Burr, MS Account Book, 272, 273; *NYGBR*, 67 (1936), 118-120; 35 *NJA*, 181, and 5 (2 ser.) *NJA*, 37, 244, 398; *APS Proc.*, 94 (1950), 279-80.

HS

James Jauncey, Jr.

JAMES JAUNCEY, JR., A.B., A.M. 1766, merchant and public official, was the brother of William Jauncey (A.B. 1761). He was born, probably in 1747, at the home of his parents, Maria Smith and her husband, James Jauncey, Sr., one of New York City's wealthiest merchants. After graduating from the College, James, Jr., like William, joined his father's business.

The Jaunceys were merchants who had close official and other ties with London, and perhaps for that reason they were among the leading Tories in the colony. James, Jr., was particularly close to the British after his marriage on November 20, 1773, to Eleanor Elliot, a daughter of Sir Andrew Elliot, once the collector of the Port of New York, and the niece of Sir Gilbert Elliot, a member of the king's privy council and one of the most violently anti-American members of Parliament. Jauncey's in-laws also included the officer who was second-in-command of the British fleet in New York in 1778 and the British minister in Berlin.

In March 1774, Andrew Elliot moved to have his son-in-law named master of the rolls in the royal government of New York. The post, with its salary of £300 per year plus large fees and perquisites, was just below the chief justice of the province in the pecking order on the governor's council. Elliot connived with Councilor William Smith to have young Jauncey's name submitted as part of a plan to undermine the dominant influence of the DeLanceys. And while the nomination was greeted with derision because of Jauncey's youth, the anti-De-Lancey members of the council combined to approve the appointment. As evidence of Jauncey's promising abilities, Smith reminded the council that the young man had just published an admirable pamphlet. If such a pamphlet did exist, it has not survived. The DeLancey objections, that the work was on a metaphysical subject about which no one knew anything and that it had probably been written by "the President of the New Jersey College" anyway, had no effect.

Smith was satisfied that Jauncey's appointment would cause lasting animosity between the Jauncey and DeLancey families. Since the Jaunceys were already unpopular, the loss of DeLancey support would probably mean that James, Sr., would lose his assembly seat. And Smith was also sure that the young master of the rolls would be under heavy fire from the provincial bar while taking the brunt of popular opposition to lawyers. The DeLanceys in turn would be forced to ally with the bar and the "Liberty Boys"—an unstable union that would weaken both partners.

In August 1776, General Washington ordered the expulsion of the Jauncey family from New York. James, Jr., wrote to his old acquaintance Gouverneur Morris to ask what charges were made against him, but Morris refused to intercede. James, Sr., William, and James, Jr., were detained in New Rochelle, New York, where they promised to travel to Connecticut for permanent detention. On the strength of that promise, Washington removed their guard and they were allowed to proceed on their own. The Connecticut Committee of Safety allowed the elder Jauncey to bring his wife and his son's wife from Westchester, New York, to Middletown, Connecticut, at the end of August. For the rest of 1776, James, Jr., and his father-in-law appealed to the New York and Connecticut Committees of Safety to allow the family to return home because no specific charges had ever been made against them. In December, the New York committee refused because it suspected that young Jauncey still claimed his title as a member of the council and because of his relationship to Sir Gilbert Elliot. In fact, the royal governor of New York, William Tryon, continued to regard Jauncey as a councilor throughout his captivity. The Connecticut committee was more lenient. On December 20, the Jaunceys were allowed to go home after promising not to take up arms against the Americans or to report any intelligence they had gathered in Connecticut to the British. No sooner was Jauncey back in New York, however, than he violated his parole by reporting to Tryon all he knew about what he claimed was the waning revolutionary ardor in Connecticut. In May, Washington considered releasing James Jauncey, Jr., from his parole in exchange for the freedom of an American prisoner. But there was no time to execute the plan. Jauncey died on August 8, 1777. He and his wife had no children.

SOURCES: J. O. Brown, *Jaunceys of New York* (1876), 18-19, and 19n, 21; marriage: *New York Marriages*, 203; political stance of N.Y. merchants: V. D. Harrington, *N.Y. Merchant on the Eve of the Rev.* (1935), 350-51; appointment as master of the rolls: T. Jones, *Hist. N.Y. during Rev. War* (1879), II, 12; B. Mason, *Road to Independence* (1966), 18-19; political implications of that appointment, and service in Council: W.H.B. Savine, ed., *Historical Memoirs of William Smith . . . 16 March 1763-9 July 1776* (1956), 172, 174-76, 209, 216, 219, 222; arrest, detention, and parole: Force, *Am. Arch.* (5 ser.), I, 1189; III, 368, 370, 908, 1205, 1321, 1391, 1514; Washington, *Writings*, v, 440-41; Washington's exchange plan: ibid., VIII, 44; *Doc. Col. Hist. N.Y.*, VIII, 685.

RAH

John Lathrop

JOHN LATHROP, A.B., A.M. Harvard 1768, D.D. Edinburgh 1785, Congregational and Unitarian clergyman, was born in Norwich, Connecticut, on May 6, 1739, the son of Mary Kelly, and her husband, William Lathrop, a farmer. Having studied medicine before entering the College, once at the College John turned instead to preparation for the ministry. Upon graduation he read theology with Eleazar Wheelock (Yale 1733) and taught for a year or two at Wheelock's Indian Charity School at Lebanon, Connecticut. His students included Uncas, "the last of the Mohegans," whom he described as "a fat fellow, of dull intellectual parts." Eager, like his mentor Wheelock, "to extend the knowledge of salvation to the heathen nations," Lathrop went in search of converts among the Indians.

On December 24, 1765, the Windham Association of Connecticut licensed Lathrop and sent him off to the First Church of Reading. There, and at other local churches, he preached on a trial basis and aspired to prove his orthodoxy. Yet he was never entirely comfortable with the rigid Calvinism in which he had been reared, and as he grew older he became even less comfortable with it. The apparent result was that to his Reading congregants he proved himself less than orthodox.

John Lathrop, A.B. 1763

In March 1768 Lathrop became a supply preacher for the Reverend Samuel Checkley (Harvard 1743), failing minister of Boston's Old North Church. Checkley died shortly thereafter, and on May 18, 1768, Lathrop was ordained as his successor at Old North. A rousing sermon on the Boston Massacre, delivered the day after the event of March 5, 1770, won him lasting public attention. While most other Boston clergymen scrupulously refrained from comment, deferring to lay orators, Lathrop declaimed boldly on "Innocent Blood Crying to God from the Streets of Boston." Although he refused to place blame, at least formally, on the British, his views were sufficiently pointed to stir the wrath of English critics, to whom he responded.

Lathrop was, however, by nature a gentle and peace-loving soul; as late as December 1774 he neither expected nor wanted revolution to break out. When it did, he became an ardent patriot. Forced to flee British-occupied Boston in 1775, he served as pastor of a Providence congregation. The next year Lathrop returned to Boston, only to discover that his Old North Church, "a model of the first architecture in New England," had been demolished by the British for use as fuel. Lathrop and his parishioners re-assembed at the New Brick Church, whose pastor, Ebenezer Pemberton (Harvard 1721), was in poor health. In May 1779 the two congregations merged, and adopted as their common name the former formal title of Old North, the "Second Church of Boston." Lathrop became their pastor and remained there for the rest of his life.

As minister of Old North, both before and after its merger, Lathrop was entitled to membership on Harvard's Board of Overseers, and he served on the board for forty-eight years until his death. During the last eleven of those years he served as the secretary of the board. In 1778 he became a Fellow of the Harvard Corporation as well. For his service Harvard awarded him an honorary A.M. in 1768 and would have granted him an honorary doctorate too, had the modesty of his reputation as a theologian not barred the way. Edinburgh, however, faced no such qualms and sold him a doctorate in 1785.

Lathrop was married twice: on January 30, 1771, to Mary Wheatley, and, following her death in 1778, to Elizabeth Checkley Sayer on September 14, 1780. She died in 1809. Together, his two wives bore him a dozen children.

By the beginning of the nineteenth century, Lathrop had become increasingly Unitarian in theology and increasingly Federalist in politics. If the intellectual and ideological climate of Boston inspired these changes, so too did Lathrop's inordinately sunny disposition, which invariably overcame any temporary doubts about the future of mankind and the future of America. "The state of things is *now*," he proclaimed in 1784, "more favorable to human happiness than at any former period since the Christian religion was established." Reason, "that principle which the Author of our existence implanted in our breath," would preserve that achievement.

Lathrop's sermons, according to a contemporary, were brief, "practical," and "generally obvious to ordinary minds"—and for all three reasons proved highly popular. Tall, dark-eyed, and gray-haired, he made an impressive appearance whatever the intellectual rigor of his remarks. The considerable influence that Lathrop exercised on his congregation and associates was, in the words of that same contemporary, due finally "rather to his uniformly judicious course than to any remarkable intellectual endowments or acquirements."

In addition to his service to Harvard, Lathrop served as president of both the Society of Promoting Christian Knowledge and the Massachusetts Congregational Charitable Society; as vice-president of both the Massachusetts Bible Society and the Society for Propagating the Gospel among the Indians in North America; and as a member of the American Academy of Arts and Sciences. He was also active in the

Massachusetts Humane Society, the Massachusetts Charitable Fire Society, and the Boston School Committee. Such reform enterprises won him the praise of, among others, George Washington and Benjamin Rush (A.B. 1760). For these "works of Humanity," Lathrop told his Humane Society colleagues, "we shall receive the full reward of our labours, when those who found relief from our hand . . . shall rise up and call us Blessed."

On January 4, 1816, Lathrop died of what his doctors termed lung fever. He was buried with an elaborate funeral.

SOURCES: Vital data: Lathrop File, PUA; *Norwich Vital Records*, I, 70; Sprague, *Annals*, VIII, 68-72; *Sibley's Harvard Graduates*, XV, 428-436; *Innocent Blood Crying to God* (1771); quotations: Uncas: *MHS Col.*, IX, 88; Wheelock: *Memoirs of the Rev. Eleazar Wheelock* (1811), 164; 1784 optimism: *A Discourse on the Peace* (1784); reason: *A Discourse, Preached on March the Fifth, 1778* (1778); reform: *A Discourse before the Humane Society* (1787); Rush: Butterfield, *Rush Letters*, I, 468, 483; Washington, *Writings*, XXIX, 422, XXX, 4.

PUBLICATIONS: STE and Sh-Sh #s 6618, 6619, 6620, 6621, 6622, 6623, 17889, 25822, 25823, 25824, 25825, 28907, 28908, 35076, 35077.

HS

Joseph Lyon

JOSEPH LYON, A.B., farmer, was born in Newark, New Jersey, in 1741, the son of Joseph Lyon and his wife Mary Cook. The father was a farmer and a one-time sloop captain as well. Young Joseph was a great-grandson of Henry Lyon, one of Newark's and Elizabeth's first settlers.

Like his father, Joseph spent most of his life at Lyons Farms, an Essex County agricultural community established by Henry Lyon midway between Newark and Elizabeth. Though he apparently aspired to the ministry, what a contemporary described as a "weakness of the lungs" ruled this out. Nevertheless, he did succeed his father as an elder of Elizabeth's First Presbyterian Church, a position he held for thirty years. A nineteenth-century historian of that church describes Lyon as having the appearance and the demeanor of a "Christian Pilgrim"—tall, slender, humble, patient, generous, even angelic.

Lyon married twice: in 1766, to Rachel Crane, and following her death in 1792, to Sarah Crane, who, though probably related to Rachel, was not her sister. Rachel bore him three children, but Sarah bore him none.

Lyon enthusiastically supported the Revolution, which he later described as a "glorious revolution in favor of liberty and religion." He joined the Newark Committee of Observation at its organization in

1774. At least as appealing to him, however, was membership in the Elizabeth Library Association, which he helped found in 1792.

In 1799 Lyon published a small book entitled *Miscellaneous Essays*. Written as letters to a friend, all the essays at once lamented the "general declension" of the day—as evidenced in denominational discord, lax discipline, and various immoralities—yet held out the prospect of a Second Coming as early as the very next year, at the start of the new century. Hence the "shaking" of the "foundations" of faith then at hand might, Lyon believed, ultimately yield national if not universal unity and progress. Whatever might occur, Lyon's confidence in the new national government remained firm.

Lyon died in Elizabeth on May 14, 1821, and was buried in the First Presbyterian Church's yard. The inventory of his personal property came to $71.11, one half of which he left to his wife, who he stipulated could remain in his home six months after his death.

SOURCES: Vital data: Joseph Lyon File, PUA; S. E. Lyon, ed., *Lyon Memorial* (1907), II; S. R. Winans, "Biographical Sketches of the Elders in . . . the First Presbyterian Church of Elizabeth, New Jersey," MS, PPPrHi; *Minutes of the Prov. Congress . . . of the State of N.J.* (1879), 38; Elizabeth Lib. Assoc.: Hatfield, *Elizabeth*; will: MS, N.J. State Lib., Trenton.

HS

Obadiah Noble

OBADIAH NOBLE, A.B., A.M. Dartmouth 1773, Congregational clergyman, farmer, and public official, was born in Sheffield, Massachusetts, on September 6, 1739, the son of Obadiah Noble and his wife Mary Bosworth. On November 5, 1771, he was ordained as first pastor of the Congregational Church of Orford, New Hampshire, which he had helped organize. He remained as pastor until he was dismissed, apparently for lack of funds, on December 31, 1777.

For at least the last two years of his pastorate, Noble spent considerable time as chaplain of the New Hampshire militia. He was present at the surrender at Saratoga and probably at other engagements. The extent to which Noble inspired the American troops is unclear. Philip Fithian (A.B. 1772), who heard him read a military sermon, found Noble to be a moving speaker.

In 1777 or 1778 Noble moved to Tinmouth, in Rutland County, Vermont. There he acquired the farm of a man who had been killed as a suspected Tory. When Rutland County became formally organized, Noble served as its first court clerk from 1781 to 1789 and as its first justice of the peace from 1789.

A contemporary described Noble as "a man of great benevolence," of "medium size with broad shoulder, full deep breast, muscular frame, stout neck, full face, dark eyes, and dark hair." He lived to be 89, dying at Tinmouth on February 19, 1829. He had outlived his eighteen College classmates. His wife, Rebecca White, whom he married on August 11, 1774, died four years after her husband. They had three sons, one of whom, also named Obadiah, succeeded his father as a Rutland County justice of the peace and later became a state senator.

SOURCES: Vital data: Obadiah Noble File, PUA; Alexander, *Princeton*, 86; Giger, Memoirs, I; L. M. Boltwood, *Hist. and Genealogy of Family of Thomas Noble of Westfield, Mass.* (1878), 392-93; H. P. Smith and W. S. Rann, *Hist. of Rutland Cty., Vt.* (1886), 824-825; *Fithian Journal*, II, 192.

HS

William Paterson

WILLIAM PATERSON, A.B., A.M. 1766, LL.D. 1805, LL.D. also Univ. State of N.Y., 1792, Dartmouth, 1805, Harvard, 1806, lawyer and public official, was born in County Antrim, Ireland, on December 24, 1745, the son of Richard Paterson and his wife Mary. Paterson's family migrated to America in 1747. After some wandering, his father, a tinplate-maker and peddler, settled in 1750 in Princeton, where he achieved a more than modest prosperity as a storekeeper and land dealer. William saw Nassau Hall arise one hundred yards from his home, entered the College's Latin grammar school on May 1, 1757, and joined the freshman class in 1759. It was an association that would last a lifetime; he would later serve for sixteen years as a trustee of the College. On graduation Paterson delivered a "Cliosophic" oration (a word made up by himself to mean "in praise of wisdom") and joined in 1765 with friends still in the College to found the Well-Meaning Club, which lasted until 1768, when it was disbanded by the College authorities. He was instrumental in persuading the authorities to revive the club in 1770 as the Cliosophic Society, one of the earliest of permanent student literary and debating societies.

In 1763 Paterson signed himself on for a five-year legal apprenticeship to Richard Stockton (A.B. 1748), while continuing his informal education in the Well-Meaning Club. In 1766 he was awarded the A.M. and delivered what a New York newspaper called "an excellent Oration on Patriotism . . . in which Elegance of Composition, and Grace and Force Action were equally conspicuous." Legal education completed, he moved to rural New Bromley, Hunterdon County, to set himself up in a law practice. It did not flourish. In 1772 Paterson

William Paterson, A.B. 1763
BY EDWARD LUDLOW MOONEY

moved to Raritan, Somerset County, New Jersey, where for the next three years he taught law to a few apprentices and spent as much time running a branch of the family store as practicing his profession. Law and shopkeeping made a happy combination: customers who did not pay the merchant's bills found themselves pursued as far as New Jersey's highest court by the lawyer.

Paterson was not involved in active opposition to the royal government in the early 1770s. He appears to have followed rather than to have led his friends and associates (mostly Whigs) in their actions and ideological development. In 1775 and 1776 he was sent as a delegate from Somerset County to the revolutionary New Jersey Provincial Congress. There his reliability, his capacity for hard work, and his organizational ability quickly became evident. An evaluation written a decade and a half later describes the impression he made throughout his career: Paterson "is one of those kind of Men whose powers break in upon you, and create wonder and astonishment. He is a Man of great Modesty, with looks that bespeak talents of no great extent, but he is a Classic, a Lawyer, and an Orator,—and of a disposition so favourable to his advancement that every one seemed ready to exhalt him with their praises." Chosen attorney-general of the new state in September 1776, he prosecuted Loyalists vigorously and established a lucrative law practice among the wealthiest and most important men of the state. At the beginning of the Revolution he was an obscure country lawyer; at its end he was a leader of the legal profession, living with his family and slaves on a 350-acre estate (confiscated from a Loyalist) on the banks of the Raritan River.

Paterson's wartime prosecution of Loyalists did not extend to the family of his wife, Cornelia Bell, whom he married in 1779. The Patersons had three children. The oldest, also Cornelia, married Stephen Van Rensselaer, the patroon. After his wife's death in 1785 Paterson married Euphemia White.

Ambition bred success. Paterson was elected to the Continental Congress in November 1780, but in June 1781 declined to serve because of other duties. In 1787 he served as one of New Jersey's delegates to the Constitutional Convention in Philadelphia. There he presented the "New Jersey Plan" (the actual authorship is uncertain), which drew attention to the situation of small states. At home he fought hard for the adoption of the new constitution. In March 1789, Paterson was elected to the United States Senate. A strong supporter of Hamiltonian policies, Paterson's most significant role in the Senate was the assistance he gave to Oliver Ellsworth (A.B. 1766), a fellow-Cliosophian, in drafting the Judiciary Act of 1789, the basis of the present federal legal system. Elected governor of New Jersey on October 30, 1790, Paterson resigned his Senate seat two weeks later. As governor of New Jersey he supported the founding of a newly planned industrial city at the falls of the Passaic, which was named for him. In 1792 he began a codification of the laws of the state and a remodeling of its court system.

In 1793 President Washington appointed Paterson an associate justice of the United States Supreme Court. It was the beginning of wearying years of traveling to sit on circuit courts. In his decisions Paterson was a strong nationalist, enunciating the principle of judicial review eight years before John Marshall. In the late 1790s Paterson became famous—or notorious—as the "avenger of Federalism" in a number of trials brought under the sedition laws. He acted as both judge and, in effect, prosecutor in the trial of congressman Matthew Lyon for seditious libel.

Paterson's public and private life reflected the Whig ideology he had imbibed at Princeton. "Republicanism," he once explained, "delights

in virtue, which is an active principle, and excites to honesty and industry, and of course is opposed to idleness and sloth. The equalizing
of property by the strong hand of power would be a tax upon the
active and industrious man for the support of the sluggard . . . That nation, however," he went on, "bids fairest to attain the summit of political prosperity and happiness, in which property, especially if it be of
a landed nature, is fairly equally diffused among the people."

Paterson's health began to fail in the summer of 1806. In September
he set for a New York spa in hopes of a cure, but died en route at the
home of his daughter, Cornelia Van Rensselaer. Ambition, industry,
a steady talent and the opportunity opened by a revolution brought
the tin-plate-maker's son from County Antrim to burial in the vault of
the Manor House of the Van Rensselaers.

SOURCES: No good full length biography of Paterson exists, but see: G. S. Wood,
William Paterson of N.J. (1933); sketches: J. P. Boyd, "William Paterson, Forerunner of John Marshall," in Thorp, *Eighteen from Princeton*; M. Kraus, "William Paterson," in L. Friedman and F. L. Israel, eds., *Justices of the U.S. Supreme Court*
(1969), I, 163-82; L. B. Rosenberg, "William Paterson: N.J.'s Nation-Maker," *N.J.
Hist.*, 85 (1967), 7-40; R. C. Haskett's "William Paterson, Counselor at Law," (Ph.D.
diss., Princeton U., 1951), is exhaustive and revealing on Paterson's early life; attendance at CNJ grammar school: Aaron Burr, MS Account Book, 116-17.

Mss: DLC, MHi, NjHi, NjP, NjR, NN

Tapping Reeve

TAPPING REEVE, A.B., A.M. 1766, LL.D. 1813, Middlebury 1808, lawyer, legal educator and public official, was born at Brookhaven, Long
Island, on September 20, 1744, the son of Deborah Tapping (or Top-
ping), second wife of Abner Reeve (Yale 1731), a Presbyterian clergyman. Although the father spent the last twenty-six years of his life as
the respected pastor of the First Congregational Church in Brattleboro, Vermont, during Tapping's youth he was dismissed from two
pulpits because of extended periods of alcoholism.

After graduation Reeve moved to Elizabethtown, New Jersey,
where he was employed by Timothy Edwards (A.B. 1757) as tutor to
Edwards's niece and nephew, Sarah (Sally) and Aaron Burr (A.B.
1772), the orphaned children of the College's second president, Aaron
Burr. In the fall of 1766 a Latin grammar school sponsored by the
Presbyterian church opened in Elizabethtown, with Reeve and Ebenezer Pemberton (A.B. 1765) as the school's first masters. The enterprise was a success, so much so that the College's trustees called Reeve
back to Princeton in September 1769, to serve as tutor to the freshman

class. Reeve resigned his post the following September and traveled north to Hartford, Connecticut, where he studied law with Jesse Root (A.B. 1756).

Admitted to the Connecticut bar in 1772, Reeve on June 21 of the same year married his former pupil, Sally Burr, in a ceremony held in Stockbridge, Massachusetts, where Sally's guardian, Timothy Edwards, had recently settled. After their marriage, the Reeves moved to Litchfield, Connecticut, where they remained for the rest of their lives. In neighboring Bethlehem, Sally Reeve's young brother Aaron, recently graduated from the College, was studying divinity with the theologian Joseph Bellamy. Giving up thoughts of the ministry, in the spring of 1773 young Burr moved in with the Reeves in Litchfield. While Burr may have studied law with Reeve, as has often been stated, most of his legal training was carried on with Thomas Smith (A.B. 1754). Reeve was intensely devoted to his wife, a chronic asthmatic who needed constant care and attention. He built a special large-windowed room onto their house in order to provide Sally with an abundance of fresh air. One child, Aaron Burr Reeve (Yale 1802), was born to the couple.

Reeve quickly established a successful law practice, which was interrupted by the Revolution. In December 1776 the Connecticut Assembly appointed Reeve, along with his former mentor Jesse Root and Oliver Ellsworth (A.B. 1766), as members of a committee "to arouse the people" of Connecticut in support of the Revolution. Although Reeve accepted an officer's commission in the army, he saw no active duty.

During the war legal business languished. Reeve, like many other lawyers, began to take young men into his office to train them for the law. The students grew in number; Reeve systematized his teaching; and, by 1784, he had established, almost inadvertently, the first and most famous independent American law school. By 1798 over two hundred aspiring lawyers had passed through Reeve's course. In that year he hired James Gould (Yale 1791), a graduate of his school, as associate lecturer. By the time the school closed in 1833 over one thousand scholars had attended it: at least fifty-two from Princeton, over two hundred from Yale, thirty-five from Harvard, twenty-nine from Brown, and twenty-four each from Columbia, Dartmouth and Williams. Sources differ, but one estimate has it that Reeve's school produced six members of the national cabinet, two vice presidents of the United States (Aaron Burr and John C. Calhoun), twenty-eight United States senators and 101 congressmen, three justices of the Supreme Court, and ten state governors.

Litchfield's canopy of elms and elegantly foursquare facades shel-
tered intense political and religious passions. The town was a nest of
Federalism in its most concentrated form, and Reeve was one of its
most outspoken proponents. Beginning as a firm supporter of the constitution, Reeve's defense during the late 1790s and early 1800s of the
"Standing Order" (the establishment) in his state and his attacks on
Jeffersonian Republicanism in the nation became ever more strident.
Often signing himself "Phocion" (after the ancient Greek general condemned to death by the democratic party in Athens on a false charge
of treason), his many newspaper attacks, published in the Litchfield
Monitor, reached their culmination not long after Jefferson's assumption of the presidency, on December 2, 1801:

> . . . the Virginians having gained an absolute ascendancy in our
> Councils, they are now, through the medium of their President,
> who professes himself to be at the head of their party, stabbing
> the Constitution to its vitals.—My Countrymen, be prevailed
> upon to examine for yourselves; and although I believe it will not
> be in your power to prevent the ruin that threatens us;—and that
> our privileges, both Civil and Religious, are destined, by the
> Righteous Governor of the Universe, provoked by our rebellion
> against him, to be swallowed up in the frightful, yawning gulph
> of Atheism: Yet I conjure you not to be made subservient to your
> own ruin,—not to plant thorns under your dying pillows, by lis-
> tening to the syren songs of Jacobinism.

Reeve's articles helped to light a long fuse. The explosion came in
1806 when Pierpont Edwards (A.B. 1768), a Jeffersonian, newly appointed United States district judge for Connecticut, and uncle of
Sally Reeve, decided to repay the Federalists in kind by launching
prosecutions for libel against the United States. Federal grand jurors
shortly returned indictments for seditious libel against Reeve (on the
basis of the article quoted above) and several other critics of President
Jefferson. The president remained aloof. Edwards (one would like to
know whether or not he realized his original charge would involve
members of his own family) refused to issue a warrant for Reeve's arrest, and the case was not prosecuted.

Reeve's attack on Jefferson, Virginia, and atheism contained elements other than simple Federalist bile; he sought also to preserve
what he thought were New England's habits of piety, virtue, and sobriety. In 1781 Reeve had participated in a landmark case involving the
abolition of slavery in Massachusetts; throughout his career he was
noted for his defense of fugitive slaves. Instrumental in bringing the

evangelist Lyman Beecher to a pulpit in Litchfield, Reeve (perhaps with memories of his own father), helped found a local temperance group. In 1812 he was among the leaders of a Connecticut society concerned with the promotion of good morals and the suppression of vice. He was active too in the Connecticut Bible Society.

Reeve did not confine his activities to teaching, polemics, and moralizing. He served Litchfield County as a justice of the peace in every year from 1783 through 1798. Twice nominated for Congress (in 1790 and 1792), he did not win election, though he served on the Connecticut Council in 1792. In 1798 Reeve was made a justice of Connecticut's superior court, sitting until 1814, when he became chief justice of the supreme court of errors. Forced to retire because of age in 1815, Reeve turned his hand to the composition of legal texts to increase his reduced income. His major work, accounted by Roscoe Pound the beginning of "American text writing as a significant force in our legal development," was published in 1816. Entitled *The Law of Baron and Femme; of Parent and Child; of Guardian and Ward; of Master and Servant; and of the Powers of the Courts of Chancery. With an Essay on the Terms Heir, Heirs, and Heirs of the Body,* it went through four editions and was familiarly known to generations of law students as "Reeve's Domestic Relations."

Reeve's own domestic relations were shattered in 1797 with the death of delicate, diminutive Sally Reeve. On April 30 of the following year Reeve married his housekeeper, Betsey Thompson. A neighbor, Catherine Beecher, left a vivid record of the new household:

> Judge and Mrs. Reeve were as peculiar in their personal appearance as in their character. He had a pair of soft dark eyes of rare beauty, a beaming expression of intelligence and benevolence, while his soft gray hair fell in silver tresses to his shoulders in a style peculiar to himself. His figure was large and portly, and his manners gentle and dignified. His voice was singular, having failed for some unknown cause, so that he always spoke in a whisper, and yet so distinctly that a hundred students at once could take notes as he delivered his law lectures.
>
> Mrs. Reeve was the largest woman I ever saw, with a full ruddy face, that had no pretensions to beauty; but her strong and cultivated mind, her warm and generous feelings, and her remarkable conversational powers made her a universal favorite. She was both droll and witty, while she made so much sport of her own personal appearance that it removed all feeling of its disadvantages.

At this time Judge Reeve had taken home the widow and infant boy of his only child, [Aaron] Burr Reeve, who died [1809] just before father's removal to Litchfield. Young Mrs. Reeve was a tall, graceful, and very beautiful woman, and little [Tapping] Burr Reeve one of the most perfect specimens of infant beauty.

Reeve died in Litchfield on December 13, 1823. "Oh Judge Reeve, what a man he was!" his pastor Lyman Beecher wrote. "When I get to heaven, and meet him there, what a shaking of hands there will be!"

SOURCES: Sketches: *DAB*; D. C. Kilbourn, *Bench and Bar of Litchfield County* (1909), 42-45; D. H. Fischer, *Rev. of Am. Conservatism* (1965), 290-91; Lyman Beecher, in *Christian Spectator* (Feb. 1827), 62-71; father: Dexter, *Yale Biographies*, I, 434-45; N. S. Prime, *Hist. of Long Island* (1845), 228-29; Elizabethtown tutoring: Hatfield, *Elizabeth*, 519-20; Elizabethtown academy: 25 *NJA*, 227-28; CNJ tutor: MS CNJ Trustees' Minutes, I, Sept. 29, 1769, and Sept. 26, 1770; relations with Sally and Aaron Burr: H. S. Parmet and M. B. Hecht: *Aaron Burr* (1967), 13-16; marriage date: *NYGBR*, 72 (1941), 218; Conn. public career: *Rec. State Conn.*, I, v-ix; Litchfield Law School: S. H. Fisher, *The Litchfield Law School, 1775-1833* (1933); A. Z. Reed, *Training for the Public Profession of the Law* (1921), 128-33; Pound quotation: R. Pound, *Formative Era of Am. Law* (1938), 140; libel case: L. Levy, *Jefferson and Civil Liberties* (1963), 60-66; pro-abolition: *WMQ*, 25 (1968), 619; Catherine and Lyman Beecher quotations: B. M. Cross, ed., *Autobiography of Lyman Beecher* (1961), 156, 162-63.

MSS: CtHi, PHi

PUBLICATIONS: above and Sh-Sh #45478; Sh-Co #s 2950, 22043

John Simpson

JOHN SIMPSON, A.B., A.M. 1766, Presbyterian clergyman, was born about 1740 in New Jersey, the son of Archibald Simpson, a Scots Irishman. During his years at the College, his classmates expressed their disapproval of the Stamp Act by wearing homespun clothing and delivering passionate discourses on patriotism and "Liberty." Afterward his career as a minister and militant advocate of American independence mirrored these early enthusiasms. Following two years of theological study, the Presbytery of New Brunswick licensed him in 1770. For the next two years he preached in East Town, New Jersey. Then the Synod of Philadelphia assigned him to missionary work on the southern frontier. Temporarily leaving behind his wife, Mary Remer, whom he married in 1765, Simpson went into the sparsely settled areas of Virginia, North Carolina, and South Carolina. He soon became the permanent minister of the Presbyterians at Fishing Creek, South Carolina, and was ordained by the Presbytery of Orange in 1773.

As his congregation's first regular minister, Simpson struggled to bring the essentials of order to a rural parish. Besides enforcing the piety and strict restraints of the Sabbath, he insisted that the laity pass a written examination on religious doctrine. To insure that the next generation was equally prepared, he encouraged the education of each child admitted to the church. Only when the minister tried to introduce Isaac Watts's hymnal and discourage the singing of traditional tunes such as "Dublin," "Isle of Wite," and "London" did conflict develop. Shortly thereafter, the congregation further divided between Whigs and Tories. Simpson was also involved in a struggle to attain a royal charter for Queen's College in Charlotte, North Carolina, the nearest town to his church. Along with his classmates Waightstill Avery (A.B. 1766) and Hezekiah Balch (A.B. 1766), he hoped that an institution of higher education would further the prosperity of the new settlements.

In July 1776, Simpson gave his support to a proclamation by the North Carolina Committee of Safety that refused to respect the tax or police powers of the English government. He not only became a trustee of Queen's College, appropriately renamed Liberty Hall Academy, but also joined the revolutionary army commanded by General Sumter and fought in the battles of Beckhamville and Mobley's. During the British retaliation against the rebellious citizenry, Simpson's house and belongings were burned.

With the end of the hostilities, Simpson helped organize the Synod of South Carolina, and in 1790 accepted the ministerial duties at a church in Pendleton. Amid the plantation economy of the state, Simpson apparently achieved a measure of prosperity and prestige through the ownership of five slaves. Near the end of his life Simpson began to see in the current revivals the continuation and probably the culmination of his career. Together with ministers from several denominations, he preached to quickly assembled camp meetings scattered across the countryside. He died in 1808 and left behind his wife and seven children.

SOURCES: University environment: Wertenbaker, *Princeton*, 30-40, *N.J. Gaz.*, Oct. 2, 1766; family background, church career, military service: *Southern Presbyterian Review*, April 1853, 547-558; Liberty College, revolutionary politics: *St. Rec. N.C.*, 24 (1905), 30; *Am. Arch.* (5 ser.), I, 1366; slaves: *U.S. Census 1790, S.C.*, 13.

LLM

William Mackay Tennent

WILLIAM MACKAY TENNENT, A.B., D.D. Yale 1794, Congregational and Presbyterian clergyman, was born at White Clay Creek, New Castle County, Delaware on January 1, 1744, the eldest son of Martha Mackay (or Macky) and Charles Tennent. The father, a Presbyterian clergyman who had been educated at the Log College, was the youngest son of William Tennent I, the famous New Side Presbyterian evangelist.

After graduation young William studied for the ministry, possibly with his father. Licensed by the Presbytery of Lewes in May 1770, Tennent was called to the Congregational church at Greenfield, Connecticut, in 1772 and ordained there on June 17. In September of the following year Tennent married Susanna Rodgers, a daughter of the Reverend John Rodgers of New York City, a trustee of the College.

As early as July 11, 1776, Tennent was serving as a chaplain to Brigadier General David Waterbury's Connecticut militia units. Tennent may have been among the troops at Fort Ticonderoga in July of that year, but this is uncertain. It has been said that Tennent, though "greatly beloved by all his acquaintances" was "not popular as a preacher." His record, however, seems to belie this. When his uncle, William Tennent, Jr. (II), of Freehold, New Jersey, died in 1777, William Mackay was asked to succeed to the pastorship of that important Presbyterian congregation. Tennent declined; his Connecticut church promptly raised his salary. His surviving sermons seem neither more nor less "popular" than those of his peers—indeed, they are more fluid and moving than most.

In 1781 Tennent accepted a call from the Presbyterian church in Abington, Montgomery County, Pennsylvania, where he spent the rest of his life. Tennent and his wife had one child, born on January 22, 1793, twenty years after their marriage. The infant girl lived less than four months. Tennent and his wife were very close. "Friday evening brought me to our habitation & I found all well," he wrote to her on April 18, 1796, in a typical letter. "*Nimble-Toes* remarkably glad to see me but he was disappointed by your absence. He is in good health— but his spirits not high. In this respect a little like his master."

Tennent's activities extended far beyond his parish. He became a trustee of the new Norristown Academy in 1804. In 1797 he assumed the important post of moderator of the Presbyterian General Assembly, and in late 1800 made an extensive tour of Delaware and the eastern shore of Maryland in order to raise funds for the body. (The trip netted $1,476.) He also served as a very active trustee of the College from 1785 to 1808. After the gutting of Nassau Hall by fire in 1802 Tennent was among the trustees who made grueling trips to raise funds for rebuilding. The task was often discouraging. "In this country where I hoped for much I shall get next to nothing," he wrote to his wife from Somerset County, Maryland, on June 10, 1803. "Have rode many miles in it & pressed hard but . . . have received less than $60. This has been occasioned by the unfinished state of a large & elegant Academy lately erected in the County & in which are at present upwards of 60 students. The richest inhabitants altho' formerly my disciples absolutely decline doing any thing for me." Their warm hospitality toward Tennent did not compensate for his efforts.

Tennent was still raising funds for the College in 1805. On July 15 of that year he wrote thus to his wife from Dover, Delaware: "I have been and shall be careful as you & your good father have kindly directed with respect to the heat. For some days have rode in my gown & a pair of nankeen pantaloons so spruce that [you] will be at least pleased with my caution. Your resolut[io]n not to let me ever go again so long from home is a testimony of [tha]t tender friendship for w[hich] I shall always be in debt to the best of wives. One thing I promise you—I will never go on a begging tour again." He never did.

Tennent died at Abington on December 2, 1810. The Reverend Ashbel Green (A.B. 1783) of Philadelphia, shortly to become president of the College, preached the funeral sermon.

SOURCES: Brief sketches of Tennent and father: Sprague, *Annals*, III, 26; Greenfield pastorate: E. B. MacRury, *MORE About the Hill, Greenfield Hill* (1968), 330; Freehold call: M. A. Tennent, *Light in Darkness* (1971), 113; preaching popularity: Alexander and Carnahan, Notes of Distinguished Graduates, MS, NjP; quality of sermons: see four MS sermons, 1800-1807, PPPrHi; chaplaincy: Force, *Am. Arch.* (5 ser.), I, 195; Ticonderoga: J. T. Headly, *Chaplains and Clergy of the Rev.* (1864), 376; Abington pastorate: T. W. Bean, *Hist. of Montgomery County* (1884), 686; Norristown Acad.: *Bull. of the Hist. Soc. of Montgomery County, Pa.*, 12 (1959-61), 28; quotations: all from MS letters, PPPrHi; funeral sermon: Green, *The Life and Death of the Righteous* (1811).

Mss: PHi, PPPrHi

James Watt

JAMES WATT, A.B., A.M. 1766, Presbyterian clergyman, was born at St. George Hundred, New Castle County, Delaware, on March 12, 1743, the son of Mary and Robert Watt. After graduation Watt studied for the ministry. The Presbytery of Lewes licensed him to preach on July 30, 1767. In May of the following year the Presbyterian church at Cold Spring, Cape May County, New Jersey, asked Watt to settle permanently there as its pastor. Ordained under the auspices of the First Presbytery of Philadelphia at Greenwich, New Jersey, on April 23, 1770, Watt was installed at the Cold Spring church on May 12. The congregation gave him a salary of £55 per year, but supplemented this with a parsonage and the use of a plantation owned by the church. A few months after his installation, on October 22, Watt married Rachel Hand of Cape May. After Rachel's death in 1782 Watt married a woman named Hannah, whose last name has not been discovered. Before her death on April 12, 1785, Hannah bore him a daughter who lived only four months.

Watt was reported to be "celebrated for his humor, fond of anecdote and liberal attachment to the good things of the world." One day Watt, two other clergymen and some summer vacationers set off from Cape May in whaleboats on a devilfish-harpooning expedition. The clergymen struck a devilfish that pulled their boat along at a terrifying pace. One clergyman suggested that they all join in prayer, at which Watt burst into laughter. When all parties were safely ashore Watt was asked what he thought had been so funny about the situation. "The peril *was* imminent, perhaps," Watt replied, "but for my life I could not help laughing at the idea of the devil carrying off three ministers!" Watt was not all chuckles. His congregation increased during his ministry and was swept by a revival in 1780. Watt died on November 19, 1789. At the time of his death his church was £150 in arrears on his salary. He left this money to the church for the use of the poor. Aside from some personal bequests, he left all the rest of what appears to have been considerable property to his young niece, Ann Watt, who had been living with him. "If disinterested kindness and integrity, justice and truth deserve the tributary tear—Here it is claimed," reads the inscription on his gravestone.

SOURCES: Alexander, *Princeton*; considerable material: James Watt File, PUA; marriages: P. S. Howe, *Mayflower Pilgrim Descendants in Cape May County* (1921), 388; quotation and anecdote: R. C. Alexander, *Ho! For Cape Island!* (1956), 13-14; will: MS, N.J. State Lib., Trenton.

Simon Williams

SIMON WILLIAMS, A.B., A.M. 1766, Presbyterian clergyman, was born about 1733 in Trim, the county of Meath and province of Leicester, Ireland, probably to wealthy parents. At the age of sixteen, according to family recollection, Simon fled Ireland with his bride-to-be, Maria Floyd, the daughter of John Floyd, a captain in the British army. Because her parents refused to permit a union with one beneath her social class, the couple married in London, England, in 1749. They soon sailed for Jamaica, where Simon taught school for eight years and his first four children were born. Moving to Philadelphia in 1760, Simon came under the influence of Gilbert Tennent's preaching. He became so committed to the New Light that he tutored in two revivalist schools, one in West Nottingham, Maryland under the Reverend Samuel Finley, the other in Fagg's Manor, Pennsylvania, run by the Reverend Samuel Blair. In addition, Simon named his next two sons after his mentors: Samuel Finley and Gilbert Tennent Williams. Both grew up to be New England ministers. Simon also followed Samuel Finley to the College of New Jersey when Finley became the president in 1761, and upon graduation taught at an English school sponsored by the College. On October 17, 1764, he was licensed by the Presbytery of New Brunswick and served a brief time at a church in Deerfield, New Jersey.

Williams secured a more permanent position when the minister in Windham, New Hampshire, was dismissed due to conduct unbecoming a "christian." Accepting the call for an "orthodox" minister, Williams was ordained by the Boston Presbytery in 1766 and settled into a congregation of Scotch-Irish where he remained for twenty-seven years at an annual salary of £70. In one of his early sermons there he asked his congregation to accept his "affective labor attended with various sufferings and mournful trials of one kind or another . . . that I may leave my bones in your graveyard till the glorious day of appearance." He labored not in vain, for in 1769 the Old and New Light factions reunited under his leadership. At the formation of the Presbytery of Londonderry, Williams represented Windham and became a member of the Boston Synod. But during the 1770s, perhaps earlier, he thought that immorality and Deism so endangered the citizenry that the world was seeing the "latter days." In 1774 he wrote, that while the previous generation brought a reformed religion, a glorious Empire and sagacious patriotism to this "flourishing American world," its heirs had endangered the glorious "union of church and state" by their "infectious moral conduct." Only by being "born again," only by letting in the spirit of self-sacrifice could the dead be "redeemed" and the "resurrection come." The members of his church must have agreed, because the proclamation was signed by over a hundred citizens of Windham.

One way of cleansing the land was to join the revolutionary struggle against what Williams later called the "venality and tyranny of England." In April 1776, he along with almost all the citizens of Windham signed a proclamation of the New Hampshire Committee of Safety opposing "the hostile proceedings of the British fleets and Armies against the United American Colonies." After the war Williams opened an academy for the instruction of youth in Windham, his pupils paying either with agricultural produce or currency. Among his prominent students was the Reverend Joseph McKeen, the first president of Bowdoin College. However, in 1783 Williams once again began to record evidences of his people's decline. The younger generation was not only disgracing the sabbath with intemperate habits gleaned from the writings of English nobles, but the "infamous country habit" of sleeping together before marriage was widespread. To expurgate these "crimes" the self and all public agencies needed regeneration. A few years later, he complained that this atmosphere even endangered his "school of the prophets." Near the end of his life Williams went partially insane. He died on November 10, 1793, leaving behind his wife and ten children. When Maria Williams's death came in 1803, the town placed an epitaph over their common grave which proclaimed that "this spot is made sacred by their dust."

SOURCES: Sketch: L. A. Morrison, *Hist. of Windham in New Hamphire* (1883), 75, 91, 125-56, 813-18; early teaching: *Pa. Jour.*, Nov. 10, 1763; writings of 1774: "Introduction" to Thomas Blackwell, *Forma Sacra* (1774); declension of 1783: introduction to *Bath Kol, Voice from the Wilderness* (1783); endangered academy: Williams to ?, May 27, 1788, MS Gratz Col., PHi.

LLM

Joseph Worth

JOSEPH WORTH, A.B., has not been identified. Genealogies have not proved useful. The College's alumnus appears to have been neither a member of the numerous Worth family of the island of Nantucket, the young North Carolina army officer who died in 1777, nor the Philadelphia cutlery importer of that name. He was probably a member of the Worth family of Middlesex and Hunterdon counties, New Jersey. William Worth, a stone mason (whose father was named Joseph), oversaw the building of Nassau Hall in the 1750s and a mill owned by the family stood just off the road between Princeton and Lawrenceville. There is record of a Joseph Worth as witness to a will made in Maidenhead (now Lawrenceville), New Jersey in 1767. But the only certain facts discovered concerning the alumnus are that he was listed as living in the College's catalogue of 1789 and as dead in the catalogue of 1792.

SOURCES: Will witness: 33 *NJA*, 210; William Worth: H. L. Savage, ed., *Nassau Hall, 1756-1956* (1956), 7-8.

CLASS OF 1764

Thomas Alkin, A.B.

Thomas John Claggett, A.B.

William Foster, A.B.

Nathaniel Hazard, A.B.

John Lawrence, A.B.

Samuel Leake, A.B.

John McCrery, A.B.

Alexander Miller, A.B.

David Platt, A.B.

Joseph Smith, A.B.

Thomas Tredwell, A.B.

James Tuttle, A.B.

Andrew Wilson, A.B.

William Woodhull, A.B.

Thomas Alkin

THOMAS ALKIN, A.B., was an Anglican clergyman. No information concerning either his parentage or background has been discovered. Shortly after graduation Alkin traveled to England, where he was ordained by the Bishop of London in the Chapel Royal on February 23-24, 1766. Upon the recommendation of Lord Baltimore to Governor Sharpe of Maryland, he was sent in October 1766 to St. John's Parish, which encompassed, wholly or partly, both Queen Anne and Caroline counties. On February 25, 1767, he became a "curate on probation" at St. John's, and on July 7, 1769, he became its rector. During his tenure as rector "parish houses" were built at Nine Bridges and at Tuckahoe Bridges at a total cost of £1075. On March 2, 1767, Alkin married Ellen Middleton. The last entry in the vestry minutes that mentions his name is dated February 12, 1771. The *Maryland Gazette* of April 1, 1773, notes his having "lately died."

SOURCES: Some vital data: Thomas Alkin File, PUA; ordination: *AASP*, 83 (1973), 109; career: N. W. Rightmyer, *Maryland's Established Church* (1956), 156-57; F. Emory, *Queen Anne's Cty., Md.* (1950), 142, 223.

Thomas John Claggett

THOMAS JOHN CLAGGETT, A.B., A.M. 1773, D.D. 1787, Anglican and Episcopal clergyman and planter, was born on October 2, 1743, at the village of White's Landing on the Patuxent River in Prince Georges County, Maryland, the son of Elizabeth Gantt and Samuel Claggett. In middle life the father, a substantial planter, decided to become an Anglican clergyman, studied for the ministry, and in 1747 traveled to England to be ordained. On his return he served in various Maryland parishes until his death in 1756, when Thomas John was thirteen years old. Young Claggett inherited the five-hundred-acre family farm, "Croom," and became the ward of his uncle Edward Gantt. Claggett was prepared for college by another uncle, the Reverend John Eversfield, an Anglican.

Claggett entered the College at the age of seventeen. In an English debate at his commencement he attacked the thesis. "He has not one true virtue who has not every one." Visiting in Princeton, the great English evangelist George Whitefield delivered the sermon at the commencement ceremonies. He also gave what a New York newspaper described as "a very striking and animated Exhortation to the Young

Thomas John Claggett, A.B. 1764

Gentlemen who were Candidates for the Honours of the College."
Claggett was so impressed by Whitefield's performance that in later
years he often tried to imitate it.

After graduation Claggett returned to Prince Georges County,
Maryland, where he studied for the ministry with his uncle John Eversfield, rector of what was at that time probably the wealthiest and
most prominent Anglican parish in the province. In the spring of
1767, Claggett sailed for England and was ordained by the Bishop of
London on October 11, 1767. About six feet four inches tall, Claggett
cut a large, imposing figure. He was an amiable man, described as
"friendly, open, frank, engaging Mr. Clagett [sic], a native of Maryland, educated in a college of the Jerseys," by a young Englishman
who was ordained at the same time as he. Claggett remained in England for a few months after his ordination in order to continue his
studies and to visit various English relatives.

Early in 1768 Claggett returned to Maryland, soon receiving a
curacy worth £100 per year. And Governor Sharpe of Maryland

promised more to come. "I really would advise you," Claggett wrote
to an English friend on July 1, "if you do not meet with that encouragement which I am sure your merit deserves, to take a trip over, you
might easily get a recommendation from Lord Baltimore to our governor. . . . Merit in your country has long since (I am sorry to say it) lost
its sterling value. . . . I am very anxious to see an able and good ministry in this province, too many of my brethren at present being a shock-
ing set (to say nothing worse of them) having neither abilities, a sense
of the importance of their duty, nor (what is worse than all,) an inclination to perform it."

Claggett's own duties expanded on March 16, 1769, when Maryland's governor appointed him curate of All Saints' Parish in Calvert
County. In the following July he was inducted as rector. It was probably at about this time that he married his first cousin, Mary Gantt.
The couple had at least six children. "I am now, Sir, settled for life, I
believe," he wrote to his English friend on September 19, 1769. America seemed to him to be lacking in only one thing: "The Presbyterian
religion gains ground, & seems to flourish; & most probably the whole
continent will be presbyterianized if we do not obtain an able & faithful bishop from our mother country." But it would take a Revolution
for America to acquire a bishop.

In the early 1770s Claggett was engrossed by his parochial duties.
He found the church in his parish a ruin; by 1775 he had built a new
one that endured well into the twentieth century. The Revolution presented Claggett, like all the clergy in Maryland's established church,
with a conflict of loyalties between king and country. Preferring not
to abjure his ordination oath, late in 1776 Claggett retired to "Croom"
in St. George's County, for two years. From 1778 to 1780 he officiated
in his home parish, St. Paul's, being named rector there in 1780. He
held the post until 1786, when he took charge of both St. James Parish
in Anne Arundel County and All Saints', his old parish in Calvert
County.

The latter decades of the eighteenth century were trying ones for
what had been the Church of England, and in few places more than
in Maryland. The legal status of the church was unclear; governmental
financial support of the clergy was stopped, and many ministers left
the state. During the 1780s Claggett, most often behind the scenes, was
extremely active in the reorganization of the church in Maryland. On
May 31, 1792, a convention of Maryland's Protestant Episcopal clergy
meeting at Annapolis elected Claggett the first Episcopal bishop of
Maryland. His consecration—the first held in America—took place at

Trinity Church in New York City on the following September 17. After his election Claggett resigned his rectorates in Anne Arundel and Calvert counties and moved back to "Croom." There, in addition to his episcopal duties, he served St. Paul's Church as rector until 1808.

The main reasons for Claggett's elevation appear to have been that he was amiable, noncontroversial, and possessed of private means. He received no salary during his twenty-four years as bishop, nor did he ever receive compensation equal to the expenses he incurred in executing his duties. The size of the fortune that supported his activities is difficult to estimate. He increased the size of "Croom" to over 700 acres, but it seems to have been a relatively small operation, since in 1790 the federal censustaker recorded him as owning only seven slaves. However, in his will Claggett disposed of several farms and town lots in various parts of his state, as well as some securities. (He had either sold or emancipated his slaves by then, since none is mentioned in the document.)

After his consecration Claggett entered upon his new post vigorously, traveling about the state to confirm thousands of communicants. At public ceremonial functions he usually appeared clad in bishop's mitre and robes, which sometimes frightened small children, who were not used to seeing Americans in such fancy dress. In 1800 he served as first chaplain to the United States Senate after it moved from Philadelphia to Washington. During his term as bishop, Claggett acted mainly as a mediator, successfully remaining above the various factions ("Low" and "High" church) that developed within his denomination. Claggett's later years were shadowed by gout and nervous difficulties, which often interfered with his ability to travel to church functions. He resigned his St. Paul's rectorate in 1808. In 1814 the election of a suffragan bishop relieved him of many burdensome duties. Claggett died at "Croom" on August 2, 1816.

SOURCES: Full biogr: G. B. Utley, *Life and Times of Thomas John Claggett* (1913); also: J. N. Norton, *Life of Bishop Claggett* (1858); sketches: Sprague, *Annals*, v, 251-55; N. W. Rightmeyer, *Maryland's Established Church* (1956), 170-71; commencement debate: Samuel Finley, Acct. of Commencement of 1764, MS, NjP; Whitefield's exhortation: *N.Y. Mercury*, Oct. 8, 1764; corresp. with English friend: John Nicols, *Illustrations of the Literary Hist. of the 18th Century* (1828), v, 850-59; church conflicts: E. C. Chorley, *Men and Movements in the Am. Episcopal Church* (1950), 260-62; slaves: *U.S. Census of 1790, Md.*, 10; will: copy, T. J. Claggett File, PUA. Date of marriage usually given as 1775/76; for earlier date see letter of L.B.K. Claggett, Jan. 4, 1919, Claggett File, PUA.

PUBLICATIONS: Sh-Sh #s 8195, 10149, 37252

Mss: MdHi

William Foster

WILLIAM FOSTER, A.B., Presbyterian clergyman, was born in Little Britain in Lancaster County, Pennsylvania, in 1740, the son of Alexander Foster, an Irish immigrant. Foster was the first student to take the stage in the Latin syllogistic debates held at his commencement. William was licensed by the Presbytery of New Castle on April 21, 1767. After declining the calls of two other Pennsylvania congregations, he was ordained at the Presbyterian Church of Upper Octorara in Chester County on October 19, 1768.

Upper Octorara was Foster's only pulpit. He purchased a 250-acre farm a short distance east of the church in 1770 and lived there with his family for the rest of his life. His wife, Hannah Blair, whom he married in 1768, was a sister of the Reverend Samuel Blair (A.B. 1760) and a sister-in-law of the Reverend John Carmichael (A.B. 1759). They had four sons and four daughters.

Foster's ability at preserving the unity of his congregation won him popularity and respect. His congregation was still smoldering over the Old Side–New Side controversy, a conflict his predecessor had only begun to settle. A less drastic instance of Foster's ability to mediate dissension was his success in introducing new hymns into church services without irremediably offending the "Old Guard." Among his other activities, he occasionally taught theology to students, including Nathaniel Sample (A.B. 1776), and in 1779 opened a Latin grammar school, which lasted for three years.

Foster preached frequently and eagerly in support of the Revolution and spurred more than one young man to enlist. Indeed, so fervent was his commitment that the British tried, unsuccessfully, to capture him and burn his church. A typical statement of his indicates why they felt provoked: "There is nothing can afford such solid and rational comfort in any undertaking, as a firm and unshaken confidence that the Lord Jehovah is on our side, and the cause we engage in, is the cause of God."

Foster died on September 30, 1780, at his farm home, after a brief illness brought on by exposure to heavy rainfall. His death at 40, although meticulously described by John Carmichael as unusually peaceful, was deeply mourned by his flock as well as by his family.

Foster composed his will the day before he died. It provided that "My son Samuel [is] to be made a scholar." Samuel became a prominent Pennsylvania lawyer. William's library of 104 books, which "for that day was large and well selected," was appraised at £3,004 in inflated Continental currency and subsequently sold for £69 in specie. Foster's personal effects were appraised £26,743; his four slaves, at £8,100. His farm land was divided among his wife and his two eldest sons, Samuel and Alexander.

SOURCES: Vital data: William Foster File, PUA; Sprague, *Annals*, III, 202; Webster, Brief Sketches, Bk. 2; J. S. Futhey and J. Cope, *Hist. of Chester County, Pa.* (1881), 250; sketch and will: J. S. Futhey, *Hist. Discourse delivered on the Occasion of the One Hundred and Fifteenth Anniversary of the Upper Octorara Presbyterian Church, Chester County, Pa.* (1870); quotation: Foster, *True Fortitude Delineated* (1776).

PUBLICATIONS: STE   HS

Nathaniel Hazard

NATHANIEL HAZARD, A.B., A.M. Yale 1770, merchant and ironmonger, brother of Joseph Hazard (Class of 1774), was born on July 18, 1748, probably in New York City, the sixth child and first son of Elizabeth Drummey (or Drummie) and her husband, Nathaniel Hazard. The father was a prosperous New York merchant, leading Presbyterian layman, and close friend of Joseph Bellamy, the Connecticut New Light theologian. Samuel Hazard, the father's brother, became a trustee of the College in the year of young Nathaniel's birth.

Hazard's father died a few months after the son's graduation from College. Young Nathaniel was left £400 payable at the age of twenty-one and a part-interest in various of his father's properties. Hazard was still a minor; among his guardians was James Jauncey, one of the wealthiest merchants in New York, a friend of Joseph Bellamy's, and the father of two of the College's alumni. Most likely, Hazard's guardians saw to it that he was apprenticed to a New York merchant house. He experienced something of public affairs as well, recalling years later "that when a Stripling, I used to attend the Debates of the Assembly."

When British forces occupied New York City in September 1776, Hazard, his mother, and younger brothers fled to Newtown, Connecticut, where he appears to have spent the war years. A request the family made to the Connecticut legislature to move clothing and furnishings stored at Smithtown, Long Island, to Newtown was refused.

After the peace Hazard returned to New York City and established himself in business. He served as an agent for White Matlock's steel furnace and appears to have dealt as well in porter, beer, and snuff on a fairly extensive scale. In 1784 he was prominent enough to become one of the first members of the state Chamber of Commerce. In 1785 Hazard published in New York a pamphlet, *Observations on the Peculiar Case of the Whig Merchants Indebted to Great Britain at the Commencement of the Late War Sent to Congress Sept. 1779*, in which he pointed out that merchants had given wholehearted support to the Revolution and that, because of the peculiar nature of their capital, had been—unlike landowners—particularly hard hit by the conflict. He urged that Congress assume the debts merchants owed the British, indicating that his alone amounted to £20,000. In 1787 the New York Common Council appointed him as one of two commissioners charged with the management of real property belonging to the city. It was probably at about this time that Hazard married Maria (or Mary) Robinson, daughter of Colonel Joseph Robinson, who served as surrogate of Queen's County from 1784 to 1815. The couple had two children, Maria and Nathaniel. The federal censustaker of 1790 found Hazard living in New York's East Ward in a household of eight persons that included one slave.

Merchants usually leave little mark in the historical record, and Hazard is no exception. Evidence for most of his career is, at best, fragmentary. In 1786 Hazard dabbled in politics, sounding out Alexander Hamilton on the attitude of Hamilton's prominent father-in-law, General Philip Schuyler, toward the problems of New York City merchants. In 1790 he presented Hamilton with a detailed plan for a lottery designed to alleviate the national debt. In March 1791, at the time Hamilton was composing his *Report on Manufactures*, merchants and manufacturers from many parts of the country wrote to him describing conditions and prospects in their areas. Hazard contributed a disorganized account of the amount of excise that might be raised from the goods he dealt in. Then, in October and November 1791, Hazard exploded in a kind of fit of politicking. He wrote to New Jersey's Governor William Paterson (A.B. 1763), suggesting that an edition of former New Jersey Governor William Livingston's writings should be published and enclosing essays on roads and canals that he wanted published in New Jersey newspapers. In November Hazard made a trip to Connecticut, where he met and conferred with Pierpont Edwards (A.B. 1768), whom he claimed as an old friend, Tapping Reeve (A.B. 1763), and other political leaders. In a very lengthy and gossipy letter Hazard gave Hamilton a complete account of the political situation in Connecticut, with an emphasis on how it affected Burr, the nephew and brother-in-law respectively of Edwards and Reeve, both friends of Hamilton. Burr, Hazard told Hamilton, "has an Address not resistable by common Clay; he has Penetration, Fire, incessant Per-

severance, animatedly active Execution, & could if so unwise, as to
pursue so wrong a Course, mar Councils & Systems, more I suspect
than any Individual in either House."

What reply, if any, Hamilton made to Hazard's extraordinary pro-
duction has not been discovered. Nor is the aim of Hazard's peculiar
excursion into politics clear. Among his brothers-in-law was his classmate Thomas Tredwell, a leading Antifederalist and strong supporter
of New York's Governor George Clinton. In his correspondence with
Hamilton Hazard insinuated that he was a Federalist and strongly
opposed to Clinton. He may have been playing a double game; or, he
may simply have been on a fishing expedition. In any case, no further
record of him has been found except the date of his death on June 2,
1798.

SOURCES: Vital data: T. R. Hazard, *Recollections of Olden Times* (1879), 231, 260;
F. B. Mather, *Refugees of 1776 from Long Island to Conn.* (1913), 671, 529; father's
will: *N.Y. Wills*, VI, 366-68; "when a Stripling": Hazard to Hamilton, Apr. 21, 1786,
Hamilton Papers, III, 663, 664-65; pamphlet: *Observations on the Peculiar Case of
the Whig Merchants Indebted to Great Britain* . . . (1785); Ch. of Com.: J. G. Wilson, *Memorial Hist. of the City of N.Y.* (1893), III, 16; *U.S. Census of 1790, N.Y.*,
119; *N.Y. Common Council Minutes*, I, 293; Hazard to Paterson, Oct. 5, 1791, MS,
NjP; *Hamilton Papers*, VIII and IX.

John Lawrence

JOHN LAWRENCE, A.B., M.B. College of Philadelphia 1768, physician,
was born in Monmouth County, New Jersey, in 1747, one of the seven
children of Mary Hartshorne, wife of John Lawrence, a well-to-do citizen who served as judge and surveyor for his county and also drew in
1743 the "Lawrence line" separating East and West Jersey.

After graduation Lawrence joined the first medical class to be matriculated at the College of Philadelphia. On June 21, 1768, he, along
with John Archer (A.B. 1760) and David Cowell (A.B. 1763) was one
of the eight recipients of the first medical diplomas awarded in North
America. Lawrence was chosen to deliver the Latin oration that
opened the ceremonies. It was composed in the style of the Roman
rhetorician Quintilian, whose works served as the main oratorical
model for the students during Lawrence's undergraduate years. Very
conscious of the historical significance of the occasion, Lawrence re-
viewed the history of medicine from the time of the Mesopotamians to
contemporary Britain. "And now the bright dawn of our own day appears," he concluded. "We rejoice that our own native physicians, truly
in the manner of ancient scholars, have left home and travelled to far

John Lawrence, A.B. 1764
BY THOMAS SULLY

off countries and brought home the elements of every kind of instruction which has to do with the advancement of medicine."

After receiving his degree, Lawrence returned to New Jersey and established himself in Monmouth County. He built up a very large practice that extended into every part of his own county and into Middlesex County as well. In 1775 he moved to Perth Amboy, where he met with equal professional success.

The revolutionary years were not happy ones for Lawrence. Both his father and his brother Elisha were prominent Loyalists, appointed by General Howe to administer to New Jersey Whigs who wished to defect from the American cause oaths of allegiance to the crown. Lawrence himself was taken into custody by Whig forces on July 8, 1776, and placed on a parole that confined him to a six-mile radius of Morristown. Lawrence was sorely missed by his patients. "Sundry Ladies at Perth-Amboy," chief among them Elizabeth Franklin, wife of New Jersey's royal governor William Franklin, petitioned General Washington for Lawrence's release, declaring that "they apprehend fatal and melancholy consequences to themselves and families, and to the inhabitants in general, if they should be deprived of Doctor Lawrence's skill in his profession, as his attendance is hourly necessary to several patients now much indisposed, who will be left helpless if he be removed, as no other practitioner resides in that place." Washington politely refused the request.

At some time not long after this, Lawrence went within the British lines and remained for the rest of the war in New York City. There he continued to practice medicine, treating among others Governor Franklin and various Loyalist members of the Livingston and Delancey families. He also commanded a local militia unit formed to defend the city against the Whigs. At the peace Lawrence did not, like his brother Elisha (who had been a colonel of a Loyalist army unit) leave the United States. Instead, he returned to New Jersey, settling in the Mulberry section of Upper Freehold. Although some of his property had been confiscated during the war, Lawrence was rumored to be independently wealthy and must have been, for he never resumed his practice. When his father died in 1790 Lawrence inherited an indeterminable amount of property.

Lawrence never married, living the life of country squire with his two spinster sisters. A fine horseman, his favorite pastime was foxhunting. He was reputed to have been "full of life and mirth," and he must have been, for he once survived treatment for an illness which consisted of seventeen bleedings. Very fond of games, he died in Trenton on April 29, 1830, while playing chess. His personal property was inventoried at $2,127. He left all of it to his sisters.

SOURCES: Sketches: M. B. Gordon, *Aesculapius Comes to the Colonies* (1949), 376-77; S. Wickes, *Hist. Med. in N.J.*, 306-10 (includes extracts from account book); E. A. Jones, *Loyalists of N.J.* (1927), 124-25; College of Philadelphia oration: *Trans. & Studies of the Col. of Physicians of Phil.*, 25 (1957), 41-52; father's will: 26 *NJA*, 222; parole and ladies' petition: Force, *Am. Arch.* (4 ser.), VI, 1640, 1641, 1647; father and brother: R. M. Calhoon, *Loyalists in Rev. Am.* (1973), 363; will and inventory: MS, N.J. State Lib., Trenton.

Samuel Leake

SAMUEL LEAKE, A.B., Presbyterian clergyman, was born in 1733, the son of Judith Mask and her husband, Walter Leake, probably at "Rocky Springs," the family home in Goochland County, Virginia. The circumstances that brought Leake to the College at the age of thirty or more have not been discovered.

After graduation Leake returned to Virginia. He was licensed to preach by the Presbytery of Hanover meeting at Tinkling Spring, Virginia, on April 18, 1766. Leake proved popular as an apprentice preacher in various Virginia pulpits, Early in 1770 he accepted a call to settle permanently as joint pastor of Presbyterian churches at Rich Cove and North Garden, Albemarle County, and was ordained on May 3, 1770. It was probably at about this time that Leake married Elizabeth Morris of Henrico County. The couple had three daughters, all of whom, according to a nineteenth-century memorialist, possessed "the amiable disposition of their father." Active in church affairs, Leake also kept a school in his home and was one of the founding trustees of Hampden-Sidney College. He died in Albemarle County on December 2, 1775.

SOURCES: Parentage: D. F. Wulfeck, *Marriages of Some Virginia Residents, 1607-1800* (1 ser.), 4 (1964), 134; "Rocky Springs": W. C. Harllee, *Kinfolks* (1934), I, 253; career: Foote, *Sketches, Va.,* II, 87-88; wife and children: E. Wood, *Albemarle County* (1901), 249; school: H. M. Wilson, *The Tinkling Spring* (1954), 239; Hampden-Sidney: *VMHB*, 6 (1899), 174.

John McCrery

JOHN McCRERY, A.B., A.M. 1773, Presbyterian clergyman, was born in 1732 or 1733. McCrery took part in the public disputations held at his commencement. He went on to study theology. Licensed by the New Castle Presbytery on July 31, 1766, McCrery was ordained at the Presbyterian churches of both White Clay Creek and Head of Christiana, Delaware, on May 10, 1769. Although McCrery remained pastor of both churches until the end of his life, he continued to supply a number of other churches throughout Pennsylvania, Virginia, and North Carolina.

On May 21, 1783, McCrery was elected to a year-long term as moderator of the Synod of New York and Philadelphia. His bid eight years later for the post of moderator of the recently formed Presbyterian General Assembly proved less successful: McCrery was decisively defeated by the Reverend John Woodhull (A.B. 1766) of Freehold, New Jersey. McCrery was nevertheless described during the electoral proceedings as "a godly and evangelical man."

McCrery made his permanent home at Mill Creek, Delaware. He and his wife had two sons and three daughters. The last years of his life were plagued by illness. In letters to Ashbel Green (A.B. 1783) in

1799 he lamented being "so wholly cut off from the House of God and from . . . my ministry" and prayed for an opportunity to preach just once more. "The brink of the grave is a trying place," he observed eighteen months before his death, on June 18, 1800, at Head of Christiana.

SOURCES: Vital data: John McCrery File, PUA; Webster, Brief Sketches, Bk. 2; J. L. Vallandigham and S. A. Gayley, *Hist. of Presbytery of New Castle . . . 1717 to 1888* (1889); *JPHS*, 2 (1913-1914), 392, 394; J. W. Alexander, *Life of Archibald Alexander* (1834), 96; letters: Gratz Col., PHi.

HS

Alexander Miller

ALEXANDER MILLER, A.B., A.M. 1768, Presbyterian clergyman and schoolmaster, was born in New Castle County, Delaware, on August 26, 1739, the son of Susanna Roddy and her husband, Abraham Miller, immigrants from Ireland. When Miller was twelve years old his family moved to Maryland, where Alexander was prepared for the College by the Reverend James Finley, brother of President Samuel Finley, at East Nottingham. At his commencement Miller defended the proposition "All dreams are not useless and insignificant" in an English disputation with his classmate Thomas Tredwell.

After graduation Miller studied for the ministry in New York City with the Reverend John Rodgers, a trustee of the College. Licensed by the Presbytery of New York in May 1768, over the following two years Miller acted as a supply preacher at various places, including an eight-month stint in the Presbytery of Donegal in Pennsylvania. Ordained by the Presbytery of New York in 1770, Miller preached at various churches along the Hudson Valley. In Schenectady, New York, Presbyterians were attempting to form a church. Miller accepted a call to serve as their permanent pastor and was installed at the new church in 1771.

Miller's Schenectady pastorate seems to have passed uneventfully except for a clash with the Freemasons, who were very strong in the area. Invited to preach to the Masons on a "moral subject," Miller managed to alienate them. The sermon, in effect, proselytized for Presbyterianism. Moreover, Miller concluded by making insinuations about Masonic meetings: "I have my Suspicions and Jealousies, respecting both the conduct of your Societies in general, and the Warrantableness of entering into them in the manner which I believe to be the Practice. How you conduct yourselves, Gentlemen, I know not."

However, he concluded, young men in social meetings, "act more like Infernal Spirits than like Men or Christians." A Mason responded with a vituperative letter; Miller published the letter along with his sermon and let the public decide.

Besides his Schenectady church Miller also preached at neighboring congregations at Currie's Bush and Remsen's Bush. The Revolution scattered Miller's congregations, and in 1781 he moved to New Jersey, where he conducted an academy in Hackensack. On July 2, 1783, he was installed as pastor of the Presbyterian church at South Hanover, Morris County, New Jersey. On April 26, 1786, Miller married Elizabeth Ayres of Morristown. The couple had five children. Obviously well-regarded by his peers, Miller served as moderator of the Synod of New York and Philadelphia in the year of his marriage, and from 1785 to 1795 as a trustee of the College. But affairs at home in South Hanover went less smoothly. In 1785 Miller's congregation asked him to accept a salary of £100 per year (modest for the time). The congregation declared that it would request Miller's dismissal if he did not accept, for it could not subscribe more. The matter was not resolved; Miller left the church either in 1786 or 1787. It took the congregation three years to find another minister.

Miller soon moved to Wallkill, Ulster County, New York, where he became head of an already established classical academy. He ran the academy for some time, and later moved to Albany. There he taught and preached. He published a sermon on the death of Washington in 1800 and another, giving strong if qualified support to the union of the Congregational and Presbyterian churches, in the following year. Though Miller does not appear to have held a permanent pulpit in these years, he became a member of the Presbytery of Albany in 1796 and presided at some of its meetings. At some time after 1802 Miller migrated northwest to St. Lawrence County, where two of his children had made their homes. He eventually settled down in Hague (now Morristown), New York. There he helped to organize churches and continued to preach almost to the time of his death on January 14, 1820.

SOURCES: "Memoir of Rev. Alexander Miller," *Christian Herald*, 7 (June 17, 1820), 97-99; commencement oration: Samuel Finley, Account of Commencement of 1764, MS, NjP; early career: *Presbyterian Records*; Schenectady: G. S. Roberts, *Old Schenectady* (n.d.), 106-107; Masons: Miller, *Sermon Preached at Schenectady* . . . (1775); South Hanover pastorate: *Hist. of Morris Cty., N.J.* (1882), 207; Albany Presbytery: *JPHS*, 3 (1905-1906), 228, 234.

PUBLICATIONS: above, and: *A Sermon Occasioned by the Death of . . . Washington* . . . (1800); *An Essay on Church Government* (1801).

David Platt

DAVID PLATT, A.B., was born in Huntington, Long Island, on July 13, 1746, the second of the three sons of Zophar Platt and his wife, Rebecca Wood. The father was a well-to-do physician who served in various local public offices and also as a deacon and elder of the Presbyterian church at Huntington. After graduation young Platt returned to Huntington, where he died on January 19, 1768. News of his death reached Princeton in time to be included in the College's first catalogue, published in 1770. Two of Platt's sisters married (at different times) Robert Ogden (A.B. 1765).

SOURCES: Vital data: Charles Platt, Jr., *Platt Genealogy* (1963), 82; father: ibid., pp. 131-2; F. G. Mather, *Refugees of 1776 from L.I. to Conn.* (1913), 509-10; R. Davidson, *Historical Discourse . . . First Christian Church . . . Huntington, L.I.* (1866), 41.

Joseph Smith

JOSEPH SMITH, A.B., Presbyterian clergyman, was born in West Nottingham, Maryland, in 1736. At his College commencement Smith participated in the Latin debate. Licensed by the Presbytery of New Castle on August 4, 1767, he was ordained for its Lower Brandywine, Delaware, church on April 19, 1769. He remained there until August 1772, when he resigned in the wake of a dispute over the site of a new church. Declining calls from the congregations of Rocky Creek and Long Cane in South Carolina, where he had preached in 1771 and 1772 on missionary tours of the South, Smith accepted a one-year appointment as supply preacher of his former congregation. By the time of his resignation, Smith had married Esther Cummins of Cecil County, Maryland, and she had given birth to the first of their three sons and five daughters.

In August 1773 Smith became pastor of the Second Presbyterian Church of Wilmington, Delaware. After its merger in October 1774 with his former church at Lower Brandywine, he became pastor of the united congregation. In April 1778 the British advance on Delaware prompted the flight of Smith and his family to the "Barrens of York" in Pennsylvania. Two years earlier the excitement of the battle of Brandywine near their home had caused Mrs. Smith to give birth prematurely, but safely, to their fourth child.

Smith remained in the Barrens for more than two years, preaching with characteristic enthusiasm and success. Periodic visits to Western

Pennsylvania produced a joint call, in June 1780, from the Buffalo and Cross Creek Congregations of Washington County. Two hundred and four persons, many of them prominent in local affairs, signed the petition, and each congregation agreed to pay half of his $600.00 yearly salary. Smith accepted the call and remained pastor until his death a dozen years later. During much of that time he directed and sustained a powerful revival movement.

Despite the burden of his duties, Smith managed to preach throughout western Pennsylvania and to inspire revivals there as well—even though, as nineteenth-century historian James Alexander put it, few of the local Scottish Presbyterians "had much faith in these sudden awakenings" and most of them assumed that "these religious commotions would pass away." In September 1781, Smith and three other Presbyterian ministers—John McMillan (A.B. 1772), James Power (A.B. 1766), and Thaddeus Dod (A.B. 1773)—formed the new Presbytery of Redstone, which embraced the entire region west of the Alleghenies. The region was so "unexplored" religiously that it was not divided into other presbyteries until 1793, and until Smith's visit in August 1784 even Pittsburgh had seen no Presbyterian minister since 1775. For their efforts, the four ministers were called the "Four Presbyterian Horsemen of Western Pennsylvania," Smith himself being singled out as "Hell-Fire Smith."

Smith's effectiveness as a revivalist won him widespread respect, and many aspiring ministers regularly sought his assistance in improving their own talents. To accommodate their demands he opened a classical school in his Buffalo, Pennsylvania, home in 1785. "The Study," as it was called, outgrew its quarters and was moved a few miles away to Chartiers, near Canonsburg. In 1791 it merged with the equally new Canonsburg Academy, and out of that merger grew Jefferson College, and in turn Washington and Jefferson College. After Smith's death the academy was directed for a time by Thaddeus Dod.

Smith was tall, slender, fair-complexioned and, despite his powerful and moving oratory, not very robust. He worried greatly about the state not only of his flock's souls but of his own family's as well, and he spent many nightly vigils by the foot of his bed praying on their behalf. Worn out by so much anxiety and activity, Smith died of "inflamation of the brain" on April 19, 1792, at his Buffalo home. Because his death was nevertheless unexpected, his parishioners observed only afterward that his last sermon, delivered at Cross Creek on the first Sunday in April, had subtly summarized his twelve years of work there and at Buffalo.

Smith was survived by his wife and all eight of his children. Although the hundreds of acres of land he owned in Washington County probably provided a comfortable source of income for his family, the Bible which Smith willed to each of his children was, in his words, "ten thousand times" more valuable than any material possession. Still, he left a "respectable patrimony" for each and, in addition, left £70 in gold to support his son David's ministerial training. David amply fulfilled those expectations by joining the Presbytery of Redstone shortly after his father's death and by preaching in its congregations for several years. Another son died while preparing for the ministry, and all four of his daughters who reached adulthood married ministers as well.

Smith's only known published work was "A Sermon on the Character and Preaching of the Reverend Mr. Whitefield," which appeared posthumously and as a prefix to Whitefield's *Fifteen Sermons* (New York, 1794). Smith praised Whitefield profusely, not only for his style and his substance but also for blessing a degenerate world "with another reformation."

SOURCES: Vital data: Joseph Smith File, PUA; Sprague, *Annals*, III, 274-80: Webster, Brief Sketches, Bk. I; *Presbyterian Mag.*, III (1853); *Hist. Presbytery of Washington* (1889), 395; *Hist. Presbytery of Redstone* (1889), 5; *Pa. Arch.* (3 ser.), XXII (1898), 768; XXVI (1899), 604, 607; *JPHS*, 10 (1919-1920), 57-83; W. W. McKinney, *Early Pittsburgh Presby.* (1938); Alexander: J. S. Alexander, *Life of Archibald Alexander* (1854), 52; Washington and Jefferson College: U.S. Bur. Educ., *Circular of Information*, 18 (1902), 236-37.

                                                                          HS

Thomas Tredwell

THOMAS TREDWELL, A.B., A.M. 1773, lawyer and public official, was born at Smithtown, Long Island, on February 6, 1743, the eldest of the four children of Mary Platt, wife of Timothy Tredwell, a carpenter, prosperous farmer, and substantial landowner. The family had been prominent locally since the seventeenth century. At his commencement Tredwell took the negative in an English debate with his classmate Alexander Miller on the proposition, "All dreams are not useless and insignificant."

One account has it that after graduation Tredwell studied law with Robert R. Livingston, future Chancellor of New York. Since Livingston did not graduate from King's College until 1765, this seems unlikely. If Tredwell did read law with a member of the Livingston family it was most probably with the Chancellor's father of the same name. On October 26, 1765, Tredwell married Ann Hazard, daughter of a prosperous New York City merchant and a sister of Tredwell's class-mate, Nathaniel Hazard. Despite the paralysis that struck Ann Tred-well about 1770, the couple had at least thirteen children, six of whom died in infancy.

After finishing his studies Tredwell returned to Suffolk County, Long Island, and established a legal practice. It must have been a suc-cessful one, for in 1776 he was supporting a large household of fifteen people, which included six slaves. Tredwell was an early adherent of the Whig cause. When Smithtown formed a three-member Committee of Correspondence on August 9, 1774, he was a member. In 1775 Tred-well signed the local association boycotting the importation of British goods, became a member of a Committee of Safety and of a committee charged with raising troops. Elected to the New York Provincial Con-gress, in January 1776 he was appointed to confer with General Wash-ington about military supplies on Long Island. Later in the year he served on a committee charged with investigating "disaffected per-sons." Through his public service Tredwell became widely known in the province. By June 1776, New York's future governor George Clin-ton, in an association that would last for many years, was referring to Tredwell as his "friend."

When British forces occupied Long Island after the American defeat in the battle of Long Island late in the summer of 1776 Tredwell, like many of his Whig neighbors, took refuge in Connecticut. He served as a member of the New York convention that met at Kingston in 1777 to draw up a constitution for the new state. Along with Peter R. Living-ston (Class of 1758), Tredwell was one of two delegates to vote in op-position to the document. Livingston, the Loyalist diarist William Smith recorded, rejected it "because it was too levelling & . . . [Tred-well] because it is not enough so & particularly because all Elections are not to be by Ballot." Tredwell's action here presaged his future po-litical stance. Voting by ballot protected the citizen's privacy and thus his independence, while the more common *viva voce* voting laid thou-sands of New York tenant farmers open to economic and other pres-sures from the great Hudson Valley landlords.

During the war Tredwell acted as a clerk to Captain Nathaniel Platt's Company. He served too as a justice of the New York court of probates from 1777 to 1787. A member of the New York Assembly from 1777 to 1783, Tredwell was accounted by Alexander Hamilton, who described him as "a sensible and an honest man," as one of the five leading members of that body.

With the peace, Tredwell returned to Long Island. Shortly there-after he moved to New York City, where he appears to have remained until about 1786, when he once more returned to Long Island, settling this time in Huntington. In 1787 he was made first surrogate of Suffolk County, a post he held until 1791. Elected to the New York Senate, Tredwell took his seat on February 23, 1788. He served in the Senate through 1789, consistently voting the Antifederalist, Clintonian, line.

Tredwell was a delegate to the New York convention that met in 1788 to consider ratification of the new federal constitution. During his by then long and influential public career Tredwell's words had never entered the public record. The 1788 convention almost proved to be the great exception. Tredwell wrote a speech, but never delivered it. "Sir, little accustomed to speak in public," he began,

> and always inclined, in such an assembly as this, to be a hearer rather than a speaker, on a less important occasion than the present I should have contented myself with a silent vote; but when I consider the nature of this dispute, that it is a contest, not between little states and great states, (as we have been told), [but] between little folks and great folks, between patriotism and ambition, between freedom and power; not so much between the navigating and non-navigating states, as between navigating and non-navigating individuals . . . that I cannot be totally silent on the occasion, lest lisping babes should be taught to curse my name, as a betrayer of their freedom and happiness.

In a classic expression of the Antifederalist mentality, Tredwell continued:

> In this Constitution, sir, we have departed widely from the principles and political faith of '76, when the spirit of liberty ran high, and danger put a curb on ambition. Here we find no security for the rights of individuals, no security for the existence of our state governments; here is no bill of rights, no proper restriction of power; our lives, our property, and our consciences, are left wholly at the mercy of the legislature, and the powers of the judiciary may be extended to any degree short of almighty. Sir, in this Constitution we have not only neglected,—we have done worse,— we have openly violated, our faith,—that is, our public faith.

Tredwell's friends were undoubtedly aware of his sentiments. He followed his undelivered speech with elaborate maneuvers designed to amend the constitution. He and his fellow Antifederalists, however, ultimately were defeated, and New York ratified the constitution. Back in the state senate, Tredwell led the fight for the adoption of a Bill of Rights.

In the state gubernatorial campaign of 1789 Tredwell was among the most active supporters of the incumbent, George Clinton. Signing himself "Brutus," he wrote an article for a New York City newspaper defending the governor against charges of corruption, and claiming that Clinton's fortune was the result of simple republican frugality.

In 1790 Tredwell ran for the United States Congress from Long Island. The Antifederalist vote was hopelessly split, and Tredwell ran fourth in a field of five. In the spring of the following year, the Federalist incumbent died. Tredwell made another try for Congress and was elected.

As was his custom, Tredwell never made a speech in Congress. But his voting record reveals him to have been an early and especially strong ally of James Madison (A.B. 1771). In the first session of the Second Congress, which met from October 1791 to May 1792, a small group of men voted together consistently, casting their votes with Madison, around whom the nascent Democratic-Republican party was beginning to coalesce. Out of thirty-five roll call votes recorded in that session Tredwell voted the same as Madison twenty-six times—more than any other congressman from a northern state. Tredwell's Long Island constituency apparently approved of his record, for he won an overwhelming reelection to Congress in January 1793.

Tredwell was among the original proprietors of the Plattsburgh Patent in Clinton County on the shores of Lake Champlain. His landholdings there amounted to at least 1,120 acres, and probably a good deal more. Late in 1794 he moved to a place about four miles north of Plattsburgh that later was named Beekmanstown. Tredwell was immediately put forward by Clinton County Republicans as their congressional candidate from the Van Rensselaer–Clinton district. However, the Federalist patroon, Stephen Van Rensselaer, saw that his tenants voted for his candidate, and Tredwell was resoundingly defeated.

While the federal censustaker of 1790 recorded Tredwell as the owner of twelve slaves, one account has it that he was accompanied to his new home in Clinton County by at least forty slaves. Whatever the truth, the issue of slavery was one on which Tredwell did not follow the practice of either Jefferson or Madison. He had objected to slavery during the debates on the federal constitution in 1788:

> There is no other clause in this Constitution, which, though there is no prospect of getting it amended, I think ought not to be passed over in silence, lest such a silence should be construed into a tacit approbation of it. I mean the clause which restricts the gen-

eral government from putting a stop, for a number of years, to a commerce which is a stain to the commerce of any civilized nation, and has already blackened half the plains of America with a race of wretches made so by our cruel policy and avarice, and which appears to me to be already repugnant to every principle of humanity, morality, religion, and good society.

As good as his rhetoric, not long after his arrival in Clinton County, Tredwell emancipated his slaves and settled them at a place called "Richland" (later known as "Nigger Hill") a few miles north of his own holdings.

Tredwell's wife died in 1798, and in 1800 he married Mary Conklin Hedges, a widow of East Hampton, Long Island. Tredwell returned to public office once more in 1803. In the Democratic–Republican electoral sweep in April of that year, he was elected to the New York Senate. In February 1804 he was appointed one of the three members of the Senate's powerful council of appointment. Tredwell served in the legislature until 1807, when he appears to have retired from the larger public stage. Appointed a surrogate of Clinton County in 1807, he held the post until his death. Tredwell's favorite activity was horseback riding. Despite having his left eye put out by a twig he continued the pastime until late in life. He died at his home near the shores of Lake Champlain on December 30, 1831.

SOURCES: The name was sometimes spelled Treadwell; geneal. and basic data: *NY-GBR*, 43 (1912), 138-40; F. G. Mather, *Refugees of 1776 from Long Island to Conn.* (1913), 607-608; commencement: Samuel Finley, MS Account of Commencement of 1764, NjP; Clinton's "friend": *Clinton Papers*, I, 239-41; Smith quotation: W.H.W. Sabine, ed., *Historical Memoirs of William Smith, 1776-1778* (1958), 121; Hamilton quotation: *Hamilton Papers*, III, 139-40; general N.Y. pol. career: A. F. Young, *Democratic-Republicans of N.Y.* (1967); E. W. Spaulding, *N.Y. in the Critical Period* (1932); J. D. Hammond, *Hist. of Political Parties in the State of N.Y.* (1850), I; also *N.Y. State General Assembly Journals, 1782* (1782), 50, 60, 84, 99-100, 103, 106, 107; ibid. (1783), 1, 107, 167; *N.Y. State Senate Journals, 1778* (1788), 62. 68-69, 70-71; ibid., for Twelfth Session (1789), 6, 10, 14-16, 20ff., 54-55, 77ff.; opposition to Constitution: *WMQ*, 20 (1963), 30; R. A. Rutland, *Birth of the Bill of Rights* (1955), 177-79; anticonstitution and antislavery quotations: J. Elliot, *Debates on the Federal Constitution* (1901), II, 396, 401, 402; non-deliverance of speech: L. G. De Pauw, *The Eleventh Pillar* (1966), 197n.; record in Congress: N. E. Cunningham, *The Jeffersonian Republicans* (1957), 22-23, 271; Clinton County lands: F. McDonald, *We the People* (1958), 307; slaves: *U.S. Census of 1790, N.Y.*, 152.

James Tuttle

JAMES TUTTLE, A.B., A.M. 1768, Presbyterian clergyman, was born in Hanover, Morris County, New Jersey, on May 7, 1742, the son of Abigail Nutman, wife of Colonel Joseph Tuttle, a wealthy farmer and prominent county official. The family had been in America since the emigration of William and Elizabeth Tuttle from England in 1635.

James was prepared for the College, and after graduation for the ministry, by the Reverend Jacob Green (Harvard 1744), trustee and sometime vice-president of the College and pastor of the Hanover Presbyterian Church, to which his family belonged. At commencement Tuttle defended (in English) the Socratic thesis "He has not one true virtue who has not every one."

Licensed by the Presbytery of New York early in 1767, he was ordained in April of that same year and settled as pastor of the Presbyterian churches of Parsippany and Rockaway, both in Morris County, New Jersey. Tuttle was Rockaway's first pastor and was paid £60 for his half-time position. His Rockaway congregants built a parsonage expressly for him and his wife Anna, who was the daughter of Jacob Green and the sister of President Ashbel Green (A.B. 1783). They had married on February 2, 1767.

As a preacher, Tuttle was respected and popular despite his proclivity for long and scholarly sermons. His tenure, however, was brief: in 1770 he became ill, and on Christmas Day of that year he died. The death a few weeks earlier of his only child, a son Benajah, may have speeded James's own passing. Anna returned to her father's house in Hanover and herself died of consumption three or four years later.

Tuttle's will was probated on January 28, 1771. He left £100 to his wife and any remaining money to his father, who survived him by nearly twenty years. His land he wanted sold. The inscription on his tombstone reads: "This man of God had a short race but swift, he ran far in little time. Few exceeded him in sweetness of Temper, Tenderness of conscience and fidelity in his ministerial work and the End of this man was Peace."

SOURCES: Vital data: James Tuttle File, PUA; Webster, Brief Sketches, Bk. 1; Rec. Pres. Church, 365, 377, 391, 401, 412; NJHSP, 58 (1940), 3-17; 37 NJA (1942), 365; Hist. Morris County, N.J. (1882), 343; J. F. Tuttle, Annals Morris Cty. (1876), 80; NJHS Coll., 9 (1916), 203-204; J. P. Crayon, Rockaway Records (1902), 49, 62; will: 34 NJA (1931), 534.

HS

Andrew Wilson

ANDREW WILSON, A.B., A.M. 1774, bore a name that was extremely common in eighteenth-century America. Only three things are certain about the College's alumnus: he was listed as being "of New Jersey" when he received his A.M. in 1774, as being alive at the time of the publication of the College's catalogue of 1773, and as being dead at the time of the next catalogue, published in 1786. The Andrew Wilson described below seems the most likely among many men of the same name to have been the alumnus.

This Andrew Wilson was the son of Hannah and Peter Wilson of Amwell, Hunterdon County, New Jersey, who may have come from Bucks County, Pennsylvania. In 1769 Wilson married Sarah Anderson, daughter of Captain John Anderson, a well-to-do citizen of Maidenhead (now Lawrenceville), New Jersey. Anderson died late in 1773, leaving an estate inventoried at £5,971. Wilson, along with Samuel Tucker, later a prominent Whig leader in Trenton, was named an executor of Anderson's estate. His father-in-law also left Wilson lands and a house in New Brunswick and appointed Wilson and Samuel Tucker guardians of his young son, Samuel Anderson. Wilson's wife was left her father's "wench, Polly."

Not only his father-in-law but many of his neighbors regarded Wilson as a man to be trusted. He served as executor for many estates in the early 1770s. But late in 1775 Wilson himself fell ill, and signed his will on January 16, 1776. His wife had probably predeceased him, for she is not mentioned in the document. In his will Wilson specified that his "son" Samuel—quite probably his ward and nephew, Samuel Anderson—was to be cared for by Wilson's mother, who was left £30 per year to cover expenses as well as Wilson's household goods. When he came of age Samuel was to receive a Negro woman, silver spoons, and a bookcase. Wilson specified too that Samuel was to be sent to college. Wilson's other major legacies included £650 to nieces and nephews. Samuel Tucker was made an executor of his estate. Wilson died at some time between the signing of his will and March 9, 1776, when the will was probated.

SOURCES: The name was sometimes spelled "Willson." The CNJ graduate was probably not the Samuel Wilson who, citing President Witherspoon as a reference, advertised (N.Y. Gaz., July 3) a Latin grammar school in Morristown, N.J. in 1775. This Andrew Wilson may have been a recent immigrant from Scotland. See Andrew Wilson File, PUA. Award of A.M.: Pa. Journals, Oct. 12, 1774; Wilson's father's will: 34 NJA, 589; marriage: GMNJ, 22 (1947), 38; Anderson's will: 34 NJA, 16-17; Samuel Tucker: J. P. Snell, Hist. of Somerset and Hunterdon Counties (1881), 27, 30, 203; Wilson's will: 34 NJA, 588-89.

William Woodhull

WILLIAM WOODHULL, A.B., A.M. 1785, Presbyterian clergyman, politician and public official, older brother of John Woodhull (A.B. 1767)

William Woodhull, A.B. 1764

was born in Miller's Place, Suffolk County, New York, on December 3, 1741, the first of the ten children of John and Elizabeth Woodhull. The father, descended from a wealthy Long Island family, was a prosperous landowner and judge. William not only was the first of a long line of Woodhulls to attend the College but also distinguished himself in a public debate at commencement. After graduation he went to East Hampton, Long Island, where he studied theology with Samuel Buell (Yale 1741) and married Elizabeth Hedges on May 3, 1767. In the same year he was licensed by the Suffolk Presbytery, and for the next few months preached at a church at Black River, New Jersey. Then the Succassuna church in Morris County, New Jersey, called him to service at an annual salary of £40, and William was ordained by the New York Presbytery in 1769. For seven years William resided, taught school, and preached in the town of Chester, an area already noted for its iron foundries and mining.

The coming of the colonial revolt turned Woodhull's career toward political affairs. In 1775 he signed an "Associator's Oath" that protested the crown's activities in Massachusetts Bay and resolved "never to become slaves" to the British ministry. Elected in May 1776 to the third provincial congress meeting at Burlington, Woodhull became one of the majority that decided upon the arrest of Governor William Franklin, the drafting of a state constitution, and the casting of the state's vote in Congress for independence. He was also appointed by the legislature to purchase clothing in Hunterdon and Morris counties for the use of the army.

Clearly, Woodhull served his constituents well during the next three years, for he later became a public official in the new political order. He was justice of the peace in Roxbury, Morris County, New Jersey from 1780 to 1811, then became a judge on the New Jersey circuit court from 1808 to 1824. When he died at the age of 84 on October 24, 1824, he left behind his wife and ten children. His descendants continued to play an active part in the civic and religious life of New Jersey.

SOURCES: Sketch: E. F. Cooley, *Genealogy of the Early Settlers in Trenton and Ewing* (1883), 306-311; M. G. Woodhull and F. B. Stevens, *Goodhull Genealogy* (1904), 44, 85, 86, 302, 310; judicial and political career, nature of Chester: *Hist. of Morris County, N.J.* (1882), 182, 212, 254, 367; *Minutes of the Provincial Congress and the Council of Safety of N.J.* (1879), 446-550; Samuel Finley, Description of 1764 Commencement, MS, NjP.

LLM

CLASS OF 1765

John Bacon, A.B.

John Bay, A.B.

Joel Benedict, A.B.

Joseph Chambers, A.B.

George Corbin, A.B.

Gershom Craven, A.B.

William Davies, A.B.

Jonathan Edwards, Jr., A.B.

Joseph Finley, A.B.

Samuel Finley, Jr., A.B.

Richard Goodman, A.B.

Robert Halstead, A.B.

Richard Hutson, A.B.

Samuel Kirkland, A.B.

Alexander McCausland, A.B.

Alexander Mitchel, A.B.

Jonathan Ogden, A.B.

Robert Ogden, III, A.B.

Henry Parkinson, A.B.

Ebenezer Pemberton, A.B.

Edward Pope, A.B.

David Ramsay, A.B.

Theodore (Dirck) Romeyn, A.B.

Jacob Rush, A.B.

John Staples, A.B.

Henry Stevenson, A.B.

Alexander Thayer, A.B.

Jacob Van Arsdale, A.B.

Stephen Voorhees, A.B.

Ralph Wheelock

Samuel Williams, A.B.

Simeon Williams, A.B.

John Bacon

JOHN BACON, A.B., A.M. 1768, Harvard 1771, Presbyterian clergyman, public official, and farmer, was born in Canterbury, Connecticut, on April 9, 1738, the son of Ruth Spaulding and her husband, John Bacon. After graduation from the College young Bacon studied for the ministry and on July 30, 1767, was licensed by the Presbytery of Lewes, Delaware. On June 23 of the following year he was ordained by the presbytery as an itinerant preacher.

From then until August 7, 1771, Bacon served Presbyterian churches in Delaware and on Maryland's Eastern Shore. "The climate being unfavorable to my health," he later recalled, "I declined settling with any particular people, but supplied two vacant congregations alternately . . . during the whole of that time, I lived in the greatest harmony and friendship."

Bacon received a dismissal from the presbytery in order to accept a three-month probationary appointment as pastor of Boston's Old South Church. Anxious to counteract Harvard's liberal Congregationalists, the Church sought orthodox replacements for the recently deceased Reverend Joseph Sewell (Harvard 1707) and the recently resigned Reverend Samuel Blair (A.B. 1760), themselves both theologically respectable. Bacon had been an acknowledged Hopkinsian who insisted that "for the baptism of children one of the parents must be in full communion—and if they don't come to the Lords Supper, neither they nor their children have baptism." Despite these convictions, he decided to accept Old South's practice of the Half-Way Covenant.

On September 25, 1771, Bacon was installed as co-pastor with the Reverend John Hunt (Harvard 1764), and on the following November 4 he married Elizabeth, the daughter of Ezekial Goldthwait of Boston and the widow of another predecessor at Old South, the Reverend Alexander Cumming (Harvard 1747). The couple had a son and a daughter and managed easily on Bacon's weekly salary of £2 13s. The family lived in the church parsonage.

By virtue of his position as pastor of Old South, Bacon, in October 1771, became an Overseer of Harvard College and simultaneously received an honorary A.M. That same year he became a member of the Boston schools visitation committee. His growing stature, however, suffered a setback when, in the fall of 1771, he read to his congregation the Thanksgiving Proclamation of Governor Thomas Hutchinson. Unknown to Bacon, the Whigs had decided to denounce the proclamation because it called for a day of thanksgiving for the preservation of civil and religious liberties. Bacon was immediately condemned, in the words of a street ballad, as "wrapt with a Tory clan." Once Sam Adams and other leading Whigs learned of the political innocence that had apparently led Bacon to read the document, they ceased challenging his patriotism. Still, suspicion lingered among his congregation, partly because of the warm relations of his father-in-law, Ezekial Goldthwait, with Governor Hutchinson.

Unfortunately, Bacon's ministerial career faced additional difficulties. His "argumentative" and "severe" preaching stood in sharp contrast to Hunt's "affectionate, modest, sweet, and pacific" pulpit style. More important, his insistence on rigid Hopkinsian orthodoxy aroused his parishioners' ire. Bacon's refusal to temper his unsettling remarks about original sin and likely damnation, even in the presence of children, won him little parental support or respect. As a contemporary poet put it:

> Where Hunt can trace out means of grace as leading to conversion;
> ... Hopkin's scheme is Bacon's theme and strange was his assertion.
> For *strive*, said he, a saint to be, and *worse you will become.*

Bacon's announcement in August 1774 that he could no longer accept the Half-Way Covenant proved to be the turning point. A special church committee recommended that Bacon be dismissed without prejudice and that, in the interest of fairness, his controversial sermons be printed at Old South's expense. On January 25, 1775, the congregation approved the report. Bacon made a prolonged defense and sought trial by local clergy, but neighboring ministers refused him one, and he was dismissed on February 8, 1775. Six years later, at his request, his former parishioners publicly declared their confidence in and respect for him as a person, stressing that only certain doctrinal differences had forced his departure. "During the time he was with the Church," the report stated, "his conversation and deportment was evidently such as became the gospel."

Nevertheless, and much to his surprise, Bacon was unable to obtain another pulpit. Instead, he occasionally supplied congregations near his birthplace in the Canterbury, Connecticut, area, to which he had returned. Eventually, he became a prosperous farmer in Stockbridge, Massachusetts, and a familiar sight in his chaise.

Yet even in retirement religious controversy plagued him. Bacon entered the dispute involving the Reverend Stephen West's (Yale 1755) effort to bar from communion a member of his Stockbridge Congregational church whose husband had used profanity. Bacon supported

West against the attacks of the Reverend Joseph Huntington (Yale 1762) and wrote vigorously and extensively on West's behalf.

Bacon simultaneously engaged again in political controversy, but this time with more positive results than he had achieved in 1771. Elected Stockbridge's delegate to the Massachusetts House of Representatives in 1777, in the Constitutional Convention of 1778 he forcefully condemned a proposed clause denying the vote to "Negroes, Indians, and Mulattoes." "Are they not Americans?" he asked. "Were they not (most of them at least) born in this country? Is it not a fact, that those who are not natives of America, were forced here by us, contrary, not only to their own wills, but to every principle of justice and humanity?" The clause was retained, but the constitution itself was rejected (for other reasons), and a new constitution without the offending clause was adopted in 1780.

Bacon's humanitarian efforts probably helped him win election, in 1779, to the first of twelve terms in the Massachusetts House of Representatives, the last of which ended in 1817. Interspersed with these terms were ten terms, beginning in 1782, in the Massachusetts Senate. During the last of them, which ended in 1807, he was elected Senate president.

In 1783, Bacon was appointed a justice of the peace for Berkshire County, Massachusetts. Two years later he became a member of the quorum. Five years after that, in 1790, he became a justice of the court of common pleas, and from 1807 until 1811 he served as its chief justice.

Bacon's renewed respectability certainly played a part in his role in 1780 as one of the incorporators of the American Academy of Arts and Sciences; and in 1786, in his election to the Williams College Board of Trustees, where he served until 1804.

Bacon's political stance changed over the years. An initial supporter of the federal constitution, he changed his mind sometime in 1787 and thereby infuriated Theodore Sedgwick, a leading proponent of ratification who may have been instrumental in Bacon's first judicial appointment. Sedgwick, moreover, did not hesitate to publish a report in the Stockbridge area proclaiming Bacon's continued enthusiasm for the constitution despite personal knowledge to the contrary. In retaliation, Bacon campaigned throughout the area against the constitution, declaring that the new government would favor the wealthy and the powerful, especially lawyers, and that it would disarm the public in favor of a standing army. By 1789, however, Bacon could confess to Elbridge Gerry that "since the Constitution has been ratified, every Citizen ought to support it. . . . I do not feel assured that, had the Constitution been rejected, we should have been in a better situation, at present, than what we now are."

Nevertheless, by the mid-1790s, Bacon had become increasingly critical not only of the constitution but of the Federalist party as well. Specific targets of his characteristically harsh criticism included duelling, the Alien and Sedition Acts, the United States Treasury Department, the Circuit Courts, and the Congress. His election to the last of these in 1801, following his defeat as the Democrat-Republican candidate for lieutenant governor of Massachusetts, did not temper his outbursts. Federalist Loring Andrews called him "as bitter an enemy, at heart, to the federal government and its measures, as any man in existance—and as d——d a Jacobin as ever met in any conclave of sedition within the limits of United States." In 1804 he served as a presidential elector and voted, not surprisingly, for Jefferson.

Bacon died at his Stockbridge home on October 25, 1820. His wife died a year later. His son Ezekial (Yale 1794), a lawyer, had nearly as wide-ranging a career of public service as his father.

SOURCES: Vital data: John Bacon File, PUA; *DAB*; Sibley's *Harvard Graduates*, XVI, 120-25; *Biog. Direct. Amer. Congresses*, 500; Sprague, *Annals*, I, 686; "the climate": *Illustrations Illustrated* (1781); "for the baptism": Stiles, *Literary Diary*, I, 86; H. A. Hill, *Hist. of Old South Church* (1890), II, passim; preaching to children: A. M. Earle, ed., *Diary of Anna Green Winslow* (1894), 2-4 chaise: S. C. Sedgwick and C. S. Marquand, *Stockbridge* (1939), 168; G. H. Moore, *Hist. of Slavery in Mass.* (1866), 187-91; Williams College trustee: C. Durfee, *Hist. of Williams College* (1860), 87-88; attitude toward federal constitution: R. J. Taylor, *Western Mass. in the Rev.* (1954), 93, 95, 169-170; J. T. Main, *The Antifederalists* (1961), 202; record in Congress: *Annals of Congress* (1851), XI, XII; Ezekial: Dexter, *Yale Biographies*, V, 99-103.

PUBLICATIONS: STE and Hill, II, 591-93   HS

John Bay

JOHN BAY, A.B., ~~A.M. 1765~~, lawyer and public official, was born in Maryland on August 15, 1743, the son of William Bay. The father's Huguenot parents had been forced to flee France in 1685 at the revocation of the Edict of Nantes. After graduation from the College John moved to Albany, New York, where he taught school and read law. Although he did not open a law office until 1781, by which time he had moved to nearby Claverack, New York, Bay had probably already practiced law during the 1770s.

From at least 1775 to 1780, however, public service took up much of his time, and that service was largely in the cause of the Revolution. Bay served simultaneously as secretary of the Claverack Committee of Safety, secretary pro tempore of the Albany Committee of Correspondence, and deputy of the Provincial Congress of New York. In June of that same year he bought 400 pounds of powder for the Continental army. In 1779 and 1780 and again in 1788, 1794, and 1795 he was elected to the New York State Assembly. There he served on a committee to evaluate laws about to expire and to propose new laws. In 1788 he was a delegate to the state's ratifying convention at Poughkeepsie. Finally, from 1796 to 1813 he served as a presidential elector. It is therefore unlikely that he was the same John Bay who enlisted as a mere private in both the First Company, Second Regiment, and the Albany County militia, Eighth Regiment, during the Revolution.

Bay's legislative record mirrored the influence of his mentor, long-term Governor George Clinton, for it bore the indelible stamp of, first, Antifederalism and, later, emerging Republicanism. Bay thus voted regularly to support the Revolution, to confiscate Tory lands, to tax the predominantly Federalist large landowners, to alleviate the plight of their tenants, and to retain significant state power under the new United States constitution. He also opposed the nomination of Alexander Hamilton as New York delegate to the last Congress under the Articles of Confederation and that of Rufus King as United States Senator from New York under the federal constitution.

About 1772 Bay married Ann Williams of Albany. They had four sons and a daughter and lived at Claverack in a mansion constructed on a large tract of land—the result of Bay's thriving legal practice. At least two of their sons were baptized in the Claverack Dutch Reformed Church. A third, William, entered the College in 1792 but did not graduate.

Bay was described by contemporaries as a man of intelligence, integrity, and eloquence. He died at Claverack on June 10, 1818.

SOURCES: Vital data: John Bay File, PUA; 24 *NJA*, 633; P. F. Miller, *A Group of Great Lawyers of Columbia County, N.Y.* (1904), 58-60; legislative record: *Journal of the Assembly of the State of New York*, title varies, issues for 3rd, 4th, 12th, 17th, 18th Sessions, 1779, 1780, 1788, 1794, 1795.

HS

Joel Benedict

JOEL BENEDICT, A.B., A.M. 1768, D.D. Union 1808, Dartmouth 1814, Congregational clergyman, was born in North Salem, Westchester County, New York, on January 8, 1745, the son of Agnes Tyler and

Peter Benedict. The family had been in America at least since the emigration of Thomas Benedict from England in 1639.

At the College Joel was a founding member of the Well-Meaning Club, forerunner of the Cliosophic Society. According to the Reverend Eliphalet Nott, Benedict's son-in-law, former student, and the president of Union College, Benedict "was distinguished at College, as he was afterwards through life, for his love of the classics and mathematics—in which departments he had few equals." Another contemporary reported years later that Benedict's "reading of Latin poetry, even when he was in College, was so remarkable that the Professors sometimes set him to reading Virgil merely for their own gratification."

At some time after graduation Benedict went south to teach school but returned home within a year or two because of the ill health that plagued him throughout his life. Having already determined to enter the ministry, Benedict then left for Connecticut to study with the Reverend Joseph Bellamy, the New Light theologian. His elder brother Abner (Yale 1769) joined him a short time later. Benedict studied Hebrew, which he called "the language of the angels," in order to be able

Joel Benedict, A.B. 1765

to read Scripture in its original tongue. Gradually he became an out-standing Biblical scholar.

A notebook of Benedict's records a conversation with Bellamy "on the downfall of Anti-Christ." The close relationship between teacher and student that it suggests is confirmed by two warm letters from Benedict to Bellamy seeking advice on various theological issues.

In 1769 Benedict was licensed as a Congregational minister by the Association of Litchfield, where Bellamy taught. He then served the association's parent body, the Connecticut General Association, as a theological instructor. Throughout most of 1770 Benedict preached at churches in Massachusetts and Maine but declined a call to Maine's Sheepscot (Newcastle) congregation, which was torn between Presby-terianism and Congregationalism.

On November 25, 1770, Benedict was called to the Congregational church of Newent (now Lisbon) in New London County, Connecticut, and on February 21, 1771, was ordained as its pastor. The congregation had previously been racked by the Old Light/New Light dispute, and the refusal of the Reverend Benjamin Lord (Yale 1714) to attend the ceremonies only reflected the fact, Lord being a prominent Norwich, Connecticut, Old Light. Diehards like Lord aside, by 1770 the two sides had been reconciled and had agreed to hire Benedict and to pay him through voluntary contributions. Benedict himself, a contempo-rary recalled, "kept aloof from all extremes . . . and made little of any other authority in matters of religion than that of the Great Master Himself." He never allowed theological differences to preclude per-sonal friendships. "Whenever you put up a petition for young minis-ters," Benedict wrote Bellamy in 1769, "let one request be that *they may be prudent.*"

On May 16, 1771, Benedict married Sarah McKnown of Boston. She bore him four sons and seven daughters. Her husband's continuing poor health and long periods of convalescence greatly increased her parental and domestic responsibilities. Although poor health barred his actual participation in the Revolution, Benedict was nevertheless a strong supporter, publicly as well as privately.

Benedict's health in part prompted his resignation from his Newent congregation in April 1782. Two other factors were involved: the in-adequacy of his salary and persistent theological divisions. Benedict spent the following two years recuperating at North Salem, New York, preaching occasionally in the locality. By December 1784 he felt suf-ficiently recovered to accept a call from the Congregational church of Plainfield in Windham County, Connecticut, where he remained for the rest of his life. Like Newent, Plainfield had been struck by Old

Light/New Light disputes, but the tensions had apparently disappeared entirely by the time he took up his post.

At Plainfield, Benedict's persuasive, if restrained, preaching and his regular pastoral visits to congregants increased his reputation and his membership rolls alike. He managed to fulfill both tasks despite recurring ill health. A theological debate he reluctantly held in 1791 with an itinerant evangelist enhanced his reputation, for the debate was resolved in Benedict's favor—at least so Benedict claimed in a letter to his brother. Perhaps the most momentous event during his tenure at Plainfield was not of his making: on September 23, 1815, a gale leveled the congregation's thirty-year-old church.

In addition to his regular pastoral activities Benedict was preceptor in Plainfield's Academy, which was organized in 1784, the year he arrived. There, as elsewhere, he won not only the respect but also the affection of his students. Benedict may have preached for a time at the Presbyterian church of Bethlehem, Orange County, New York, sometime after 1787. In 1796 he was appointed a missionary for the General Association of Connecticut.

Benedict preached on the next-to-last Sabbath of his life, then fell ill of pleurisy, and died on February 13, 1816. Eliphalet Nott delivered the funeral sermon. In his only publication, a sermon preached at the funeral of the Reverend Levi Hart of Preston, Connecticut in 1808, Benedict argued that the righteous as well as the wicked must die. For it is exactly the passing of the righteous that teaches all men that their existence has a higher purpose and that they are destined for a world beyond their present one. "We are [all] in a probationary state, and must soon end it." In short, Benedict urged the calm acceptance of death, and he apparently practiced what he preached.

Sources: Vital data: Joel Benedict File, PUA; Sprague, *Annals*, I, 682-85; *NEHGR*, 23 (1869), 307, and 24 (1870), 335; C. R. Williams, *The Cliosophic Society* (1916), 15; Dexter, *Yale Biographies*, III, 316-18; L. Bacon et al., *Contributions to the Ecclesiastical Hist. of Conn.* (1861), 165, 318, 416, 463, 518; C. M. Clark, *Hist. of the Congregational Churches in Maine* (1926), 136-37; Stiles, *Literary Diary*, I, 58, 59, and III, 247-48; E. M. Ruttenber and L. H. Clark, *Hist. of Orange County. N.Y.* (1881), 767; *NYGBR*, 45 (1914), 272; W. G. McLoughlin, *New England Dissent* (1971), II, 961; letters: MSS, Gratz Col., PHi, and Webster/Bellamy Transcripts, PPPrHi; funeral sermon: *A Sermon Delivered at the Funeral of the Rev. Levi Hart* (1809), 26.

HS

Joseph Chambers

JOSEPH CHAMBERS, A.B., schoolmaster, was born in Philadelphia. All information discovered about Chambers is contained in three letters

written by the Reverend William Smith, Anglican Provost of the College of Philadelphia, in 1768. On April 24 Smith informed the Bishop
of London "that one M^r. Chambers, born in this Town, educated a
Presbyterian in New Jersey College, hath gone into Maryland, got a
title to a [Anglican] Curacy . . . and some of the Maryland Clergy to
sign his Credentials, deceaved, I suppose, by his College Certificate,
which is full; but it is three years since he left College and they know
nothing of Him during that time, he having been in this province, nor
yet the Cause of his leaving the Presbyterians, nor a very high charge
against him at Lancaster about a month ago, in this Province, which
made him quit that and go to Maryland."

Smith told the bishop that the charge against Chambers was bas-
tardy and pleaded that the bishop not confirm him in holy orders until
a full investigation was made. Two weeks later Smith's investigation
was completed. He reported that on February 16, Mary Kalleren, a
Lancaster servant-girl, had deposed that " 'the Bastard child, where-
with she is pregnant, was begotten upon her by Joseph Chambers, late
of Lancaster, Schoolmaster, who is the Father and none else.' " Smith
included other particulars, and added that Chambers had spent some
time in Newark, New Jersey, before moving to Lancaster. A resident
of that town reported to Smith of Chambers that "this is not the first
crime of the sort in him. In short, he is a person of no valuable qualifications, has read nothing and can scarce write three lines correctly.
His passions are violent and his conceit insufferable. He seems to prefer a life of Dissipation to anything serious, and discovers a fondness
for Drink, Gaming and Low Company." Smith's warnings to the
bishop must have got back to Chambers, for in a letter of October 28
to an English correspondent, Smith wrote: "That worthless man Joseph Chambers is, I hear, gone to Ireland to try for orders. Can nothing be done to prevent it? Pray write to some of the Bishops to put
them on their guard it if is not too late."

No notice of Chambers has been found in the records of the Church
of Ireland, nor has any further information about him been discovered. Smith was worried about the moral character of the Anglican
clergy in America and about the increasing number of Presbyterian
youths taking Anglican orders. Although Smith was given to hyper-
bole, there seems little reason to doubt the veracity of his reports
about Chambers. Chambers was first listed as dead in the College's
catalogue of 1804.

SOURCES: Smith to Bishop of London, Apr. 24 and May 6, 1768, H. W. Smith, *ed.,*
Life and Correspondence of the Rev. William Smith, D.D. (1880), I, 413-15; Smith
to secretary of S.P.G., Oct. 22, 1768, W. S. Perry, ed., *Hist. Collections . . . Am. Col.*
Church (1969 ed.), II, 436.

George Corbin

GEORGE CORBIN, A.B., in all probability was the landowner and public official George Corbin of Accomac County, Virginia, son of Coventon (Covington) Corbin and his second wife Barbara Drummond. Although specific confirmation for his identification is lacking, no other of the Corbins found in a widespread search could have attended the College at this time. The date of birth has not been established, but his parents were married at some time after 1738 and before 1742, when a child of theirs was buried on the property overlooking Chincoteague Bay that is graced by a handsome residence known in recent years as Corbin Hall, probably built by George Corbin about 1787. The father, who died August 30, 1778, at the age of 67, and the mother, who died September 25, 1756, are also buried there with tombstones erected by their son. Coventon Corbin, who became one of the more substantial residents of the county, was the son of Ralph Corbin and the grandson of George Corbin, a surgeon residing at the beginning of the century in Northampton County. If the great-grandson of this George Corbin graduated from the College at the normal age of twenty, he would have been born about 1745.

Corbin is listed among the graduate members of the Cliosophic Society, and so presumably was associated with William Paterson (A.B. 1763), Oliver Ellsworth (A.B. 1766), Luther Martin (A.B. 1766), and others in the organization of the Well-Meaning Club in 1765. No other details of his career at the College seem to be known.

After graduation, Corbin's career remains for a time as sketchy as his stay in the College. He is listed as having taken an oath of allegiance to the king together with his father in September 1773, though the occasion has not been discovered. On December 24, 1774, he became a member of the Accomac Committee created in response to the recommendations of the recent Continental Congress for a boycott of British imports. From 1779 to 1781 he served as acting lieutenant for the county, none too happily if we may accept surviving correspondence with Governors Jefferson and Nelson and Colonel William Davies (A.B. 1765), a classmate who in the spring of 1781 had become Virginia's commissioner of war.

In 1781 Corbin was succeeded as county lieutenant by his nephew Colonel John Cropper, revolutionary soldier and son of a sister, Sabra Corbin, by her marriage to Sebastian Cropper. Scattered references suggest that he may have been attorney for the state in 1788, and that in August 1781 he served as judge advocate in the court martial of the Reverend John Lyon before a court presided over by Colonel John

Cropper. The fullest record of Corbin's activity has been preserved in a number of real estate transfers indicating that he belonged to a family of property, and that his own activity was greater after he had become the heir to his father in 1778. The major part of the property on Chincoteague Bay seems to have been accumulated by him. His standing among the leading citizens of the county is indicated by his subscription of £30 in 1783 for support of Washington Academy, built *College in Chesterton,* near Princess Anne, in Somerset County, Maryland, a *Kent County in Maryland's Eastern Shore,* project jointly undertaken by residents of that county and of Accomac County in Virginia. In 1786 by act of the state assembly Corbin became, together with Isaac Avery, a former Anglican minister he probably had known in college, one of nine trustees for Margaret Academy, a separate educational venture that would achieve an important measure of success in the nineteenth century.

The record of Corbin's personal life is especially sparse. Not even the name of his wife has been discovered, nor of any surviving children other than his daughter Agnes Drummond, who was married to John S. Ker and who inherited the bulk of Corbin's property upon his death in 1793.

SOURCES: R. T. Whitelaw, *Virginia's Eastern Shore* (2 vols., 1951), *passim*, has been the principal source of information, but see especially pp. 927, 1042, 1045, 1048, 1233, 1267, 1278, 1356, 1360-64 for family and principal properties; oath: *VMHB*, 5 (1898), 103; Committee: *WMQ* (1 ser.), 5 (1896), 252; service as lieutenant of county: *Jefferson Papers*, see Index v. 1-6, and *Cal. Va. St. Pap.*, II, 339-41, 511; III, 149, 245; ibid., II, 305 for judge advocate, and IV, 470, for attorney; Washington College: *MHM* 6 (1911), 172; Margaret Academy: Whitelaw, 733-34, 1024, and Hening, *Statutes*, XII, 364; *md. Hist. mag. (VI) (1911), "Washington College, 1783," 164-179.* WFC

Gershom Craven

GERSHOM CRAVEN, A.B., physician, was born in Middletown, Hunterdon County, New Jersey, on February 2, 1746, the fifth of the eight children of Thomas Craven and his wife Elizabeth Walling. The father, a schoolmaster, was born in London in 1709 and emigrated to Pennsylvania in 1728, and taught in several New Jersey villages before his death in 1775. After graduation from the College, young Gershom studied for a time at the newly constituted Medical Faculty of the College of Philadelphia, but did not remain to take his degree.

Craven established a practice at the village of Ringoes in Hunterdon County, New Jersey, in 1771. The first "regular-bred" physician at the place, he was remembered by a local historian as being "popular, persistent and successful." On June 9, 1774, Craven married Rebecca

Quick in an Anglican ceremony. The couple had thirteen children. The only certainty concerning Craven's activities during the Revolution is that he served as a surgeon in the 2nd Regiment of the Hunterdon County militia. After the war Craven apparently pursued his profession quietly in Ringoes. He retired in 1812, when he was completely disabled by paralysis. He died on May 3, 1819, and was buried in St. Andrew's churchyard in Ringoes. The inventory of his personal property amounted to $384.32.

SOURCES: Geneal., marriage, and children: *GMNJ*, 21 (1946), 57-61; addit. information: Gershom Craven File, PUA; Ringoes practice: J. P. Snell, *Hist. of Hunterdon and Somerset Counties* (1881), 224, 225; militia surgeon: Wickes, *Hist. of Med. N.J.*, 223; inventory: MS, N.J. State Lib., Trenton.

William Davies

WILLIAM DAVIES, A.B., A.M. 1768, was born in 1749 at Hanover, Virginia, the oldest of three sons, including John Rodgers Davies (A.B. 1769), of Samuel Davies, fourth president of the College, and Jane Holt, his second wife and the daughter of John Holt of Williamsburg who subsequently became a printer and publisher in Connecticut and New York. William presumably moved from Hanover to Princeton with the family in the summer of 1759, when his father assumed the presidency. The father's death early in 1761 left the widow with five children very largely dependent upon subscriptions collected in Philadelphia and New York for their support and education. William completed his studies at Nassau Hall with the largest class yet graduated from the College, and one that included three others who were sons of presidents of the College: Jonathan Edwards, Joseph Finley, and Samuel Finley.

According to tradition, after his father's death William had become the ward of Richard Stockton (A.B. 1748), with whom he subsequently read law, possibly supporting himself in part by teaching in the grammar school. Perhaps it was some time after he qualified for the master's degree that he returned to his native state, to which his mother and two younger sisters seem to have returned earlier. He settled at Norfolk, where on December 17, 1771, he was one of six lawyers who signed an agreement binding themselves to undertake no cause before the courts without receipt of their fees.

Nothing else seems to be known of his activity there before July 6, 1774, when he signed as clerk a series of resolutions adopted at a meeting of the "Freeholders, Merchants, Traders, and other inhabitants of the County and Borough of Norfolk" in support of the block-aded port of Boston, of a forthcoming convention at Williamsburg of the "late burgesses," of the calling of a continental congress, and of a general association for the boycott of British imports. In the following February the *Virginia Gazette* reported him as secretary of the "Committee of Observation" that on the 7th of the month had censored a Dr. Alexander Gordon for breaking the association adopted by the Continental Congress in the preceding October. In July 1775 he was secretary of the Norfolk Committee of Safety.

Late in September 1775 he received a commission as captain in the 1st Virginia Regiment of the Continental Line. His promotion to major in March 1777 and to the ranks of lieutenant-colonel and colonel in 1778, with varying regimental assignments, testifies to the quality of his continuing service as a continental officer. After Baron von Steuben's appointment in the spring of 1778 as inspector-general of the army, Davies became one of four sub-inspectors and won the enduring confidence of the baron. This led perhaps to the especially heavy responsibilities he assumed during the difficult last year of the war for the defense of his own state in the face of invasions by Benedict Arnold and Lord Cornwallis. In the fall of 1780 General Nathaniel Greene succeeded Gates in command of the southern army and von Steuben came south with him. On his way to the Carolinas Greene left von Steuben in Virginia, which the two of them had judged to be the likeliest source of men and materials for the strengthening of the southern army. Davies was promptly given charge of a base at Chesterfield Courthouse that was of critical importance in plans for organizing and equipping fresh troops.

The head of the Virginia Board of War having resigned in the spring of 1781 under circumstances suggesting a need for stronger leadership, Governor Thomas Jefferson selected Davies to succeed him, which he did on March 27, approximately six months before the final victory at Yorktown. He served as the state's commissioner of war until late in 1782. In an assignment that was in no way easy, and amidst troubled relationships among other officials with whom he had to deal, Davies so conducted his office that he retained the full confidence of Jefferson, Greene, von Steuben, and Thomas Nelson, who in June 1781 succeeded Jefferson as governor.

Davies's reputation as a man of ability and integrity undoubtedly explains his selection in 1788 to serve as agent for the state in the settlement of claims between Virginia and the United States. A complex problem, often found at the very center of political controversy, with which the Congress and the states had been struggling since 1782, it remained far from fully resolved when the new federal government was inaugurated in 1789. Over the course of several years, Davies was often away from his home in Virginia, much of the time at first in New York and then in Philadelphia. The generally satisfactory settlement ultimately achieved for Virginia is in no small measure attributable to him.

For a man of his accomplishments the record of his personal life seems to be surprisingly and disappointingly incomplete. He married a Mary Murray, widow of Alexander Gordon of Petersburg, and apparently was survived by a daughter Mary Ann, but no record has been found of when the marriage occurred. It is reported that after he was mustered out of the army in 1783, he practiced law in Petersburg. However, when the first federal census was taken in 1790 his residence seems to have been Norfolk. And there is reason for believing that he was the William Davies appointed collector of the port by President Adams in December 1800, and the William Davies, "late collector of this port," who was reported as having died in Mecklenburg by a Norfolk newspaper of December 23, 1805.

SOURCES: Family and personal details: Maclean, *History*, esp. I, 245-46; G. W. Pilcher, *Samuel Davies* (1971); R. C. McCullough, *Yesterday When It Is Past* (1957); file PUA. Ashbel Green, writing in 1822 and quoted by Maclean, said that Davies had died in Virginia "a few years since," which argues that the year 1837 sometimes found for his death is an error. Another year given at times is 1814, but a letter of 1802 referring to "Colonel Davies, the collector," and evidence that William Davies in that year subscribed in support of a Presbyterian church in Norfolk, helps persuade one that he actually died in 1805. See *Calendar Va. St. Papers*, IX, 316, 340; and *Lower Norfolk County . . . Antiquary*, V, Pt. 2, 66. For his relatively voluminous official correspondence, see *Calendar Va. St. Papers*, passim but esp. IV-VI; *Jefferson Papers*, IV-VI (and for circumstances of appointment to War Office, editorial note on V, 205); and *Official Letters of the Governors of the State of Virginia* (1928, 1929) II and III; military career: J. H. Gwathmey, *Historical Register of Virginians in the Rev.* (1938). See also *Madison Papers*, III, 32n.; D. Malone, *Jefferson the Virginian* (1948), 333, 348-49; and E. J. Ferguson, *Power of the Purse* (1961), 215-16, 314-15, 323-24.

WFC

Jonathan Edwards, Jr.

JONATHAN EDWARDS, JR., A.B., A.M. 1768, D.D. 1785, A.M. Yale 1769, Congregational clergyman and college president, was born in Northampton, Massachusetts, on May 26, 1745, the son of Sarah Pierpont, wife of Jonathan Edwards, third president of the College. Jonathan was one of three Edwards brothers to attend the College, the others being Timothy (A.B. 1757) and Pierpont (A.B. 1768).

Jonathan Edwards, Jr., A.B. 1765
BY REUBEN MOULTHROP

"When I was but six years of age," Edwards wrote in 1788, "my father removed with his family to *Stockbridge*, which at that time, was inhabited by [Mohican] Indians almost solely; as there were in the town but twelve families of whites or Anglo-Americans, and perhaps one hundred fifty families of Indians. The Indians being the nearest neighbours, I constantly associated with them; their boys were my daily school-mates and play-fellows. Out of my father's house, I seldom heard any language spoken, beside the Indian. By these means I acquired the knowledge of that language, and a great facility in speaking it. It became more familiar to me than my mother tongue. I knew the names of some things in Indian, which I did not know in English; even all my thoughts ran in Indian. . . . When I was in my tenth year, my father sent me among the six nations [i.e., the Iroquois], with a design that I should learn their language, and thus become qualified to be a missionary among them. But on account of the war with France, which then existed, I continued among them but about six months."

When Edwards's parents died suddenly in 1758, the cost of young Jonathan's education was assumed by friends. He was prepared at the College's grammar school and matriculated in the College itself in November 1761. He was, apparently, precocious. Jacob Rush, a classmate, told his brother Benjamin (A.B. 1760) that when Edwards was in College "Dr. Finley often submitted to be taught by him, especially in the mathematics." Edwards also underwent a religious conversion in Princeton, drawing up an elaborate compact between himself and God. At his graduation, a Pennsylvania newspaper reported, Edwards delivered "with great Propriety and Spirit" a pre-commencement Latin oration "On the Evils to which a People is Liable, when involved in debt."

Shortly after commencement Edwards left Princeton to study theology with the two most prominent exponents of his father's ideas. During the winter months of 1765 he lived with the theologian Samuel Hopkins in Great Barrington, Massachusetts. He left Hopkins in the spring of 1766 to study with the theologian Joseph Bellamy in Bethlehem, Connecticut. In later years Edwards would become the chief exponent of the intellectual tradition represented by his father, Hopkins, and Bellamy. To the "New Divinity" school of theology he contributed little more than the first full modern statement of the "governmental theory" of the atonement. His major significance was in his role as a rigid upholder and defender of the ideas of the New Divinity against a spreading Arminianism on the one hand, and the Old Calvinists, or heirs to the Half-Way Covenant on the other.

Licensed to preach in October 1766, Edwards soon returned to the College. There, with time out for occasional preaching in pulpits in New Jersey, New York, and Connecticut, he served as tutor in languages and logic. In December 1768 Edwards was called to the White Haven Church, which had been formed out of New Haven's First Church in 1742 by a New Light secession. In 1760 the church had returned to the practice of the Half-Way Covenant, which permitted the baptism of the children of members not in full communion. Edwards would have none of it. Within eight months after his arrival in New Haven, a dissident group of "Old Calvinists" broke away and constituted a new church. The issue remained a constant point of contention throughout Edwards's New Haven pastorate.

Edwards and his congregation were in complete agreement on one issue: he and they gave total support to the Revolution. During a British raid on New Haven, a good deal of his property was destroyed. But as the years went by the membership in Edwards's church steadily dwindled. His doctrinal rigorousness, his dry preaching, and his chilly personality led some to Anglicanism, others to less demanding churches. Edwards's personal life was marred by tragedy. In 1770 he married Mary Porter of New Haven. The couple had four children. In 1782 Mary Edwards was drowned in a bizarre accident. Edwards later married Mary Sabin of New Haven.

During his New Haven years, a flood of essays and sermons poured from Edwards's pen. They were not limited to theological matters. As early as 1773–1774 Edwards was writing newspaper articles critical of slavery. In 1791 he published a pamphlet attacking slavery that was apparently widely circulated. "Should we be willing, that the Africans or any other nation should purchase us, our wives and children, transport us into Africa and there sell us into perpetual and absolute slavery?" he asked. "Great Britain in her late attempt to enslave America, committed a very small crime indeed in comparison with the crime of those who enslave the Africans." But to a South Carolina minister who in 1798 asked for advice after reading his words, Edwards could only reply: "Thirty [years] ago Connecticut was involved in as great darkness concerning the rights of the Negroes, as South Carolina is now. . . . I can advise neither to abdicate the ministry, nor to remove to some distant region, nor yet to expose yourself to a prosecution for sedition." Talk quietly among your friends and colleagues against slavery, Edwards counseled.

In 1795 Edwards's difficulties with his congregation came to an end. "This day the Society at White Haven had a Meeting," President Ezra Stiles of Yale noted in his diary on April 13. "They are dissatisfied with Dr Edwards, and voted 22 for & 15 against his Dismission. Appointed a Committee to confer with him on Terms of Dismission. He has been 26 years in the Ministry. No objection against his Conduct or moral Character, but dissatisfied with his Mode of Preaching & Rigidity in Church Discipline especially as to Terms of Communion & Baptisms, & his refusing to commune with the other two Congregational Churches in Town, with which that Church wish for free & open Communion."

Edwards shortly took up a new pastorate in what he called the "remote situation" of a small mission church at North Colebrook, Connecticut. There he remained until 1799, when he was asked to succeed John Blair Smith (A.B. 1773) as second president of Union College at Schenectady, New York. At Union Edwards led a successful building program and tightened control over student life. He was also extremely active in laying plans that led to the union of the Congregational and Presbyterian churches. He died in Schenectady on August 1, 1801, too soon to see his work either in the college or the church come to fruition.

Some have seen parallels in the careers of the junior and the senior Edwards—both were theologians, both were college presidents. Such parallels obscure more than they reveal. The senior Edwards was the greatest theologian in the reformed tradition since John Calvin. The junior Edwards was an intellectual conservator—and not a particularly original one at that. The senior Edwards's few weeks as a college president were inconsequential in his career and the affairs of the College; the junior Edwards had a strong and immediate effect on his institution. There was, however, one striking coincidence in the lives of both men: father and son preached on the first Sunday of the years of their deaths from the text, "This year thou shalt die."

SOURCES: Full biography: J.R.L. Ferm, "Jonathan Edwards the Younger and the American Reformed Tradition," Ph.D. diss., Yale University, 1959; among sketches see: *DAB*; Tryon Edwards, "Memoir," in *Works*, I, below; autobiographical fragment: Edwards, "Preface" to *Observations on the Language of the Muhhekaneew Indians* (1788); Jacob Rush remark: Butterfield, *Rush Letters*, 369; commencement: *Pa. Gaz.*, Oct. 10, 1765; slavery quotations: Edwards, *The Injustice and Impolicy of the Slave Trade . . .* (1791), 4, 24; slavery letter: Edwards to Rev. Robert Wilson, Nov. 16, 1798, MS, PPPrHi; Stiles quotation: *Literary Diary*, III, 562; Union: A.V.V. Raymond, *Union University* (1907), I, 70-71, and F. B. Hough, *Historical Sketch of Union College* (1876), 10-11.

PUBLICATIONS: STE and also, Tryon Edwards, ed., *The Works of Jonathan Edwards, D.D.*, 2 vols, Andover, 1842.

MSS: CtHC, CtY, NjP, PPPrHi, PHi, PYHi, MNtcA, Conn. Missionary Society

Joseph Finley

JOSEPH FINLEY, A.B., physician, was born at West Nottingham, Maryland, about 1746, the first son and second child of Samuel Finley, an Irish-born Presbyterian clergyman and schoolmaster, by his first wife, Sarah Hall. The father became the fifth president of the College in 1761 and moved his family to Princeton. President Finley died the year after Joseph's graduation from the College. The surviving members of his family appear to have moved to Philadelphia, where young Joseph studied medicine. He may have had time to establish a practice in the city before his death, which occurred at some time between 1770 and 1776. He had not married.

SOURCES: *A Finley Genealogy: A Compilation* (1905), 4. The alumnus is sometimes confused with his cousin, Joseph Lewis Finley (A.B. 1775).

Samuel Finley, Jr.

SAMUEL FINLEY, JR., A.B., physician, was the second son of the College's fifth president, the Irish-born Presbyterian clergyman Samuel Finley, and his first wife, Sarah Hall. Finley was born on June 11, 1748, at West Nottingham, Maryland, where for many years his father conducted an academy that was, in effect, a preparatory school for the College. The family moved to Princeton when the father became president of the College in 1761.

After graduation Finley studied medicine, most likely in Philadelphia. During the Revolution he served as a surgeon with the American army. Finley spent the winter of 1776–1777 with his younger brother, Dr. James E. B. Finley, at the army hospital at Bethlehem, Pennsylvania. Supplies were short, conditions difficult, and on February 17, 1778, both brothers signed a letter protesting conditions at the hospital. The letter was used as a weapon in the campaign of their cousin, Dr. Benjamin Rush (A.B. 1760), to unseat Dr. William Shippen (A.B. 1754), director general of the army's medical services. On April 8, 1778, Finley was appointed surgeon to the Fourteenth Massachusetts Regiment of the Continental line. He served with that unit until he was transferred to the Seventh Massachusetts Regiment on January 1, 1781. He remained on active duty until June 3, 1783.

After the war, Finley moved to New York City and established a medical practice. He was a member of the Society of the Cincinnati, a controversial hereditary organization of former army officers. Finley returned briefly to active duty during the quasi-war with France, serving from September 4, 1799, until April 1, 1800, as a surgeon with the 12th United States Infantry Regiment. His return to military service may have brought on an illness, for he died at his home in Yonkers, New York, early in 1801. He had never married.

SOURCES: Basic data: *A Finley Genealogy: A Compilation* (1905), 4-5; B. A. Whittemore, *Memorials of the Mass. Soc. of the Cincinnati* (1964), 187; mentions: L. C. Duncan, *Medical Men in Am. Rev.* (1971 ed.), 184, 199, 305, 393; Bethlehem hosp.: Butterfield, *Rush Letters*, 201-202; death: *NYGBR*, 59 (1928), 136.

Richard Goodman

RICHARD GOODMAN, A.B., farmer, was born on April 14, 1748, at West Hartford, Connecticut, the son of Joanna Wadsworth and Timothy Goodman, a farmer. The high point of Goodman's public career ap-

pears to have come during the College's commencement exercises on
September 25, 1765. A Pennsylvania newspaper reported the event
thus: "After . . . two Disputes, a short Intermediate Oration, for the
Sake of Variety, was introduced by Mr. Richard Goodman, in which
he pointed out the Difference between the Eloquence of Cicero, and
that of Demosthenes, with their peculiar Excellencies; his Delivery
very well examplified his Subject."

After graduation Goodman returned to West Hartford and farmed.
In 1771 Goodman married Nancy Seymour, daughter of Timothy Seymour of New Haven. The couple had thirteen children before Nancy's
death in 1792. In September 1773, both of the Goodmans became full
members of West Hartford's Congregational church. A flag and mark-
er on Goodman's grave in West Hartford indicate that he was a participant in the Revolutionary War, but no record of his service has
been discovered. He may have been the Richard Goodman who was
paid £2.1s.6d by the Connecticut treasurer in 1783 for carrying an express message, or the Richard Goodman who was listed in May 1788
as one of the founding members of the Governor's Independent Volunteer Troop of Horse Guards. Goodman died in West Hartford on April
8, 1834. In his will he divided his household goods and money (4s.6d.)
among his ten surviving children.

SOURCES: [Edward Goodman], Genealogical Notes on the Goodman Family, 1741-
1868, p. 6, MS, Conn. State Lib., Hartford; commencement: *Pa. Gaz.*, Oct. 10, 1765;
wife, children: D. L. Jacobus, *A Hist. of the Seymour Family* (1939), 128; church:
West Hartford First Church records, 1:102, MS, Conn. St. Lib.; grave: cemetery inscriptions, West Hartford 126, Cemetery 2, p. 36. MS, Conn. St. Lib.; message and
Horse Guards: *Rec. State Conn.*, V, 90; VI, 442; will: MS, Probate Record File, Conn.
St. Lib.

Robert Halsted

ROBERT HALSTED, A.B., A.M. 1768, physician, was born on September 13, 1746, at Halsted Point, Elizabethtown, New Jersey, the first of
the twelve children of Rebecca Ogden, wife of Caleb Halsted. The father, a farmer, had an income sizable enough to provide his sons with
a good education. Three of them attained positions of public stature:
Caleb Halsted, Jr., became a surgeon and mayor in Elizabeth, New
Jersey; William became the sheriff of Essex County in 1790; Matthias
served as a general in the Continental army. Upon the father's death
in 1784, he left £1,200 to his family.

When Robert came to Nassau Hall in 1762, he was the first of a long
line of Halsteds to attend the college. He began his medical appren-

ticeship in Elizabethtown, New Jersey. There he also set up a practice that lasted sixty years, attended the Presbyterian church on a regular basis, and became noted for his strict moral piety. On April 15, 1773, he married Mary Wiley, who came from a Rhode Island Baptist family. They had five children, among them Job Stockton Halsted (A.M. Hon. 1823). With Mary's death in 1786, Robert married again on October 11, 1787. His second wife was Mary Mills, the daughter of the Reverend William Mills (A.B. 1756); the couple had five children, among them Matthias Ogden Halsted (A.B. 1810).

The coming of the Revolution found Robert a firm Whig. In 1776 he joined the New Jersey militia at Fort Lee. As company surgeon, he attended to the sick with very limited supplies of medical equipment. When Fort Lee fell to the English, a tragic loss for the revolutionary armies, Robert was taken prisoner on November 18, 1776. During the next five years he was confined in the Old Sugar House, Liberty Street, New York City amid cramped, disease-ridden conditions. Only when he was exchanged in 1781 did Robert return to his family and reestablish his practice in Elizabethtown, where he remained until his death on November 25, 1825. He was buried in the First Presbyterian church-yard, leaving behind his wife and ten children. One son, Matthias Ogden Halsted, became one of the richest and most respected merchants in Elizabethtown.

SOURCES: Family, military career: Wheeler, *Ogden Family*, 87-88, 141; *Biog. and Geneal. Hist. of Newark and Essex Cty., N.J.* (1890), 123-25; father's will: 35 *NJA*, 135; medical career, religious piety: Wickes, *Hist. of Medicine, N.J.*, 272-73; conditions at Ft. Lee: H. B. Carrington, *Battles of the Am. Rev.*, 49, 232; New York City prisons: T. J. Wertenbaker, *Father Knickerbocker Rebels* (1940), 106.

LLM

Richard Hutson

RICHARD HUTSON, A.B., A.M. 1784, lawyer, public official, and planter, was born in Prince William Parish, South Carolina, either on August 27, 1747, or on July 9, 1748, the son of Mary Woodward and her husband, William Hutson. The father, born in England, was destined for the law by his father, an Anglican clergyman. After difficulties with his family the father fled to America and joined a troupe of actors. Converted by George Whitefield's preaching, he became a clergyman, serving as pastor of the Independent (Congregational/Presbyterian) Church in St. William's Parish from 1743 to 1757, and from 1757 to 1760 as pastor of Charleston's Independent Church. The father died

Richard Hutson, A.B. 1765
ATTRIBUTED TO JAMES EARL

on May 26, 1760, leaving to young Richard a substantial but indeterminable amount of property as well as "all family pictures and books."

After graduation Hutson studied law, probably in South Carolina, for he had returned to that province by 1766, when he purchased four slaves from his brother-in-law, Colonel Isaac Hayne. Hutson began the practice of law in Charleston, where he was a member of his father's old church, which by the 1770s had as its pastor William Tennent III (A.B. 1758). The congregation included a number of prominent Whig leaders, among them Hutson's classmate, Dr. David Ramsay.

Hutson owned a plantation along the Stono River in St. Andrew's Parish near Charleston. In January 1775 he was appointed to St. Andrew's committee to enforce the association formed to boycott the importation of British goods. When the British attacked Charleston in 1776, Hutson served in the militia and later in the year was elected to the South Carolina Assembly, which elevated him to the Council. As befitted a member of the Independent Church, Hutson was active in the drive to disestablish the Church of England, writing in January

1777 to advise his brother-in-law Hayne to be sure to attend the assembly to press the religious Dissenters' cause.

Elected to the Continental Congress on January 22, 1778, Hutson took his seat on April 13, serving intermittently until June 1779. In Congress he was a member of several minor committees and joined the other South Carolina delegates in attempts to preserve southern influence and to exclude free Negroes from the "privileges and immunities" clause of the Articles of Confederation. Though Hutson and his fellow South Carolina delegates worried about their authority, they ultimately signed the Articles.

Back in Charleston by 1780, Hutson served on the privy council and was present at the capitulation of the city to the British in May of that year. Among the South Carolinians seized by the British for refusing to swear allegiance to the crown, Hutson was put aboard a prison ship and sent to St. Augustine for internment. There he was imprisoned in a room with his fellow alumni James Hamden Thomson (A.B. 1761) and Dr. David Ramsay.

Released in July 1781, Hutson was sent north to Philadelphia. At about the time his ship was passing Charleston, Hutson's brother-in-law, Colonel Isaac Hayne, was being hanged there by the British in a case which would become one of the *causes célèbres* of the Revolution. Back in South Carolina by 1782, Hutson was elected to the assembly and in February of the same year became lieutenant-governor of his state.

In 1783 Hutson became the first Intendant (mayor) of Charleston. The city was in a volatile mood in 1783–1784. Early in 1783 the legislature allowed British merchants to stay on after the British evacuation in order to clear up their affairs. It was also surprisingly lenient toward Loyalists. But when news of the Treaty of Peace, which provided for the payment of debts by Americans to British merchants reached the city, trouble broke out. Several minor riots against the "Tories" and British occurred. The mobs were composed of disbanded soldiers, artisans, and sailors. Disturbances continued throughout 1783–1784. The exact course of events has yet to be completely unraveled, but it appears that Hutson and the South Carolina Council managed to split the unruly elements in the population into different factions. In an election that was framed in terms of "Aristocracy" versus "Democracy," Hutson—on the "Aristocratic" side—was reelected as Intendant in September 1784. The events surrounding the election included a bizarre plot to kill Hutson and other officials. Hutson's success in quelling the disturbances won the praise of the visiting Latin American patriot, Francisco de Miranda. "Good judgement, considerable education, and a love of the sciences, society, and humanity are the qualities of this affable person," wrote Miranda of Hutson.

When South Carolina's chancery, or equity, court was organized in 1784, Hutson was elected one of the first chancellors. He became senior judge of the court in 1791, resigning in 1793. He also served in the South Carolina House of Representatives in 1789. A member of the South Carolina convention called in 1787 to consider the federal constitution, he voted for its adoption. He was involved in nonpolitical affairs as well. In 1784 he joined Charles C. Pinckney and others in founding the Mount Sion Society to promote educational facilities in South Carolina. In 1793 Dr. David Ramsay wrote favorably of an oration Hutson had recently given on "the utility of studying Latin & Greek."

Hutson suffered financial losses during and after the war. Still, in 1790 he owned 264 acres of land valued at $3,214 and seventeen slaves. Hutson died in Charleston on April 12, 1795, never having married.

SOURCES: Sketch: *DAB*; geneal.: *SCHGM*, 9 (1908), 128; father and many details of career scattered throughout: E. McCrady, *Hist. of South Carolina* (1969 ed.), I-III; all early sources give 1748 as birthdate, but for 1747 birthdate see: "Register Kept by the Rev. Wm. Hutson," *SCHGM*, 37 (1936), 26; father's will: C. T. Moore, *Abstracts of the Wills of S.C.* (1969), 10; 1766 slaves: *SCHGM*, 12 (1911), 19; early rev. activities: W. E. Hemphill, ed., *Extracts from the Journals of the Prov. Congr. of S.C.* (1962), 147-48; Cont. Congr.: *LMCC*, III-IV; and, W. M. Dabney and M. Dargan, *William Henry Drayton & the Am. Rev.* (1962), 147-48; St. Augustine: *SCHGM*, 33 (1932); Isaac Hayne: *DAB*; Intendancy: R. Walsh, *Charleston's Sons of Liberty* (1959), 120-21; Miranda: J. S. Ezell, ed., *The New Democracy in America* (1963), 31; M. Jensen, *The New Nation* (1965), 275-77; plot: A. S. Edwards, ed., *Jour. of the Privy Council, 1783-1789* (1971), 136; Mt. Sion Soc.: C. G. Singer, *S.C. in the Confederation* (1941), 26; R. L. Brunhouse, ed., *David Ramsay, 1749-1815*, APS *Trans.*, 55 (1965), 135; property: F. McDonald, *We the People* (1958), 220.

Mss: PHi

Samuel Kirkland

SAMUEL KIRKLAND, A.B., A.M. Yale 1768, Dartmouth 1773, Congregational clergyman and missionary, was born at Norwich, Connecticut, on November 20, 1741, the tenth of the twelve children of Daniel Kirtland (Yale 1720) and his wife Hannah Perkins. The father, a Congregational clergyman, was dismissed from his pulpit in 1753 amid rumors of mental derangement. He found another pulpit, but soon lost that too. The circumstances of his dismissals are now obscure; they may have had theological overtones, for he was a New Light. In 1760 young Kirkland (he changed the spelling of the family name at some time in the late 1760s) entered Moor's Indian Charity School in Leb-

Samuel Kirkland, A.B. 1765
BY AUGUSTUS ROCKWELL

anon, Connecticut. Run by Eleazar Wheelock (Yale 1733), the school
had been founded to train white and Indian missionaries. Determined
to become a missionary himself, Kirkland learned the Mohawk tongue
from Indian youths at the school, among them the later-famous leader,
Joseph Brant. The superintendant of Indian affairs, Sir William Johnson, encouraged Kirkland's goals. "Mr. Kirkland's intention of learning
the Mohawk language I much approve of," Johnson wrote to Wheelock
from the New York frontier, "as after acquiring it he could when qualified, be of vast service to them as a clergyman."

Wheelock and others thought that to become properly qualified
Kirkland first needed to attend a college. Accordingly, he set off for
Princeton in the fall of 1762, arriving on November 7. "This college,"
Kirkland wrote back to Wheelock, "is in a flourishing Situation. The
Labours of Mr *President* & *Tutors* for its welfare are indefatigable."
Kirkland reported that at Nassau Hall he "met with kind Reception;
was admitted into the Sophomore Class, upon your desire and without
an examination, as I told Revd Mr Finley and the Tutors, that if I were

examined, I should not attempt to stand for the Sophomore Class, as I knew myself to be in no measure prepared as to the Languages. . . . I recite with my class in Geography; in the Greek Testament at present by myself to S^m Blair, our tutor; I shall likely joyn with them in *Longinus*, in the Spring; and in those Latin authors which they shall study. I am very highly favoured."

Kirkland quickly caught up with his peers. He kept a watchful eye on his classmate, epileptic Ralph Wheelock, Eleazar's son, and sent careful reports on Ralph's condition back to Connecticut. And, as a charity scholar, he also kept a careful eye on his accounts: One year's tuition and board cost him £17.7s.6d. He underwent inoculation against smallpox, but indulged himself a bit, spending 1s.4d. for a quart of rum and 4s.2d. for pipes and tobacco. "Kirkland, for whom you have been concerned," President Finley wrote to Wheelock, "gives me pleasure, and raises my hopes, It grieves me, that his circumstances are so strait."

When his class graduated in September 1765, Kirkland received his degree *in absentia*. He had left Princeton in January to embark on a mission among the Seneca Indians in western New York. It was a major challenge, which Kirkland met with the fortitude and competence that marked his whole life. He learned the Seneca language and gradually overcame the Indians' suspicion of the first Protestant missionary to appear among them. But it was a gruelling ordeal, and when Sir William Johnson in May 1765 saw Kirkland for the first time in several months, he exclaimed, "Good God, Mr. Kirkland, you look like a whipping post!"

In 1766 Kirkland left the frontier for Connecticut, where he was ordained at Lebanon on June 19. On the same day the Connecticut Board of Correspondents for the Honorable Society in Scotland for Propagating Christian Knowledge commissioned him its missionary to the Indians, without assigning him to any particular people. Whether on his own initiative or Wheelock's, when Kirkland returned to western New York in July 1766, he did not take up his old post with the Senecas but settled instead among the Oneidas and their dependents, the Tuscaroras. Kirkland established residence at one of the Oneida "castles," Kanonwalohule. He would remain in the area for the greater part of his life. He quickly learned the Oneida language and was soon instructing them in their own tongue. Kirkland immediately began a campaign to wean his flock from liquor and met with some success. But life was dismally hard. "From week to week," he wrote to Wheelock in 1767, "I am obliged to go eeling with the Indians at Oneida Lake for my subsistence. I have lain and slept with them till I am lousy as a Dog—feasted and starved with them as their Luck depends upon Wind & Weather. It should be asked, why they don't support me, the Answer is ready, they can't support themselves."

As time went by, financial support from Wheelock seemed ever more inadequate to Kirkland, particularly after September 1769, when he married Jerusha Bingham, a niece of Wheelock. Six children were born to the couple. The first two were twins, named George Whitefield and John Thornton. The latter became twelfth president of Harvard in 1810. In 1770 Kirkland began delicate negotiations aimed at achieving independence from Wheelock and securing a steady salary by switching his allegiance to the Boston, rather than the Connecticut, commissioners of the Scottish society. His efforts were successful. The Boston commissioners gave him an annual allowance of £100 (part of it contributed by Harvard College). Support came from a new source as well, when the oldest English missionary organization, the New-England Company, made a handsome donation. Over the years Kirkland collected funds sufficient to build a saw mill, blacksmith shop, and to make other improvements in Oneida life.

By 1771 people from seven different villages were attending Kirkland's services, and he preached to others as well. Kirkland never relaxed his New Light standards: only the truly converted were admitted to full church membership, and, abjuring the Half-Way Covenant, he refused to baptize the children of members not in full communion. He gradually achieved a commanding position among the Oneidas. They sat patiently through his three Sunday sermons and other services, which often ran on until midnight. Kirkland also became the chief figure to whom the Indians referred their civil and personal disputes. After 1772 he spent much of his time alone for, because of troubled conditions on the frontier, in that year he bought his wife a farm in Stockbridge, Massachusetts. There she lived for many years, raising their children. Kirkland made several visits home every year.

As the events leading to the Revolution unfolded, Kirkland took on a new role. He became a central figure in Whig efforts to keep the Iroquois neutral in the conflict between Britain and the colonies. He met with at least partial success, for the Oneidas and Tuscaroras remained loyal to the colonies. During the war, the Oneidas were scattered and Kirkland himself served as a brigade chaplain, accompanying General Sullivan on his 1779 campaign to subdue the Indians in western Pennsylvania and New York. After the war the Scottish society reconfirmed him in his missionary work, Congress rewarded him substantially for his services, and Harvard gave him an outright grant of over £300.

By the 1780s and 1790s the Country of the Six Nations was fast becoming a far different land from the rude wilderness Kirkland had first visited in the 1760s. In those years Indian territory was reduced at a rapid rate as white settlers filtered into the region. Kirkland's position changed with that of his area. In 1790 the Indians and New York state confirmed him and his two sons in a grant of 4,000 acres of land about twelve miles south of Utica. He built a house and moved his family there. Over the next dozen or so years he continued his ministry to the Indians and often served the federal government in negotiating with various tribes. Family and professional difficulties sometimes preoccupied him: the bankruptcy of a son, the death of his wife (in 1796 he took a second wife, Mary Donelly of Stockbridge), the phasing out of its American activities by the Scottish society, and the growth of "pagan" sects among the Indians. But Kirkland was now a landed proprietor, and possessed of a new dream.

Kirkland concluded about 1792 that the only hope for Indian survival lay in their adoption of white culture. The best instrument to achieve this aim, he thought, would be a school for both Indians and whites:

> A serious consideration of the premises, the importance of education, an[d] early improvement and cultivation of the human mind, together with the situation of the frontier settlements of this part of the state, tho' extensive and flourishing, destitute of any well-regulated seminary of learning, have determined us to contribute of the ability wherewith our Heavenly Benefactor hath blessed us, towards laying the foundation of a *Free School*, or *Academy*, in the town of Whitestown and County of Herkimer, contiguous to the Oneida Nation of Indians, for the mutual benefit of the young flourishing settlements in said County and the various tribes of confederate Indians, agreeably to the respective plans proposed for said Seminary.

Kirkland promoted his plan vigorously, donated 300 acres of his land to the academy, and in January 1793 the state of New York chartered Hamilton Oneida Academy. (Alexander Hamilton appears to have contributed only his name to the institution.)

Kirkland lived to see his school flourish, and contributed much of his own money to it. He died on February 28, 1808. Over the years Hamilton came to serve the white settlers more than the Indians. It was rechartered in 1812 as Hamilton College. In 1968 Hamilton opened a coordinate woman's school named Kirkland College in honor of its founder.

SOURCES: Sketches: *DAB* and esp., W. Thorp, "Samuel Kirkland: Missionary to the Six Nations," in Thorp, ed., *Lives of Eighteen from Princeton* (1946), 24-50; S. K. Lothrop, *Life of Samuel Kirkland* (1848); B. Graymount, *Iroquois in the Am. Rev.* (1972), passim; R. F. Berkhofer, *Salvation and the Savage* (1965), passim; father: Dexter, *Yale Biographies*, I, 227-28; quotations: Johnson: D. McClure and E. Parish *Memoirs of the Rev. Eleazar Wheelock* (1811), 229; "flourishing situation": Kirkland to E. Wheelock (hereafter E.W.), Jan. 20, 1763, Wheelock MSS, "eeling": E. W. to friends in Boston, quoting Kirkland, July 27, 1767, ibid.; W. Kellaway, *The New England Company* (1961), 268; plan for Hamilton: *Doc. Hist. of Hamilton College* (1922), 50.

MSS: MH; MHi; NCH; NhD

Alexander McCausland

ALEXANDER MCCAUSLAND, A.B., has not been identified. In the eighteenth century there were extensive families of this name in what are now Maine and West Virginia. The alumnus was first listed as dead in the College's catalogue of 1785.

Alexander Mitchel

ALEXANDER MITCHEL, A.B., Presbyterian clergyman, was born in 1731. After graduation Mitchel taught for two years at the Mattisonia Grammar School in Lower Freehold, Monmouth County, New Jersey. During this time, he studied theology and was licensed by the New Brunswick Presbytery in 1767. Called by the Tinicum Church in Bucks County, Pennsylvania, Mitchel was ordained by the First Philadelphia Presbytery in April 1768. In that year he also married Jane Cochrane of Cochranville, Pennsylvania. Over the next seventeen years Mitchel gradually increased his land holdings from six acres in 1771 to 200 acres and three black servants in 1782. With the coming of the Revolution Mitchel took the Whig side. It is possible that he was the Alexander Mitchel who served as a private in the Bucks County Militia from 1776 to 1783. If so, shortly after his discharge, Mitchel resigned from his pastorate at the Tinicum Church.

Replacing William Foster (A.B. 1764), Mitchel was installed on December 14, 1785, at the Octorara Presbyterian church, Chester County, Pennsylvania, and also accepted a position as part-time pastor in the nearby Doe Run congregation. In addition to tending his farm, Mitchel saw his duties among his predominately Scots-Irish parishioners as "the improvement of the minds," and "reform of the hearts to make the people good." Early in his ministry, he introduced the Watts Hymnal and Psalms, while presiding over the material improvement of the church building. But in the 1790s Mitchel became deeply disturbed by what he regarded as the community's moral decline. When some of the congregation participated in a late-night ball, a contemporary recalled that on the next Sunday, the minister "gave them a regular tearing up about it." The crisis reached such proportions that Mitchel was locked out of his pulpit. Only when he asked the local presbytery to investigate "some unhappy difficulties existing between him and the congregation" was the conflict resolved: Mitchel left his pastorate in April 1796, and no permanent minister held the post until 1810. For the rest of his life, Mitchel served the more conservative Doe Run church. He died on December 6, 1812, and was buried in Octorara, presumably leaving behind no offspring.

SOURCES: Family: *Pa. Arch.* (2 ser.), II, 206; *PMHB*, 3 (1879), 242; W.W.H. Davis, *Bucks County History* (1920), I, 311; career: A. Harris, *A Biographical Hist. of Lancaster County* (1872), 211-12; J. S. Futhey, *Historical Discourse on the Octorara Church* (1870), 91-100; *Bucks County Hist. Soc. Col.*, IV (1917), 110-13; economic success: *Pa. Arch.* (3 ser.), XVII, 89, 426; XII, 88, 191, 256, 465; XX, 172, 629; possible military career: *Pa. Arch.* (5 ser.), II, 358; VI (1906), 63, 418; comments on a minister's duties: Mitchel, "A Sermon Occasioned by the Death of the Reverend Robert Smith," MS, PPPrHi.

LLM

Jonathan Ogden

JONATHAN OGDEN, A.B., is difficult to identify with absolute certainty, but there is little reason to doubt that he was the oldest child and son, born November 16, 1743, of Stephen Ogden and his wife Elizabeth Whitaker. The father was a native of Elizabethtown in Essex County, New Jersey, and E. F. Hatfield's usually reliable history of that place describes Jonathan, together with his cousin and classmate Robert Ogden, as being "of this town." At some time, however, before his death Stephen Ogden had moved, possibly as early as 1753, to Basking Ridge in Somerset County, where he died early in January 1764. No record of Jonathan's performance in the College has survived other than the fact of his graduation on September 25 in a class of thirty-one young men, all but a few of them wearing homespun clothing in protest against the recently enacted Stamp Act.

What Jonathan Ogden was doing and where he was situated for a decade after his graduation remain unknown. On June 15, 1774, he was married to Abigail Gardner, and on May 4, 1775, the two of them renewed their covenant as members of the Presbyterian church of Morristown, located in Morris County, New Jersey, not far above Basking Ridge. He became one of the more active members of the congregation, serving from time to time over the course of three decades beginning in 1790 as clerk of the parish, trustee of the church, and late in life as moderator of a parish meeting. That he was one of the more substantial residents of the township is indicated by the £1,200 invested at interest credited to him by a tax list of 1780, by his liberal contribution for the purchase of the "Morristown Green," a gift to the town made on the condition that it would remain open space, and by his participation in the organization of a local bank. From 1802 to 1804 he represented the county in the state assembly, and from 1805 to 1812 he was a justice of the county court.

Ogden died on January 14, 1825, and his wife just over two weeks afterward. The couple had at least six children and possibly seven, of whom one died in infancy.

SOURCES: Hatfield, *Elizabeth* (1868), 519, 570; Wheeler, *Ogden Family* (1907), 73, 114 especially; *Hist. of the First Presbyterian Church, Morristown* (n.d.); *GMNJ*, 46 (1971), 44, for tax list. There were many Ogdens, and among them the name Jonathan enjoyed a continuing popularity. One Jonathan (1748-1845) became a Loyalist who settled in New Brunswick, Canada, according to L. Sabine, *Biographical Sketches*, II, 126. The date of birth makes it possible but unlikely that he graduated from the College in 1765.

WFC

Robert Ogden, III

ROBERT OGDEN, III, A.B., A.M. 1768, lawyer and public official, was born in Elizabethtown, New Jersey, on March 23, 1746, the fourth child and first son of Phebe Hatfield and her husband, Robert Ogden, Jr., a prosperous and prominent lawyer and active Presbyterian layman who was a trustee of the College from 1764 to 1786. The father also served as speaker of the New Jersey Assembly from 1763 to 1765 and was a delegate to the Stamp Act Congress. Robert's younger brother, Aaron Ogden, received his A.B. in 1773. In College Ogden was a founding member of the Well-Meaning Society, forerunner of the Cliosophic Society.

After graduation Ogden remained in Princeton to read law with Richard Stockton (A.B. 1748). While still there he began a correspondence with Sarah Platt of Huntington, Long Island. The correspondence ripened into romance, and the couple was married on May 19, 1772. Many of Odgen's letters are concerned—in fact, almost

Robert Ogden, III, A.B. 1765

obsessed—with the health or the deaths of various relatives. The pre-occupation was understandable: a fall as a boy had left Ogden without the use of his right arm, and he was severely afflicted by asthma throughout his life.

Ogden was licensed to practice law on June 21, 1770. In April 1772 Governor William Franklin appointed Ogden a surrogate, in place of his father, who had just resigned the post. The younger Ogden soon became known in Elizabethtown and beyond as "the honest lawyer." His chronic ill health did not prevent him from taking a leading role on the Whig side in the early stages of the Revolution. Appointed to the Essex County Committee of Correspondence on December 1, 1774, by February 1776 he was serving as its chairman. Ogden's father acted as a commissary to the American forces early in the Revolution, but his health failed and he turned over his duties to the younger Ogden. By late 1776 the son's health too had begun to fail. His wife and children moved to Morristown, New Jersey, in October of that year, and Ogden was left behind in Elizabethtown. "Robert is and has been very poorly this fall," Ogden's father wrote to one of Ogden's brothers-in-law,

Francis Barber (A.B. 1767), on October 26. At some time during the next few months Ogden, both for reasons of health and to escape the raids of British and Loyalist troops, moved to mountainous north Jersey, settling first in Morristown and then in New Providence. His movements during the Revolution are difficult to trace. He appears to have been now in Sussex County, now in Elizabethtown. Either he or his father served on the New Jersey council for Sussex County in 1778 and 1779. On September 3, 1779, Ogden was appointed clerk to two Essex County courts. The following year he was made one of the twelve New Jersey sergeants-at-law, and in October 1781 became clerk of Essex County.

Ogden's wife died in childbirth on January 21, 1782. The couple had had five children, among them another Robert (A.B. 1793). On March 12, 1786, Ogden married Hannah Platt, a sister of his first wife. Six children were born of this marriage. In the year of his second marriage Ogden gave up his prosperous Elizabethtown law practice to his brother Aaron in exchange for property in Sussex County, where he settled for the rest of his life. His parents had moved there earlier, his mother naming their place "Sparta." (It is now called Ogdensburg; the present Sparta is about four miles south of the original.) Ogden became one of the most prominent citizens of his county. He served as a delegate to the New Jersey convention called to consider the federal constitution in 1787 (he supported its adoption), and in 1790 represented Sussex County in the state legislature.

Ogden's principal concern in his later years was the Presbyterian church, particularly the local one, which he served both as elder and president of the board of trustees. When a minister was not available, Ogden officiated at church services. His imposing house was a center for his area. A visitor described it as being complete with "a well-stocked larder, plenty of servants, abundance of fruit, and a pious, good family to entertain you."

By 1810 Ogden had sold or given away the ten slaves he had once owned. But he still had many active years before him. His 1824 diary records his pleasure in the revivals held in that year in his neighborhood. In 1825 he served as president of the Sussex County Bible Society. Ogden died at the home of a daughter on February 14, 1826. He left a substantial, but indeterminable, amount of property. His legacies included one of $400 to the Princeton Theological Seminary to endow a professorship there.

SOURCES: Sketches: Wheeler, *Ogden Family*, 131-32; J. P. Snell, *Hist. of Sussex and Warren Counties, N.J.* (1881), 178-79; T. F. Chambers, *Proc. of the Centennial Anniversary of the Presbyterian Church at Sparta, N.J.* (1887); A. A. Haines, *Hardys-*

ton Memorial (1888), which contains extracts from diary; considerable correspondence with wives and other misc. MSS, NjP; Com. of Corresp.: 29 *NJA*, 546; Force, *Am. Arch.* (4 ser.), V, 307; commissary: T. Thayer, *As We Were* (1964), 121; health quotation: Hatfield, *Elizabeth*, 445; court clerk: 3 (2 ser.) *NJA*, 598; 5 (2 ser.) *NJA*, 306; will and inventory: MSS, N.J. State Lib., Trenton.

Mss: NjP

Henry Parkinson

HENRY PARKINSON, A.B., schoolmaster, was born in Londonberry, Ireland, in 1741, the son of Esther Wood and William Parkinson. Three years later the family emigrated to America, where they settled in Londonderry, New Hampshire. At some time before Henry entered the College the family moved to New Jersey, possibly to Princeton itself.

At the College Henry was a diligent student. His undergraduate exercise book, which still survives, is clearly and meticulously divided into sections on Ontology, Pneumatology, Moral Philosophy, Logick, and Algebra. Each section contains from 114 to 589 numbered questions and answers. Parkinson made no personal comments on his studies.

Parkinson tutored his younger brother Reuben for the College, but family financial problems, together with the outbreak of the Revolution, prevented Reuben's entry. Shortly after the Battle of Lexington Henry returned to New Hampshire and enlisted as a private in the Londonderry company of the Continental army. The company became part of the First New Hampshire Infantry Regiment, and on July 6, 1775, Parkinson became regimental quartermaster. On January 1, 1776, he was commissioned second lieutenant and regimental quartermaster of the Fifth Continental Infantry, positions he retained until the expiration of his commission in June 1777. Parkinson's uncompromising patriotism was confirmed on March 4, 1777, in the testimony he offered against a fellow officer who on January 1 had tried to persuade him to desert to the British army.

Upon leaving military service Parkinson went to Francestown, New Hampshire. There he served for one year as chairman of its Committee of Safety and for three years as its town clerk. On September 17, 1778, he married Janet McCurdy of Londonderry, New Hampshire; she bore him three sons and six daughters. From 1781 to 1784 he ran a Latin grammar school at Pembroke, New Hampshire, and from 1784 to 1794 he conducted another at Concord, New Hampshire.

In 1794 Parkinson moved to Canterbury, New Hampshire, where he remained until his death. It was there that he acquired his reputation as an outstanding teacher. Years later, one of his pupils recalled that of the sixty students in Parkinson's class in his day, "every one . . . liked him as a teacher. His order was excellent and his explanations perfect." Another remembered that "he was exceedingly fond of his books, and when indoors usually had one in hand." Living on a farm, he simultaneously operated both a grist mill and a clothing mill.

The income Parkinson received from his school, his farm, and his mills apparently could not sustain him and his wife in old age. Citing "reduced circumstances in life," he applied for a government pension for military service on April 17, 1818, and was granted $20.00 per month. Barely two years later, on May 23, 1820, he died. His funeral was extremely well attended by neighbors and distant friends alike. A notice in the *Concord Patriot* a month later praised Parkinson's military and educational attainments. The Latin inscription on his tombstone in Canterbury indicated his deepest loyalties and affections: "Ireland gave me birth; America reared me; Nassau Hall educated me."

SOURCES: Vital data: Henry Parkinson File, PUA; *Som. Cty. Hist. Quart.*, VI (1917), 258-62; E. L. Parker, *Hist. of Londonderry, N.H.* (1851), 336-37; J. O. Lyford, *Hist. of . . . Canterbury, N.H.* (1912), II, 276-77; College exercise book: MS NjP; military service and pension: Revolutionary War Miscellaneous Numbered Records, #3502 (MS File), National Archives, Washington, D.C.; reputation as teacher: *Granite Monthly*, 5 (1882), 218.

HS

Ebenezer Pemberton

EBENEZER PEMBERTON, A.B., A.M. 1768, Yale 1781, Dartmouth 1782, Harvard 1787, LL.D. Allegheny 1817, schoolmaster, was born in Newport, Rhode Island about 1747, the son of Mary Leach and Judge Samuel Pemberton. When Ebenezer was seven years old he was sent to Boston to be educated by his uncle, also Ebenezer Pemberton (Harvard 1721), pastor of the New Brick Church and a founder both of the Log College and the College of New Jersey. A Philadelphia newspaper reported that at his commencement young Ebenezer delivered an "elegant valedictory Oration on PATRIOTISM." In the year after his graduation Pemberton served as a master in the College's grammar school, and spent 1766–1769 teaching at the Latin grammar school in Elizabethtown, New Jersey. In 1767 he returned to Princeton, where he acted as tutor to the freshman class until 1769. Almost sixty years later James Madison (A.B. 1771), one of his pupils, still remembered Pemberton's teaching favorably.

After leaving Princeton in 1769 Pemberton went to Newport, Rhode Island. There he studied theology with the Reverend Samuel Hopkins, a leader of the New Divinity school of theology and one of the main developers of the thought of Jonathan Edwards. Along with one Jabez Denison, a Baptist, Pemberton also kept a charity school sponsored by, among others, Ezra Stiles, minister to Newport's Second Congregational Church. Charles Chauncy (Harvard 1721), a Boston minister with Arminian leanings, was appalled by the choice of Pemberton as instructor in the charity school. Pemberton, Chauncy wrote to Stiles, "is as thorow a fatalist, and bigot to the whole scheme connected wth it, as Mr Hopkins. Dr Witherspoon has a sad time of it; as the New-Jersey College is the foundation of their [theological] corruption." Stiles was not put off by Pemberton's theology. He frequently catechized the pupils in the charity school and sent his son Isaac to a Latin grammar school conducted by Pemberton.

Pemberton's uncle Ebenezer wanted him to become a clergyman and made this a condition of Pemberton's inheriting the uncle's large library and considerable estate. But Pemberton, according to a family history, "from his physical sensibility and religious scruples could never be persuaded to preach." (The uncle ended by leaving his library to the College of New Jersey.) Instead, Pemberton went to Elizabethtown, New Jersey, to read law with William Livingston (Yale 1741), an early friend of the College and later the first governor of the state of New Jersey. Pemberton probably left Newport in July 1773 for his name does not appear in Ezra Stiles's diary after that time.

One account has it that Pemberton began the practice of law in Newport in 1777. This seems unlikely: the city was occupied by the British in 1776, its economy was destroyed, and much of its population dispersed. In about 1778 Pemberton moved to Plainfield, Connecticut, where his mother lived. There he became a founder of and preceptor in the town's academy. He did not remain long, soon moving to Windham to keep school and doing some private tutoring in Newport from time to time.

In 1786 the trustees of the Phillips Academy at Andover, Massachusetts, offered Pemberton a life-time contract as principal of the youthful institution. Pemberton at first refused, but when the trustees modified their offer to permit him to resign if he should so choose, he accepted. He received a very substantial salary at Andover: £140 per year.

At Andover Pemberton was a complete success. His predecessor, Eliphalet Pearson (Harvard 1773), a bluff, autocratic man who ruled more by terror than persuasion, had established the academy on a strong foundation. To pupils who knew both men, Pemberton seemed almost Pearson's opposite. One student, Josiah Quincy (Harvard 1790) described Pemberton as "mild, gentle, conciliatory, and kind, inspiring affection and exciting neither fear nor awe, while he preserved and supported discipline, he made himself beloved and respected by his pupils." Under Pemberton the deportment of the students improved and the academy prospered. Visiting Andover in February 1789, William Bentley, a minister from Salem, described the academy thus:

> It is an elegant building, situated upon a hill, in free air. In the front are enclosed two rooms, designed for private Schools, & a Library, &c. Between there you pass into the academy. Between 40 or 50 youth were present under the Preceptor M^r E Pemberton. . . . The Preceptor is an amiable man & communicative. His abilities are admirable for his profession.

Admirable or not, Pemberton resigned his post about three and a half years later, in October 1793. He gave ill-health as the reason; it seems more likely that differences with certain members of the Phillips family prompted the move. Shortly thereafter Pemberton opened an academy of his own in Billerica, Massachusetts, not far from Andover. The Andover branch of the Phillips family was annoyed. The Andover academy declined, overshadowed for a time by other academies and by private schools such as Pemberton's.

On December 6, 1796, Pemberton married Elizabeth Whitwell, a daughter of the Reverend William Whitwell (A.B. 1758). The couple had at least six children. Although the facilities at the Billerica school were not as fine as those at Andover, the school prospered. Visiting it about 1807 President Timothy Dwight of Yale described it as "a respectable academy under the direction of Mr. Pemberton, an instructor of the first reputation."

Not long after Dwight's visit a group of Bostonians asked Pemberton to open a school for their children. He pulled up stakes in Billerica—where he had been a deacon of the First Congregational Church—and opened a school in what is now Washington Street, Boston. It too was successful. About 1825 his former students raised an annuity that allowed him to retire comfortably. Attended by two of his daughters, Pemberton spent his last years in Boston, where he died on June 25, 1835.

SOURCES: Sketch: *Sibley's Harvard Graduates*, XVI, 197-200, which differs in several important respects from the above; uncle Ebenezer: ibid., VI, 535-46; commencement: *Pa. Gaz.*, Oct. 10, 1765; Elizabethtown gr. school: 25 *NJA*, 227; CNJ tutor and gr. school: MS Trustees' Minutes, I; Madison memory: *Madison Papers*, I, 45, 47n; Chauncy quotation: Stiles, *Itineraries*, 451; Newport charity and grammar schools: Stiles, *Literary Diary*, I, 195, 200, 216, 260, 394; ministry: *Records of the Pemberton Family* (1890), 14-15; Phillips Andover: C. M. Fuess, *An Old New England School* (1917), 98-112; Andover description: Bentley, *Diaries*, I, 117, and ibid., II, 231 for Billerica school; Dwight quotation: T. Dwight, *Travels in New England and New York* (1969 ed.), I, 285.

Edward Pope

EDWARD POPE, A.B., lawyer and public official, was born in Sandwich, Massachusetts, on February 15, 1740, the oldest son of Thomas Pope and his wife, Thankful Dillingham. The family later moved to Dartmouth, Massachusetts, where Pope was raised and whence he entered Harvard College in 1761. Harvard was dear, Princeton was cheap, and in his sophomore year Pope, along with his classmate Simeon Williams, transferred from Harvard to the College of New Jersey. Both youths left Cambridge, the Harvard faculty recorded, "for Saving Cost."

After graduation Pope read law and then settled in what is now the town of Acushnet, Massachusetts. In the spring of 1768 he married Elizabeth Ballard of Boston. The couple attended Dartmouth's First Congregational Church and had one daughter before Elizabeth's death in November 1781. In June 1785, Pope married Mrs. Elizabeth Greenleaf Eliot, a Boston widow. Two sons and a daughter were born of the second union.

Pope's law practice was successful, and he soon rose to local prominence. In 1772 he became a justice of the peace and a major in the Bristol County militia. He must have been an evenhanded man, for after an affray between Dartmouth townspeople and the British navy in 1775 it was Pope who defended the British seamen and counseled moderation. This action did not prejudice him with the Whigs, for in August 1775, the revolutionary government made him naval officer of the Port of Dartmouth. He served Dartmouth as a selectman, and in 1776, from 1778 to 1781, and in 1783–1784, the town sent him as its representative to the Massachusetts General Court.

In November 1778, a British raiding party burned Pope's house and captured him. He did not defend the British this time, but escaped and invested in three privateers, which proved not to be as profitable as his flourishing law practice. Dartmouth's port was incorporated as New

Bedford in 1787, and Pope became the town's leading citizen, serving on the school committee and as an incorporator of the Bedford Bank. In 1797 he was appointed to Bristol County's court of common pleas and when the federal government was organized, Pope was named revenue collector and inspector of the port of New Bedford. He served in both posts until August 1808, when he was removed because of laxness in enforcing the embargo laws. He retained the support of his neighbors, who elected him as a Federalist to the Massachusetts Senate in 1810–1811. Pope had built himself a fine mansion in New Bedford, where he died on June 10, 1818. His death was duly noted in the next catalogue published by the College.

SOURCES: Marriage, children: D. P. Worden et al., *Genealogy of Thomas Pope* (1917), 23; sketch: *Sibley's Harvard Graduates*, XVI, 203-205, which does not mention the CNJ A.B. However, no contemporary Edward Pope who has been found other than the above could have attended CNJ.

David Ramsay

DAVID RAMSAY, A.B., M.B. Pennsylvania 1773, M.D. 1780, Yale 1789, physician, legislator, and historian, was born April 2, 1749, in Lancaster County, Pennsylvania, the youngest of three sons of Jane Montgomery and James Ramsay to graduate from the College, the others being William (A.B. 1754) and Nathaniel (A.B. 1767). The father had emigrated from Ireland and supported a "numerous family" by farming.

Admitted to the College with sophomore standing, after graduating David taught school, first on the Eastern Shore of Maryland and later in Virginia. In 1770 he enrolled in the Medical College at Philadelphia, where he came under the influence especially of Dr. Benjamin Rush (A.B. 1760). He received his bachelor's degree in July 1773, but only after several years of practice did he qualify for the M.D. with a thesis entitled *De Fluore Alba*.

On leaving medical school, Ramsay settled briefly in Cecil County, Maryland. In the spring of 1774 he moved to Charleston, S.C., where he quickly won professional success. He became an influential member of the Independent Church of Charleston, of which he would write an informative history near the end of his life, and which in 1774 had as its minister William Tennent (A.B. 1758). In February 1775 he married Sabina Ellis, daughter of a local merchant with prospects of "a pretty fortune" of her own that were terminated by her death in June 1776.

In Charleston Ramsay promptly became a politically active Whig.

David Ramsay, A.B. 1765
BY CHARLES WILLSON PEALE

His first known publication was *A Sermon on Tea*, written in 1774 with a text from St. Paul: "Touch not, Taste not, Handle Not." After reading Tom Paine's anonymously published *Common Sense*, he wrote enthusiastically to Rush in Philadelphia for the author's name. He had become surgeon to a local militia unit in 1775, and in the fall of 1776 he was elected to the state legislature, where with only a few intervals he continued to be an active and influential member until 1790. On July 4, 1778, he delivered at Charleston an address "On the Advantages of American Independence." He later claimed, possibly correctly, that this was the first of all Fourth of July orations. Having served briefly in the field during the campaigns ending with the British reduction of Charleston in 1780, he spent almost a year in prison at St. Augustine. In 1782–1783 and again in 1785–1786 he represented South Carolina in the Congress. He responded enthusiastically to the calling of the Constitutional Convention of 1787, and was a member of the state convention that ratified the new constitution in 1788. His political career ended in 1796 after three terms as a member of the state senate, of which he was the presiding officer in each term.

The chief political disappointment in Ramsay's career came in 1788 with his defeat as a candidate for a seat in the new national Congress. This reversal has been attributed in part to his views on slavery. As his letters to Rush repeatedly indicate, he disliked the institution, as much for its effect upon the master as upon the slave. In a letter of 1779 he confidently predicted "that there will not be a slave in these states fifty years hence." In the same letter he rejected the idea that the slave was fit for employment as a soldier, but attributed his inadequacies for this purpose to the conditioning slavery had imposed upon him. In 1788 he opposed an effort to repeal a law of 1787 which prohibited the foreign slave trade for a period of three years. How early he himself may have been the owner of slaves cannot be said, but the census of 1790 showed him the possessor of six, perhaps as the result of his third marriage.

In 1783 Ramsay married Frances, daughter of President Witherspoon of Princeton. She died in December 1784, a few days following the birth of John Witherspoon Ramsay (A.B. 1803). In 1787 he married Martha Laurens, daughter of Henry Laurens, wealthy merchant, planter, and revolutionary leader. By this marriage eleven children were born, including David (A.B. 1812) and James (A.B. 1814). Ramsay's third wife was a woman of exceptional talent, education, and piety whose spiritual diary was published by her husband with a biographical preface as *Memoirs of the Life of Martha Laurens Ramsey* shortly after her death in 1811.

Ramsay is chiefly remembered as historian of the Revolution. His two-voume *History of the Revolution of South Carolina*, published in 1785 at Trenton, drew favorable attention both in this country and overseas. Broader in scope than its short title suggests, the *History* includes an account of the southern military campaigns to the surrender of Cornwallis at Yorktown. Jefferson, in France as American ambassador, was instrumental in securing its translation and publication in a French edition in 1787. To Ramsay, Jefferson expressed a hope that his history might be matched by histories of comparable quality for the middle and eastern states to provide the basis for a general history of the Revolution. But Ramsay was unwilling to wait. In 1789 he published at Philadelphia a two-volume *History of the American Revolution*, which by 1795 had been republished in London and Dublin and translated into Dutch and German for publication on the continent.

Ramsay's reputation as a historian has undergone startling changes. It was the historian, rather than the physician, who in his own day won the recognition that came with election to membership in the Massachusetts Historical Society, the American Antiquarian Society, and the American Philosophical Society. But at the beginning of the present century it was charged that much of his history was plagiarized. It is true that Ramsay did not always cite his sources, that in his usually hurried act of composition he at times transcribed the words of others with omission of quotation marks, and that he leaned heavily, as did other contemporaries, upon the *Annual Register*, an English Whig publication, for his narrative of the war. More recently, however, responsible scholars have raised the question of whether the writer of an earlier age is to be judged by the much more rigid standards of a later time; turning back to Ramsay's history, they have found much of merit and interest in it, such as the documents he had an opportunity to consult and include as a result of his public service, and the value of his comments upon the life and time through which he moved so actively. Ramsay's history, of course, was as much a part of the Revolution as it was a history of it. He wrote with a purpose, and the purpose, to quote from a memoir by President Samuel Stanhope Smith of Princeton, was that of "a decided and active friend of his country, and of freedom."

Once committed to the writing of history, Ramsay continued. He extended his history of South Carolina through the year 1808 in a two-volume work he published in 1809. His *History of the Revolution* became the basis for a *History of the United States*, covering the same period of time, that was published posthumously, with an addendum by President Smith "and Other Literary Gentlemen" that carried the story through the Treaty of Ghent. At the time of his death a few months after the battle of New Orleans, according to Smith, Ramsay was collecting material for a biography of Andrew Jackson. Had he lived to complete it, it might have known the popularity his biography of George Washington, a panegyric first published in 1807, enjoyed through many years.

Much of Ramsay's writing in his later years represents an almost frantic attempt to rescue his personal fortune from the effects of what Smith sadly described as a "want of judgment in the affairs of the world." He fell a victim to the speculative fevers besetting many of his contemporaries, and lost heavily.

A man of enormous energy and Puritanical habits, Ramsay remained an active practitioner of medicine. A "rigid disciple of Rush," according to Stanhope Smith, he believed firmly in the "single vigorous remedy." Actively concerned with the problems of public health, he was a founder of the Charleston Medical Society. "A Review of the

Improvements, Progress and State of Medicine in the XVIIIth Century," a paper read before the Society "on the first day of the XIXth Century" and published at its request, still commands respectful attention.

Ramsay was shot in the back on Broad Street, Charleston, early in the afternoon of May 6, 1815 by a deranged man who nursed a grievance against the doctor for an earlier diagnosis of his mental state. Death came the second day afterward.

SOURCES: The principal source of information is *David Ramsay, 1749-1815: Selections From His Writings*, with Introduction and Notes by Robert L. Brunhouse, *APS Trans.* (new ser.), 55, Pt. 4, 1965. The introduction is the fullest of biographical accounts; the larger part of the work consists of Ramsay's correspondence, especially with Benjamin Rush. In the concluding section there are reprints of Ramsay's *Sermon on Tea*, the July 4 oration of 1778, another of 1794, and the essay on medicine in the eighteenth century. An appendix carries full bibliographical listings, with helpful comments, of Ramsay's published works; see too: Brunhouse, "David Ramsay's Publication Problems, 1787-1808," *Papers of the Bibliographical Society of America*, 39 (1945), 51-67. A memoir by R. Y. Hayne, first published in *Analectic Magazine*, 6 (1815) and reproduced in substance at the front of Ramsay's *Washington* (Ithaca, 1840), is the principal source for Ramsay's early life. This is helpfully supplemented by the memoir of his brother-in-law Samuel Stanhope Smith that prefaces Ramsay's *History of the United States* in Volume I of the second edition (Philadelphia, 1818). Robert L. Meriwether's article in the *DAB* is by an authority on the history of South Carolina, and is appreciative of parts of Ramsay's history of that state. See also Page Smith, "David Ramsay and the Causes of the American Revolution," *WMQ* (3 ser.), 17 (1960), 51-77; William Raymond Smith, *History as Argument: Three Patriot Historians of the American Revolution* (1966); and C. G. Sellers, Jr., "The Am. Rev.: Southern Founders of A National Tradition," in A. S. Link and R. W. Patrick, eds., *Writing Southern History* (1965), 38-66.

WFC

Theodore (Dirck) Romeyn

THEODORE (DIRCK) ROMEYN, A.B., D.D. Queen's (later Rutgers) 1789, Dutch Reformed clergyman and educator, was born in Hackensack, New Jersey, on January 12, 1745, the son of Rachel Vreeland and her husband, Nicholas Romeyn. An elder son named Dirck had died shortly after birth in 1736, and young Theodore was usually known as Dirck in turn. By the age of nine the younger Dirck manifested religious inclinations and at age sixteen or seventeen made a public profession of faith. At about this time Romeyn began studying for the ministry— first, with a brother, the Reverend Thomas Romeyn (A.M. 1765), pastor of the Dutch Reformed Churches on the Delaware, and later with the Reverend John M. Goetschius, pastor of the Dutch Reformed churches of Hackensack and Schralenburgh, New Jersey.

Dirck entered the College as a junior. His closest friend there was his classmate, Jonathan Edwards, Jr., who with Dirck's support, later became president of Union College. On September 24, 1765, the day before his graduation, Romeyn signed a petition to the Grand Lodge of Freemasons of Massachusetts for a Princeton lodge. The request was not granted, and the founding later that year of the Cliosophic Society, of which he became a graduate member, may have been a response to the rejection.

After graduation Romeyn studied briefly again with John Goetschius and in May 1766 was licensed and ordained by the Dutch Reformed Church in America, which had only recently won the right to ordain its own ministers from the Classis of Amsterdam. The ordination followed Romeyn's acceptance of a joint call from three Ulster County, New York, churches: Rochester, Wawarsing, and Marbletown.

On June 11, 1767, Romeyn married Elizabeth Brodhead of Ulster County, the daughter of Wessel Brodhead, a well-to-do Ulster landowner. The couple had a son and a daughter.

Romeyn remained in Ulster County until 1775. During the last two years of his tenure he also supplied the Dutch Reformed churches of Red Hook Landing and Rhinebeck Flats, both in Dutchess County. He declined regular calls from several congregations in New York, New Jersey, and Pennsylvania. In October 1775, however, he received a joint call from the Dutch Reformed churches of Hackensack, his home congregation, and Schralenburgh, both in Bergen County. Although he had declined two previous calls from them, he accepted their third and was installed in May 1776. His hesitation may have been due to internal disputes that had wracked both churches for years and that had by no means been finally resolved by 1776.

The dispute was caused by the long-standing division of the Dutch Reformed Church in America into two wings. The reform wing, or Coetus, sought independence from the Classis of Amsterdam. The conservative wing, or Conferentie, sought to maintain traditional ties with Europe, particularly the ordination of all Dutch Reformed ministers by the Classis. Because neither the Hackensack nor the Schralenburgh congregations could resolve their differences, since 1744 each had hired two pastors, one from each wing. The practice continued with Romeyn, a supporter of the Coetus party. He alternated in the two pulpits with the Reverend Warmoldus Kuyper, a staunch Conferentie supporter. The Coetus partisan whom Romeyn succeeded was his former mentor, John Goetschius, who had died in 1774.

Political as well as religious disputes divided the two congregations.

The Coetus faction, Romeyn among them, contained many zealous Whigs. The Conferentie was composed of equally zealous Loyalists. In late November 1776 the Conferentie conspired with British troops then occupying Hackensack to raid Romeyn's home while he and his family were away visiting friends. The British, according to a modern historian, "emptied the barns of their hay and grain, drove off the domine's milk cows, and carried away his furniture and his clothes, one of the greedy thieves even ripping the brass locks from the doors." Romeyn immediately moved his family to New Paltz, New York, but made several visits throughout the war to his two congregations. In so doing he risked his life and more than once narrowly escaped ambush by Loyalists. Rather than accept safer pulpits elsewhere, he insisted upon serving his remaining parishioners. To avoid detection he lodged each night of his stay with a different friend. In March 1780 his luck nearly ran out: the British unexpectedly raided a friend's home at which he was staying and took prisoner several of its inhabitants; only the proximity of the chimney, and his quick decision to hide behind it, saved him. His own churches were used almost exclusively by the Tory Conferentie and were thereby saved from the fate that befell his parsonage. Both in gratitude for his extraordinary efforts on their behalf, and in hopes of retaining his services, his congregations sent him £25.18s in 1778.

In addition to his pastoral duties, Romeyn regularly reported to General Washington and his staff on British troop movements in New Jersey and New York. On November 3, 1780, for example, he received a letter from Washington himself requesting confirmation of a suspected British "embarkation under the command of Sir Henry Clinton . . . at New York." The next day Romeyn sent intelligence to Washington of twelve British warships in the East River and of the British impressment of able-bodied Americans for an apparent embarkation. Coincidentally, perhaps, Romeyn's character and appearance—"reserved, self-confident, of aristocratic temperament"—were likened by contemporaries to Washington's. The British, however, called him "the Rebel Parson."

After the Revolution Romeyn returned with his family to Hackensack and resumed his joint ministerial obligations. Reportedly, he displayed far less animus toward his formerly Loyalist Conferentie parishioners than did most of his Whig Coetus parishioners. In 1784 he resigned from his posts—in part because of continued internal theological and political dissension, in part because of an inadequate salary and an unfulfilled promise of reimbursement.

Shortly before leaving, Romeyn declined the first of two calls to the presidency of fledgling Queen's College in New Brunswick. He wanted neither to live in New Brunswick nor to be the pastor of its Dutch Reformed church, an additional responsibility stipulated by the Queen's trustees and indeed a necessary supplement to the meagre proposed presidential salary. Instead, Romeyn left New Jersey to become the seventh pastor of the First Dutch Reformed Church of Schenectady, New York, and, in addition, to engage in various educational activities.

Romeyn was installed in Schenectady in November 1784. His initial annual salary of $350 was raised to $500 in 1796 and to $625 in 1798. He also received a home, pasture for cows and horses, and seventy cords of firewood yearly. In 1794 he was granted an assistant pastor, the Reverend Jacob Sickles (Columbia 1792), to handle his growing responsibilities and the growing number of parishioners, who numbered 2,500 by that time. Sickles remained for two years before accepting a pulpit of his own.

Though its battles were tame compared with those of the New Jersey churches, Romeyn's Schenectady congregation was divided over the use of Dutch or English in the service. The older members favored Dutch; the younger members preferred English. Romeyn used both. In 1799 he purchased eight English Bibles to increase the use of English, but every third Sunday he conducted the service entirely in Dutch.

Strongly aware of the need for institutions of higher education in the Schenectady area, Romeyn played a major role in founding Schenectady Academy in 1785. He served as the first chairman of its Board of Trustees. A decade later the academy became Union College, and he became a Union trustee. His various educational efforts led to his being named, on April 13, 1787, a New York State Regent, a post he held until 1796. Several years after his death New York Governor DeWitt Clinton addressed the following letter to Romeyn's son, the Reverend John B. Romeyn:

> When the Legislature met in New York, . . . your excellent father attended the Regents of the University, to solicit the establishment of a College at Schenectady. Powerful opposition was made by Albany. . . . I have no doubt but that the weight and respectability of your father's character procured a decision in favour of Schenectady. . . . There was something in his manner peculiarly dignified and benevolent, calculated to create veneration as well as affection, and it made an impression on my mind that will never be erased.

In June 1794 Romeyn attended the First General Synod of the Dutch Reformed Church in America and was appointed to its educational committee. Three years later he became one of the synod's professors of theology and held the position for the rest of his life. The professorships had been established in 1784 as the first step in the creation of a seminary independent of Queen's College. Romeyn himself had expressed support for such an institution in a letter of October 1783. He also helped draft the synod's constitution and spent years working and reworking its provisions.

In 1801 Romeyn suffered a stroke. Severely impairing his speech, though not his physical mobility, it forced him to restrict his activities. By the end of the year, however, he had regained some vocal abilities and was able to preach every Sunday. With his concurrence, the First Reformed Church hired another assistant pastor. Romeyn performed no more public services thereafter, though he continued to tutor theological students. Romeyn died in Schralenburgh, *Bergen County, New Jersey,* on April 16, 1804. In accordance with his wishes all those present at his funeral were "given a glass or two of wine" before his body was "layed out."

SOURCES: Vital data: Dirck Romeyn File, PUA; Sprague, *Annals*, IX, 46-51; *Appleton's Amer. Biog.*, V, 315; L. B. Sebring, "Dirck Romeyn," unpub. MS, Union College (1938); namesake: 24 *NJA*, 637n; Masonic Lodge: Richard Stockton File, PUA; Cliosophic Society: C. R. Williams, *Cliosophic Society* (1916), 15; Ulster Cty. churches: *Proc. Ulster Cty. Hist. Soc.* (1937-1938), 57-58; A. T. Clearwater, *Hist. Ulster Cty.* (1907), 345; Wessel Brodhead will: Sebring, 214; Hackensack and Schralenburgh religious and political conflicts: T. B. Romeyn, *First Reformed Church at Hackensack* (1870), 49-66; A. C. Leiby, *Revolutionary War in Hackensack Valley* (1962), passim; "zealous partisan": Leiby, 84; "emptied the barn": ibid.; letter from Wash.: Washington, *Writings*, XX, 286-287; "reserved": Demarest, *Hist. Rutgers College* (1924), 55, 154, 159; R. P. McCormick, *Rutgers* (1966), 19, 22; Schenectady church: G. S. Roberts, *Old Schenectady* (n.d.), 86-89; Schenectady Academy and Union College: F. B. Hough, *Hist. Sketch Union College* (1876), 7n; *One Hundredth Anniversary Union College* (1897), 38, 93; A. V. Raymond, *Union Univ.* (1907), I, 12-18, 32-33; Clinton letter: Sprague, 48; General Synod: *NJHSP*, 73 (1955), 34; Demarest, 155-56; McCormick, 11-12; funeral: Sebring, 197, Raymond, 15.

Mss: NHi   HS

Jacob Rush

JACOB RUSH, A.B., A.M. 1768, LL.D. 1804, lawyer and public official, was born on November 24, 1747, in Byberry township, just above Philadelphia, the son of John Rush, farmer and gunsmith, and his wife Susanna Hall. Jacob was the younger brother of Benjamin Rush (A.B.

1760), and the two of them were prepared for college, through the enterprise of their widowed mother after the father's death in 1751, at Samuel Finley's Nottingham Academy, located on the upper edge of Maryland. Jacob probably came to Princeton in 1761 with Finley, who had married his mother's sister and who in that year succeeded Samuel Davies as president of the College. During his years as a student Jacob is reported to have acquired a reputation as a parliamentarian and he probably enjoyed some reputation also as an orator, for on the day of his graduation the morning exercises, according to a Philadelphia newspaper, "were closed with an Oration on *Liberty*, pronounced with Beauty and Propriety by Mr. Jacob Rush." Three years later, when he was awarded his second degree, the press credited him with "a very emphatical exhibition on true greatness." Among his classmates, it can be noted, David Ramsay later claimed to have been an intimate friend.

After graduation Jacob presumably read law, for in 1769 he had been admitted to practice in Philadelphia and the nearby courts of Chester and Berks counties. With the aid of his older brother he jour-

Jacob Rush, A.B. 1765

neyed to England in the fall of 1770, under a plan to spend two years at one of the Inns of Court, "in order to finish his studies in the law." He had returned to Philadelphia by January 1773, when he was admitted to practice before the supreme court of the province. Rush's activity prior to the coming of the Revolution remains uncertain, except that presumably he was quietly (and perhaps not too profitably) engaged in the practice of law. At some time before the outbreak of war he had run up a bill of £35 with Charles Dilly, London bookseller, for lawbooks, a bill still unpaid for a while after the Revolution. As a young man he was described as rotund of build and shy in manner (except apparently when on the speaker's platform), and obviously he yielded prominence in the historical developments preceding the Revolution to his more flamboyant brother. In July 1776 he acted as secretary to John Hancock, then president of the Congress. Thereafter he apparently served as an assistant to Charles Thomson, secretary of the Congress, until his choice as deputy secretary on November 7, 1777, a post he resigned on January 28, 1778. On January 24, 1777, Benjamin Rush wrote to his wife from Baltimore, where the Congress had fled in the preceding December through fear that the British might capture Philadelphia. He reported that his "brother lodges in a tavern and perfectly harmonizes with me in complaining of Baltimore." After the British evacuation of Philadelphia in the spring of 1778, Rush evidently resumed his practice there, having spent a part of the intervening time perhaps on a farm he is reported to have owned outside Philadelphia.

Rush had been married on November 17, 1777, to Mary Wrench. A native of the Chesapeake Eastern Shore, she had moved to Philadelphia, where she gained enough reputation as painter of miniature portraits to support her mother and a younger brother. She is said to have painted only female subjects, out of modesty, and to have dropped the art entirely after her marriage because it was no longer necessary. The marriage lasted until her death in 1806. There were five children, all girls, four of whom survived their father.

No evidence of significant political activity, aside from his service to Congress, has been found prior to Rush's election to the state assembly in October 1782 as one of the Republican majority. No doubt, he had for some time shared with his brother and other critics of the state constitution of 1776 views that grouped him with the Republicans, whose hope for constitutional reform was not to be achieved until 1790. That he was a person of some political importance is suggested by the fact that he was attacked in a newspaper prior to his reelection in 1783 as "a needy practitioner of the law, who has been long gaping with rotundity of belly, vacant, and open mouth, for an office." He was charged with possession of a slanderous pen, but that Benjamin may have been the true target of this attack is suggested by the author's additional charge that Jacob perhaps was only "the imputed father, compelled by a busy and overbearing brother to stand midwife to the ebullitions of his own violent and distempered fancy." Jacob's legislative career was terminated on March 20, 1784, when he resigned in order to accept appointment as an associate justice of the state's supreme court. During the bitter debate over the new federal constitution, he was attacked in the Antifederalist press, but more perhaps because of his brother's known support of the document than for any act of his own.

For nearly thirty-six years after 1784, until his death on January 5, 1820, Jacob Rush served the state through a succession of appointments as a judge, and over time he acquired in his own right more than a little fame. In 1791, after seven years on the supreme court, he was in effect demoted when Thomas Mifflin, the state's first governor under the constitution of 1790, failed to reseat him on that court and instead appointed him as the presiding judge for the third judicial district. One of five districts established by act of the legislature, it embraced Berks, Northampton, Luzerne, and Northumberland counties. This made him a country judge who was required to move from county seat to county seat, where with the aid of less qualified associate judges he presided over a wide range of judicial actions, criminal and civil. His pay was $500 plus travel expenses, and in order to reduce the burden of travel Rush moved his residence to Reading. His brother charged that the demotion was attributable to his own opposition to Mifflin's election. In 1806 the city and county of Philadelphia was made a separate district, and Judge Rush was reassigned to it. It was in Philadelphia, where he had grown up, that he died.

Judge Rush became famous for his charges to grand juries, some of which were published in newspapers, on occasion at the request of the grand jury itself. In keeping with the custom of the time, the charge to the jury might range over a wide variety of topics—political, philosophical, and moral, as well as legal. The problems of checking immorality had a special interest for Rush, and in 1803 a selection of charges delivered by him on this general subject between 1796 and 1802 was published at the instance of a group of Philadelphia ministers headed by Ashbel Green (A.B. 1783), later president of the College. An appendix carried the main body of the state's statute of 1794 on vice and immorality, which dealt with sabbath-breaking, swearing, gambling, drunkenness, duelling, cock-fighting, and other such popular "vices." There can be no question as to Judge Rush's willingness, as his charges repeatedly demonstrate, to enforce this law. He firmly believed that the social order depended upon maintaining "the purest precepts of morality." He saw in the Christian religion, and the teachings of Scripture, a *"part* of the *law* of the *land."* One finds no reason for doubting that his admonitions reflected deep-rooted convictions, but it is also evident that he had been alarmed by Tom Paine's *Age of Reason* and other evidence of the spread of an "infidelity" related in his own mind to the course of the French Revolution. He was a stern judge, and had no reluctance in overriding his lay associates on the bench insofar as he was able to do so. On one occasion this characteristic led to an unsuccessful attempt to impeach him.

In politics he was a Federalist, who condemned the Whiskey Rebellion of 1794 and the Fries Rebellion of 1799, both of which brought forth firm charges to grand juries on the need to uphold the law. He welcomed the Alien and Sedition Acts of 1798, and when diplomatic relations with France were severed that year he congratulated the jurors of Berks County upon the declaration "of our independence of France," and the hope of a "perpetual exemption from the baneful effects of her morals, her religion and her politics." There is evidence that by this time he entertained some doubts about Federalist political leaders in his own state, but it is impossible here to state what may have been his later political course. An effort by the state legislature to provide a remedy for crowded court dockets by encouraging arbitration of issues outside the courts brought from the judge's nephew, Richard Rush (A.B. 1797), an able published argument in 1809 for expansion, instead, of the court system, a question of obvious interest to the Judge, but it carried no indication that the uncle influenced its composition.

It is also difficult to say what course Rush's religious convictions may have followed. His father had been Anglican, and his own strong beliefs had been nurtured under a Presbyterian aegis. There is evidence that his experience in Reading, where he reported in 1798 that there was no "English" minister and that a cooperative effort with leaders of the two German churches to secure a minister who also could officiate in the English language had failed, weakened his sense of identification with any one denomination. This may help to explain a strange piece he wrote in 1818, which was published at Philadelphia in 1819 as *An Inquiry into the Doctrine of Christian Baptism, with a View to Unite Christians of Every Denomination at the Lord's Supper, Exhibiting Some Objections to the Baptism of Adults and Infants. . . .*

SOURCES: Informative, especially on later career: L. Richards, "Hon. Jacob Rush, of the Pennsylvania Judiciary," *PMHB*, 39 (1915), 53-68; as in life, Jacob continues in the shadow of his famous brother, see: Rush, *Autobiography*, 28, 78; early years: Butterfield, *Rush Letters*, passim, 44 for sketch, 76 for trip to England and quote, 131 for Baltimore and quote, 917n for Mifflin's prejudice; D. F. Hawke, *Benjamin Rush* (1971), 38, 84, 97, 261 for assembly, and 266 for reelection and quotations; for college years, Mills, *Life at Princeton College*, 36; *Pa. Gaz.*, Oct. 10, 1765; *Pa. Chronicle*, Oct. 12, 1768; R. L. Brunhouse, *David Ramsay* (1965), 55; marriage: C. C. Sellers, *Charles Willson Peale* (1969), 102-103; lawyer: J. H. Martin, *Bench and Bar of Philadelphia* (1883), 239, 242, 308, and F. M. Eastman, *Courts and Lawyers of Pa.* (1922), 2, 555-56; Congress: *JCC*, VII, 176n; IX, 872-73, 875; X, 94n, 95, 96, 108, this last a warrant for pay as deputy with a deduction for a month's absence, probably at time of wedding; Force, *Am. Arch.* (5 ser.), I, 34; *Papers of the C.C.*, No. 78, XIX, 201-204, indicates he resigned because of "a very disagreeable" development in his personal affairs; tax lists for 1782 and 1784 indicate that his farm of 125 acres was in Lower Dublin township of Philadelphia County (*Pa. Arch.* [3 ser.], XVI, 113, 584), and if this identification is correct the census of 1790 shows a household of 2 free white males over 16, 7 free white females, and 3 other free persons, all of which raises unresolved questions.

PUBLICATIONS: Sh-Sh #s 5005, 6000, 7214, 11307, 21248, 35823, 49337

Mss: the family correspondence of Benjamin Rush probably contains a number of his letters for the period of his residence in Reading. One written to his brother on May 28, 1798, contains interesting comments upon the burdens of a district judge, "the Nabobs of the federal party," and the local religious situation. See Benjamin Rush Family Letters, Part II, v. 34, p. 54, Ridgeway Lib., Library Co. of Philadelphia.

WFC

John Staples

JOHN STAPLES, A.B., Congregational clergyman, was born in Taunton, Massachusetts, on April 23, 1742, to Seth Staples, a shoemaker and a Taunton public official, and his wife Hannah Standish. Young Staples early came under the influence of the Reverend Eleazar Wheelock (Yale 1733), founder of Moor's Indian Charity School in Lebanon, Connecticut, and its successor, Dartmouth College. Staples may have attended Wheelock's school. While at Nassau Hall he expressed his undying gratitude to Wheelock in extraordinarily fulsome terms. Staples entered the College's freshman class on probation in the summer of 1761. However, he was forced to drop back a year. "He had lost so much Time and the class was pretty forward in their Studies, so that I was afraid to admit him absolutely," tutor Jeremiah Halsey (A.B. 1752) explained to Wheelock. "This Fall," Halsey continued, "upon Examination He appeared so much behind the Class, notwithstanding He had been industrious, that it was unanimously agreed upon as best, that He should stay another year."

After graduation Staples prepared for the ministry and was licensed by Connecticut's Windham Association. On April 17, 1772, he was ordained pastor of the Second Congregational Church of Canterbury, Connecticut. He held this, his first and only pulpit, until his death more than thirty years later. On August 13, 1772, he married Susannah Perkins. She bore him eleven children. Throughout his tenure at Canterbury Staples and his family lived in a house he built himself.

(handwritten margin note:) sister of Nathan Perkins (A.B. 1770) + Matthew Perkins (Class of 1777)

The Second Congregational Church was only a year old when Staples became its minister. Its members had seceded from Canterbury's First Congregational Church less for doctrinal reasons than for geographical ones. For the location of the First Church in eastern Canterbury had proved inconvenient for the increasing number of parishioners who were moving westward. The division within the First Church led in 1771 to the dismissal of its long-time pastor, the Reverend James Cogswell. Cogswell nevertheless assisted Staples in sustaining the Second Congregational Church and in 1799 persuaded Staples to join his newly formed Eastern Association of Windham County. Along with hard work and a reputation for piety and integrity, Cogswell's initial guidance enabled Staples to lead a church that, according to a nineteenth-century historian, was "generally united and prosperous from the first."

"Priest Staples," as he was affectionately called by his parishioners, died in Canterbury on February 15, 1804, from illness supposedly brought on by "not putting on his wig when visiting a dying woman in the night time." His widow and children continued to live in the family home for a number of years thereafter. Of his children, the most notable was Seth Perkins Staples (Yale 1797). A prominent lawyer in both New Haven and New York, in 1818 he established in New Haven what later became the Yale Law School.

SOURCES: Vital data: John Staples File, PUA; H. E. Staples, "Staples Family," typescript, MSS, NN (n.d.), I, 65, 89-90, 518; Staples to Wheelock, Dec. 12, 1761, and Halsey to Wheelock, Feb. 12, 1762, Wheelock MSS; *Quarter Millennial Celebration of City of Taunton, Mass.* (1889), 370, 378, 379, 387; S. H. Emery, *Ministry of Taunton* (1853), II, 4; Canterbury Congregationalism: E. D. Larned, *Hist. Windham Cty., Conn.* (1880), II, 42, 44, 232; L. Bacon, *Contributions to Ecclesiastical Hist. of Conn.* (1861), 337, 503; quotations: Bacon, 503; Staples, 89, ibid.

HS

Henry Stevenson

HENRY STEVENSON, A.B., has not been identified. He was listed as dead in the College's first catalogue, published in 1770. Extensive investigation has failed to establish a relationship between the alumnus and the well-known Baltimore physician, Dr. Henry Stevenson.

Alexander Thayer

ALEXANDER THAYER, A.B., Congregational clergyman and farmer, was born on January 25, 1743, in Mendon, Worcester County, Massachusetts, to Abigail Sumner and her husband, William Thayer, a third-generation New Englander. Alexander entered Harvard in 1761, but transferred as a sophomore to the College of New Jersey. After graduation he apparently studied theology, receiving a license to preach from the Mendon Conference on June 28, 1768. Two years later Thayer replaced the deceased Reverend Silas Bigelow (Harvard 1756) as the minister of the First Congregational Church in the recently incorporated town of Paxton, Worcester County, Massachusetts. Here he was ordained on November 28, 1770, and on August 18, 1773, married Abigail Boulding of Holliston, Massachusetts. In May 1775 the townspeople elected Thayer as their representative to the provincial congress. But Massachusetts' long history of excluding ministers from civil affairs led a Committee of the Congress to deny both Thayer and the Reverend Caleb Curtis (A.B. 1754) of Charlton their seats.

No further record of Thayer has been found until his dismissal from the Paxton ministry on August 14, 1782. Although past commentators have attributed this action to Thayer's "Loyalist opinions," it appears unlikely that in a highly patriotic town the citizenry would tolerate a Tory preacher over the entire revolutionary period. A more probable explanation is the economic depression and political conflict that followed the war. In the year of Thayer's discharge, he complained that his salary of £66 was inadequate; but it was a bad time to be asking for more money. In 1782 the towns of Worcester County officially protested against inflation, high taxes, and the costs of supporting the state government in Massachusetts. Whether Thayer sided with the resistance to officialdom remains unknown. What is certain is that Paxton had trouble supporting a minister after Thayer's departure: his replacement was discharged after only two years. Antagonism to Boston's established leaders also continued into the time of Shays' Rebellion four years later, and was shown in the area's resistance to the ratification of the new federal constitution. After leaving Paxton, Thayer began farming in Holliston, the home of his wife's family. He died there on September 25, 1807, and was buried in the Central Cemetery, leaving behind his wife and seven children. His tombstone states that he received an A.M. degree; however, no record of it has been found.

SOURCES: Sketch: for Loyalist interpretation, see: *Sibley's Harvard Graduates*, XVI, 245; family background, church career, loyalist opinions: M. Blake, *A Centurial Hist. of the Mendon Association* (1853), 218; provincial congress: W. Lincoln, ed.,

Journal of the Mass. Provincial Congress (1838), 313-15; Paxton and Shays' Rebellion: J. Nelson, *Worcester County* (1934), I, 217, 257-58; D. H. Hurd, *Hist. of Worcester County* (1889), I, 568-84; R. Taylor, *Western Massachusetts in the Revolution* (1954), 168-77.

LLM

Jacob Van Arsdale

JACOB VAN ARSDALE, A.B., A.M. 1768, Presbyterian clergyman, was born on February 8, 1745, in Hillsborough Township, Somerset County, New Jersey, the sixth child of Jannitz Hendricks and Philip Van Arsdale. The father was a prosperous farmer who divided his estate among five sons, leaving to Jacob £150. After graduation from the College, Jacob studied theology with William Tennent in Freehold, Monmouth County, New Jersey. There he married Mary, the daughter of Dirck Sutphin, a wealthy member of the Old Tennent Church. Licensed by the New Brunswick Presbytery in April 1768, he supplied pulpits in the surrounding area for the next three years. When William Tennent introduced him to the Presbyterian congregation in Kingston, Somerset County, New Jersey, this prestigious parish not far from Princeton called Van Arsdale to be their permanent minister. He was ordained by the Presbytery of New Brunswick, and served in Kingston until 1775. Then in December he resigned to accept a ministerial position at the First Presbyterian Church in Springfield, Essex (now part of Union) County, New Jersey, at the salary of $250 a year. An agreement with the church's trustees demonstrated that Van Arsdale was a shrewd bargainer. The congregation supplied him with a house, firewood, and a $1,500 bond that he in turn would never redeem if they "promptly every year" paid his salary. Clearly the union was a happy one, for the minister spent the rest of his life in Springfield, where he raised five children and owned at least one slave.

During the Revolution, Van Arsdale supported the Whigs and suffered dearly for it. In the campaign of 1776, he asked General MacDougall to keep his troops in the area to protect the inhabitants against the British. But as Washington's army retreated through New Jersey, the commander-in-chief staying briefly at Van Arsdale's home, the entire state was left at the mercy of the enemy. The government fled and the royal troops raided the countryside, burning most of the houses in Springfield as well as Van Arsdale's church. For the remainder of the conflict the congregation met in a barn. Van Arsdale accepted a year-to-year allowance from his parishioners. Shortly after the war the townsmen donated their time, effort, and materials to rebuild their house of worship. In addition to continuing his ministerial duties, Van Arsdale served as a trustee of the College from 1793 to 1802. He died on October 24, 1803, and was buried in the Springfield cemetery.

SOURCES: Family background, father's will: *NYGBR*, 81 (1950), 229, 38 *NJA*, 378; church career: E.V.D. Wight, *Hist. of Kingston Church* (1952), 24-27; W. W. Clayton, *Hist. of Union and Middlesex Counties* (1882), 368-71; Rev. War activities: Force, *Am. Arch.* (5 ser.), III, 1297; *NJHSP* (1921), VI, 167.

*See sketch of son Elias Van Arsdale (H B. 1791)
in Vol. IV*   LLM

Stephen Voorhees

STEPHEN VOORHEES, A.B., A.M. 1768, Dutch Reformed and Presbyterian clergyman, was born in 1740 at Six Mile Run, Somerset County, New Jersey, to Sarah and Isaac Voorhees. After graduation, Voorhees, assisted by Francis Barber (A.B. 1767), established a Latin grammar school in Hackensack, New Jersey. In 1769, he moved the school to New York City, where he began recruiting youths to study the classical languages. Three years later, he left teaching for the ministry. Licensed by the Dutch Reformed Church in 1772, he joined that part of the denomination that was breaking from Holland and introducing the use of English into the local congregations, an issue that wracked the denomination for a generation. Receiving a call from the Dutch Reformed church in Poughkeepsie, Dutchess County, New York, he was ordained early in 1773. Here he married Elizabeth Mathewman, who died a few years later in childbirth. The Poughkeepsie ministry began a controversy which would plague Voorhees's entire career. His desire to use English in church ceremonies and records divided the congregation. Only his resignation in 1776 healed the schism.

Almost immediately he accepted a new parish in Red Hook Landing, Dutchess County, New York. While he and his congregation supported the Whig cause in the Revolution, their political agreement could not assuage the conflict arising from Voorhees's use of the English language. Forced to step down in 1780, he took over the Dutch church in Rhinebeck Flatts, Dutchess County, New York. There the controversy over the use of Dutch or English continued, culminating with Voorhees's departure in 1785 for a new congregation in Philipsburg (or Tarrytown), Westchester County, New York. There the conflict once again arose, ending with the dismissal of the "radical" minister in 1788. Voorhees then decided to shed his affiliation with the Dutch church and return to New Jersey where more "liberal views might prevail." Sometime during this period of flux, Voorhees married his second wife, Elizabeth Clausen. They had three children. After four years of seeming ministerial inactivity, he began supplying pulpits for the New Brunswick Presbytery. Even though he had difficulties receiving the proper financial maintenance, he began serving on a regular basis the Kingston Presbyterian Church in Kingston, New Jersey. Voorhees died in Assunpink, New Jersey, on November 23, 1796.

SOURCES: Family background: E. W. Van Voorhis, *Genealogy of the Van Voorhis Family* (1888), II, 357-58; *Historical Handbook of the Van Voorhis Family* (1935), 58-59; grammar school: *N.Y. Gaz.*, Oct. 9, 1769; *N.Y. Jour.*, Jan. 4, 1768; career: C. E. Corwin, *Manual of the Reformed Church in America* (1922), 563; F. Hasbrouck, ed., *Hist. of Dutchess County, N.Y.* (1909), 446; H. H. Morse, *Historic Old Rhinebeck* (1908), 132-34; E. M. Bacon, *Chronicles of Tarrytown and Sleepy Hollow* (1898), 49-53; E. Van Dyke Wight, *Hist. of the Kingston Pres. Church* (1952), 25-28.

LLM

Ralph Wheelock

RALPH WHEELOCK, schoolmaster and college tutor, was born at Lebanon Crank, Connecticut, on August 18, 1742, the third child and first surviving son of Sarah Davenport and Eleazar Wheelock (Yale 1733). The mother was a sister of James Davenport (Yale 1732), one of the most notorious itinerant preachers of the Great Awakening. The father, also a leader of the Great Awakening, was a Congregational clergyman and founder of both Moor's Indian Charity School and its successor, Dartmouth College.

Wheelock was his father's favorite child, the intended heir to his enterprises, and an epileptic. Admitted to the College in the winter of 1761–1762, Wheelock was placed in the freshman class. "He enjoys his health," tutor Jeremiah Halsey (A.B. 1752) reported to Wheelock's father on February 12, 1762, "as well as can be expected, all things considered, and I hope the Disadvantage he is under in this Respect, will not be so great hereafter." The "disadvantage," however, grew ever more intense over the next three years. "Your Son is still weakly," President Samuel Finley reported in August, 1763, "for now & then He has a bad fit, & I fear his ability in point of Health for him, lest his Indisposition shou'd cause his making a disadvantageous appearance upon ye yearly Examination which approaches."

Whatever Wheelock's performance in his examinations, the next few months were not easy ones for him. "I am . . . able to follow my Studies," he wrote to his father in the following April, "tho my Spirits are much gone; my Health going, & my worldly comforts as few as they ever were. . . . My Class-mates from whom I received such injurious

Treatment last summer have been very compl[a]isant since my return." President Finley was less complaisant. Wheelock was due to
receive his degree in 1764, but Finley felt that he was not yet qualified:
"To give him a Degree without standing an Examination with his class,
wou'd be inferior, wou'd check a spirit of study, as they [the other stu-
dents] wou'd imagine partiality, &c. It can be no dishonour to him, not
to have a Degree with's Class, as all know the obstacles he has met
with." Finley recommended that Ralph spend another year in the
College.

Rather than improving, by March 1765, Wheelock's situation had
deteriorated. In that month he had a tooth pulled, which brought on
a succession of three fits. Finley explained to the father that Ralph had
become "so discouraged by his Fits, that he lately, of his own accord,
proposed going to Yale College, which I immediately consented to."
Miserable, Ralph wrote to his father: "I am convinced that Life does
not sute me." But by April or May he had recovered sufficiently to proceed to New Haven, where Yale, in an unusual private commencement
ceremony, awarded him the A.B. a few months later.

After receiving his degree Wheelock returned to his family's home
in Lebanon. There he taught in his father's Indian Charity School for
two years. In 1766, 1767, and 1768, Wheelock's father sent him on missions among the Oneida Indians in New York. These were ill-advised
moves, though the father did not realize it at the time. Wheelock managed to cast aspersions on the successful work of Samuel Kirkland
(A.B. 1765) among the Indians. He alienated the Oneidas personally
by his overbearing conduct and by beating their children, whom he
was supposed to teach, for every trifle. He barely managed to avoid a
physical confrontation with Oneida leaders. "Take care brother!" they
advised him. "Learn yourself, to understand the word of God before
you undertake to teach and govern others."

In 1770 Wheelock moved with his family to Hanover, New Hampshire, where his father established Dartmouth College. Named one of
Dartmouth's two tutors. Wheelock's illness grew ever more severe. In
1771 he was forced to give up teaching. Over the next two or three
years Wheelock seems to have traveled from place to place about New
England, lodging with relatives and vainly seeking cures for his malady. In hopes of raising Ralph's spirits, when a New Hampshire militia
regiment was formed in 1774 the elder Wheelock saw that Ralph was
appointed an officer. He saw no service. The last direct reference to
Wheelock among his family's correspondence came on April 10, 1778,
when a sister in Hartford reported to their father that he had wan-
dered westward after a visit. "I am concerned that I hear nothing from

him," she wrote. It was probably at about this time that Wheelock, whose mental stability had come near collapse, was placed under permanent restraint in Hanover.

Wheelock's father died in 1779. "To my loving and afflicted son Ralph or Radulphus Wheelock," part of his will reads "(who has been by the holy hand of God upon him rendered useless a great part of his life and is reduced to such a state that there is little prospect he will ever be able to get into any business . . .) I give fifty pounds lawful money for his support so long as he shall live." Ralph was also left a small farm adjoining Dartmouth College and his mother's silver tankard. With considerable sacrifice, Dartmouth's trustees faithfully paid Wheelock's annuity until his death on February 7, 1817.

SOURCES: Sketch: Dexter, *Yale Biographies*, III, 159-60; sketch, Oneida quotation, father's will: J. D. McCallum, *Eleazar Wheelock* (1939), 126-28, 208-15; all other direct quotations drawn from Wheelock MSS as follows: J. Halsey to E. Wheelock (hereafter E. W.), Feb. 12, 1762; S. Finley to E. W., Aug. 19, 1763; R. Wheelock to E. W., Apr. 4, 1764; Finley to E. W., Aug. 20, 1764, and Mar. 12, 1765; R. Wheelock to E. W., Mar. 27, 1765; Ruth Patten to E. W., Apr. 10, 1778.

Samuel Williams

SAMUEL WILLIAMS, A.B., bore a name that was extremely common in eighteenth-century America. The only certain fact about the Princeton alumnus is that he was listed as dead in the College's first catalogue, published in 1770. Of the many contemporary Samuel Williamses, one appears most likely to have been the alumnus. This Samuel Williams was born in Lebanon, Connecticut, on December 11, 1746, the youngest of the eleven children of Deborah Throop, wife of Samuel Williams. After graduation, young Williams returned to Lebanon, where he died on August 21, 1768. He was buried in the town's Old Cemetery.

SOURCES: Parentage, birth and death dates: S. W. Williams, *Gen. & Hist. of the Family of Williams* (1847), 145; gravestone inscription: *NEHGR*, 74 (1920), 112.

Simeon Williams

SIMEON WILLIAMS, A.B., A.M. 1774, Harvard 1769, Congregational clergyman, was born on June 30, 1743, at Easton, Bristol County, Massachusetts, the son of Deacon Simeon Williams and his wife Zipporah Crane. Williams first attended Harvard, but when his parents could no longer afford the fees, he left in his sophomore year for "saving charge." During his time in Princeton, Williams joined the Well-Meaning Club, forerunner of the Cliosophic Society. After graduation he was asked to preach at the Second Congregational Church in the small farming town of Weymouth, Suffolk County, Massachusetts, one of the oldest settlements in the province. For over two years the parish had been interviewing candidates to fill their pulpit. Although Williams impressed them with his abilities and was called, there remained the vexing question of adequate support. Not satisfied with the original offer of £73 annually and a £133 settlement fee, Williams bargained with the town for more. Finally they agreed to give him twelve cords of wood yearly "when he shall marry and have a family." Satisfied with their offer, Williams wrote, "Gentlemen—I accept your invitation to the work of the ministry and expect a maintenance." He was ordained on October 26, 1768. On September 1, 1770, Williams married Anna, daughter of the Reverend Joseph Crocker (Harvard 1734) of Eastham, Barnstable County, Massachusetts. They subsequently had seven children.

On December 23, 1774, Williams signed with his fellow townsmen a "Solemn League and Covenant" not to purchase or consume tea. Despite a wartime consensus in support of the American cause, serious problems developed between Williams and his parishioners. Due to the inflation of the period, he asked that his remuneration be adjusted in proportion to the accelerating prices. When the town granted his request, Williams received on December 1779 a £1,366 increase in salary. The next year the town gave him £6,190. Only when Williams once again was supplied with hard money did his pay return to its regular £73 in 1781. After the war, prosperity returned to Williams's parish, and a very elaborate meetinghouse replaced the old church in 1785.

At the turn of the century, however, a decline in congregational numbers set in. From a high enrollment of 105 members in the church, only 63 were present to grace Williams's last years. A sympathetic witness attributed this to the "floods of French infidelity" spreading over the area. But it was also due to the effective (if not formal) disestablishment of the state church as well as the attraction of competing sects. When in 1813 the precinct no longer taxed everyone in the town for the support of the Second Congregational Church, at least five new denominations officially appeared. The Baptists and the Methodists housed their worshippers in much more humble abodes; the more prosperous Unitarians and Universalists drew away some of Williams's congregation. Amid these troubles, in 1811 Williams claimed that "bodily infirmities" inhibited the full performance of duty and that he wished the aid of an assistant. On December 18, 1818, William Tyler (Brown 1809) was ordained as co-pastor and immediately tried to heighten interest in the church through innovations such as the town's first total abstinence society. After serving the longest ministerial term in the history of the town, Williams died on May 31, 1819.

SOURCES: Sketch: *Sibley's Harvard Graduates*, XVI, 272-73; family background, Weymouth ecclesiastical history, problem of pay: H. H. Joy, *Hist. of Weymouth* (1923), I, 230-40; revolution in Weymouth, Solemn League and Covenant: C. F. Adams, Jr., *Settlement of Weymouth*, 58-59, 70-73.

LLM

CLASS OF 1766

Waightstill Avery, A.B.

Hezekiah Balch, A.B.

Hezekiah James Balch, A.B.

Joseph Burt, A.B.

Caleb Chase, A.B.

Jonathan Cheever, A.B.

Daniel Cunyngham Clymer, A.B.

Ebenezer Cowell, Jr., A.B.

Samuel Edmiston, A.B.

Oliver Ellsworth, A.B.

John Haley, A.B.

Joseph Hasbrouck, A.B.

Moses Haslett, A.B.

David Howell, A.B.

Daniel Jones, A.B.

Solomon Kellogg, A.B.

Josiah Lewis, A.B.

Peter Van Brugh Livingston, Jr., A.B.

Daniel McCalla, A.B.

John MacPherson, A.B.

Luther Martin, A.B.

Nathaniel Niles, A.B.

James Power, A.B.

Isaac Skillman, A.B.

Samuel Smith, A.B.

William Smith, A.B.

Alpheus Spring, A.B.

Benjamin Stelle, A.B.

Micah Townsend, A.B.

John Woodhull, A.B.

Joseph Woodman, A.B.

Waightstill Avery

WAIGHTSTILL AVERY, A.B., A.M. 1771, lawyer, was born at Groton, Connecticut, on May 10, 1741, the tenth child of Jerusha Morgan and her husband, Humphrey Avery, a substantial resident of New London County, selectman, justice of the peace, and sometime deputy in the General Assembly. He studied in a school at Hempstead, Long Island, conducted by the Anglican Reverend Samuel Seabury (Harvard 1724). Avery was initially enrolled at Yale, but on July 27, 1764, President Thomas Clap recorded that he and Oliver Ellsworth (A.B. 1766) "at the request of their respective parents" had been dismissed from the college. Both young men transferred to Nassau Hall, where they became roommates and members of the Well-Meaning Club. Avery graduated at the head of his class, and at the commencement of 1766 he delivered, according to a New York newspaper, "an elegant Latin Funeral Oration" on the recent death of President Finley.

Avery remained in Princeton for a year in charge of the grammar school, and subsequently read law with Littleton Dennis, a prominent lawyer and planter of Maryland's Eastern Shore. Early in 1769 he set out on a journey that seems to have had the purpose of settlement on the western frontier of North Carolina, at the time one of the most rapidly growing of the thirteen colonies. In April he settled in Charlotte, county seat of Mecklenburg County, after a three-month trip in which he virtually crossed the province twice and made the acquaintance of most of its leading inhabitants, including Governor William Tryon, who licensed him for the practice of law. Success in his profession seems to have come immediately. Traveling by horseback from court to court through neighboring counties, and quickly qualified to appear at the bar of superior as well as inferior courts, he pled causes both criminal and civil as did "country" lawyers for generations to come. The fees, limited by law, were not large. During six months in 1772 he recorded 120 of them for a total of £164, a comfortable income for the time and place but hardly enough to promise that the practice of law alone would win him the wealth he later acquired.

A devout and informed Calvinist who could describe a sermon by an Anglican minister as "a well-connected cunning Arminian discourse," Avery found a growing company of fellow Presbyterians in Mecklenburg, including his classmate the Reverend Hezekiah J. Balch. These Presbyterians have been credited as the chief sponsors of Queen's College in Charlotte, an academy chartered by the legislature in January 1771. Among the fourteen trustees named in the act were both Balch and Avery. Governor Tryon's support of the charter may help to explain Avery's opposition to the Regulators, whose movement of protest against officeholders and lawyers reached its climax in the Battle of Alamance during the following spring. Similarly, the disallowance of the charter by the king, together with another act intended to enlarge the right of Presbyterian ministers to perform marriage ceremonies, may help to explain Avery's later identification with the cause of American independence. In any case, he remained a stout supporter of the "Church of Scotland," as on occasion he described it when speaking of its rights in relation to the Church of England, and of Liberty Hall, as Queen's College was renamed in 1777.

Avery, together with Balch and Ephraim Brevard (A.B. 1768), has been listed among the "signers" of the "Mecklenburg Declaration of Independence," which bears the date of May 20, 1775. Modern scholarship has seriously challenged the authenticity of the document, attributing its text to faulty recollections many years later of a meeting, on May 31, 1775, called by the Mecklenburg Committee of Safety, which adopted a highly significant set of resolves. These stopped short of a declaration of independence, but did affirm that commissions from the king had become "null and void" and prescribed "certain rules and regulations for the internal government of this country" pending action by the Provincial Congress "under the direction of the great Continental Congress." The ablest defender of the "Mecklenburg Declaration" has attributed to Avery the authorship of these resolves.

Avery sat for Mecklenburg in the third North Carolina Congress assembled on August 20, 1775, and was chosen by it a member of the provincial council. He attended the congress in April 1776, and again in November, when he became a member of the committee charged with drafting a bill of rights and a constitution for the state. It is assumed that the instructions given the Mecklenburg delegation, in Avery's handwriting, helped to shape this first of the state's constitutions. Some have attributed to him a special influence in the provision which committed the state to the support of education, including "one or more Universities." Whatever the fact, he lived to serve as a trustee of the recently established University of North Carolina from 1795 to 1804.

Over the years extending into the 1790s Avery repeatedly sat in the general assembly. In 1777 he was one of four commissioners who, with commissioners from Virginia, negotiated a treaty of cession with the Cherokee Indians sometimes known as Avery's Treaty. He became the state's first attorney general in 1778, an office he resigned the following year to take up residence on the plantation in Jones County belonging to a newly acquired wife, a young widow named Leah Probart Franks, whom he married on October 3, 1778. Appointed colonel in the local militia, Avery saw active duty, with doubtful distinction, when Cornwallis invaded the state. In the fall of 1780 his law office in Charlotte, with library and papers, was burned by the British.

After the war Avery fled the malaria-ridden area of eastern Carolina to the newly created Burke County, in the far west of the state. There, with a sharp eye for good "river-bottom" land, he acquired thousands of acres (he paid taxes in 1818 on 13,000 in Burke County alone); built Swan Ponds, described by a traveler in 1795 as one of the "finest Country seats" in the state; and continued to practice law along a circuit that led at times across the mountains to Jonesboro, in Tennessee, until a fall from his horse in 1801 left him unable to walk. It was at Jonesboro in 1788 that Avery evidently had a duel with young Andrew Jackson that happily did no harm to either party. When Avery began to acquire slaves cannot be said, but the census of 1790 showed that he possessed 24, the largest number in the county, and in 1818 he owned 25 taxable slaves between the ages of 12 and 50. He died on March 15, 1821, leaving land and slaves to each of three daughters and the bulk of his estate to an only son, Isaac Thomas Avery.

By moving to the western frontier of colonial America, this son of New England had become a southern gentleman, a wealthy slaveholder commonly known as Colonel Avery, but to the end he remained true to his Puritan ancestry. In his will he declared "All may be assured that no part of what is here devised was acquired by horse racing, gambling or betting of any kind, but by sober, honest industry," and expressed the hope that "the same will not be squandered or desecrated by idleness and extravagance of any kind."

SOURCES: The sketch leans heavily on E. W. Phifer, "Saga of a Burke County Family," *NCHR*, 39 (1962), 1-17, from which the quotation from will is taken. For family: H. DeL. Sweet, *Averys of Groton* (1894); E. M. and C. Avery, *Groton Avery Clan* (1912,) 156, 230, 235; and Isaac Avery file, PUA; dismissal from Yale: W. G. Brown, *Life of Oliver Ellsworth* (1905); and for law practice: C. Eaton, "Mirror of the Southern Colonial Lawyer," *WMQ*, 8 (1951), 520-34. His public career is easily followed through Weeks' *Index* of the colonial and state *Records*. See especially W. H. Hoyt, *Mecklenburg Declaration of Independence* (1907); J. H. Moore, *Defence of the Mecklenburg Declaration of Independence* (1908); and R.D.W. Connor's judicious discussion of the issue in his *Hist. of North Carolina* (1919), I, 394n. For Cherokee Treaty, *NCHR*, 8 (1931), 55-116. His journal for 1769 and a fee book are in the Wisconsin Historical Society.

WFC

Hezekiah Balch

HEZEKIAH BALCH, A.B., A.M. 1774, D.D. Williams 1806, Presbyterian clergyman and educator, was born on Deer Creek, Harford County, Maryland, in March 1741, the son of John Balch, who is said to have moved his family to North Carolina in 1763, though confirmation of this has not been found. He was a first cousin of his classmate Hezekiah James Balch. According to one source Balch was admitted to the College in 1758 on the recommendation of the Reverend John Rodgers, later one of the trustees. If Balch did indeed go to Princeton in that year it would have been as a student in the grammar school rather than in the College.

After graduation Balch studied for the ministry. Licensed to preach by the Presbytery of New Castle in 1769, he was ordained the following year by the Presbytery of Hanover. He probably was the Hezekiah Balch who with five others successfully petitioned the synod that year for the organization of a new Presbytery of Orange for the area south of Virginia. It was most likely during this period that Balch married Hannah Lewis of North Carolina. The couple had six children.

From the beginning of his ministry Balch seems to have been something of an itinerant. There is evidence that he served congregations on the frontier of South Carolina, and over the course of more than a decade he is found identified successively with the presbyteries, in addition to Orange (which he represented at the synod of 1774), of Donegal (which he represented in 1775 and 1781), and Hanover, to which he was dismissed by Donegal in 1782. About 1783 Balch moved west to the area that later became the state of Tennessee. There he founded churches and bought a plantation three miles south of Greeneville.

In his new home Balch quickly became involved in the controversy attending the effort to launch the abortive state of Franklin. A convention held in December 1784 had drafted a constitution that was subject to ratification by a second convention meeting at Greeneville in November 1785. Balch seems not to have been a member of the convention but to have gained the floor as a spectator to denounce an effort to substitute a markedly different draft with enough vigor as to have become involved in a continuing and bitter controversy.

In 1785 Balch, along with Samuel Doak (A.B. 1775), became one of the founding members of the Presbytery of Abingdon. Balch and Doak launched a strong campaign to introduce the use of Isaac Watts's hymns into Tennessee churches, a movement that met strong resistance from their more conservative parishioners. Balch opened the first session of the Abingdon Presbytery with a sermon called *Gospel Liberty in Singing the Praises of God, Stated, Illustrated, and Urged,* which was later printed.

In the early 1790s Balch's interests shifted to education. On September 3, 1794, the territorial legislature chartered Greeneville College, to be located on Balch's plantation. At the first meeting of the board of trustees the following February Balch was chosen president. Shortly thereafter he set out on a fund-raising tour. Beginning in Charleston, South Carolina, Balch moved up the Atlantic coast, preaching and begging for his college as far as Portland, Maine. Back in Tennessee in time for the second meeting of the board of trustees on May 12, 1796, Balch reported that he had raised $1,352 in cash, $350 in subscriptions, and had been given many books and some mathematical equipment. The trustees voted to give Balch half the money he had raised as recompense (he accepted only half of this) and to erect an eight-room building. Balch gave 154 acres of his own land to the college.

Balch had neglected to tell the trustees of the most important item he had picked up on his trip to the east: the ideas of Samuel Hopkins, a key figure in the New Divinity school of New England theology. Hopkins's most important contribution to this intellectual tradition, Sidney Ahlstrom has succinctly written, was "his identification of sin and self-love, and his very forceful exposition of its Edwardsean corollary that true virtue consists in 'disinterested benevolence,' even unto complete willingness to be damned if it be for the greater glory of God." Upon his return to Tennessee Balch immediately began to preach this doctrine. It aroused a storm of theological controversy in his predominantly conservative, Old Side Presbyterian area, one that drove him into an endless series of church trials and that interfered seriously with the firm establishment of Greeneville College.

Balch's methods of promulgating the New Divinity were not quiet. His tone is suggested in a public statement of his creed that he published in a Knoxville newspaper in 1796: "I believe the essence of all true religion in Heaven & on Earth consists in *disinterested Benevolence*, by which I mean *loving God for his own glory & our neighbors as ourselves* & our *selves* as our neighbors. . . . I believe that we ought to have charity that is love for all the Affricans [sic] Cherokees, Papists, Universalists, Arminians, Socinians, Pelagians, Antinomians, Arians, Quakers, Methodists, Baptists & even for the Presbyterians. . . . I say we ought to love them as we do ourselves, and that this kind of Charity instead of being Hell-born charaty [sic] is the very essence of holiness and that whoever quarrels at this kind of charity . . . gives evident proof, of a bad heart or a stupid head."

Balch's Hopkinsian doctrines led to a long series of squabbles among Presbyterians. He was brought to trial before the General Assembly in 1798. That body declared that "Mr Balch is erronious [sic] in making disinterested Benevolence the only diffinition [sic] of Holiness or true Religion; because this may perplex the mind of those not accustomed to abstract Speculation—is questionable in itself . . . on the whole we recommend that Mr Balch be required to acknowledge that he was wrong in the publication of his creed."

Balch did not recant. Controversy and the division of one presbytery into another along Hopkinsian and anti-Hopkinsian lines continued in Balch's area for the rest of his life. Eastern Tennessee became the only redoubt of the New Divinity in the south. The views of Samuel Hopkins were spread throughout the immediate area and beyond by graduates of Greeneville College, particularly after Balch was joined in 1805 in his work as minister and teacher by the Reverend Charles Coffin (Harvard 1793), a more temperate Hopkinsian. The college itself was little more than an academy until 1802. Late in the nineteenth century it merged with what is now Tusculum College.

Balch's later years were seriously disturbed by the recurrent mental illnesses of his wife. After her death in about 1808 Balch married Ann Luckey. Balch himself died after a short illness in April 1810.

SOURCES: Family: see Hezekiah James Balch; sketch: Sprague, *Annals*, III, 308-19; Franklin: J.G.M. Ramsey, *Annals of Tenn.* (1853), 323; S. C. Williams, *Hist. of the Lost State of Franklin* (1924), esp. 91-93; T. P. Abernethy, *From Frontier to Plantation in Tenn.* (1932), 76; bitterness of controversy: S. J. Folmsbee et al., *Tennessee* (1969), 84, 124; Greeneville College: A. E. Ragan, *A Hist. of Tusculum College* (1945), 1-35; Hopkinsianism: S. E. Ahlstrom, *A Religious Hist. of the Am. People* (1972), 408; Balch and Hopkinsianism in south: W. B. Posey, *Presbyterian Church in the Old Southwest* (1952), 19n, 31, 51-52; E. T. Thompson, *Presbyterians in the South* (1963), 114, 353-55, 409; Balch's creed: *Knoxville Gaz.*, July 15, 1796 (copy at PPPrHi); General Assembly: "Copy of the Transactions of the General Assembly in Relation to Mr. Balch's Creed, May 27, 1798," MS, PPPrHi.

PUBLICATIONS: see text

MSS: PHi

Hezekiah James Balch

HEZEKIAH JAMES BALCH, A.B., A.M. 1774, Presbyterian clergyman, brother of Stephen Bloomer Balch (A.B. 1774), and first cousin of a classmate who also bore the name Hezekiah Balch, was born in 1746 on Deer Creek, Harford County, Maryland, the fifth child and first son of Anne Goodwyn and her husband, James Balch. He was licensed to preach in 1767 by the Presbytery of Donegal in Pennsylvania, and ordained by the same Presbytery in 1770. He had settled in western North Carolina in 1769, where he had charge of two congregations at Rocky River and Poplar Tent, near to Charlotte, county seat of Mecklenburg County.

He may have been the Hezekiah Balch who in 1770 was instrumental in the establishment of a new Presbytery of Orange with jurisdiction over congregations in the Carolinas. He almost certainly was the Hezekiah Balch who in 1771, together with Waightstill Avery (A.B. 1766), became one of the original trustees of Queen's College, an academy located in Charlotte and headed at first by Joseph Alexander (A.B. 1760).

The name of Hezekiah James Balch, like that of Avery and Ephraim Brevard (A.B. 1768), is found among the "signers" of the "Mecklenburg Declaration of Independence," to which has been assigned the date of May 20, 1775. The document probably found both its text and date much later in the faulty memory of a meeting called by the local Committee of Safety which persuaded the assembled citizenry to adopt the Mecklenburg Resolves of May 31, 1775. The tradition recorded in the controversial literature on the subject of the "Mecklenburg Declaration" has Balch serving as one of the initial speakers on the occasion of the assumed earlier meeting of May 19-20. Perhaps in fact he performed that service at the meeting that adopted the resolves of May 31, one of the more radical papers to emerge from the response outside New England to the beginning of the War of Independence in the preceding month at Lexington.

Balch died early in 1776, having never married.

SOURCES: Family: T. W. Balch, *Balch Genealogica* (1907); "Mecklenburg Declaration": sources cited for Waightstill Avery, and W. H. Hoyt, ed., *Papers of Archibald D. Murphy* (1914), II, 198. In *Col. Rec. N.C.*, 8, 487, the name of the trustee for Queen's College is given as Hezekiah T. Balch, probably through an error of transcription; in the act of 1777 that renamed the Academy Liberty Hall (ibid., 24, 30-32) no Balch appears among the names of trustees, an omission fitting with the known date of death for Hezekiah James. Orange Presbytery: *NCHR*, 44 (1967), 381.

WFC

Joseph Burt

JOSEPH BURT, A.B., has not been identified. The only certain facts discovered about him are that while at the College he was a member of the Well-Meaning Club, forerunner of the Cliosophic Society, and that he was listed as living in the College's catalogue of 1770 and as dead in the catalogue of 1773. He was not the Joseph Burt of Northfield, Massachusetts, who is incorrectly awarded a Princeton A.B. in volume sixteen of *Sibley's Harvard Graduates*. The Burt family was numerous in Hunterdon County, New Jersey, and although it is impossible to identify him with any certainty in surviving records, the alumnus may well have belonged to it. However, an equally good chance exists that he came from Connecticut.

SOURCES: *Gen. Cat. American Whig-Cliosophic Soc.* (n.d.), 27; N.J. possibility: W. L. Burt, *Descendents of Richard Burt of Taunton, Mass.* (1944), 20; Conn. possibility: R. H. Burnham, *Genealogical Records of Henry & Ulalia Burt* (1892), 52.

Caleb Chase

CALEB CHASE, A.B., schoolteacher, innkeeper, and public official, was born in Newbury, Massachusetts, on July 28, 1746, the son of Mary Morse and her husband, Joseph Chase, a farmer. Caleb was the youngest of eleven children. Some time after graduation from the College he moved to Gorham, Maine, where he taught school from 1769 to 1779. He married Joanna Whitney of York, Maine, on December 31, 1769, and the first of their twelve children—six sons and six daughters—was born a year later.

Besides teaching school, Chase operated Gorham's first licensed inn. His twin vocations were likely the source of the popularity that won him election as town treasurer in 1772 and as town clerk four years later. His term in each position was for two years. Chase also helped found Gorham's Committee of Correspondence in 1772, and he represented Gorham in the Massachusetts House of Representatives (Maine was still part of Massachusetts) in 1776 and 1777. In the last he served on three committees: one to which a letter from the selectmen of Winslow was referred; one for viewing seaports south of Boston, and one for inspecting the impression of bills of credit.

In 1779 Chase moved to Concord, New Hampshire. As in Gorham, he was successively a schoolteacher, an innkeeper, and a public official —again, serving first as town treasurer, in 1787, and then as town clerk, from 1788 until 1796. In 1796 he moved to Thornton, New Hampshire, and remained there until he died on February 14, 1810.

SOURCES: Vital data: Caleb Chase File, PUA; *Vital Rec. Newbury, Mass.* (1911), I, 87: J. C. Chase and G. W. Chamberlain, *Seven Generations of Descendants of Aquila and Thomas Chase* (1928), 58, 101; J. Pierce, *Hist. of Town of Gorham, Me.* (1862), 12, 113, 158, 228, 231; H. D. McClellan, *Hist. of Gorham, Me.* (1903), 140, 225, 318, 373; *Concord Town Rec.* (1894), 233, 234, 241, 249, 256, 264, 269, 276, 280, 287, 532, 534; J. O. Lyford, *Hist. of Concord, N.H.* (1903), II, 1226; *Jour. of Mass. House of Rep.,* 1776, 1777.

HS

Jonathan Cheever

JONATHAN CHEEVER, A.B., was probably the Jonathan Cheever born in 1744 to Nancy and Ezekiel Cheever of Morristown, Morris County, New Jersey. The father was a Morris County freeholder who died in 1775. The father's will of April 13, 1775, left an indeterminable amount of money to Jonathan and two other survivors. It is possible that Cheever's share of the inheritance enabled him to become a physician, for he is referred to as "Dr." in some wills of the period. For a man of this possible profession, his almost complete absence from the public record is peculiar. Like his parents, Cheever belonged to the First Presbyterian Church of Morristown. When the church sought subscriptions to support the College in 1769, he contributed £1, one of the smaller gifts. Cheever died on October 14, 1794, at age fifty.

SOURCES: Vital data: Jonathan Cheever File, PUA; *Hist. of the First Pres. Church of Morristown, N.J.* (n.d.), Pt. II, 36; *GMNJ*, 16 (1941), 62; *NJA*, 34 (1931), 89-90; *Hist. Morris Cty., N.J.* (1882), 148; A. M. Sherman, *Historic Morristown, N.J.* (1905), 110.

HS

Daniel Cunyngham Clymer

DANIEL CUNYNGHAM CLYMER, A.B., lawyer and public official, was born in Philadelphia on April 6, 1748, the son of Ann Judith Roberdeau and her husband William Clymer, a ship's captain and privateer. Daniel was baptized in Anglican Christ Church on July 12 of that year. The father was lost at sea while Clymer was a boy; the responsibility for his upbringing was assumed by his uncle, Daniel Roberdeau, a prosperous and politically popular Philadelphia merchant, who entered Clymer in the Academy of Philadelphia in 1755.

After graduation from the College Clymer studied law. In 1768 his Uncle Roberdeau reported to *his* uncle, Daniel Cunyngham, a merchant of St. Christopher's, that "my nephew, now out of town, is studying the law, having had all the advantages of a good education; having obtained by examination in one of our seminaries the Degree of Bachelor of Arts, promises fair for making, I hope, a tolerable figure in his profession." Clymer was admitted to the practice of law in Chester County, Pennsylvania, in September 1769. Admission to the Philadelphia bar followed in October the following year.

For much of his life Clymer's career was overshadowed—and, doubtlessly, assisted—by those of his Uncle Roberdeau and of his first

cousin, George Clymer. The former became a member of the Continental Congress and a general in the revolutionary army; the latter
was a signer of the Declaration of Independence and a member of the
Constitutional Convention. Daniel Clymer's role in the affairs of his
time was considerably more modest. As the Revolution approached,
he was among the earliest to join the Philadelphia Association that
boycotted the importation of British goods. On May 2, 1775, he joined
the second battalion of Philadelphia militia and the following year became a lieutenant colonel in the Rifle Battalion of the Philadelphia Associators. Late in 1777 Clymer was appointed deputy commissary general of prisoners of the Continental army. He appears to have served
in the post only until early in 1778. In 1777 he also served for an indeterminable period as a commissioner of claims for the treasury. At
some time in 1778 Clymer moved to Berks County, Pennsylvania,
where his mother lived on the family's lands. He established a law
practice in Reading and for many years maintained an office in Philadelphia as well. In either 1781 or 1788 Clymer married Ann Weidner
of Berks County. A daughter and two sons were born to the couple.

In 1783–1784 Clymer was elected to the Pennsylvania Assembly as
representative from Berks County. He served in the same office again
in 1787 and in 1791. Closely allied with those opposed to Pennsylvania's constitution of 1776, throughout his career in the assembly
Clymer supported the chartering of the Bank of North American and,
in 1787, the calling of a Pennsylvania convention to ratify the federal
constitution. Speaking in support of the constitution, he said:

> If it is the interest of a few individuals to keep up the weak and
> shattered government [i.e., the Confederation], which brings on
> us the contempt of every surrounding tribe, and the reproach and
> obloquy of every nation, let them exert their opposition; but it will
> be all in vain, for should this House refuse, I think it the duty of
> the people, as they value their present and future welfare, to come
> forward, and to do that justice to themselves, which others would
> deny them.

Pennsylvania ratified the federal constitution, although Clymer was
not a member of the convention that did so.

During the 1790s Clymer appears to have practiced law in and
about Reading. He owned a 250-acre farm near Morgantown, where
he lived with his family much of the time. He was involved in commercial as well as professional pursuits, for the property included a
limestone quarry, kiln, and distillery. A candidate for Congress on the
Democratic-Republican ticket in 1798, he was defeated (3,356 votes to

797) by a Federalist, Joseph Hiester, who later became governor of Pennsylvania. It was Clymer's last venture into politics. He died in Reading on January 25, 1810.

SOURCES: Basic source is: R. Buchanan, *Genealogy of the Roberdeau Family* (1876), 130-32, from which most of sketch by R. E. Brooke in *Hist. Review of Berks County*, 4 (1938), 2-5, is drawn; see too: J. M. Martin, *Bench and Bar of Philadelphia* (1883), 257; scattered refs. to mil. career and property holdings in *Pa. Arch.*, passim; Constit. quotation: J. B. McMaster and F. D. Stone, eds., *Penn. & the Fed. Constit.* (1888), 38-39; 1798 campaign: B. A. Fryer, *Congressional Hist. of Berks (Pa.) District* (1939), 14-15.

MSS: PHi

Ebenezer Cowell, Jr.

EBENEZER COWELL, JR., A.B., lawyer and public official, was born in 1743, probably in Dorchester, Massachusetts, the second son of Sarah and Ebenezer Cowell. The father, a smith who worked largely with guns, locks, and so forth, moved to Trenton, New Jersey, about 1761, shortly after the death of his brother David (Harvard 1732), first Presbyterian minister in Trenton and a trustee of the College. In New Jersey the father prospered through his business and also through extensive land dealings. Young Ebenezer was the second of his sons to attend the College, the first being David (A.B. 1763).

After graduation Cowell studied law, probably with Abraham Cottman of Trenton. On November 30, 1769, he was licensed as an attorney. He lived in Trenton with his brother David, and his name seldom appeared in the public record. But the Revolution brought a change in Cowell's affairs. On July 18, 1776, he petitioned New Jersey's provincial congress to the effect that the "High Sheriff of the County of Hunterdon, had refused to receive and execute two writs issued under the authority of the people, pursuant to the ordinance of this Convention." Ordered to appear before the Congress, the sheriff declared that he declined to act as sheriff "under the authority of the people," and resigned. The incident may have brought Cowell to the attention of the new government. On the following September 7 he was appointed clerk of the pleas for Hunterdon County, a post he held until 1794. Cowell's work brought him into contact with William Paterson (A.B. 1763), who shortly became the new state's attorney general. Cowell represented the attorney general in state cases when Paterson was unable to appear personally, and was often employed by Paterson in his private cases in the same capacity.

After his retirement Cowell lived alone in Trenton. On February 17,

1817, the following notice appeared in the *Trenton Federalist*: "Died. In this city on the night of the 14th inst. Ebenezer Cowell Esq. formerly clerk of the pleas of Hunterdon Co. On the morning of the 15th he was found dead in the house, where he resided, and probably perished in consequence of the weather." Cowell died intestate. His personal property was inventoried at $77.10. The most valuable ($50) item he had was an eight-volume set of the statutes of Great Britain. He also left scattered pieces of real estate, which were divided among his relatives.

SOURCES: Brief sketch, father, family, and inventory: W. Nelson, *N.J. Biog. and Geneal. Notes* (1916), 79-81; residence: *A Hist. of Trenton* (1929), II, 602; petition: *Minutes of the Provincial Congress and the Council of Safety of the State of N.J.* (1879), 513; for association with Paterson: R. C. Haskett, "William Paterson, Attorney General of N.J.," *WMQ*, 12 (1950), 29 n14.

Samuel Edmiston

SAMUEL EDMISTON, A.B., A.M. 1775, physician, was born on July 7, 1746. Although neither his parentage nor place of birth has been discovered, it seems more than likely that he came from the area of Maryland adjoining Chester County, Pennsylvania. Tracing his career has proved difficult. While Edmiston himself always spelled his name "Edmiston," in contemporary records he is alluded to variously as "Edmondson," "Edmonson," or "Edmunson." Moreover, he had two contemporaries of the same name, one a Pennsylvania surveyor, the other a Virginia clergyman.

After graduation Edmiston studied medicine, probably by apprenticing himself to an established physician. No trace of his career has been discovered until June 1776, when he became quartermaster of the 4th Maryland Battalion of the Flying Camp. He served with the unit through December. On May 16, 1777, Benjamin Rush (A.B. 1760) appointed him a second surgeon in the military hospitals under Rush's command. On September 20, 1781, Congress elevated Edmiston to the position of "Physician and Surgeon of the Hospitals of the United States." He held the post until the end of the war.

In August 1783, Edmiston married Martha Blair, a daughter of the Reverend Samuel Blair of Fagg's Manor, Chester County, Pennsylvania. (Four other of the College's alumni also married Blair's daughters.) The couple had an indeterminate number of children. In 1790 the federal censustaker found Edmiston living in Londonderry town-

ship, Chester County, where he apparently practiced medicine until
his death in 1816.

SOURCES: Birth and death dates: F. G. Hoenstine, comp., *The 1955 Year Book of the
Pa. Soc. Sons of the Am. Rev.* (1956), 691; sketches: Alexander, *Princeton,* 105-106;
J. S. Futhey and G. Cope, *Hist. of Chester County, Pa.* (1881), 529; military ser-
vice: Heitman, 164; *U.S. Census of 1790, Pa.,* 67.

Oliver Ellsworth

OLIVER ELLSWORTH, A.B., LL.D. 1797, Yale 1790, Dartmouth 1797;
lawyer, member of Continental Congress, Constitutional Convention,
and first U.S. Senate, and third chief justice of the United States, was
born in Windsor, Connecticut, on April 29, 1745, the second son of
Jemina Leavitt and her husband, David Ellsworth, a substantial farmer. Little is known of his youth except that he was intended by his
father for the ministry, and that he was prepared for college by the

Oliver Ellsworth, A.B. 1766

Reverend Joseph Bellamy, New Light minister and disciple of Jonathan Edwards.

Ellsworth entered Yale in 1762, but after two years he transferred to Nassau Hall. The specific occasion for this transfer is uncertain. It occurred during the extremely stormy last years of President Thomas Clap's administration in New Haven, and there is evidence that Ellsworth more than once became a victim of the severe discipline for which Clap was noted. The president recorded on July 27, 1764, that Ellsworth and Waightstill Avery (A.B. 1766) were dismissed from the college "at the desire of their respective parents." That the choice for continuing their education should have fallen to the College of New Jersey is not surprising, for it had at the time a strong following in New England.

The record of Ellsworth's two years at Princeton is almost as sparse as that for his youth. As might be expected, he roomed with Avery. Contrary to what has often been stated, he did not graduate with highest honors. Tradition assigns to him a chief role in the organization of the Well-Meaning Society, forerunner of the Cliosophic Literary Society of 1770.

After graduation Ellsworth returned to Connecticut, where for a time he studied theology with the Reverend John Smalley (Yale 1756) of New Britain, but later turned to the study of law and was admitted to practice in 1771. His training in the law seems to have been skimpy, and at first he struggled to establish a reputation; but after moving his practice to Hartford in 1775 he quickly attained rank among the leading advocates of the state. Tall, possessed of a commanding appearance, meticulous in dress, and quick and effective in speech, he won clients in large numbers and invested his fees shrewdly, thereby acquiring a substantial though probably not a great fortune. In 1772 he had married Abigail Wolcott of East Windsor. Of the seven children apparently born to this marriage, one died in infancy, Oliver, Jr., died in 1805, and three other sons and two daughters survived their father.

Ellsworth began his long career of public service as deputy for Windsor in the General Assembly from 1773 to 1775. With the outbreak of hostilities in this last year he became a member of a committee of five charged with superintendence of military expenditures, and in 1779 a member of the Council of Safety, which with the governor, oversaw all military activities of the state. Appointed state attorney for Hartford County in 1777, he held the office until 1785. In 1780 he was elevated to the Governor's Council, a position he also held until 1785, when he began a term of four years as judge of the superior court.

Perhaps his commitment to the responsibilities of state office explains the delay of a year in taking the seat in the Continental Congress to which he was first elected in 1777, as well as his less than perfect record of attendance through the nearly five years of service in that body after taking his seat on October 8, 1778. It is difficult to assess this part of his career. As with other members of the Congress, he was named to a number of committees, some of them important. In view of his subsequent career, there is special interest in his membership in the committee whose report gave shape to "The Court of Appeals in Cases of Capture," which the Congress established in May 1780 with a jurisdiction in maritime cases later taken over by the supreme court. More immediately significant was the acquaintance with the nation's problems that persuaded Ellsworth of a need to strengthen the central government. Toward the end of his last term, in the summer of 1783, he wrote Governor Jonathan Trumbull from Princeton, where the Congress was then sitting: "There must, Sir, be a revenue some how established that can be relied on & applied for national purposes as the exigencies arise, independent of the will or views of a single State, or it will be impossible to support national faith or national existence." As for the risk that Congress might abuse the proposed addition to its powers, he felt it "better to hazard something than to hazard all."

Ellsworth returned to the national political scene in 1787 as one of the three Connecticut delegates to the Constitutional Convention. His part in its deliberations is chiefly remembered for the most famous of the convention's compromises, the so-called Connecticut Compromise, which proposed equal representation for the states in the Senate after it had been decided that seats in the lower house would be apportioned according to population. Although Ellsworth cannot be assigned full credit for this strategic proposal, it is true that the convention's decision came on a motion he made. He also was one of the five members of a committee of detail charged on July 24 with the writing of a draft constitution in keeping with resolutions previously adopted. Having returned home before the end of the convention, he did not sign the document, but he vigorously supported ratification by his own state both in the public press and as an influential member of the ratifying convention meeting early in 1788. Among other arguments he employed was a forecast of the exercise of judicial review by the federal courts. Should the United States "overleap their limits," he declared, "the judicial department is a constitutional check." With the new constitution in force, Ellsworth was elected to the Senate, in the "first class" and so for a term of two years. Reelected, he served in the Senate to the time of his appointment to the supreme court.

Ellsworth deserves to be remembered chiefly for the Judiciary Act of 1789. The constitution had left much to the discretion of congress in its simple statement that "The judicial Power of the United States shall be vested in one supreme Court, and in such inferior Courts as the Congress may from time to time ordain and establish." Chairman of the Senate committee appointed for drafting the requisite legislation, Ellsworth has been credited both by contemporaries and modern scholars with the dominant influence in framing a bill to which the federal judiciary in its broad outlines continues to adhere.

Ellsworth was commissioned chief justice of the United States on March 4, 1796, after John Rutledge, successor to John Jay, failed to win confirmation by the Senate and after William Cushing, a member of the court, declined the post. His term in the office was short, less than four years, and illness kept him from sitting in more than one session. Nevertheless, it has been suggested that he was the first chief justice to assert leadership of the court.

A thorough-going Federalist in his support of Hamilton's measures during Washington's first administration, Ellsworth also managed through a period of factional strife among Federalist leaders to retain the confidence of President John Adams. In 1799 Adams appointed him head of a commission of three, including at Ellsworth's suggestion William R. Davie (A.B. 1776), to negotiate a settlement of differences with France in the hope of ending the quasi-war that recently had been heated up by the famous XYZ Affair. The convention that was negotiated with Napoleon in 1800 did not secure for the United States all that was hoped, but it was a significant step toward ending the prospect of open warfare with a former ally, and toward preparing the way for the Louisiana Purchase of 1803.

Ellsworth returned home in 1801, after a visit to England and with his uncertain health finally broken. He had resigned as chief justice while abroad. He died at Windsor on November 26, 1807.

It seems altogether appropriate that Ellsworth should have been remembered by the nation he long served chiefly for one of the more famous compromises in its history, for his political instincts were well developed. At the same time, he was a man of strong conviction and determination. Aaron Burr (A.B. 1772), who was no friend, is reported to have declared that if "Ellsworth had happened to spell the name of the Deity with two d's, it would have taken the Senate three weeks to expunge the superfluous letter." His sons were educated at Yale, and he himself became a fellow of the Yale Corporation, but he has not been forgotten in Princeton. When the Pyne Library (now East Pyne Building) was completed in 1897, its west tower was decorated with figures representing four eminent Princetonians: McCosh, Witherspoon, Madison, and Ellsworth.

SOURCES: W. G. Brown, *Life of Oliver Ellsworth* (1905), though dated in its point of view, is informative and generally dependable. Helpful brief accounts are found in the *DAB*; L. Friedman and F. L. Israel, eds., *Justices of the United States Supreme Court* (1969), 1; and D. D. Egbert, *Princeton Portraits* (1947). The sketch in K. B. Umbreit, *Our Eleven Chief Justices* (1938), is at points misleading. A. DeConde, *The Quasi-War: The Politics and Diplomacy of the Undeclared War with France 1797-1801* (1966) provides the most authoritative account of the French mission. J. Goebel, Jr., *Antecedents and Beginnings to 1801* (1971), first volume of the Holmes history of the Supreme Court, is similarly authoritative on the Judiciary Act and the years of Ellsworth's service on the court.

WFC

John Haley

JOHN HALEY, A.B., remains one of the more obscure of the early graduates of the College. On Commencement Day, September 24, 1766, according to a New York newspaper, he "closed the Exercises of the Batchelors with a very spirited nervous Harangue on *Liberty*, towards the Close of which he also paid the just Tribute of Gratitude to the Memory" of President Finley, who had died during the summer. Two days later his name was one of ten subscribed to a diploma ("Given in Plain-Dealing Hall, in Nassau Hall, September 26, 1776") awarded his classmate Joseph Hasbrouck in testimony that he was a member of the Plain-Dealing Club who had "conducted himself with great propriety while connected with us." Haley thus can be identified as a member of the club that was the forerunner of the American Whig Society. But all other questions about his identity lack firm answers.

The family name was not uncommon in colonial America, and the name John was all too common. Records reveal the presence of Haleys in New England, Virginia, and Pennsylvania, where there was more than one John Haley. Of these, it seems most likely that the College's alumnus was the John Haley who was admitted to the practice of law at Philadelphia on October 15, 1772, who became clerk of the city court on June 11, 1777, and of the orphans' court on September 15 of the same year, and who died on March 12, 1786, a date confirmed by the fact that both of these clerkships were filled by his successor on March 24, 1786. That he had begun his practice of law as early as 1769 is indicated by his listing, together with Jacob Rush (A.B. 1765) and Daniel Clymer (A.B. 1766), among the attorneys practicing in Chester County in that year. There is also an indication that he died in this county, but no information has been found as to his parentage, place of birth, marriage, or descendants. A John Haley shown by the census of 1790 to have been a resident of Roxborough Township in Philadelphia County may or may not have been related.

SOURCES: Commencement: *N.Y. Gaz.*, Oct. 2, 1766; diploma: G. M. Giger, *Centennial Hist. Clio* (1865), 11; practice and offices: J. H. Martin, *Bench and Bar of Phil.* (1885), xv, 61, 71, 239, 242, 274.

Mss: PHi   WFC

Joseph Hasbrouck

JOSEPH HASBROUCK, A.B., A.M. 1770, farmer and public official, was born in Kingston in Ulster County, New York, on March 3, 1744, the son of Catherine Bruyn and her husband, Abraham Hasbrouck. Joseph's great-grandfather, the first Abraham Hasbrouck, a Huguenot, left his native France and after several years in Germany, Holland, and England emigrated to America in 1675. As one of the earliest settlers in what became Ulster County and as a founder of the town of New Paltz, he acquired at once substantial landholdings in Ulster County and a reputation for public service. The Hasbroucks became one of the most prominent families in New York State and sent several sons to Princeton, Joseph's brother James (A.B. 1773) among them.

After graduation from the College, where he was a member of the Plain-Dealing Club, Joseph apparently returned home to tend his family's lands. He was probably the Joseph Hasbrouck who served on the Ulster County road commission in the years just before the Revolution, a position filled at the beginning of the eighteenth century by his grandfather, the first Joseph Hasbrouck.

At the outbreak of the Revolution, Hasbrouck became an officer in the Ulster County militia. His initial rank may have been captain. In any case by 1775 he had become a major in the Third Ulster Regiment, and by 1778 he had risen to lieutenant colonel. Either during or after the Revolution he became a brigadier general in the state militia and was thereafter often called "General Joe." His military record included not only several major engagements but the supervision of at least one major court-martial as well. In addition, he served as treasurer of the Ulster Committee of Safety, and his farm became a supply depot for the Continental army.

After the Revolution Hasbrouck returned home to his growing family. He had married Elizabeth Bevier on March 25, 1773; she bore him eight children, seven sons and one daughter. One of them, Louis, graduated from the College in 1797. All of Joseph's sons except Louis were baptized in the New Paltz Dutch Reformed Church, which the Hasbrouck family had helped found. Joseph served as a Deacon of the church from 1782, the date of his baptism, until 1785.

In 1786 Hasbrouck was elected to the New York State Assembly from Ulster County. Upon his father's death in 1791, Joseph, as the eldest son, inherited the family farmhouse and several hundred acres of land in Guilford in Ulster County. He also inherited a large general store that his father had established in Kingston. He returned to the New York Assembly in 1791 and 1792. In 1793 he moved up to the New York State Senate, where he served till 1796. During those same three years Hasbrouck also served on the legislature's council of appointment. His years in the legislature continued the traditions of his father and his great-grandfather.

Although Hasbrouck's attendance record in the legislature was considerably less than perfect, when present he did conform to Ulster County's—and Governor George Clinton's—Antifederalist line. Thus he voted to confiscate Tory properties, to require aspiring lawyers to sign loyalty oaths, to restrict the salaries of state and local officials, and to limit state government expenditures in general. Hasbrouck died on February 26, 1808, at his Guilford home.

SOURCES: Vital data: Joseph Hasbrouck File, PUA; *NYGBR*, 71 (1940), 13-21, 154, 358, and 72 (1941), 37-38; R. LeFevre, *Hist. of New Paltz, N.Y.* (1903), 375, 377, 382-385; *Rec. Reformed Dutch Church of New Paltz* (1896), 1-2, 68, 75, 128, 137, 143, 150, 158, 166; A. T. Clearwater, *Hist. of Ulster Cty., N.Y.* (1907), 255, 334; J. N. Beam, *Amer. Whig Society* (1933), 9, 111; Force, *Am. Arch.* (4 ser.), IV, 307, and VI, 1274; (5 ser.), III, 505, 506, 1126, 1262; *Ulster Çty., N.Y., Wills* (1906), II, 83-89; *Rec. Road Commissioners of Ulster Co.* (1940), I, 1, 95, and II, 3, 7, 54, 55, 90; legislative record: *Journal of the Assembly of the State of New York*, title varies, issues for 9th, 14th, 15th Sessions, 1786, 1791, 1792; and *Journal of the Senate of the State of New York*, title varies, issues for 16th, 17th, 18th, 19th Sessions, 1793, 1794, 1795, 1796.

HS

Moses Haslett

MOSES HASLETT, A.B., A.M. 1788, physician, was born about 1739. Neither his parentage nor place of origin has been discovered. After graduation Haslett studied medicine. By 1771 he had established himself in the rapidly expanding city of Baltimore, at first in association with the English-born, Oxford-educated Dr. Henry Stevenson, who had the reputation of being the most successful inoculator in the colonies.

Haslett left no record of political involvement, but a 1779 association with Dr. John Boyd (A.B. 1757) in readjusting the fee schedule for

Baltimore medical men suggests a Whiggish outlook, as does his membership in Baltimore's First Presbyterian Church. About 1779 Haslett married a woman named Sarah, whose last name has not been discovered. The couple had three sons baptized in their church and may have had other children as well. Haslett's practice was mainly among Baltimore's poor, and he apparently owned no slaves.

In the 1780s Haslett entered into partnership with one John Ross. The disintegration of the partnership in February 1789 was the occasion for violent recriminations between the two in Baltimore newspapers. Haslett's temper appears to have been restored by July of the following year, when he was among the signers of a Baltimore petition calling for the establishment of a humane society in the city. Haslett died in Baltimore on February 29, 1796. A Baltimore newspaper described him as "well known in this Town as a long established physician. His skill, his modest worth, and Kind solicitude for his friends will long be remembered by those who have had occasion for his services."

SOURCES: E. F. Cordell, *Medical Annals of Md.* (1903), 12, 13, 34, 656, 668, 669; Stevenson: M. B. Gordon, *Aesculapius Comes to the Colonies* (1949), 234; assoc. with Stevenson: *Va. Gaz.* (Rind), Sept. 5, 1771; poor: T. W. Griffiths, *Annals of Baltimore* (1824), 59; church: *MHM*, 35 (1940), 258; wife, children: "First Presby. Ch.: Baptisms, Marriages & Deaths from 1767," MS, MdHi; obit.; Baltimore *Telegraphe*, Mar. 4, 1796.

David Howell

DAVID HOWELL, A.B., A.M. Rhode Island College and College of Philadelphia 1769, Yale 1772, LL.D. Rhode Island College 1793, college tutor and professor, lawyer, and public official, was born in Morristown, New Jersey, on January 1, 1747, the son of Aaron and Mary Howell. Young Howell prepared for college at the Reverend Isaac Eaton's academy in Hopewell, New Jersey, the first Baptist institution of its kind in the colonies. Among his schoolmates was James Manning (A.B. 1762), founder and first president of Rhode Island College (later Brown University). In the summer before his graduation Howell requested Manning's advice about his future career. From Warren, Rhode Island, where his new college was just becoming established, Manning suggested that Howell look north. "I would advise you to see me before you engage elsewhere," he wrote to Howell. "A taste for learning is greatly upon the increase in this Colony."

Howell followed Manning's advice, joining him in Warren not long after his commencement. On his own authority Manning shortly ap-

David Howell, A.B. 1766
BY JAMES SULLIVAN LINCOLN AFTER TRUMBULL

pointed Howell as Rhode Island College's first tutor. The position was confirmed by the college's corporation the following year, and Howell was granted the salary of £72 per year. Manning and his trustees had ambitious plans for their college, which moved to Providence in 1770. In 1769 they named Howell Professor of Mathematics and Natural Philosophy—a position warranted by neither Howell's background nor the college's equipment. But Howell performed more than creditably over the next decade. "Although experimental philosophy was the direct object of my profession," Howell wrote in a 1779 review of his academic career, "yet the other branches of learning were devolved upon me." The other branches turned out to be Latin, Greek, and somewhat surprisingly, law. From his initial appointment until the end of his life, Rhode Island College remained one of Howell's central concerns. He resigned his professorship in 1779 because of wartime disruptions, but in the following year was appointed secretary of the corporation, a post he filled until 1806. Elected a fellow of the corporation in 1772, he held the position until his death. In 1791–1792, after

Manning's death, Howell acted as interim president of the college, and from 1790 to 1824 held the title of Professor of Jurisprudence.

Howell, somehow, had been admitted to the practice of law in Rhode Island as early as 1768. "The parent of science, and my favorite theme," he called the law in 1779. In fact, law and public office were the two main poles of Howell's mature career. Howell's first public appointment came in February 1777, when he was sent by his state to Baltimore to present Rhode Island's accounts for reimbursement to the Continental Congress. Howell served his state in other minor capacities as well and in May 1779 was elected a deputy from Providence to the Rhode Island legislature. In 1780 and 1781 he served as a justice of the court of common pleas for Providence County and in May of the latter year was appointed fifth justice of the state superior court.

Howell's rise to more than local importance was sparked by events taking place far away from Rhode Island. In February 1781, the Continental Congress requested the states to grant it the power to levy a five percent impost on the value of most imported articles. The need for such a national revenue seemed urgent, and as an amendment to the powers conferred upon the government by the Articles of Confederation the proposal needed the unanimous assent of the states to be adopted. By the end of the year eight states had approved the measure, by early 1782, three more. But by then the military pressures that had seemed so urgent a year before had lessened in force. In the spring of 1782 Howell began to publish a series of articles in a Providence newspaper opposing the impost. In them he discussed matters that went beyond the impost itself and raised essential constitutional issues—namely, the power of Congress to tax the states, a power that it had not been granted under the Articles of Confederation. "This grant is to be irrevocable," Howell charged in April 1782. It would become "fixed as fate, and no more in the power of the respective legislatures of the several states than the elements, the seasons, or the planetary bodies: And whatever may be our wishes or prayers afterwards, when this important act is once passed, it will be like *Adam's fall*, unalterable, and affect not only ourselves, but all our posterity.—It will be like *Pandora's box*, once opened, never to close." Howell's articles found wide support in Rhode Island, and in May 1782 his state sent him as its representative to Congress.

By the time Howell arrived in Congress, the impost had taken on a new aspect. It had become a central tool in the drive by Robert Morris, head of the office of finance, and others, to establish a stronger national government by means of taxation. Howell became the leading opponent of this policy in Congress. Part of his—and his state's—opposition to the impost arose from the fear that Rhode Island, whose economy was bound up with the importation and subsequent export of various goods, would end by bearing a heavier tax burden than the agrarian states. But opposition sprang in equal measure from the mainspring of the American Revolution—the pervasive fear of an overbearing central government. Howell followed the wishes of his constituents to the letter, constantly attacking the impost and advising his state not to agree to it. Despite Rhode Island's recalcitrance in passing the Impost of 1781, in September 1782, Congress determined to make an emergency call upon the states for over a million dollars to pay interest on the public debt. Howell, predictably, resisted the move, advising rejection by the Rhode Island legislature, which it did in November. Privately, Howell wrote to his state's officials that negotiations with foreign powers were at such a stage that a loan could be secured and that the congressional requisition was thus unnecessary. Meanwhile, on December 6, a special congressional committee set off to try in person to persuade the Rhode Island legislature to change its mind. Reaching New York, the committee discovered to its surprise that Virginia, for reasons even today obscure, had repealed its earlier act of accession to the tax measure. It seemed that singlehandedly Howell and Rhode Island had reversed Congress's course. But neither Howell nor his state had heard the last of the affair. Howell's private letter to his state describing diplomatic relations was published in a Rhode Island, and then in a New York, newspaper. Congress claimed that this was a breach of secrecy and determined to rebuke Howell. Howell claimed that he had every right to send information to his constituents and claimed freedom of speech. Congress ended by complaining strongly to Rhode Island—which, in turn, gave Howell complete support.

If Howell enraged some of his congressional colleagues, he puzzled foreigners unfamiliar with the democratic style of Rhode Island's politics. Visiting President Manning in the 1780s, the South American patriot Francisco de Miranda reported meeting "Mr. David Howell, a member of Congress and an educated man, beneath the cloak of a simplicity almost vulgar." But Howell's "cloak" apparently suited Rhode Island perfectly: "You must not suffer yourself to be Hortey," the Providence merchant John Brown advised his son in 1782, "high-minded nor so proud as to look Down on those of a Smaller kind of Mortalls but learn so much of the Courtyer as to please the poore as well as the rich. Mr. Howall is a good Exampler."

Howell's later years in Congress were less stormy than his first. He became a warm admirer of Thomas Jefferson, working with him close-

ly on the Ordinance of 1784, which organized the territories of the Old
Northwest. This was a measure dear to Howell's heart, for in the impost controversy he had linked the cession to Congress of western
lands by states who possessed tham to the possible subsequent sale of
these lands to liquidate the public debt. Recent historians have credited Howell with having a significant influence on the framing of the
ordinance.

Howell remained always the simple republican. He celebrated Congress's removal from Philadelphia and chafed over the frivolity of the
members when it assembled at Annapolis. But when Congress settled
for a time at Princeton, meeting in the College's library, Howell found
his native state and his alma mater completely to his liking. He even
suggested to friends in Rhode Island that Princeton would make an
excellent capital for the nation: "There are some considerations of
weight in favour of this State and even of this Spot. It is nearly in the
center of the population and wealth of the U.S. This is a small State
and therefore its influence is not to be feared. It never will be a very
wealthy State, not being calculated for commerce: it may therefore
preserve the purity of its manner as long as any; and even its
Liberty[,] for corruption follows luxury, and Luxury wealth."

Howell's service in Congress ended in 1785, and he returned to his
law practice in Providence. In May 1786, he was appointed to the
Rhode Island Superior Court. Shortly thereafter he became embroiled
once again in controversy. In a complex situation, Rhode Island had
passed a law requiring that its paper currency be accepted as legal
tender. The law imposed severe penalties on those who did not comply. In September 1786, a section of the law was tested before Rhode
Island's superior court in a case later famous in American constitutional history, Trevett v. Weeden, which for many generations was
considered a precedent in the development of judicial review. In fact,
Howell and the other justices merely decided not to take cognizance
of the case. Rhode Island's General Assembly, however, mistakenly
thought that the court had overruled it and called the justices before
it. In his nonjudicial testimony before the assembly Howell declared
that the legislature was setting itself up as the superior court and that
the paper money force act was in fact unconstitutional and uninforce-
able. The assembly, understandably enough, did not return Howell to
the superior court for another term.

Barred from the bench, Howell's interests turned toward philan-
thropy. In February 1789, he was a founder and became the first president of the Providence Abolition Society, an extremely active organization in the early 1790s. He was also a strong advocate of the ratifica-

tion of the federal constitution. "Since the adoption of the Federal Constitution by this state," he wrote to Thomas Jefferson in June 1790, "I can inform my friends that I am alive, and make mention of the place where I live with more pleasure, than I could before. For, indeed, life would be scarcely worth having if one should be condemned to Spend it under such a Government as we have lately experienced."

Howell appears to have been reduced to somewhat straightened circumstances in the early 1790s. He lived on a farm outside Providence and occupied himself with his law practice, Rhode Island College, and his family. On September 30, 1770, he had married Mary Brown, daughter of Jeremiah Brown, a Baptist clergyman. (Howell himself was a Baptist, but not a full church member.) The couple had five children, two sons and three daughters.

In 1796 President Washington appointed Howell to the commission charged with establishing the border between Canada and the United States under the provisions of Jay's Treaty. Howell was absent from public office for the next decade and a half. In 1811 his eldest son, Jeremiah Brown Howell, a Federalist, was elected United States Senator from Rhode Island. In the following year President James Madison (A.B. 1771) appointed the senior Howell United States district judge for Rhode Island. Howell served in the post until his death in Providence on July 29, 1824.

SOURCES: Sketches: *DAB*; D. H. Fischer, *Rev. of Am. Conservatism* (1965), 279-80; connections with R.I. College: R. A. Guild, *Early Hist. of Brown Univ.* (1897), passim and p. 66 for Manning quotation; W. C. Bronson, *Hist. of Brown Univ.* (1914); early R.I. pol. career: R. C. Vaccaro, "The Politics of David Howell of R.I. in the period of the Confederation," (M.A. thesis, Columbia Univ., 1947); impost controversy: J. T. Main, *The Antifederalists* (1961), 72-102 (Howell remarks *re* same from *Prov. Gaz.*, April 13, 1782, as quoted here, p. 81, n. 30); E. J. Ferguson, *The Power of the Purse* (1961), 146-76; C. L. Ver Steeg, *Robert Morris* (1954), 111-31; *LMCC*, VII-VIII; *Madison Papers*, V-VI; W. R. Staples, *R.I. in the Continental Congress* (1870), passim; E. C. Burnett, *The Continental Congress* (1941), 530-35; Miranda quotation: J. S. Ezell, ed., *The New Democracy in America* (1963), 151; J. Brown quotation: *R.I. Hist. Soc. Col.*, 34 (1941), 53; Ordinance of 1784: *WMQ*, 29 (1972), 231-62; Princeton as capital: Howell to Moses Brown, Aug. 24, 1783, *LMCC* VII, 279; see too VIII, 841; Trevett *v.* Weedon: esp. P. T. Conley, "R.I.'s Paper Money Issue and Trevett *v.* Weedon (1786)," *R.I. Hist.*, 30 (1971), 95-108; same, and 1790 constit. quotation: *Jefferson Papers*, XVI, esp. Boyd's notes, 445-54; abolition soc.: *R.I. Hist.*, 21 (1962), 33-48; obit.: *Prov. Gaz.*, July 31, 1824.

MSS: RPB

Daniel Jones

DANIEL JONES, A.B., Presbyterian clergyman, was born in 1744. His parentage has not been discovered. In 1766 he became a graduate member of the Well-Meaning Society, forerunner of the Cliosophic Society. At the commencement of that year, a Philadelphia newspaper reported, Jones "pronounced a very animated Harangue on Oratory, and beautifully exemplified his Subject with all the graces of Elocution and Action, which very agreeably relaxed the Attention of the Assembly, which might otherwise have been fatigued by unmixed Disputation alone."

Although Jones was licensed by the Presbytery of New Castle in 1769 or 1770, a combination of poor health and a long sea voyage undertaken to improve it delayed his ordination until August 21, 1783, when he was ordained *sine titulo*. Because of the state of his health it is unlikely that he was the Daniel Jones who served in several Pennsylvania militia units during the Revolution. From 1781 until 1785 Jones lived in Philadelphia and probably served as a supply preacher for local Presbyterian churches. He may have been the Reverend Daniel Jones who during these years speculated in land in several outlying counties, purchasing up to 300 acres at a time. In the absence of a permanent pastorate, Jones moved to Carlisle, Pennsylvania, in 1786, where for the rest of his life he served its presbytery, again as a supply preacher. That presbytery was eventually divided, and the part of it in which he resided continued to bear the name Carlisle Presbytery.

Benjamin Rush (A.B. 1760), Jones's apparent friend and admirer, tried to secure a professorship of oratory for him at Dickinson College, but evidently failed to do so. In a letter of August 20, 1785, to John Montgomery, a Dickinson College charter trustee, Rush wrote: "The Reverend Mr. Jones talks of setting up a lodging house at Carlisle. Do stop him on his return from Warm Springs and try to *fix* him. He will draw pupils from this city [Philadelphia]. We may allow him hereafter £25 a year for teaching our boys to *read* and *speak* properly." The letter was followed by another, in April 1786, to all the Dickinson College trustees: "The Reverend Mr. Jones, who is now settled in Carlisle, has a high character in this place for reading and speaking the English language correctly and agreeably. Should the trustees think proper to honor him with a professorship of oratory, I am persuaded it might tend to draw pupils from this city. I dare say he would be contented with a salary not exceeding £40 or £50 per annum if his business were confined only to teaching our boys to read and to speak well." Nothing came of Rush's recommendation, nor has anything more been discovered of Jones's career. He died at Carlisle on April 8, 1814.

SOURCES: Vital data: Daniel Jones File, PUA; Webster, Brief Sketches, Bk. 2, MS, PPPrHi; commencement oration: *N.Y. Gaz.*, Oct. 2, 1766; affiliation with Presbytery of New Castle: *Rec. Pres. Church*; possible military service: *Pa. Arch.* (6 ser.), 1

"... the Rev. Daniel Jones, whose elocution had rendered him famous ..." sometimes preached for Ashbel Green in Phil. in late 1780's, see Green, Life, 193

(1906), 491, 644; 2 (1906), 533, 609; possible land speculation: references scattered throughout *Pa. Arch.* (3 ser.); affiliation with Presbytery of Carlisle: *Centennial Memorial of Presbytery of Carlisle, Pa.* (1889), I, 105, 106, 440, 441; Rush letters: Butterfield, *Rush Letters*, I, 361-63, 382.

HS

Solomon Kellogg

SOLOMON KELLOGG, A.B., A.M. Yale 1770, was born in Colchester, Connecticut on July 14, 1744, the oldest son of Mary Lewis and her husband, Aaron Kellogg. The father probably was a tavern-keeper. At the College young Kellogg joined the Well-Meaning Club, forerunner of the Cliosophic Society. Along with Richard Stockon (A.B. 1748), Dirck Romeyn (A.B. 1765), and his classmate Oliver Ellsworth, Kellogg also signed in September 1765 a petition addressed to the Grand Lodge of Freemasons of Massachusetts requesting permission to establish a lodge in Princeton. The request was not granted; the founding of the Cliosophic Society may well have been the students' answer to the denial.

After graduation Kellogg returned to Colchester. His occupation has not been discovered, but his award by Yale of an honorary A.M. suggests that he may have been reading law, for the degree normally was granted only to professional men of good character. Kellogg died in Colchester on August 9, 1773. Listed as "Captain Solomon Kellogg," his death was considered noteworthy enough to be reported in newspapers in Boston and in New London. Kellogg, apparently, had never married.

SOURCES: Parentage: *NEHGR*, 48 (1894), 64; father's occupation: *New London Hist. Soc. Col.*, 1 (1901), 370, 388; Masonic petition: copy in Dirck Romeyn File, PUA, extracts in J. H. Tasch, *Freemasonry in the Thirteen Colonies* (1927), 54; death notices: *Boston News-Letter*, Aug. 19, 1773, and *New London Gaz.*, Aug. 13, 1773.

Josiah Lewis

JOSIAH LEWIS, A.B., was a Presbyterian clergyman. His parentage has not been determined, but he is said on good authority to have been prepared for college along with Ephraim Brevard, William C. Houston, and Adlai Osborne (all A.B. 1768) at "Crowfield Academy" in Rowan County, North Carolina. He may well have come from that province.

Lewis studied for the ministry after graduation and was licensed to preach by the Presbytery of New Castle on August 11, 1768. The presbytery ordained Lewis *sine titulo* at Fagg's Manor, Pennsylvania, on August 1, 1770. The Synod of New York and Philadelphia then ordered Lewis to act as a supply preacher on the southern frontier. He was directed to spend six months at Long Cane, South Carolina, three months at Briar Creek, Georgia, and three months at his discretion in the Carolinas. Lewis complied with the synod's order. He must have made a favorable impression on the various congregations in the south, for subsequently several requested the synod to send Lewis back to them.

Lewis returned to the south, but at what date and under what circumstances are difficult to determine. In 1773 the synod transferred Lewis from the jurisdiction of the Presbytery of New Castle to that of the Presbytery of Lewes, a small and somewhat obscure body in southern Delaware. One source states that Lewis served as pastor of the Presbyterian church at Blackwater, Sussex County, Delaware, from 1771 to 1774, but some doubt about this exists. Lewis seems, in fact, never to have taken up the Delaware pastorate. In May 1779, the synod recorded that Lewis had yet to attend a meeting of the Lewes Presbytery, having "removed to a distant part; and as some reports have arisen to the disadvantage of his moral character, the Synod do hereby order the Lewestown Presbytery to take cognizance of Mr. Lewis in the premises, and make a report at the next meeting of the Synod."

No report was forthcoming, for the Delaware people had lost track of Lewis. He appears to have moved south to one of the communities in which he had preached on his earlier missionary trip. In about 1773 Lewis married one Susannah, whose last name has not been discovered. However, the fact that the couple named the first of their four children Jonathan Rees Lewis suggests a connection with the families of Thomas Reese (A.B. 1768) or Oliver Reese (A.B. 1772), both Carolina clergymen.

In 1773 a large area of former Cherokee land in Georgia was opened to white settlement. Many communities in North and South Carolina— among them the one at Long Cane, where Lewis had preached—made applications for land. Several groups were granted property in what was then St. George's Parish on the Savannah River. Lewis and his family were associated with one of the groups.

Barely settled in Georgia, Lewis was shortly involved in the Revolution. On July 2, 1776, Georgia's Council of Safety appointed "ye Rev. Josiah Lewis" one of the magistrates for St. George's Parish. Whether Lewis was a practicing clergyman at the time or not is uncertain. His designation as "reverend" suggests that he was, although by this time the Presbyterians had lost track of him. A very faint possibility exists that Lewis may have become a Baptist, although no record of him has been found in the sources of that denomination.

For most of the Revolution much of Georgia was occupied by British forces, and few records from the period survive. It is certain, however, that Lewis served for a time as chaplain with an American army unit. On January 8, 1782, listed simply as "Josiah Lewis, Esquire," he was named registrar of probates for his area of Georgia, by then renamed Burke County. He died on November 10, 1783. On the basis of his military service his widow made a successful claim for 1,000 acres of land in Georgia.

SOURCES: Sketch: Webster, MS Brief Sketches, PPPrHi; col. prep.: Foote, *Sketches, N.C.,* 434; career: *Minutes of the Synod of New York and Phila.* (1841) passim: *Pres. Records* (1841), 390, 403-404; Del. pastorate: Weis, *Col. Clergy of Md., Del., & Ga.,* 78; Ga. settlers: J. E. Callaway, *Early Settlement of Ga.* (1948), 62-63; Ga. appointments: A. D. Candler, ed., *Rev. Recs. of the State of Ga.* (1908), I 149, and III, 54; wife, children, war claims: L. M. Knight, *Georgia's Roster of the Rev.* (1920), 110; possible Baptist: *Lewis Letter,* 16 (1905-1906), 80; date of death: *DAR Patriot Index* (1966), 414.

Peter Van Brugh Livingston, Jr.

PETER VAN BRUGH LIVINGSTON, JR., A.B., merchant, was born either in his parents' mansion on Dyke Street in Manhattan or at their country villa on Brooklyn Heights. He was baptized in the Dutch Reformed church in New York City on March 13, 1751. He was the third son and fifth child of Christina Ten Broeck and her husband, Philip Livingston (Yale 1731), a wealthy merchant who served as speaker of the New York Assembly in 1765 and later became a signer of the Declaration of Independence. Peter's older brother, Philip Philip Livingston, graduated from the College in 1758; a younger brother, Henry Philip, received the A.B. in 1776. The Livingstons lacked imagination in christening their sons: Peter had both an uncle and a first cousin of the same name.

Still only a boy, after graduation Livingston moved to Jamaica in the West Indies, where his family owned considerable property and was profitably engaged in commerce. His older brother had preceded him there, and Peter probably joined Philip Philip in learning the business. In 1770 Livingston boarded a ship in Kingston in order to make a visit to his family in New York. He never reached the mainland, dying on

July 4 while still at sea. News of his death reached Princeton quickly, for he was listed as dead in the College's first catalogue, published in 1770.

SOURCES: E. B. Livingston, *Livingstons of Livingston Manor* (1910), 551-52; father: Dexter, *Yale Biographies*, I, 582-85; death notice: *N.Y. Post-Boy*, Aug. 6, 1770.

Daniel McCalla

DANIEL McCALLA, A.B., D.D. College of South Carolina 1808, Presbyterian and Congregational clergyman, was born in Neshaminy, Bucks County, Pennsylvania, on July 23, 1748. His parentage has not been discovered. McCalla prepared for the College at the Reverend John Blair's Latin grammar school at Fagg's Manor, Pennsylvania. According to a nineteenth-century historian, he acquired there "a very decided taste for classical learning" and "high reputation as a scholar," both of which he maintained throughout his years at the College.

After graduation McCalla was encouraged by several prominent Philadelphians to open an academy in the city. In preparation for teaching he studied medicine, modern languages, and theology, the last in connection with his simultaneous preparation for the ministry. On July 20, 1772, McCalla was licensed by the First Presbytery of Philadelphia, and two years later, after numerous inquiries by other congregations, he was ordained by the united Presbyterian churches of New Providence and Charleston, Pennsylvania. He was their first joint pastor, his predecessors at Charleston having included both Benjamin Chestnut (A.B. 1748) and John Carmichael (A.B. 1759).

McCalla served diligently and enthusiastically until the beginning of the Revolution, when he turned his energies to support of the American cause. As a nineteenth-century historian wrote, "he stood ready to obey any summons, whatever sacrifice it might involve, which he should receive from his country." Such a summons came in 1776, and from General William Thompson, who had McCalla appointed chaplain of his Second Pennsylvania Battalion on January 16, 1776. It was, however, the Continental Congress that actually appointed him, and he was the first and last chaplain so appointed. Thereafter chaplains were named directly by regimental commanders.

In early June 1776 Thompson's battalion was ordered to Canada and shortly after its arrival met defeat by the British at Three Rivers, Quebec. During the engagement McCalla reportedly waded through swampland "side by side" with General Thompson and "moved with him into the fire." Many men were killed or wounded, and Thompson, McCalla, and hundreds of others were captured. As prisoners, they spent several months on a prison ship, where they were subjected to harsh treatment.

In late 1776 McCalla was freed on parole and was allowed to return to his congregation. Yet within a short time of his return he preached what local British authorities deemed an inflammatory sermon and was forced to flee to Virginia. Following an exchange of other prisoners the following year, his parole was ended.

McCalla settled in Hanover, Virginia, where he served as both pastor of its Presbyterian church and principal of its Washington Henry Academy, which he had founded. There he was assisted by the Reverend John Blair (A.B. 1775), nephew of McCalla's former teacher. Once again, McCalla proved popular in both pursuits. In addition, he met and in April 1778 married Eliza Todd, the daughter of the Reverend John Todd (A.B. 1749) of Louisa County, Virginia.

McCalla's successes were marred by rumors of excessive drinking. These recurrent indiscretions "subjected him to severe remark, and finally brought him into some [unspecified] difficulties" with the Hanover Presbytery, within whose territory he lived and worked. Since his formal affiliation remained with the Philadelphia Presbytery, it was apparently not until Hanover Presbyterians had brought the problem to the attention of Philadelphia Presbyterians that McCalla felt compelled to act in 1788: he "very suddenly removed" to South Carolina.

McCalla settled in Christ's Church Parish near Charleston and for the rest of his life served its Wappetaw Congregational Church— faithfully, zealously, and without incident or even suspicion of any kind. The honorary degree which the College of South Carolina bestowed upon him in 1808 confirmed his high standing within the state.

Of the sermons he delivered at Wappetaw, three were published during his lifetime—in 1791, 1799, and 1800—and they and several others were published posthumously as his collected works. His sermons condemned the theater as a "vicious" destroyer of morals; dismissed Paine's *Age of Reason* as "the most contemptible performance . . . that ever was obtruded on the world on the side of infidelity"; viewed the French Revolution with "a mixture of admiration and terror"; criticized President John Adams, "Chief Servant of the United States of America," for excessive favoritism toward Britain; and defended Thomas Jefferson as a genuine Republican and a dedicated public servant whose particular religious beliefs were his private business and not subject to outside scrutiny.

McCalla and his wife had only one child, Jane, who married Dr.

(cousin)

John R. Witherspoon (A.B. 1794), a nephew of President Witherspoon. Her untimely death at twenty-seven in February 1808 hastened Mc-Calla's own on April 6, 1809, and that of his wife on November 3 of the same year. The memory of McCalla lived on in his grandson, who bore the name Daniel McCalla Witherspoon (A.B. 1825).

A sermon delivered by the Reverend William Hollinshead upon Mc-Calla's death characterized him as "a graceful figure; polite, easy, and engaging in his manners; entertaining and improving in conversation; of a lively fancy and a generous heart; of unfettered liberality and un-dissembled candour; . . . a friend to mankind; but peculiarly attached to men of science and religion." An editorial from the April 12, 1809, Charleston *City Gazette and Daily Advertiser* lamented that "in him Religion has lost one of her brightest ornaments and truth an able de-fender." Finally, his Wappetaw congregation erected a monument in his honor and inscribed on it a "testimony of affection and respect for the memory of their late worthy pastor."

SOURCES: Vital data: Daniel McCalla File, PUA; Sprague, *Annals*, III, 320-22; Web-ster, MS Sketches, Bk. I, PPPrHi; *Appleton's Amer. Biog.*, IV, 76; Charleston, Pa., Presbyterian pastors: J. S. Futhey and G. Cope, *Hist. of Chester Cty., Pa.* (1881), 249; T. W. Bean, *Hist. of Montgomery Cty., Pa.* (1884), 1053; military service: *Pa. Arch.* (2 ser.), 10 (1880), 51; *PMHB*, 8 (1884), 113; J. T. Headley, *Chaplains and Clergy of the Rev.* (1864), 277; Washington Henry Academy: *WMQ*, 2 (1945), 367; marriage: M. H. Harris, *Hist. of Louisa Cty., Va.* (1936), 233; Christ's Church Par-ish: M. Webber, *Register of Christ Church Parish, S.C.*, 22 (1921), 17-18; 1791, 1799, 1800 sermons: see STE; quotations from *Works: The Works of the Rev. Dan-iel McCalla* (1810), I, 32-33, 124-25; II, 5; I, 271; II, 104; II, 322; death of daughter: *SCHM*, 25 (1924), 140; Hollinshead sermon: *Works*, I, 16; newspaper editorial: *SCHM*, 33 (1932), 68; Wappetaw monument: *SCHM*, 25 (1924), 140.

PUBLICATIONS: see above and STE   HS

John MacPherson

JOHN MACPHERSON, A.B., A.M. 1770, lawyer and army officer, was the son of Captain John MacPherson and his wife, Margaret Rodgers. The mother was a sister of the Reverend John Rodgers, a prominent Pres-byterian clergyman who became a trustee of the College in 1765. The father, a Scotsman, made a fortune as a privateer during the Seven Years War and began in 1761 the construction of "Mount Pleasant," one of the finest Georgian mansions in the northern colonies. Still standing, it is located in what is now Philadelphia's Fairmount Park.

Some confusion exists concerning young MacPherson's birthdate. Most sources, with some puzzlement, give it as 1754, which is mani-

John MacPherson, A.B. 1766
BY EDITH MANN

festly impossible. However Luther Martin, a classmate, once recalled that he and MacPherson "graduated together;—about the same age." Since Martin was born in 1748, the same year of birth seems likely for MacPherson.

MacPherson's father entered him in the Academy of Philadelphia in 1757. He entered the grammar school connected with Nassau Hall about 1761 and presumably matriculated in the College itself about a year later. In College he was one of the founders of the Plain-Dealing Club, forerunner of the American Whig Society. MacPherson made many friends at Princeton, perhaps the closest being William Paterson (A.B. 1763), founder of the competing Well-Meaning Club who remained in Princeton after graduation to study law with Richard Stockton (A.B. 1748). A New York newspaper reported that at his commencement "MacPherson began the Exercises of the Afternoon by very judiciously pointing out the *Difference between ancient and modern Learning,* in an elegant and well pronounced Discourse on the Subject."

After receiving his diploma MacPherson returned to Philadelphia, where he indentured himself as legal apprentice to John Dickinson, soon to be famous as author of the *Farmer's Letters*. He also began a long exchange of letters with William Paterson. The correspondence is typical of countless exchanges between recent college graduates that survive in various collections in many parts of the United States. MacPherson and Paterson exchanged gossip on common acquaintances, discussed their legal studies, speculated about various young ladies, and, in general, supplied each other with mutual reinforcement as they made their ways from youth into their adult roles.

In 1769 MacPherson complained with a certain pride about his mentor, Dickinson: "Is it not hard that I who had made trouble with the Farmer's Letters (for I copied the whole once, & some part twice) than Mr Dickinson should have only labour (not a single fee) for my pains?" The visit to Philadelphia in May 1770 by the great evangelist George Whitefield filled MacPherson with admiration and slightly disguised ambition: "He is in my opinion the greatest Speaker I ever heard, & were I as good in that way, I would quit law for gospel, & the study of Coke for the study of Clarke. Sed non sumus quod esse volumus, & I must be content to plod on, happy, if in my way I can be what the honest Knight of La Mancha wished to be, the righter of wrongs & redresser of injuries."

In June 1770, MacPherson's mother died. His father then made plans for a trip to Britain—a voyage for which MacPherson hoped Dickinson would release him from his indenture. But he remained in Philadelphia, reporting to Paterson that he had been admitted to practice in the court of common pleas on January 1, 1771, and thus had "no expectation of seeing England soon." But June saw him on the high seas, and in September he arrived in Scotland. He made his way south from Edinburgh to London, once there describing carefully to Paterson the Inns of Court, St. Paul's, Drury Lane, and Covent Garden.

MacPherson's stay in England lasted until late spring 1773. Returning to Philadelphia about June 1, he found establishing himself as a lawyer dispiriting. "If I do not take more money than I have done," he wrote to Paterson in August, "I fancy I may turn travelling merchant, or novel writer, or essayist, or itinerent preacher, or itinerent player, or poet, or physician or—any thing with a greater prospect or Advantage than I have at present." Paterson's reply was sanguine: "I know of no young lawyer, unless abetted by Party of Influence, that has any great run of Practice. Have Patience—the Prospect will brighten as you advance in Life."

MacPherson had little patience. He moved to New Castle, Delaware and began what appears to have been a moderately prosperous practice, though a 1774 bid to follow George Read as attorney general of the Lower Counties (Delaware) did not meet with success. But within a year MacPherson had given up law for war.

In June 1775, the Continental Congress appointed one of its members, Philip Schuyler of New York, as Major General to serve under Washington. Schuyler was placed in command of the Northern Division, which consisted of New York. Shortly after his appointment Schuyler made MacPherson his aide-de-camp with the rank of captain. The Revolution split the MacPherson family; John and his father were strong Whigs, while William, an older brother, who had long been a regular officer in the British army, remained in its service. John's appointment may have been due to the influence of his former mentor, Dickinson, for both Schuyler and Dickinson were Whigs of a conservative stamp. MacPherson spent the late summer and early fall of 1775 assisting Schuyler in strengthening various New York military installations and in preparing for an American invasion of Canada. In October Schuyler fell ill and was forced to hand over his immediate command to Brigadier General Richard Montgomery. MacPherson was shortly appointed one of Montgomery's two aides-de-camp, the other being Aaron Burr (A.B. 1772).

MacPherson accompanied Montgomery on the march to Quebec, but found that administrative work was not to his taste. "The happiness I experience while in yours, and since I have been of General Montgomery's family," he wrote to Schuyler on December 6, "is lessened when I reflect that I am but half a soldier, as being at headquarters exempts me from many fatigues which others undergo. This, and a natural desire of rising, which is, I believe, common to every one, lead me to request the favor of such a commission as you think I deserve." But MacPherson would soon become a "full" soldier.

On December 31, 1775, the American forces made their initial assault on the city of Quebec. Shortly before going into battle MacPherson wrote the following letter to be delivered to his father in case of his death:

My Dear Father:

If you receive this it will be the last this hand shall ever write you. Orders are given for a general storm on Quebec this night, and Heaven only knows what will be my fate. But, whatever it may be, I cannot resist the inclination I feel to assure you that I experience no reluctance in this cause to venture a life which I consider as only lent to be used when my country demands it. In moments like these such an assertion will not be thought a boast by any one, by my father I am sure it cannot. It is needless to tell that my prayers are for the happiness of the family and for its preservation in this general confusion. Should Providence in its wisdom call me from rendering the little assistance I might to my country, I could wish my brother did not continue in the service of her enemies."

Along with General Montgomery, MacPherson was killed a few hours later. Before news of his death had reached Philadelphia Congress, on Philip Schuyler's recommendation, promoted him to the rank of major. One of MacPherson's last wishes was fulfilled. His brother William eventually resigned from the British army. On January 1, 1779, the Supreme Executive Council of Pennsylvania recommended and Congress approved William's appointment as major in the American army, "in regard to the memory of his brother Major John MacPherson, who fell before the walls of Quebec, as well as in consideration of his own merit."

SOURCES: Parentage, father, Mt. Pleasant, and Dec. 30, 1775 letter: T. W. Glenn, *Some Colonial Mansions* (1900), 445-83; H. D. Eberlein and H. M. Lippincott, *Colonial Homes of Philadelphia* (1912), 113-17; grammar school, L. Martin quotation: *MHM*, 50 (1955), 154; commencement: *N.Y. Gaz.*, Oct. 2, 1766; letters from Paterson: MSS, NjP; letters to Paterson: copies at NjP; some originals, PHi; some printed in *PMHB*, 23 (1899), 51-59; New Castle practice: W. T. Read, *Life and Correspondence of George Read* (1870), 140; Schuyler and Dec. 6, 1775 letter: B. J. Lossing, *Life and Times of Philip Schuyler* (1883), 1, 345, 487, 498; several accts. of death: K. Roberts, *March to Quebec* (1938); brother's appointment: *PMHB*, 5 (1881), 89-90. In 1903 Paterson's letters to MacPherson were published by W. Jay Mills in a bowdlerized and inaccurate edition called *Glimpses of Colonial Society and the Life at Princeton College 1766-1773*. For the reliability of this volume, see: R. C. Haskett, "Princeton Before the Revolution: Notes on a Source," *WMQ*, 6 (1949), 90-93.

MSS: PHi

Luther Martin

LUTHER MARTIN, A.B., A.M. 1769, lawyer and public official, was born about February 9, 1748, on his father's New Jersey farm, located above the Raritan River in the neighborhood of Piscataway. He was the third son in a family of nine children of Benjamin Martin and his wife Hannah, whose maiden name is unknown. Writing in 1802, Luther recalled that "in my thirteenth year, and in the month of August, I was sent to Princeton College, where I entered the grammar school" to begin "the first Rudiments of the Latin language." If by his "thirteenth year" he meant the year following his twelfth birthday, his enrollment fell in 1760, but it may have been in 1761, as is suggested by the immediately

Luther Martin, A.B. 1766
BY ROBERT FIELD

following statement that "in September, five years next after, I received the honours of the College." At the time of his graduation, he tells us, "I wanted near five months of being nineteen years of age."

It is not known when Martin was admitted to the College, nor with what standing, but he reported that he studied both Hebrew and French, and that of the latter he became a "tolerable master." His claim to have graduated as "the *first* in the languages, and *second to none* in the *sciences*" probably was an exaggeration, for he was not salutatorian of his class. Among the friendships formed at Princeton, Martin gave special emphasis to those with his classmate John MacPherson and with William Paterson (A.B. 1763). Martin became a member of the Well-Meaning Club, and so is numbered among the founders of the Cliosophic Society.

In the spring of 1767 Martin became the master of a school at Queenstown in Queen Anne's County, Maryland. He held that post until 1770, when he moved down the Eastern Shore to Somerset County, apparently with a view to studying law, which he already had begun to read in such spare time as he had. A later charge that he left Queenstown because of scandalous conduct lacks confirmation, but he did leave behind unpaid debts, and perhaps for this reason he agreed to succeed in the summer of 1770 David Ramsay (A.B. 1765) as master of a grammar school at Onancock in Accomac County on the Eastern Shore of Virginia. He continued in this position until August 1771.

Shortly thereafter Martin sustained at Williamsburg the examination required for the practice of law in Virginia, and in September he qualified as an attorney in Accomac County. During the next year he toured northwestern Virginia in the evident hope of finding a likely location for his practice, but in the end he settled in Maryland's Somerset County, where he resided and practiced in the courts of both Virginia and Maryland until his appointment as attorney-general of the latter state in 1778. In the spring of that year he moved to Baltimore.

Martin early identified with the Whig cause. Elected in the fall of 1774 to the Somerset Committee of Observation for enforcement of the boycott of British imports, he sat for his county in December at the third meeting of the provincial convention. When Howe was moving up the Chesapeake late in the summer of 1777, Martin through letters to the newspapers and a broadside warned his countrymen against the General's promises of amnesty and of protection for the king's "WELL DISPOSED SUBJECTS." The office of attorney-general widened Martin's circle of acquaintances among leading citizens of the state and improved his opportunities for private practice, which the office did not preclude. He continued as attorney-general until 1805. As a member of the Baltimore Light Dragoons, a company of some fifty mounted gentlemen, Martin caught a brief glimpse of the war early in the summer of 1781, when the Dragoons rode south to assist Lafayette on the Virginia peninsula, but official duties soon called him back to Maryland and he apparently saw no action.

Elected to Congress in December 1784, Martin did not serve, a fact often overlooked, and so his first appearance on the national political scene was as a member of the Constitutional Convention of 1787. Having been elected on May 26, he took his seat on June 9, just as the convention, sitting as a committee of the whole house, faced one of its more serious crises. The question was whether the rule of equal representation by state should be abandoned for the principle of representation in proportion to population. It is impossible to say what specific contribution he may have made to the drafting of the Paterson or New Jersey Plan, which supported equality among the states and was submitted on June 15 to the convention, still in committee, but historians have assumed that it was significant. After the rejection of this plan on

June 19, the issue continued to hang like a threatening cloud over the deliberations of the convention, now in formal session, and when on June 27 the question no longer could be avoided, Martin sorely tried the patience of his colleagues by speaking for more than three hours and then announcing that he would have more to say on the following day. On the 28th Martin completed his remarks "with much diffuseness & considerable vehemence," noted James Madison (A.B. 1771), who responded at some length himself, and the day's debate ended with Franklin's famous and unavailing suggestion that the convention resort to prayer. On the next day it was decided that representation in the lower house would be in proportion to population.

Martin had failed even to carry his own delegation, but he probably should be credited in part for the sober mood in which the convention on July 2 designated a committee of one delegate from each state to search for a possible basis of compromise. It is significant that Martin was chosen to represent Maryland on this committee, which incidentally included four other graduates of Nassau Hall: Gunning Bedford of Delaware (A.B. 1771), William R. Davie of North Carolina (A.B. 1776), Oliver Ellsworth (A.B. 1766), and William Paterson. The committee's recommendation, submitted on July 5, was to balance proportional representation in the lower house of Congress with equality among the states in the upper branch, and this was the decision the convention finally made.

No other member held more extreme views regarding the rights of the states than did Martin, who insisted, in Madison's succinct summary, "that the General Government was meant merely to preserve the State Governments, not to govern individuals." But Martin was more than an irresponsible obstructionist. He favored additional powers for the central government, though within the framework of a union perpetuating the basic assumptions written into the Articles of Confederation. Having remained an active member of the convention until September 4, he returned home to lead the opposition to ratification of the new constitution. His "Genuine Information," originally a report in November to the Maryland legislature, spells out in great detail his views. But once again Martin lost. The ratifying convention, of which he was a member, adopted the constitution by a decisive vote of 63 to 11 in April 1788.

The remainder of Martin's life is an almost unbelievable combination of professional success and personal tragedy. By the testimony of Chief Justice Roger B. Taney, himself a Marylander, Martin had become by the end of the century "the acknowledged and undisputed head" of the bar in Maryland. Nor was his reputation limited to his own state. Having qualified for practice before the United States Supreme Court in 1791, he repeatedly appeared over the course of many years in some of the more important proceedings of the federal courts. In 1805 he was one of the defense attorneys in the abortive impeachment of Justice Samuel Chase, a native of Somerset County with whom Martin long had been acquainted and politically associated. Two years later he had a prominent part in the defense of Aaron Burr (A.B. 1772) before Chief Justice John Marshall at Richmond.

Martin achieved success at the bar despite a number of personal deficiencies, chief of which was a weakness for hard drink. In 1801 a Baltimore newspaper reported as a remarkable fact that he had been in Washington for an entire week without having once been seen drunk on the streets. Justice Taney reported that Martin often appeared in court intoxicated, that his dress was "a compound of the fine and the coarse" and at times soiled, that his voice was unmusical, that his arguments were "unreasonably long," and that in his speech he delighted "in using vulgarisms which were never heard except among the colored servants or the ignorant and uneducated whites." To this summation Taney added: "He was as coarse and unseemly at a dinner-table, in his manner of eating, as he was in everything." But the Justice also reported that Martin was an "accomplished scholar" who "wrote with classical correctness and great strength." Those who may be puzzled as to the man's extraordinary achievements at the bar are perhaps best advised to fall back on Henry Adams's description of him as a "notorious reprobate genius."

A part of Martin's personal difficulties can be attributed to the misfortunes he suffered in his family. He was married on December 25, 1783, to Maria Cresap, daughter of Captain Michael Cresap, a prominent frontiersman whom Martin had met on his westward tour in 1772. The couple apparently lived well in Baltimore. Although Martin's income from his law practice may have been less than the $12,000 he claimed in 1800, it must have been substantial. He had speculated in confiscated Loyalist property, and at the time of the Constitutional Convention his holding of public securities was substantial. The census of 1790 shows that he owned six slaves, a fact lending additional interest to the opposition he expressed in the convention to both the slave trade and slavery. Of the five children born to the marriage, two died in early childhood, and his wife died in November 1796 after a long struggle with cancer, leaving Martin with three young daughters.

It was little over six months later that Martin launched a famous attack in the public print upon Thomas Jefferson. In the *Notes on Virginia* Jefferson had included the "speech" by a Mingo Indian chieftain named Logan which charged "Colonel Cresp" with the murder in 1774 of Logan's entire family. It had been printed in a number of places as an example of Indian oratory, but Martin blamed Jefferson for its circulation in what he insisted was an unwarranted attack upon his father-in-law. The eight letters addressed to Jefferson, and immediately printed in the newspapers, reveal above all that Martin could be as intemperate with words as with the bottle, and that he had acquired a deep hatred of Jefferson. This hatred has been used as a simple explanation for Martin's identification with the Federalists, but it may be too simple. He was not alone among the Antifederalists of 1788 in Maryland, and elsewhere, who later became Federalists. Jefferson, who naturally attributed Martin's action to political motives, withheld public reply until 1800, when he published an *Appendix* to the *Notes* embodying information he meanwhile had accumulated.

Soon thereafter Martin was involved in another public controversy, this time with a son-in-law. In January 1802 Richard R. Keene (A.B. 1795), who had clerked in Martin's office and resided in his home, eloped with one of his daughters, then fifteen years of age. Before this, at the beginning of December 1801, Martin had circulated a printed notice *To the Citizens of Baltimore* of a plan to publish "a variety of letters" between the two men for correction of gross misrepresentations he charged to Keene. As good as his word and against the advice of friends, Martin published four angrily rambling pamphlets under the title of *Modern Gratitude* before Keene felt compelled to respond in June 1802 with a published account of his own. Of the two accounts the latter is the more sane and so the more persuasive, but fortunately for historians Keene's charge of scandalous conduct in 1770 provoked Martin into publishing a largely autobiographical fifth number of *Modern Gratitude*. Keene's wife died as early as 1807. Her sister Maria, who was blamed by Keene for the trouble, after an unhappy marriage and separation from her husband suffered mental derangement through many years.

It usually has been assumed that Martin's friendship with Burr dated from the Chase impeachment trial, over which Burr presided as vice president and in which Martin effectively pled for a strict construction of the "high Crimes and Misdemeanors" clause of the Constitution. His first identification with litigation arising from the Burr Conspiracy came in February 1807, when he successfully appealed to the supreme court for the release from prison of Erich Bollman and Samuel Swarthwout, agents of Burr who had been arrested in New Orleans by General James Wilkinson. Martin was probably firmly convinced of Burr's innocence of treason, which he insisted must be narrowly defined, but President Jefferson's special message to Congress on January 22 affirming that Burr's guilt had been "placed beyond question" was in itself enough to explain Martin's enlistment with the defense. His suspicion of Jefferson was fully reciprocated by the president, who advised the government attorney in Richmond that "this unprincipled & impudent federal bull-dog" was probably guilty at least of misprision of treason. Martin is reported to have served without fee. He was among those who provided security for Burr's bail, and after the jury failed to convict, he again became surety for Burr's bail pending a trial in Ohio on a misdemeanor charge. When Burr fled to England the bond was forfeited.

This default helps to explain Burr's unusual kindness to Martin in his last years. Martin's health broke in the summer of 1819, when he suffered a stroke. By his own confession in 1802 he had never been "an aeconomist of any thing but *time*," and with his health collapsed also his fortune, such as it may then have been. He had served as the chief judge of a Baltimore court from 1813 to 1816, and his return to the office of attorney-general in 1818 could have been intended to provide him financial support, as it did until his resignation in 1822. In that year the Maryland legislature adopted an extraordinary resolution imposing a $5 annual license fee upon every practicing attorney in the state for the benefit of Luther Martin. Burr on hearing of Martin's plight took him into his home in New York City, where incapacitated physically and mentally he lived for more than three years. He died on July 10, 1826, and was buried in New York.

SOURCES: P. S. Clarkson and R. S. Jett, *Luther Martin* (1970), is the only biography and the authority followed here except where otherwise noted. Number 5 of *Modern Gratitude* remains the chief source for Martin's early career, but it has to be used with care, and see C. R. Williams, *Cliosophic Society* (1916), 1-13; W. J. Mills, *Life at Princeton College* (1903), 141-43; and PUA file. Sketches: *DAB*; H. P. Goddard, *Md. Hist. Fund Pubs.*, 24 (1887), 9-42. Congress: *LMCC*, VII, lxvii; Constitutional Convention: Charles Warren, *Making of the Constitution* (1928); M. Farrand, *Framing of the Constitution* (1913), 93, 120 and 209; G. Hunt, Madison's *Journal* (1908), I, 248-261; M. Farrand, *Records of the Federal Convention*, III, 172-232 for "Genuine Information"; P. A. Crowl, "Anti-Federalism in Maryland," *WMQ*, 4 (1947), 446-69; E. D. Obrecht, "Influence of Luther Martin in the Making of the Constitution," *MHM*, 27 (1932), 173-90, 280-96; McDonald, *We the People*, 69-70, 90, for economic interests. Taney's comments are found in Appendix C of Clarkson and Jett; Adams's quotation from his *John Randolph*, 140. See also C. Warren, *Supreme Court in U.S. History* (1923), I, 56. The account of attack on Jefferson follows D. Malone, *Jefferson and His Time*, III, 346-52, except for the error as to the time of death for Martin's wife; and for *Appendix*, see W. H. Peden, *Notes* (1955), 226-58. Earlier publication of Logan's speech, see I. Brant, *James Madison*, I, 281-84. For the Chase and Burr trials: C. Evans, *Report of the Trial of . . . Chase* (1805), and D. Robertson, *Reports of the Trials of . . . Burr* (1808), together with W. H. Safford, *The Blennerhassett Papers* (1864), esp. 377-79; H. S. Parmet and M. B.

Hecht, *Aaron Burr* (1967), 290-94; S. H. Wandell and M. Minnigerode, *Aaron Burr* (1925), II, 308; T. P. Abernethy, *Burr Conspiracy*, 227-49; and D. Malone, *Jefferson and His Time*, V, 312-16, 330-31, 337, 348-49. In the College catalogues after 1812 Martin is listed as holding the LL.D. degree, but a search of the Trustees' minutes indicates that it was not awarded by Princeton.

Mss: MdHi   WFC

Nathaniel Niles

NATHANIEL NILES, A.B., A.M. 1769, Harvard 1772, Dartmouth 1791, preacher, public official, inventor and businessman, was born at South Kingston, Rhode Island, on April 3, 1741, a son of Sarah Niles and her husband and first cousin, Judge Samuel Niles (Harvard 1731), a farmer and a leading citizen of Braintree, Massachusetts. Young Nathaniel was prepared for college in Braintree by Joseph Marsh (Harvard 1728) and entered Harvard College in the summer of 1761. For reasons now unknown, Niles transferred to the College of New Jersey the following year. His younger brother Samuel (A.B. 1769) joined him at Princeton in 1765. Inclined to endless theological disputations, in College the brothers were known as "Botheration Primus" and "Botheration Secundus" by their fellow students.

After graduation Niles briefly studied law and medicine and took up schoolteaching in New York City for a time. Finally deciding upon the ministry, he traveled to Bethlehem, Connecticut, to study with the New Light theologian Joseph Bellamy. Licensed to preach on April 25, 1769, in the early 1770s Niles began speaking from various pulpits in Massachusetts and Connecticut without being called permanently to any of them. However, he was very much in demand as a visiting preacher and several of his sermons were printed. While preaching at the Congregational church in Charlestown, Massachusetts, in 1772, Niles so impressed a large proportion of the communicants that they urged him to stay. Since such a move would have split the congregation, Niles did not accept, continuing instead to preach in other New England pulpits. Theologically, Niles was a moderate follower of the New Divinity thinker Samuel Hopkins, a position that attracted neither rigid Calvinists nor those Congregationalists who were sliding toward Arminianism, a forerunner of Unitarianism. In later years Niles used to say of this part of his life that he had "had seventeen calls, but they were all to go away."

Niles was an early and enthusiastic supporter of the Revolution.

Hearing news of Bunker Hill he wrote a poem, "The American Hero," which was later set to music. Said to have been a widely popular anthem, sung from meetinghouse to tavern, its last verse forces a certain admiration for the vocal abilities of eighteenth-century Americans:

> Life, for my Country and the Cause of Freedom,
> Is but a Trifle for a Worm to part with;
> And if preserved in so great a Contest,
> Life is redoubled.

Niles's greatest service to the American cause came through his connection with the family of his wife, Elizabeth Lothrop of Norwich, Connecticut, whom he married about 1774. The wife's father was a substantial millowner. As the Revolution developed, the American forces were in desperate need of woolen cloth. Before the Revolution, the wire used for making wool cards had been imported. Niles invented a successful new method of making wire from iron bars in the Lothrop mills. Not only did the Connecticut Assembly advance him money to develop his plans, but the townspeople of Norwich elected him to that body from 1779 to 1781.

By 1782 competition from illegal imports and impending peace made it apparent that the end of war would mean the end of American wiremaking. Niles took his profits and bought a large section of land in what later became West Fairlee, Orange County, Vermont. He built a house, barn, and mill on his property and settled a group of families from Norwich on it as well. He became the commanding figure in the area, serving as preacher, lawyer and physician to the settlers. In his house he always maintained a special room in which to tinker with gadgets and to conduct scientific experiments. Although never ordained, he joined the local ministerial association and dominated it. He shortly became a leading figure in what was still the Republic of Vermont. Appointed to Vermont's supreme court in 1784, he served until 1788; in 1784 he also became speaker of Vermont's House of Representatives. In 1785 he joined the Vermont Council and the Council of Censors, serving again in 1787 and 1789. In about 1784 Niles's wife died after bearing him four children. On November 22, 1787, Niles married Mrs. Elizabeth Marston Watson of Plymouth, Massachusetts, a well-known literary and theological figure. The couple had five children. Niles, in keeping with his ardent democratic beliefs, persuaded his wife to discard her fashionable wardrobe and dress in simple republican homespun.

Niles was a strong supporter of the federal constitution, and in a 1791 convention urged Vermont to adopt it:

Let every member, says he, state his objections freely, and let every argument be duly attended to—but suffer not division of sentiment to prevail in community if possible to avoid it. It is a certain truth that warm spirits exist among us—these warm spirits may be heated, and being heated may diffuse their warmth to others, and by so doing may kindle a flame in society the effect of which may be destructive to its peace.

Vermont sent Niles to Congress as its first representative in 1791. He served until defeated by a Federalist in 1794. He became the leader of the Jeffersonian Republicans in his state, speaking out vigorously against banks, slavery, and the Hartford Convention of 1814. He served in the Vermont House of Representatives from 1800 to 1803, leaving it in that year to spend six years on the governor's council. As presidential elector he voted for Jefferson in 1804 and for Madison in 1813. He was a delegate to Vermont's convention for the revision of its constitution in 1814.

Niles was an active trustee of Dartmouth College from 1794 until 1820. From the day of his election to the board, he was a thorn in President John Wheelock's side. As an historian of Dartmouth describes it, Niles "was critical of the scholarship of the president, he doubted his theological soundness, and, most of all, he had scant patience with the Wheelock pretense to complete dominance over the institution and his obvious belief that the trustees held in its organization a very minor role. John Wheelock returned this aversion with interest." The feud culminated in the investigation, which contemporaries credited Niles with inspiring, of Dartmouth by the New Hampshire legislature and the subsequent celebrated Dartmouth College Case. It was his last conspicuous public engagement. Niles spent his later years developing his theology. "Niles is the same man he ever was," a contemporary wrote in 1811, "Is a high Democrat and an Hopkinsian. . . . He is a very sensible man, but is Niles yet." He died at West Fairlee on October 31, 1828.

SOURCES: Sketches: *Congregational Quarterly*, v (1863), 33-41, from which "American Hero" quotation is drawn; *DAB*; *Sibley's Harvard Graduates*, XVI, 390-97, from which "Niles yet" quotation is drawn; quotation *re* fed. constit.: *Rec. of the Gov. and Council of the State of Vermont*, III (1875), 479; Dartmouth quotation: L. B. Richardson, *History of Dartmouth College* (1932), I, 225-26; see too: S. J. Novak, "The College in the Dartmouth College Case: A Reinterpretation," *NEQ*, 47 (1974), 550-63; theology: A Heimert, *Religion and the Am. Mind* (1966), passim.

PUBLICATIONS: STE and Sh-Sh #s 1055, 18238, & Sh-Co #2555.

Mss: PHi

James Power

JAMES POWER, A.B., D.D. Jefferson College 1808, Presbyterian clergy-man, was born in Nottingham, Chester County, Pennsylvania, in 1746, the son of "a substantial farmer" who had emigrated from Ireland at an early age. James prepared for the College at the Reverend Samuel Finley's Nottingham Academy and graduated from the College in the last year of Finley's presidency. That same year Power visited Finley on his deathbed in Philadelphia, and according to a nineteenth-century historian "the affecting scene left a powerful and enduring impression in his mind." The visit probably inspired Power to become a minister, and he began studying theology with Finley's younger brother, the Reverend James Finley.

Ill health prolonged Power's studies, and not until June 24, 1772, was he licensed by the Presbytery of New Castle. By that time he had married Mary Tanner of East Nottingham, the daughter of an elder in James Finley's church. She eventually bore him eight daughters, three of whom married Presbyterian ministers.

From December 1772 or 1773 to the spring of 1774 Power served as a missionary to the congregations of Highbridge, Cambridge, and Oxford in Botetourt County, Virginia, but he declined a call to become their permanent pastor. In the summer of 1774 he crossed the un-mapped and challenging Allegheny Mountains and spent three months as a missionary in western Pennsylvania. At the end of his tour he returned to Nottingham, where until the spring of 1776 he was a supply preacher.

On May 23, 1776, Power was ordained *sine titulo* by the Presbytery of New Castle just before leaving for western Pennsylvania once again. This time he took with him his wife and four daughters—two of them placed in baskets on his horse, the other two on his wife's horse. He settled in Dunlap's Creek near Brownsville in Fayette County, where he had previously organized one of the first Presbyterian churches west of the Alleghenies. For the next three years he was a supply preacher for local congregations. He was the first Presbyterian clergyman to settle permanently in western Pennsylvania and was the first Presbyterian clergyman to preach a sermon and perform a baptism in Washington County. Within a short time he had become known as a dedicated and effective preacher. On each visit to a particular locale he regularly baptized thirty to forty people (once more than sixty) and performed many marriages, including one across an unfordable stream with the couple forced to remain on the other side. Moreover, he regularly returned backsliders to the fold and impressed all he met by

rarely forgetting their names or faces. "We have a considerable number of apparently pious ministers in this Western part of the world,"
wrote a Colonel James Smith to his sister after a visit with Power,
"where we lately heard nothing but the yells of savages and wolves,
etc.; but now we have the Word of God, with peace and plenty."

In 1779 Power accepted a call to become pastor of two of the Presbyterian congregations on his circuit: Mount Pleasant in Westmoreland County and Sewickley in Allegheny County. When these double
responsibilities eventually became unduly taxing, Power resigned from
Sewickley, the smaller of the two churches, on April 22, 1787. He remained, however, at Mount Pleasant, which paid him $600 annually.
Only age and infirmity compelled his retirement from Mount Pleasant
on April 15, 1817.

A sermon Power preached "to a large assembly" on August 2, 1781,
indicated support for the Revolution. "Think of ye cruel acts of ye
British parliament," he reminded his audience, "by which we and our
children ar[e] to be made slaves forever, and the money which we had
earned by the sweat of our brows taken from us without a reason rendered for so doing." Power himself may have served, presumably as
chaplain, in militia units in Chester, Cumberland, Washington, and
Westmoreland counties from 1777 to 1782. Whatever his degree of
participation in the Revolution, Power definitely engaged in combat
of another kind—against Indians. Indian attacks in western Pennsylvania were especially frequent and bloody between 1780 and 1785.
Several times Power was himself reported to have been murdered—in-
accurately, it turned out.

In September 1781 Power and three other Presbyterian ministers—
Joseph Smith (A.B. 1764), John McMillan (A.B. 1772), and Thaddeus
Dod (A.B. 1773)—formed the new Presbytery of Redstone with jurisdiction over the entire region west of the Alleghenies. Not until 1793
would other presbyteries be formed in the area.

Power was also active in the development of higher education in
western Pennsylvania. In 1786 Hugh Henry Brackenridge (A.B. 1771),
a Pittsburgh lawyer and a member of the Pennsylvania General Assembly, obtained from the assembly an act incorporating Pittsburgh
Academy, which later became the University of Pittsburgh. The act of
incorporation provided for trustees of several Christian denominations, including Power, McMillan, and Smith. Similarly, in 1802 Power,
Smith, and Dod were among those designated by the assembly as
founders and first trustees of Jefferson College (later Washington and
Jefferson College), which grew out of Canonsburg Academy, of which
Power had also been a trustee. He remained a trustee of Jefferson Col-

lege until his resignation in 1806, and he was especially close to the College's first president, the Reverend James Dunlap (A.B. 1773), who had assisted him at Dunlap's Creek in the 1770s.

Power was described by associates as "slender, erect, of a medium height, and at no period of life, corpulent." His manners, we are told, "were easy, graceful, free from affectation, and such as made him agreeable to all classes of society." His conversation was "dignified and somewhat precise" yet "sociable." His dress was "always plain, and at the same time remarkably neat." In his preaching Power was soft-spoken and restrained, yet he enunciated so clearly that he reached as many parishioners as his more oratorical colleagues, and he spoke so appealingly that he made as many converts as they did. The welfare of children was a special concern of his, and he devoted much time to individual youths and groups of youths.

"In his doctrines," a colleague noted, Power "was of the same school with the Tennants, Davies, Robert Smith, and Samuel Finley."

Power died at his home in Mount Pleasant on August 5, 1830, leaving to his wife and children a large farm that had permitted him to live comfortably and respectably despite the limited income he received as a minister. He may also have been the James Power who in the late 1780s and 1790s acquired several hundred acres of land in Cumberland and Westmoreland Counties.

SOURCES: Vital data: James Power File, PUA; Webster, MS Brief Sketches, PPPrHi; Sprague, *Annals*, III, 326-30; "a substantial farmer": Sprague, 326; relationship with Samuel Finley: J. A. Alexander and J. Carnahan, Notes of Distinguished Grads., MS, NjP; "the affecting scene": *Presbyterian Encyclopaedia*, 629; R. Webster, *Hist. Presbytery of Washington, Pa.* (1889), 392; ordination and settlement in western Pa.: *Hist. Presbytery of Redstone* (1889), 3-5, 25, 34; *JPHS*, 10 (1919-1920), 62-64; W. W. McKinney, *Early Pittsburgh Presbyterianism* (1938), 45, 50, 51; Washington Co. firsts: D. Elliot, *Life of Rev. Elisha Macurdy* (1848), 287; Mt. Pleasant and Sewickley churches: F. T. Nevin, *Village of Sewickley, Pa.* (1929), 12, 20, 27; *JPHS*, 10 (1919-1920), 63; farm and possible landholdings: *Pa. Arch.* (3 ser.), 24 (1898), 746, 747, and 26 (1899), 487; 1781 sermon: "A Preparatory Sermon," typescript copy of MS, PPPrHi; possibly military service: references in *Pa. Arch.* (3 ser.), XXII, (5 ser.), IV, V, VI; (6 ser.), II; D. R. Guthrie, *John McMillan* (1952), 41; work in higher education: A. B. Young, *The Voice That Speaketh Clear* (1957), 1-7; H.T.W. Coleman, *Banners in the Wilderness* (1956), 2, 15, 63, 231; McKinney, 54-55; character: quotations from Sprague, 327; 1768 sermon: "A Compend of Theology," typescript copy of MS, PPPrHi.

HS

Isaac Skillman

ISSAC SKILLMAN, A.B., A.M. Rhode Island College 1774, D.D. 1798, Baptist clergyman, was born in Somerset, New Jersey, in 1740, the son of Isaac Skillman, a shoemaker. His mother was possibly a member of the New Jersey branch of the Beekman family. Young Isaac prepared for the College at the Reverend Isaac Eaton's academy in Hopewell, New Jersey. The academy was the first Baptist institution of its kind in the colonies and sent several of its graduates to Nassau Hall.

Shortly after his graduation, in January 1767, Skillman was hired by James Beekman, a wealthy New York City merchant, as tutor to Beekman's sons William (A.B. 1773), Abraham (Class of 1774), and James (Class of 1776), at a salary of £27.10 per year. Skillman remained with the Beekmans only until May 1767, when he set up a school of his own in New York City. He conducted the school at least until 1770, when he began to study for the ministry. In 1772 or 1773 he was ordained by the Philadelphia Association at the First Baptist Church of Philadelphia. At the ceremony the sermon was delivered by the Reverend James Manning (A.B. 1762), the first president of Rhode Island College (later Brown University). In September 1773 Skillman became pastor of the Second Baptist Church of Boston, having earlier declined a call to Hopewell's Baptist church.

In the course of his fourteen years in Boston, Skillman became a prominent preacher. He was appointed to the standing committee of New England Baptists, to the Warren Association committee of grievances, and to the association's committee on publications. During his service on these committees, he opposed discriminatory practices against Baptists. He also opposed the publication, by the Warren Association, of spelling books containing rival religious doctrines to those of the association.

In October 1787 Skillman resigned from the Second Baptist Church in order to become pastor of the Salem, New Jersey, Baptist Church, which had recently built a new sanctuary. His ordination, however, did not take place until the fall of 1790, and he spent the three years in between as a supply preacher for Salem. The cause of the delay may have been his unwillingness to sign the detailed contract with the congregation that he finally did sign in 1790. In return for an annual salary of £125 he was expected to preach at all funerals, to preach twice on Sundays in summer, to visit each member family of the congregation at least twice a year, not to leave the area without the congregation's consent, and in case of disputes to accept arbitration by the Baptist churches of Cumberland and Wilmington.

According to a nineteenth-century historian, Skillman proved to be "a man of learning and abilities, but never very popular as a preacher." However, William Bentley, the Congregationalist minister of Salem, Mass., recorded in his diary that of the three New England preachers whom he heard lecture in Boston in April 1785, he "very much preferred" Skillman. During his years at Salem, moreover, Skillman added fifty-seven new members to the congregation. Still, the lengthy and quite satirical "Ballad of Boston Ministers" of 1774 offered the following unkind assessment of him: "If there's another ghostly brother, [called] a baptist teacher, let that atone for passing o'er this preacher." That Skillman's name was the last one mentioned in the ballad indicated his standing in the eyes of its author.

On June 7 or 8, 1799, Skillman died suddenly, leaving no will. He had never married. An inventory of his estate by Abraham and Cornelius Skillman found only personal effects. His passing was reportedly "deeply lamented."

SOURCES: Vital data: Isaac Skillman File, PUA; Sprague, *Annals*, VI, 453; *NYGBR*, 37 (1906), 91, 94-95, 281; T. S. Griffiths, *Hist. of Baptists in N.J.* (1904), 46-48; *NJA*, 27 (1905), 538; tutoring and school: P. L. White, *Beekmans of N.Y.* (1956), 479-82; W. Nelson, *N.J. Biog. and Geneal. Notes* (1916), 192; New England activities: R. A. Guild, *Life, Times, and Correspondence of James Manning* (1864), 330; Guild, *Chaplain Smith and the Baptists* (1885), 142, 302, 310; Guild, *Early Hist. of Brown Univ.* (1897), 261, 380; W. G. McLoughlin, *New England Dissent* (1972), 771; Salem contract: Griffiths, 46-47; quotations: "a man of learning": Sprague; "very much preferred": *Diary of W. Bentley* (1905), I, 19; "Ballad of Boston Ministers": *NEHGR*, 13 (1859), 132; "deeply lamented": Griffiths, 48; will: *NJA*, 38 (1944), 330.

HS

Samuel Smith

SAMUEL SMITH, A.B., A.M., physician, was born in New York City on July 24, 1745, the twelfth of the fourteen children of Mary Het and her husband, William Smith. The father, a prominent Presbyterian layman, was a prosperous lawyer and one of the founding trustees of the College. Samuel was the third of his sons to attend the College, the others being Thomas (A.B. 1754) and James (A.B. 1757).

In 1767 Smith enrolled in the newly constituted medical department of King's College in New York. At the same time his older brother James returned from study abroad to become the institution's first Professor of Chemistry and Materia Medica. Smith did not complete his course at King's, but the fact that he was awarded the A.M. suggests that he was considered a qualified professional man.

Some of Smith's sisters married into South Carolina families. Smith himself went to Charleston, whether with the intention of settling permanently or for an extended visit has not been discovered. He died there on August 10, 1771. A South Carolina newspaper described him as "a young Gentleman highly valued and esteemed by all who had the Pleasure of his Acquaintance." In his will he left legacies to his sisters and his books and manuscripts "on physic and surgery" to his brother James. He was buried in the graveyard of Charleston's Presbyterian "Circular Church."

SOURCES: Vital data: W. S. Pelletreau, *Wills of the Smith Families* (1898), 124; *NYGBR*, 4 (1873), 99; M. H. Thomas, *Columbia Univ. Officers and Alumni* (1936), 107; obituary notice: *S.C. and Am. General Gaz.*, Aug. 12, 1771; will: C. T. Moore, *Abstracts of Wills of . . . S.C.* (1969), 153. The CNJ Catalogue of 1770 lists Smith as the holder of an A.M., but the college that bestowed the degree has not been determined.

William Smith

WILLIAM SMITH, A.B., M.B. College of Philadelphia 1771, druggist and surgeon, was born in Philadelphia in 1746, the youngest son of Mary Harrison and her husband, Samuel Smith, a prosperous and prominent merchant and a founding trustee of Philadelphia's Second Presbyterian Church. In 1756 young William entered the academy connected with the College of Philadelphia. He was preceded at Princeton by his older brother, Jonathan Bayard Smith (A.B. 1760).

Smith's activities immediately after graduation have not been discovered, but in 1769 he enrolled in the medical department of the College of Philadelphia, receiving his degree in 1771. Not long thereafter he became a junior partner in the drug firm of Lehman and Smith at "The Sign of the Rising Sun" in Philadelphia. He was active in medical affairs as well, serving as secretary of the American Medical Society in 1771.

Smith was elected a member of Philadelphia's Committee of Correspondence on May 20, 1774. But involvement in the Revolution did not prevent him from making an advantageous marriage. On November 30, 1775, he married Ann Young, granddaughter of Thomas Graeme, an extremely wealthy physician and former member of the Pennsylvania Council. The ceremony took place at his wife's family's impressive country seat, "Graeme Park," about eighteen miles northeast of Philadelphia. Four children were born to the couple.

On August 20, 1776, Smith was appointed druggist by Congress, with a mandate "to receive and deliver all Medicines, Instruments and shop Furniture, for the benefit of the United States." Styled "continental druggist," Smith over the next fourteen months received several thousand dollars from Congress in payment for medical supplies. After the summer of 1777 he appears to have given up his post as continental druggist and entered upon active duty as a surgeon in the General Hospital at Bethlehem, Pennsylvania. On February 17, 1778, along with other medical men at the hospital—including Samuel Finley, Jr. (A.B. 1765), and Robert R. Henry (A.B. 1776)—he signed a memorial to Congress accusing Dr. William Shippen (A.B. 1754), director general of medical services for the American army, of gross maladministration. The length of time that Smith remained on active military service is uncertain, but by June 1781 he was petitioning Congress for half-pay due to him as a supernumerary.

Smith's wife died on April 4, 1780. His involvement with her family continued for many years thereafter, causing him no little nuisance. Ann Smith's aunt, Elizabeth Graeme Ferguson, once a leading Philadelphia hostess, had inherited the family seat, Graeme Park. Mrs. Ferguson's husband was a Loyalist; she herself came close to having her property confiscated by Whig leaders. Smith—along with many other prominent Philadelphians—constantly lobbied with the Pennsylvania legislature to secure her safe title to her lands. In 1791 Smith finally purchased Graeme Park, permitting Mrs. Ferguson to stay on for several years after the sale. In the meantime, Smith remarried. He and his second wife, Letitia Corey, had three children.

In 1782 Smith reentered the drug business, advertising in the *Pennsylvania Gazette* on January 16 that his new medicinal shop, located in Third Street, would be called "The Sign of the Unicorn and Mortar." Active in civic affairs, Smith was a member of Philadelphia's St. Andrew's Society and in January 1792 was elected to the American Philosophical Society. In the same year he became one of the organizers and first directors of the Insurance Company of North America. Nothing has been discovered of Smith's later years. He died at his home in Sansom Street in Philadelphia at 4:30 on the afternoon of May 16, 1822.

Sources: Vital data: F. W. Leach, "Old Philadelphia Families," Philadelphia *North American*, Aug. 14, 1912; C. P. Keith, *Provincial Councillors of Pa.* (1883), 165; Med. Soc.: *Pa. Chronicle*, Oct. 28, 1771; "Rising Sun": *Pa. Gaz.*, Sept. 30, 1772; Com. of Corresp.: *Cal. of Va. State Papers*, VIII (1890), 45; Graeme Park: H. D. Eberlein and H. M. Lippincott, *Colonial Homes of Philadelphia* (1912), 298-304; cont. druggist and army service: *JCC*, V, 673; VII, 274; XX, 690; anti-Shippen petition: L. C. Duncan, *Medical Men in the Am. Rev.* (1970 ed.), 282-83; Elizabeth Graeme Ferguson: *DAB*; several letters of Smith to Mrs. Ferguson: *PMHB*, 39 (1915); Ins. Co. N.A.: M. James, *Biography of a Business* (1942), 39; death notice: *Poulson's Am. Daily Advertiser*, May 17, 1822. Smith is often credited with a 1784 CNJ A.M. The actual recipient of the degree in that year was William Smith (A.B. 1774) of New York.

Mss: PHi

Alpheus Spring

ALPHEUS SPRING, A.B., A.M. Dartmouth 1785, was born on May 10, 1739, in Watertown, Middlesex County, Massachusetts. He was the eleventh child of Kezia Convers and her husband, Henry Spring, who served Watertown as a constable and baptized his children in the town's Congregational church. Alpheus's older brother Marshall graduated from Harvard in 1762, and while there was described as "as Big a Fop as any in College." Alpheus was not a fop. Instead, in College he entertained dreams of missionary work among the Indians. "There is a young Gentleman whose name is *Spring*," Ralph Wheelock (Class of 1765), wrote from Nassau Hall, "of good Family, but destitute of a fortune, sustains a very Religious character, who has manifested a desire once & again of improving his tallents, in doing service for ye Kingdom of J[esus] Ch[rist] among ye Savages, & he knows of no other Objection to oppose it, but his Mothers fear." Spring's mother's fears must have prevailed, for after graduation he studied theology in Kittery, Maine, with the Reverend John Rogers (Harvard 1711), a vehement New Light preacher who had disrupted the New England ecclesiastical establishment during the Great Awakening. When Rogers prepared to retire, he requested that his church, the Second Parish of Kittery, located in nearby Eliot, call Spring to its pulpit. Spring was ordained on June 28, 1768, and on May 18 of the following year married Sarah, the daughter of Simon Frost (Harvard 1729). The couple had three children.

Spring's brother Marshall, a physician, became one of the richest professional men in Massachusetts and a prominent Republican politician. Although Alpheus lived in relative obscurity, he brought an end to the controversies that had surrounded John Rogers's ministry. In his fifty-third year, Parson Spring succumbed to a fever and died suddenly on June 14, 1791. He was buried in Kittery.

SOURCES: *Genealogies . . . of the Early Settlers of Watertown, Mass.* (1855), I, 44; *Watertown Records*, IV (1906), 144, 185; V (1908), 52; Ralph Wheelock to Eleazar Wheelock, Feb. 12, 1765, Wheelock MSS; marriage: *NEHGR*, 10 (1856), 46; John Rogers and Marshall Spring: *Sibley's Harvard Graduates*, V, 580-83; XV, 294-97; career: Sprague, *Annals*, VIII, 262; Stiles, *Literary Diary*, II, 203; death: *Boston Independent Chronicle*, June 30, 1791.

LLM

Benjamin Stelle

BENJAMIN STELLE, A.B., A. M. Rhode Island College 1774, schoolmaster and businessman, was born in Piscataway, Middlesex County, New

Jersey, in 1746, the son of Christiana Clarkson and her husband, the Reverend Isaac Stelle, pastor of Piscataway's Stelton Baptist Church. Benjamin's great-grandfather, a Huguenot named Poncet Stelle, came to America sometime between 1675 and 1680.

Benjamin prepared for the College at the academy of the Reverend Isaac Eaton in Hopewell, New Jersey. The academy was the first Baptist institution of its kind in the colonies and sent several of its graduates to the College.

Shortly after graduation from the College, Stelle moved to Providence, Rhode Island, where he established a Latin grammar school. He was aided in recruiting students by the Reverend James Manning (A.B. 1762), who was not only a native of Piscataway and a close friend of the Stelle family but, more importantly, the first president of Rhode Island College (later Brown University) and the leading Baptist educator of the day. Manning, whose school and college were then located in Warren, Rhode Island, assured the parents of prospective students that Stelle's "proficiency is . . . as good as common, and his character fair and free from blots." Manning nevertheless expected that Stelle would find Newport a more receptive community for the school, and the citizens of Newport themselves sought Stelle. Yet Stelle received a surprisingly warm reception in Providence and soon had as many students as he could comfortably handle—about twenty. By July 1766, Manning was writing that Stelle "gives good satisfaction and is much esteemed by the gentlemen of the town."

Indeed, the schoolmaster was so successful—and enterprising—that in the spring of 1767 he advertised in the *Providence Gazette* "to open a school for the instruction of young ladies, in the knowledge of writing and arithmetic." Beginning on May 20, Stelle would, for a fee of "two dollars for scholar," hold two sessions a day, 6:00–7:30 A.M. and 4:30–6:00 P.M., for a term of four months. The school apparently opened and, as in the case of the classical school, promptly inspired proposals for another school—a night school for "all persons who have a mind to come, or send their children."

Stelle's educational conglomerate prospered until early in 1770, when, for various religious, financial, and personal reasons, Manning moved both his College and its Latin grammar school from Warren to Providence. Apparently, Manning's competition proved too great, and Stelle's "school system" collapsed. Yet rather than despair, Stelle "betook himself to other paths of usefulness." He became joint owner, with Benjamin Bowen, of both a chocolate mill and an apothecary shop, the latter in central Providence. As an advertisement of August

1770 indicated, the two enterprises complemented each other: the shop offered a full assortment not only of medicines, "Chymical and Galenical," but also of chocolate, sold "by the Pound, Box, or Hundred weight."

Not surprisingly, Stelle gradually became a prominent Providence citizen. In 1771 he was asked to subscribe to the Rhode Island College building fund and contributed £7.10. In 1774 he was elected first clerk of the Charitable Baptist Society, and in the same year he was awarded an honorary A.M. from Rhode Island College.

From the very outset of the Revolution, Stelle was an active, enthusiastic Whig. On November 1, 1775, he became adjutant to the newly formed Rhode Island State Regiment of Colonel William Richmond and Major Benjamin Tallman. In that post he remained at least until 1777. From June 1, 1779, to April 1, 1781, he was deputy paymaster of the same unit. Stelle also supervised the exchange of prisoners of war with the British that took place on Block Island in November 1776. In May of the following year he received £39.10 from his state government as compensation "for effects lost" as a result of that expedition.

Stelle's ties to Rhode Island College remained strong throughout his lifetime. They were not merely religious and geographic; they were also familial. First, Huldak Crawford, his wife since 1768, was a first or second cousin of Ann Carter, the first wife of Nicholas Brown, after whom Rhode Island College was later renamed. Second, three years after his wife's death in 1798, Brown married Stelle's younger daughter Mary, one of his two children. The marriage ceremony itself took place in Stelle's home, which had been the Crawford family home—and in addition one of Providence's most fashionable addresses. As a result of Stelle's long residence there, the house eventually became known as the Benjamin Stelle House.

Stelle died in Providence on the afternoon of Sunday, January 17, 1819, at age seventy-three.

SOURCES: Vital data: Benjamin Stelle File, PUA; Giger, Memoirs, 1; NYGBR, 44 (1913), 61-69, 107-114; attendance at Hopewell Academy: R. A. Guild, Early Hist. of Brown University (1897), 10; Manning and Stelle family: Guild, Life, Times, and Correspondence of James Manning (1864), 36, 84-85; W. G. McLoughlin, New England Dissent (1971), I, 507; Manning quotations: G. S. Kimball, Providence in Colonial Times (1912), 342; E. Field, State of Rhode Island and Providence Plantations . . . A History (1902), III, 634, 637, 638; Crawford/Stelle House: R.I. Hist., 10 (1951), 46; wartime service: S. G. Arnold, Hist. of State of Rhode Island (1894), II, 359, 391, 413; Force, Am. Arch. (5 ser.), III, 1087; R.I. Hist. Soc. Coll., 6 (1867), 177; R.I. Col. Rec., 8 (1863), 256; death notice: Providence Gaz., Jan. 23, 1819.

HS

Micah Townsend

MICAH TOWNSEND, A.B., lawyer and public official, was born at Cedar Swamp, Oyster Bay, Long Island, on May 13, 1749, the son of Elizabeth Platt and Micajah Townsend, a well-to-do farmer. Micah prepared for the College with a local clergyman and entered the College as a freshman.

After graduation Townsend read law in New York City with Thomas Jones, a future New York supreme court justice. On April 6, 1770, he was admitted to the New York bar and on June 14 of that year became a master Mason. From then until 1776 he practiced law in White Plains, Westchester County.

Early in 1776 Townsend became clerk of the Westchester County Committee of Safety. In June he enlisted in the county militia as a captain and was assigned a fifty-man unit. From July until October his unit awaited the British at the mouth of the Croton River in Westchester County. When the British neared in overwhelming numbers, Townsend and his men broke camp, set fire to several White Plains homes, and thereby managed to avoid what would have been certain defeat. The deliberate destruction of his neighbors' homes did not endear Townsend to the citizens of White Plains. Shortly thereafter he moved to Brattleboro, Vermont. There, in 1778, he became both a commissioner and a clerk of Cumberland County and a year later became a Vermont representative to the New York Assembly.

On August 15, 1778, Townsend married Mary Wells of Brattleboro. The couple had five daughters and three sons. Mary was the daughter of Samuel Wells, and her father, a prominent Loyalist, may have been responsible for Townsend's conversion, in about 1781, to Loyalism and to Vermont independence. Prior to 1781 he had been a confidant of New York Governor George Clinton and Clinton's official representative in numerous negotiations with those Vermonters seeking independence.

Townsend frequently warned Clinton about the increasing size of Vermont's rebel militia, which was led by Ira and Ethan Allen, and their increasing determination to wage war, if necessary, to win freedom, which meant ownership of their own land above all. In June 1779 he wrote Clinton that Congress must take up the jurisdictional dispute at once and obtain a permanent settlement. In the interim, New York must supply men and arms to loyal "Yorkers" in Vermont. Otherwise, "Vermont is favored and will infallibly maintain their [sic] independence." Townsend himself brought before Congress a petition, signed by ten Vermont town committees, opposing independence.

In a letter to Clinton on April 10, 1780, he stressed the impatience of Yorkers with Clinton and the Congress and noted that many were changing allegiances to Vermont. Sometime in the next year, convinced that New York would never seriously negotiate, Townsend changed his own allegiance. He took an oath of Vermont citizenship and promptly became the first lawyer in the state and a most successful practitioner. "I have hitherto acted from motives purely disinterested," he had written Clinton in 1779, "and have only had a consciousness of that for my reward."

Townsend was immediately appointed or elected to several prestigious public posts and later to others: in 1781 to the State House of Representatives—Vermont by then claiming to be an independent state—to a judgeship and registry of probate in Windham County, and to the Secretaryship of State of Vermont; and in 1785 to the Vermont Council of Censors, which had been established to revise the 1777 Vermont constitution. Townsend's legal acumen made him the logical choice for council secretary and thus the council's leading draftsman. In 1784 Townsend's official duties won him both a franking privilege for state-related business and the right to hold lotteries and to raise money for a Brattleboro bridge. The extensive lands, furniture, and moneys that he inherited upon his father's death in 1781 likely enabled him to devote so much time to public service.

Three incidents suggest that Townsend's status both before and after his switch to the side of Loyalism and of Vermont was precarious. First, in May 1779 Townsend and thirty-five other military officers from Brattleboro, Putney, and Westminster, each bearing New York State commissions, were arrested by Vermont officials for having refused induction into the new Vermont state militia. As a prominent lawyer, Townsend became the leader of the group, demanded impartial proceedings, and pleaded not guilty on behalf of all of them. All, however, were found guilty, and Townsend paid a £20 fine. Second, on a visit to Long Island in May 1781 he "met with abuse" in New York City at the hands of Loyalist refugees from Westchester County who resented his military exploits against them five years earlier. Fearing for his life on his way back from Long Island, he took a different route back to Vermont. "A thousand pounds," he wrote Governor Clinton, "would not tempt me to a similar visit." Finally, in July 1784 Townsend was nevertheless in New York City again, and this time was arrested on charges of having served as a Vermont official and thus having broken with New York State. He was obliged to pay £2,000, but was compensated with the commissions an outraged Vermont legislature permitted him to keep from the sale of Vermont lands owned by New York citizens.

In 1788 Townsend retired from his public offices but remained in Brattleboro. In 1801 he moved to Guilford, Vermont, where he stayed less than a year before moving to Farnham in Lower Canada. The British government granted him and his wife 1,200 acres in compensation for losses sustained by Samuel Wells during the Revolution. At Farnham he lived quietly, spending as much time in religious matters as in domestic ones. Indeed, for the last thirty years of his life he, an Episcopalian, practiced daily devotions.

In 1816 Townsend and his wife moved to Clarenceville in Lower Canada to live with their son, the Reverend Micajah Townsend. At Clarenceville Micah served briefly as a justice of the peace and as "judicial commissioner for the trial of small causes." Most of his time, however, he gardened, read, and meditated. The death of his wife on June 27, 1831, provoked an anticipation of his own passing, which came, after a fever, on April 23, 1832.

SOURCES: Vital data: Micah Townsend File, PUA; B. H. Hall, *Hist. of Eastern Vt.* (1865), I-II, passim; O. Hufeland, *Westchester Co. During the Amer. Rev.* (1926), 444; Force, *Am. Arch.* (5 ser.), III, 214; Vermont independence movement: C. Williamson, *Vt. in Quandary, 1763-1825* (1949); letters to Clinton: *Clinton Papers*, v, 68-70, 595-96 and 112; *Coll. Vt. Hist. Soc.* (1871), 97; W.H.W. Sabine, *Hist. Memoirs Wm. Smith* (1971), 398, 405, 407; M. R. Cabot, *Annals of Brattleboro, Vt.* (1921), I, 128; C. M. Thompson, *Independent Vt.* (1942), 438-40, 445; lottery privilege: *Vt. Hist.*, 35 (1967), 48-49; inheritance from father: *NYHS Col.*, x (1902), 231-33.

HS

John Woodhull

JOHN WOODHULL, A.B., D.D. Yale 1798, Presbyterian clergyman and educator, younger brother of William Woodhull (A.B. 1763), was born in Miller's Place, Suffolk County, New York, on January 26, 1744, the second of ten children of Elizabeth Smith and John Woodhull. The father descended from an established Long Island family, and was in his own right a prominent landholder, judge and Presbyterian layman. The younger John attended the grammar school in Orange, New Jersey, run by his maternal uncle Caleb Smith (Yale 1743), the College's first tutor and later a trustee. When John went to Nassau Hall in 1762, he was swept up in a student revival, made a confession of faith to the president and later joined the Well-Meaning Club. After graduation he spent two years in theological training with John Blair at Fagg's Manor, Pennsylvania, and received his license from the New Castle Presbytery on August 10, 1768. In his subsequent ministry, Woodhull became noted for persuasive speaking, strict habits of punctuality, and what in later years he called "abundant labors for Christ." When called by the Leacock congregation in Lancaster, Pennsylvania, and ordained by the New Castle Presbytery on August 1, 1770, Woodhull's acceptance sermon described the means to self-"perfection." Ministers must reject indolence, vanity and the pleasures of the senses, demanding, in turn, that the world be similarly converted. Shortly after being installed, Woodhull married Sarah Spafford, stepdaughter of the famous revivalist Gilbert Tennent, on May 28, 1772. Setting up residence on a 130-acre farm named Harmony Hall, the Woodhulls began to raise four of six children who survived infancy. Two sons were named after the Tennents, Gilbert and William, while another, George Spafford (A.B. 1790) became a minister and trustee of the College.

The Revolution awakened John's deepest sympathies. Early in the war, he called for a state militia to purge the land of an English enemy "more cruel than the savages." He then served as a chaplain in the 5th Lancaster Battalion, a unit that included men from his church. In let-

John Woodhull, A.B. 1766
BY EDWARD LUDLOW MOONEY

ters to his wife in the summer of 1778 he described preaching to the soldiers before the battles of Long Island and Monmouth, as well as his fervent prayers that "God may grant us victory." At the end of his military service in 1779, he accepted the pastorate of the Old Tennent Church in Freehold, Monmouth County, New Jersey, succeeding William Tennent II. In a Thanksgiving sermon of 1789, Woodhull hailed the victory over England and the new federal constitution as evidence that the nation was God's chosen Israel. Just when tyranny threatened to overwhelm the world's last repository of true religion, Washington had become, like Moses and Joshua, God's agent in bringing on the "latter days." Yet though "RIGHTEOUSNESS EXALTETH A NATION" with prosperity and happiness, America could still be forsaken, if her people chose the "forbidden way" of vice.

During this period, Woodhull established a grammar school in Freehold, New Jersey. In 1780 he became a trustee of the College. He served as vice president of the Board of Trustees from 1821 to 1824. Woodhull also took an active part in the administrative affairs of the church. In 1788 he moderated the last Synod of New York and Pennsylvania, and also the new General Assembly in 1791. When he died on November 24, 1824, he left a sizable estate to his wife and children.

SOURCES: Sketch: M. G. Woodhull, *Woodhull Genealogy* (1904), 128-32; general character and funeral sermon: Isaac Brown, "A Sermon Preached at Freehold, Nov. 25, 1825, on the Death of Reverend John Woodhull," MS, PPPrHi; ordination sermon: John Woodhull, "An Ordination Sermon," *The New Jersey Preacher*, ed. G. Woodhull, I. V. Brown (1813), 54-60; Lancaster estate and tombstone: W. Buyers, "The Reverend John Woodhull," *Papers Read Before the Lancaster County Hist. Soc.*, 43 (1939), 131-36; Revolutionary War sermon: John Woodhull, "Friends and Countrymen," MS, PPPrHi; letters from the war: John Woodhull to Sarah Woodhull, Aug. through Sept., MSS, NjP; sermon of 1779: John Woodhull, *Sermon on the Day of Public Thanksgiving* (1790); financial condition at death: H. B. Woodhull, "A Sketch of John Woodhull," MS, NjP; will: MS, N.J. State Lib., Trenton.

PUBLICATIONS: STE

MSS: NjP, PPPrHi   LLM

Joseph Woodman

JOSEPH WOODMAN, A.B., Congregational clergyman, was born on August 22, 1748, at West Newbury, Essex County, Massachusetts, the son of Anna and John Woodman, a prosperous shipowner, landholder, and former soldier. A few years after graduation, on March 8, 1771, Woodman married Mrs. Esther Whittemore Hall, a young widow. Of this marriage eleven children were born. Described by contemporaries as a man of "commanding personal presence and dignified bearing," Woodman was called to the pulpit of the First Congregational Church in Sanbornton, New Hampshire. His annual salary of $200 included $80 worth of labor and the rights to the town's two-acre parsonage lot. Ordained on November 13, 1771, Woodman assisted in building both his home and Sanbornton's first meetinghouse. During the next thirty-five years, Woodman regularly attended to the duties of his office.

Like the majority of his fellow-townsmen, Woodman was an active Whig, dedicated to resisting the encroachment of British "tyranny." He was found participating in a county meeting of January 17, 1775. On July 3, 1776, he was the first citizen of the town to sign a petition demanding that "all men notoriously disaffected to the cause of America" be disarmed and pledging support to the struggle against royal authority. Shortly thereafter he enlisted as a chaplain in the militia, serving for a little over a year. Thereafter, the sacrifices he made for the cause included a sizable cut in salary for the duration of the conflict. With the coming of peace, Woodman rejected proposed changes in the state constitution because it failed to make sufficient provision for the support of the church.

Seeing in the American nation, rather than in any one church, the repository of Christian "order and virtue," Woodman militantly advocated the nation's defense against internal and external enemies. Speaking before a military society at Concord, New Hampshire, on August 19, 1794, he expressed sympathy with the embattled French Republic in its war with monarchical and "popish" foes, and depicted America as the world's asylum for the oppressed. Its ultimate hope— the coming of the millennium—depended upon the prospect that the members of a citizen army would purge their hearts of "vice, immorality and profanity." Timely appeals of this sort made Woodman a popular speaker, as evidenced by his addressing in Concord on November 7, 1803 an assemblage composed of the governor, members of the house of representatives and senate.

Despite Woodman's preaching in behalf of a harmonious society, his last years were filled with discord within his own congregation. In 1803, after an epidemic disease had reduced his capacity to fulfill his duties, the town declared that it wanted to terminate his contract and sell the parsonage land. Woodman refused to agree. Only when the church was closed for most of 1806 did he grudgingly yield to the town's demands. Explaining that the present conflict gave him "reason to lament the little success which has attended my ministry," he agreed to retire rather than have the parish divided and exposed to ministers without the "proper credentials." On September 28, 1807, Woodman died and was buried in the churchyard. Shortly thereafter the parsonage land was auctioned off to the highest bidder.

Sources: Family background: *Vital Records of Newbury* (1911), I, 554; J. J. Curier, *Old Newbury* (1896), 592; *Early Coastwise and Foreign Shipping of Salem* (1927), vols. 63, 62; church career, revolutionary and political activities, controversy in Sanbornton, family: M. T. Runnels, *Hist. of Sanbornton* (1882), I-II; sermon on religious tolerance: Woodman: *A Sermon on Christian Candour* (1792), 1-15; sermon on defense: Woodman, *A Discourse Delivered by the Particular Desire of the Military Society* (1794), 1-25.

Publications: STE & Sh-Sh #s 1680, 3584, 5611.   LLM

CLASS OF 1767

Isaac Avery

Francis Barber, A.B.

Zephaniah Briggs

Samuel Cunningham, A.B.

Francis Curtis, A.B.

Richard Devens, A.B.

Jacob I. Hasbrouck, A.B.

Elias Jones, A.B.

Asarelah Morse

Nathaniel Ramsay, A.B.

William Schenck, A.B.

Samuel Witham Stockton, A.B.

Josiah Stoddard, A.B.

Hugh Vance, A.B.

Isaac Avery

ISAAC AVERY, Anglican clergyman and public official, the younger brother of Waightstill Avery (A.B. 1766), was born October 27, 1743, at Groton, Connecticut, the eleventh child of Humphrey and Jerusha Morgan Avery. Evidence of his attendance at the College is slight but convincing. He is listed among the "sub-graduate" members of the Cliosophic Society under the year 1765, which is to say that he presumably belonged to its forerunner, the Well-Meaning Club. Even more persuasive is the fact that, when he was ordained a priest by the bishop of London on October 18, 1769, he was described as "Isaac Avery of the College of New Jersey." The University has no record of the time of his entrance or of the award of a degree to him.

His career as a clergyman may have been as short as apparently was his stay in college. The record of his ordination indicates an assignment in Virginia, where he has been listed as rector of Hungars Parish, Northampton County, in 1769. The parish had another rector by 1772. A list of carriage owners in that county for 1776 is headed by the Reverend Isaac Avery, and in May 1778 his right to a seat in the House of Delegates was challenged because of the provision in the state's constitution prohibiting the election to either House of Assembly of "ministers of the Gospel of every denomination." In the following October, the House concluded that he was not a minister of the Church of England and so was eligible for his seat.

That Avery resided on the Eastern Shore of Virginia before his ordination is indicated by his marriage to Esther, widow of Thomas Preeson, on May 4, 1768. His wife was still living in 1779, but no evidence of children born to this marriage has been found. He was married a second time on June 7, 1785, to Margaret Stringer, daughter of Hillary Stringer, member of one of the county's older families. At least two sons and two daughters were born to this union. Through his marriages, Avery was aided in acquiring a number of properties, enough to make him a substantial resident of the county without marking him as a man of true wealth.

His prompt and continuing identification with the Whig cause is evident from his membership in county committees as early as December 1774, his appointment as naval officer for the Northampton district in 1777, and his elevation to the rank of colonel in the militia and the office of the county lieutenant in 1778, this last a position he resigned in March 1781. He became sheriff in 1787, and more than once sat in the General Assembly. That he had gained some standing in state politics is indicated by the support he received in 1789 for election, without success, to the first U.S. Congress.

Like other clergymen, Avery may have taught school at times. In any case, his interest in education is attested by the fact that he was one of the trustees to whom the General Assembly in 1786 granted a charter for the establishment of an academy in Northampton County. He thus became one of the founders of Margaret Academy, which finally opened its doors in 1807. A real estate transaction indicates that he was still living in 1818; another that he was dead by 1822.

SOURCES: See Waightstill Avery; geneal. of family connections, PUA; Whig-Clio General Cat.; R. T. Whitelaw, *Virginia's Eastern Shore* (1951); Tyler's *Quarterly*, 1 (1919-20), 193; *VMHB*, 14 (1906-7), 54; 26 (1918), 156; 30 (1922), 288; *WMQ*, 5 (1896-97), 246; 6 (1897-98); 26 (1917-18), 75; 7 (1927), 260; *Journal* Va. C. of State, I, 356, II, 91, 213, IV, 125; *Jefferson Papers*, v, 153-54; J. H. Gwathmey, *Register of Virginians in the Revolution* (1938), 28; Hening, *Statutes*, XII, 364-65.

WFC

Francis Barber

FRANCIS BARBER, A.B., A.M. 1770, schoolmaster and army officer, was born in Princeton on November 26, 1750, the oldest son of Jane Fraser (Frazer, Frasher) and Patrick Barber. From County Longford, Ireland, probably minor gentry fallen upon hard times, the parents settled in Princeton not long before Francis's birth. He was the first of their children to be born in the New World. By 1758 the father was prosperous enough to make a small donation to the College and in 1762 contributed £5 to the minister's salary. In 1764 he purchased a 200-acre farm near his relations, the Clinton family, in what is now Ulster County, New York, and moved his family there. Left behind at Nassau Hall was young Francis, who seems to have been intended for the church by his parents.

Within four months of his graduation Barber set himself up, in association with Stephen Van Voorhees (A.B. 1765), as a schoolmaster in Hackensack, a place, they advertised, that was "healthy, pleasant and inviting; it abounds with innocent and necessary pleasure and amusement: But, at the same time, youth are very little exposed to vice, or dangerous examples to corrupt their morals." Although Van Voorhees dropped out of the venture in 1769, the school was apparently a success—so much so that the Visitors of the Latin grammar school associated with the First Presbyterian Church in Elizabethtown chose Barber, late in 1771, to succeed Joseph Periam (A.B. 1762) as master.

Again Barber met with success in teaching. Among his best pupils

Francis Barber, A.B. 1767

was young Alexander Hamilton, whom he prepared for King's College in less than a year. Barber fit well into the Whig-Presbyterian circles of Elizabethtown. Within a year after taking up his post there, in January 1773, he married Mary Ogden, one of the twenty-two children of Robert Ogden, a member of his board of visitors. It was a short marriage, for Mary was dead by October. Barber left town for a time, but by March 1774 was back teaching school.

Barber followed his Whig relatives in opposition to the Crown: January 1776 saw him a lieutenant in a local militia unit. Two weeks later he was commissioned a major in Colonel Elias Dayton's 3rd New Jersey Battalion. Commanding schoolboys seems to have prepared Barber well for commanding troops. "Major Barber is worth his weight in gold to this continent," Dayton declared by the end of the year.

For the rest of his years the army was the center of Barber's life. The indispensable, always-reliable junior officer, staff and line, he carried out orders effectively and was a model for others. ("I set out for Camp the day after tomorrow. My stay is ended short but I might purchase a longer Stay at too dear a stake. A Character is much easier lost than procured.") He participated in the Trenton-Princeton campaign, served at Brandywine and was wounded at Germantown. In March 1778, he married again. His second wife, Anne ("Nancy") Ogden, was a cousin of his first. Three children were born to the couple, among them George Clinton Barber (A.B. 1796). A few months after his re-marriage Barber was wounded again in the battle of Monmouth. He recovered rapidly. ("My wound is in a very promising situation. The most I apprehend from it is a broken rib. I have not the least sickness, neither has my wound inflammation.") By 1779 he had recovered enough to join General John Sullivan's punitive expedition against the Indians of western New York.

Barber served in several other important engagements during the war. He has long been credited by historians with playing a major role in quelling the mutiny of the New Jersey line in February 1781. His concern with the mutinies is undeniable. Our soldiers, he complained to Elias Dayton in that month, "are exceedingly altered for worse; from being almost the most orderly & subordinate soldiers in the army, they are become a set of drunken and unworthy fellows. The situation of an officer among them is rendered more disagreeable than any other calling in life, even the most menial, can possibly be." However the most recent scholarship on the subject suggests that Barber's role in restoring order to the army was minor at most.

Perhaps the former schoolmaster longed again for the classroom. By now he had a family. "It is my principle and glory to devote my-self to the most important service of my country, but my dear Sir, my circumstances in point of family affairs [go] very illy with this un-dertaking," he wrote to Dayton in April 1781. He missed Nancy: "if you have not the most rich and honorable you have the most fond & faithful husband on earth." He missed his children: "Do they grow well? Is Poll handsome? Can she sit or stand alone? What does George principally talk about. I beg you give me some anecdotes of him & her."

Barber saw more action, leading his men at Yorktown. In April 1782, he joined his regiment at the military encampment at Newburgh, New York, not far from his parents' home. Possibly he had time there to discuss the religious matters that he had often talked about with fellow officers. Some of them had found Barber's views odd. Barber "acknowledges a supreme being," one officer reported in 1776, "that he is the Creator, upholder and universal governor of the universe; and that he not only permits, but orders and directs every incident that happens among men. . . . But why . . . [God] should order and direct sin to enter into the world, thereby making the human race miserable, . . . [Barber] says is best known to . . . [God] for the display of his divine attributes."

Barber was not predestined to enjoy peacetime. Scheduled to take his wife to tea with Martha Washington on February 11, 1783, he was killed on the way back to his quarters to prepare for the visit. "As he passed thro' the Woods," one of Washington's secretaries reported to General von Steuben, "some Soldiers were felling a Tree & did not perceive him—& whether owing to the sudden fright or what I know not, instead of putting spurs to his Horse and pushing on—he attempted to turn back but had not time, the Tree Crushed both him & Horse—his death was instant for he uttered not a groan nor shewed the least sign of life—when the Soldiers who ran to him immediately took him out—thus has an unhappy accident deprived the Army of one of its most excellent Officers—Society of one of its best members —his family (a Wife and three Children) are inexpressibly afflicted —indeed the whole Army are exceedingly affected—there is no man who was so generally beloved."

SOURCES: Most complete sketch: *NYGBR*, 62 (1931), 3-22; see too: *DAB*, and, B. Mitchell, *Alexander Hamilton: Youth to Maturity* (1957), 41-45; Hackensack school: *N.Y. Jour.*, Jan. 14, 1768; Elizabethtown acad.: *N.Y. Gaz.*, Jan. 6, 1772: "character" and "wound" quotations: Barber to Robert Ogden, May 26 and July 10, 1778, MSS, NjP; "soldiers" quotation: Barber to Dayton, Feb. 28, 1781, MS, Gratz Col., PHi; mutinies: C. Van Doren, *Mutiny in January* (1943); "family" quotation: Barber to Dayton, Apr. 10, 1781, MS, Dreer Col., PHi; Barber to "Nancy" Barber, June 16, 1781, MS, Dreer Col., PHi; religion quotation: "Jour. of Lt. Ebenezer Elmer," *NJ-HSP* (1 ser.) 2 (1846-47), 185; acct. of death: *NYGBR*, 62 (1931), 10-11.

MSS: NjHi, NjP, PHi

Zephaniah Briggs

ZEPHANIAH BRIGGS, Congregational clergyman and merchant, was born on December 28, 1742, at Rochester, Massachusetts, the first of the seven children of Thankful Burgess, wife of Cornelius Briggs. In 1765, the father willed a salt meadow to Zephaniah, who sold it the same year. Presumably these funds supported Briggs at Nassau Hall. However, in April 1765, he transferred from Princeton to Harvard. President Finley wrote a letter to President Holyoke of Harvard recommending Briggs, deeming him of "advantageous character." He entered Harvard's sophomore class on April 17, 1765, and received a Samuel Browne scholarship. In his senior year, Briggs participated in the student rebellion of 1766 that erupted seemingly over the quality of butter served in the dining rooms and the expulsion of a fellow student. Briggs was among those who left the chapel early to present the pro-testors' case to the Overseers, but he later signed a letter of apology to the president. The incident did not impair his standing, for he re-ceived his A.B. from Harvard in 1767, then wrote a master's thesis en-titled "Aquatic Animals are as Liable to Disease as Land Animals."

Starting in 1770 Briggs began a period of itinerant preaching. He supplied several Congregational churches in Connecticut and Mas-sachusetts, among them Great Barrington and Scarborough, but he ap-parently did not receive an acceptable offer. In 1772, he settled as a merchant in Northborough, Middlesex County, Massachusetts. There he married Margaret, daughter of Thomas Lambert of Reading. The Briggses were known for their hospitality; some of the town's most prosperous families dined at their home. When the local minister was rendered homeless by a fire in 1780, his family moved in with the Briggses. Briggs died childless in 1782.

SOURCES: Parentage: E. A. Hannibal, *John Briggs of Sandwich, Mass.* (1962), 10, 34, 35; sketch: *Sibley's Harvard Graduates*, XVI, 448-49; butter rebellion: *Pub. Col. Soc. Mass.*, 10 (1905), 54-57; career in Northborough: J. C. Kent, *Northborough History* (1921), 44, 45.

LLM

Samuel Cunningham

SAMUEL CUNNINGHAM, A.B., A.M. 1774, bore a name that was common in eighteenth-century America. Samuel Cunninghams contemporary with the College's alumnus have been found in almost every colony in North America. However, the only certain fact concerning the graduate is that when he received his A.M. in 1774 he was described as "of New-Jersey." No Samuel Cunninghams have been found in New Jersey records of the period. Cunningham's death was never noted in the College's catalogues.

SOURCES: A.M.: *Pa. Journal*, Oct. 12, 1774.

Francis Curtis

FRANCIS CURTIS, A.B., has not been identified in an intensive genealog-ical search. Men of that name have been found in Massachusetts, Con-necticut, New Jersey, Pennsylvania, and South Carolina, but none can be connected with any assurance to the College. Curtis was listed as living in the College's catalogue of 1804 and as dead in the next catalogue published in 1808.

Richard Devens

RICHARD DEVENS, A.B., A.M. 1771, college tutor, was born at Charlestown, Massachusetts on October 23, 1749, the son of Mary Townsend and her husband, Richard Devens, a prosperous merchant who later played a prominent part during the Revolution in Massachusetts. Devens "early discovered a taste for books, and a genius for the sciences," a memorialist later recalled. "While at the publick school in his native town, so singular was his progress in the rudiments of knowledge there taught, that he attracted the particular notice of his master; who often, and with earnestness, urged his affectionate father to give him a collegiate education. His father consented, and . . . [Devens] accordingly, having passed through the usual preparatory studies, was admitted a member of the college at Princetown, in New-Jersey, in the year 1764." Devens did extremely well at the College. As the highest ranking scholar in the class, he served as Latin Salutatorian at his commencement.

Shortly after graduation Devens joined the staff of the Latin grammar school conducted in association with the Presbyterian church in Elizabethtown, New Jersey. The school's Visitors advertised that Devens had been hired "in order to instruct Youth in the several Branches of the Mathematicks, both theoretical and practical, without Detriment to the Students in the Languages." The College's trustees thought so well of Devens that in 1770 he was appointed tutor in mathematics and returned to Princeton. In October 1772 the teaching of an elective course in Hebrew to pre-divinity students was added to to his duties. But over the succeeding months Devens became ill and in April 1773 resigned his post. He had recovered by the following fall, when William Bradford (A.B. 1772) informed James Madison (A.B. 1771) that after resigning his tutorship Devens "had retired to New England. There he spent the summer in galloping pegasus [i.e., in writing poetry] and publishing poems. He has now taken refuge again in the arms of his Alma Mater & was elected Tutor." It was probably during this summer that Devens wrote his poem *A Paraphrase on Some Parts of the Book of Job*, which was later published.

Although Devens's return to the College as a tutor lasted for only eight months, it was most likely then that he composed and delivered two addresses to the College's divinity students. Both emphasize the main impulse that had led to the College's founding in 1746—the New Light evangelists' insistence on the necessity of a converted ministry. Early in the spring of 1774 Devens suffered a nervous breakdown, and the trustees found it necessary to dismiss him. Devens was sent back to Charlestown. He never recovered. "From that time to the present" a contemporary wrote in 1795, "he has continued an affecting, living monument to parents and near connexions, to be cautious how they place their affection too ardently on a promising child or brother, or suffer their hopes to be too much elevated, when brilliant talents appear to tempt them. Suddenly, as in this instance, may their complacent love be changed into affectionate pity, and their fairest prospects succeeded with hopeless disappointment." Devens died in Charlestown in 1835.

SOURCES: Richard Devens File, PUA; brief biog., probably by a relative, from which quotations are drawn: "Preface," to Devens, *A Paraphrase on Some Parts of the Book of Job* (1795), iii-v; Elizabethtown school: *N.Y. Mercury*, Dec. 21, 1767 (supplement); CNJ: MS Trustees' Minutes, I, entries for Oct. 2, 1772; Apr. 21 and Oct. 1, 1773; and for Apr. 19, 1774; Bradford to Madison, Nov. 5, 1773, *Madison Papers*, I, 98.

PUBLICATIONS: See above and STE

Jacob I. Hasbrouck

JACOB I. HASBROUCK, A.B., farmer, was born in Marbleton Township, Ulster County, New York, on February 19, 1749, the son of Mary Bruyn, wife of Isaac Hasbrouck. Jacob's great-grandfather, Jean Hasbrouck, a Huguenot, emigrated from his native France to America in 1672. Jean and his brother Abraham were among the earliest settlers in what became Ulster County, New York. The family they founded there became one of the most prominent in the state. Jacob was one of several of their descendants to attend the College.

Jacob may have been tutored for the College by Henricus Frelinghuysen, brother of Jacobus Frelinghuysen (A.B. 1750). On May 27 of the year after graduation Hasbrouck married Sarah DuBois of New Paltz and established a home near Stone Ridge in Marbleton Township. There he and his wife raised at least twelve children, all but two of them sons. Hasbrouck spent the bulk of his time tending his father's extensive lands in Ulster County. As the eldest son, he apparently inherited most of them upon his father's death, intestate, in 1789. Indicative of Jacob's substantial responsibilities for those lands is the contention of a family historian that, contrary to an earlier account, Jacob probably remained home during the Revolution to tend them rather than joining his four younger brothers in combat.

The Hasbrouck family had been active in public affairs since its arrival in America, and Jacob carried on that tradition, if more modestly than some of his relations. He was a signer of New York State's Articles of Association and was probably the Jacob Hasbrouck who served as an Ulster County road commissioner in the early 1770s.

Hasbrouck died on June 21, 1818. His will, drawn up that same day, was probated on September 15, 1818. Hasbrouck left his wife most of his domestic goods and divided his lands and bonds among his children.

SOURCES: Vital data: Jacob Hasbrouck File, PUA; *NYGBR*, 73 (1942), 287-88; R. LeFevre, *Hist. of New Paltz, N.Y.* (1903), 368-69, 400, 402-404; *Ulster Co., N.Y., Wills* (1906), I, 170-71, and II, 181-82; *Rec. Road Commissioners of Ulster Co.* (1940), II, 10, 12, 43.

HS

Elias Jones

ELIAS JONES, A.B., was a Congregational clergyman. His parentage has not been discovered. At College he joined the Well-Meaning Society, forerunner of the Cliosophic Society. Immediately after graduation, in October 1767, Jones was hired by James Beekman, a wealthy New York City merchant, to succeed Isaac Skillman (A.B. 1766) as tutor to Beekman's sons William (A.B. 1773), Abraham (Class of 1774), and James (Class of 1776) at a salary of £30 per year. Jones remained with the Beekmans until the fall of 1769, when the boys went off to Princeton. He was also studying for the ministry, for at some time after he left New York he became affiliated with the Congregational church in Halifax, Nova Scotia.

Described as a "young man of prepossessing manner and address and fine talents for the pulpit," in 1777 Jones was among the several candidates for the pulpit at the Congregational church in Taunton, Bristol County, Massachusetts. The town was exceedingly careful in its choice, since, of its last two ministers, one had been dismissed in 1768 for drunkenness, while the other, Caleb Barnum (A.B. 1757), had recently died. With the concurrence of the town meeting, the pastors of seven neighboring churches examined Jones's qualifications. One of his powerful sponsors was Ezra Stiles, shortly to become president of Yale, who spoke in behalf of the young man. The Taunton Council called Jones on April 15 and ordained him on October 22, 1777.

Two years later, Jones "fell into error," most likely moral delin-
quency, and was dismissed from his pulpit. In his farewell sermon,
Jones quoted the biblical psalm proclaiming "Have pity, Lord, forgive;
Let a repenting sinner live." Nothing can be discerned of Jones until
October 15, 1788, when he became grammar master in a Kentucky
school recently created by the merger of the Transylvania Seminary
and the Lexington Grammar School. Yet because he attracted only a
few students, on October 15, 1789, the trustees dismissed him. Nothing more has been discovered of his life.

SOURCES: P. L. White, *The Beekmans of N.Y.* (1956), 480, 482; S. H. Emery, *The
Ministry of Taunton* (1853), II, 30-33; Stiles's sponsorship: *Literary Diary*, II, 145,
221; schoolteaching: *PMHB*, 35 (1911), 351.

LLM

Asarelah Morse

ASARELAH MORSE, a Congregational clergyman, was born in Falmouth,
Barnstable County, Massachusettes, on January 16, 1745, the son of
Thankful Crocker and Theodore Morse, a sea captain. After spending
three years at the College, Morse and a fellow student, Samuel Parker
(Class of 1768), requested admission to Harvard in October 1766.
They gave no reason, but their removal was probably due to the death
of President Finley. They brought with them recommendations from
acting College President William Tennent II but were nevertheless
asked to take Harvard's entrance examinations. Parker temporarily
refused but Morse, "after some demur," agreed to stand for admission
as a senior Sophister. "Upon which," continue the Harvard Faculty
Records, "we proceeded to Examine him in Horace, Tully, Xenophons
Cycopaedia, Logick and the use of the Globes, but as to the Hebrew,
he told us, That in their College none were obliged to learn it, and
none did attend those Instructions but such as chose to do it, and that
having no Inclination to it he had never attended those Instructions.
And having examin'd him after some considerable Debate upon, it
was voted, That he shou'd be admitted."

Morse received both his A.B. and his A.M. from Harvard in 1767.
After graduation Morse preached in Douglas and Marlborough, Massachusetts until late in 1770, when he accepted a call from the united
Congregational Churches of Annapolis and Granville, Nova Scotia.
On July 13, 1771, following several months of trial preaching, he was
ordained as their first joint pastor. The two parishes covered a very
large territory, and Morse came near to ruining his health in his efforts
to minister to both. However, a memorialist later remembered him as

maintaining "uniform display of christian graces and ministerial qualifications." When the congregations were finally separated Morse remained with Granville.

On July 4, 1774, Morse married Hepzibah Hall of Yarmouth, Massachusetts. The couple had a son and three daughters. The Reverend
Jacob Bailey (Harvard 1755), the Anglican missionary at Annapolis,
called Hepzibah a woman of "good sense, modesty, and discretion."
He also reported that she was far more tolerant of persons of other denominations than her husband, whom Bailey, perhaps in a fit of theological pique, called "not very remarkable for wisdom or prudence."

The Revolution posed a number of dilemmas for Morse and his
parishioners. Most of them were native Americans and "Americans in
political sentiment and feeling" as well. They therefore felt less and
less comfortable as more and more fellow patriots left Nova Scotia for
native soil and as more and more Loyalists left the rebellious colonies
for Nova Scotia. By the end of the Revolution most of Morse's congregation also wished to return home, and he consequently secured a dismission in November 1783.

After a brief stay in Brewster, Massachusetts, Morse moved to Tisbury, Martha's Vineyard, Massachusetts, in July 1784. Tisbury's Congregational church eagerly sought his services, and in return for an
annual salary of £170 and use of the parsonage, on October 22, 1784,
he accepted its call. He was installed on December 1 and remained at
Tisbury until his retirement.

In Tisbury Morse faced a congregation that was on the verge of
schism. He devoted himself and his health to preventing it. But in 1799,
after prolonged debate over the division of the parish into two units,
Morse decided to resign his pulpit and move to the mainland. He settled
his family near Wayland, Massachusetts, where he died on April 25,
1803.

SOURCES: Vital data: Asarelah Morse File, PUA; *Sibley's Harvard Graduates*, XVI,
509-11; Nova Scotia pastorate: W. A. Calnek, *Hist. of Cty. of Annapolis, N.S.* (1897),
302, 554; A. W. Savary, *Supplement Hist. of Cty. of Annapolis* (1913), 35; "uniform
display": Boston *Columbian Centinel*, May 11, 1803, 1; Jacob Bailey quotation:
Sibley, 510; "Americans in political sentiment": *Centinel*, May 11, 1803, 2; Tisbury
pastorate: C. E. Banks, "Annals of Tisbury," *Hist. of Martha's Vineyard* (1966), II,
35-6.

HS

Nathaniel Ramsay

NATHANIEL RAMSAY, A.B., A.M. 1771, lawyer, soldier, and public official, was born on May 1, 1741, in East Drumore Township, Lancas-

ter County, Pennsylvania, the second son of Jane Montgomery and her husband, James Ramsay, a farmer and emigrant from Ireland. Nathaniel was preceded at the College by his older brother William (A.B. 1754), who became a Presbyterian clergyman, and by his younger brother David (A.B. 1765), who became a physician and a noted historian of the Revolution.

After graduation Ramsay read law and on March 14, 1771, was admitted to practice in Cecil County, Maryland. In the same year he married Margaret Jane ("Jenny") Peale, widow of a Baltimore merchant and a sister of the painter Charles Willson Peale. Ramsay's early legal practice was probably modest, for when he placed an order for some law texts with an Annapolis bookseller in 1774 he frugally specified that they should be, if possible, second-hand copies. Still, by 1775 Ramsay was well-enough known to be elected one of the five Cecil County delegates to a Maryland convention called to consider British policies. There Ramsay served on a committee concerned with encouraging domestic manufactures and on one specifically involved with the

Nathaniel Ramsay, A.B. 1767
BY CHARLES WILLSON PEALE

manufacture of saltpetre. On July 26 he signed the Proclamation of the Freemen of Maryland protesting British measures. Visiting Ramsay in November 1775, his brother-in-law Peale found him talking of raising a military company. On January 2, 1776, Ramsay was elected captain of a Maryland battalion that on January 14 became part of Smallwood's Maryland Regiment. The regiment in turn became part of the Continental army in July and saw its first action and tasted defeat at the battle of Long Island in August.

Back in Baltimore by the winter, Ramsay joined a group of zealous patriots known as the Whig Club, which caused a great stir by its haphazard persecution of suspected Loyalists. Appointed a lieutenant colonel in the Maryland regulars in March 1777, Ramsay saw action at Chadd's Ford. Accompanied by his wife, he joined Washington's forces and spent the winter of 1777–1778 in a cozy log hut at Valley Forge. The Ramsays' quarters became something of a social center for other officers. Early in the summer of 1778 Ramsay and his men set off in pursuit of the British forces evacuating Philadelphia. When the American and British forces met in New Jersey at the battle of Monmouth on June 28, Ramsay performed heroically, helping to stem the British advance caused by General Charles Lee's "retreat." Ramsay's family had lived in fear that his height (6 feet 3 inches) would make him a prime target for the enemy. Their fears were realized at Monmouth. Severely wounded in the melee, he was captured by the enemy. Placed on parole, Ramsay was taken to Princeton, where he was nursed by the Sergeant family.

Now a British prisoner, Ramsay was sent to New York City after his recovery and then to Long Island along with other captured officers of the Maryland line. His captivity was not harsh; he was joined in New York by his wife. Despite efforts by the American authorities and a continuing campaign waged by Charles Peale, Ramsay was not released until December 1780.

Although Ramsay volunteered for further service after his release, his old unit was far away. On leaving New York the Ramsays went to Philadelphia, where they lingered for the summer, visiting with Peale. The family was rising in the world; Nathaniel's father was serving as a member of the Pennsylvania Assembly from York. Ramsay was declared supernumerary on July 1, 1781, and granted half-pay by Congress. By 1783 the Ramsays had settled themselves in a handsome house in Baltimore. Ramsay became extremely active in the affairs, state and national, of the Society of the Cincinnati, a hereditary association of former army officers that became the object of considerable public controversy. In 1785 Ramsay was elected to the Maryland legis-

lature from Cecil County. On November 6, 1785, his state sent him as
its representative to the Continental Congress. There he joined his
younger brother David, who was a representative from South Carolina. Reelected, his service in Congress extended through June 1787.

Ramsay supported the new federal constitution and in 1789 made
a bid to run as a Federalist for the new Congress. Although he had
a good deal of local support, he was bumped from the ticket by Maryland's leading Federalists and resigned from the House of Delegates.
Ramsay himself admitted that he was not sufficiently well-known
throughout the state and that a game leg would preclude extensive
campaigning. Compensation came when President Washington appointed him United States marshal for Maryland. In December 1794,
he was named naval officer for the District of Baltimore, a post he held
under Presidents Washington and Adams and, although a Federalist,
under Jefferson, Madison and Monroe as well.

Ramsay's activities were not limited to law and public service. On
settling in Baltimore after the Revolution he had become an agent
for confiscated Loyalist estates and is said to have profited substantially
from the post. In March 1786, he paid £1,750 for an estate at Carpenter Point (otherwise "Carpoint") on the eastern side of Chesapeake
Bay in Cecil County a few miles south of the mouth of the Susquehanna. In 1790 he purchased another property, 400-acre Clay Fall, for
£580. The Carpoint place was a fishery rich in shad and herring and
was also famous for its ducks. Ramsay's operation there must have
been extensive, for in the federal census of 1790 he was recorded as the
owner of twenty-six slaves. (Since, as federal marshal Ramsay himself
was responsible for the census, the number was probably accurate.)
The childless Ramsays spent part of the year in Baltimore and part
of the year at Carpoint, which Ramsay loved. However pleasant, the
place was low and swampy, and early in 1788 Jenny Ramsay fell ill
and died. About 1790 Ramsay married Charlotte Hall. As became a
lawyer and former legislator, he named his short-lived first son Mon-
tesquieu. Four more children, three of whom lived to maturity, were
born to the couple.

Ramsay's death on October 23, 1817, was the occasion for handsome tributes in Maryland newspapers to the last man in Baltimore
to wear a cocked hat. "A noble heart and a great mind—an enlarged
mind—such as few men possess," Charles Peale noted on hearing the
news. In his will Ramsay divided his various properties among his
wife, children and grandchildren, remembering "nieces in Charlestown, South Carolina, daughters of my late unfortunate brother, Dr.

Ramsay." To a daughter he left his pew in Baltimore's First Presbyterian Church, in whose graveyard he was buried.

SOURCES: Sketches: *DAB*; G. Johnston, *Hist. of Cecil County, Md.* (1881), 321-22,
537-56; *Md. Hist. Fund Pubs.*, 24 (1887), 45-60; E. Boyle, *Biogr. Sketches of Distinguished Marylanders* (1877), 140-45; law books: *MHM*, 34 (1939), 136; first
wife, relations with Peales: C. C. Sellers, *Charles Willson Peale* (1969); Monmouth,
capture, U.S. marshall: *Hamilton Papers*, I, II, XIII, XV; Washington, *Writings*, XV,
XVIII, XIX, XX; S. S. Smith, *Battle of Monmouth* (1964), 19; Whig Club: *MHM*, 36
(1941), 139-49; Cont. Congr.: *JCC*, XXX-XXXII; *LMCC*, VIII; campaign of 1788-89:
MHM, 57 (1962), 207; ibid., 63 (1968), 16; children: W. W. Bronson, *Account . . .
of the Descendants of Col. Thomas White, of Md.* (1879), 136; slaves: *U.S. Census
of 1790, Md.*, 46; obituary: *Md. Gaz.*, Nov. 6, 1817; will: A. W. Burns, *Md. Wills:
Baltimore County Book No. 10* (n.d.), 80.

Mss: MdHi

William Schenck

WILLIAM SCHENCK, A.B., Presbyterian and Dutch Reformed clergyman,
was born on October 13, 1740, in Allentown, Monmouth County, New
Jersey, the seventh of the eight children of Mary Couwenhoven and her
husband, Koert Schenck. The father, a third-generation colonial, was a
prosperous landholder and elder in the Dutch Reformed church, where
William was baptized. After graduation from the College, the younger
Schenck studied theology with the trustee of the College, William Tennent II, in Freehold, Monmouth County, New Jersey. There on March
7, 1768, he married Tennent's granddaughter Anna, whose father, Robert Cumming, was the sheriff of Monmouth County. The couple had
nine children, four daughters and five sons. Licensed by the New
Brunswick Presbytery in 1771, Schenck became known as an "energetic" and "dignified" evangelical preacher. When called by the Allentown Presbyterian church, Schenck returned to his hometown and was
ordained there by the Presbytery of New Brunswick in 1772. With the
coming of the Revolution, Schenck supported the Whig cause, most
likely serving for a brief period as a chaplain in the Continental army.
Driven from their home by the British in 1777, the family fled to
safety in Pennsylvania.

In that year, Schenck accepted a new pastorate in the Dutch Reformed church at Southampton, Bucks County, Pennsylvania, at a
salary of approximately £100 yearly. Here William Tennent's widow
joined them in their home, where she died in 1780. Shortly thereafter, Schenck resigned from his Southampton ministry and was installed on May 3, 1780, at the Pittsgrove Presbyterian Church in Salem

County, New Jersey. Six years later, he went to Ballston, a recently chartered town in New York. As the minister of the Ballston Presbyterian Church, Schenck preached in those surrounding communities without churches of their own. Apparently moderately prosperous, he owned one slave in 1790. In 1793, Schenck once again moved, this time to a Presbyterian church in Huntington, Suffolk County, New York, where his family was noted for its Federalist political sympathies. Although Huntington might have appeared to have been his last parish, Schenck responded to the call of his son William, a land developer, militia general, and politician, to join him on a new frontier. So in 1817, the seventy-year-old minister took his family to Franklin County, Ohio. Appropriate to a new settlement, Schenck established a "Union" church, which welcomed all peoples, embraced all denominations, and avoided doctrinal niceties. Schenck died on September 1, 1822, and was buried in Franklin.

SOURCES: Family background: *NYGBR*, 81 (1950), 172; baptism: *NJGM*, 24 (1949), 48; Tennent relationship: *PMHB*, (1882), VI, 374, VII, 115; church career, salary, Revolutionary War activities: *Rec. Pres. Church*, 411, 425; MS Biography of William Schenck, n.d., Schenck File, PUA; Alexander Schenck, *Reverend William Schenck, His Ancestry and Descendants* (1883), 40-55; slave ownership: *U.S. Census of 1790*, N.Y., 18; Ohio venture, Federalist sympathies: *Ohio State Arch. and Hist. Quart.*, 47 (1938), 309, 363-66, 371.

LLM

Samuel Witham Stockton

SAMUEL WITHAM STOCKTON, A.B., A.M. 1770, lawyer and public official, was born in Princeton, New Jersey, on February 4, 1751, the youngest son of Abigail Phillips and Judge John Stockton, a well-to-do landowner, public official, and early patron of the College. Stockton's eldest brother, Richard, was a member of the College's first graduating class. Where Samuel prepared for the College has not been discovered, but it probably was at the grammar school connected with Nassau Hall.

After graduation Stockton studied law, most likely with his brother Richard. A Philadelphia newspaper reported that on receiving his A.M. in 1770 Stockton "delivered an English Oration on 'Ambition'; in which he took Occasion to introduce a particularly complimentary Address to Governor *Franklin*, who was pleased to honour the Commencement with his presence." Licensed to practice law in New Jersey in September 1772, Stockton soon came to feel that changing affairs in the province offered little scope for his own ambitions. He decided to make a trip to England. "The probability of there being little or no business in the law way in this Country for a good while & the advice & approbation of my brother together with the prospect of greater improvement has determined me," he explained on September 1, 1775, to his brother-in-law, Elisha Boudinot, whom he tried to persuade to accompany him. Boudinot remained at home.

Stockton's arrival in England did not come at a propitious moment. Within a few months his brother Richard had signed the Declaration of Independence. Precisely what Stockton did in England cannot now be determined, but somewhat over two years after his arrival there he explained that he had "given the best of my small services to turn the mad & destructive current of ministerial measures pursued against my country, by contradictory false representations given by interested tools, & dinning in the ears of [the] ministry the injustice & fatality of their plans."

By October 1778, when Stockton wrote this letter, he had been in Germany for six months. In May 1777 Congress had appointed William Lee of Virginia, previously sheriff and alderman of London and a business partner of Stephen Sayre (A.B. 1757), as American commissioner to the courts of Prussia and Austria. Lee shortly made Stockton his secretary. The post was not an enviable one. Neither Prussia nor Austria was disposed to recognize the United States, and Lee also became entangled in the quarrel between the American commissioners to France, Silas Deane and Benjamin Franklin. Lee's one accomplishment was the negotiation of a secret treaty of commerce between the United States and Holland. Though not ratified by either party, the treaty eventually became the *causus belli* for hostilities between Britain and Holland.

Early in 1779 Lee dispatched Stockton back to America with a copy of the treaty and complaints that he did not have money enough to afford a secretary. Declaring that he had already given Stockton 3,732 livres, he recommended that Congress pay Stockton the balance due him. "Justice calls upon me to say," Lee wrote, "that he merits consideration and esteem for his zeal and readiness to serve his country, whenever it was in his power, and therefore I am sure Congress will render him ample retribution."

Stockton arrived in Boston in December 1779. A New Jersey newspaper proudly reported that it was "happy to hear from several quarters that he has uniformly distinguished himself in different parts of Europe as a firm and zealous Friend to the Liberties of his Country, we therefore presume his own State will claim the advantages of his future services." After completing his business with Congress, Stockton settled in Trenton and began a long career that would make him one of the more distinguished citizens of the town. In 1781 he became clerk of Hunterdon County and secretary of the New-Jersey Society for Promoting Agriculture, Commerce and Arts. His brother-in-law Elias Boudinot became president of the Continental Congress and some of the lustre reflected on Stockton. When Congress was threatened by unruly troops in February 1783, Stockton publicly invited it to locate in Trenton. It was probably at about this time that Stockton married Catherine Cox, daughter of a prominent Trenton family. The couple had at least three children, among them John Cox Stockton (A.B. 1804). Besides his legal practice, Stockton was involved with two land companies, the Miami Company and the New Jersey Land Company.

When a New Jersey convention met in Trenton in December 1787 to consider adoption of the new federal constitution, Stockton served as its secretary. Though not a delegate, he warmly supported its ratification and followed with close attention the debates about it in various states. Stockton made constant efforts to obtain public appointments. When William Churchill Houston (A.B. 1768), who had held the lucrative (£1,200 to £1,500 per year) post of clerk to the New Jersey Supreme Court, died in 1788, Stockton lobbied actively but unsuccessfully for the position. ("It is an important post for me, perhaps for my life . . . my duty to a young family induces me to wish for it. . . . I am very conveniently situated for 3 years at least in the house I now live in—having annexed to it the best and largest office for ye publick Records by far of any in this town.") When the new Congress was organized Stockton lobbied with equal vigor and lack of success for the post of clerk to the House of Representatives. Stockton had more success in local affairs. A senior warden of the Trenton lodge of Freemasons in July 1789, by January 1794 he was Grand Master of the organization. He became an alderman of Trenton in 1792 and finally achieved state office in 1794, when he became New Jersey's secretary of state.

Through the early 1790s Stockton fretted about federal assumption of state debts. He favored the policy, but was worried about the justice being done to small creditors. Always involved in the affairs of his far-flung family, during the yellow fever epidemic that swept Philadelphia in 1793 he gave shelter to his niece Julia Stockton Rush, wife of Benjamin Rush (A.B. 1760), and her children.

Stockton died intestate on June 27, 1795. A local historian described the event thus: "While going to Philadelphia in company with his son, in his own carriage, he saw in the neighborhood of Bristol some very fine cherries, and in an effort to get them from the trees, he fell, and so injured his skull that he died in a few days from the effects of it." Stockton's Presbyterian pastor, James Francis Armstrong (A.B. 1773), preached the funeral sermon. His widow later married the Reverend Nathaniel Harris (A.B. 1788).

SOURCES: Full sketch: M. Rubincam, "Samuel Witham Stockton, of N.J.," *NJHSP*, 60 (1942), 98-116; A.M. oration: *Pa. Chronicle*, Oct. 8-15, 1770; trip to England, account of stay: Stockton to Elisha Boudinot, Sept. 1, 1775, and Oct. 26, 1778, MSS, NjP; William Lee: *DAB*; Lee quotation: J. Sparks, ed., *Diplomatic Corresp. of the Am. Rev.* (1829), II, 338; return home quotation: *N.J. Gaz.*, Dec. 8, 1779; Trenton and other local affairs: 5 (2 ser.) *NJA*, 289, 306; land affairs and N.J. clerkship: R. P. McCormick, *Experiment in Independence* (1950), 97-98, 231n, 232n; clerkship quotation: Stockton to Elisha Boudinot, Aug. 15, 1788, MS, NjP; fed. constit.: J. Elliot, ed., *Debates on the Federal Constitution* (1901), I, 320-21, and Stockton to Elisha Boudinot, June 27, 1788, MS, NjP; H. of Reps.: H. Wynkoop to R. Beattie, Apr. 2, 1789, *PMHB*, 38 (1914), 15; Masonry: J. H. Hough, *Origin of Masonry . . . in N.J.* (1870); assumption: Stockton to Elias Boudinot, Mar. 11 and Apr. 26, 1790, MSS, NjP; family: Butterfield, *Rush Letters*, 604, 642; account of death: J. O. Raum, *Hist. of the City of Trenton* (1871), 75.

Mss: NjP

Josiah Stoddard

JOSIAH STODDARD, A.B., A.M. 1770, army officer, was born in Salisbury, Connecticut, on December 2, 1747, the son of Sarah Robbarts and Josiah Stoddard, the fairly prosperous (he left an estate valued at £731) proprietor of an ironworks, town clerk, and sometime deputy to the Connecticut General Assembly. A member of Salisbury's Congregational church, the father was apparently of a religious turn of mind, for an inventory of his estate made shortly after his death listed many books by divines such as Jonathan Edwards, Joseph Bellamy, and Isaac Watts.

Left a saddle and £100 on his father's death in 1764, young Stoddard may have used the money to put himself through the College, where he joined the Well-Meaning Club, forerunner of the Cliosophic Society. After graduation he seems to have used his saddle to good effect, for his friends lost track of him. "Pray what has become of Stoddard?" wrote William Paterson (A.B. 1763) to Dirck Romeyn (A.B. 1765) in August 1770. Wherever he had been, Stoddard was back in Salisbury by August 22, 1774, when he was appointed to the town's Committee of Correspondence. In May of the following year he was one of the participants in the American capture of Ticonderoga. In May 1776, he was commissioned a second lieutenant in Bradley's Connecticut state regiment. When Colonel Elisha Sheldon of Connecticut organized the Second Regiment of Continental Light Dragoons in December 1776, Stoddard put his saddle to use again, becoming a captain in the unit. Stoddard appears occasionally in records of the Revolution, now delivering 500 guineas from Congress to George Washington, now being advised by the general not to reprieve a deserter from his company.

Stoddard's health failed late in 1778. His physicians recommended that he travel to France to recover his health. Stoddard requested furlough from Washington. Since this was the first occasion that a regular officer had asked to leave the United States, Washington referred the matter to Congress, which granted Stoddard leave. Stoddard apparently did not manage to make the voyage, but died unmarried on August 24, 1779. In May, shortly before his death, the Connecticut legislature passed an act forbidding duelling as a direct result of a quarrel between Stoddard and William Nichols (Yale 1762) that had originated in the Ticonderoga campaign of 1775.

SOURCES: Father, Com. of Corresp.: D. W. Patterson, *John Stoddard of Wethersfield Conn.* (1873), 33, 51; mother: Salisbury Vital Records, vol. 7, p. 204, Barbour Col., Conn. State Lib., Hartford; father's will and inventory: MS, Probate Record File, Conn. St. Lib.; Paterson letter: Mills, *Life at Princeton College*, 147; military appointment: *Rec. Col. Conn.*, XV; further mil. career: *Washington Writings*, XII-XIV; duelling: *Rec. State Conn.*, II; Nichols: Dexter, *Yale Biographies*, II, 765.

Hugh Vance

HUGH VANCE, A.B., was a Presbyterian clergyman. No certain information concerning his parentage has been discovered. However, in the 1740s an extensive Vance family, which included a schoolmaster, belonged to one of Virginia's earliest Presbyterian congregations at Tuscarora, in the northwestern part of the colony. The College's alumnus may well have been a member of this family. After graduation Vance studied theology with the Reverend Robert Smith at Pequea, Pennsylvania. Licensed by the Presbytery of Donegal, which embraced much of western Pennsylvania and northwestern Virginia, on October 13, 1769, he was called to fill the pulpits in the churches of the frontier settlements of Tuscarora and Back Creek, Virginia, in 1770. (Back Creek, now called Black Creek, is roughly midway between present Martinsburg and Berkeley Springs, West Virginia.)

Little record of Vance's career has survived. Visiting him in May 1775, Philip Fithian (A.B. 1772), found him living "at the Foot of the North-Mountain, in a pleasant Situation—Partakes, I observe, of the

Virginian Spirit, & hands round the 'Sociable Bowl.' " No bowls were handed round in the following month, when Fithian recorded that he "rode to Mr. Vance's Meeting-House at Back-Creek. The sacrament was administered—Ninety-three Communicants! A vast Assembly!" Over the years Vance occasionally attended meetings of his presbytery, but aside from signing a 1776 petition calling for religious toleration and the disestablishment of the Anglican Church in Virginia, he appears to have taken little part in affairs outside his area. Visiting Vance in September 1791, a Presbyterian missionary found him "upon the borders of the grave in the last stage of consumption." Vance died on December 31 of that year. No record of a wife or children has beeen found.

Sources: Possible family: H. M. Wilson, *The Tinkling Spring* (1954), 296; sketches: Alexander, *Princeton*, 120; Webster, ms Brief Sketches, PPPrHi; Fithian, *Journal*, ii, 11, 32; toleration: *VMHB*, 18 (1910), 260; *Centennial Memorial of the Presbytery of Carlisle* (1889), i, 97, 99, 426-27, 452-53.

CLASS OF 1768

Robert Blackwell, A.B.

Ephraim Brevard, A.B.

Samuel Culbertson, A.B.

Pierpont Edwards, A.B.

William Churchill Houston,
    A.B.

Isaac Knowles

Adlai Osborne, A.B.

Samuel Parker

Thomas Reese, A.B.

Michael Sebring, A.B.

Thomas Smith, A.B.

Isaac Story, A.B.

Elias Van Bunschooten, A.B.

Benjamin West

Robert Blackwell

ROBERT BLACKWELL, A.B., A.M. 1782, A.B. King's 1770, D.D. Pennsylvania 1788, Anglican and Episcopal clergyman and sometime surgeon, was born near Newtown, Long Island, on May 6, 1748, the eldest son of Frances Sackett and Colonel Jacob Blackwell, a moderately well-to-do landowner. The family's properties included Blackwell's Island in Manhattan's East River. Although an active Anglican, the father was not prejudiced toward religious dissenters: in 1758 he donated land for a Presbyterian church and school in Blooming Grove, New York. Robert prepared for college at Rudge's Classical School at Hallett's Cove, Long Island, and in New York City. At his commencement he delivered what a Philadelphia newspaper described as "a judicious Harangue on Genius."

Blackwell's own genius led him to the Anglican ministry. After graduation he acted as a tutor to New York's Philipse family and studied divinity, probably with the Reverend Samuel Auchmuty, rector of New York City's Trinity Church. He may have studied medicine as well. In 1771 Auchmuty recommended Blackwell to Richard Peters, rector of Christ Church and St. Peter's Church in Philadelphia. "Though . . . not very showy," Auchmuty wrote "yet he will make a solid . . . minister. . . . He is a lump of good nature and very diligent when he has anything to do." Auchmuty suggested that Blackwell might be suitable for the dormant Anglican missionary post in southwest New Jersey's Gloucester County. As added inducement, Auchmuty noted that Blackwell "is a single man, and at his first setting off a small income will suffice him." Blackwell made a trip to Gloucester County to see if it suited him and agreed to serve there. Plans were put in motion to appoint him to the position. He sailed for England and on June 11, 1772, was ordained by the Bishop of London in the chapel in Fulham Palace.

Blackwell returned to America immediately. On November 19 for the tiny salary of £50 per year he took charge of churches at Colestown, Gloucester and Greenwich, New Jersey, as a missionary for the English Society for the Propagation of the Gospel in Foreign Parts. Each congregation numbered about forty communicants. "My people, in general," he reported to the S.P.G. on April 4, 1774, "are not so zealous in promoting the interest of the Church as I could wish them; at Waterford [Colestown] they are too much tinctured with Quakerism, & at the new Church at Greenwich with Methodism. . . . I exercise much gentleness towards them, endeavouring to reclaim them rather by conviction than reproof."

Somewhat over a year later, in November 1775, Blackwell reported to England once again. The situation in New Jersey, he wrote, was one of "general confusion. There is very little hope of inculcating divine truths in the hearts of men, when they are eagerly engaged in worldly matters, that appear to them of the greatest moment. In this dark time of distress, may God of his infinite mercy, as he hitherto hath done, preserve our church from the attempts of designing, wicked men." Blackwell's letter was, in fact, somewhat disingenuous. Back on Long Island his father had become chairman of the local Committee of Correspondence in 1774 and in the following year was a member of the New York convention that selected delegates to the Second Continental Congress. In 1776, when British troops invaded Long Island, he fled to New Jersey. Blackwell himself was the only Anglican clergyman in New Jersey to take the American side in the Revolution. When hostilities began, he simply omitted prayers for the king and continued as usual. When the British passed through Gloucester County in 1777 Blackwell left his parishes and joined the American army at Valley Forge. Back in England, the S.P.G. struck him off its list of missionaries. From 1777 to 1780 Blackwell served as both chaplain and surgeon in the First Pennsylvania Brigade under the command of General Anthony Wayne.

On January 17, 1780, Blackwell married one of his former parishioners, Rebecca Harrison, daughter of a long-prominent family of Gloucester County landowners. He resigned from the army not long thereafter. In 1781 Blackwell was called to assist the Reverend William White as rector of Philadelphia's United Churches of Christ Church and St. Peter's at a salary of £150 per year. He must have performed satisfactorily in his new parish, for on September 19 his salary was raised to £350 and the post was made permanent. Blackwell served as White's assistant for the next thirty years.

On February 25, 1782, Rebecca Blackwell died in childbirth. The following year Blackwell married a wealthy Philadelphia widow who may have been a cousin of his first wife, Mrs. Hannah Bingham Benezet, sister of William Bingham, one of the richest men in North America. If any children were born to the couple, none survived. A memorialist once claimed that Blackwell's wife's "ample fortune joined with his own" made him "not only the richest clergyman in the country but one of the richest men in Philadelphia." In fact, although he was made an executor of his father's estate, Blackwell received only a £10 legacy in his father's 1779 will. But the Blackwells lived in a world and on a scale far beyond those of most clerical families. Blackwell's sister-in-law, Anne Willing Bingham, was the queen of Philadel-

phia society during the years that the city served as the nation's capital. The Binghams' Philadelphia home, "Mansion House," was modeled
on that of the Duke of Manchester—"the dimensions of the original
being somewhat enlarged in the copy," an English visitor observed.
The Blackwells themselves lived in a fine mansion on Pine Street. A
daughter of Blackwell's first marriage, named like her mother Rebecca, married George Willing, a brother of Anne Willing Bingham.
Blackwell built the couple a fine townhouse that was connected by a
common garden to his own home.

Blackwell counted George Washington and many members of Congress among his congregation. Hannah Blackwell had literary tastes,
and the couple entertained widely. Blackwell developed something
of the reputation of "court preacher" to Federalist Philadelphia. But
Blackwell's wealth and social position did not hamper his clerical or
civic duties. Among the organizers of the Protestant Episcopal
Church in America, he served as a representative for Pennsylvania to all
general conventions held from 1785 to 1809, as well as acting as treasurer of various general and diocesan committees and as a member of
the Corporation for the Relief of Widows and Orphans of the Episcopal clergy from 1783 to 1831. He was a member of the American
Philosophical Society and of the Society for Political Inquiries, a manager of the Philadelphia Dispensary, and from 1780 to 1822 a trustee
of the University of Pennsylvania.

In 1793, when Philadelphia was devastated by yellow fever, Blackwell
remained at his post until September 23, when he was struck by
the disease. His wife rushed him to Gloucester in hopes of recovery.
Dr. Benjamin Rush (A.B. 1760) dispatched John Redman Coxe, one
of his apprentices, to treat Blackwell by means of repeated bleedings
and purges of mercury. Then, according to Rush, an old patient of
Dr. Adam Kuhn "went down to Gloucester and begged Mrs. Blackwell
in the most pathetic terms not to consent to his being bled again. Mrs.
Blackwell acted with firmness and propriety, and submitted to the
subsequent bleedings with full confidence of their being proper,
though advised only by Mr. Coxe." Blackwell recovered from the
disease but perhaps not from its cure: his health was significantly impaired for the rest of his long life. In 1811 Blackwell resigned his
pastoral duties. He spent his retirement in study and gardening and
died in Philadelphia on February 12, 1831. In his will he left a legacy
founding a scholarship at New York's General Theological Seminary.

SOURCES: Some vital data: Robert Blackwell File, PUA; sketch, printing some primary material: R. W. Bronson, *Inscriptions in St. Peter's Church Yard, Philadelphia* (1879), 543-50; sketch, "lump of good nature" quotation: H. D. Eberlein and

H. M. Lippincott, *Colonial Homes of Philadelphia* (1912), 42-47; sketch: N. R. Burr, *Anglican Church in N.J.* (1954), 585-86; Blooming Grove church: ENOS AYRES sketch; commencement: *Pa. Chronicle,* Sept. 28, 1768; Blackwell to S.P.G., Apr. 4, 1774, and June 26, 1775, Records of the S.P.G. Letter Series B, vol. 24, numbers 16, 17, Microfilm, NjP; father in Rev.: J. Riker, *Annals of Newtown* (1852), 176-77, 180, 194, 249-50; "only Anglican clergyman": W. W. Manross, *Hist. of the Am. Episcopal Church* (1950), 181; army record: L. C. Duncan, *Medical Men in Am. Rev.* (1970), 383; "Oaths of Allegiance and Fidelity, 1778," Record Book 167, p. 118, MS, War Dept. Col. of Rev. War Records, National Archives, Washington, D.C.; the Binghams: *DAB*; father's will: *N.Y. Wills*, X, 5; Harrison-Willing relation: *PMHB*, 5 (1881), 452-53; yellow fever: J. H. Powell, *Bring Out Your Dead* (1949), 252-53; Butterfield, *Rush Letters*, 683, 718, 722, 723, 728.

Mss: PHi

Ephraim Brevard

EPHRAIM BREVARD, A.B., physician, was born in Cecil County, Maryland, about 1744, the son of John Brevard and Jane McWhorter, sister of Alexander McWhorter (A.B. 1757). His paternal grandfather, also named John, apparently was a Huguenot who fled from France to Ireland and subsequently migrated to Maryland, where through the better part of two decades he is found as a landowner and active member of the Presbyterian Church. Ephraim's father moved with his family and two of his brothers, perhaps in 1747, to the frontier of North Carolina, becoming in 1749 a justice of the peace in the area that soon became Anson County, as he did in 1753 of Rowan County.

Ephraim attended school at "Crowfield Academy" in western Carolina, and it has been said that he and his classmate Adlai Osborne, first cousins through their mothers, received further schooling in Prince Edward County, Virginia, but conclusive evidence seems to be lacking. There is also a question regarding the assumption that the two of them first enrolled at the College in 1766, in view of the fact that Luther Martin (A.B. 1766) later described Brevard as a person with whom he had been "most intimately acquainted" at Princeton. After graduation Brevard taught school at Back Creek, Somerset County, Maryland.

When he took up residence in Mecklenburg County of North Carolina, is uncertain. Equally uncertain is the answer to the question of when, where, and how he received his medical training. No evidence has been found that he held the M.D. degree, and so it is assumed that such training as he had was acquired through an apprenticeship. It is possible that he studied with David Ramsay (A.B. 1765), as often has been said, but this seems doubtful in view of what is known of Ramsay's early career.

Brevard won his place in history by serving as clerk of the Mecklenburg Committee of Safety and signing in that capacity its justly famous resolves of May 31, 1775. He also has been listed among the "signers" of the "Mecklenburg Declaration of Independence," a document of doubtful authenticity that has been assigned the date of May 20, 1775. In the highly controversial literature relating to this last, he has at times been credited with the authorship of both documents. But it can be said with assurance only that the resolves, described by the royal governor as surpassing all the "treasonable publications that the inflammatory spirits of this Continent have yet produced," were made public over his signature.

In December 1776 Brevard was appointed justice of the peace for Mecklenburg County, and he seems to have been active in later years on the local court. He became a trustee in 1777 of Liberty Hall, as the academy which had been in existence for several years was then renamed. Some time later, perhaps in 1779, he was sent with Samuel E. McCorkle (A.B. 1772) to New Jersey on a successful mission to persuade his uncle, Alexander McWhorter, to accept the presidency of the academy. Late in 1779 or early in 1780, he became a surgeon with the 1st North Carolina Regiment, and so a prisoner of the British with the fall of Charleston on May 12, 1780. To his imprisonment has been attributed the illness that ended his life probably in 1781 but possibly in 1782.

His will, dated July 20, 1781, left all his property, including two male slaves, to Martha, a minor and sole surviving child by a marriage to the daughter of Colonel Thomas Polk. A few days before the will was written, he had been elected to represent the state in the Continental Congress, but he did not take the seat.

SOURCES: The many sketches of his life scattered through the literature on the Mecklenburg Declaration, and found in local histories, are repetitious and must be used with care. The best evidence on the family is in *Pennsylvania Genealogical Magazine*, 16 (1948), 91-95; on its migration to Carolina: R. W. Ramsey, *Carolina Cradle* (1964). See sketch of WAIGHTSTILL AVERY; Luther Martin's recollections: *MHM*, 50 (1955), 158, 161, 162, which reveal an acquaintance with David Ramsay, who was about to depart the Eastern Shore for his medical studies in Philadelphia; Liberty Hall: *NCHR*, 6 (1929), 403-406; F. A. Berg, *Encyclopedia of Continental Army Units* (1972); will: Ephraim Brevard File, PUA. See also Adlai Osborne File, PUA.

WFC

Samuel Culbertson

SAMUEL CULBERTSON, A.B., physician, may have been the son born in 1744 to John Culbertson and Mary Rogers, who were married in Phil-

adelphia's First Presbyterian Church in 1731. But since several Pennsylvania contemporaries bore the same name as the alumnus, his parentage cannot be established with any certainty. By 1775 Culbertson's
family was living in the recently settled and extremely fertile Kish-
nicoquillas Valley in what is now Mifflin County, Pennsylvania. Visiting there in August of that year, Philip Fithian (A.B. 1772) made the
following entry in his Journal:

> Afternoon I walked over to Mr. Cuthbertson's, half a Mile. He
> has a large, well-improved Farm. This present Season he reap'd
> nine Hundred Dozen Sheaves of wheat, & one Hundred Dozen of
> Rye!

> One of his Sons, is an Alumnus of fair Nassau-Hall. He is now
> at Home, a Doctor of Physick. Seems to be an intelligent, plea-
> sant, improved Youth. How pleasant it is to talk of pleasant Times!
> We enumerated all the Exercises, Amusements, & Fooleries we
> once took a Part in—Our Sorrow too, & Reluctance at leaving it;
> but chiefly parting with our Brother-grown Class Mates."

Culbertson went on to inquire of Fithian about John Beatty (A.B.
1769). "Indeed . . . he has two fine Sister's, *Polley & Betsey*," Culbertson
said. He then went on to recount the following anecdote:

> [The sisters] lived in Bucks County in this Province—I was
> there a Week after I left College; their Father was in Scotland;
> The Girls led us as brisk a Country Dance as we were able to fol-
> low, all the Week through—They had a curious musical Clock
> —They lived genteelly, & merrily —Our Sport however at last was
> stopped by the Presence of a Clergyman; one [Enoch] Green —He
> came to preach, & *Betsey* told me he had something more in His
> head than Preaching —He was a slim Man, wore a large Wig
> said little, read his Sermon, &c—I took my Leave on Monday
> Morning, with this Green, of the two uncommonly merry Miss
> Beatties, & rode down to Philadelphia.

Fithian did not mention to Culbertson that he had been prepared
for college by Green, nor that he was planning to marry Betsey Beatty
in October. As Fithian left the area he did note that Culbertson and
his mother were about to set off on a trip to Albany—the only
other certain item of information concerning Culbertson discovered.
However, he was probably the Samuel Culbertson who served as a surgeon with the 12th Virginia Regiment of the Continental Line from

March, 1777 to April 21, 1778. All trace of Culbertson after this date has eluded recent family genealogists.

SOURCES: Possible parentage and mention: L. R. Culbertson, *Genealogy of the Culbertson and Culberson Families* (1923), 19, 95; Fithian, *Journal*, II, 96-97, 99, 101, 108; Va. regiment: L. C. Duncan, *Medical Men in the Am. Rev.* (1970), 390.

Pierpont Edwards

PIERPONT EDWARDS, A.B., A.M. 1781, lawyer and public official, was born in Northampton, Massachusetts, on April 8, 1750, the eleventh and youngest child of Sarah Pierpont and Jonathan Edwards, third president of the College. In the year of Pierpont's birth, his family moved to the Indian village of Stockbridge, Massachusetts. Pierpont was only eight years old when both his parents died suddenly in 1758. Where he spent the succeeding two or three years has not been discovered. In

Pierpont Edwards, A.B. 1768
BY REMBRANDT PEALE

1760 Pierpont's oldest brother Timothy (A.B. 1753) married Rhoda Ogden of Elizabethtown, New Jersey, set up housekeeping in the Edwards house in Stockbridge, and assumed guardianship of Pierpont, his brother Jonathan, Jr. (A.B. 1765), the other Edwards children, and the orphaned children of his sister Esther—Sally Burr and Aaron Burr, Jr. (A.B. 1772). When Timothy and Rhoda Edwards returned from Stockbridge to live in Elizabethtown about two years later, Pierpont accompanied them. The Burr children, only four and six years, respectively, younger than Pierpont must have seemed more like sister and brother than niece and nephew. Timothy and Rhoda Edwards saw that Pierpont was prepared for the College—most likely at the academy in town run by Tapping Reeve (A.B. 1763).

Pierpont matriculated in the College in 1764. While there he joined the Well-Meaning Club, forerunner of the Cliosophic Society. At his commencement Pierpont delivered a Latin oration on "Civil Liberty," a subject that would remain a life-long preoccupation. Shortly after graduation Edwards went to Middletown, Connecticut, to study law with Judge Seth Wetmore, husband of his aunt Hannah Edwards. The following year he returned to Elizabethtown to marry Frances Ogden, a cousin of his brother Timothy's wife. Shortly thereafter Edwards and his bride moved to New Haven, Connecticut, where he had many Pierpont connections and where his brother Jonathan had just been installed as a Congregational clergyman. Pierpont and Frances Edwards had ten children, among them John Stark (A.B. 1796) and Henry Waggaman (A.B. 1797), who became a governor of Connecticut, The Edwardses' daughter Henrietta Frances married Eli Whitney, inventor of the cotton gin.

Admitted to the New Haven bar in 1771, Edwards quickly built a successful law practice. By May 1774 he was a member of the New Haven Committee of Correspondence. In 1775 he became a member of the Second Company of the Governor's Footguards, a unit captained by Benedict Arnold, then a merchant-storekeeper of New Haven. On April 22, 1776, in response to news of Concord and Lexington, the guards were speedily mobilized and, after a public exhortation by Jonathan Edwards, Jr., set out for Cambridge. The details of Pierpont Edwards's military career have not been discovered, although it is known that he took part in at least two battles.

As early as October 1776 Edwards was involved with others in fitting out a ship to be used as a privateer. In the spring of the following year he joined Arnold in pursuit of British forces after their raid on Danbury. Later in the same year he was elected for the first time, along with Samuel Bishop, Jr., with whom he would long be associated in politics and business, as New Haven's deputy in the Connecticut legislature.

During the Revolution New Haven's economy was severely disrupted and the town itself invaded by the British. The homes of Pierpont and his brother Jonathan were singled out for looting. While it is likely that Edwards spent most of the war years building up his law practice, he was also involved in trading ventures with the West Indies. After the war Edwards supported amnesty to former Tories with the hope of bringing Loyalist New York merchants and their capital to New Haven. In 1782 he was nominated to stand for election to Congress. Though he was not elected then, nor in the following year, when he was again nominated, in 1784 he was elected to both the New Haven Common Council and the Connecticut legislature and became the first Grand Master of the Grand Lodge of Freemasons of Connecticut. In October 1787, he was elected to Congress for a term of one year, succeeding the Reverend William Samuel Johnson, who became president of Columbia College in that year. (Edwards's daughter Susanna married Johnson's son in 1791.) The only record of his congressional service that appears to have survived is a letter complaining of his state's failure to supply him with funds to get to New York. Meanwhile, from 1787 to 1790, Edwards served as speaker of the Connecticut House of Representatives and was a delegate to the Connecticut convention called to consider ratification of the federal constitution, which he strongly supported.

In 1790 Edwards's political career appears to have suffered a setback. In August he and his followers attacked the aged Roger Sherman, United States Senator from Connecticut. A bitter newspaper war between Edwards and his followers, and Sherman's supporters ensued. Edwards was elected to the United States Congress in the fall of 1790, but suddenly, and inexplicably, resigned his seat without serving. He left himself no fallback position, for at the same time he resigned the speakership of the Connecticut house. By the end of the year he was left with only membership on a committee to confer on the Milford and Stratford ferry.

The reasons for Edwards's reversal of fortune are unclear. He may simply have retired from public life to repair his private affairs. It is more likely that in the incoherent factionalism of the Connecticut politics of the period Edwards's faction had momentarily lost out. But the drift of Edwards's future ideological commitments—and of the future of nascent party politics in his state—was made plain in a letter Edwards wrote less than two years later: "A dissatisfaction with the Vice-President [John Adams], which is extensive though not general in the eastern states," he told a Philadelphia correspondent,

> induces a wish to fill that office with a character more unexceptionable. Many suppose that a too strong tendency to aristocracy is a trait in Mr. Adams's character; I am of the number of those who entertain this idea.
>
> We are not without hope from New England, that, even here, something can be done, but our greatest hopes are from those friends to true republican liberty who live South of us.
>
> There certainly are symptoms in our present court and courtiers that are alarming. A disposition to treat with coldness those who, from an honest regard to the preservation of real liberty can not blindly devote their interest to the support of all their measures, points out the danger of unconditionally advocating their schemes, and sound the alarm to those who mean to guard against the first advances of tyranny.
>
> To preserve our liberties, we think a watchful reasonable jealousy is necessary, and we shall always endeavour to tread upon the line which divides stupidity on the one hand, and zeal without knowledge of the other.

Such Antifederalism was Jeffersonian republicanism in embryo. It stood little chance of success in the Connecticut of the 1790s, where the established church and a conservative older generation of politicians constituted a "standing order" opposed to change and prone to look upon opposition of any sort as little short of "infidelity" or "libertinism." ("As well attempt to revolutionize the kingdom of heaven as the state of Connecticut," Edwards once remarked.) Through the 1790s Edwards maneuvered in Connecticut and in the nation, most often in concert with his nephew, Aaron Burr, to establish the emerging Republican party.

In the 1790s Edwards was involved in many nonpolitical activities. When Connecticut ceded its western lands in 1795, he was among the largest purchasers of shares in the company formed to exploit the Western Reserve. While his brother Jonathan, on the east side of New Haven, wrote pamphlets and articles attacking slavery, Pierpont lived comfortably on the west side of town, attended by two slaves. He was active in cultural affairs, conferring with President Stiles on a suitable New Haven monument to John Dixwell, the regicide, and was among the founders of the Connecticut Academy of Arts and Sciences.

By 1799–1800 Edwards was at the head of the New Haven bar and ready once again to attempt to topple the old order. As the Jeffersonians organized in Connecticut, faction developed into party. The Republican campaign of 1800 began with a meeting in Edwards's home in New Haven. The victory of Thomas Jefferson and Aaron Burr was followed by the formation of a full-scale Republican party organization in the state, with Edwards and his old associates, the Bishop family, its foremost leaders. Federalist opposition was furious. "The federalists here," Edwards informed President Jefferson "do not consider themselves conquered; they are putting every faculty to the torture to effect the overthrow of your republican Administration. Our leading federalists are all royalists; they think as our Clergy do 'Moses and Aaron here walk together.' The Throne and the alter have here entered into an alliance offensive and defensive. If they cannot effect a change in the administration, they are resolved to divide the Union."

Edwards's political career brought him rewards in the form of a United States judgeship in 1806. He began inauspiciously enough by persecuting Federalist journalists as vigorously as they had harried Republicans. He even found himself in the anomalous position of having to refuse to issue a warrant for the arrest of his nephew, Judge Tapping Reeve, a virulent Federalist who had been indicted for libel against Jefferson in a case that Edwards himself had initiated.

Edwards's later career on the bench was less partisan. After the death of his wife in 1800, he married Mary Tucker and moved to near Bridgeport, Connecticut. He was one of the chief founders of the "Toleration Party" in Connecticut. The main aim of the party was to secure religious freedom in the state and to replace the charter of Charles II still in the early nineteenth century serving as the state's fundamental law, with a modern constitution. Edwards's work culminated in 1818 when he became chairman of the committee charged by the state constitutional convention with producing a new basic frame of government for the state. He saw that the Congregational church was disestablished and that a wide range of civil liberties was secured for the people of Connecticut. It was a fitting climax to a career which had begun with his 1768 Princeton commencement oration on "Civil Liberty." Edwards died in Bridgeport on April 14, 1826.

Edwards's posthumous reputation has been curious. In the nineteenth century he came to be known as the "Great Connecticut Adulterer." This gossip found its way in the *DAB* and other scholarly accounts as well. (Cf. E. S. Morgan, *The Gentle Puritan* [1962], 415, where Edwards is characterized as "a notorious libertine and as free in theology as in morals," and Collier, above, 302-309n.) These charges rest, first, on some mid-nineteenth-century remarks of the Utopian communitarian, John Humphrey Noyes, no enemy to adultery, and second, on the erroneous identification of Edwards with a character in Hannah Webster Foster's 1797 novel, *The Couqette: or the History of Eliza Wharton. A Novel founded on Fact* (see esp. Boston, 1855, ed.). The misidentification of Edwards with the character in the novel is pointed out in Mrs. Dall, *The Romance of the Association . . .* (1875), and in C. K. Bolton, *The Elizabeth Whitman Mystery at the Old Bell Tavern in Danvers* (1912).

More serious is the following passage in the most recent article on Edwards (Smith, below, 14-15):

> Mrs. Edwards had a younger sister, Mary Cozzens Ogden, who was born in Elizabethtown, Nov. 25, 1764. During the Revolution this young and attractive girl went to New Haven to visit her sister. When she was fifteen years old she became the mother of a child [Sarah, b. Dec. 11, 1780], and less than two years more of another child [Horace, b. Aug. 12, 1782] these children were reared in the Edwards household and became known by the name of Edwards because Pierpont was their father. (*New Haven Vital Statistics; Vineland Hist. Mag.*, Oct. 1928, p. 90.)

Pierpont's paternity seems unlikely for three reasons: (1) I can find no reference to the children in the *New Haven Vital Statistics*; (2) the *Vineland Historical Magazine* reference is to a bible printed in 1864, hardly a reliable source; and (3) such affairs were seldom kept secret. In 1781 Edwards received an honorary degree from Princeton. While it is possible that he fathered Mary Ogden's children, it seems wildly improbable that the College would have awarded him the A.M. for having done so.

SOURCES: Sketches: *DAB*; E. Y. Smith, "The Descendants of William Edwards," *NYGBR*, 91 (1960), 6-16; E. E. Atwater, *Hist. of the City of New Haven* (1887), sketch and local pol. career, 243-44, 40, 81, 82; for family background see TIMOTHY EDWARDS; commencement: *Pa. Gaz.*, Oct. 12, 1768; Arnold: W. M. Wallace, *Traitorous Hero: The Life and Times of Benedict Arnold* (1954), 35-41; Conn. public career: *Rec. State Conn.*, I-IX; Stiles, *Literary Diary*, III, 111, 483-84; C. Collier, *Roger Sherman's Connecticut* (1971), 308-15; Cont. Congress: *LMCC*, VIII, 713; letter to Jefferson: *AHR*, 3 (1897-98), 276; Edwards's post-1800 pol. career can be pieced together from: R. J. Purcell, *Conn. in Transition* (1918); D. Malone, *Jefferson the President* (1970), 75-81; N. E. Cunningham, Jr., *The Jeffersonian Republicans* (1957), 201-10, and Cunningham, *The Jeffersonian Republicans in Power* (1963), 19, 22-23, 125-26, 127, 131, 227-28; slaves: *U.S. Census of 1790, Conn.*, 104.

William Churchill Houston

WILLIAM CHURCHILL HOUSTON, A.B., A.M. 1771, college tutor and professor, lawyer and public official, was born in 1746 in the Sumter district of South Carolina, the son of Archibald Houston and his wife Margaret. The father was a small planter who in 1753 received patents on land in what was then Anson County, North Carolina. He moved his family there and over the years achieved a modest prosperity, patenting 500 acres of land in Mecklenburg County in 1764. In the federal census of 1790 he was listed as the owner of three slaves and was carefully styled "Captain" Archibald Houston. Young William is said to have been prepared for college at Crowfield Academy along with his classmates Ephraim Brevard and Adlai Osborne, though conclusive proof of his attendance is lacking.

Several of the College's alumni were active in Houston's area of North Carolina, and it seems probable that one of them directed him to Nassau Hall. A strong tradition asserts that Houston early determined upon a professional career and that to help him achieve his goal his father provided him with a patrimony of a horse and £50, with which he set off for New Jersey. Houston must have carried extraordinarily strong recommendations from North Carolina, for on his arrival in Princeton he was appointed a master in the College's Latin grammar school, a position that enabled him to pay for his undergraduate education.

Although Houston won no honors in College, he made a strong enough impression on the authorities to be appointed master of the grammar school immediately upon graduation, in 1768–1769. It was John Witherspoon's first year in America, and young Houston must have seemed promising to the new president. In the following year Houston was made the College's librarian and curator of its philosophical (i.e., scientific) apparatus and advanced to the extremely responsible position of tutor to the junior class. Among his students was James Madison (A.B. 1771). Using Madison as intermediary, Houston generously secured grammars for Madison's former tutor, Thomas Martin (A.B. 1762), who had directed the young Virginian toward Nassau Hall.

Shortly after his arrival in New Jersey, President Witherspoon determined to augment the College's excellence in every sphere, particularly natural science. In September 1769, the College's trustees created the post of Professor of Mathematics and Natural Philosophy. The position was not to be occupied until funds sufficient for its support

had been raised. At the same time the trustees appointed a committee
to determine the needs of the College for scientific apparatus. Among
the most advanced scientific teaching machines of the day was the
orrery, or planetarium—an elaborate working model of the solar
system. Hearing that David Rittenhouse, the famed instrument-maker,
was building an orrery, Witherspoon rushed to the Philadelphia
suburbs and secured the machine for Nassau Hall, snatching it from
under the nose of the head of the College of Philadelphia.

Rittenhouse's orrery arrived in Princeton in 1771, and Houston was
shortly promoted to the position of Professor of Mathematics and Natural Philosophy at the generous salary of £125 per year. It was a
widely publicized coup both for the College and for Houston. Little
record of Houston as a teacher survives, except for a 1773 comment
by an undergraduate, William Smith (A.B. 1774), in a letter to Philip
Fithian (A.B. 1773). "Mr. Houston," Smith wrote, "is trying to instill
philosophy into our heads, and I assure you I dont think it by any
means a disagreeable study." Smith's future father-in-law, John Adams,
left a fuller description. On his way to the Continental Congress
in August 1774, Adams stopped at Princeton, where Houston (referred
to by Adams as "Mr. Euston") acted as his guide:

> Mr. Euston . . . shewed us the Library. It is not large, but has
> some good Books. He then led us into the Apparatus. Here we saw
> a most beautiful Machine, an Orrery, or Planetarium, constructed
> by Mr. Writtenhouse of Philadelphia. It exhibits allmost every
> Motion in the astronomical World. The Motions of the Sun and
> all the Planetts with all their Satellites. The Eclipses of the Sun
> and Moon &c. He shewed us another orrery, which exhibits the
> true Inclination of the orbit of each of the Planetts to the Plane
> of the Ecliptic. He then shewed Us the electrical Apparatus,
> which is the most compleat and elegant that I have seen. He
> charged the Bottle and attempted an Experiment, but the State of
> the Air was not favourable.

Adams went on to add that President Witherspoon was "as high a
Son of Liberty, as any Man in America." He noted too that, though
"the Schollars sing as badly as the Presbyterians at New York," they
also were Sons of Liberty. Like his students, Houston was a Son of
Liberty. The revolutionary years would nip his budding scientific career and turn him toward new pursuits.

In 1775 and 1776 Houston served as deputy secretary to the Continental Congress. His duties sent him north to the besieged Boston
area, where he met his opposite number from the Harvard faculty, the

scientist John Winthrop, then serving on the Massachusetts Council. "I had a safe but not a very comfortable journey home," Houston reported to Winthrop in December 1775. "Broke my sulky about 13 miles from Providence, brought it forward and sold it at that Place, came on Horseback to New London; acrossed the Sound to Long Island in Terror of being chased . . . travelled through the Island, the West end of which is the very Land of the Sons of Belial, where there are 4 Tories to a Whig."

Back in the Land of Promise, on February 28, 1776, Houston was appointed a captain in the Second Regiment of Foot of the Somerset County militia. But President Witherspoon's attendance at the Continental Congress made Houston's presence at the College imperative. Explaining that "from his connexion with the college in the absence of Dr. Witherspoon, and other circumstances, he cannot pay the due attention to his company," Houston resigned his commission on August 17. However, he retained his seat in the provincial congress and served in the New Jersey Assembly from 1777 to 1779. During the early revolutionary years it was Houston, more than anyone else, who held together the College—at one point reduced to only ten students. On May 25, 1779, Houston himself was elected to the Continental Congress, where he served intermittently until 1785. His mathematical talents were put to good use in Congress, for although he served on the standing committees for war, foreign affairs, and the post office, most of his committee assignments involved taxes and other financial matters. In 1781 he wrote an extensive essay on taxes, in which he urged the taxation of luxuries such as silver plate, hunting dogs, blooded race horses, pleasure carriages, and servants in livery. Describing slavery as "a Disgrace to any Government," he urged that the peculiar institution be taxed too. Meanwhile, he took up the study of law with Richard Stockton (A.B. 1748) and in 1781 was admitted to the New Jersey bar. It was probably at about this time that Houston married Jane Smith, a daughter of the Reverend Caleb Smith (Yale 1743) of Orange, New Jersey, and granddaughter of Jonathan Dickinson, the College's first president. The couple had five children, four of whom lived to maturity.

In 1781 Houston was appointed clerk to the New Jersey Supreme Court, a post he held until his death. In the same year he declined the federal post of comptroller of the treasury, though he drew up the national budget for the army, navy, and civil affairs in that year. Somehow, he also managed to draw up plans for graduate instruction at Princeton in theology and law at the same time. In the following year Houston moved to Trenton, where he took over the affairs of his wife's cousin, Jonathan Dickinson Sergeant (A.B. 1762), and became a leading member of the local Presbyterian church. His concern with national issues did not cease: in 1782 he served as a commissioner in the landmark dispute between Connecticut and Pennsylvania over lands in the Wyoming Valley and from 1782 to 1785 he acted as receiver for Continental taxes in New Jersey. During his 1784-1785 term in Congress his main activity appears to have been promoting John Fitch's steamboat.

In 1783 Houston resigned both his professorship in the College and his post as treasurer, which he had held since 1779. His legal practice and public duties engrossed more and more of his energies. Judging by the mass of his papers now in the Princeton University Library, his law practice was extensive. Affairs of state seldom let him rest. In 1786 New Jersey appointed him one of its delegates to the Annapolis Convention, though some question exists as to whether Houston's health permitted him to attend. In 1787 the New Jersey legislature elected Houston one of its delegates to the Constitutional Convention. It is uncertain how regularly Houston, by then very ill, attended the convention's sessions, since a Georgia delegate was also named William Houston. He does, however, appear to be the William Houston who moved to make the president of the United States eligible for more than one term in office.

Houston was not among the signers of the constitution, probably because of his advancing tuberculosis. However, he did sign the letter transmitting the constitution to his state. In August 1788, Houston began a trip south in hopes of recovering his health. He died suddenly on the twelfth of that month at an inn in Frankford, Pennsylvania. His funeral was held from the Philadelphia home of Jonathan Dickinson Sergeant; he was buried in the graveyard of the city's Second Presbyterian Church. Throughout his public career he had adhered strictly to his code of simple republican virtue. "No man can pretend to make this office on its present footing his principal business," Houston had written to Robert Morris, the financier, on being appointed Continental tax receiver in 1783. "I have never viewed this or any other publick office in the Light of a mere Bargain of Profit." He followed his ideals, for an inventory of his personal property made shortly after his death totaled only a little over £271.

SOURCES: More an appreciation than a biography, but containing much primary material, is: T. G. Glenn, *William Churchill Houston, 1746-1788* (1903); sketches: *DAB*; 26 *NJA*, 289-91; father's slaves: *U.S. Census of 1790, N.C.*, 160; college prep.: Foote, *Sketches, N.C.*, 434; Martin: *Madison Papers*, 1, 43, 45; orrery & professorship: H. C. Rice, Jr., *The Rittenhouse Orrery* (1954); B. Hindle, *Pursuit of Science in Rev. Am.* (1956), 91 (Houston mistakenly called a Scot); *WMQ*, 6 (1949), 60;

Smith quotation: *Fithian Journal*, I, 34; Adams quotation: Butterfield, ed., *Adams Papers*, II, 112-13; Houston to Winthrop, Dec. 27, 1775, ALS, NjP; College in Rev.: V. L. Collins, *President Witherspoon* (1925), I-II; public career: *Minutes of the [N.J.] Council of Safety* (1872), passim; *Minutes of the [N.J.] Provincial Congress & Council of Safety* (1879), 395, 541; J. F. Hageman, *History of Princeton* (1879), I, 93; *LMCC*, IV-V, VIII; E. C. Burnett, *The Continental Congress* (1941), 451, 475, 490; R. P. McCormick, *Experiment in Independence* (1950), passim; McCormick, *N.J. from Colony to State* (1964), 170-71; *WMQ*, 26 (1969), 527; Houston to Morris, May 17, 1783, ALS, NjP; estate inventory: MS, NjP.

MSS: NjHi, NjP, PHi

Isaac Knowles

ISAAC KNOWLES, Congregational clergyman and merchant, was born on June 3, 1741, in that part of Eastham that is now part of the town of Orleans on Cape Cod, Massachusetts, the fifth of the eight children of Rebecca Dillingham and Amos Knowles. The father seems to have been prosperous and served his town as a selectman. Young Isaac entered the College's freshman class in 1764. For reasons now unknown, Knowles left Princeton after one year in the College and on October 25, 1765, requested admission to Harvard. He was placed in Harvard's sophomore class and received his A.B. in 1768. The A.M. was awarded in due course in 1771.

After leaving Cambridge Knowles preached to various congregations in Nova Scotia, along the Penobscot River in Maine, and finally for a time at Sandwich on Cape Cod. He was never formally ordained. On September 6, 1775, Knowles registered his intention of marrying Mrs. Deliverance Bassett Hall, a widow of Sandwich. The couple had at least five children.

Knowles's allegiance wavered in the early stages of the Revolution. Late in 1777 he went with a group of Loyalists to Rhode Island to join the British. But he changed his mind, returned home, and in February 1778 found himself imprisoned for his refusal to take the oath of allegiance to Massachusetts. Knowles apparently did not preach after his release. On his father's death in 1784 he inherited the family homestead and until 1794 was active as a trader in Sandwich. In that year he made a trip to Troy, New York, sold his Massachusetts property and settled permanently in New York. In Troy he was known as a merchant, trader, or a gentleman, but when he died on February 5, 1818, his newspaper obituary called him "the Reverend."

SOURCES: Fuller sketch: *Sibley's Harvard Graduates*, XVII, 56-57; father and father's will: *NEHGR*, 79 (1925), 389-91.

Adlai Osborne

ADLAI OSBORNE, A.B., planter and public official, was born June 4, 1744, probably in Lancaster County, Pennsylvania, the son of Alexander Osborne, a native of New Jersey, and his wife Agnes MacWhorter, sister of both Alexander MacWhorter (A.B. 1757) and of Jane, the mother of Adlai's classmate Ephraim Brevard. The father moved the family to North Carolina in or about 1749, when he became one of the first justices of the peace in an area designated as Anson County in 1750. When that county was divided in 1753 for the purpose of creating its upper part as Rowan County, he again became one of the original justices of the county. Until his death in 1776, Alexander Osborne remained a leading and influential man on the Carolina frontier, as local magistrate, sometime representative in the provincial assembly, and colonel in command of the Rowan militia at the time of the Regulator troubles.

Adlai was prepared for college at "Crowfield Academy," located only a few miles from his father's residence. It has been said that he and Brevard received further schooling in Prince Edward County, Virginia, but there are reasons for doubting this. There is a question too as to just when he and Brevard were admitted to the College; it may have been in 1766 but it could have been earlier. There can be no question, however, that by his senior year Osborne had become a careful and industrious scholar. An exercise book of his, kept through that year in a very neat and legible hand, was presented to the Princeton University Library in 1960 by Ralph C. DeMange (A.B. 1904) in memory of his son, Lt. Ewing Anthony DeMange of the Class of 1945 (the fifth in a line of descent beginning with Adlai Osborne to have attended Princeton) who was killed at Iwo Jima on March 5, 1945. The book follows the conventional form of query and answer through such subjects as Metaphysics, Ontology, Natural Theology, and Moral Philosophy, this last with 502 questions and answers being decidedly the longest single section. It is one of the earliest student notebooks in the library's possession.

After graduation, Osborne returned to North Carolina, where for a time he may have read law and where, perhaps in 1770, he signed the "Redressors" Association in opposition to the Regulators. As early as 1772 he secured a commission as clerk of the Rowan County court, and through many years thereafter (as late as 1809, according to a local history) he displayed a marked talent for holding the office of clerk to any court, inferior or superior, sitting in Salisbury, the county seat. When the Whigs moved in 1774 to form a county committee for rallying opposition to British policy, he became its clerk and soon a full member. As the committee developed into a Committee of Safety in 1775, he was especially active in collecting the stores of war (tradition has the county magazine located in his own home), in putting pressure on local residents for support of the American cause, and as a member of the patriot militia, in which he became lieutenant-colonel.

The surviving public record indicates that he remained active chiefly in his own locality, but that he achieved more than local prominence is indicated by the fact that he twice was elected to represent the state in the Congress, in 1784 and 1785. In neither instance did he actually serve. He was a member of the state's second ratifying convention of 1789, and was counted among the majority that finally brought North Carolina into the new federal union.

In the same year he became one of the original trustees of the University of North Carolina. His long-term interest in education is shown by his inclusion in 1777 among the trustees of Liberty Hall, as the academy formerly known as Queen's College in Charlotte was reconstituted in that year by the state legislature. Again, when Liberty Hall fell into "an entire state of decay" after 1780, he was one of those who secured in succession to it the incorporation in 1784 of an academy to be located in Salisbury. The records of the University trustees show that through the years after 1789 he remained an active and working member of the board. Through the difficult first years, when finance was the critical problem, he served as attorney for the board in more than one district of the state for the purpose of collecting certain revenues assigned by the legislature to the University. He evidently remained a member of the board to his death.

Osborne obviously was a prospeous man, though it is impossible to speak specifically regarding his economic enterprises. As an only son he undoubtedly inherited substantial properties from his father, and that he added to these is evident from the fact that, whereas his father in 1768 had owned four slaves, he possessed nineteen when the federal census was taken in 1790, which made him one of the largest slaveholders in his county, then Iredell. He had been married on January 30, 1771, to Margaret Lloyd, and so into one of the more prominent families of Orange County. All told, eleven children were born to this union, one of them named in 1786 for Ephraim Brevard. Osborne died December 16, 1814, and was buried in Centre Churchyard, near Mount Mourne in Iredell County.

SOURCES: For family and move to Carolina, Adlai Osborne File, PUA; R. W. Ramsey, *Carolina Cradle* (1964); for his public career, Weeks *Index* to colonial and state *Records of* N.C.; *LMCC*, VII, VIII; R.D.W. Connor, *Documentary Hist. of the Univ. of N.C., 1776-1799* (1953); J. Rumple, *Hist. of Rowan County* (1881, 1929).

WFC

Samuel Parker

SAMUEL PARKER, a Congregational clergyman, was born at West Barnstable, Massachusetts, on November 18, 1740 or 1742. The identity of his parents has not been discovered. The death of President Samuel Finley and the College's difficulties in finding a new president led Parker and Asarelah Morse (Class of 1767) to request admission to Harvard in October 1766. Morse took the entrance examination and was admitted to Harvard's senior class. However Parker, the Harvard faculty recorded, "refus'd to Stand an Examination, upon which he was told We had nothing to say to him and that he had no further Business here." Later in the day, hearing of Morse's admission, Parker reappeared and presented himself for examination: "Upon which We proceeded to examine him, in Tully, Homer, Logick and the use of the Globes, after deliberating upon the Matter, it was agreed, That He shou'd be admitted a Student of Harvard College and into the junior Sophisters Class." Parker roomed with Morse and received his A.B. from Harvard in 1768. Award of the A.M. followed in 1771.

After graduation Parker returned to Barnstable County and began to preach to the people of the minister-less First Congregational Church in the tiny fishing village of Provincetown at the tip of Cape Cod. On December 7, 1773, the people of the town asked him to settle as their permanent pastor. They offered him a salary of £66.13s.7d. per year lawful money, a frame for his house and half the building of it, a meadow for two cows, and his firewood. The Massachusetts General Court guaranteed to supplement his low salary by £45 annually for twelve years. Parker's formal ordination followed on January 20, 1774.

Because of its exposed position, most of Provincetown's inhabitants deserted their village during the Revolution. Although Parker appears to have seen little or no active service, he was listed as a chaplain on the rolls of a Massachusetts company of artillery. Peace brought prosperity to the town and apparently to Parker as well. On January 14, 1785, he married Mrs. Mary Smith, who died on November 20 of the same year, about two weeks after the birth of the couple's son, Samuel. The early years of Parker's ministry were successful. Visiting Provincetown in 1800, President Timothy Dwight of Yale described Parker as "much, and deservedly, respected by his people; and his public labors are very generally attended. This undoubtedly, is a prime source of the sobriety and decency conspicuous among the inhabitants." Three years later, in January 1803, Parker remarried. His second wife was Eunice Hinckley of Barnstable, daughter of Isaac Hinckley (Harvard 1740). The couple had one daughter, Eliza Davis.

Parker's later years were shadowed by the rise of new, non-Calvinist, denominations in Provincetown. The town voted to place a Methodist minister in Parker's pulpit when he was unable to officiate. Many members of his congregation joined the Methodists or the Universalists. But when Parker died on April 11, 1811, his parishioners united to give him an elaborate and well-attended funeral.

SOURCES: Sketch: N.W.P. Smith, *The Provincetown Book* (1922), 120-21, 211; *Sibley's Harvard Graduates*, XVII, 76-77; Sibley gives 1740 birthyear, *NEHGR*, 46 (1892), 206, gives 1742; Timothy Dwight, *Travels in New-England and New-York* (1969 ed.), III, 64; account of funeral: *Columbian Centinel*, May 1, 1811.

Thomas Reese

THOMAS REESE, A.B., A.M. 1771, D.D. 1794, Presbyterian clergyman and schoolmaster, was born in Pennsylvania in 1742, the son of Susan Ruth Polk and her husband David Reese, a farmer. When Thomas was quite young, the family moved to Mecklenburg County, North Carolina. Thomas prepared for the College at the county's Latin grammar school, so-called Queen's College, headed by the Reverend Joseph Alexander (A.B. 1760).

After graduation from the College Reese taught at the academy in Back Creek, Somerset County, Maryland. A fellow teacher was Ephraim Brevard (A.B. 1768). Luther Martin (A.B. 1766), a mutual friend, was favorably impressed with the performance of these two "most worthy, respectable young gentlemen."

In the early 1770s Reese began preparations for the ministry and was both licensed and ordained by the Presbytery of Orange, in 1773. In that year he accepted a call from the Salem Church of South Carolina's Sumter District, where, until the British invasion of South Carolina in 1780, "he continued in the quiet and faithful discharge of his duties." It was likewise in 1773 that Reese married Jane Harris of Mecklenburg. Their family eventually grew to four sons, including Edwin (A.B. 1794), and three daughters. Like Reese's father, Jane's father, Robert Harris, was later listed among the signers of the "Mecklenburg Declaration of Independence"—an indication that they were remembered in the county for Whiggish sentiments in 1775.

Following the British invasion of the state, Reese fled with his family to Mecklenburg County. There he preached against the enemy, read printed handbills of news before local audiences, and in the words of a nineteenth-century historian, "used his pen for his country."

The advent of peace in 1782 brought Reese back to his Salem congregation, a post he eagerly resumed. His duties included providing medical as well as spiritual comfort to his parishioners. According to a contemporary, Reese had "read many medical authors, and being conversant with physicians, he had acquired a pretty good knowledge of Southern diseases." In addition to these responsibilities, Reese ran a Latin grammar school and numbered among his pupils John R. Witherspoon (A.B. 1794), a nephew of President Witherspoon. Having studied at the school for five years (1787–1792), John later recalled his former teacher fondly: "As a teacher, he had a peculiar facility for communicating knowledge and the happy talent of commanding respect without severity." From 1777 on Reese also served with several other graduates of Nassau Hall as a trustee of Liberty Hall, successor to Queen's College.

After nearly two decades as its pastor, Reese left Salem Church. He was formally released on May 26, 1792. In part he resigned because of poor health and the need for a change of climate, but the move was also spurred by a dispute over the introduction of Isaac Watts's hymns. A nineteenth-century historian adds that the conflict "was enhanced by a certain sarcastic jeu d'esprit in which Dr. Reese indulged." In his farewell sermon, *Steadfastness in Religion* (1793), which Reese delivered as "a monument of his gratitude," he implored his parishioners to "hold fast" to Christianity and to withstand the many temptations to abandon it. "Patience, courage, and perseverance in a good cause command respect and merit applause. . . . The cause of religion is not only good, but infinitely important and interesting." And it is "the cause which shall finally prevail."

Leaving Salem, Reese accepted a joint call from the Presbyterian churches of Hopewell and Carmel in the Pendleton District of South Carolina, located along the Seneca River. Formerly territory belonging to the Cherokee Indians, this land was ceded to the United States by a 1777 treaty, and following the construction of a major wagon road the district had attracted many settlers. Reese divided his time equally between the two congregations. Hopewell, the smaller of the two, he deemed the "more liberal in sentiment."

Reese spent much of the last decade of his life writing on the religious and philosophical themes he had pondered since his student days. Publishing the bulk of what he wrote would have cost too much, but what he did publish won him respect as "the most finished writer of that day" among southern Presbyterians. The honorary doctorate the College conferred upon him in 1794 reflected his stature.

Reese's most prominent work was probably his *Essay on the Influence of Religion on Civil Society* (1788). In it he argued that religion had always been and would always remain crucial for the preservation of peace and order among mankind. The proposition applied not least to his own day, in which "the general neglect of religion which prevails among us, is one great, if not the chief cause, why our laws are so feeble in their operation." Had Reese's work "come from the east side of the Atlantic, and made its appearance with the name of some European divine," it would, lamented David Ramsay (A.B. 1765), have gone through two or more editions instead of only one. "The execution of the work would have been reputable to the pen of Warburton; but coming from the woods of Carolina, and an unknown writer, it fell still-born from the press in Charleston."

One of Reese's sermons was included in *The American Preacher* (1791), a collection of sermons by America's most respected divines. He was the only contributor south of Virginia to be so honored. Here, in "The Character of Haman," Reese argued that the lives of evil men like Haman were as valuable as character studies as those of good men, for "they exhibit in their lives, a striking proof of the depravity of human nature; and by viewing their characters, drawn agreeably to truth and nature, . . . we are led to abhor their vices, and shun those wicked courses which, if persisted in, must end in misery and ruin."

Besides preaching and writing, Reese also lectured to local blacks on religion and defended the institution of slavery against the criticisms of the Reverend W. C. Davis, who in 1794 denounced all Christians who owned slaves.

Reese's tenure at Hopewell and Carmel was brief. Already weak when he arrived, he could not overcome an attack of rabies and died at his home in August 1796. Ramsay wrote of him that "he left behind him the character of a distinguished scholar, and an eminently pious man." The epitaph on Reese's tombstone reads in part: "Exemplary in all the social relations of life, as a son, husband, father, and citizen, he lived beloved, and died lamented."

SOURCES: Vital data: Thomas Reese File, PUA; Sprague, *Annals*, III, 331-32; G. Howe, *Hist. of Pres. Church in S.C.* (1883), I, 411, 492, 593, 636-39; Webster, Brief Sketches, Bk. III, MS, PPPrHi; *Appleton's Amer. Biog.*, V, 213; L. Martin quotation: L. Martin, *Modern Gratitude* (1801-1802), 38; "used his pen for his country": Foote, *Sketches, N.C.*, 415; also 246; "read many medical authors": Howe, I, 639; Witherspoon quotation: ibid.; also J. B. O'Neall, *Bench and Bar of S.C.* (1859), II, 223; Liberty Hall Academy: *NCHR*, 6 (1929), 404; "was enhanced by": Howe, I, 593; farewell sermon: *Steadfastness in Religion* (1793), 4-5; "more liberal in sentiment": B. A. Klosky, *The Pendleton Legacy* (1971), 24; also 30-31; "the most finished writer": Howe, I, 638; Ramsay quotation: *Hist. S.C.* (1809), II, 506; "The Character of Haman": *The American Preacher* (1791), II, 324; E. T. Thompson, *Presbyterians in the South* (1963), 336.

PUBLICATIONS: see above and STE.   HS

Michael Sebring

MICHAEL SEBRING, A.B., M.B. King's 1771, was a fledgling physician. Although there were many members of the Sebring family in Somerset and Hunterdon counties, New Jersey, and a smaller branch, mainly minor merchants, on Long Island, Michael's parentage has not been discovered. In College Sebring joined the Well-Meaning Society, fore-runner of the Cliosophic Society. After graduation he matriculated in the newly formed medical department of King's College in New York City, receiving his degree in 1771. He died shortly thereafter and was listed as dead in the College's second catalogue, published in 1773.

SOURCES: N.J. Sebrings: *Som. Cty. Hist. Quart.*, III (1914), 118-24; N.Y. branch: *NYGBR*, passim; Whig-Clio *Gen. Cat.*, 27; M. H. Thomas, *Columbia Univ. Off. and Alumni 1754-1857* (1936), 106.

Thomas Smith

THOMAS SMITH, A.B., was a Presbyterian clergyman. No information concerning his origin has been discovered. After graduation from the College Smith studied for the ministry. On October 19, 1770, he was licensed by the Presbytery of New Castle. He preached among the sur-rounding churches and seems to have been popular. Not only did the Lewes Presbytery request that he be transferred to its jurisdiction in 1773, but he accepted a joint call from two churches in June of that year. The first, St. George Church in New Castle County, Delaware, was a former New Light congregation created during the Great Awak-ening. Smith was ordained there on June 23, 1773. The second was the Middletown church in the same county, which he resigned in 1775. He may have been the Thomas Smith who married Ruth Evans of Prince George County, Maryland on August 18, 1777. Smith resigned his St. George's pastorate on December 8, 1787. In 1788 he represented the New Castle Presbytery in the General Assembly. On June 9, 1789, Smith accepted the joint pastorate of the Pencader Presbyterian church at Glasgow, New Castle County, Delaware, and his old church at Mid-dletown. He served both churches until his death on January 25, 1792. He was buried in Middletown.

SOURCES: Career: Webster, Brief Sketches, MS, PPPrHi; J. L. Vallandigham, *Hist. of the Presbytery of New Castle* (n.d. [1888]), 14; S. A. Gayley, *Historical Sketch of the Presbytery of New Castle* (1888), 10, 17; possible marriage: *NEHGR*, 73 (1919), 134.

LLM

Isaac Story

ISAAC STORY, A.B., A.M. 1771, Congregational clergyman and business-man, was born in Boston, Massachusetts, on September 9, 1749, the son of Joanna Appleton and William Story, a lawyer and public official. It was "on account of the strong savor of Arminianism supposed to haunt the walls" that William objected to his elder son Elisha's going to Har-vard, and this objection may also have prompted the decision to send Isaac to the College of New Jersey. At the College Isaac joined the Well-Meaning Club, precursor of the Cliosophic Society, and at his commencement delivered "an elegant valedictory oration on pa-triotism."

After graduation Story prepared for the Congregational ministry and on May 1, 1771, was ordained pastor of the Second Congrega-tional Church of Marblehead, Massachusetts. In his letter of accep-tance Story acknowledged that he had intended "not to settle in any place until I had a much greater progress in Divine studies," but that consultations with his parents, his friends, and Heaven had changed his mind. He nevertheless insisted upon assurances that he be allowed to pursue "a frequent [intellectual] interchange with [other] min-isters."

Among the officials who participated in the ordination ceremonies were the Reverend William Whitwell (A.B. 1758), the Reverend Na-thaniel Whitaker (A.B. 1752), and the Reverend Ebenezer Pemberton (Harvard 1721), who delivered the ordination sermon.

Story served as co-pastor to the Reverend Simon Bradstreet (Har-vard 1728), who had recently become ill. Upon Bradstreet's death on October 5, 1771, Story assumed full responsibility himself. Sometime within the next two years he married Bradstreet's daughter Rebecca, who had inherited her father's home and also his fine library. She bore her husband five sons and six daughters.

On a thanksgiving day in 1774 Story delivered a sermon entitled "The Love of Country," which won him considerable prominence. All Americans, he declared, should resist any infringement on their free-dom. "If we are to love a neighbor as ourselves, we ought to love the public better than self. And, of consequence, we ought to be ready, when the exigencies of the state require it, to expose our reputation, our interest, and our lives for its good." To privileged Americans— those of "superior abilities, and more advantageous circumstances, whether possessed by birth or accident"—Story assigned the special obligations of leading the people and defining the common goal.

Story's concern for those of supposedly "superior abilities" may have stemmed in part from the treatment his father had received at the hands of the Boston mob nearly a decade earlier. For on the evening of August 25, 1765, the mob that plundered the home of Governor Hutchinson also attacked the office of William Story, then registrar at the court of admiralty. The attack came despite Story's advertisement in that day's newspapers denying allegations that he had written unfavorable reports of the Boston merchants. The mob destroyed many private and public papers and extensively damaged his office and his house. The father, who was a vigorous opponent of the Stamp Act, was eventually compensated for some of his losses and later lived with Isaac in Marblehead.

Isaac himself continued to preach on behalf of the Revolution throughout the course of the war. During the 1770s he served as a trustee of the Marblehead public schools. Story's tenure at Marblehead was lengthy but troubled. There was, in fact, a certain strain of nonconformity in the family. Problems arose first with the Reverend Ebenezer Hubbard (Harvard 1777), pastor of Marblehead's First Congregational Church. In December 1787 and again in August 1788 Story had apparently attended evangelical meetings without Hubbard's knowledge or consent, and many of Story's own parishioners expressed their disapproval by boycotting Sunday services. When, after the disclosure of his presence at the second meeting, Story exchanged pulpits with the Reverend Daniel Hopkins (Yale 1758), he stirred only further wrath. Reportedly, he offered "the most humble concessions, and a full acknowledgement of his error." Nevertheless, his popularity continued to wane.

Story's relations with Hubbard became increasingly difficult. From 1785, two years after Hubbard's ordination at Marblehead, until 1800, when Hubbard died, Story did not once preach in Hubbard's church. Though he did preach there on October 26, 1800, the very Sunday after Hubbard's death, he did not receive a call. "The smart of discipline," a contemporary observed, "has kept Story from our Association."

By February 1802 Story's disputes within his own congregation had grown so heated that many members were avoiding communion altogether and muttering that their pastor had become "a little insane." Allegations of illicit property acquisitions and of plagiarism of the sermons of New York ministers severely undermined his status. Story felt compelled to resign. He did so, however, only on condition that he be paid a $400 gratuity. "When I was a boy," recalled a Marblehead resident in 1885, "I remember hearing an old deacon say, 'Yes, we raised that amount in fifteen minutes.' And it is also said that $400 was converted into coppers and paid him in that coin." Although Story reportedly wished to retain some formal ties to his church, in order to retain certain tax exemptions, the negotiations fell through. The consequent tax burden must have been, in the words of a contemporary, "heavy upon his impertinence."

Story left the ministry for unspecified "secular business." Within a decade after his departure the Second Congregational Church had become Unitarian and Story himself had become an Episcopalian. Politically, Story was an enthusiastic Federalist. In a sermon delivered on February 19, 1795, he praised Washington for keeping the United States out of European affairs while increasing American trade and prosperity. Involvement in foreign affairs would, he predicted, lead to a massive, unwanted immigration of persons with "the vicious habits of the old countries." The sufferings of American seamen taken prisoner by North African pirates moved him deeply, and he preached and solicited contributions on their behalf four days earlier: "If you have feelings becoming the dignity of your nature," he declared, "give; if you are the sincere friends of your country, give; if you would establish grounds for the most pleasing retrospection, give."

The deaths of his father in 1799, of his elder brothers Elisha (father of Justice Joseph Story) and William in 1805 and 1806, and of his son Isaac (a lawyer) in 1803 marred his last years. (Several of his other children had died in infancy years earlier.)

Story died in Marblehead on October 23, 1816. In his will he left his furniture and his clothes to his wife; the children of his daughter Hannah and her husband William Whitwell (son of William Whitwell, A.B. 1758) received $1,279.21; and his other grandchildren were left a portion of his estate.

SOURCES: Vital data: Isaac Story File, PUA; S. Roads, *Hist. and Traditions and Marblehead, Mass.* (1880), 342, 245, 279; S. P. Hathaway, Jr., "Second Congregational Church in Marblehead," *Essex Instit. Hist. Col.,* 22 (1885); F. A. Gardner, "Elisha Story of Boston," ibid., 51 (1915), 41-42; A. Heimert, *Religion and the American Mind* (1966), 468-69, 473; E. S. and H. Morgan, *The Stamp Act Crisis* (1953), 166; Bentley, *Diaries,* I-III, passim.

PUBLICATIONS: see STE   HS

Elias Van Bunschooten

ELIAS VAN BUNSCHOOTEN, A.B., Dutch Reformed clergyman, was born on October 26, 1738, at New Hackensack, Dutchess County, New York, to Antic and Teunis Van Bunschooten, a Dutch immigrant, church deacon and wealthy farmer. After graduation Van Bunschooten studied theology with Hermannus Meyer of Kingston, New York, and received his license in 1773. That year he was called by the Dutch Reformed Church in Schaghticoke, Rensselaer County, New York, and was ordained. There he gained a reputation for strict piety. A contemporary recalled that

> He was a person about six feet in height, neat and stately in carriage, and was a man of great sternness of character. His manner in the pulpit was earnest and impressive, and his sermons highly evangelical. He preached in both Dutch and English. In his intercourse with his neighbors he displayed a parsimony that was harsh and miserly, dealing justice rather than mercy.

Van Bunschooten always insisted in paying for services, demanding in all exchanges of money a balanced account.

In August 1785, three churches of the Kittatinny Valley asked him to be their common minister. Resigning his former parish, he accepted their offer of £100 yearly salary. His duties now involved periodically riding down the old mine road to serve the churches of Minisink, Sullivan County, and Magagkamack, Orange County, New York, in addition to Wallpack, Sussex County, New Jersey. Van Bunschooten also took on in August 1788 the church located at the Clove (now Port Jervis), New York, where he bought a 700-acre farm on which he built a house and mill. During these years he again served numerous neighborhood parishes. In June 1794 he participated in a committee of the General Synod investigating the training of ministers for the Dutch Reformed Church. When the revival of 1803 spread over the countryside, Van Bunschooten was an active participant. Perhaps it was a similar fervor that encouraged him to respond favorably to a request for a sizable donation to the Dutch Reformed Church. In the midst of the proceedings of the General Synod in June 1814, Van Bunschooten walked to the head of the assembly and laid on the table ten bonds worth $13,800 and $800 in cash. The money was to be placed in trust with the trustees of Queen's College (Rutgers) for the education of ministerial students, with the surplus to go to Queen's itself. It was the largest gift the future Rutgers had ever received. Van Bunschooten left the institution another $3,000 in his will.

Neither Van Bunschooten nor any of his four brothers ever married. After he died on June 10, 1815, a monument was erected over his grave at Clove. On its side was this simple inscription: "He persevered in a good profession of faith, and a holy and exemplary life."

SOURCES: Full sketch: *The New Brunswick Review*, I (1855), 573-95; contemporary account: 26 *NJA*, 288; visiting other churches: S. Reynolds, *Hist. of the First Presbyterian Church, Wilkes Barre, Pa.* (1898), 14; committee work in synod: *NJHSP*, 73 (1955), 34; Rutgers donation, possessions in Clove: W.H.S. Demarest, *Hist. of Rutgers College* (1924), 246-49, R. P. McCormick, *Rutgers, A Bicentennial History* (1966), 33, 69.

LLM

Benjamin West

BENJAMIN WEST, lawyer and sometime public official, was born on Martha's Vineyard, Massachusetts, April 8, 1746, the tenth child and sixth son of the twelve children born to the Reverend Thomas West and his wife Drusilla Presbury. In 1748 Benjamin moved with the family to the town of Dorchester, where he grew up. Both his father and an older brother, Samuel, attended Harvard, and this seems to have been from the first the objective of Benjamin. He came to Princeton, apparently in the fall of 1764, with the financial assistance of his brother and on the advice "that young men were admitted into Nassau col-

Benjamin West, Class of 1768

lege, who, although not properly fitted to take their standing with their class, were allowed by attending the school connected with the college, to try whether they could not, in the course of a few months, so far gain upon their class, as to be properly admitted to their standing in it." Samuel's "Family Anecdotes," composed late in life, continues: "My brother was admitted on this ground—soon made good his standing, and took his place accordingly."

There may be some question as to whether this means that he "took his place" as a member of the freshman class in the College before leaving Princeton, after a year of residence during which he contracted smallpox through inoculation. It can only be said that such an advancement at the time was possible, and that he left Nassau Hall, in his brother's words, "having acquired some reputation as a scholar" and with the purpose of enrolling at Harvard for "greater convenience of communication with his friends." He carried the recommendation of President Finley and was admitted at Harvard with sophomore standing on October 7, 1765. He received the A.B. there with his class in 1768.

Having taught school at Worcester for two years, studied divinity with his brother in preparation for the ministry, and abandoned that career after preaching eight sermons in 1771, he read law at Lancaster with Abel Willard and in 1773 settled at Charlestown, New Hampshire. Wartime conditions soon increased the difficulty of establishing a new law practice, and late in 1779 he journeyed to Charleston, South Carolina, to become a tutor in a planter's family. There he felt a strong distaste for both the climate and the society into which he had moved, as also for the war moving then into that area (as a member of a "light-horse company" he became briefly a prisoner of the British), and by late summer of 1779 he was back in New Hampshire, once more at Charlestown. As the war drew to its end, he was on the way to a position of distinguished leadership in the New Hampshire bar.

Daniel Webster later described West as "one of the most successful advocates, if not the most successful, that ever practiced" in the state. His great strength seems to have been a quiet and persuasive way of explaining the evidence to a jury. His contemporaries judged him not to be especially learned in the law itself, and he was reported to have agreed, with the explanation that he had quit studying the law when he began to practice it.

Other descriptions indicate that he was tall, modest but urbane, unfailingly courteous, and witty, personal qualities that help to explain the frequency with which he was called to public office. More difficult to comprehend is his repeated refusal to heed the call. He served for many years after 1786 as justice of the peace and of the quorum in the county of his residence, but among the offices he refused was election to Congress in 1781 and 1789, appointment as attorney-general of the state in 1786, and membership in New Hampshire's delegation to the Constitutional Convention of 1787. He sat, however, in the state's ratifying convention and voted for the adoption of the new national constitution, and from that time to his death he remained a staunch Federalist. He also served as presidential elector in the elections of 1808 and 1812. In addition, he was one of an unofficial delegation representing parts of New Hampshire in the Hartford Convention of 1814. Tradition has it that in this last instance a friend undertook to dissuade him on the ground that he might be charged with treason, and that he replied that "if that be so, I shall consider myself fortunate that I, who am old and useless, shall be the means of saving the neck of a younger and better man."

When he did agree to sit with a deliberative assembly, it is said that he consistently refused to speak from the floor, whether because of diffidence, as his friends were inclined to assume, or for some more calculated reason of his own. On one occasion he reportedly explained, "If people who never heard me now think well of me, I am unwilling by my own act to destroy that opinion."

To the time of his death on July 29, 1817, he persisted in wearing the eighteenth-century dress of powdered wig and knee breeches. He had closed out his law practice in 1805, presumably having accumulated the means for a comfortable subsistence. What he may have gained through investment in the construction of a bridge at Charlestown and one of the New Hampshire turnpikes is problematical. His will provided for his second wife, Fanny Atherton and the widow of William Gordon at the time of their marriage on September 3, 1806, and left property valued at $5,000 to the local church. His first wife was Mary (Polly), the eldest daughter of Reverend Thaddeus Maccarty of Worcester, whom he married on January 8, 1781, and who died in 1803. Neither marriage brought children.

SOURCES: Sketches: *Sibley's Harvard Graduates*, XVII, 106-12, one of Shipton's best; C. H. Bell, *Bench and Bar of N.H.* (1894), 727-29, source for Webster quotation and the two attributed to West; A. S. Batchellor, *Early State Papers of N.H.* (1891), XX, 847-48, XXII (1893), 859-64; and S. L. Knapp, *Sketches of Eminent Lawyers, Statesmen, and Men of Letters* (1821), 245-72, which quotes at length from Samuel West's "Family Anecdotes," including the critically important passages relating to Benjamin's stay of "one year" at Nassau Hall. For quotations above from this source see p. 252.

WFC

APPENDIX

BY JANE E. WEBER

PLACE OF BIRTH

British Isles

Hugh Bay '50
John Brown '49
John Carmichael '59
Benjamin Chestnut '48
Robert Cooper '63
Hugh Henry '48
Robert Henry '51
Alexander Huston '60
Samuel Kennedy '54
Hugh Knox '54

James Leslie '59
Henry Parkinson '65
William Paterson '63
Francis Peppard '62
John Rosburgh '61
Robert Ross '51
Daniel Thane '48
John Todd '49
Simon Williams '63
John Wright '52

Connecticut

Isaac Avery '67
Waightstill Avery '66
John Bacon '65
Jonathan Badger '51
Caleb Barnum '57
James Beard '50
Noah Benedict '57
Thaddeus Burr '55
Benjamin Chapman '54
John Close '63
Caleb Curtis '57
Ebenezer Davenport '62
Oliver Ellsworth '66
Daniel Farrand '50
Richard Goodman '65
Richard Crouch Graham '60
Elnathan Gregory '57
Benjamin Hait '54
William Hanna '58
John Hulbert '62

David Hull '56
John Huntington '59
Solomon Kellogg '66
Enos Kelsey '60
Samuel Kirkland '65
John Lathrop '63
Ralph Pomeroy '58
Ammi Ruhamah Robbins '60
Jesse Root '56
Benajah Roots '54
Samuel Spencer '59
Josiah Stoddard '67
Josiah Thatcher '60
Amos Thompson '60
Noah Wadhams '54
Ralph Wheelock '65
Eliezer Whittlesey '49
Jesse Williams '58
Samuel Williams '65

Delaware

Samuel Eakin '63
Alexander MacWhorter '57
Alexander Miller '64

William Mackay Tennent '63
James Watt '63

Maryland

Joseph Alexander '60
John Archer '60
Hezekiah Balch '66
Hezekiah James Balch '66
John Bay '65
Ephraim Brevard '68
Thomas John Claggett '64

John Ewing '54
Joseph Finley '65
Samuel Finley, Jr. '65
Edward Gantt '62
Isaac Handy '61
John Harris '53
Joseph Smith '64

Massachusetts

Moses Barrett '54
Zephaniah Briggs '67
William Burnet Browne '60
Caleb Chase '66
David Cowell '63
Ebenezer Cowell '66
William Crawford '55
Richard Devens '67
Jonathan Edwards, Jr. '65
Pierpont Edwards '68
Timothy Edwards '57
Ezekiel Emerson '63
Peter Faneuil '57
Isaac Knowles '68
Isaac Livermore '56
Samuel Livermore '52
William Livermore '56
Samuel MacClintock '51
Asarelah Morse '67
Obadiah Noble '63
Ebenezer Noyes '59

Joshua Noyes '59
Nathaniel Noyes '59
Samuel Parker '68
Thomas Pierce '59
Edward Pope '65
Josiah Sherman '54
Nathaniel Sherman '53
Alpheus Spring '66
John Staples '65
Isaac Story '68
Alexander Thayer '65
James Hamden Thomson '61
David Thurston '51
Benjamin West '68
Caleb White '62
William Whitwell '58
Elijah Williams '53
Simeon Williams '65
Jahleel Woodbridge '61
Joseph Woodman '66

New Hampshire

John Houston '53

Henry Sherburne '59

New Jersey

Isaac Allen '62
Enos Ayres '48
Absalom Bainbridge '62
Jonathan Baldwin '55
Moses Baldwin '57
Francis Barber '67
William Burnet '49
Stephen Camp '56
Jabez Campfield '59
Israel Canfield '53
Jonathan Cheever '66
John Clark '59
Samuel Clark '51
Gershom Craven '65
Jacobus Frelinghuysen '50
Alexander Gordon '51
Enoch Green '60
Jeremiah Halsey '52
Robert Halstead '65
Noah Hart '63
Thomas Henderson '61
David Howell '66
Jacob Ker '58
Nathan Ker '61
John Johnston '58
Philip Johnston '59
John Lawrence '64
John Lefferty '61
Gerhardus Leydekker '55

Cornelius Low '52
Nicholas Low '57
James Lyon '59
Joseph Lyon '63
John McCrea '62
Benjamin McDowell '61
James Manning '62
Nathaniel Manning '62
Alexander Martin '56
Luther Martin '66
Thomas Martin '62
John Moffat '49
Isaac Ogden '58
Jonathan Ogden '65
Josiah Ogden '56
Lewis Ogden '53
Robert Ogden '65
Jonathan Odell '54
Samuel Parkhurst '57
Nathaniel Potter '53
Joseph Reed '57
Thomas Reynolds '59
Theodore Romeyn '65
William Schenck '67
Nathaniel Scudder '51
Jonathan Dickinson Sergeant '62
John Simpson '63
Isaac Skillman '66
Samuel Sloan '61

Isaac Smith '55
Jasper Smith '58
Thomas Smith '58
Benjamin Stelle '66
Richard Stockton '48
Samuel Witham Stockton '67
John Van Brugh Tennent '58
William Tennent, Jr. '58
Joseph Tichenor '58
William Thomson '54
James Tuttle '64

Jacob Van Arsdale '65
Jacob Van Buskirk '59
Lawrence Van Derveer '61
Johannes Martinus Van Harlingen '60
Stephen Voorhees '65
Henry Wells '57
Andrew Wilson '64
Benjamin Woodruff '53
Joseph Woodruff '53
Jacob Woolley '62

New York

Nicholas Bayard '57
Joel Benedict '65
Robert Blackwell '68
John Borkuloe '58
Benoni Bradner '55
Daniel Isaac Browne '53
Abner Brush '57
Wheeler Case '55
Alexander Clinton '50
Benjamin Conklin '55
Peter Winne Douw '58
Jacob I. Hasbrouck '67
Joseph Hasbrouck '66
Nathaniel Hazard '64
Ezra Horton '54
Thomas Hun '57
David Jamison '53
James Jauncey '63
William Jauncey '61
Peter R. Livingston '58
Peter Van Brugh Livingston, Jr. '66
Philip Peter Livingston '58
Philip Philip Livingston '58
Walter Livingston '59
Nehemiah Ludlum '62

David Mathews '54
John Dyer Mercier '62
William Mills '56
John Milner '58
David Platt '64
Benjamin Youngs Prime '51
James Reeve '54
Tapping Reeve '63
Azel Roe '56
Stephen Sayre '57
Hezekiah Smith '62
James Smith '57
Jeffrey Smith '56
Samuel Smith '66
Thomas Smith '54
Smith Stratton '55
Micah Townsend '66
Dirck Ten Broeck '58
Thomas Tredwell '64
Elias Van Bunschooten '68
Jeremiah Van Rensselaer '58
Abner Wells '57
Nathaniel Whitaker '52
John Woodhull '66
William Woodhull '64

North Carolina

Josiah Lewis '66

Pennsylvania

Hugh Alison '62
James Anderson '59
Samuel Blair '60
James Boyd '63
John Boyd '57
David Caldwell '61
Joseph Chambers '65
Daniel Cunyngham Clymer '66
John Craighead '63
Samuel Culbertson '68
George Duffield '52
Samuel Edmiston '66
William Foster '64

John Haley '66
John Hanna '55
Robert Harris '53
Ebenezer Hazard '62
John Hoge '49
Hugh McAden '53
Daniel McCalla '66
John McKesson '53
John MacPherson '66
Joseph Montgomery '55
Adlai Osborne '68
James Power '66
David Purviance '54

Pennsylvania (cont.)
David Ramsay '65
Nathaniel Ramsay '67
William Ramsay '54
Thomas Reese '68
Benjamin Rush '60
Jacob Rush '65
Thomas Ruston '62

John Shippen '58
Joseph Shippen '53
William Shippen, Jr. '54
John Slemmons '60
Jonathan Bayard Smith '60
William Smith '66
Joseph Treat '57
Henry Wynkoop '60

Rhode Island
Nathaniel Niles '66

Ebenezer Pemberton '65

South Carolina
William Churchill Houston '68

Richard Hutson '65

Virginia
James Caldwell '59
George Corbin '65
William Davies '65

James Hunt '59
Samuel Leake '64
David Rice '61

Unknown
Thomas Alkin '64
Joseph Burt '66
Samuel Cunningham '67
Francis Curtis '67
Edmund Davis '62
David Gillespie '61
John Harris '62
Moses Haslett '66
Daniel Jones '66
Elias Jones '67
Thomas Kennedy '49
William Kirkpatrick '57
Alexander McCausland '65
Thomas McCracken '61
John McCrery '64
Henry Martin '51
Alexander Mitchel '65
Simeon Mitchell '50

Morrow '62
Samuel Nivins '59
Sylvanus Osborn '54
James Paterson '58
Joseph Peck '56
Joseph Periam '62
Israel Read '48
Michael Sebring '68
Dickinson Shepherd '62
David Smith '57
Thomas Smith '68
Henry Stevenson '65
John Strain '57
Samuel Taylor '57
Isaac Townsend '55
Hugh Vance '67
Barnet Wait '59
Joseph Worth '63

PLACE OF PRIMARY RESIDENCE*

Connecticut
Jonathan Badger '51
Moses Barrett '54
James Beard '50
Joel Benedict '65
Noah Benedict '57
Thaddeus Burr '55
Benjamin Chapman '54

Samuel Clark '51
Ebenezer Davenport '62
Jonathan Edwards, Jr. '65
Pierpont Edwards '68
Oliver Ellsworth '66
Daniel Farrand '50
Richard Goodman '65

* Since many subjects moved several times during their lives, no listing of this nature can be definitive. For instance, after residing for much of his life in Virginia, John Brown '49 spent the latter years of his career in Kentucky.

Ezra Horton 54
Solomon Kellogg '66
Sylvanus Osborn '54
Joseph Peck '56
Ralph Pomeroy '58
Tapping Reeve '63
Ammi Ruhamah Robbins '60
Jesse Root '56
Benajah Roots '54

Robert Ross '51
Nathaniel Sherman '53
Josiah Sherman '54
John Staples '65
Josiah Stoddard '67
Noah Wadhams '54
Ralph Wheelock '65
Jesse Williams '58
Samuel Williams '65

Delaware

Alexander Huston '60
John McCrery '64
John MacPherson '66

David Purviance '54
Thomas Smith '68
Daniel Thane '48

Georgia

Josiah Lewis '66

Ireland

Benjamin McDowell '61

Maine

William Crawford '55
Ezekiel Emerson '63
William Livermore '56
James Lyon '59

Thomas Pierce '59
Alpheus Spring '66
Josiah Thatcher '60

Maryland

Thomas Alkin '64
John Archer '60
Hugh Bay '50
John Boyd '57
Thomas John Claggett '64
Edward Gantt '62
Isaac Handy '61
William Hanna '58

Moses Haslett '66
Hugh Henry '48
James Hunt '59
Jacob Ker '58
Thomas McCracken '61
Luther Martin '66
Nathaniel Ramsay '67
Samuel Sloan '61

Massachusetts

John Bacon '65
Moses Baldwin '57
Caleb Barnum '57
Zephaniah Briggs '67
Benjamin Conklin '55
Caleb Curtis '57
Richard Devens '67
Timothy Edwards '57
Peter Faneuil '57
Richard Crouch Graham '60
John Hulbert '62
John Huntington '59
Elias Jones '67
John Lathrop '63
Asarelah Morse '67
Joshua Noyes '59
Samuel Parker '68

Ebenezer Pemberton '65
Edward Pope '65
Nathaniel Potter '53
Isaac Skillman '66
Hezekiah Smith '62
Isaac Story '68
Alexander Thayer '65
David Thurston '51
Barnet Wait '59
Henry Wells '57
Nathaniel Whitaker '52
Caleb White '62
William Whitwell '58
Elijah Williams '53
Simeon Williams '65
Jahleel Woodbridge '61

New Hampshire

Caleb Chase '66
John Houston '53
Samuel Livermore '52
Samuel McClintock '51
Ebenezer Noyes '59
Nathaniel Noyes '59

Henry Parkinson '65
Henry Sherburne '59
Benjamin West '68
Simon Williams '63
Joseph Woodman '66

New Jersey

Isaac Allen '62
Jonathan Baldwin '55
Francis Barber '67
Daniel Isaac Browne '53
William Burnet '49
James Caldwell '59
Stephen Camp '56
Jabez Campfield '59
Israel Canfield '53
Jonathan Cheever '66
David Cowell '63
Ebenezer Cowell '66
Gershom Craven '65
Samuel Cunningham '67
Edmund Davis '62
Alexander Gordon '51
Enoch Green '60
Benjamin Hait '54
Jeremiah Halsey '52
Robert Halstead '65
John Hanna '55
Noah Hart '63
Thomas Henderson '61
William Churchill Houston '68
David Jamison '53
John Johnston '58
Philip Johnston '59
Enos Kelsey '60
Samuel Kennedy '54
William Kirkpatrick '57
John Lawrence '64
John Lefferty '61
Gerhardus Leydekker '55
Isaac Livermore '56
Cornelius Low '52

Nehemiah Ludlum '62
Joseph Lyon '63
Alexander MacWhorter '57
Jonathan Odell '54
Isaac Ogden '58
Jonathan Ogden '65
Josiah Ogden '56
Lewis Ogden '53
Robert Ogden '65
William Paterson '63
Francis Peppard '62
Joseph Periam '62
Israel Read '48
Thomas Reynolds '59
Azel Roe '56
Stephen Sayre '57
Nathaniel Scudder '51
Isaac Smith '55
Jasper Smith '58
Thomas Smith '58
Richard Stockton '48
Samuel Witham Stockton '67
William Thomson '54
Joseph Tichenor '58
James Tuttle '64
Jacob Van Arsdale '65
Lawrence Van Derveer '61
Johannes Martinus Van Harlingen '60
James Watt '63
Andrew Wilson '64
John Woodhull '66
William Woodhull '64
Benjamin Woodruff '53
Joseph Woodruff '53

New York

Enos Ayres '48
Absalom Bainbridge '62
John Bay '65
Nicholas Bayard '57
John Borkuloe '58
Benoni Bradner '55
Abner Brush '57
Wheeler Case '55
Alexander Clinton '50

John Close '63
Peter Winne Douw '58
Samuel Finley, Jr. '65
Jacobus Frelinghuysen '50
Elnathan Gregory '57
Jacob I. Hasbrouck '67
Joseph Hasbrouck '66
Nathaniel Hazard '64
Thomas Hun '57

James Jauncey '63
William Jauncey '61
Nathan Ker '61
Samuel Kirkland '65
Isaac Knowles '68
James Leslie '59
Peter R. Livingston '58
Philip Peter Livingston '58
Walter Livingston '59
Nicholas Low '57
John McCrea '62
John McKesson '53
David Mathews '54
John Dyer Mercier '62
Alexander Miller '64
William Mills '56
John Moffat '49
Samuel Parkhurst '57

David Platt '64
Benjamin Youngs Prime '51
James Reeve '54
Theodore Romeyn '65
James Smith '57
Jeffrey Smith '56
Samuel Smith '66
Thomas Smith '54
Smith Stratton '55
Dirck Ten Broeck '58
John Van Brugh Tennent '58
Joseph Treat '57
Thomas Tredwell '64
Elias Van Bunschooten '68
Jeremiah Van Rensselaer '58
Stephen Voorhees '65
Abner Wells '57

North Carolina

Waightstill Avery '66
Hezekiah James Balch '66
Ephraim Brevard '68
David Caldwell '61

Hugh McAden '53
Alexander Martin '56
Adlai Osborne '68
Samuel Spencer '59

Pennsylvania

James Anderson '59
Robert Blackwell '68
Samuel Blair '60
James Boyd '63
John Carmichael '59
Joseph Chambers '65
Benjamin Chestnut '48
John Clark '59
Daniel Cunyngham Clymer '66
Robert Cooper '63
John Craighead '63
Samuel Culbertson '68
George Duffield '52
Samuel Eakin '63
Samuel Edmiston '66
John Ewing '54
Joseph Finley '65
William Foster '64
John Haley '66
Robert Harris '53
Ebenezer Hazard '62
Daniel Jones '66
Henry Martin '51

Alexander Mitchel '65
Joseph Montgomery '55
James Power '66
Joseph Reed '57
John Rosburgh '61
Benjamin Rush '60
Jacob Rush '65
Thomas Ruston '62
William Schenck '67
Jonathan Dickinson Sergeant '62
John Shippen '58
Joseph Shippen '53
William Shippen, Jr. '54
John Slemmons '60
Jonathan Bayard Smith '60
Joseph Smith '64
William Smith '66
John Strain '57
William Mackay Tennent '63
Jacob Van Buskirk '59
Eliezer Whittlesey '49
Henry Wynkoop '60

Rhode Island

David Howell '66
James Manning '62

Benjamin Stelle '66

South Carolina

Joseph Alexander '60
Hugh Alison '61
David Gillespie '61
John Harris '53
Richard Hutson '65
Daniel McCalla '66

David Ramsay '65
Thomas Reese '68
John Simpson '63
David Smith '57
William Tennent, Jr. '58
James Hamden Thomson '61

Tennessee

Hezekiah Balch '66

Vermont

Nathaniel Niles '66
Obadiah Noble '63

Micah Townsend '66

Virginia

Isaac Avery '67
John Brown '49
William Burnet Browne '60
George Corbin '65
William Davies '65
Robert Henry '51
John Hoge '49
Samuel Leake '64
Nathaniel Manning '62

Thomas Martin '62
John Milner '58
Simeon Mitchell '50
David Rice '61
Amos Thompson '60
John Todd '49
Hugh Vance '67
John Wright '52

West Indies

Hugh Knox '54
Peter Van Brugh Livingston, Jr. '66

Philip Philip Livingston '58

Unknown

Joseph Burt '66
Francis Curtis '67
John Harris '62
David Hull '56
Thomas Kennedy '49
Alexander McCausland '65
Morrow '62
Samuel Nivins '59

James Paterson '58
Michael Sebring '68
Dickinson Shepherd '62
Henry Stevenson '65
Samuel Taylor '57
Isaac Townsend '55
Jacob Woolley '62
Joseph Worth '63

PROFESSIONAL OCCUPATIONS

Ministry

ANGLICAN

Thomas Alkin '64
Isaac Avery '67
Robert Blackwell '68
Thomas John Claggett '64
William Hanna '58

Nathaniel Manning '62
Thomas Martin '62
John Milner '58
Jonathan Odell '54
Samuel Sloan '61

BAPTIST

James Manning '62
Isaac Skillman '66

Hezekiah Smith '62

CONGREGATIONAL

Caleb Barnum '57
Moses Barrett '54
Joel Benedict '65
Noah Benedict '57
Zephaniah Briggs '67
Benjamin Chapman '54
Samuel Clark '51
Benjamin Conklin '55
Caleb Curtis '57
Ebenezer Davenport '62
Jonathan Edwards, Jr. '65
Daniel Farrand '50
Richard Crouch Graham '60
Elnathan Gregory '57
Ezra Horton '54
Elias Jones '67
Samuel Kirkland '65
Isaac Knowles '68
John Lathrop '63
Samuel MacClintock '51
Asarelah Morse '67

Obadiah Noble '63
Nathaniel Noyes '59
Sylvanus Osborn '54
Samuel Parker '68
Nathaniel Potter '53
Ammi Ruhamah Robbins '60
Benajah Roots '54
Robert Ross '51
Josiah Sherman '54
Nathaniel Sherman '53
Alpheus Spring '66
John Staples '65
Isaac Story '68
Josiah Thatcher '60
Alexander Thayer '65
David Thurston '51
Noah Wadhams '54
William Whitwell '58
Simeon Williams '65
Joseph Woodman '66

DUTCH REFORMED

Jacobus Frelinghuysen '50
Gerhardus Leydekker '55
Theodore Romeyn '65

Elias Van Bunschooten '68
Johannes Martinus Van Harlingen '60
Stephen Voorhees '65

LUTHERAN

Jacob Van Buskirk '59

PRESBYTERIAN

Joseph Alexander '60
Hugh Alison '61
James Anderson '59
Enos Ayres '48
John Bacon '65
Hezekiah Balch '66
Hezekiah James Balch '66
Moses Baldwin '57
Samuel Blair '60
James Boyd '63
Benoni Bradner '55
John Brown '49
Abner Brush '57
David Caldwell '61
James Caldwell '59
John Carmichael '59
Wheeler Case '55
Benjamin Chestnut '48
John Clark '59
John Close '63
Robert Cooper '63
John Craighead '63
George Duffield '52

Samuel Eakin '63
Ezekiel Emerson '63
John Ewing '54
William Foster '64
Enoch Green '60
Benjamin Hait '54
Jeremiah Halsey '52
John Hanna '55
John Harris '53
Hugh Henry '48
Robert Henry '51
John Hoge '49
John Houston '53
James Hunt '59
John Huntington '59
Alexander Huston '60
Daniel Jones '66
Samuel Kennedy '54
Jacob Ker '58
Nathan Ker '61
William Kirkpatrick '57
Hugh Knox '54
Samuel Leake '64

PRESBYTERIAN (cont.)
Josiah Lewis '66
James Lyon '59
Hugh McAden '53
Daniel McCalla '66
Thomas McCracken '61
John McCrery '64
Benjamin McDowell '61
Alexander MacWhorter '57
Henry Martin '51
Alexander Miller '64
William Mills '56
Alexander Mitchel '65
John Moffat '49
Joseph Montgomery '55
Samuel Parkhurst '57
Joseph Peck '56
Francis Peppard '62
Thomas Pierce '59
James Power '66
David Purviance '54
Israel Read '48
William Ramsay '54
Thomas Reese '68
David Rice '61
Azel Roe '56

Law

Isaac Allen '62
Waightstill Avery '66
John Bay '65
James Beard '50
Daniel Isaac Brown '53
Daniel Cunyngham Clymer '66
Ebenezer Cowell '66
William Davies '65
Pierpont Edwards '68
Oliver Ellsworth '66
John Haley '66
Isaac Handy '61
William Churchill Houston '68
David Howell '66
Richard Hutson '65
Solomon Kellogg '66
John Lefferty '61
Samuel Livermore '52
William Livermore '56
Philip Peter Livingston '58
Walter Livingston '59
Cornelius Low '52
John McCrea '62
John McKesson '53
John MacPherson '66

*Medicine**

John Archer '60
Absalom Bainbridge '62

John Rosburgh '61
William Schenck '67
John Simpson '63
John Slemmons '60
Joseph Smith '64
Thomas Smith '58
Thomas Smith '68
John Strain '57
Smith Stratton '55
William Tennent, Jr. '58
William Mackay Tennent '63
Daniel Thane '48
Amos Thompson '60
John Todd '49
Joseph Treat '57
James Tuttle '64
Jacob Van Arsdale '65
Hugh Vance '67
James Watt '63
Nathaniel Whitaker '52
Eliezer Whittlesey '49
Simon Williams '63
John Woodhull '66
William Woodhull '64
Benjamin Woodruff '53
John Wright '52

Alexander Martin '56
Luther Martin '66
David Mathews '54
Isaac Ogden '58
Lewis Ogden '53
Robert Ogden '65
William Paterson '63
Ralph Pomeroy '58
Edward Pope '65
Nathaniel Ramsay '67
Joseph Reed '57
Tapping Reeve '63
Jesse Root '56
Jacob Rush '65
Jonathan Dickinson Sergeant '62
Jasper Smith '58
Thomas Smith '54
Samuel Spencer '59
Richard Stockton '48
Samuel Witham Stockton '67
William Thomson '54
Micah Townsend '66
Thomas Tredwell '64
Benjamin West '68

Hugh Bay '50
John Boyd '57

Ephraim Brevard '68
William Burnet '49
Stephen Camp '56
Jabez Campfield '59
Jonathan Cheever '66
Alexander Clinton '50
David Cowell '63
Gershom Craven '65
William Crawford '55
Samuel Culbertson '68
Samuel Edmiston '66
Joseph Finley '65
Samuel Finley '65
Edward Gantt '62
Robert Halstead '65
Robert Harris '53
Noah Hart '63
Moses Haslett '66
Thomas Henderson '61
John Hulbert '62

John Lawrence '64
Nehemiah Ludlam '62
Ebenezer Noyes '59
Benjamin Youngs Prime '51
David Ramsay '65
Benjamin Rush '60
Thomas Ruston '62
Nathaniel Scudder '51
Michael Sebring '68
John Shippen '58
William Shippen, Jr. '54
Isaac Smith '55
James Smith '57
Samuel Smith '66
William Smith '66
John Van Brugh Tennent '58
Lawrence Van Derveer '61
Barnet Wait '59
Henry Wells '57
Jesse Williams '58

School Masters

Jonathan Badger '51
Francis Barber '67
Joseph Chambers '65
Caleb Chase '66
Edmund Davis '62
Richard Devens '67
David Gillespie '61
Alexander Gordon '51
James Leslie '59

Isaac Livermore '56
Joshua Noyes '59
Henry Parkinson '65
Ebenezer Pemberton '65
Joseph Periam '62
David Smith '57
James Hamden Thomson '61
Ralph Wheelock '65

HOLDERS OF MAJOR PUBLIC OFFICES

Members of Provincial Congresses,
1774–1776

Jonathan Baldwin '55
John Bay '65
Daniel Isaac Browne '53
David Caldwell '61
Caleb Curtis '57
Timothy Edwards '57
John Harris '53
William Churchill Houston '68
Enos Kelsey '60
Peter R. Livingston '58
Walter Livingston '59
John McKesson '53
Alexander Martin '56
Luther Martin '66

Isaac Ogden '58
Lewis Ogden '53
William Paterson '63
Thomas Reynolds '59
Benjamin Rush '60
Jonathan Dickinson Sergeant '62
Jasper Smith '58
Thomas Smith '54
Samuel Spencer '59
William Tennent, Jr. '58
Thomas Tredwell '64
Jahleel Woodbridge '61
William Woodhull '64
Henry Wynkoop '60

* Lines between the traditional divisions of the medical profession were indistinct in eighteenth century America. This listing includes men who functioned as apothecaries, surgeons, and physicians.

Members of State Legislatures

Isaac Avery '67
Waightstill Avery '66
John Bacon '65
John Bay '65
Nicholas Bayard '57
James Beard '50
Thaddeus Burr '55
Caleb Chase '66
Daniel Cunyngham Clymer '66
Caleb Curtis '57
Pierpont Edwards '68
Oliver Ellsworth '66
Jacob Hasbrouck '66
Thomas Henderson '61
William Churchill Houston '68
David Howell '66
John Hulbert '62
Thomas Hun '57
Richard Hutson '65
John Johnston '58
Samuel Livermore '52
Peter R. Livingston '58

Philip Philip Livingston '58
Walter Livingston '59
Alexander Martin '56
Joseph Montgomery '55
Nathaniel Niles '66
Jonathan Ogden '65
Robert Ogden '65
Edward Pope '65
David Ramsay '65
Nathaniel Ramsay '67
Joseph Reed '57
Jesse Root '56
Jacob Rush '65
Nathaniel Scudder '51
Jeffrey Smith '56
Samuel Spencer '59
William Tennent, Jr. '58
Josiah Thatcher '60
Micah Townsend '66
Thomas Tredwell '64
Jesse Williams '58
Jahleel Woodbridge '61

State Governors

Alexander Martin '56

William Paterson '63

State Judges

Samuel Livermore '52
Isaac Smith '55
Jesse Root '56
Samuel Spencer '59
Henry Wynkoop '60
Tapping Reeve '63

William Woodhull '64
Richard Hutson '65
Jacob Rush '65
Oliver Ellsworth '66
David Howell '66
Nathaniel Niles '66

State Attorneys-General

Waightstill Avery '66
Samuel Livermore '52
Luther Martin '66

William Paterson '63
Jonathan Dickinson Sergeant '62

Other High State Offices

James Caldwell '59
Timothy Edwards '57
Oliver Ellsworth '66
Thomas Henderson '61
Richard Hutson '65
Nathaniel Niles '66
Robert Ogden '65

Joseph Reed '57
Tapping Reeve '63
Jonathan Bayard Smith '60
Samuel Spencer '59
Richard Stockton '48
Samuel Witham Stockton '67
Micah Townsend '66

*Members of the
Continental Congress*

William Burnet '49
Pierpont Edwards '68
Oliver Ellsworth '66

William Churchill Houston '68
David Howell '66
Richard Hutson '65

Samuel Livermore '52
Walter Livingston '59
James Manning '62
Alexander Martin '56
Joseph Montgomery '55
David Ramsay '65
Nathaniel Ramsay '67
Joseph Reed '57

Jesse Root '56
Benjamin Rush '60
Nathaniel Scudder '51
Jonathan Dickinson Sergeant '62
Jonathan Bayard Smith '60
Richard Stockton '48
Henry Wynkoop '60

Postmaster General
Ebenezer Hazard '62

*Members of the
Constitutional Convention of 1787*
Oliver Ellsworth '66
William Churchill Houston '68
Alexander Martin '56

Luther Martin '66
William Paterson '63

*Members of
State Ratifying Conventions*
John Bay '65
Thaddeus Burr '55
David Caldwell '61
Caleb Curtis '57
Pierpont Edwards '68
Richard Hutson '65
Samuel Livermore '52
Philip Peter Livingston '58
Nicholas Low '57

Nathaniel Niles '66
Robert Ogden '65
Adlai Osborne '68
David Ramsay '65
Benjamin Rush '60
Samuel Spencer '59
Benjamin West '68
Henry Wynkoop '60

Members of U.S. Senate
Oliver Ellsworth '66
Samuel Livermore '52

Alexander Martin '56
William Paterson '63

*Members of
U.S. House of Representatives*
John Archer '60
Thomas Henderson '61
Samuel Livermore '52
Nathaniel Niles '66

Isaac Smith '55
Thomas Tredwell '64
Henry Wynkoop '60

Justices of U.S. Supreme Court
Oliver Ellsworth '66

William Paterson '63

U.S. District Judges
Pierpont Edwards '68

David Howell '66

Presidential Electors
John Archer '60
John Bacon '65
John Bay '65
Thaddeus Burr '55
Thomas Henderson '61

Nathaniel Niles '66
Jesse Root '56
Isaac Smith '55
Benjamin West '68

Those Performing Some Form of Military Service During the War of Independence

Joseph Alexander '60
John Archer '60
Isaac Avery '67
Waightstill Avery '66
Francis Barber '67
Caleb Barnum '57*
John Bay '65
James Beard '50
Robert Blackwell '68*
Samuel Blair '60*
Benoni Bradner '55
Ephraim Brevard '68
William Burnet '49
James Caldwell '59*
Jabez Campfield '59
John Carmichael '59*
John Close '63*
Daniel Cunyngham Clymer '66
Robert Cooper '63*
George Corbin '65
David Cowell '63
John Craighead '63*
Gershom Craven '65
William Crawford '55*
Samuel Culbertson '68
William Davies '65
George Duffield '52*
Samuel Eakin '63*
Samuel Edmiston '66
Pierpont Edwards '68
Samuel Finley, Jr. '65
Enoch Green '60*
Benjamin Hait '54*
Robert Halstead '65
William Hanna '58*
Joseph Hasbrouck '66
Thomas Henderson '61
William Churchill Houston '68
Richard Hutson '65
Philip Johnston '59
Samuel Kirkland '65*
Josiah Lewis '66*
Peter R. Livingston '58
Walter Livingston '59
James Lyon '59
Daniel McCalla '66*
Samuel MacClintock '51*

John McCrea '62
John MacPherson '66
Alexander MacWhorter '57*
Alexander Martin '56
Luther Martin '66
John Dyer Mercier '62
Alexander Mitchel '65
Joseph Montgomery '55*
Nathaniel Niles '66
Obadiah Noble '63*
Samuel Parker '68*
Henry Parkinson '65
Joseph Periam '62
Ralph Pomeroy '58
Edward Pope '65
James Power '66*
David Ramsay '65
Nathaniel Ramsay '67
Joseph Reed '57
Thomas Reynolds '59
Ammi Ruhamah Robbins '60*
Jesse Root '56
John Rosburgh '61*
Benjamin Rush '60
William Schenck '67*
Nathaniel Scudder '51
Josiah Sherman '54*
William Shippen, Jr. '54
John Simpson '63
Hezekiah Smith '62*
Isaac Smith '55
Jeffrey Smith '56
Jonathan Bayard Smith '60
William Smith '66
Samuel Spencer '59
Benjamin Stelle '66
Josiah Stoddard '67
Dirck Ten Broeck '58
William Mackay Tennent '63*
Amos Thompson '60*
John Todd '49*
Micah Townsend '66
Joseph Treat '57*
Barnet Wait '59
Jahleel Woodbridge '61
John Woodhull '66*
Joseph Woodman '66*

* Indicates service as chaplain.

PROFESSED LOYALISTS

Isaac Allen '62
Absalom Bainbridge '62
Daniel Isaac Browne '53
James Jauncey, Jr. '63

Gerhardus Leydekker '55
David Mathews '54
Jonathan Odell '54
Isaac Ogden '58

INDEX

BY JANE E. WEBER

A single date within parentheses indicates the Class to which a person belonged. The names of all matriculates for whom a sketch is included in this volume are listed in italic type, as is the location of the sketch, which follows immediately after the name. In the case of identical family names the subject's relation to the student is indicated thus: (father) or (son), etc. Place names often can be made specific, especially in areas outside New England, only by including within parentheses the name of the county.

INDEX 681

Bedford Co., VA, 355
Bedminster (Somerset), NJ, 55, 352
Beecher, Catherine, 443
Beecher, Lyman, 443, 444
Beekman, Abraham (1774), 591, 615
Beekman, Catherine, 274
Beekman, Eva, 387
Beekman, James (1776), 591, 615
Beekman, James (father), 591, 615
Beekman, William (1773), 591, 615
Beekmanstown (Clinton), NY, 471
Belcher, Jonathan, xvii, 11, 57, 89, 288, 385n
Belden, Eunice, 241
Belknap, Jeremy, 382
Bell, Cornelia, 439
Bellamy, Joseph, 3, 23, 24, 31, 45, 82, 94, 115, 117, 178, 189, 198, 217, 218, 225, 260, 315, 348, 401, 402, 441, 458, 484, 494, 556, 585
Benedict, Abner, 484
Benedict, Daniel, 177
Benedict, Joel (1765), *483–86*
Benedict, Noah (1757), *177–78*
Benedict, Peter, 484
Benedict, Thomas, 484
Benezet, Hannah Bingham, 632
Bennet, Rhoda, 178
Bensalem (Bucks), PA, 419
Benson, Maritjie, 143
Bentley, William, 63, 255, 515, 591
Berkeley Co., VA, 377
Berks Co., PA, 552
Berkshire Co., MA, 481
Berlin, NJ, 5
Bethel, MD, 266
Bethlehem, CT, 115, 190, 218, 494, 585
Bethlehem, NJ, 142, 266
Bethlehem (Orange), NY, 137, 399, 486
Bethlehem, PA, 497
Bethune, Mary, 186
Bevier, Elizabeth, 560
Bigelow, Silas, 532
Big Spring, PA, 51
Billerica, MA, 515
Bingham, Anne Willing, 632
Bingham, Jerusha, 505
Bingham, William, 632
Birt, Hester, 155
Bishop, Samuel, Jr., 639
Bishop, Sarah, 375
Black, John, 320
Black, Samuel, 64
Black River, NJ, 475
Blackwater (Sussex), DE, 570
Blackwell, Jacob, 3, 4, 631, 632

Blackwell, Robert (1768), *631–34*, 3
Blackwood, John, 4
Blackwood (Gloucester), NJ, 4
Bladensburgh, MD, 269
Blair, Elizabeth, 51
Blair, Hannah, 457
Blair, John, 20, 77, 304, 358, 572, 573, 600
Blair, Martha, 554
Blair, Mary, 355
Blair, Sally, 265
Blair, Samuel (1760), *302–306*, 195, 355, 457, 479, 504
Blair, Samuel (father), 5, 51, 265, 303, 355, 449, 554
Blooming Grove, NY, 3, 4, 134, 135, 199, 631
Boardman, Daniel, 30
Boardman, Jerusha, 30
Bollman, Erich, 583
Bonaparte, Joseph, 208
Bordentown, NJ, 208
Borkuloe, Harmanus, 223
Borkuloe, John (1758), *223*
Boston, MA, 54, 81, 195, 231, 253, 254, 304, 433, 434, 479, 515, 591, 655
Boston, Presbytery of, 73, 171
Bostwick, David, 215
Bostwick, Hannah, 163
Bosworth, Mary, 436
Boudinot, Annis, 7, 96
Boudinot, Elias, 7, 150, 216, 249, 260, 624
Boudinot, Elisha, 196, 623
Boulding, Abigail, 532
Bound Brook, NJ, 6, 125
Bowdoin College, 450
Bowen, Benjamin, 596
Bowes, Nicholas, 82
Bowes, Theodosia, 200
Boyce, Rachel, 145
Boyd, Ann, 179
Boyd, James (1763), *419*
Boyd, Jane, 419
Boyd, John (1757), *178–80*, 561
Brackenridge, Hugh Henry (1771), 589
Bradford, Ann, 395
Bradford, William (d. 1752), 395
Bradford, William, 397
Bradford, William (1772), 165, 613
Bradner, Benoni (1755), *134–35*, 4, 160, 199
Bradner, John, 134
Bradner, John (son of Benoni), 134
Bradstreet, Rebecca, 655
Bradstreet, Simon, 655

Library of Congress Cataloging in Publication Data

McLachlan, James, 1932–
  Princetonians, 1748–1768.

  Includes index.
  1. Princeton University—Alumni.   I. Title.
LD4601.M32   378.749'67   76-4063
ISBN 0-691-04639-5